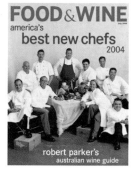

# FOOD & WINE
## annual cookbook 2005

## FOOD & WINE ANNUAL COOKBOOK 2005

EDITOR **Kate Heddings**
SENIOR EDITOR **Colleen McKinney**
SENIOR DESIGNER **Andrew Haug**
LAYOUT AND PRODUCTION **Katharine Clark**
COPY EDITOR **Lisa Leventer**
EDITORIAL ASSISTANT **Kiri Tannenbaum**

SENIOR VICE PRESIDENT, CHIEF MARKETING OFFICER **Mark V. Stanich**
VICE PRESIDENT, BOOKS AND PRODUCTS **Marshall Corey**
DIRECTOR, BRANDED PRODUCTS AND SERVICES **Tom Mastrocola**
MARKETING MANAGER **Bruce Spanier**
CORPORATE PRODUCTION MANAGER **Stuart Handelman**
SENIOR OPERATIONS MANAGER **Phil Black**
BUSINESS MANAGER **Doreen Camardi**

### FRONT COVER

Salmon with Scotch Bonnet–Herb Sauce and Onion Toasts, p. 167
PHOTOGRAPH BY Dana Gallagher
FOOD STYLING BY Kevin Crafts

### BACK COVER

PHOTOGRAPHS BY Tina Rupp
FOOD STYLING (SOUP) BY Jee Levin, (CHICKEN) BY Alison Attenborough

### FLAP PHOTOGRAPHS

DANA COWIN PORTRAIT BY Andrew French
KATE HEDDINGS PORTRAIT BY Andrew French

## AMERICAN EXPRESS PUBLISHING CORPORATION

ISBN 1-932624-01-5
ISSN 1097-1564

Published by American Express Publishing Corporation
1120 Avenue of the Americas, New York, New York 10036

Manufactured in the United States of America

## FOOD & WINE MAGAZINE

VICE PRESIDENT/EDITOR IN CHIEF **Dana Cowin**
CREATIVE DIRECTOR **Stephen Scoble**
MANAGING EDITOR **Mary Ellen Ward**
EXECUTIVE EDITOR **Pamela Kaufman**
EXECUTIVE FOOD EDITOR **Tina Ujlaki**
WINE EDITOR **Lettie Teague**

### FEATURES

FEATURES EDITOR **Michelle Shih**
TRAVEL EDITOR **Salma Abdelnour**
SENIOR EDITOR **Kate Krader**
ASSOCIATE STYLE EDITOR **Charlotte Druckman**
ASSISTANT STYLE EDITOR **Lauren Fister**
EDITORIAL ASSISTANTS **Ann Pepi, Ratha Tep**

### FOOD

SENIOR EDITORS **Lily Barberio, Kate Heddings, Jane Sigal**
TEST KITCHEN SUPERVISOR **Marcia Kiesel**
SENIOR TEST KITCHEN ASSOCIATE **Grace Parisi**
KITCHEN ASSISTANT **Jim Standard**

### ART

ART DIRECTOR **Patricia Sanchez**
PHOTO EDITOR **Fredrika Stjärne**
PRODUCTION MANAGER **Matt Carson**
SENIOR DESIGNER **Andrew Haug**
ASSOCIATE PHOTO EDITOR **Lucy Schaeffer**
ASSISTANT PHOTO EDITOR **Lisa S. Kim**
PRODUCTION ASSISTANT **Katharine Clark**

### COPY & RESEARCH

ASSISTANT MANAGING EDITOR **William Loob**
COPY EDITORS **Ann Lien, Maggie Robbins**
ASSISTANT EDITORS **Jen Murphy, Stacey Nield**

EDITORIAL BUSINESS ASSISTANT **Jessica Magnusen-DiFusco**

# FOOD & WINE

## annual cookbook 2005

### an entire year of recipes

FOOD&WINE
BOOKS

American Express Publishing Corporation, New York

FOR TIPS ON SHELLING LOBSTER, SEE P. 200

1   starters P. 8

2   salads P. 30

3   soups P. 50

4   pasta P. 72

5   poultry P. 88

6   beef + lamb P. 120

7   pork + veal P. 142

8   fish P. 160

# contents

foreword P. 7

wine pairings P. 362

recipe index P. 374

chefs + cooks P. 402

9   shellfish P. 182

10   vegetables P. 202

11   potatoes, grains + more P. 228

12   breads, pizzas + sandwiches P. 246

13   breakfast + brunch P. 264

14   pies + fruit desserts P. 278

15   cakes, cookies + more P. 306

16   sauces + condiments P. 342

17   drinks P. 352

This cookbook contains an entire year of recipes—more than 650—from the pages of FOOD & WINE Magazine. We're proud to say that it's an exceptionally well-rounded batch, with a terrific range of dishes.

You'll see more than 100 excellent fast recipes for weeknight cooking (like Chicken Piccata with Artichokes and Olives or Grilled Skirt Steak with Chimichurri Sauce) and almost as many slower, more ambitious ones to try on a mellow Sunday afternoon (Cassoulet with Bacon, Andouille and Country Ribs or Slow-Braised Lamb Shanks). There are plenty of riffs on American classics (Cherrystone Clam Chowder with Corn or Warm Succotash Salad) as well as lots of recipes that use global flavors in inventive and delicious ways (Vietnamese Pork Meatball Sandwiches or Crispy Roast Chicken with Shallots and Miso Gravy).

New to this year's collection, as a preview of our forthcoming cocktail book, is a generous supply of fun, tasty drinks from top bars, lounges and restaurants, like the Ice Wine Martini from Blue Martini in Birmingham, Michigan, and the Sugar Baby from The Sam Bar in Houston.

Every year our editors look through the recipe collection and struggle to narrow down their list of favorites, and this time was no different. You'll see our picks marked with an orange dot. Our wine pairing guide has been expanded to include entire new categories of readily-available wines, such as Grüner Veltliner—a sommelier's favorite that is especially food-friendly. Finally, you'll note dozens of useful tips scattered throughout the book, covering kitchen equipment, pantry essentials and cooking shortcuts.

The 2005 annual cookbook reflects an entire year of work by the F&W staff, as we tested, tasted and retested recipes again and again. We hope you'll enjoy these dishes as much as we have.

Editor in Chief
FOOD & WINE Magazine

Editor
FOOD & WINE Cookbooks

**SMOKY DEVILED EGGS, P. 14**

# starters

1

IDAHO POTATO CHIPS

FIERY CARROT DIP

### Idaho Potato Chips

**ACTIVE: 50 MIN; TOTAL: 2 HR 50 MIN**

8 SERVINGS ●

5 Idaho baking potatoes, peeled
Kosher salt
Vegetable oil, for frying

**1.** Using a mandoline, slice the potatoes $\frac{1}{16}$ inch thick. Rinse the slices under cold water and put them in a large bowl with 2 tablespoons of salt. Toss to distribute the salt, add cold water to cover and let stand for 1 hour.

**2.** Drain the potatoes and return them to the bowl. Add water to cover and let soak for 1 more hour. Drain and pat dry.

**3.** In a large pot, heat 2 inches of oil over moderately high heat until it registers 350° when tested with a candy or deep-fry thermometer. Working in small batches, fry the potato slices, stirring a few times, until golden, about 4 minutes. With a slotted spoon, transfer the potato chips to paper towels to drain. Sprinkle with salt and serve. —*Russ Pillar*

**MAKE AHEAD** The chips can be stored in an airtight container overnight.

### Fiery Carrot Dip

**ACTIVE: 15 MIN; TOTAL: 35 MIN**

8 SERVINGS ● ●

2 pounds carrots, cut into 3-inch lengths
¼ cup plus 2 tablespoons extra-virgin olive oil
¼ cup red wine vinegar
3 medium garlic cloves, very finely chopped
1 tablespoon honey (optional)
1¼ teaspoons *harissa* or other chile paste
1½ teaspoons ground cumin or caraway
½ teaspoon ground ginger
Salt
¼ pound feta cheese, crumbled (about 1 cup)
3 pitted black olives

**1.** Bring a large saucepan of salted water to a boil. Add the carrots and cook over moderately high heat until tender, about 20 minutes. Drain.

**2.** Transfer the carrots to a food processor. Add the olive oil, vinegar, garlic, honey, *harissa,* cumin and ginger and process to a smooth puree. Season the dip with salt.

**3.** Scrape the carrot dip onto a platter or into a serving bowl. Scatter the feta cheese and olives on top and serve. —*Nadia Roden*

**MAKE AHEAD** The dip can be refrigerated, tightly covered, for 2 days. Serve at room temperature.

## Warm Crab Dip with Fresh Herbs

**TOTAL: 30 MIN**

12 SERVINGS ● ●

- 4 tablespoons unsalted butter
- 1 large shallot, minced
- 1 tablespoon dry vermouth
- ¾ cup cream cheese (6 ounces), softened
- ¼ cup crème fraîche or heavy cream
- ¼ cup mayonnaise
- 2 tablespoons Dijon mustard
- 3 tablespoons minced chives
- 2 teaspoons finely chopped tarragon

Salt

Cayenne pepper

- 1½ pounds jumbo lump crabmeat, picked over to remove any bits of shell
- ⅔ cup coarse dry bread crumbs

Pita chips or toasted baguette slices

**1.** In a medium skillet, melt 1 tablespoon of the butter. Add the shallot and cook over moderate heat until just beginning to brown, 4 minutes. Add the vermouth and cook until nearly evaporated, about 1 minute. Remove from the heat and stir in the cream cheese, crème fraîche, mayonnaise, mustard, chives and tarragon. Season lightly with salt and cayenne and scrape into a large bowl. Stir in the crabmeat, breaking it up slightly with a spoon. Spread the crab dip in a shallow baking dish or 12 shallow ramekins.

**2.** Preheat the broiler. Position a rack 10 inches from the heat. In a small glass bowl, melt the remaining 3 tablespoons of butter in a microwave on high heat. Stir in the bread crumbs and a pinch of salt. Sprinkle the buttery crumbs over the crab dip and broil until the dip is heated through and the topping is golden, about 2 minutes; shift the baking dish for even browning. Serve warm with pita chips or toasted baguette slices.
—*Grace Parisi*

**MAKE AHEAD** The recipe can be prepared through Step 1 and refrigerated overnight. Return to room temperature before broiling.

**WINE** Dry, light, crisp Champagne.

## Crudités with Creamy Pistachio Dip

**TOTAL: 25 MIN**

40 SERVINGS ● ● ●

- 1½ cups raw unsalted shelled pistachios (7 ounces)
- 1 large shallot, minced
- ¼ cup Champagne vinegar or white wine vinegar
- 1 cup mayonnaise
- 2 tablespoons fresh lemon juice
- 1 large garlic clove, minced
- ½ cup extra-virgin olive oil
- 2 cups crème fraîche
- ¼ cup minced flat-leaf parsley
- 2 tablespoons minced tarragon

Salt and freshly ground pepper

- 10 large Belgian endives, preferably red and green varieties, separated into leaves, or very thinly sliced black radishes

**1.** Preheat the oven to 350°. Spread the pistachios on a large, rimmed baking sheet and toast for 8 minutes. Let cool. Transfer the pistachios to a food processor and pulse until coarsely ground.

**2.** Meanwhile, in a small bowl, soak the shallot in the vinegar for 10 minutes. In a large bowl, whisk the mayonnaise with the lemon juice and garlic. Gradually whisk in the olive oil until thickened.

**3.** Drain the shallot and stir it into the mayonnaise along with the crème fraîche, parsley and tarragon. Stir in the ground pistachios and season with salt and pepper. Scrape the dip into a bowl or several ramekins and serve with the endive spears. —*Naomi Hebberoy*

**MAKE AHEAD** The creamy pistachio dip can be refrigerated overnight.

**WINE** Dry, fruity sparkling wine.

## Indian-Spiced Edamame

**TOTAL: 15 MIN**

8 SERVINGS ● ● ● ●

- 2 pounds fresh or frozen edamame (soybeans in their pods; see Note)
- 2 tablespoons extra-virgin olive oil
- 1 teaspoon pickle masala or pure chile powder (see Note)

Sea salt and freshly ground pepper

In a large steamer basket, steam the edamame, covered, until tender, about 5 minutes. Transfer to a bowl and toss with the oil and pickle masala. Season with salt and pepper. —*Daniel Orr*

**NOTE** You can buy frozen edamame at most supermarkets. Both pickle masala, a blend of ground spices used to make spicy Indian relishes, and pure chile powder are available at Kalustyan's, 800-352-3451 or kalustyans.com.

**MAKE AHEAD** The steamed edamame can be made up to 3 hours ahead.

## Toasted Rosemary Pecans

**ACTIVE: 5 MIN; TOTAL: 45 MIN**

8 SERVINGS ●

- 4 cups pecan halves (1 pound)
- 4 tablespoons unsalted butter, melted
- 1½ teaspoons salt
- 1 teaspoon dried rosemary, crushed
- ½ teaspoon sugar

Preheat the oven to 250°. Spread the pecans on a large, rimmed baking sheet. Bake for 15 minutes, shifting the baking sheet halfway through for even coloring, or until lightly toasted. Drizzle the butter over the pecans, then sprinkle with the salt, rosemary and sugar and toss to coat. Bake for 15 minutes longer, shifting the pan halfway through, or until well browned and crisp. Transfer to paper towels and let cool. —*Mary Lynn Van Wyck*

**MAKE AHEAD** The pecans can be stored in an airtight container for up to 2 weeks.

# starters

## Celery Root–Potato Pancakes with Green Apple Sour Cream

**TOTAL: 30 MIN**

**4 SERVINGS** ● ●

- 2 small baking potatoes (about ¾ pound total), peeled
- 1 small onion
- 1 medium celery root (about 1¼ pounds), peeled
- 2 large eggs
- ¼ cup all-purpose flour
- 1½ teaspoons salt

Vegetable oil, for frying

- 2 Granny Smith apples, 1 peeled, 1 cored and very thinly sliced crosswise
- ½ cup sour cream

**1.** Line 2 wire racks with paper towels. Using the large holes of a box grater or the shredding disk of a food processor, grate the potatoes and onion. Working over a small bowl, squeeze the liquid out of the potato and onion and transfer the grated vegetables to a medium bowl. Let the liquid stand for 1 minute, then pour it off, leaving the potato starch at the bottom of the bowl. Scrape the starch into the potato shreds. Grate the celery root and add it to the potatoes along with the eggs, flour and salt.

## ingredient

Fresh ginger adds a spicy-sweet kick to dishes like the Chickpea Blinis on this page. But you rarely use an entire root for a recipe. Tightly wrapped in plastic and refrigerated, unpeeled ginger can last up to 3 weeks. Stored in the freezer, however, it keeps for up to 6 months—and it's easier to grate when frozen.

**2.** In each of 2 large nonstick skillets, heat ¼ inch of oil until shimmering. For each pancake, add a scant ¼ cup of the batter to a skillet and flatten slightly with the back of the measuring cup; you should be able to fit 8 pancakes in each skillet. Cook the pancakes over moderately high heat until golden and crisp, about 3 minutes per side. Transfer them to the prepared wire racks to drain.

**3.** Meanwhile, grate the whole apple and squeeze until dry; transfer it to a small bowl. Stir in the sour cream. Spoon the apple sour cream onto the pancakes, garnish with the apple slices and serve. —*Bill Telepan*

**WINE** Round-textured Sémillon.

## Sesame-Coated Sweet Potato Croquettes

**TOTAL: 50 MIN**

**MAKES ABOUT 30 CROQUETTES**

- 1½ pounds sweet potatoes, peeled and cut into 2-inch chunks

Salt

- ¼ cup plus 2 tablespoons cornstarch
- 1 tablespoon sugar
- ½ teaspoon cinnamon
- ½ teaspoon ground allspice
- 6 ounces extra-sharp Cheddar cheese, shredded (2 cups)

One 2-ounce jar sesame seeds (¾ cup)

Vegetable oil, for frying

**1.** Put the sweet potatoes in a medium saucepan, cover with water and bring to a boil. Add a large pinch of salt and simmer over moderately high heat until tender, about 20 minutes. Drain the sweet potatoes and return them to the pan. Shake the pan over high heat to dry out the potatoes, about 1 minute.

**2.** Mash the cooked sweet potatoes until smooth. Stir in the cornstarch, sugar, cinnamon, allspice and Cheddar cheese. Season the mixture with salt.

**3.** Put the sesame seeds in a shallow bowl. Using your hands, roll the sweet potato mixture into 1-inch balls. Roll the balls in the seeds until thoroughly coated and transfer the balls to a large plate or rimmed baking sheet.

**4.** In each of 2 large skillets, heat ¼ inch of oil. Add the sweet potato balls and fry over moderate heat until golden brown all over, about 1 minute per side. Drain on paper towels and serve warm or at room temperature. —*Portia de Smidt*

**MAKE AHEAD** The coated sweet potato balls can be refrigerated overnight. Remove them from the refrigerator at least 30 minutes before frying.

**WINE** Dry, mineral-flavored Chenin Blanc.

## Chickpea Blinis with Pineapple-Mint Relish

**TOTAL: 1 HR**

**MAKES ABOUT 30 BLINIS**

Chickpea flour, also called *besan,* is commonly used in India as an alternative to wheat flour in fritters, dumplings and spicy breads.

- ¾ cup chickpea flour
- 1 teaspoon salt
- ¾ teaspoon fennel seeds
- ½ teaspoon caraway seeds
- ¼ teaspoon turmeric
- ⅛ teaspoon freshly ground black pepper
- ⅛ teaspoon crushed red pepper
- ⅛ teaspoon baking soda
- 1 small onion, minced
- 1 shallot, minced
- 1 garlic clove, minced
- 1 small green chile, seeded and minced
- 2 tablespoons minced cilantro leaves
- 2 teaspoons finely grated peeled fresh ginger
- ¾ cup water
- 4 tablespoons unsalted butter

Pineapple-Mint Relish (recipe follows)

1. Preheat the oven to 250°. In a medium bowl, combine the chickpea flour with the salt, fennel and caraway seeds, turmeric, black pepper, crushed red pepper and baking soda. In another smaller bowl, combine the onion, shallot, garlic, green chile, cilantro and ginger with the water. Add the onion mixture to the dry ingredients and stir just until moistened but still lumpy.

2. Melt the butter in a small saucepan. Skim off the foam, then pour the clear melted butter into a heatproof measuring cup, stopping when you reach the milky residue.

3. Heat 1 tablespoon of the clarified butter in a very large nonstick skillet. Add scant tablespoonfuls of the blini batter ½ inch apart and cook over moderately high heat until golden on the bottoms, about 1 minute. Flip the blinis and cook until set, about 1 minute longer. Transfer to a large baking sheet in a single layer and keep warm in the oven. Repeat with the remaining batter, brushing the skillet with clarified butter between batches. Serve with the Pineapple-Mint Relish. —*Akasha Richmond*

**WINE** Light, soft Chenin Blanc.

### PINEAPPLE-MINT RELISH

**ACTIVE: 30 MIN; TOTAL: 1 HR**

MAKES 1½ CUPS ● ●

- 1 cup finely diced fresh pineapple
- ¼ cup very finely diced white onion
- ¼ cup very finely diced red bell pepper
- 1 small serrano or jalapeño chile, seeded and minced
- 2 tablespoons finely chopped mint leaves
- 1 tablespoon fresh lime juice
- 1 teaspoon sugar

Pinch of kosher salt

In a medium bowl, combine all of the ingredients and refrigerate until chilled, about 1 hour. —*A.R.*

**CELERY ROOT–POTATO PANCAKES**

**SESAME-COATED SWEET POTATO CROQUETTES**

# starters

## Creamy Fried Mozzarella Balls

**TOTAL: 45 MIN**

10 SERVINGS

- 1 **pound salted mozzarella, cut into 1-inch pieces**
- 2 **large eggs, lightly beaten**
- 3 **tablespoons all-purpose flour, plus more for dusting**

**Salt**

**Vegetable oil, for frying**

**1.** In a food processor, puree the mozzarella to a creamy paste. Add the eggs, the 3 tablespoons of flour and ¼ teaspoon of salt; process until combined.

**2.** Line a large baking sheet with wax paper and generously dust it with flour. Shape rounded teaspoons of the cheese mixture into ¾- to 1-inch balls, then roll them in the flour on the baking sheet.

**3.** In a large, deep skillet, heat 1 inch of oil to 350°. Line a wire rack with paper towels. Roll the mozzarella balls in the flour again. Fry them in batches, stirring once, until golden, about 5 minutes; some may burst open. Transfer them to the paper-lined rack. Sprinkle with salt and serve. —*Rafaella Giamundo*

**WINE** Tart, peppery Grüner Veltliner.

## Crispy Fried Chicken Livers

**TOTAL: 30 MIN**

6 SERVINGS ●

- 2 **cups *panko* or coarse bread crumbs (see Note)**
- 1 **cup all-purpose flour**

**Salt and freshly ground pepper**

- 2 **large eggs**
- ⅓ **cup milk**
- 1 **pound chicken livers, trimmed and halved**

**Vegetable oil, for frying**

**Lemon wedges, for serving**

**1.** In a food processor, process the *panko* until fine. Transfer to a pie plate. In another pie plate, season the flour with salt and pepper. In a medium bowl, whisk the eggs with the milk.

**2.** Working in batches, dredge a few livers at a time in the flour, then dip them into the egg mixture. Coat them with the *panko* and transfer to a large plate.

**3.** In a large skillet, heat ¼ inch of oil until shimmering. Add half of the livers and cook over moderately high heat, turning once, until browned and crisp, about 5 minutes. Drain on paper towels. Repeat with the remaining chicken livers. Transfer to plates and serve with the lemon wedges. —*Ashley Christensen*

**NOTE** *Panko* (Japanese bread crumbs) is available in most supermarkets, specialty food stores and Asian markets.

**WINE** Ripe, oaky Chardonnay.

## Rustic Chicken Liver Mousse

**ACTIVE: 45 MIN; TOTAL: 3 HR**

20 SERVINGS ● ●

- 1 **pound chicken livers, trimmed**
- ¼ **cup brandy**
- 2 **bay leaves**
- 4 **garlic cloves, 2 crushed, 2 thinly sliced**
- 2 **tablespoons extra-virgin olive oil**
- 1 **medium red onion, very finely chopped**
- 4 **ounces thinly sliced pancetta, coarsely chopped**
- 1 **anchovy, chopped**
- 2 **teaspoons tomato paste**
- 3 **tablespoons balsamic vinegar**
- ½ **cup sweet vermouth**
- 1 **cup heavy cream**
- 1 **teaspoon chopped thyme**
- 1 **teaspoon chopped sage**

**Salt and freshly ground pepper**

**Toasted baguette slices and Spiced Prune Chutney (p. 350), for serving**

**1.** In a medium bowl, toss the chicken livers with the brandy, bay leaves and crushed garlic; let marinate at room temperature for 2 hours or refrigerate for up to 8 hours. Drain the livers and pat dry; discard the bay leaves and garlic.

**2.** In a large, deep skillet, heat the oil. Add the onion, pancetta, anchovy and sliced garlic and cook over moderately high heat, stirring, until the onion and garlic are softened, 8 minutes. Add the tomato paste and stir for 1 minute. Stir in the livers. Add the vinegar and cook until nearly evaporated. Add the vermouth and cook until it is nearly evaporated and the livers are just pink within, 3 minutes. Scrape the mixture into a food processor; let cool slightly.

**3.** Add the cream, thyme and sage to the skillet and cook over moderately high heat, stirring, until the cream is reduced to ½ cup, about 8 minutes. Pour into the food processor and puree. Press the mousse through a fine sieve set over a bowl; season with salt and pepper. Press plastic wrap directly onto the surface of the mousse and refrigerate until chilled. Serve with toasted baguette slices and the Spiced Prune Chutney. —*Tommy Habetz*

**MAKE AHEAD** The mousse can be refrigerated for up to 5 days.

**WINE** Tart, low-tannin Barbera.

## Smoky Deviled Eggs

**TOTAL: 35 MIN**

8 SERVINGS ●

Smoky Spanish *pimentón* makes these eggs distinctive. It is available at specialty food stores.

- 12 **large eggs**
- ¼ **cup plus 2 tablespoons crème fraîche**
- 3 **tablespoons mayonnaise**
- 3 **tablespoons finely chopped cornichons**
- 2 **tablespoons chopped red onion**

**Salt and freshly ground black pepper**

**Freshly ground white pepper**

- ½ **teaspoon smoked *pimentón* (Spanish paprika)**

**1.** In a large saucepan, cover the eggs with cold water and bring to a boil over high heat; boil for 1 minute. Remove from the heat, cover and let stand for 10 minutes.

**2.** Drain the eggs and cool them under cold running water, shaking the pan vigorously to crack the shells. Add ice cubes to the pan and let stand until the eggs are cool. Drain and peel the eggs.

**3.** Halve the eggs lengthwise. Gently remove the yolks and transfer them to a food processor. Add the crème fraîche and mayonnaise and process until smooth. Transfer to a bowl, stir in the finely chopped cornichons and onion and season with salt, black pepper and white pepper.

**4.** Arrange the egg-white halves cut side up on a serving plate. Using a teaspoon or a pastry bag fitted with a star tip, fill the cavities with the yolk mixture. Sprinkle with the *pimentón* and serve.

—*Ashley Christensen*

**MAKE AHEAD** The deviled eggs can be refrigerated overnight. Sprinkle with the *pimentón* just before serving.

**WINE** Dry, rich Champagne.

## Stuffed Shiitake Mushrooms
**TOTAL: 30 MIN**
6 SERVINGS ● ●

- 2 tablespoons soy sauce
- 2 tablespoons rice vinegar
- ½ teaspoon Asian chili-garlic sauce
- 4 teaspoons minced fresh ginger
- 1 pound ground pork
- ½ cup minced water chestnuts
- 2 scallions, white and tender green parts only, very thinly sliced
- 1 tablespoon cornstarch
- 1 large garlic clove, minced
- 1½ teaspoons kosher salt
- ½ teaspoon white pepper
- Twelve 3-inch shiitake mushrooms with rounded caps, stemmed
- 2 tablespoons vegetable oil

**1.** Preheat the oven to 425°. In a small bowl, blend the soy sauce, rice vinegar, chili-garlic sauce and 2 teaspoons of the minced ginger.

**2.** In a large bowl, gently mix the ground pork with the minced water chestnuts, sliced scallions, cornstarch, garlic, salt, white pepper and remaining 2 teaspoons of minced ginger. Fill the mushroom caps with the pork mixture.

**3.** In a very large, ovenproof nonstick skillet, heat the oil. Add the shiitake, pork side down, and cook over high heat until browned, 3 minutes. Turn and cook for 1 minute. Transfer the skillet to the oven and bake for 7 minutes, or until the pork is cooked. Serve with the dipping sauce.

—*Grace Parisi*

**WINE** Dry, fruity sparkling wine.

## Zucchini "Sandwiches" with Herbed Goat Cheese
**ACTIVE: 30 MIN; TOTAL: 1 HR**
8 SERVINGS ● ●

These faux sandwiches of zucchini slices filled with cheese are a fun and elegant beginning to a summer dinner.

- 2 large zucchini (about 10 ounces each), halved crosswise
- 1 red bell pepper
- ½ pound soft mild goat cheese
- ¼ cup pitted Calamata olives, coarsely chopped
- 3 tablespoons chopped basil
- 2 tablespoons chopped mint
- 2 tablespoons chopped parsley
- 1 tablespoon chopped tarragon
- 2 tablespoons fruity extra-virgin olive oil
- 2 tablespoons coarsely chopped capers
- 1 teaspoon grated lemon zest
- 1 teaspoon coarsely ground black pepper
- Salt

**1.** Light a gas or charcoal grill. Using a mandoline or a sharp knife, cut the zucchini lengthwise into ¼-inch-thick slices. Grill the zucchini over high heat, turning once, until barely tender, about 3 minutes. Transfer to a wire rack to cool, then refrigerate until chilled. Meanwhile, grill the bell pepper until blackened all over. Transfer to a bowl, cover with plastic wrap and let cool. Peel the pepper and cut it into very thin strips.

**2.** In a medium bowl, using a fork or the back of a wooden spoon, mash the goat cheese until smooth. Stir in the olives, basil, mint, parsley, tarragon, olive oil, capers, lemon zest and black pepper. Season with salt.

**3.** Transfer half of the zucchini slices to a work surface and pat dry if necessary. Spread each one with 1½ tablespoons of the herbed goat cheese and top with the remaining zucchini slices. Season lightly with salt and garnish each sandwich with a strip of roasted red pepper.

—*Daniel Orr*

**MAKE AHEAD** The sandwiches can be refrigerated for up to 4 hours. Season and garnish before serving.

**WINE** Lively, assertive Sauvignon Blanc.

## Prosciutto, Tomato and Olive Bruschetta
**TOTAL: 35 MIN**
8 SERVINGS ●

- 2 pints cherry or grape tomatoes, quartered
- 2 garlic cloves, minced
- ¼ cup finely chopped basil
- 10 oil-cured black olives, pitted and finely chopped
- 6 tablespoons extra-virgin olive oil
- Salt and freshly ground pepper
- Eight ½-inch-thick slices of peasant bread, toasted
- 8 thin slices of prosciutto

In a medium bowl, toss the tomatoes with the garlic, basil, olives, olive oil and salt and pepper. Let stand until juicy, about 15 minutes. Mound the tomato mixture on the toasts, top with the slices of prosciutto and serve at once.

—*Steven Wagner*

**WINE** Light, spicy Pinot Grigio.

# starters

## Caviar and Potato Salad Tartlets

**ACTIVE: 30 MIN; TOTAL: 1 HR**

**6 SERVINGS** ●

You can use store-bought frozen all-butter puff pastry or buy the pastry shells from a local bakery for these tartlets. They are delicious with any kind of caviar, from beluga to salmon.

- ½ pound medium Yukon Gold potatoes
- Salt
- ½ pound frozen all-butter puff pastry dough, thawed and well chilled
- 1 large egg beaten with 1 tablespoon water
- ¼ cup plain whole-milk yogurt
- ½ cup crème fraîche or sour cream
- 1½ tablespoons water
- 1 tablespoon thinly sliced scallion, white and tender green parts only
- 1 tablespoon minced onion
- 1 tablespoon chopped flat-leaf parsley
- ½ tablespoon cider vinegar
- Freshly ground pepper
- 1 hard-cooked large egg
- About 2 ounces beluga or osetra caviar or 4 ounces salmon caviar
- 2 tablespoons minced chives
- Lemon wedges, for serving

## ingredient

**HOMEMADE CRÈME FRAÎCHE**

Tangy, nutty and velvety-textured, the crème fraîche sold in the U.S. is rather like a luxe sour cream. It's easy to make your own: **COMBINE** 1 cup heavy cream with 2 tablespoons buttermilk in a glass jar or bowl. Cover and let sit at room temperature for 8 to 24 hours, or until thick and creamy. Stir and use.

**1.** Preheat the oven to 400°. Line a large baking sheet with parchment paper. Put the potatoes in a medium saucepan and add enough cold water to cover them by 2 inches. Bring the potatoes to a boil over high heat. Add 1 tablespoon of salt, reduce the heat to moderate and boil the potatoes until tender, about 25 minutes. Drain the potatoes and let cool slightly, then peel and cut them into ¼-inch dice. Transfer to a medium bowl.

**2.** Meanwhile, on a lightly floured work surface, roll out the puff pastry ⅛ inch thick. Using a 3-inch round biscuit cutter, cut out 6 rounds. Using a 2½-inch round biscuit cutter, make a deep indentation in the center of each round without cutting all the way through. Set the rounds on the prepared baking sheet. Prick the inside rounds all over with a fork, then brush the pastry rounds all over with the egg wash. Bake the pastry shells for 18 minutes, or until they are browned and puffed. Let cool slightly on the baking sheet. Using a paring knife, cut around and lift out the centers of the pastry shells and reserve.

**3.** In a large bowl, blend the yogurt with 2 tablespoons of the crème fraîche, the water, scallion, onion, parsley and vinegar. Fold in the diced potatoes. Season the potato salad with salt and pepper.

**4.** Halve the hard-cooked egg. Push the white through a fine sieve set over a small bowl. Repeat with the egg yolk over another small bowl.

**5.** Arrange the pastry shells on a platter. Spoon the potato salad into the shells and top each tartlet with 1 tablespoon of crème fraîche and a small dollop of caviar. Sprinkle the sieved egg white and yolk over the caviar, followed by the minced chives. Top the tartlets with the reserved pastry lids, tipping them on a diagonal so you can see the garnished potato salad. Serve at once, with lemon wedges. —Jean-Claude Szurdak

**MAKE AHEAD** The pastry shells can be stored in an airtight container overnight. Recrisp in a 350° oven. The potato salad can be refrigerated overnight. Let return to room temperature before using.
**WINE** Dry, light, crisp Champagne.

## Goat Cheese Panna Cotta with Tomato Salad

**TOTAL: 15 MIN, PLUS 2 HR CHILLING**

**8 SERVINGS** ●

- 1 quart half-and-half
- 1 tablespoon unflavored gelatin (from 2 envelopes)
- ½ pound fresh goat cheese, softened
- Salt
- 1 pint cherry tomatoes, preferably Sweet 100s, halved
- 1 pound medium tomatoes, cut into wedges
- ¼ cup extra-virgin olive oil
- 1 small shallot, minced
- 1 tablespoon minced chives
- 1 tablespoon finely chopped basil
- Freshly ground pepper
- Boiling water
- 1 cup baby arugula leaves

**1.** Pour 1 cup of the half-and-half into a medium bowl. Sprinkle the gelatin all over the surface and let stand until dissolved, about 5 minutes.

**2.** In a medium saucepan, combine the remaining 3 cups of half-and-half with the goat cheese and a large pinch of salt and whisk over moderate heat just until the mixture is hot to the touch and the cheese has melted. Whisk the goat cheese cream into the gelatin cream until blended. Pour the panna cotta into eight 4-ounce ramekins and refrigerate until set, about 2 hours.

**3.** Meanwhile, in a large bowl, toss the tomatoes with the olive oil, shallot, chives and basil and season with salt and pepper. Let stand at room temperature for 1 hour, stirring occasionally.

**4.** Pour about 3 inches of boiling water into a shallow heatproof bowl. Dip the bottom of each ramekin into the water for 5 seconds, then invert the ramekins onto plates and shake to unmold the panna cottas. Spoon the salad over and around each panna cotta, top with the arugula and serve. —*Christian Shaffer*

**MAKE AHEAD** The panna cottas can be made through Step 2 and refrigerated for up to 2 days.

**WINE** Round-textured Sémillon.

### Warm Onion Flans with Fresh Tomato Sauce

**ACTIVE: 25 MIN; TOTAL: 1 HR 35 MIN**
**4 SERVINGS** ●

These flans (and other egg-thickened custards) benefit from being cooked in a water bath, where they are surrounded by gentle, moist heat. Any small glass, metal or ceramic baking dish can be used to fashion the water bath, as long as it's at least 2 inches deep. For even cooking, it's best if the ramekins fit snugly in the water bath and if the water reaches at least halfway up their sides.

ONION FLANS
- 2 tablespoons unsalted butter
- 1 large onion, thinly sliced (2½ cups)
- 1 garlic clove, smashed
- 1 cup water
- 3 large eggs, beaten
- ½ cup heavy cream
- ½ teaspoon salt
- ¼ teaspoon freshly ground pepper

TOMATO SAUCE
- 2 tablespoons pure olive oil
- 1 small onion, finely chopped
- 3 garlic cloves, unpeeled
- 1½ pounds fresh tomatoes, cut into 2-inch chunks
- 1 thyme sprig
- 1 oregano sprig
- 1 teaspoon salt
- ½ teaspoon freshly ground pepper
- 2 tablespoons minced chives

**1.** MAKE THE ONION FLANS: Preheat the oven to 325°. Butter four ½-cup ramekins and set them in a baking dish that holds them snugly.

**2.** In a large saucepan, melt the butter. Add the onion and garlic and cook over moderate heat, stirring occasionally, until softened, about 10 minutes. Add the water and bring to a boil. Cover and simmer over moderately low heat until the onion is very tender, about 25 minutes. Uncover and boil over high heat until any excess liquid has evaporated, about 2 minutes.

**3.** Set a food mill fitted with the fine disk over a medium bowl. Transfer the onion mixture to the mill and puree. Whisk the eggs, heavy cream, salt and pepper into the puree, then pour the onion custard into the prepared ramekins. Add enough tepid water to the baking dish to reach halfway up the sides of the ramekins. Bake the flans for 35 minutes, or until almost firm but still loose in the center; if the water in the baking dish simmers, add a few ice cubes to cool it down.

**4.** MEANWHILE, MAKE THE TOMATO SAUCE: In a medium saucepan, heat the olive oil. Add the chopped onion and garlic cloves and cook over moderate heat, stirring, until fragrant, about 2 minutes. Add the tomatoes, thyme and oregano sprigs, salt and pepper, cover and cook over moderate heat for about 10 minutes. Set a food mill fitted with the coarse disk over a medium bowl. Add the tomato sauce and work it through the mill. Transfer the tomato sauce to a small saucepan and keep warm.

**5.** Remove the ramekins from the water bath and wipe the bottoms and sides dry. Run a small, sharp knife around each flan to loosen it, then invert the flans onto plates. Spoon the tomato sauce around the flans and sprinkle with the chives. Serve right away.
—*Jacques Pépin*

**MAKE AHEAD** The flans can be baked early in the day and gently rewarmed in their ramekins before serving. The tomato sauce can be refrigerated for up to 2 days and reheated gently.

**WINE** Light, fruity Beaujolais.

### Tangy Spinach Pastries

**ACTIVE: 25 MIN; TOTAL: 1 HR**
**6 SERVINGS** ● ●

The light olive-oil pastry for these Lebanese turnovers has only four ingredients and does not need to rise.

PASTRY
- 1 cup all-purpose flour
- ¼ teaspoon salt
- 2 tablespoons extra-virgin olive oil
- About ⅓ cup water

SPINACH FILLING
- 1 small onion, minced
- 1 tablespoon ground sumac (see Note) or fresh lemon juice
- Salt and freshly ground pepper
- One 10-ounce package frozen chopped spinach, thawed and squeezed dry
- 1 tablespoon pine nuts
- 1 tablespoon fresh lemon juice
- 1 tablespoon extra-virgin olive oil

# strategy

**HORS D'OEUVRES**    TIP

**COUNT ON SERVING** about 8 hors d'oeuvres per person per hour.
**CHOOSE** as many make-ahead dishes as possible.
**MIX IT UP!** Offer warm pastries next to room-temperature dips; crunchy nuts alongside creamy cheeses; rich pâtés with lowfat crudités; spicy shrimp with sweet croquettes; and cured and smoked meats next to interesting vegetarian options.

# starters

1. MAKE THE PASTRY: In a medium bowl, whisk the flour with the salt and make a well in the center. Add the olive oil and work it in with your fingers until the flour is evenly moistened. Add ⅓ cup of water and stir until a rough dough forms. Pinch the dough together; add another tablespoon of water if the dough seems too dry. Cover the dough with plastic wrap and let rest for 10 minutes.

2. Turn the dough out onto an unfloured work surface and knead until smooth, 5 minutes. Cut the dough into 6 pieces; cover with a moistened paper towel.

3. MAKE THE SPINACH FILLING: In a medium bowl, toss the onion with the sumac and a generous pinch each of salt and pepper. Add the spinach and stir in the pine nuts, lemon juice and olive oil. Season with salt and pepper.

4. Preheat the oven to 450°. Line a large baking sheet with parchment paper. On an unfloured work surface, roll out each piece of dough to a 6-inch round ⅛ inch thick. Spoon some of the spinach filling onto the center of each pastry round and fold into half-moons. Pinch the seams to seal and transfer the spinach pastries to the baking sheet. Bake for 18 minutes, or until golden. Serve warm or at room temperature. —*Anissa Helou*

**NOTE** Sumac is a fruity, tangy spice that is sold ground or as whole dried berries. It is available at Middle Eastern markets.

**MAKE AHEAD** The unbaked spinach pastries can be frozen for up to 1 month. The baked pastries can be refrigerated for up to 2 days.

**WINE** Tangy, crisp Vernaccia.

## Mini Tartes Flambées

**TOTAL: 30 MIN**

**MAKES 30 MINI TARTES** ●

These are bite-size versions of *tarte flambée,* a traditional Alsatian tart.

> 6 egg roll wrappers
> Extra-virgin olive oil, for brushing
> ¼ pound smoked slab bacon, cut into 1-by-¼-inch sticks
> 3 tablespoons sour cream
> Salt and freshly ground pepper
> 1 small onion, quartered lengthwise and very thinly sliced crosswise

1. Preheat the oven to 375°. Using a 2-inch round biscuit cutter, stamp out about 30 rounds from the egg roll wrappers. Brush the rounds lightly on both sides with olive oil and arrange them on a baking sheet. Toast in the center of the oven for about 5 minutes, or until lightly browned. Pat off any excess oil with paper towels; let the crisps cool.

2. Meanwhile, bring a small saucepan of water to a boil. Add the bacon and simmer for 1 minute. Drain and pat dry.

3. In a small bowl, season the sour cream with salt and pepper and mix well. Spread the sour cream on the rounds and top with the onion and bacon; season with pepper. Return the rounds to the baking sheet and bake for about 5 minutes, until the bottoms are browned and the bacon is hot. Transfer the tarte flambées to a platter and serve. —*Gabriel Kreuther*

**WINE** Dry, full-flavored Alsace Riesling.

## Caramelized Onion and Gruyère Tart

**ACTIVE: 1 HR; TOTAL: 2 HR**

**6 TO 8 SERVINGS** ● ●

> 1 tablespoon unsalted butter
> 1 tablespoon vegetable oil
> 2 large onions, halved and thinly sliced
> ¼ cup dry Marsala
> Salt and freshly ground white pepper
> Buttery Cornmeal Pastry (p. 249)
> 6 ounces Gruyère cheese, coarsely shredded (1½ cups)

1. In a large skillet, melt the butter in the oil. Add the onions, cover and cook over moderate heat, stirring, until softened, about 12 minutes. Uncover the skillet and cook, stirring occasionally, until the onions are very soft and well browned, about 45 minutes longer; add a little water as necessary to prevent the onions from sticking. Add the Marsala and cook until the liquid is nearly evaporated. Season the onions with salt and white pepper and transfer to a medium bowl.

2. Meanwhile, preheat the oven to 375°. On a lightly floured work surface, roll out the Buttery Cornmeal Pastry to a 13-inch round, ⅛ inch thick. Wrap the dough around the rolling pin and drape it into a 10-inch fluted tart pan with a removable bottom, pressing the dough to fit. Run the rolling pin over the rim to trim off the overhang. Prick the bottom of the tart shell with a fork and refrigerate until chilled, at least 10 minutes.

3. Line the tart shell with foil and fill with pie weights or dried beans. Bake in the center of the oven for about 25 minutes, or until the edge is golden and the center is nearly set. Remove the foil and weights, cover the edge with foil and bake for 5 minutes longer, until the shell is cooked through and golden.

4. Sprinkle the Gruyère into the baked tart shell and spread the onions on top. Bake for 10 minutes, or until the cheese

# ingredient

**TIP** **WORKING WITH PHYLLO**

Tissue-thin phyllo is an elegant edible wrapper, but working with it can be tricky. Here are some tips. **KEEP THE SHEETS COVERED** with plastic wrap, then a damp towel; don't expose them to air for more than 1 minute or they will dry out. **BRUSH THE EDGES** with melted butter first, then the center. Remember to brush the last sheet. **NEVER REFREEZE** thawed phyllo. It will become too brittle to use.

**CARAMELIZED ONION AND GRUYÈRE TART**

**TURKISH CIGARS**

is melted and the onions are sizzling and slightly browned. Let cool for 15 minutes. Unmold the tart, cut it into wedges and serve warm. —*Ashley Christensen*

**MAKE AHEAD** The finished tart can be refrigerated, covered, overnight. Rewarm in the oven before serving.

**WINE** Ripe, oaky Chardonnay.

### Turkish Cigars

**TOTAL: 40 MIN; TOTAL: 1 HR 10 MIN**
**MAKES 32 CIGARS**

- 14 ounces feta cheese
- 2 large eggs, beaten
- ½ cup finely chopped mixed herbs, such as mint, flat-leaf parsley and dill
- Salt and freshly ground pepper
- 16 sheets phyllo dough
- 6 tablespoons unsalted butter, melted

**1.** Preheat the oven to 350°. In a medium bowl, blend the feta with the eggs and the mixed herbs and season with salt and pepper.

**2.** Have 2 large, rimmed baking sheets ready. Work with 2 sheets of phyllo at a time, keeping the remaining sheets covered with a damp towel. Set 1 sheet of phyllo on a work surface and brush its entire surface with some of the melted butter. Press a second sheet of phyllo on top of the first and brush it with butter. Using a very sharp knife, cut the phyllo lengthwise into 4 even rectangles.

**3.** Spread 1 tablespoon of the feta cheese and herb filling along the short end of one of the phyllo rectangles, leaving about ½ inch on each side. Roll up the phyllo, neatly tucking in the ends one-third of the way up to enclose the filling, then continue to roll up the phyllo with

the sides open. Transfer the rolled-up cigar, seam side down, to a large, rimmed baking sheet and brush with more of the melted butter. Repeat with the remaining phyllo dough, feta cheese and herb filling and melted butter. Keep the rolled-up cigars on the baking sheet covered with plastic wrap or a very lightly damp towel.

**4.** Bake the cigars for about 30 minutes, or until they are golden brown and crisp; switch the baking sheets halfway through for even browning. Transfer to a platter or large shallow bowl. Serve the cigars hot or at room temperature.
—*Nadia Roden*

**MAKE AHEAD** The cigars can be assembled up to 4 hours ahead. Cover them with plastic wrap and refrigerate. Bake just before serving.

**WINE** Light, dry Soave or similar white.

● FAST   ● HEALTHY   ● MAKE AHEAD   ● STAFF FAVORITE

19

**TUNA ROLLS WITH SHALLOT-WASABI SAUCE**

**SMOKED SALMON–STUFFED PUFFS**

## Tuna Rolls with Roasted Shallot–Wasabi Sauce

**ACTIVE: 1 HR; TOTAL: 2 HR 15 MIN**

**4 TO 6 SERVINGS** ●

**SHALLOT-WASABI SAUCE**

**Kosher salt**

4 large shallots

2 teaspoons wasabi powder

2 teaspoons hot water

1 tablespoon fresh lemon juice

1 tablespoon soy sauce

1 tablespoon vegetable oil

¼ teaspoon Asian sesame oil

**TUNA ROLLS**

1 pound sushi-grade tuna, finely diced

⅓ cup mayonnaise (see Note)

2 teaspoons *sambal oelek* or other Asian chili sauce

**Kosher salt**

10 ounces baby spinach, rinsed

1 tablespoon sesame seeds

1 scallion, minced

¼ teaspoon Asian sesame oil

8 sheets of phyllo dough

2 tablespoons unsalted butter, melted

**Vegetable oil, for frying**

**1. MAKE THE SHALLOT-WASABI SAUCE:** Preheat the oven to 325°. Spread a ½-inch layer of salt in a pie plate. Set the shallots in the salt, root end down. Bake for 1 hour, or until very tender. Let cool slightly, then peel.

**2.** In a bowl, mix the wasabi powder with the hot water. Cover and let stand for 5 minutes. Scrape the wasabi into a mini processor, add the roasted shallots, lemon juice, soy sauce, vegetable oil and sesame oil and puree. Season with salt.

**3. MAKE THE TUNA ROLLS:** In a bowl, mix the tuna with the mayonnaise and *sambal oelek;* season with salt.

**4.** Set a large skillet over moderately high heat. Add the spinach a handful at a time and cook, stirring, until just wilted. Transfer the spinach to a colander and let it cool, then squeeze out any excess liquid. Coarsely chop the spinach and transfer it to a bowl.

**5.** In a skillet, toast the sesame seeds over moderately high heat, stirring, until golden brown, about 1 minute. Transfer to a mortar and let cool completely, then coarsely grind. Stir the sesame seeds into the spinach along with the scallion and sesame oil; season with salt.

**6.** Stack 4 sheets of the phyllo dough on top of each other on a work surface. Brush the top sheet with melted butter and cut the stacked phyllo into 6 squares; work with 1 square at a time and keep the rest covered with plastic wrap. Spoon about 3 tablespoons of the tuna and 1 tablespoon of the spinach on the lower third of the phyllo square. Fold the phyllo up and over the filling and roll up tightly, pushing the phyllo in at the sides to form an even cylinder. Brush the seal with butter. Transfer to a baking sheet and refrigerate uncovered. Repeat with the remaining phyllo, butter and filling to make a total of 12 rolls.

**7.** In a medium skillet, heat ¼ inch of vegetable oil. Add 2 of the tuna rolls and fry over high heat, turning to brown on all four sides, about 2 minutes. Transfer the rolls to a cutting board. Repeat with the remaining rolls, adding more vegetable oil if necessary and reducing the heat if the rolls brown too quickly. Slice each roll into 4 pieces and arrange on a platter. Spoon ½ teaspoon of the shallot-wasabi sauce on top of each slice and serve immediately. —*Marc Orfaly*

**NOTE** If possible, use homemade mayonnaise or a Japanese brand, like Kewpie, which is available at Asian markets.

**MAKE AHEAD** The shallot-wasabi sauce can be refrigerated overnight; return to room temperature before serving. The tuna rolls can be refrigerated for up to 4 hours before frying.

**WINE** Bright, citrusy Riesling.

## Smoked Salmon–Stuffed Puffs

**TOTAL: 1 HR**

**10 TO 12 SERVINGS** ●

**PUFFS**

- 1 **cup water**
- 1 **stick (4 ounces) unsalted butter, cut into tablespoons**
- 1 **teaspoon kosher salt**
- 1 **cup all-purpose flour**
- 4 **large eggs**
- 2 **tablespoons poppy seeds**

**FILLING**

- ½ **pound sliced smoked salmon**
- ¼ **pound cream cheese, softened**
- 6 **tablespoons sour cream**
- 1 **teaspoon Dijon mustard**
- 1 **small garlic clove**

**Tabasco sauce**

**1. MAKE THE PUFFS:** Preheat the oven to 400° and position 2 racks in the upper and lower thirds. Lightly grease 2 large, rimmed baking sheets.

**2.** In a medium saucepan, bring the water, butter and salt to a boil. Off the heat, add the flour and, using a wooden spoon, stir vigorously until combined. Return to the heat and cook over moderate heat, stirring constantly, for 1 minute. Scrape the mixture into a bowl and, using an electric mixer, beat at medium speed for 1 minute. Add the eggs 1 at a time, beating well after each addition, until the mixture is a thick, smooth and shiny dough.

**3.** Transfer the dough to a pastry bag fitted with a ½-inch plain tip. Pipe 1-inch mounds onto the prepared baking sheets about ¾ inch apart. Using lightly moistened fingertips, smooth the tops. Sprinkle the tops with the poppy seeds and bake for 20 minutes, shifting the pans halfway through, until the puffs are risen and golden. Lower the oven to 250°.

**4.** With the tip of a knife, poke a hole into the side of each puff and return to the baking sheet. Bake for 10 minutes longer, with the oven door slightly ajar, to dry out the centers. Transfer to a rack and let cool.

**5. MEANWHILE, MAKE THE FILLING:** In a food processor, combine the smoked salmon with the cream cheese, sour cream, mustard and garlic and process until smooth; season with Tabasco. Transfer the filling to a pastry bag fitted with a ¼-inch tip. Pipe the filling into the holes in the sides of the puffs and transfer to a serving plate. Serve right away. —*Gabriel Kreuther*

**MAKE AHEAD** The unfilled baked puffs can be frozen for up to 1 month; recrisp in a 325° oven. The filling can be refrigerated for up to 3 days.

**WINE** Dry, light, crisp Champagne.

## Smoked Salmon Spirals

**ACTIVE: 45 MIN; TOTAL: 1 HR 45 MIN**

**MAKES 3 DOZEN SPIRALS** ●

- ¾ **cup all-purpose flour**
- **Pinch of salt**
- **Pinch of sugar**
- 1 **cup milk**
- 2 **large eggs, beaten**
- 2 **tablespoons unsalted butter, melted**
- ½ **cup mayonnaise**
- ¼ **cup chopped dill, plus 36 sprigs**

# ingredient

**SMOKED FISH** | **TIP**

Fish like salmon and trout can be smoked in two different ways.

**HOT-SMOKING** cooks the fish at a very low temperature while it soaks up flavor; the flesh of the fish becomes opaque.

**COLD-SMOKING** involves curing the fish with salt and sometimes sugar before exposing it to smoke that has cooled. The flesh becomes shiny and translucent and can be sliced very thinly.

# starters

1 teaspoon finely grated lemon zest
1 teaspoon fresh lemon juice
Salt and freshly ground pepper
Vegetable oil
½ pound thinly sliced smoked
salmon
2 tablespoons very finely chopped
red onion

1. In a medium bowl, whisk the flour with the salt and sugar. Whisk in the milk, followed by the eggs and then the butter. Refrigerate the crêpe batter for 1 hour.
2. In a small bowl, blend the mayonnaise with the chopped dill, lemon zest and juice and season with salt and freshly ground pepper.
3. Heat a 6-inch nonstick skillet (measured across the bottom). Lightly oil a paper towel and use it to grease the skillet. Add about 3 tablespoons of the crêpe batter to the skillet, swirl to coat the bottom of the pan and pour the excess batter back into the bowl of batter. Cook the crêpe over moderately high heat until browned around the edge, about 1 minute. Flip the crêpe and cook for about 30 seconds longer; transfer the crêpe to a baking sheet. Repeat with

# method

TIP

## CLEANING SHRIMP

If the shrimp are frozen, don't defrost them completely; they'll be easier to shell. Begin at the large end of the shrimp.
BREAK OPEN the soft shell and peel it—with the attached legs— away from the flesh.
PINCH OFF the tail unless your recipe specifies to leave it intact.
RUN THE TIP OF A SMALL KNIFE along the back of the shrimp and lift out the intestinal vein.

the remaining crêpe batter, rubbing the skillet with oil as needed and reducing the heat to moderate if the skillet gets too hot. You should have 18 crêpes, but you'll need only 16.

4. On a work surface, arrange 4 crêpes overlapping to make a row that measures 19 inches. Arrange a second row of 4 overlapping crêpes just below to form a neat 19-by-9-inch rectangle. Spread half of the smoked salmon slices over the lower row of crêpes. Starting at the bottom of the rectangle, roll up the crêpes neatly and tightly around the salmon. Trim the ends and slice the roll crosswise into 1-inch spirals. Repeat with the remaining crêpes and salmon. Transfer the spirals to a large platter.
5. Dot ½ teaspoon of the dill mayonnaise on each spiral, sprinkle with red onion and top with a dill sprig. Secure each spiral with a toothpick and serve. —*Alex Freij*
**MAKE AHEAD** The crêpes can be refrigerated for up to 6 hours before slicing.
**WINE** Dry, rich Champagne.

## Smoked Salmon Soufflés with Gingered Salad
ACTIVE: 35 MIN; TOTAL: 1 HR
6 SERVINGS

1 cup Pinot Gris
2 tablespoons unsalted butter
¼ cup all-purpose flour
¾ cup milk
4 large eggs, separated
¼ cup cream cheese, softened
4 ounces hot-smoked salmon or poached fresh salmon, flaked
Salt and freshly ground black pepper
Cayenne pepper
Large pinch of cream of tartar
2½ tablespoons extra-virgin olive oil
2 tablespoons fresh lemon juice
1 small shallot, chopped
1 tablespoon honey
1½ teaspoons finely grated fresh ginger

1 teaspoon finely grated orange zest
½ teaspoon finely grated lemon zest
½ teaspoon Asian sesame oil
Mesclun, yellow cherry tomatoes and boiled small red potatoes, for serving

1. Preheat the oven to 375°. Butter six 1-cup ramekins. In a medium saucepan, boil the wine over high heat until reduced to 2 tablespoons, about 6 minutes; transfer to a bowl. Melt the butter in the saucepan and stir in the flour. Add the milk and bring to a boil, whisking constantly. Cook over low heat, whisking often, for 5 minutes. Transfer to a large bowl and beat in the egg yolks and cream cheese. Fold in the salmon and reduced wine. Season with salt, black pepper and cayenne pepper; cover.
2. In a large bowl, beat the egg whites with the cream of tartar until firm peaks form. Gently fold one-third of the egg whites into the salmon mixture, then fold in the rest. Spoon into the prepared ramekins and bake the soufflés in the center of the oven for 20 minutes, or until puffed and browned. Let them cool slightly; the soufflés will sink.
3. Meanwhile, in a blender, combine the olive oil, lemon juice, shallot, honey, ginger, orange and lemon zests and sesame oil; blend until smooth. Season with salt and pepper. Toss with some mesclun, tomatoes and potatoes. Carefully unmold the soufflés and serve with the salad. —*Gina Gallo and Bruce Riezenman*
**WINE** Dry, medium-bodied Pinot Gris.

## Armagnac-Doused Shrimp
TOTAL: 30 MIN
MAKES 8 HORS D'OEUVRES ● ●
This cooked dish uses French Armagnac yet is based on the Chinese recipe for drunken shrimp. If you can find tiny, whole, live shrimp in Chinatown, stir-fry them shell and all.

¼ cup Armagnac or other brandy
1 pound medium shrimp,
  shelled and deveined
Salt and freshly ground pepper
¼ cup vegetable oil

1. In a shallow dish, add the Armagnac to the shrimp, toss to coat and marinate for 15 minutes.
2. Remove the shrimp from the marinade and drain lightly on paper towels. Season with salt and pepper.
3. In a large skillet, heat 2 tablespoons of the oil. Add half of the shrimp and stir-fry over high heat until browned on both sides and cooked through, about 1 minute total. Transfer to a platter and repeat with the remaining oil and shrimp. Serve immediately. —*Zak Pelaccio*
WINE Dry, crisp sparkling wine.

## Mexican Shrimp Cocktail

TOTAL: 25 MIN
4 SERVINGS ● ●
1¼ pounds shelled and deveined medium shrimp
½ cup ketchup
¼ cup coarsely chopped cilantro
2 tablespoons drained prepared horseradish
1 large Hass avocado, peeled and cut into ½-inch dice
Salt and freshly ground pepper

1. In a medium saucepan of boiling salted water, cook the shrimp for 1 minute, or until opaque throughout. Drain the shrimp and spread them on a baking sheet. Let cool in the refrigerator for about 10 minutes.
2. Meanwhile, in a medium bowl, mix the ketchup with the cilantro and horseradish. Fold in the cooled shrimp and the avocado and season with salt and pepper. Transfer to bowls and serve right away. —*Jamie Samford*
SERVE WITH Tortilla chips and fresh lime wedges.
WINE High-acid, savory Vermentino.

## Shrimp Tempura with Miso Mayonnaise

TOTAL: 30 MIN
8 SERVINGS ●
The sparkling water in the tempura batter makes the crust amazingly light. The most efficient way to prepare the tempura is to dip the shrimp two at a time in the batter using both hands and drop them into the oil.

Vegetable oil, for frying
½ cup mayonnaise
2 tablespoons fresh lemon juice
2 tablespoons white miso (see p. 107)
1 tablespoon Cointreau or other orange liqueur
1 teaspoon Asian chili paste
1 teaspoon finely grated orange zest
1 cup all-purpose flour
1 teaspoon salt
1 cup cold sparkling water
½ cup ice water
1 large egg, lightly beaten
1½ pounds shelled and deveined medium shrimp
Cornstarch, for dredging
2 tablespoons finely chopped chives

1. In a medium saucepan, heat 1 inch of vegetable oil to 350°. Set a large wire rack over a baking sheet and place it near the stove.
2. In a small bowl, whisk together the mayonnaise, lemon juice, miso, Cointreau, chili paste and orange zest.
3. In a medium bowl, stir together the flour and salt. Add the sparkling water, ice water and lightly beaten egg and stir with a fork just until blended; the batter can be a little lumpy.
4. Working close to the hot oil, dredge 8 shrimp in cornstarch, shaking off any excess. Holding a shrimp or two in each hand, swirl them quickly through the batter and carefully drop them into the

oil. Repeat with the remaining dredged shrimp. Fry until the tempura crust is golden brown, about 1½ minutes. Using a long-handled slotted spoon, transfer the shrimp to the rack to drain. Repeat with the remaining shrimp.
5. Arrange the shrimp on a large platter, sprinkle with the chives and serve immediately with the miso mayonnaise.
—*Masaharu Morimoto*
MAKE AHEAD The miso mayonnaise can be refrigerated for up to 2 days.
WINE Full-bodied, fragrant Viognier.

## Shrimp BLTs

TOTAL: 30 MIN
MAKES 30 HORS D'OEUVRES ● ●
1 baguette, cut crosswise into thirty ¼-inch-thick slices
1 tablespoon pure olive oil
¼ pound thinly sliced pancetta
¾ pound cooked shrimp, coarsely chopped
½ cup plus 2 tablespoons mayonnaise, plus more for spreading
2 tablespoons coarsely chopped basil
1½ tablespoons fresh lemon juice
Salt and freshly ground pepper
3 ounces baby arugula
4 small plum tomatoes, thinly sliced crosswise

1. Preheat the oven to 350°. Spread the baguette slices on a large, rimmed baking sheet and bake for about 8 minutes, or until just crisp. Let cool.
2. In a large skillet, heat the olive oil until shimmering. Add the pancetta slices in an even layer and cook over moderate heat until crisp and browned, about 2 minutes per side. Drain the pancetta on paper towels and crumble.
3. In a medium bowl, mix the chopped, cooked shrimp with the mayonnaise, basil and lemon juice and season with salt and pepper.

# starters

**4.** Spread a thin layer of mayonnaise on each of the baguette slices. Top with an arugula leaf, a tomato slice and a scant tablespoon of the shrimp salad. Sprinkle with the pancetta and serve. —*Alex Freij*

**MAKE AHEAD** The shrimp salad can be refrigerated for up to 2 days.

**WINE** Medium-bodied, round Pinot Blanc.

## Shrimp and Chicken Summer Rolls

**TOTAL: 1 HR 15 MIN**

**MAKES 12 ROLLS** ●

The healthy elegance of Vietnamese cooking is exemplified in these *goi cuon*, or salad rolls, often called summer rolls. Round, dried rice-paper wrappers, reconstituted in water until soft but still chewy, are stuffed with lean chicken and shrimp, delicate rice noodles and lots of greens. It's a light dish but full of flavor. Be sure to have extra rice-paper wrappers on hand to replace any that tear while you're filling them.

**DIPPING SAUCE**

- 3 tablespoons sugar
- ⅓ cup water
- ¼ cup fresh lime juice
- 3 tablespoons Asian fish sauce
- 2 Thai or serrano chiles, thinly sliced
- 1 small garlic clove, mashed to a paste with a fork
- 1½ tablespoons finely chopped cilantro

**SUMMER ROLLS**

- 18 large shrimp (about 10 ounces)
- 4 ounces rice vermicelli, soaked in warm water for 15 minutes and drained

Twelve 8-inch rice-paper wrappers
- 12 small red leaf lettuce leaves, ribs removed
- 3 tablespoons hoisin sauce
- 2 cups shredded skinless cooked chicken breast meat (¾ pound)
- 36 large mint leaves

Twelve 6-inch chives

**1. MAKE THE DIPPING SAUCE:** In a small microwavable bowl, combine the sugar and water and microwave on high power just until the sugar is dissolved. Let cool, then stir in the remaining dipping sauce ingredients. Let stand at room temperature for 30 minutes.

**2. MEANWHILE, MAKE THE SUMMER ROLLS:** Fill a medium bowl with ice water. In a medium saucepan of boiling salted water, cook the shrimp until pink, 2 minutes. Using a slotted spoon, transfer the shrimp to the ice water to cool. Peel and devein the shrimp, then pat dry and halve lengthwise.

**3.** Return the cooking water to a boil. Add the soaked rice vermicelli and cook until tender, about 2 minutes. Drain and rinse under cool running water. Drain again and pat dry with paper towels. Using scissors, cut the noodles into 2-inch lengths.

**4.** Fill a bowl with hot water. Add 3 rice-paper wrappers, 1 at a time, and let soak until slightly softened but still a bit stiff, about 30 seconds; transfer to a work surface. Rub each wrapper with a little water until completely pliable, then blot dry with paper towels. Place 1 lettuce leaf on the lower third of each wrapper. Brush with a little of the hoisin and top with 3 shrimp halves, a scant 3 tablespoons of the shredded chicken and 3 mint leaves. Fold up the bottom edge of the wrapper, then fold the ends in and roll over once. Place a chive on the wrapper and continue to roll into a tight cylinder. Place the finished rolls on a large platter and cover with lightly moistened paper towels while you soak, fill and roll the remaining wrappers. Cut each roll in half diagonally, arrange them on the platter and serve with the dipping sauce. —*Anya von Bremzen*

**MAKE AHEAD** The dipping sauce can be refrigerated for up to 4 days.

**WINE** Soft, off-dry Riesling.

## Tuna and Green Olive Empanadas

**ACTIVE: 45 MIN; TOTAL: 2 HR 30 MIN**

**MAKES 12 EMPANADAS**

This recipe works double time, making more filling than is needed for the empanadas. Toss the leftover filling with pasta or use it to top crostini; it will last a few days in the refrigerator.

- ¼ cup extra-virgin olive oil
- 1 large onion, finely chopped
- 1 bay leaf
- 2 medium tomatoes, seeded and minced
- ½ rounded teaspoon smoked *Pimentón* (Spanish paprika)

One 6-ounce can tuna packed in olive oil, drained
- ½ cup pitted green olives, coarsely chopped
- 1 large hard-cooked egg, coarsely chopped
- 1 tablespoon chopped flat-leaf parsley

Kosher salt

Two 14-ounce packages puff pastry
- 1 large egg
- 2 tablespoons whole milk

**1.** Heat the olive oil in a large skillet until shimmering. Add the onion and bay leaf and cook over moderate heat, stirring occasionally, until the onion is softened and beginning to brown, about 12 minutes. Add the tomatoes and *pimentón* to the onions and cook, stirring occasionally, for 10 minutes. Remove from the heat and let cool. Discard the bay leaf.

**2.** In a medium bowl, using a fork or the side of a wooden spoon, lightly break up the tuna. Add the chopped olives, egg and parsley and stir in the tomato-onion mixture. Season with salt and refrigerate until cool, about 30 minutes.

**3.** Unfold the puff pastry on a lightly floured work surface. Using a 4½-inch biscuit cutter, cut the pastry into 12 rounds. Using a rolling pin, lightly roll out each round to a 5-inch diameter.

TUNA AND GREEN OLIVE EMPANADA, ALONGSIDE APPLE SALAD WITH CABRALES CHEESE (P. 36)

# starters

**4.** Spoon 2 tablespoons of the tuna-and-olive filling onto one side of each pastry round. Fold the pastry over the filling and press the edges with the tines of a fork to seal decoratively.

**5.** Line 2 baking sheets with parchment paper and set 6 empanadas on each sheet. Cover with plastic wrap and refrigerate for at least 30 minutes, or until the empanadas are chilled.

## ingredient

TIP

### GREEK STARTERS

F&W tasted 30 different kinds of Greek starters to find these favorite brands.

**DIVINA** specializes in estate-grown olives, like the juicy, earthy, black Mt. Pelions from the western slopes of their namesake mountain. The dolmas—Sultana grape leaves stuffed with long-grain rice flavored with lemon, dill and mint—are exceptional (FoodMatch; 800-350-3411).

**MOREA** makes a peppery, fruity extra-virgin olive oil from Koroneiko olives hand-picked in the south of Greece. Morea's olives include green Halkidikis, purplish Calamatas and rare blond Hondroelias (World Pantry; 866-972-6879 or worldpantry.com).

**MT. VIKOS** offers baked gigandes—giant white beans slow-cooked with tomatoes and roasted red peppers. The company also sells fabulous cheeses: luscious, creamy manouri and kefalotyri, a hard cheese with a caramel-like flavor (Salumeria Italiana; 800-400-5916 or salumeriaitaliana.com).

**6.** Preheat the oven to 400° and place 2 racks in the center. In a bowl, whisk the egg with the milk. Brush the empanadas with the egg wash. Bake for 30 minutes, or until deep golden brown. Let cool for 5 minutes before serving. —*José Andrés*

**MAKE AHEAD** The unbaked empanadas can be wrapped in plastic and refrigerated for up to 2 days or frozen for up to 1 month.

**WINE** Lively, assertive Sauvignon Blanc.

## Broiled Sardines with Mustard-Shallot Crumbs

**TOTAL: 20 MIN**

**6 SERVINGS** ●

- ⅓ cup fine dry bread crumbs
- 2½ tablespoons whole-grain mustard
- 2 tablespoons finely chopped flat-leaf parsley
- 1½ tablespoons unsalted butter, softened
- 1 small shallot, thinly sliced, slices separated into rings
- ¼ teaspoon crushed red pepper

Salt

- ½ cup heavy cream

Four 4- to 4½-ounce cans large sardines in olive oil—drained, halved lengthwise and boned

**1.** Preheat the broiler. In a medium bowl, combine the bread crumbs with 1½ tablespoons of the mustard and the parsley, butter, shallot and crushed red pepper. Season lightly with salt.

**2.** In a medium, shallow baking dish, whisk the heavy cream with the remaining 1 tablespoon of mustard.

**3.** Arrange the sardines in the baking dish skin side down. Scatter the bread-crumb mixture on top. Broil the sardines 6 inches from the heat for 1 minute and 30 seconds, or until heated through and golden brown. Serve at once. —*Marcia Kiesel*

**WINE** Lively, assertive Sauvignon Blanc.

## Lemony Smoked Trout Salad in Red Endive Scoops

**TOTAL: 25 MIN**

**MAKES 32 HORS D'OEUVRES** ● ●

- 1 small head frisée lettuce
- ¾ cup mayonnaise
- 1 tablespoon fresh lemon juice
- 2 teaspoons Dijon mustard
- 1 large scallion, white and tender green parts only, minced
- 10 ounces skinless smoked trout fillets, shredded

Freshly ground pepper

- 32 red endive leaves, or 1 medium head radicchio, leaves torn into 2-inch pieces

**1.** Reserve 32 small frisée leaves for garnish. Coarsely chop 1 cup of the frisée; reserve the rest for another use. In a medium bowl, blend the mayonnaise with the lemon juice, mustard and scallion. Fold in the trout and chopped frisée and season with pepper.

**2.** Arrange the endive leaves on a platter. Mound 1 tablespoon of the smoked trout salad on each leaf, garnish with the reserved frisée leaves and serve. —*Alex Freij*

**MAKE AHEAD** The smoked trout salad can be refrigerated for up to 2 days.

**WINE** Dry, full-flavored Alsace Riesling.

## Scallops Steamed in Sake and Riesling

**TOTAL: 30 MIN**

**8 SERVINGS** ● ● ●

- 2 tablespoons sake
- 2 tablespoons Riesling
- 2 tablespoons oyster sauce
- 24 sea scallops (about 1½ pounds)

Salt and freshly ground pepper

- ⅓ cup peanut oil
- 4 large scallions, white and tender green parts only, thinly sliced on the diagonal
- 2 tablespoons finely julienned peeled ginger

**LEMONY SMOKED TROUT SALAD**

**SPICY TUNA RILLETTES**

**1.** Set a two-tiered bamboo steamer in a wok or in a large saucepan or skillet over 2 inches of boiling water; alternatively, use a large, wide steamer.

**2.** In a small bowl, blend the sake, Riesling and oyster sauce. Arrange the scallops on two 9-inch glass pie plates and season them with salt and pepper. Spoon the sauce mixture over the scallops. Steam the scallops over high heat until they are just cooked through, about 3 minutes. (If using a large, wide steamer, steam the scallops in 2 batches.)

**3.** Meanwhile, heat the oil in a skillet until almost smoking. As soon as the scallops are done, add the scallions and ginger to the hot oil, stir and remove from the heat. Spoon the mixture over the scallops and serve. —*Masaharu Morimoto*

**SERVE WITH** Steamed rice.

**WINE** Bright, citrusy Riesling.

## Spicy Tuna Rillettes

**TOTAL: 30 MIN**

**MAKES 2½ CUPS** ● ●

Rillettes is a traditional spread made from meat, poultry or fish that has been slowly cooked with fat, then mashed and packed into a crock or ramekin. This tuna rillettes is a twist on that classic.

¾ pound fatty tuna belly
½ cup finely chopped
    cilantro leaves
½ cup finely chopped scallions
4 tablespoons unsalted
    butter, softened
10 brined green peppercorns,
    drained and finely chopped
½ tablespoon fresh lemon juice
½ teaspoon cayenne pepper
½ cup heavy cream
Salt
Crackers or toasts, for serving

**1.** Fit a medium pot with a steamer basket. Add 1 inch of water to the pot and bring to a boil. Add the tuna belly and steam until cooked through, about 8 minutes. Let cool, then flake the cooked tuna into a medium bowl; don't remove the fat. Gently stir in the cilantro, scallions, butter, peppercorns, lemon juice and cayenne pepper.

**2.** In a small bowl, beat the heavy cream until stiff. Fold the whipped cream into the tuna mixture and season with salt. Transfer the rillettes to a crock and serve at room temperature or slightly chilled, with crackers or toasted baguette slices. —*Pascal Rigo*

**MAKE AHEAD** The tuna rillettes can be refrigerated for up to 2 days. Let stand at room temperature for about 30 minutes before serving.

**WINE** Dry, mineral-flavored Chenin Blanc.

# starters

## Crab and Corn Beignets

**TOTAL: 40 MIN**

MAKES 40 BEIGNETS ●

- 1 small red bell pepper
- ½ cup all-purpose flour
- 2 tablespoons cornmeal
- ½ teaspoon baking powder

Kosher salt and freshly ground pepper

- ⅓ cup milk
- 1 large egg, lightly beaten
- ½ pound cooked crabmeat, picked over
- ½ cup fresh corn kernels
- 1 scallion, minced
- ½ cup mayonnaise
- 1 tablespoon chopped basil
- 1 tablespoon chopped cilantro
- 1 tablespoon fresh lemon juice
- ½ teaspoon chopped tarragon
- 1 teaspoon Dijon mustard

Vegetable oil, for frying

**1.** Char the red pepper directly over a gas flame or under the broiler, turning frequently, until blackened and blistered on all sides. Transfer to a plate to cool for about 10 minutes. Discard the blackened skin, stem and seeds and cut the pepper into ¼-inch dice.

**2.** In a large bowl, whisk the flour with the cornmeal, baking powder, ¾ teaspoon of salt and ¼ teaspoon of pepper. Stir in the milk and egg. Fold in the crabmeat, corn, scallion and diced red pepper. Let the beignet batter rest for about 10 minutes.

**3.** In a small bowl, blend the mayonnaise with the basil, cilantro, lemon juice, tarragon and mustard and season with salt and pepper.

**4.** Preheat the oven to 300°. Set a rack over a baking sheet. In a large skillet, heat 1½ inches of oil to 350°. Cook the beignets without crowding the pan: Drop rounded teaspoons of the batter into the hot oil and fry until golden, about 1 minute per side. Drain on the rack and keep warm in the oven while you fry the rest.

Repeat with the remaining batter, adjusting the heat if the beignets brown too quickly. Transfer the beignets to a platter and serve with the herbed mayonnaise.
—Alex Freij

**MAKE AHEAD** The batter and the mayonnaise can be refrigerated overnight.

**WINE** Dry, full-flavored Alsace Riesling.

## Parmesan-Dusted Meatballs

**ACTIVE: 25 MIN; TOTAL: 1 HR**

MAKES 40 MEATBALLS ● ●

- ⅓ cup long-grain rice
- 1 pound ground pork
- ½ cup fine dry bread crumbs
- 2 large eggs, beaten
- 1½ teaspoons kosher salt
- ½ teaspoon freshly ground pepper
- 2 garlic cloves, minced
- ¼ cup extra-virgin olive oil
- 1 small onion, finely chopped
- ½ teaspoon crushed red pepper
- 1 large tomato, finely chopped
- ¾ cup freshly grated Parmesan cheese
- 2 tablespoons finely chopped flat-leaf parsley

**1.** Bring a small saucepan of water to a boil. Add the rice and cook over moderately high heat, stirring occasionally, until tender, about 12 minutes. Drain and let cool.

**2.** In a large bowl, combine the ground pork with the cooked rice, bread crumbs, eggs, salt, pepper and half of the garlic. Blend thoroughly with your hands. Wet your hands and roll the mixture into 1-inch meatballs.

**3.** In a large skillet, heat the olive oil. Add the onion, crushed red pepper and the remaining garlic and cook over moderate heat until the onion is softened, about 4 minutes. Add the tomato and cook, stirring occasionally, until saucy, about 5 minutes. Add the meatballs, cover and cook over moderately low heat, carefully

turning the meatballs a few times, until firm and cooked through, about 10 minutes. Using tongs, transfer the meatballs to a rimmed baking sheet to cool.

**4.** In a small, shallow bowl, combine the Parmesan and parsley. Roll the meatballs in the herb-cheese mixture to coat, then transfer the meatballs to a platter, skewer with toothpicks and serve.
—Alex Freij

**MAKE AHEAD** The meatballs can be prepared through Step 3 and refrigerated overnight.

**WINE** Simple, fruity Chianti or Sangiovese.

## Roasted Persimmons Wrapped in Pancetta

**TOTAL: 30 MIN**

20 SERVINGS ●

- 42 thin slices of pancetta (about 1¼ pounds), or 21 slices of bacon, halved crosswise
- 7 Fuyu persimmons, peeled, each cut into 6 wedges

Salt and freshly ground pepper

Balsamic vinegar, preferably aged at least 10 years

**1.** Preheat the oven to 450°. Lay the pancetta slices on 2 large, rimmed baking sheets. Bake for 3 minutes, or until they are heated through and softened. Transfer the pancetta to a large plate. Wipe off the baking sheets.

**2.** Season the persimmon wedges with salt and pepper and wrap each one with a slice of pancetta. Secure with toothpicks, if needed. Arrange the wrapped persimmons on the baking sheets. Bake 1 sheet at a time in the center of the oven for 4 minutes, or until the pancetta is crisp. Transfer to a platter, drizzle with the balsamic vinegar and serve.
—Morgan Brownlow

**MAKE AHEAD** Wrap the persimmon wedges earlier in the day and refrigerate them until ready to bake.

**WINE** Light, spicy Pinot Grigio.

CRAB AND CORN BEIGNETS

ESCAROLE AND FRESH HERB SALAD WITH APPLES AND POMEGRANATE, P. 35

# salads

ICEBERG WEDGES WITH BLUE CHEESE DRESSING

CRISP WINTER SALAD WITH GINGER-GARLIC VINAIGRETTE

### Iceberg Wedges with Blue Cheese Dressing

TOTAL: 20 MIN

6 SERVINGS ●

- 4 ounces Roquefort cheese, crumbled (1 cup)
- ⅔ cup sour cream
- ⅔ cup mayonnaise
- ¼ cup fresh lemon juice
- 2 scallions, minced
- ½ teaspoon chopped thyme
- ½ teaspoon finely grated lemon zest
- 1 tablespoon plus 2 teaspoons chopped flat-leaf parsley

Salt and freshly ground pepper

- 6 large wedges of iceberg lettuce (1½ heads)
- 6 radishes, very thinly sliced

1. In a bowl, using the back of a fork, lightly mash the Roquefort with the sour cream and mayonnaise. Stir in the lemon juice, scallions, thyme, lemon zest and 2 teaspoons of the chopped flat-leaf parsley. Season the blue cheese dressing with salt and pepper.

2. Set the iceberg lettuce wedges on a chilled serving platter. Spoon a generous amount of the blue cheese dressing over each lettuce wedge. Top with the thinly sliced radishes and the remaining 1 tablespoon of chopped parsley and serve. —*Tom Douglas*

### Fresh Green Salad with Citrus Vinaigrette

TOTAL: 30 MIN

8 SERVINGS ● ●

Zest and juice of 1 lemon

- 3 navel oranges, 1 zested
- 1 teaspoon Dijon mustard
- ¼ cup extra-virgin olive oil

Salt and freshly ground pepper

- 2 ruby red grapefruits
- 14 ounces mesclun
- ¼ cup finely chopped flat-leaf parsley

1. In a small bowl, combine the lemon zest with the lemon juice and orange zest. Squeeze the juice from the zested orange into the bowl. Whisk in the mustard and olive oil and season the vinaigrette with salt and pepper.

2. Using a sharp knife, remove the peel and bitter white pith from the remaining 2 oranges and the grapefruits. Working over a plate, cut between the membranes to release the segments.

3. In a large bowl, toss the mesclun with the chopped parsley and the citrus vinaigrette; season the salad with salt and pepper. Add the citrus segments to the greens and serve right away. —*Pascal Rigo*

## Lefty's Green Salad
TOTAL: 20 MIN
8 SERVINGS ● ●
- 2 tablespoons fresh lemon juice
- 1½ tablespoons sherry vinegar
- ½ teaspoon dry mustard
- Pinch of five-spice powder
- 1½ tablespoons minced shallot
- 1 small garlic clove, minced
- ¼ cup plus 2 tablespoons extra-virgin olive oil
- Salt and freshly ground pepper
- 1 pound mixed baby greens
- ¼ cup cilantro leaves
- ¼ cup celery leaves
- ¼ cup flat-leaf parsley leaves
- ¼ cup chives (in 1-inch pieces)

In a large bowl, whisk the lemon juice with the vinegar, mustard, five-spice powder, shallot and garlic. Slowly whisk in the olive oil and season with salt and pepper. Add the baby greens, cilantro, celery leaves, parsley and chives and toss to coat. Season with salt and pepper, toss again and serve. —*Daniel Orr*

## Crisp Winter Salad with Ginger-Garlic Vinaigrette
TOTAL: 20 MIN
4 TO 6 SERVINGS ● ●
- 1 head radicchio (7 ounces), cored and finely shredded
- 6 Belgian endives, sliced crosswise ¼ inch thick
- ¼ cup extra-virgin olive oil
- 2 garlic cloves, minced
- 1 tablespoon minced fresh ginger
- 2 tablespoons rice vinegar
- Salt

In a large bowl, toss the radicchio and endives. In a skillet, heat the olive oil. Add the garlic and ginger and cook over moderate heat until fragrant, about 2 minutes. Remove from the heat and add the vinegar. Stir and pour over the salad. Sprinkle with salt, toss well and serve. —*Naomi Duguid and Jeffrey Alford*

## Lemony Greens with Olive Oil and Olives
TOTAL: 15 MIN
4 TO 6 SERVINGS ● ● ●
- 1¼ pounds young spinach
- Extra-virgin olive oil
- 2 lemons, 1 juiced, 1 sliced
- Salt
- Assorted Greek olives

In a large skillet of boiling salted water, cook the spinach for 3 minutes. Drain well in a colander and transfer to a bowl. Add olive oil and a little lemon juice and toss the spinach to coat; season with salt and, if necessary, more lemon juice and olive oil. Scatter the olives on top, garnish with the lemon slices and serve warm or at room temperature. —*Diane Kochilas*

## Endive Salad with Grainy-Mustard Vinaigrette
TOTAL: 20 MIN
6 SERVINGS ● ●
This mustardy dressing is so good it's worth doubling the recipe and refrigerating the extra for later in the week.
- 2 tablespoons French whole-grain mustard
- 1 tablespoon sherry vinegar
- 1 tablespoon fresh lemon juice
- ¼ cup extra-virgin olive oil
- ¼ cup canola oil
- Salt and freshly ground pepper
- 3 large white Belgian endives, separated into spears
- 3 large red Belgian endives, separated into spears, or 3 heads radicchio, torn into bite-size pieces

In a large bowl, whisk the mustard with the vinegar and lemon juice. Gradually whisk in the olive and canola oils and season with salt and pepper. Add the white and red endive spears and toss gently to coat. Serve right away. —*Geoffrey Zakarian*

## Mixed Lettuces with Orange Vinaigrette and Candied Pecans
TOTAL: 25 MIN
8 SERVINGS ● ●
- 1½ cups pecan halves (6 ounces)
- 3 tablespoons sugar
- 2 tablespoons pure maple syrup
- ¼ teaspoon cayenne pepper
- Kosher salt
- 1 head each butter and red leaf lettuces, torn into bite-size pieces
- Seeds from 1 large pomegranate
- 3 tablespoons Champagne or white wine vinegar
- 1 tablespoon grated orange zest
- ⅓ cup extra-virgin olive oil
- Freshly ground black pepper

**1.** In a nonstick skillet, toast the pecans over moderately low heat, stirring, until golden, 8 minutes. Add the sugar, maple syrup, cayenne and a pinch of salt and stir until coated, 2 minutes; let cool.

**2.** In a large bowl, toss the lettuces with the pomegranate seeds. In a small bowl, combine the vinegar and zest. Whisk in the oil and season with salt and black pepper. Toss the salad with the dressing, add the pecans and serve. —*Russ Pillar*

## Mixed Greens with Nuts and Dried Fruit
TOTAL: 25 MIN
12 SERVINGS ● ●
- 1 cup walnuts (4 ounces)
- 1 cup pecan halves (4 ounces)
- 1 large shallot, minced
- ¼ cup sherry vinegar
- 1 tablespoon Dijon mustard
- 6 tablespoons extra-virgin olive oil
- ¼ cup walnut oil
- Salt and freshly ground pepper
- Four 5-ounce bags washed salad greens, such as mixed baby greens, arugula and spinach
- 1 cup dried pears, julienned (4 ounces)
- 1 cup dried cranberries (4 ounces)

ASPARAGUS SALAD WITH TOASTED WALNUTS AND GOAT CHEESE

1. Preheat the oven to 350°. Spread the nuts on a large baking sheet and bake for 10 minutes, or until golden and fragrant. Let cool, then coarsely chop.

2. In a large bowl, combine the shallot, vinegar and mustard. Whisk in the olive oil and walnut oil in a thin, steady stream. Season with salt and pepper.

3. Add the mixed greens, nuts and dried pears and cranberries to the bowl and toss. Serve immediately. —*Grace Parisi*

**MAKE AHEAD** The dressing can be refrigerated for up to 3 days.

### Mixed Greens with Spiced Pears and Almonds

**TOTAL: 45 MIN**

8 SERVINGS

Indian spices can overwhelm delicate foods like mixed greens. Temper the flavors by using the spices sparingly, as in this recipe.

- ¼ teaspoon cayenne pepper
- ¼ teaspoon ground coriander
- ¼ teaspoon ground cumin
- Kosher salt
- 1 tablespoon canola oil
- 1 cup blanched almonds (5 ounces)
- 1 tablespoon unsalted butter
- ¾ teaspoon turmeric
- 1 tablespoon wildflower honey
- 2 large Bosc pears—peeled, cored and cut into ½-inch wedges
- 2 tablespoons white balsamic vinegar
- ¼ cup extra-virgin olive oil
- Freshly ground black pepper
- 8 ounces mixed greens
- 4 ounces goat blue cheese, crumbled (¾ cup)

1. In a medium bowl, mix the cayenne, coriander, cumin and ¼ teaspoon of salt. In a medium skillet, heat the canola oil. Add the almonds and cook over moderate heat, stirring constantly, until golden, about 2 minutes. Add the hot nuts to the spices and toss to coat. Spread the nuts on a plate and let cool.

2. Melt the butter in a large nonstick skillet. When the foam subsides, add the turmeric and cook over moderately high heat until fragrant, about 30 seconds. Add 2 teaspoons of the honey and stir until melted. Add the pears in a single layer, season with a pinch of salt and cook, turning once, until softened and lightly browned, about 3 minutes. Transfer the pears to a plate.

3. In a large bowl, whisk the vinegar with the remaining 1 teaspoon of honey. Whisk in the olive oil and season with salt and black pepper. Add the greens and blue cheese, season with salt and black pepper and toss to coat. Top with the spiced almonds and pears and serve.
—*Akasha Richmond*

### Asparagus Salad with Toasted Walnuts and Goat Cheese

**TOTAL: 30 MIN**

6 SERVINGS ●

- 1 cup walnut halves (4 ounces)
- ½ teaspoon fennel seeds
- 2 pounds medium asparagus
- ¼ cup extra-virgin olive oil
- 1½ tablespoons sherry vinegar
- 1 large scallion, white and light green parts only, very finely chopped
- 1 tablespoon chopped tarragon
- 1 tablespoon chopped mint
- Salt and freshly ground pepper
- 4 ounces goat cheese, such as Bûcheron, rind removed, cheese crumbled

1. Preheat the oven to 350°. Spread the walnuts on a small baking sheet and bake them for 8 minutes, or until lightly toasted. Transfer to a plate to cool, then break in half lengthwise.

2. Meanwhile, in a small skillet, toast the fennel seeds over moderately high heat until fragrant and golden, about 20 seconds. Transfer to a work surface and let cool, then finely chop.

3. Pour ½ inch of water into a large pot fitted with a large steamer basket and bring to a boil. Discard the tough ends from the asparagus and add the spears to the steamer; cover and steam over high heat until just tender, about 4 minutes. Transfer to paper towels and pat dry. Let cool to room temperature, then cut on the diagonal into 2-inch lengths.

4. Meanwhile, in a large bowl, whisk the olive oil with the vinegar, scallion, tarragon, mint and chopped fennel seeds. Season with salt and pepper.

5. Add the asparagus and walnuts to the bowl and toss. Add the goat cheese. Season with salt and pepper, transfer to plates and serve. —*Marcia Kiesel*

### Escarole and Fresh Herb Salad with Apples and Pomegranate

**TOTAL: 20 MIN**

10 SERVINGS ● ●

When working with pomegranates, cut them in quarters, bend back the peels and pry out the seeds. Discard any membrane that's still attached to the seeds.

- 3 tablespoons fresh lemon juice
- 2 tablespoons plain whole milk yogurt
- 1 tablespoon soy sauce
- 1 garlic clove, minced
- ¼ cup plus 2 tablespoons extra-virgin olive oil
- Salt and freshly ground pepper
- 2 heads escarole, tough dark leaves discarded, inner leaves torn
- 1 cup flat-leaf parsley leaves
- ⅓ cup snipped chives
- ¼ cup tarragon leaves
- 2 tablespoons small mint leaves
- 2 scallions, white and light green parts only, cut into 1½-inch lengths and sliced lengthwise
- 2 Granny Smith apples—quartered, cored and thinly sliced
- 1 cup pomegranate seeds (from 1 large pomegranate)

# salads

In a large salad bowl, whisk the lemon juice, yogurt, soy sauce and garlic until blended. Whisk in the olive oil in a thin stream and season the vinaigrette with salt and pepper. Add the escarole, parsley, chives, tarragon, mint, scallions and apples and toss until evenly coated. Sprinkle the pomegranate seeds on top and serve right away. —*Gabriel Kreuther*

# ingredient

**1 L'ABBÉ ROUS BANYULS VINEGAR** Made from a sherrylike wine ($18 for 17.6 ounces; 877-337-2491 or chefshop.com).
**2 MARTIN POURET CHARDONNAY VINEGAR** From France's last great Orléans artisan ($13 for 17.6 ounces; 888-212-3224 or formaggiokitchen.com).
**3 WENTE VINEYARDS CHAMPAGNE VINEGAR** Subtle and grapey ($10 for 12.7 ounces; 925-456-2305 or wentevineyards.com).
**4 NIEBAUM-COPPOLA CABERNET VINEGAR** A mild, barrel-aged wine vinegar ($13 for 6.8 ounces; 800-575-9927 or niebaum-coppola.com).

## Apple Salad with Cabrales Cheese and Toasted Almonds
**TOTAL: 40 MIN**
6 SERVINGS

- 1 cup blanched almonds (5 ounces)
- 7 medium garlic cloves
- ¼ cup extra-virgin olive oil
- 2 tablespoons sherry vinegar
- 1 tablespoon very finely chopped shallot

Kosher salt and freshly ground black pepper
- 3 large Granny Smith apples
- 2 tablespoons chopped chives
- 5 ounces Cabrales cheese, crumbled

**1.** Preheat the oven to 350°. Spread the almonds on a baking sheet and bake for 10 minutes, or until lightly toasted. Let cool, then coarsely chop.
**2.** In a small saucepan, cook the garlic cloves in the olive oil over moderately high heat until golden, about 5 minutes. Remove from the heat and let cool.
**3.** Transfer the garlic and oil to a blender. Add the vinegar and shallot, season with salt and pepper and blend until smooth.
**4.** Halve and core the apples, then cut them into ¼-inch matchsticks. In a large bowl, toss the apples with the almonds, chives and dressing. Top the salad with the crumbled Cabrales and serve.
—*José Andrés*

## Frisée Salad with Pears, Blue Cheese and Hazelnuts
**TOTAL: 20 MIN**
4 SERVINGS ●

- ¼ cup hazelnut oil
- 2 tablespoons red wine vinegar

Salt and freshly ground pepper
- 1 medium head radicchio, torn into bite-size pieces
- 1 medium head frisée, torn into bite-size pieces
- 1 medium endive, cut crosswise into 1-inch pieces

- 2 ripe Bartlett pears, each cored and cut into 8 wedges
- 4 ounces blue cheese, crumbled (1 cup)
- ½ cup salted roasted hazelnuts, coarsely chopped

In a large bowl, whisk the hazelnut oil with the red wine vinegar and season with salt and pepper. Add the radicchio, frisée and endive and toss until coated. Add the pears, blue cheese and hazelnuts, season with salt and pepper, toss gently and serve. —*Bill Telepan*

## Frisée and Endive Salad with Pears and Blue Cheese
**TOTAL: 30 MIN**
10 SERVINGS ● ●
This salty, sweet and crunchy salad is a light and delicious start to any meal.

- 2 tablespoons balsamic vinegar
- 1 tablespoon sherry vinegar
- 1 tablespoon minced shallot
- 1½ teaspoons Dijon mustard
- ½ cup extra-virgin olive oil
- 2 tablespoons hazelnut oil
- 2 tablespoons walnut oil
- 1 teaspoon finely chopped thyme

Salt and freshly ground pepper
- 3 heads frisée (about 1¼ pounds total), torn into bite-size pieces
- 4 large endives (about 1 pound total)—halved, cored and cut into 1-inch pieces
- 2 ripe Bartlett pears—peeled, cored and thinly sliced
- 4 ounces blue cheese, crumbled (1 cup)

In a large salad bowl, whisk the balsamic and sherry vinegars with the shallot and mustard. Slowly whisk in the olive oil, then the hazelnut and walnut oils. Add the thyme and season with salt and pepper. Add the frisée and endives and toss to coat. Add the pears and blue cheese, toss gently and serve right away.
—*Lee Hefter*

## Cantaloupe and Prosciutto Salad with Ice Wine Vinaigrette

**TOTAL: 20 MIN**

**4 SERVINGS** ●

- 2 tablespoons ice wine (eiswein) or other sweet white dessert wine
- 1 tablespoon extra-virgin olive oil
- 1 teaspoon Champagne vinegar
- 2 teaspoons balsamic vinegar, preferably aged

Salt and freshly ground pepper

One 2-pound cantaloupe—halved, seeded and cut lengthwise into ¼-inch-thick slices

- ½ pound *burrata* (cream-filled mozzarella) or fresh buffalo mozzarella, at room temperature, cut into 4 slices
- 4 thin slices of prosciutto
- 1½ ounces baby arugula (2 cups)

1. In a small bowl, combine the ice wine, olive oil and Champagne and balsamic vinegars. Season with salt and pepper.
2. In a large bowl, drizzle the cantaloupe with 1½ tablespoons of the dressing and toss to coat. Arrange the slices on plates. Set a slice of *burrata* on the melon and drizzle the plates with 1 tablespoon of the dressing. Drape a slice of prosciutto over the cheese. In the large bowl, toss the arugula with the remaining dressing. Top the salads with the arugula and serve right away. —*Eric Michel Klein*

## Tricolore Salad with Walnuts and Prosciutto

**TOTAL: 15 MIN**

**4 TO 6 SERVINGS** ●

- ¾ cup walnut halves (3 ounces)
- 1 large shallot, minced
- 2 tablespoons sherry vinegar
- 1½ teaspoons Dijon mustard
- ¼ cup plus 2 tablespoons extra-virgin olive oil

Salt and freshly ground pepper

- 3 endives, cored and cut crosswise 1 inch thick
- 1 medium radicchio—cored, halved and thinly sliced
- 1 bunch arugula, thick stems trimmed
- ¼ cup flat-leaf parsley leaves
- 3 ounces thinly sliced prosciutto, fat removed, prosciutto torn into pieces

1. Preheat the oven to 350°. Spread the walnuts in a pie plate and toast for about 8 minutes, or until fragrant and golden. Let cool to room temperature.
2. In a large bowl, combine the shallot with the vinegar and let stand for 5 minutes. Whisk in the mustard, then, in a thin stream, whisk in the oil. Season generously with salt and pepper. Add the endives, radicchio, arugula, parsley and walnuts and toss to coat. Top with the prosciutto and serve. —*Tina Ujlaki*

## Mixed Salad with Bacon, Blue Cheese and Pecans

**TOTAL: 30 MIN**

**8 SERVINGS** ●

- 1½ cups pecan halves (6 ounces)
- 8 thick slices of bacon (4 ounces)
- ⅓ cup plus 1 tablespoon cider vinegar
- 1 teaspoon Dijon mustard
- 1 garlic clove, minced

Pinch of sugar

- ⅔ cup extra-virgin olive oil

Salt and freshly ground pepper

- 2 bunches watercress (¾ pound total), tough stems discarded
- 1 pound arugula, tough stems discarded
- 1 head frisée (8 ounces), torn into bite-size pieces
- 2 large carrots, coarsely shredded
- 6 ounces blue cheese, such as Maytag, crumbled (1½ cups)
- 1 Hass avocado, cut into ½-inch dice

1. Preheat the oven to 350°. Spread the pecans in a pie plate and bake for 10 minutes, or until lightly toasted. Transfer to a plate to cool.
2. In a medium skillet, cook the bacon over moderately high heat until browned and crisp, about 7 minutes. Drain on paper towels and crumble.
3. In a small bowl, whisk the vinegar with the mustard, garlic and sugar. Slowly whisk in the olive oil and season with salt and pepper.
4. In a very large bowl, toss the watercress, arugula and frisée with the carrots and toasted pecans. Pour half of the dressing over the greens and toss. Add the blue cheese, bacon, avocado and the remaining dressing and toss. Season with salt and pepper and serve. —*Mary Lynn Van Wyck*

## Lemon and Arugula Salad with Parmesan Cheese

**TOTAL: 20 MIN**

**20 SERVINGS** ● ●

Six 4-ounce bunches arugula

- 2 lemons, sliced paper-thin

Extra-virgin olive oil, for drizzling

Salt and freshly ground pepper

- 4 ounces Parmesan cheese, shaved

In a very large bowl, toss the arugula with the lemon slices. Drizzle with the extra-virgin olive oil, season with salt and pepper and toss again. Scatter the shaved Parmesan on top of the salad and serve at once. —*Tommy Habetz*

## Arugula, Fennel and Orange Salad

**TOTAL: 20 MIN**

**6 SERVINGS** ● ●

- 3 navel oranges
- 3 tablespoons extra-virgin olive oil
- 2 tablespoons balsamic vinegar

Salt and freshly ground pepper

- 1 medium fennel bulb— trimmed, cored and thinly sliced crosswise
- 4 scallions, white and tender green parts only, thinly sliced
- 2 bunches arugula, trimmed

# salads

1. Using a sharp knife, peel the oranges, taking care to remove all of the bitter white pith; slice the oranges crosswise ¼ inch thick.

2. In a large bowl, whisk the olive oil and vinegar and season with salt and pepper. Add the fennel, scallions and arugula and toss well. Add the orange slices, season with salt and pepper and serve.
—*Steven Wagner*

## Radicchio Salad with Oranges and Fennel
**TOTAL: 30 MIN**
8 SERVINGS ● ●

- 2 large navel oranges
- 3 tablespoons extra-virgin olive oil
- 2 tablespoons red wine vinegar
- Salt and freshly ground pepper
- 1 large romaine heart, coarsely chopped
- 1 small head radicchio, finely shredded
- 1 small red onion, thinly sliced
- 1 medium fennel bulb, cored and thinly sliced lengthwise

1. Using a small, sharp knife, peel the oranges, taking care to remove all of the bitter white pith. Slice the oranges crosswise ¼ inch thick.

2. In a very large bowl, combine the olive oil with the vinegar and season with salt and pepper. Add the orange slices, romaine, radicchio, red onion and fennel and toss well. Serve right away.
—*Rachael Ray*

## Fennel Salad with Parmesan
**TOTAL: 15 MIN**
6 SERVINGS ● ●

- 3 fennel bulbs, halved lengthwise and cored, fronds reserved
- ⅓ cup chopped pitted Calamata olives
- 2 tablespoons fresh lemon juice
- 1 tablespoon capers, drained and chopped

Kosher salt and freshly ground pepper
- 3 tablespoons extra-virgin olive oil
- 2 ounces Parmesan cheese, shaved (¾ cup loosely packed)

1. Using a mandoline, thinly slice the fennel bulbs. Coarsely chop enough of the fennel fronds to equal ¼ cup.

2. In a large bowl, whisk the olives with the lemon juice, capers and ¾ teaspoon each of salt and pepper. Slowly drizzle in the olive oil, whisking constantly. Add the fennel slices and chopped fronds and toss well. Mound the salad on plates, top with the Parmesan cheese and serve.
—*Melissa Clark*

## Chopped Fennel and Olive Salad
**TOTAL: 30 MIN**
6 SERVINGS ● ●

- 2 anchovy fillets, mashed
- 1½ tablespoons fresh lemon juice
- ½ cup jarred green olives (3 ounces), pitted and chopped, plus 1½ tablespoons of brine from the jar
- ¼ cup plus 2 tablespoons extra-virgin olive oil
- 1 small seedless cucumber— peeled, halved lengthwise and cut into ½-inch dice
- ½ fennel bulb, cut into ½-inch dice
- 4 inner celery ribs, thinly sliced
- 1 medium heart of romaine, cut into ½-inch strips
- 1 medium bunch arugula, torn into bite-size pieces
- 1 small head radicchio, chopped
- Salt and freshly ground pepper
- 3 ounces Parmesan cheese, shaved (1 cup)

In a bowl, mash the anchovies and lemon juice. Whisk in the olive brine and then the oil. Add the olives, cucumber, fennel, celery, romaine, arugula and radicchio; season with salt and pepper. Top with the Parmesan shavings and serve.
—*Jody Denton*

## Chickpea Puree with Fennel Salad
**ACTIVE: 40 MIN; TOTAL: 3 HR, PLUS SOAKING**
4 SERVINGS ●

- 1 cup dried chickpeas (6½ ounces), soaked overnight or quick-soaked and drained (see Note p. 74)
- Salt
- 7 tablespoons extra-virgin olive oil, plus more for drizzling
- 1 small onion, minced
- 1 small rosemary sprig
- Pinch of dried oregano
- 1 tablespoon fresh lemon juice
- Freshly ground pepper
- 1 small fennel bulb, cored and sliced paper-thin
- Parmesan cheese shavings and crostini, for serving

1. In a medium saucepan, cover the chickpeas with water by 2 inches and bring to a boil. Simmer over moderately low heat until tender, about 2½ hours. Keep adding water as necessary so the chickpeas are always submerged in 1 inch of water. Remove them from the heat and season with salt. Drain the chickpeas, reserving the cooking liquid.

2. In a large skillet, heat 6 tablespoons of the olive oil until shimmering. Add the onion, rosemary and oregano and cook over moderate heat until softened, about 6 minutes. Add the chickpeas and 2 cups of their cooking liquid and simmer, mashing the chickpeas with a spoon, until most of the liquid has been absorbed, 5 minutes. Discard the rosemary. Press the puree through a food mill. Season with salt and keep warm.

3. In a medium bowl, mix the lemon juice with the remaining 1 tablespoon of olive oil and season with salt and pepper. Add the fennel and toss to coat. Mound the chickpea puree and fennel salad on plates. Top with Parmesan shavings, drizzle with olive oil and serve with crostini.
—*Christophe Hille*

### Turkish Chopped Salad
**TOTAL: 25 MIN**
**6 SERVINGS** ● ● ●

- 3 medium garlic cloves, minced
- 2 tablespoons extra-virgin olive oil
- 2 teaspoons pomegranate molasses
- ½ teaspoon crushed red pepper

Salt

- 2 large tomatoes, cut into ¼-inch dice
- 2 medium cucumbers—peeled, halved lengthwise, seeded and and cut into ¼-inch dice
- 2 scallions, minced
- 1 green bell pepper, cut into ¼-inch dice
- 1 red onion, cut into ¼-inch dice
- ½ cup chopped flat-leaf parsley
- ¼ cup chopped mint leaves

1. In a small bowl, combine the garlic, olive oil, molasses and crushed red pepper. Season the dressing with salt.
2. In a large bowl, toss the tomatoes with the cucumbers, scallions, bell pepper, onion, parsley and mint. Pour the dressing over the salad and toss well. Serve at once. —*Musa Dagdeviren*

**MAKE AHEAD** The salad can be refrigerated for up to 1 hour.

### Feta, Tomato and Red Onion Salad
**TOTAL: 15 MIN**
**6 SERVINGS** ● ● ●

This quick and delicious Turkish salad is a great filling for pita bread and a wonderful topping for bruschetta.

- 5 ounces French feta cheese, crumbled (1¼ cups)
- 2 large ripe tomatoes—halved, seeded and cut into ½-inch pieces, or 1½ pints cherry or grape tomatoes, halved and seeded
- 1 medium red onion, finely chopped
- 1 jalapeño, seeded and thinly sliced
- 2 tablespoons minced flat-leaf parsley
- 3 tablespoons extra-virgin olive oil

Salt

In a large bowl, gently toss the feta cheese with the tomatoes, onion, jalapeño and parsley. Drizzle the olive oil over the salad, season with salt and toss until coated. Serve the salad at room temperature. —*Anissa Helou*

**MAKE AHEAD** The salad can be covered and refrigerated for up to 4 hours. Let return to room temperature, then serve.

### Swiss Chard Salad with Garlicky Yogurt
**TOTAL: 35 MIN**
**6 SERVINGS** ● ● ●

This Cypriot salad is particularly refreshing. Instead of blanching the Swiss chard in boiling water, here you rub salt into the leaves and then wilt them in a warm skillet, thus retaining all the vibrant color and flavor.

- 1 medium red bell pepper
- 2 pounds Swiss chard, leaves only, finely chopped

Kosher salt

- 3 tablespoons extra-virgin olive oil
- 5 medium garlic cloves, minced
- 1 cup plain whole milk yogurt
- ¼ cup tahini, at room temperature
- 3 tablespoons fresh lemon juice
- ¼ teaspoon crushed red pepper
- 1 tablespoon chopped flat-leaf parsley

1. Roast the bell pepper directly over a gas flame or under a preheated broiler, turning as needed, until charred all over. Transfer to a bowl, cover and let steam for 10 minutes. Peel and seed the pepper, then cut into ¼-inch dice.
2. Put the Swiss chard in a colander set in the sink. Sprinkle 1 tablespoon of salt over the chard and rub it into the leaves with your fingers. Let stand for 1 minute, then rinse the chard and squeeze dry.
3. Heat 2 tablespoons of the oil in a large skillet. Add 2 of the minced garlic cloves and cook over moderate heat until fragrant, about 1 minute. Add the chard and cook, stirring, until tender, about 7 minutes. Add the roasted pepper and cook for 1 minute. Transfer the vegetables to a platter. Spread in an even layer; let cool.
4. In a medium bowl, mix the yogurt with the tahini, lemon juice and the remaining 3 minced garlic cloves. Season with salt. Spoon the sauce over the vegetables.
5. In a skillet, heat the remaining 1 tablespoon of olive oil. Add the crushed red pepper and cook over moderately high heat until the pepper begins to sizzle, about 10 seconds. Pour the pepper oil over the yogurt sauce, sprinkle with the parsley and serve. —*Musa Dagdeviren*

**MAKE AHEAD** The recipe can be prepared through Step 4 up to 1 day ahead. Refrigerate the vegetables and yogurt sauce separately.

# health

**THE MEDITERRANEAN DIET** **TIP**

The Mediterranean diet—with its vegetables, whole grains, fish, fresh fruit, olive oil and red wine—has blessed people in southern Greece with some of the lowest rates of heart disease and longest life expectancies in the world. But does it work elsewhere? A 2002 study published in the British medical journal *The Lancet* showed that a similar diet helped prevent heart disease in high-risk Indians. And researchers at Monash University in Australia found that Greek immigrants there who ate a traditional Greek diet—defined as a diet high in leafy greens, figs and olive oil—were less likely to die of heart disease. Foods like these are high in antioxidants, which help prevent cancer.

# salads

## Greek Salad with Garlicky Pita Toasts

**TOTAL: 30 MIN**
**6 SERVINGS** ● ●

Two 8-inch pocketless pita breads
- 2 tablespoons extra-virgin olive oil, plus more for brushing
- 1 garlic clove, halved
- 1 teaspoon dried Greek oregano, crumbled

Salt and freshly ground pepper
- 2 medium tomatoes, cut into ½-inch dice
- 1 large red onion, chopped
- 1 large green bell pepper, cut into ½-inch dice
- 1 cucumber—peeled, halved lengthwise, seeded and cut into ½-inch dice
- 12 large, cracked green olives
- 3 pickled green peppers (peperoncini), thinly sliced
- 2 pickled red cherry peppers, seeded and thinly sliced
- 2 tablespoons drained capers
- 4 ounces feta cheese, crumbled

**1.** Preheat the oven to 400°. Brush the pita breads on both sides with olive oil and bake on the oven rack until golden, about 8 minutes. Rub the toasts on both sides with the garlic and let cool.

**2.** In a large bowl, mix the 2 tablespoons of olive oil with the oregano; season with salt and pepper. Add the tomatoes, red onion, bell pepper, cucumber, olives, pickled peppers and capers and toss. Scatter the feta on top, toss lightly and serve with the toasts. —*Diane Kochilas*

## Fattoush

**TOTAL: 30 MIN**
**6 SERVINGS** ● ●

This Lebanese salad is very versatile. It's delicious with lettuce or with purslane, with bread or without. The fresh herbs are important not only to add flavor but also to hold the ground sumac, which gives the dish its distinctive taste.

- 1 large pita bread, split horizontally
- 1 large romaine heart, cut crosswise into ½-inch ribbons
- 1 bunch scallions, white and tender green parts only, thinly sliced
- 3 kirby cucumbers or 1 seedless cucumber—peeled, halved lengthwise and thinly sliced
- 1½ pints cherry or grape tomatoes, quartered
- 3 cups chopped flat-leaf parsley
- 1 cup fresh mint leaves
- 2½ tablespoons ground sumac (see Note p. 18) or fresh lemon juice
- 6 tablespoons extra-virgin olive oil

Salt and freshly ground pepper

**1.** Preheat the oven to 300°. Bake the pita bread directly on the oven rack for 10 minutes, or until dry and crisp but not browned. Let cool completely, then break into 1-inch pieces.

**2.** Meanwhile, in a large bowl, combine the romaine with the scallions, cucumbers, tomatoes, parsley, mint and ground sumac. Drizzle the olive oil over the salad, season with salt and pepper and toss to coat. Add the toasted pita bread pieces and toss again. Serve at once. —*Anissa Helou*

## Asian Coleslaw with Miso-Ginger Dressing

**TOTAL: 15 MIN**
**6 TO 8 SERVINGS** ● ● ● ●

This recipe makes twice as much dressing as the coleslaw requires. Keep the extra on hand for tossing with rice noodle salads, serving as a dip for crudités or spooning over broiled or sautéed fish.

- ¼ cup unseasoned rice vinegar
- 3 tablespoons white (*shiro*) miso (see p. 107)
- 1 tablespoon mayonnaise
- 1 tablespoon fresh lemon juice
- 1 teaspoon finely grated fresh ginger

Pinch of sugar
- ¾ cup grapeseed or vegetable oil

Salt and freshly ground pepper
- ½ small green cabbage, shredded (4 cups)
- ½ small red cabbage, shredded (4 cups)
- 4 medium carrots, shredded
- 4 radishes, shredded
- 3 large scallions, white and tender green parts only, julienned

**1.** In a food processor, combine the rice vinegar with the white miso, mayonnaise, lemon juice, grated ginger and the sugar and process until the mixture is completely smooth. With the machine on, add the grapeseed oil in a slow and steady stream; process until combined. Season the miso dressing with salt and pepper. Pour ½ cup of the dressing into a large bowl; cover and refrigerate the rest of the dressing for another use.

**2.** Add the green and red cabbage, carrots, radishes and scallions to the bowl and toss to coat thoroughly with the miso-ginger dressing. Serve the coleslaw slightly chilled or at room temperature. —*Grace Parisi*

**MAKE AHEAD** The dressing can be refrigerated for up to 1 week.

# ingredient

**TIP** **SESAME SEEDS**

The tofu salad on the opposite page calls for sesame seeds. Black sesame seeds are a striking alternative to the usual ivory variety. Unlike their pale, nutty and slightly sweet cousins, the darker seeds have a pleasant bitterness. Try using them to coat salmon, tuna or shrimp as well as tofu.

SESAME-CRUSTED TOFU SALAD

FETA, TOMATO AND RED ONION SALAD, P. 39

## Sesame-Crusted Tofu Salad with Citrus Vinaigrette

**TOTAL: 40 MIN**

**4 SERVINGS** ●

½ cup low-sodium soy sauce

2 tablespoons snipped chives

1 tablespoon very finely chopped fresh ginger

1½ teaspoons Asian sesame oil

2 garlic cloves, very finely chopped

1 small shallot, very finely chopped

½ cup sesame seeds

Two 14-ounce blocks soft tofu, drained, each cut into 6 slices

¼ cup pure olive oil

1 tablespoon sherry vinegar

1 tablespoon fresh orange juice

1 tablespoon fresh lemon juice

⅓ cup extra-virgin olive oil

Salt and freshly ground pepper

6 ounces mesclun

¼ cup mint leaves

¼ cup torn basil leaves

½ cup cherry tomatoes

**1.** In a small bowl, combine the soy sauce with the chives, ginger, sesame oil, garlic and shallot.

**2.** Spread the sesame seeds on a large plate. Press one side of each slice of tofu into the sesame seeds so the seeds adhere. In each of 2 large nonstick skillets, heat 2 tablespoons of the pure olive oil until shimmering. Add the tofu, coated side down, and cook over moderate heat until the seeds are lightly golden, about 9 minutes. Carefully flip the tofu slices, pour the soy mixture between them and simmer until the liquid thickens slightly, about 3 minutes.

**3.** Meanwhile, in a large bowl, mix the sherry vinegar with the orange juice, lemon juice and extra-virgin olive oil.

Season with salt and pepper. Add the mesclun, mint and basil leaves and toss well to coat. Mound the salad in shallow bowls or on plates and scatter the tomatoes all around. Transfer the tofu to the bowls and serve. —*Elizabeth Mendez*

## Pickled Asian Pear Salad with Creamy Lemon Dressing

**TOTAL: 30 MIN, PLUS OVERNIGHT MARINATING**

**12 SERVINGS** ● ●

3 cups water

¼ cup sugar

2 tablespoons kosher salt

1 teaspoon fennel seeds

1 lemon, halved

3 large Asian pears—halved, cored and thinly sliced lengthwise

¼ cup crème fraîche or sour cream

¼ cup fresh lemon juice

# salads

1 medium shallot, very
finely chopped

½ teaspoon finely grated lemon zest

½ cup extra-virgin olive oil

Salt and cayenne pepper

4 small heads frisée lettuce
(2 pounds), tender green and
white leaves only, torn into
bite-size pieces

4 bunches watercress (2 pounds),
thick stems discarded

1 red onion, very thinly sliced
lengthwise

6 ounces blue cheese, crumbled
(1½ cups)

1. In a medium bowl, combine the water, sugar, kosher salt and fennel seeds; stir to dissolve the sugar and salt. Squeeze the lemon halves over the water and drop them in the bowl. Add the Asian pears and stir to separate the slices. Cover the pears with a plate to keep them submerged and refrigerate overnight or for up to 2 days.

2. In a very large bowl, whisk the crème fraîche with the lemon juice, shallot and lemon zest. Gradually whisk in the olive oil and season with salt and cayenne.

# ingredient

TIP **VINAIGRETTE**

**NUT OILS** such as hazelnut and walnut are delicious in salads made with fruits like pears and papaya as well as bold greens like arugula. **BALSAMIC OR WINE VINEGARS** are great matches for nut oils (see page 36 for some of our favorites). The standard proportion for a vinaigrette is one part vinegar to three parts oil. Always season your vinaigrette with salt, to bring out the salad's flavor.

3. Drain the pear slices in a colander. Add the pears, frisée, watercress and red onion to the dressing, season with salt and cayenne and toss well to coat. Sprinkle the blue cheese over the salad and serve. —*Grace Parisi*

**MAKE AHEAD** The pickled pears, dressing and cleaned greens can be refrigerated separately for up to 2 days. Slice the onion just before serving.

**SERVE WITH** Sour Cream–Pecan Scones (p. 271).

## Spicy Green Papaya Salad

**TOTAL: 30 MIN**

8 SERVINGS ● ● ●

The classic northern Thai salad called *som tam* is often eaten with sticky rice and very small Thai eggplants, little tomatoes, crushed peanuts, dried shrimp, long beans, crispy pork and even salted crabs. This is a minimalist version, but it doesn't skimp on flavor: It's simply stunning.

½ cup fresh lime juice

2 garlic cloves, finely chopped

2 tablespoons Asian fish sauce

2 tablespoons sugar

2 Thai chiles, minced

1 tablespoon plus 1 teaspoon
minced peeled fresh ginger

2 pounds green papaya—peeled,
seeded and cut into
1¼-by-¼-inch sticks (see Note)

1 firm, barely ripe mango—peeled,
sliced off the pit and cut into
1¼-by-¼-inch sticks

¼ cup chopped cilantro

¼ cup shredded mint leaves

Salt

In a blender or food processor, puree the lime juice with the garlic, fish sauce, sugar, chiles and ginger. In a large bowl, toss the papaya with the mango, cilantro and mint. Add the dressing and toss to coat thoroughly. Season the salad with salt, toss again and serve at once. —*Zak Pelaccio*

**NOTE** You will probably have to go to Chinatown to find green (unripe) papaya. Alternatively, substitute a crisp vegetable such as jicama or celery.

**MAKE AHEAD** The green papaya salad can be refrigerated for up to 2 hours. Serve it slightly chilled.

## Papaya, Orange and Watercress Salad with Pancetta

**TOTAL: 20 MIN**

4 SERVINGS ● ●

4 ounces thinly sliced pancetta
(about 10 slices)

2 large navel oranges

3 tablespoons extra-virgin
olive oil

2 teaspoons Asian sesame oil

Salt and freshly ground black
pepper

One 2-pound papaya—peeled,
seeded and thinly sliced

6 large scallions, white and
tender green parts only,
thinly sliced

One 6-ounce bunch watercress,
tough stems discarded

1. In a large skillet, cook the pancetta over moderate heat until browned and crisp. Drain on paper towels and let cool, then coarsely crumble.

2. Peel the oranges with a sharp knife, removing all of the bitter white pith. Working over a strainer set over a bowl, cut in between the membranes to release the sections. Squeeze the membranes to extract the juice: You should have 3 tablespoons. Pour the orange juice into a jar. Add the olive and sesame oils, season with salt and pepper and shake. Halve the orange sections.

3. In a bowl, toss the papaya, scallions, watercress and orange pieces with the dressing. Season with salt and pepper, transfer to plates, garnish with the crumbled pancetta and serve. —*Martin Molteni*

SPICY GREEN PAPAYA SALAD

# salads

## Asian Eggplant Salad
**TOTAL: 30 MIN**
4 SERVINGS ● ●

- 4 medium Japanese eggplants (1¼ pounds total), peeled
- 2 tablespoons canola or peanut oil
- ½ teaspoon salt
- 2 tablespoons soy sauce
- 2 tablespoons extra-virgin olive oil
- 1 tablespoon Asian sesame oil
- 2 teaspoons finely chopped garlic
- 1 teaspoon sugar
- ¼ teaspoon Tabasco sauce
- 2 bunches watercress, tough stems removed

1. Preheat the oven to 425°. Slice the eggplants lengthwise ¼ inch thick.
2. Spread the canola oil on 2 nonstick rimmed baking sheets and add the eggplant slices in a single layer. Press lightly on the slices to coat them with oil, then turn them over and sprinkle with the salt. Bake for 20 minutes, or until the slices are soft and lightly browned.
3. In a bowl, mix the soy sauce, olive oil, sesame oil, garlic, sugar and Tabasco.
4. Arrange the watercress on a platter. Fold the eggplant slices in half or roll them up and arrange on the watercress. Drizzle the dressing over the salad and serve. —*Jacques Pépin*

## Mâche Salad with Beets
**ACTIVE: 30 MIN; TOTAL: 1 HR 30 MIN**
6 SERVINGS ●

Since mâche is such a delicate green, toss the salad just before serving it.

- 4 medium beets (1¼ pounds)
- Salt
- 2½ tablespoons white wine vinegar
- 1½ tablespoons Dijon mustard
- 1 small shallot, minced
- 2 teaspoons minced tarragon
- 3 tablespoons peanut oil
- 3 tablespoons extra-virgin olive oil
- Freshly ground pepper
- 8 ounces mâche

1. In a medium saucepan, cover the beets with water. Add a pinch of salt and bring to a boil. Simmer over moderate heat until tender, about 1 hour. Drain and let cool slightly. Peel the beets, then cut them into thick matchsticks and transfer to a bowl.
2. In a large bowl, whisk the vinegar with the mustard, shallot and tarragon. Whisk in the peanut and olive oils and season with salt and pepper.
3. Add 3 tablespoons of the vinaigrette to the beets and toss well. Add the mâche to the remaining vinaigrette and toss well. Add the beets and toss. Transfer the salad to plates and serve at once. —*Jacques Pépin*

**MAKE AHEAD** The recipe can be prepared through Step 2 up to 1 day in advance. Refrigerate both the vinaigrette and the cooked beets, whole and unpeeled.

## Cucumber Salad with Mint and Crème Fraîche
**ACTIVE: 25 MIN; TOTAL: 1 HR 30 MIN, PLUS 4 HR MARINATING**
8 SERVINGS ●

- 2 medium seedless cucumbers— peeled, halved lengthwise and sliced crosswise ¼ inch thick
- 1 teaspoon kosher salt
- ½ cup crème fraîche or sour cream
- ¼ cup minced shallots
- ¼ cup finely chopped mint
- 1 tablespoon fresh lemon juice
- ½ teaspoon finely grated lemon zest
- Freshly ground pepper

1. In a colander set over a bowl, toss the cucumbers with the salt and let stand for 1 hour. Rinse the cucumbers and pat dry.
2. In a medium bowl, mix the crème fraîche with the shallots, mint, lemon juice and zest and a generous pinch of pepper. Add the cucumbers, toss to coat and refrigerate for 4 hours. Stir the salad just before serving. —*Mary Lynn Van Wyck*

**MAKE AHEAD** The cucumber salad can be refrigerated for up to 12 hours.

## Herb-Marinated Mushroom and Celery Salad
**TOTAL: 30 MIN, PLUS 2 DAYS MARINATING**
12 SERVINGS ● ●

- 1 bottle (750 ml) dry white wine
- 1½ cups extra-virgin olive oil
- ½ cup white wine vinegar
- 16 garlic cloves, 15 coarsely chopped, 1 minced
- 4 mint sprigs
- 4 thyme sprigs
- 4 oregano sprigs
- 2 tarragon sprigs
- Kosher salt and freshly ground black pepper
- 4½ pounds mixed mushrooms— such as white button, shiitake and cremini—stems discarded, large mushrooms quartered
- 12 medium celery ribs, sliced crosswise ⅛ inch thick
- ¼ cup finely chopped flat-leaf parsley

1. In a large pot, combine the wine, olive oil, vinegar, coarsely chopped garlic and the mint, thyme, oregano and tarragon sprigs and bring to a boil. Reduce the heat to moderate and simmer for 5 minutes. Add 1 tablespoon of kosher salt and 1 teaspoon of pepper and return to a boil. Add the mushrooms; boil over moderately high heat for 2 minutes. With a slotted spoon, transfer the mushrooms to a large bowl. Boil the mushroom cooking liquid over high heat until reduced by one-third, about 10 minutes. Let the cooking liquid cool to room temperature, then season it with salt and pour it over the mushrooms. Cover and refrigerate for at least 2 days or for up to 1 week.
2. Drain the mushrooms, reserving 1 cup of the marinade. Pour the reserved marinade into a medium saucepan and boil until reduced to ⅓ cup, about 7 minutes. Transfer the marinade to a medium bowl and let cool to room temperature. Add the

minced garlic and season with salt. Stir in the celery and parsley. Spread the celery on a platter, spoon the marinated mushrooms on top and serve.
—*Marcia Kiesel*

**MAKE AHEAD** The mushrooms can marinate in the refrigerator for up to 1 week.

## Corn Bread Salad with Tomatoes and Pepper Jack Cheese

**TOTAL: 30 MIN**

4 SERVINGS ●

1 pound corn bread (not sweet), cut into 1-inch cubes
½ cup vegetable oil
1½ tablespoons dried oregano
¼ cup rice vinegar
1½ teaspoons Dijon mustard
Salt and freshly ground pepper
1½ pints cherry or grape tomatoes, halved
1½ cups shredded Pepper Jack cheese
½ cup coarsely chopped cilantro leaves
1 small red onion, very thinly sliced
½ cup toasted shelled pumpkin seeds
Lime wedges, for serving

1. Preheat the oven to 400°. Toast the corn bread cubes in a single layer on a large, rimmed baking sheet, turning once, until golden.

2. In a medium skillet, heat the oil with the oregano over low heat until fragrant, about 8 minutes. Let cool, then strain the oregano oil. In a small bowl, whisk the rice vinegar and Dijon mustard. Slowly whisk in the oregano oil and season the dressing with salt and pepper.

3. In a large bowl, combine the corn bread, tomatoes, cheese, cilantro, onion and pumpkin seeds. Add the dressing and toss well. Transfer the salad to plates and serve with lime wedges.
—*Ilene Rosen*

## Tomato Salad with Scallions and Balsamic Dressing

**ACTIVE: 25 MIN; TOTAL: 1 HR 15 MIN**

8 SERVINGS ● ●

3½ pounds large beefsteak tomatoes, peeled and thinly sliced
2 tablespoons white wine vinegar
1 tablespoon balsamic vinegar
1 teaspoon sugar
1 teaspoon paprika
½ cup extra-virgin olive oil
Salt and freshly ground pepper
6 scallions, white and tender green parts only, thinly sliced
1 cup shredded basil

Arrange the tomatoes on a large platter. In a small bowl, whisk the white wine and balsamic vinegars with the sugar and paprika. Slowly whisk in the olive oil and season with salt and pepper. Stir in the scallions and half of the basil. Pour the dressing over the tomatoes and let stand at room temperature for 1 hour. Sprinkle with the remaining basil and serve.
—*Mary Lynn Van Wyck*

## Escarole and Tomato Salad with Shaved Piave Cheese

**TOTAL: 25 MIN**

8 SERVINGS ●

2 pounds large heirloom tomatoes—cored, halved lengthwise and thickly sliced into half-moons
Salt and freshly ground pepper
½ cup extra-virgin olive oil
2 tablespoons fresh lemon juice
2 pounds escarole, inner leaves only, torn into bite-size pieces
3 cups Piave (see Note) or Asiago cheese shavings

1. On a large platter, season the tomatoes with salt and pepper. Drizzle them with ¼ cup of the olive oil and gently toss. Let stand for 10 minutes.

2. Meanwhile, in a large bowl, combine the remaining ¼ cup of oil and lemon juice. Add the escarole, season with salt and pepper and toss. Mound the escarole on a platter, top with the tomatoes, their juices and the cheese shavings and serve. —*Ashley Christensen*

**NOTE** Italian Piave, a nutty-sweet aged cow's-milk cheese, is available at specialty cheese shops.

# ingredient

**DESIGNER RADICCHIO**     **TIP**

Perhaps you thought deep maroon radicchio was exotic. Now Bella Vita Produce is importing two Italian "designer" radicchios: Castelfranco (above), which tastes mildly sweet at first, then delicately sharp; and Late Red di Treviso, with long, skinny, purple-tipped white ribs. Both are terrific in salads, or simply chopped and tossed with olive oil and salt; the sturdier Treviso can also be grilled ($14 to $20 per pound; 800-491-8482). U.S. relatives of both are showing up at farmers' markets and specialty food shops.

**TOMATO AND MOZZARELLA SALAD**

**TANGY TOMATILLO SALAD**

### Tomato and Mozzarella Salad with Frozen Balsamic Vinaigrette

**TOTAL: 20 MIN, PLUS 1 HR 30 MIN FREEZING**

6 SERVINGS

Cubes of sweet watermelon are the surprise element in this unconventional tomato and mozzarella salad topped with scrapings of tangy balsamic granita.

- ½ cup white balsamic vinegar
- 2 tablespoons water
- 2 pounds assorted tomatoes, including halved cherry, pear or grape tomatoes and large tomatoes, sliced ¼ inch thick
- 1 pound fresh mozzarella, sliced ¼ inch thick

Salt and freshly ground pepper

- 1 cup seedless watermelon cubes
- ½ cup coarsely chopped basil
- 2 tablespoons extra-virgin olive oil

**1.** In an 8-inch-square glass baking dish, mix the balsamic vinegar and water. Freeze the mixture, stirring every 20 minutes or so with a fork, until the crystals in the granita are no longer slushy, about 1½ hours.

**2.** On a large platter, arrange the sliced tomatoes and mozzarella in a slightly overlapping circle; season with salt and pepper. Scatter the cherry tomato halves, watermelon cubes and basil on top and drizzle with the olive oil. Scrape the granita over the salad with a fork and serve. —*Walter Manzke*

### Tangy Tomatillo Salad with Sun-Dried Tomatoes

**TOTAL: 35 MIN**

8 SERVINGS ● ●

Add cherry or grape tomatoes to this salad for sweetness and color.

- 1 cup loosely packed, drained oil-packed sun-dried tomatoes
- 1½ pounds large tomatillos—husked, rinsed and cut into ½-inch wedges
- 1 large jalapeño, seeded and finely chopped
- 2 teaspoons finely chopped, peeled fresh ginger
- 2 teaspoons finely chopped garlic
- 3 tablespoons extra-virgin olive oil
- 3 tablespoons fresh lemon juice

Salt and freshly ground pepper

- ⅓ cup coarsely chopped cilantro

Pat the sun-dried tomatoes with paper towels to soak up some of the oil, then chop them. Transfer to a large bowl, add the tomatillos, jalapeño, ginger, garlic, olive oil and lemon juice and toss. Season with salt and pepper. Let stand for 15 minutes or for up to 4 hours. Just before serving, add the cilantro. —*Daniel Orr*

## Salade Niçoise with Fennel-Dusted Tuna

**TOTAL: 1 HR**

8 SERVINGS ●

- 1 pound small red potatoes
- Salt
- ½ pound thin green beans
- ½ cup plus 2 tablespoons extra-virgin olive oil
- 3 tablespoons red wine vinegar
- 2 tablespoons minced parsley
- 2 tablespoons minced tarragon
- 2 garlic cloves, minced
- 1 tablespoon Dijon mustard
- 1 tablespoon fresh lemon juice
- Freshly ground pepper
- 2 tablespoons pure olive oil
- 2 pounds tuna steaks, cut ½ inch thick
- 1 teaspoon fennel pollen (see Note) or ground fennel seeds
- 10 ounces mesclun
- 16 anchovy fillets
- 1 pint cherry tomatoes, halved
- 1 cup Niçoise olives
- ¼ cup chopped chives
- 2 tablespoons drained capers
- 8 hard-cooked large eggs, quartered
- Nasturtium flowers, whole and shredded (optional)

**1.** In a large saucepan, cover the potatoes with 1½ inches of water and add a large pinch of salt. Bring to a boil and simmer the potatoes over moderately high heat for 10 minutes.

**2.** Meanwhile, put the green beans in a strainer, lower it into the simmering water in the saucepan and cook until just tender, about 4 minutes; transfer the beans to a plate to cool. Check the potatoes; they should be tender a few minutes after the beans are done. Drain and halve the potatoes, then let them cool.

**3.** In a small bowl, whisk the extra-virgin olive oil with the vinegar, parsley, tarragon, garlic, mustard and lemon juice and season with salt and pepper.

**4.** In a medium skillet, heat the pure olive oil. Season the tuna steaks with salt and pepper and dust with the fennel pollen. Cook the steaks over high heat until browned on the outside and rare within, about 1½ minutes per side. Transfer to a plate and refrigerate until slightly chilled.

**5.** In a large bowl, toss the mesclun with the potatoes, green beans, anchovies, tomatoes, olives, chives and capers. Add ¼ cup plus 2 tablespoons of the vinaigrette and toss to coat.

**6.** Mound the salad on plates. Slice the tuna ⅓ inch thick and set on top of the salads. Surround with the eggs. Scatter the nasturtiums around the plates and serve, passing the remaining vinaigrette at the table. —*Sylvie Chantecaille*

**NOTE** Fennel pollen is available at specialty food shops and from Sugar Ranch (800-821-5989 or fennelpollen.com).

**MAKE AHEAD** The recipe can be prepared through Step 3 up to 1 day in advance. Refrigerate the components separately.

## Crab Salad with Apple, Endives and Pecans

**TOTAL: 25 MIN**

4 SERVINGS ●

- 3 Belgian endives, cored and sliced crosswise ¼ inch thick
- 1 Golden Delicous apple—peeled, quartered and sliced crosswise ⅛ inch thick
- ¼ cup plus 3 tablespoons heavy cream
- 2 tablespoons ketchup
- 2 tablespoons plus 1 teaspoon red wine vinegar
- 1 tablespoon mayonnaise
- 2 teaspoons Dijon mustard
- ¾ pound lump crabmeat
- Salt and freshly ground pepper
- 1 teaspoon extra-virgin olive oil
- 2 cups packed mesclun
- ⅓ cup pecan halves, toasted and coarsely chopped

**1.** In a small bowl, toss the sliced endives and apple with 3 tablespoons of the heavy cream to coat.

**2.** In a medium bowl, whip the remaining ¼ cup of heavy cream to very soft peaks. Stir in the ketchup, 1 tablespoon of the vinegar, the mayonnaise and the mustard. Fold in the crabmeat and season with salt and pepper.

**3.** Stir 1 tablespoon of the vinegar into the endives and apples and season with salt and pepper.

**4.** In a third bowl, mix the olive oil with the remaining 1 teaspoon of vinegar; season with salt and pepper. Add the mesclun and toss with the dressing. Mound the mesclun on plates. Top with the endives and apples and then the crabmeat. Sprinkle with the toasted pecans and serve. —*Jean-Georges Vongerichten*

# health

**POWER OF VINEGAR**     **TIP**

Vinegar's value in the kitchen goes beyond flavor. Its high acidity stops the growth of bacteria and mold, which makes it an efficient preservative for everything from cucumbers to herring. Several published studies have even shown that vinegar can help kill salmonella and E. coli. Vinegar's antibacterial properties also make it an effective disinfectant for cooktops, countertops and wood and plastic cutting boards. The University of Arizona's College of Agriculture and Life Sciences recommends this method: Combine one part vinegar with five parts water, pour the solution on a surface, let it stand for a few minutes and rinse.

# salads

## Asian Spinach Salad with Sausage and Pears

**TOTAL: 30 MIN**

**4 SERVINGS** ●

¼ cup fresh lemon juice

1 teaspoon soy sauce

1 teaspoon Dijon mustard

½ teaspoon Asian sesame oil

½ cup plus 1 tablespoon vegetable oil

Salt and freshly ground pepper

2 tablespoons sesame seeds

¾ pound precooked chicken and apple sausage, cut on the diagonal into ½-inch slices

One 5-ounce bag baby spinach

2 large Asian pears—peeled, cored and thinly sliced

1. In a small bowl, whisk the lemon juice, soy sauce, mustard and sesame oil. Slowly whisk in ½ cup of the vegetable oil and season with salt and pepper.

2. In a skillet, toast the sesame seeds over high heat, shaking the pan, until fragrant, 2 minutes. Transfer to a plate. Heat the remaining 1 tablespoon of vegetable oil in the skillet. Add the sausage and cook over high heat until lightly browned, 5 minutes. Transfer to a plate to cool.

3. In a large bowl, toss the spinach, pears and sesame seeds with half of the dressing; season the salad with salt and pepper. Transfer to plates. Add the sausage to the bowl and toss with the remaining dressing. Transfer the sausage to the plates and serve. —*Ilene Rosen*

# technique

**To speed the ripening of hard avocados, put them in a paper bag and leave them out on the kitchen counter for a few days.**

## Grilled Chili-Rubbed Steak Salad with Roasted Shallot Vinaigrette

**ACTIVE: 1 HR; TOTAL: 2 HR**

**6 SERVINGS**

One 2-pound flank steak

1 tablespoon Chinese chili-garlic sauce or other chili paste

1 medium yellow onion, thinly sliced

2 rosemary sprigs

2 thyme sprigs plus 1½ teaspoons thyme leaves

1 large garlic clove, minced

½ cup plus 2 tablespoons extra-virgin olive oil

Salt and freshly ground pepper

½ pound shallots, peeled and halved

¼ cup dry sherry

¼ cup water

¼ cup plus 2 tablespoons sherry vinegar

1½ teaspoons grainy mustard

½ cup canola oil

2 medium red onions, each cut into 8 wedges

1 medium head frisée, torn into bite-size pieces

1½ cups cherry tomatoes, halved

1 cup flat-leaf parsley leaves

4 ounces blue cheese, crumbled

1. In a nonreactive baking dish, rub the flank steak with the chili-garlic sauce. Top with the sliced yellow onion, rosemary and thyme sprigs, garlic and 1 tablespoon of the olive oil. Season generously with salt and pepper and rub into the steak. Let marinate at room temperature for 1 hour or refrigerate overnight.

2. Meanwhile, preheat the oven to 375°. In a small baking dish, toss the shallots with 1 tablespoon of the olive oil and 2 tablespoons of the sherry and season with salt and pepper. Roast for 25 minutes. Add the water and bake, turning the shallots occasionally, until caramelized and softened, about 25 minutes longer. Remove from the oven and let cool. Raise the oven temperature to 400°.

3. Transfer the cooled shallots and any pan juices to a blender or food processor. Add the sherry vinegar, mustard, thyme leaves and remaining 2 tablespoons of sherry; process until smooth. With the machine on, add the remaining ½ cup of olive oil and the canola oil and process until emulsified. Season the vinaigrette with salt and pepper.

4. In a small baking dish, toss the red onions with ½ cup of the shallot vinaigrette and season lightly with salt and pepper. Roast for about 30 minutes, turning occasionally, until the onions are softened and caramelized in spots. Let cool, then separate the onion layers.

5. Meanwhile, light a grill or preheat the broiler; oil the grill grates. Discard the yellow onion and herb sprigs and grill the steak over a medium-hot fire, or broil, for about 13 minutes, turning occasionally, until charred in some spots and medium rare. Transfer the steak to a cutting board and let cool completely, then thinly slice the meat across the grain.

6. In a bowl, toss the frisée, tomatoes, parsley and roasted red onions. Add the steak, blue cheese and ½ cup of the shallot vinaigrette. Season with salt and pepper, toss gently and serve.
—*Scott Dolich*

**MAKE AHEAD** The shallot vinaigrette can be refrigerated for up to 5 days. The red onions can be roasted and the steak can be grilled 1 day ahead. Refrigerate and bring to room temperature, then slice the steak before serving.

**GRILLED CHILI-STEAK SALAD SANDWICH VARIATION** Prepare the recipe through Step 5 and toss the frisée with the parsley, roasted onions and ½ cup of the vinaigrette. Grill 12 slices of country bread. Arrange tomato slices on half of the grilled bread slices and top with the frisée salad and blue cheese. Layer the grilled steak over the salad and cheese, close the sandwiches and serve.

WARM SUCCOTASH SALAD

CHICKEN, AVOCADO AND MANGO SALAD

### Spicy Chicken, Avocado and Mango Salad

**TOTAL: 25 MIN**

**4 SERVINGS** ●

- 3 tablespoons light brown sugar
- ¼ cup water
- ¼ cup plus 2 tablespoons fresh lime juice, plus lime wedges for serving
- 1 tablespoon chili-garlic sauce
- ¼ cup vegetable oil

Salt and freshly ground pepper

One 3-pound roast chicken, skin removed, meat shredded (3 cups)

- 1 ripe mango, peeled and cut into ½-inch chunks
- 1 ripe Hass avocado, peeled and cut into ½-inch chunks
- 3 scallions, thinly sliced
- 5 ounces mesclun

In a small saucepan, bring the brown sugar and water to a boil. Transfer to a large bowl. Whisk in the lime juice and chili-garlic sauce; let cool. Whisk in the oil and season with salt and pepper. Add the chicken, mango, avocado and scallions and toss thoroughly. Add the mesclun and gently toss. Transfer the salad to plates and serve with lime wedges. —*Ilene Rosen*

### Warm Succotash Salad

**TOTAL: 30 MIN**

**4 SERVINGS** ● ●

- 2 tablespoons fresh lemon juice
- 1½ teaspoons very finely chopped thyme leaves
- 1½ teaspoons very finely chopped mint leaves
- 1 small garlic clove, minced
- ½ teaspoon grated lemon zest
- ½ teaspoon sugar
- ⅓ cup plus 1 tablespoon canola oil

Salt and freshly ground pepper

- 2 ounces mesclun
- ¼ cup halved cherry tomatoes
- 1½ cups fresh corn kernels (from 3 ears)
- 1 cup shelled edamame, thawed
- 1 red bell pepper, finely diced

**1.** In a medium bowl, combine the lemon juice, thyme, mint, garlic, lemon zest and sugar. Whisk in ⅓ cup of the oil and season with salt and pepper.

**2.** In another bowl, toss the mesclun and tomatoes with 1 tablespoon of the dressing. Mound the salad in shallow bowls.

**3.** Heat the remaining 1 tablespoon of oil in a large skillet. Add the corn, edamame and bell pepper and cook over moderately high heat until crisp-tender, about 3 minutes. Add to the dressing in the bowl, season with salt and pepper and toss. Spoon the succotash over the salad and serve. —*Lucia Watson*

LENTIL SOUP WITH SERRANO HAM AND ARUGULA, P. 62

# soups

**RADISH SOUP WITH BALSAMIC CHERRIES**

**TOMATO SOUP WITH GOAT CHEESE**

### Market Radish Soup with Balsamic Cherries

**TOTAL: 30 MIN**

4 SERVINGS ● ● ●

- 12 sour or sweet cherries, pitted and halved
- 1 teaspoon balsamic vinegar
- 1 tablespoon unsalted butter
- 2 garlic cloves, thinly sliced
- 1 small onion, finely chopped

Salt and freshly ground pepper

- 1 pound radishes (preferably White Icicle) with greens, radishes sliced
- 1 teaspoon thyme leaves
- 1 quart chicken stock or low-sodium broth

**1.** In a shallow dish, sprinkle the cherries with the balsamic vinegar.

**2.** In a large saucepan, melt the butter. Add the garlic and onion and season with salt and pepper. Cook over moderately high heat, stirring frequently, until the onion is softened, about 3 minutes. Stir in the radishes, radish greens and thyme. Add the stock and bring to a boil. Simmer over moderate heat until the radishes are tender, about 10 minutes.

**3.** Working in batches, puree the radish soup in a blender and pour it into a saucepan. Reheat the soup and season it with salt and pepper. Ladle the radish soup into bowls, top with the balsamic cherries and serve. —*Mohammad Islam*

**MAKE AHEAD** The soup can be refrigerated overnight

### Summer Tomato Soup with Herbed Goat Cheese

**ACTIVE: 30 MIN; TOTAL: 1 HR 30 MIN**

8 SERVINGS ● ●

The goat cheese with basil and cilantro mellows the soup's tomatoey bite.

- 2½ pounds red tomatoes—peeled, seeded and coarsely chopped
- 1¾ pounds kirby cucumbers, peeled and coarsely chopped
- 1 cup tomato juice
- ¼ cup extra-virgin olive oil
- 2 tablespoons fresh lemon juice
- 1 small red onion, chopped
- 5 tablespoons chopped basil
- 5 tablespoons chopped cilantro

Salt and freshly ground pepper

- 6 ounces fresh goat cheese, softened
- 12 sugar snap peas, halved
- 8 cherry tomatoes, halved
- 3 radishes, thinly sliced
- ½ Hass avocado, cut into ½-inch dice

**1.** In a large bowl, toss the chopped tomatoes with the cucumbers, tomato juice, olive oil, lemon juice, onion and

3 tablespoons each of the basil and cilantro. Working in batches, puree the vegetables in a blender. Pour the soup into another large bowl, season with salt and pepper and refrigerate until chilled.

2. Meanwhile, in a small bowl, blend the goat cheese with the remaining 2 tablespoons each of basil and cilantro and season with salt and pepper.

3. In a small saucepan of boiling salted water, cook the sugar snaps until just tender, about 1 minute. Drain and refresh under cold water, then pat dry and halve.

4. Ladle the soup into shallow bowls and spoon a dollop of herbed goat cheese into the center of each. Garnish with the sugar snaps, cherry tomatoes, radishes and avocado and serve.

—*Sylvie Chantecaille*

**MAKE AHEAD** The ungarnished soup can be refrigerated overnight.

## Hot 'n' Cold Tomato Soup

**ACTIVE: 25 MIN; TOTAL: 1 HR 10 MIN**
**6 TO 8 SERVINGS** ● ●

This soup can be served hot (with a little butter stirred in) or cold; it's delicious either way.

- ¼ cup extra-virgin olive oil
- 1 medium sweet onion, thinly sliced
- 2 garlic cloves, minced
- 4 pounds tomatoes, preferably orange Mandarin, chopped

Salt and freshly ground pepper

- 2 cups chicken stock or low-sodium broth
- 2 basil sprigs
- 2 small yellow squash, finely diced
- 2 small zucchini, finely diced
- ½ cup oil-packed sun-dried tomatoes, drained and finely chopped
- 1 tablespoon unsalted butter (optional)

Sherry vinegar, for garnish

1. In a large saucepan, heat 2 tablespoons of the olive oil. Add the onion and garlic and cook over low heat, stirring occa-sionally, until softened, about 10 minutes. Add the tomatoes, season with salt and pepper and cook over high heat, stirring, until they release their juices, about 4 minutes. Add the chicken stock and basil and bring to a boil. Reduce the heat to low and simmer the soup for 45 minutes. Discard the basil sprigs.

2. Meanwhile, in a large skillet, heat the remaining 2 tablespoons of olive oil. Add the yellow squash and zucchini and cook over moderately high heat, stirring, until crisp-tender, about 2 minutes. Stir in the sun-dried tomatoes; season with salt and pepper.

3. Set a coarse strainer over a large bowl. Working in batches, puree the tomato soup in a blender until smooth, then strain it and season with salt and pepper. If serving the soup cold, let cool to room temperature, then chill; let the squash mixture cool to room temperature, too. If serving the soup hot, return it to the saucepan, simmer until heated through and stir in the butter. Add a splash of sherry vinegar to the hot or cold soup and ladle into bowls. Spoon a little of the zucchini mixture into the center of each soup and serve. —*Josiah Citrin*

**MAKE AHEAD** The soup and cooked squash can be refrigerated separately for up to 2 days. Add the butter and vinegar before serving.

## Chilled Tomato Soup with Sweet Pea Puree

**TOTAL: 45 MIN**
**4 SERVINGS** ● ●

This gazpacho-style soup should be made with almost overripe, in-season tomatoes.

- ¾ cup fresh or thawed frozen baby peas
- 1 cup baby spinach leaves
- ½ cup extra-virgin olive oil
- 3 tablespoons fresh lemon juice
- 2 tablespoons fresh goat cheese
- 1 tablespoon freshly grated Pecorino Romano
- 1 tablespoon mint leaves
- ½ teaspoon finely grated lemon zest

Salt and freshly ground pepper

- 5 cups grape tomatoes (about 3 pints)
- 1 medium seedless cucumber— peeled, halved, and cut into large pieces
- 2 small inner celery ribs
- 1¼ cups loosely packed basil leaves
- 2 scallions, thinly sliced
- 1½ teaspoons minced garlic
- 2 teaspoons *harissa* (see Note) or other hot sauce

1. If using fresh peas, blanch them in a small pot of boiling water for 5 minutes, then drain. In a small skillet, cook the blanched or thawed frozen peas with the spinach and ¼ cup of the olive oil over high heat until the spinach is wilted, about 2 minutes. Let cool, then transfer to a blender or food processor. Add the lemon juice, goat cheese, Pecorino Romano, mint and lemon zest and puree until smooth. Season with salt and pepper and transfer to a small bowl.

2. In a blender or food processor, combine the tomatoes with the cucumber, celery and basil and puree until smooth. Strain the mixture through a fine-mesh sieve set over a bowl, pressing hard on the solids. Stir in the scallions, garlic, *harissa* and the remaining ¼ cup of olive oil. Season the soup with salt and pepper; refrigerate until chilled, at least 30 minutes or overnight.

3. Ladle the tomato soup into bowls. Drizzle with the sweet pea puree and serve the soup at once. —*Jody Denton*

**NOTE** *Harissa*, the Tunisian chili paste, is available at Middle Eastern markets and specialty food stores.

**MAKE AHEAD** The tomato soup and the pea puree can be refrigerated separately overnight.

# soups

## Chilled Cucumber Soup with Pickled Red Onion

**TOTAL: 30 MIN**
4 SERVINGS ● ● ●

To make this soup less tart, add less of the pickled red onion.

- ¼ cup rice vinegar
- ½ cup thinly sliced red onion
- 1 tablespoon sugar
- ½ red jalapeño, seeded and thinly sliced
- 3 cups plain yogurt
- 2 pounds cucumbers—peeled, seeded and chopped
- ½ cup milk
- 10 mint leaves
- 1 teaspoon ground cumin

**Salt and freshly ground white pepper**

**1.** In a small saucepan, combine the rice vinegar with the red onion, sugar and jalapeño and bring to a boil to dissolve the sugar. Transfer to a small bowl and let cool.

**2.** In a blender, working in 2 batches, puree the yogurt with the cucumbers, milk, mint and cumin. Season the soup with salt and pepper and chill for 15 minutes. Ladle into bowls and garnish with the pickled red onion and jalapeño and a drizzle of the pickling liquid.
—*Mohammad Islam*

**MAKE AHEAD** The soup can be refrigerated overnight.

## pairing

**SOUP + SAKE**

**Sake can be a great partner to soup. Cream-based, earthy soups like a chilled vichyssoise or a warm potato-leek, for instance, are best matched with a full-bodied sake like the complex Tsukasobatan Junmai.**

## Cucumber Soup with Seared Tuna Tartare

**TOTAL: 30 MIN**
4 SERVINGS ● ●

- 1 large seedless cucumber, peeled and coarsely chopped, 1 tablespoon finely diced
- ¾ cup plain low-fat yogurt
- 2 tablespoons water
- ⅛ teaspoon mild curry powder
- ⅛ teaspoon cayenne pepper
- 2 tablespoons fresh lemon juice

**Salt and freshly ground black pepper**

- 1 tablespoon extra-virgin olive oil

**One 8-ounce tuna steak**

- 3 tablespoons finely diced tomato
- 1 small shallot, minced
- 1 tablespoon snipped chives
- 1 teaspoon very finely chopped parsley

**1.** In a blender or food processor, puree the coarsely chopped cucumber with the yogurt, water, curry powder, cayenne and 1½ tablespoons of the lemon juice. Season the puree with salt and black pepper and refrigerate.

**2.** Heat 1 teaspoon of the olive oil in a small skillet until shimmering. Add the tuna and cook over high heat for 2 minutes, turning once. Let cool slightly and cut into ¼-inch dice. Toss the tuna with the diced cucumber, the tomato, shallot, chives, parsley, 2 teaspoons of olive oil and ½ tablespoon of lemon juice. Season with salt and black pepper. Pour the soup into bowls, top with the tuna mixture and serve. —*Josiah Citrin*

## Yellow Pepper and Almond Soup

**ACTIVE: 30 MIN; TOTAL: 1 HR**
6 SERVINGS ●

- 2 tablespoons unsalted butter
- 2 tablespoons extra-virgin olive oil
- 2 cups sliced blanched almonds (about 6 ounces)

**Kosher salt**

- 2 medium red onions, thinly sliced
- 2 tablespoons minced garlic
- 2 bay leaves
- 2 thyme sprigs
- ½ teaspoon crushed red pepper
- 1 large pinch saffron threads
- 4 yellow bell peppers, chopped
- 2 large carrots, thinly sliced
- 1 quart vegetable stock or canned low-sodium broth

**Sour cream and chopped parsley, for garnish**

**1.** In a large saucepan, melt the butter in 1 tablespoon of the olive oil. Add the almonds and cook over moderate heat, stirring, until golden, about 6 minutes. Transfer the almonds to a plate and sprinkle with salt.

**2.** Wipe out the saucepan and add the remaining 1 tablespoon of olive oil, the red onions and a pinch of salt. Cover and cook over low heat, stirring, until softened, about 15 minutes. Add the garlic, bay leaves, thyme, crushed red pepper and saffron and cook over moderate heat, stirring, for 3 minutes. Add the yellow peppers, carrots and vegetable stock and bring to a boil over high heat. Reduce the heat to moderately low, cover and simmer until the vegetables are softened, about 25 minutes. Discard the bay leaves and thyme.

**3.** Transfer 1 cup of the toasted almonds to a food processor and pulse until finely chopped. Add 1 cup of the vegetable cooking broth and puree. Using a slotted spoon, transfer the vegetables to the food processor and puree until smooth, adding another ½ cup of the cooking broth. Stir the puree into the remaining broth in the saucepan and season with salt. Ladle the soup into bowls. Sprinkle with the remaining toasted almonds, garnish with dollops of sour cream and the parsley and serve. —*Peter Berley*

**MAKE AHEAD** The soup can be made earlier in the day and refrigerated. Rewarm before serving.

## Asparagus Soup with Lemon-Herb Crème Fraîche

**TOTAL: 40 MIN**

6 SERVINGS ●

½ cup crème fraîche
1 tablespoon chopped parsley
2 teaspoons chopped chives
1 teaspoon chopped tarragon
1 teaspoon finely grated
  lemon zest
1 teaspoon fresh lemon juice
Kosher salt and freshly ground pepper
2 pounds medium asparagus—
  tough ends discarded,
  tips reserved, stalks
  coarsely chopped
2 tablespoons unsalted butter
1 medium onion, finely chopped
1 quart chicken stock
2 cups water

1. In a bowl, blend the crème fraîche with the parsley, chives and tarragon and the lemon zest and juice. Season with salt and pepper, then cover and refrigerate.
2. In a small saucepan of boiling salted water, cook the asparagus tips until tender; drain and transfer to a plate.
3. Melt the butter in a large saucepan. Add the onion and cook over moderate heat, stirring, until softened, 4 minutes. Add the stock and water and bring to a boil. Add the chopped asparagus and season with 1½ teaspoons of salt and a few grindings of pepper. Boil over moderately high heat until the asparagus is tender, about 10 minutes. Remove from the heat and let stand for 5 minutes.
4. Working in batches, puree the soup in a blender and pour it into a clean saucepan. Season with salt and pepper. Stir in the asparagus tips and bring to a simmer over moderate heat. Ladle the soup into warmed shallow bowls. Top with large dollops of the lemon-herb crème fraîche and serve. —*Maria Helm Sinskey*
**MAKE AHEAD** The soup can be refrigerated overnight.

## Creamy Tomato Soup with Buttery Croutons

**TOTAL: 30 MIN**

6 SERVINGS ● ●

2 tablespoons unsalted butter
2 tablespoons extra-virgin
  olive oil
1 medium onion, very thinly sliced
3 garlic cloves, smashed
5 cups canned whole tomatoes
  in their juice (from three
  14-ounce cans)
1 cup water
⅔ cup heavy cream
1 tablespoon sugar
¼ teaspoon crushed red pepper
¼ teaspoon celery seed
¼ teaspoon dried oregano
Salt and freshly ground pepper
Four ¾-inch-thick slices of white
  country bread, crusts trimmed,
  bread cut into ¾-inch dice

1. In a large saucepan, melt 1 tablespoon of the butter in 1 tablespoon of the olive oil until sizzling. Add the sliced onion and smashed garlic and cook over moderate heat, stirring occasionally, until softened, about 5 minutes. Add the tomatoes and their juice, the water, heavy cream, sugar, crushed red pepper, celery seed and oregano and season with salt and pepper. Bring the soup to a boil over high heat, breaking up the tomatoes with the back of a wooden spoon. Reduce the heat to moderate and simmer the soup for 10 minutes.
2. Meanwhile, in a small skillet, cook the remaining 1 tablespoon of butter over moderately high heat until it begins to brown, about 1 minute. Scrape the butter into a medium bowl. Add the remaining 1 tablespoon of olive oil to the skillet. Add the diced bread and cook over moderately high heat, stirring occasionally, until slightly browned, about 6 minutes. Transfer the bread to the browned butter and toss well to coat.
3. Working in batches, transfer the tomato soup to a blender or food processor and puree until smooth. Return the soup to a clean pot and rewarm if necessary. Season with salt and pepper, ladle into bowls and serve with the croutons. —*Tom Douglas*
**MAKE AHEAD** The ungarnished soup can be refrigerated overnight.

## Creamy Tomato Soup with Toasted Almonds

**TOTAL: 30 MIN**

6 SERVINGS ● ●

1 cup sliced blanched almonds
¼ cup extra-virgin olive oil
2 medium onions, very thinly sliced
4 garlic cloves, very thinly sliced
1 celery rib, very thinly sliced
Four 14½-ounce cans diced
  tomatoes
1 tablespoon tomato paste
1 tablespoon sugar
2 cups chicken stock or
  low-sodium broth
¼ teaspoon cayenne pepper
Salt and freshly ground black pepper
1 cup heavy cream
½ teaspoon finely grated
  orange zest
2 tablespoons unsalted butter

1. Preheat the oven to 350°. Spread the almonds in a pie plate and toast for 5 minutes, until golden.
2. Meanwhile, in a large soup pot, heat the olive oil until shimmering. Add the sliced onions, garlic and celery, cover and cook over moderately high heat, stirring occasionally, until softened, about 5 minutes. Uncover and cook, stirring occasionally, until the vegetables are lightly browned, about 5 minutes longer. Stir in the diced tomatoes and their juices, the tomato paste and sugar and cook for 5 minutes. Add the stock and cayenne. Season the soup with salt and black pepper and cook for 10 minutes longer.

# soups

3. In a blender, puree the soup in batches. Return the soup to the pot and stir in the cream and orange zest. Simmer over moderate heat for 2 to 3 minutes. Add the butter and stir until melted. Transfer the soup to bowls, garnish with the toasted almonds and serve. —*Maggie Pond*

**MAKE AHEAD** The ungarnished soup can be refrigerated overnight.

## Creamy Green Chile Soup
**TOTAL: 30 MIN**
4 SERVINGS ● ●
Three 6-ounce poblano chiles
Olive oil, for rubbing
  3  cups half-and-half
  8  ounces tomatillos, husked
One 5-ounce bunch cilantro, leaves
     and stems very coarsely chopped
  ¾  cup freshly grated Pecorino
     Romano cheese (3 ounces)
Salt and freshly ground pepper

1. Preheat the broiler. Rub the poblanos lightly with oil and broil for about 5 minutes as close to the heat source as possible, turning the chiles once, until they are charred all over. Transfer to a medium bowl, cover tightly with plastic wrap and let stand for 5 minutes. Rub the skin off the chiles with a paper towel and discard the stems and seeds.

2. In a medium saucepan, combine the half-and-half with the tomatillos and the roasted chiles. Simmer over moderate heat until the tomatillos are just tender, about 10 minutes. Using a slotted spoon, transfer the tomatillos and chiles to a blender. Add the cilantro and ½ cup of the half-and-half and puree until the mixture is smooth and creamy.

3. Stir the puree into the saucepan, then stir in the Pecorino Romano. Season with salt and pepper. Simmer until the cheese is melted, about 3 minutes. Ladle into bowls and serve. —*Jamie Samford*

**MAKE AHEAD** The soup can be refrigerated overnight.

## Corn Soup with Chiles and Manchego
**ACTIVE: 30 MIN; TOTAL: 1 HR 20 MIN**
4 SERVINGS ●
  6  ears of corn, kernels cut off and
     reserved, cobs reserved
  2  quarts water
  1  bay leaf
  1  Anaheim chile
  2  tablespoons vegetable oil
  3  garlic cloves, chopped
  1  medium onion, chopped
Salt and freshly ground pepper
  ½  cup half-and-half
  ½  cup shredded Manchego cheese

1. In a large saucepan, cover the corn cobs with the water and bring to a boil. Add the bay leaf and simmer over moderately low heat for 40 minutes. Strain the corn broth into a bowl.

2. Meanwhile, roast the Anaheim chile directly over a gas flame or under the broiler until charred all over. Transfer the chile to a bowl, cover with plastic wrap and let steam for 5 minutes. Discard the charred skin, the stem and the seeds and cut the chile into ¼-inch dice.

3. In a large saucepan, heat the oil. Add the garlic and onion and cook over moderate heat until softened, about 5 minutes. Add the corn kernels, season with salt and pepper and cook for 1 minute. Add the reserved corn broth and bring to a boil. Simmer the soup over low heat until the corn is tender, 10 minutes.

4. Set a strainer over a large bowl. In a food processor, puree the soup in batches until smooth; strain it into the bowl.

5. Return the soup to the saucepan, add the half-and-half and simmer for 5 minutes. Stir in the chile and season with salt and pepper. Ladle the soup into bowls, top with the Manchego and serve. —*Bob Isaacson*

**MAKE AHEAD** The soup can be refrigerated overnight. Reheat gently and add the cheese just before serving.

## Golden Gratinéed Onion Soup
**ACTIVE: 30 MIN; TOTAL: 3 HR 30 MIN**
6 SERVINGS
  2  tablespoons unsalted butter
  3  tablespoons extra-virgin olive
     oil, plus more for brushing
  3  pounds large yellow onions,
     halved lengthwise and thinly
     sliced crosswise
  2  thyme sprigs
Salt
  1  tablespoon all-purpose flour
  6  cups chicken or beef stock or
     canned low-sodium broth
Freshly ground black pepper
 12  baguette slices
1½  cups shredded Gruyère
     cheese (6 ounces)
  2  tablespoons grated
     Parmesan cheese

1. In a large enameled cast-iron casserole, melt the butter in the 3 tablespoons of olive oil until sizzling. Add the sliced onions, the thyme and ¼ teaspoon of salt and stir to combine. Cover the onions with a moistened sheet of parchment, pressing it directly onto the onions, and cover with the lid. Cook over moderately low heat, stirring occasionally, until the liquid is completely evaporated and the onions are very tender and deeply golden, 2½ to 3 hours. Sprinkle the flour over the onions and stir. Add the stock and bring to a simmer. Season with salt and pepper and cook for 10 minutes.

2. Meanwhile, preheat the oven to 350°. Brush the baguette slices on both sides with olive oil, spread them on a baking sheet and toast for 12 minutes, or until golden and crisp.

3. Preheat the broiler. Pour the soup into heatproof bowls and set them on a heavy baking sheet. In a small bowl, combine 1 cup of the Gruyère with the Parmesan. Sprinkle the remaining ½ cup of Gruyère into the soup and top with the toasted baguettes. Sprinkle the cheese mixture

**CORN SOUP WITH CHILES AND MANCHEGO**

# soups

on top and broil 8 inches from the heat for about 2 minutes, or until melted and golden, shifting the pan for even browning. Serve right away. —*Tina Ujlaki*

**MAKE AHEAD** The soup can be refrigerated for up to 4 days.

## Hearty Fennel Soup with Sausage and Gouda Croutons

**ACTIVE: 40 MIN; TOTAL: 1 HR 25 MIN**
6 SERVINGS ●

- 2 tablespoons extra-virgin olive oil
- ¾ pound sweet Italian sausage links
- 1 medium onion, thinly sliced
- 3 medium fennel bulbs—halved, cored and thinly sliced
- 2 thyme sprigs
- 6 cups chicken stock or low-sodium broth
- 1 medium zucchini, thinly sliced

Salt and freshly ground pepper

Six ¾-inch-thick baguette slices, lightly toasted

- 6 ounces medium-aged Gouda cheese, such as Prima Donna, finely shredded

**1.** Heat the olive oil in a large, heavy saucepan. Add the sausage links and cook over moderate heat until they are golden brown and just cooked through, about 10 minutes. Transfer to a plate.

**2.** Add the onion to the saucepan and cook over moderate heat until softened, about 4 minutes. Add the fennel and thyme and cook, stirring, until softened, about 5 minutes. Add the stock and simmer over moderately low heat until the fennel is very tender, about 45 minutes. Add the zucchini, cover and simmer over moderate heat until barely tender, about 2 minutes. Discard the thyme sprigs.

**3.** Working in 2 batches, puree the soup in a food processor. Return the soup to the saucepan. Thinly slice the sausage and add to the soup. Season with salt and pepper and keep warm.

**4.** Preheat the oven to 500°. Arrange the baguette toasts on a baking sheet and top them with half of the cheese. Bake for 1 minute, or until the cheese melts. Ladle the soup into shallow bowls and top with the toasts. Sprinkle the remaining cheese on the soup and serve. —*Marcia Kiesel*

**MAKE AHEAD** The soup can be refrigerated overnight. The plain toasts can be stored in an airtight container overnight.

## Gingered Carrot Soup with Crème Fraîche

**TOTAL: 30 MIN**
6 SERVINGS ● ●

- 2 tablespoons unsalted butter
- ¼ cup extra-virgin olive oil
- 1½ pounds large carrots, peeled and thinly sliced
- 1 large onion, very thinly sliced
- 2 tablespoons finely grated fresh ginger
- 4½ cups vegetable stock
- ¼ teaspoon freshly grated nutmeg

Salt and freshly ground pepper

- ¼ cup crème fraîche or sour cream
- 2 tablespoons coarsely chopped cilantro

**1.** In a medium soup pot, melt the butter in the olive oil. Add the carrots, onion and ginger, cover and cook over moderately high heat for about 8 minutes, stirring occasionally, until the vegetables just begin to soften. Add the vegetable stock and nutmeg and season liberally with salt and pepper. Cover and cook over moderate heat until the carrots and onions are very soft, about 10 minutes.

**2.** Puree the soup in batches in a blender, then return it to the soup pot. Stir in the crème fraîche and chopped cilantro and season with salt and pepper. Serve the soup in shallow bowls. —*Maggie Pond*

**MAKE AHEAD** The soup can be refrigerated for up to 2 days. Stir in the crème fraîche and cilantro before serving.

## Mushroom Soup with Chorizo and Scallions

**ACTIVE: 45 MIN; TOTAL: 1 HR 45 MIN**
10 SERVINGS
SOUP

- 4 tablespoons unsalted butter
- 4 pounds large white button mushrooms, thinly sliced
- 4 large shallots, thinly sliced
- 1 garlic clove, smashed
- 6 cups chicken stock or low-sodium broth
- 6 cups water
- 5 small thyme sprigs
- 5 parsley sprigs
- ⅓ cup heavy cream
- ¼ cup soy sauce
- 1 tablespoon cornstarch dissolved in 2 tablespoons water

Salt and freshly ground pepper
GARNISH

- ½ pound chorizo, peeled and coarsely ground in a food processor or very finely chopped
- 1 tablespoon unsalted butter
- ½ pound small white button mushrooms, quartered
- 1 bunch scallions (about 6), white and green parts only, thinly sliced

**1. MAKE THE SOUP:** In a large soup pot, melt the butter. Add three-fourths of the sliced mushrooms, the shallots and garlic and cook over moderately high heat, stirring frequently, until the mushroom liquid has evaporated and the mushrooms are lightly browned, 30 minutes.

**2.** Add the chicken stock, water, thyme and parsley and bring to a boil, scraping up any browned bits stuck to the bottom of the pot. Cover and simmer over moderately low heat for 1 hour. Strain the mushroom broth into a heatproof bowl, pressing hard on the solids with the back of a spoon. Discard the solids and wipe out the soup pot.

**3.** Return the mushroom broth to the pot. Add the remaining sliced mushrooms, bring to a boil over high heat and cook for 2 minutes. Using a slotted spoon, transfer the mushrooms to a blender. Add 1 cup of the broth and puree until smooth. Return the mushroom puree to the soup and stir in the heavy cream, soy sauce and cornstarch mixture and bring to a simmer. Cook just until the soup is slightly thickened, about 5 minutes. Season with salt and pepper.

**4.** MAKE THE GARNISH: In a large skillet, cook the ground chorizo over moderate heat until the fat is rendered, about 5 minutes. Drain the chorizo on a paper towel. Wipe out the skillet and melt the butter. Add the quartered mushrooms and cook over high heat until lightly browned, about 6 minutes. Add the scallions and chorizo and cook just until the scallions are softened, about 1 minute. Mound ¼ cup of the garnish in the center of 10 soup bowls, ladle the soup all around and serve.
—*Gabriel Kreuther*

### Potato and Wild Mushroom Soup
**TOTAL: 30 MIN**
6 SERVINGS ● ●

- ½ ounce dried oyster mushrooms (1 cup)
- 1 ounce dried shiitake mushrooms (1 cup)
- ¾ ounce dried porcini mushrooms (¾ cup)
- 3 cups hot water
- ¼ cup extra-virgin olive oil
- 2 leeks, white and tender green parts only, finely chopped
- 5 cups chicken stock or low-sodium broth
- 1 pound baking potatoes, peeled and coarsely shredded
- 1 teaspoon finely chopped thyme

Salt and freshly ground pepper

- 1½ tablespoons sherry vinegar
- 2 tablespoons unsalted butter

**HEARTY FENNEL SOUP WITH SAUSAGE**

**GINGERED CARROT SOUP WITH CRÈME FRAÎCHE**

1. Put the dried mushrooms and hot water into a microwave-safe bowl, cover with plastic and microwave for 2 minutes. Let cool slightly, then strain the mushrooms through a fine-mesh sieve, reserving the liquid. Finely chop the mushrooms.

2. Meanwhile, in a soup pot, heat the olive oil until shimmering. Add the leeks and cook over moderate heat until softened, about 5 minutes. Add the stock, shredded potato, thyme and chopped mushrooms. Slowly add the mushroom soaking liquid, stopping before you reach the grit at the bottom. Cook over moderate heat until the potatoes are almost dissolved, about 20 minutes. Season with salt and pepper. Stir in the vinegar and butter and serve in shallow bowls. —*Maggie Pond*

MAKE AHEAD The soup can be refrigerated overnight.

### Roasted Chestnut Soup

TOTAL: 30 MIN
6 SERVINGS ● ● ●

 3 tablespoons extra-virgin olive oil
 2 large onions, thinly sliced
 3 garlic cloves, thinly sliced
 4 cups chicken stock or
   low-sodium broth
One 14- to 15-ounce jar vacuum-
   packed chestnuts
1½ pounds Yukon Gold potatoes,
   peeled and very thinly sliced
 1 tablespoon chopped thyme leaves
Pinch of cinnamon
Salt and freshly ground pepper
 3 tablespoons cream sherry
 1 teaspoon fresh lemon juice

1. In a large soup pot, heat the olive oil until shimmering. Add the onions and garlic, cover and cook over moderate heat, stirring occasionally, until softened, about 5 minutes. Add the stock, chestnuts, potatoes, thyme and cinnamon; season with salt and pepper. Cover and cook over moderate heat until the potatoes are very tender and broken up, about 15 minutes.

2. In a blender, puree the soup. Return the soup to the pot and stir in the sherry and lemon juice. Ladle into shallow bowls and serve. —*Maggie Pond*

MAKE AHEAD The soup can be refrigerated for up to 2 days.

### White Bean Soup with Cauliflower

ACTIVE: 25 MIN; TOTAL: 4 HR
10 SERVINGS ● ●

 2 cups dried lima beans (14 ounces)
19 cups water
 4 large bay leaves
 4 large thyme sprigs, plus
   1 teaspoon chopped thyme
¼ cup extra-virgin olive oil
 2 tablespoons minced garlic
 1 large head cauliflower, cored
   and cut into small florets
 1 tablespoon all-purpose flour
 2 medium shallots, very
   thinly sliced
 1 teaspoon ground cumin
Salt and freshly ground pepper
½ cup Asian fish sauce
 2 Thai chiles, minced

1. In a very large saucepan, combine the lima beans with 8 cups of the water and bring to a boil. Add the bay leaves and thyme sprigs and simmer over moderately low heat, stirring occasionally, until the water is almost absorbed, about 1½ hours. Add the remaining 11 cups of water and simmer, stirring occasionally, until the lima beans are very tender, about 2 hours longer.

2. In a large skillet, heat 2 tablespoons of the olive oil. Add the garlic and cook over moderate heat until golden, 3 minutes. Add the cauliflower and cook, stirring, until well coated with the garlic and just starting to soften, 3 minutes. Add the flour and toss to coat. Stir the cauliflower into the soup, cover partially and continue to cook over moderately low heat, stirring occasionally, until the cauliflower is tender, 15 minutes.

3. Meanwhile, in a small skillet, heat the remaining 2 tablespoons of olive oil. Add the shallots and chopped thyme and cook over moderately low heat until softened, about 6 minutes. Add the cumin and cook, stirring, until fragrant, about 1 minute. Stir the mixture into the soup; season with salt and pepper.

4. In a small bowl, stir the fish sauce with the chiles. Discard the bay leaves and thyme sprigs and ladle the soup into bowls. Serve the sauce on the side. —*Naomi Duguid and Jeffrey Alford*

MAKE AHEAD The soup can be refrigerated for up to 2 days.

### Cannellini Bean and Escarole Soup

ACTIVE: 35 MIN; TOTAL: 2 HR 30 MIN,
PLUS SOAKING
4 SERVINGS ● ●

1¼ cups dried cannellini beans
   (½ pound), soaked overnight
   or quick-soaked and drained
   (see Note)
Salt
One 1-pound head escarole, cored
¼ cup extra-virgin olive oil
 1 small celery rib, finely chopped
 1 bay leaf
One 16-ounce can whole tomatoes,
   chopped, juices reserved
 2 tablespoons chopped parsley
 1 garlic clove, thinly sliced
 1 teaspoon chopped marjoram
¼ teaspoon crushed red pepper
Grilled peasant bread, for serving

1. In a medium saucepan, cover the beans with 2 inches of water and bring to a boil. Simmer over moderately low heat, stirring occasionally, until tender, 2 hours. Add water as necessary so the beans are always submerged in 1 inch of water. Remove from the heat; season with salt.

2. Meanwhile, in a large saucepan of boiling salted water, cook the escarole for 3 minutes. Drain and coarsely chop.

WHITE BEAN SOUP WITH CAULIFLOWER

**WINTER SQUASH SOUP WITH PIE SPICES**

**GARBANZO SOUP WITH CHORIZO**

**3.** In a large saucepan, heat the olive oil until shimmering. Add the celery and bay leaf and cook over low heat until the celery is softened, about 5 minutes. Add the beans, their cooking liquid, the tomatoes and their juices and simmer over moderate heat for 3 minutes. Add the escarole and simmer for 5 minutes. Discard the bay leaf. Season with salt and stir in the parsley, garlic, marjoram and crushed red pepper. Add a piece of grilled bread to each bowl, ladle in the soup and serve.
—*Christophe Hille*

**NOTE** To quick-soak beans, rinse them first. Then, in a saucepan, cover the beans with water and boil for 2 minutes. Remove the pan from the heat, cover and let the beans stand for 1 hour; drain well.

**MAKE AHEAD** The soup can be refrigerated for up to 2 days.

### Lentil Soup with Serrano Ham and Arugula
**TOTAL: 30 MIN**
6 SERVINGS ● ●

- 1½ cups lentils
- 8 cups very hot tap water
- ¼ cup plus 1 tablespoon extra-virgin olive oil
- 2 medium onions, very finely chopped
- 3 medium carrots, very thinly sliced
- 2 celery ribs, very thinly sliced
- 5 garlic cloves, 4 very thinly sliced, 1 very finely chopped
- 2 tablespoons tomato paste

Crushed red pepper

Salt and freshly ground black pepper

- 2 ounces thinly sliced Serrano ham or prosciutto, cut into ½-inch-wide strips
- 1 bunch arugula (¼ pound), thick stems discarded

**1.** In a large saucepan, cover the lentils with the water and bring to a boil.

2. Meanwhile, in a medium soup pot, heat ¼ cup of the olive oil until shimmering. Add the onions, carrots, celery and sliced garlic. Cover and cook over moderately high heat, stirring occasionally, until the vegetables are softened, 5 to 6 minutes. Carefully add the lentils and the boiling water. Add the tomato paste and ¼ teaspoon of crushed red pepper to the soup and season with salt and black pepper. Cook over moderate heat until the lentils are tender, about 20 minutes.

3. Meanwhile, in a small skillet, heat the remaining 1 tablespoon of olive oil until shimmering. Add the minced garlic and cook just until fragrant, about 30 seconds. Add the ham and a generous pinch of crushed red pepper and cook for 30 seconds. Add the arugula and cook just until wilted, 30 seconds longer. Ladle the lentil soup into shallow bowls, garnish with the garlicky ham and arugula and serve.
—Maggie Pond

### Winter Squash Soup with Pie Spices
ACTIVE: 30 MIN; TOTAL: 1 HR 30 MIN
10 SERVINGS ●

- 3½ pounds kabocha squash, halved and seeded
- 2 pounds butternut squash, halved and seeded
- 1½ pounds acorn squash, halved and seeded
- Salt and freshly ground pepper
- 2 cups water
- 7 tablespoons unsalted butter, 3 tablespoons melted
- 1 white onion, thinly sliced
- ¼ teaspoon plus 1 pinch of ground cardamom
- ¼ teaspoon plus 1 pinch of freshly grated nutmeg
- ⅛ teaspoon plus 1 pinch of ground ginger
- ⅛ teaspoon plus 1 pinch of ground cloves

- 4½ cups chicken stock or low-sodium broth
- 1 cup heavy cream
- ¾ pound peasant bread, crusts removed, bread torn into 1-inch pieces
- 1¼ cups crème fraîche

1. Preheat the oven to 350°. Season the kabocha, butternut and acorn squashes with salt and pepper and lay them cut side down on 2 large, rimmed baking sheets. Pour 1 cup of water onto each baking sheet, cover the squash with foil and bake for about 1 hour, or until tender. Let cool slightly, then scoop the flesh into a bowl. Keep the oven on.

2. In a large saucepan or casserole, melt 4 tablespoons of the butter. Add the onion and cook over moderately low heat, stirring occasionally, until softened, about 8 minutes. Add ¼ teaspoon each of the cardamom and nutmeg and ⅛ teaspoon each of the ginger and cloves and cook, stirring, until fragrant, about 2 minutes. Add the chicken stock and bring to a boil over moderately high heat. Add the squash flesh and heavy cream and simmer over moderate heat for 5 minutes. Working in batches, puree the soup in a food processor and return to the pan. Season with salt and pepper and keep warm over very low heat.

3. Meanwhile, on a large, rimmed baking sheet, toss the pieces of bread with the 3 tablespoons of melted butter. Bake for about 8 minutes, or until golden brown.

4. In a small bowl, combine the crème fraîche with the remaining pinches of cardamom, nutmeg, ginger and cloves and season with salt and pepper. Ladle the soup into bowls, dollop with the spiced crème fraîche and croutons and serve. —Lee Hefter

MAKE AHEAD The soup and spiced crème fraîche can be refrigerated separately for up to 2 days. The croutons can be stored in an airtight container.

### Garbanzo Soup with Chorizo and Smoked Paprika
TOTAL: 30 MIN
6 SERVINGS ● ●

- 1 medium link of chorizo (5 ounces), quartered lengthwise and thinly sliced crosswise
- Two 19-ounce cans chickpeas, drained well
- ½ cup water
- ¼ cup extra-virgin olive oil
- 2 medium carrots, halved lengthwise and thinly sliced
- 1 medium onion, finely chopped
- 1 garlic clove, thinly sliced
- 3 tablespoons tomato paste
- 1½ teaspoons smoked *pimentón* (see Note)
- ¼ teaspoon cayenne pepper
- 4 cups beef stock or low-sodium broth
- 1 teaspoon sugar
- Crusty bread, for serving

1. In a small skillet, cook the chorizo over moderately high heat until the meat is lightly browned and most of the fat has been rendered, 3 to 4 minutes. Drain the chorizo on paper towels.

2. In a food processor, puree half of the chickpeas with the water until smooth.

3. In a soup pot, heat the olive oil until shimmering. Add the carrots, onion and garlic, cover and cook over moderate heat until softened, about 5 minutes. Add the chorizo, tomato paste, *pimentón* and cayenne and cook, stirring, for 1 minute. Add the beef stock and sugar along with the whole and pureed chickpeas and bring to a boil. Simmer over moderate heat until the vegetables are tender, about 10 minutes. Ladle the soup into deep bowls and serve with crusty bread. —Maggie Pond

NOTE *Pimentón*, Spanish paprika, is sold at large supermarkets and specialty food shops. You can substitute 1 teaspoon of paprika mixed with ½ teaspoon of ground chipotle for the smoked *pimentón* here.

# soups

## Tangy Chickpea Soup with Olives and Anise

**TOTAL: 40 MIN**

4 SERVINGS ● ● ●

¼ cup extra-virgin olive oil, plus
　more for drizzling
1 large sweet onion, chopped
Pinch of crushed red pepper
1½ teaspoons anise seeds, crushed
4 cups chicken stock
Two 15-ounce cans chickpeas, rinsed
Salt and freshly ground pepper
3 tablespoons fresh lemon juice
1½ tablespoons Dijon mustard
½ cup finely chopped parsley
12 black or green olives

Heat the ¼ cup of olive oil in a large saucepan. Add the onion, cover partially and cook over moderate heat until it is softened, about 7 minutes. Stir in the crushed red pepper and anise and cook for 2 minutes. Add the stock and chickpeas, season with salt and pepper and simmer for 20 minutes. Stir in the lemon juice, mustard and parsley. Garnish with the olives, drizzle with olive oil and serve. —Aglaia Kremezi

**MAKE AHEAD** The soup can be refrigerated for up to 2 days.

## Chunky Summer Minestrone

**ACTIVE: 1 HR; TOTAL: 1 HR 30 MIN**

8 SERVINGS ● ●

Typically, minestrone is a hearty winter soup thickened with lots of beans and pasta. This version is much lighter. For convenience the recipe calls for frozen peas, but fresh ones would be terrific, too—just let them simmer for a few extra minutes.

⅔ cup extra-virgin olive oil, plus
　more for drizzling
2 large onions, coarsely chopped
1 cup dry white wine
4 leeks, coarsely chopped
4 celery ribs, coarsely chopped
2 bay leaves
2½ quarts cold water

8 small zucchini (about 2½ pounds
　total), halved lengthwise and
　sliced ½ inch thick
3 large garlic cloves, thinly sliced
Salt and freshly ground pepper
One 19-ounce can cannellini beans,
　drained and rinsed
1 cup frozen baby peas
½ cup chopped flat-leaf parsley
Fresh thyme leaves and shaved
　Parmesan cheese, for garnish

**1.** In a stockpot, heat ⅓ cup of the olive oil. Add the onions and cook over moderate heat until translucent, about 8 minutes. Add the wine, leeks, celery and bay leaves and cook, stirring occasionally, until the vegetables are softened, about 20 minutes. Add the water and simmer for 30 minutes. Strain the stock into a large saucepan and discard the vegetables. Keep the stock warm.

**2.** Meanwhile, in a large skillet, heat the remaining ⅓ cup of olive oil. Add the zucchini and garlic, season with salt and pepper and cook over moderate heat, stirring occasionally, until the zucchini soften, 10 minutes. Add the zucchini and the cannellini beans to the stock and simmer until the zucchini are very tender, about 10 minutes. Add the peas and parsley and simmer for 1 minute longer; season with salt and pepper.

**3.** Ladle the soup into bowls. Garnish with the thyme, Parmesan shavings and a drizzle of olive oil. —Trevor Kaufman

**MAKE AHEAD** The soup can be refrigerated for up to 2 days.

## Chicken Soup with Passatelli

**ACTIVE: 15 MIN; TOTAL: 1 HR**

6 SERVINGS

Passatelli, like gnocchi only smaller, are a dough-based, poached Italian dumpling.

2 large eggs
1 large egg yolk
1 cup freshly grated
　Parmesan cheese

¾ cup fresh bread crumbs
Finely grated zest of 1 small lemon
Pinch of freshly grated nutmeg
2 tablespoons unsalted
　butter, melted
2 quarts chicken stock
Salt

**1.** In a bowl, beat the whole eggs with the yolk. Stir in the cheese, bread crumbs, lemon zest, nutmeg and butter. Cover the dough; chill until firm. Bring the dough to room temperature before cooking.

**2.** In a large saucepan, bring the stock to a boil. Season with salt and reduce the heat so the stock simmers.

**3.** Press one-third of the dough at a time through a ricer, cutting it off in ½-inch lengths over the soup. Simmer until all of the passatelli surface, about 1 minute. Serve at once. —Fabio Trabocchi

## Hot and Sour Noodle Soup with Pork

**TOTAL: 25 MIN**

4 SERVINGS ● ●

2 ounces rice-stick noodles
　(pad thai noodles)
1 tablespoon vegetable oil
10 large shiitake mushrooms
　(about 4 ounces), stems
　discarded, caps thickly sliced
1 large garlic clove, thinly sliced
1½ teaspoons grated fresh ginger
4½ cups chicken stock or
　low-sodium broth
½ pound pork tenderloin, cut into
　2-by-½-inch strips
1½ tablespoons cider vinegar
1½ teaspoons soy sauce
1 teaspoon chile-garlic sauce
　or hot sauce
1 cup snow peas, sliced lengthwise
3 scallions, thinly sliced
½ teaspoon cornstarch dissolved
　in 1 tablespoon cold water
1 teaspoon Asian sesame oil
Salt

1. Soak the rice-stick noodles in a bowl of hot water until soft and pliable, about 5 minutes.

2. Meanwhile, in a large saucepan, heat the oil until shimmering. Add the shiitake and cook over high heat, stirring occasionally, until lightly browned, 2 to 3 minutes. Add the garlic and ginger and cook, stirring, for 30 seconds. Add the stock and bring to a boil.

3. Drain the rice-stick noodles, add them to the saucepan and cook over moderate heat, stirring occasionally, just until tender, about 3 minutes. Add the pork, vinegar, soy sauce and chile-garlic sauce and simmer until the pork is nearly cooked through, about 2 minutes. Add the snow peas, scallions and cornstarch mixture and cook until the vegetables are crisp-tender, about 1 minute. Stir in the sesame oil and season with salt. Ladle the soup into bowls and serve. —*Julie Ridlon*

### Fresh Clam and Noodle Soup

**TOTAL: 30 MIN**

6 SERVINGS ● ●

¼  cup extra-virgin olive oil, plus more for drizzling
1  large onion, finely chopped
2  medium carrots, thinly sliced
2  celery ribs, thinly sliced
4  garlic cloves, thinly sliced
One 14½-ounce can diced tomatoes
2  cups bottled clam juice
2  cups chicken stock or low-sodium broth
½  cup dry white wine
1  tablespoon tomato paste
Large pinch of saffron threads, crumbled
¼  pound thin spaghetti, broken into 1-inch pieces (1 cup)
2  pounds cockles or Manila clams, scrubbed
Three 1-inch strips of orange zest
Freshly ground pepper

1. In a soup pot, heat the ¼ cup of olive oil until shimmering. Add the onion, carrots, celery and garlic. Cover and cook over moderately high heat, stirring occasionally, until the vegetables are softened, about 5 minutes. Add the tomatoes and their juices, the clam juice, chicken stock, wine, tomato paste and saffron and bring to a boil. Add the pasta, cover and cook, stirring occasionally, until the pasta is barely tender, 6 minutes.

2. Add the cockles and orange zest and cook, uncovered, until the cockles open, about 3 minutes; discard the orange zest and any clams that do not open. Season the soup with freshly ground pepper, ladle it into bowls and drizzle with olive oil. —*Maggie Pond*

### Cherrystone Clam Chowder with Corn

**ACTIVE: 50 MIN; TOTAL: 1 HR 20 MIN**

8 SERVINGS ●

¼  pound thickly sliced bacon (5 slices)
1  cup bottled clam juice
½  cup dry white wine
1  bay leaf
40  cherrystone clams (about 8 pounds), scrubbed and rinsed
3  tablespoons unsalted butter
3  medium white or yellow onions, coarsely chopped
3  ears of corn, kernels cut off the cobs
2¼  pounds baking potatoes, peeled and cut into ¾-inch cubes
5  cups whole milk
½  cup heavy cream
Salt and freshly ground pepper

1. In a medium skillet, cook the bacon over moderate heat until it is browned and crisp, about 8 minutes. Transfer the bacon to paper towels to drain; reserve the bacon fat in the skillet. Crumble the bacon coarsely.

2. In a stockpot, combine the clam juice, wine and bay leaf; bring to a boil. Add the clams, cover and simmer over moderately high heat for 8 minutes. Transfer the clams to a bowl and discard any unopened ones.

3. Strain the clam broth through a fine-mesh sieve set over a medium bowl. Rinse out the stockpot. Remove the clams from their shells and coarsely chop them.

4. In the stockpot, melt the butter with 1 tablespoon of the reserved bacon fat. Add the onions and cook over moderate heat until softened, 4 minutes. Add the corn and potatoes and cook, stirring often, until the potatoes begin to soften, 6 minutes. Add the clam broth, cover and simmer until the corn and potatoes are very tender, about 10 minutes. Add the chopped clams, milk and cream and bring to a simmer. Season with salt and pepper. Ladle into bowls, sprinkle with the bacon and serve. —*Alexandra and Eliot Angle*

**MAKE AHEAD** The clam chowder can be refrigerated for up to 2 days.

# ingredient

**LEMONGRASS**  **TIP**

**MAKE LEMONGRASS-SCENTED TEA** by infusing a crushed stalk in a pot of boiling water for 10 minutes, then using the water to make green tea.

**GIVE GRILLED FOODS AN AROMATIC SMOKINESS** by scattering lemongrass tops over hot coals or on top of gas burners before putting food on the grill.

**ADD A SUBTLE LEMONY FLAVOR** to roast chicken or fish by lining the bottom of a roasting pan with the crushed tops of lemongrass stalks, then placing the food on top.

**WARM SOBA IN BROTH WITH TOFU**

**SOUR FISH SOUP WITH NAPA CABBAGE**

### Warm Soba in Broth with Spinach and Tofu

**TOTAL: 20 MIN**

**4 SERVINGS** ● ●

In this restorative recipe, soba is served in dashi, a broth made with bonito-tuna flakes and kombu (a kind of seaweed that's loaded with calcium, iodine and magnesium), and combined with protein-packed tofu.

- 4 large, shiitake mushrooms, stems discarded
- Vegetable oil cooking spray
- Salt and freshly ground pepper
- 2 teaspoons sugar
- 3 tablespoons low-sodium soy sauce
- 2 tablespoons mirin (see Note)
- 10 ounces soba noodles (see Note)
- 5 cups boiling water
- 2 teaspoons instant dashi or 1 tablespoon miso paste (see Note)
- 4 ounces firm tofu, cut into ½-inch dice
- 2 cups baby spinach leaves
- ¼ cup finely shredded daikon
- 1 scallion, thinly sliced
- 1 sheet nori seaweed, cut into ⅛-inch strips (see Note)

**1.** Preheat the broiler. Spray the mushroom caps with vegetable oil, season with salt and pepper and broil 6 inches from the heat, turning the caps once, until they are lightly browned and tender, 6 minutes. Let cool, then thinly slice.

**2.** In a small bowl, stir the sugar into the soy sauce and mirin until dissolved.

**3.** In a large saucepan of boiling water, cook the soba noodles, stirring once or twice, until just tender, about 8 minutes. Drain the noodles, rinse under cold water and drain again thoroughly. Add the 5 cups of boiling water and instant dashi to the saucepan. Add the tofu and shiitake and simmer just until they are heated through, about 2 minutes. Add the spinach. Transfer the soba to 4 deep bowls and spoon the dashi mixture on top. Garnish the soba with the daikon, scallion and nori and serve right away, passing the soy sauce mixture alongside. —*Anya von Bremzen*

**NOTE** Many Japanese products are now available at large supermarkets, health food stores and Asian markets. Look for soba noodles with a high percentage of buckwheat.

### Spicy Kale Chowder with Andouille Sausage
**TOTAL: 45 MIN**
12 SERVINGS ● ●
¼ cup extra-virgin olive oil
8 garlic cloves, thinly sliced
2 large onions, finely chopped
2 tablespoons very finely chopped fresh ginger
1 pound andouille sausage, sliced ¼ inch thick
One 28-ounce can Italian plum tomatoes, chopped, juices reserved
3 quarts Rich Turkey Stock (p. 112) or low-sodium chicken broth
¾ pound kale, large stems and ribs discarded, leaves coarsely chopped (8 cups)
Salt and freshly ground pepper

**1.** Heat the olive oil in a large soup pot. Add the garlic and onions and cook over moderate heat, stirring occasionally, until softened, about 12 minutes. Add the ginger and andouille and cook for 5 minutes, stirring occasionally. Add the tomatoes and their juices; bring to a boil. Add the stock and kale; return to a boil.

**2.** Reduce the heat to moderate and simmer the soup until the kale is tender, about 10 minutes. Season with salt and pepper and serve. —*Marcia Kiesel*

**MAKE AHEAD** The soup can be frozen for up to 1 month.

**SERVE WITH** Crispy Cornmeal-Gruyère Muffins (p. 271).

### Mussel Chowder with Bacon and Shiitake Mushrooms
**TOTAL: 30 MIN**
6 SERVINGS ●
6 ounces thinly sliced bacon, cut crosswise into thin strips
1 cup chopped onion
1 celery rib, chopped
2 medium Yukon Gold potatoes, cut into ½-inch dice
2 tablespoons unsalted butter
½ pound shiitake mushrooms, stems discarded, caps thinly sliced
1 tablespoon all-purpose flour
2 cups chicken stock or low-sodium broth
1 cup dry white wine
1 cup clam juice
1 cup heavy cream
1 tablespoon vegetable oil
2 pounds mussels, scrubbed
2 tablespoons chopped flat-leaf parsley
½ teaspoon hot sauce
Salt and freshly ground pepper

**1.** In a large saucepan, cook the bacon over moderately high heat until it begins to crisp. Pour off all but 2 tablespoons of the bacon fat. Add the onion, celery and potatoes and cook, stirring frequently, until the vegetables begin to soften, about 4 minutes. Add the butter and shii-take and cook for 2 minutes. Stir in the flour and cook for 1 minute, then add the stock, wine, clam juice and cream and bring to a boil. Reduce the heat, cover and simmer the chowder until the potatoes are tender, about 10 minutes.

**2.** Meanwhile, in another large sauce-pan, heat the vegetable oil over moderately high heat. Add the mussels, cover and cook, shaking the pan occasionally, until the mussels open, about 3 minutes; discard any unopened mussels. Set a fine sieve over the chowder. Using the lid to hold back the mussels, pour the mussel liquid through the sieve into the chowder.

Simmer the chowder for 1 minute longer. Stir in the parsley and season with the hot sauce and salt and pepper. Spoon the mussels into bowls, ladle the chowder on top and serve immediately. —*Tom Douglas*

### Sour Fish Soup with Napa Cabbage and Enoki Mushrooms
**TOTAL: 50 MIN**
8 SERVINGS ● ●
2 ounces cellophane noodles
2 quarts fish stock
2 scallions, thinly sliced
½ cup Asian pickled mustard greens, drained and chopped, plus ¼ cup of the pickling liquid
1½ tablespoons minced ginger
2 tablespoons rice vinegar, plus more for serving
2 tablespoons Asian fish sauce, plus more for serving
1¼ pounds shredded napa cabbage
5 ounces enoki mushrooms
1½ pounds red snapper fillets, with skin, cut crosswise into 24 slices
½ cup chopped cilantro

**1.** Using scissors, cut the cellophane noodles into 3-inch lengths. In a heat-proof bowl, cover the noodles with very hot tap water and let stand until they are clear and pliable, about 5 minutes; drain.

**2.** In a large saucepan, bring the stock, scallions, mustard-green pickling liquid, ginger and 1 tablespoon each of rice vine-gar and fish sauce to a boil. Simmer over moderately low heat for 15 minutes.

**3.** Add the cabbage and simmer over moderate heat for 10 minutes. Add the enoki mushrooms and cellophane noodles and simmer for 3 minutes.

**4.** Add the fish to the soup and simmer until barely cooked through, 2 minutes. Add the cilantro, pickled mustard greens and the remaining 1 tablespoon each of rice vinegar and fish sauce. Serve, passing additional fish sauce and vinegar at the table. —*Zak Pelaccio*

# soups

## Mediterranean Fish Soup with Garlicky Rouille

**ACTIVE: 45 MIN; TOTAL: 1 HR 30 MIN**

8 SERVINGS ●

A traditional *rouille* (French for "rust") is made with chiles, garlic, bread and olive oil. In this recipe, it's prepared with potatoes, olive oil and plenty of garlic.

- 1 medium Yukon Gold potato, peeled and cut into 1-inch cubes
- 16 garlic cloves, 8 minced, 8 halved
- 1½ cups extra-virgin olive oil, plus more for brushing

Salt

- ¼ teaspoon cayenne pepper, plus more for sprinkling
- 2 large leeks, white and tender green parts only, halved lengthwise and cut into 1-inch pieces
- 1 large onion, finely chopped
- 1 celery rib, cut into ½-inch pieces
- 1 fennel bulb—halved, cored and cut into ½-inch pieces
- ½ tablespoon coarsely ground black pepper
- ½ tablespoon ground fennel seeds
- ½ tablespoon ground cumin
- ½ teaspoon sweet paprika
- ⅛ teaspoon crumbled saffron threads
- 3 tablespoons tomato paste
- 1 cup dry white wine
- 2 quarts fish stock or 1 quart clam juice diluted with 1 quart water
- 12 thyme sprigs, tied in a bundle with kitchen string

Freshly ground black pepper

- 1½ pounds monkfish or other meaty white fish, filmy outer skin removed, fish cut into 1-inch pieces
- 1 pound skinless cod fillet, cut into 1-inch pieces
- 1 pound tuna, cut into 1-inch pieces
- 1 small baguette, thinly sliced

Pinch of dried oregano

- ½ cup freshly grated Parmesan cheese

**1.** In a medium saucepan of boiling salted water, cook the potato cubes until tender, about 15 minutes. Drain well, reserving 2 tablespoons of the potato cooking water. Transfer the potatoes to a medium bowl. Add the reserved potato cooking water and the minced garlic and mash until smooth. Whisk in 1 cup of the olive oil in a thin stream until the *rouille* is creamy. Season with salt and cayenne.

**2.** Preheat the oven to 350°. In a large soup pot, heat the remaining ½ cup of olive oil until shimmering. Add the leeks, onion, celery, fennel bulb and 6 of the halved garlic cloves and cook over high heat, stirring frequently, until the vegetables are softened and lightly browned, about 9 minutes. Add the black pepper, ground fennel, cumin, paprika, crumbled saffron and tomato paste and cook until fragrant, about 1 minute. Add the wine to the soup pot and cook until it is nearly evaporated, about 8 minutes.

**3.** Add the fish stock and thyme bundle to the pot and bring the soup to a boil. Season with salt and black pepper and simmer for 10 minutes. Add the monkfish, cod and tuna and simmer the soup until the fish is cooked through, about 8 minutes. Discard the thyme bundle.

**4.** Meanwhile, on a large, rimmed baking sheet, arrange the baguette slices. Brush the slices all over with olive oil and sprinkle on one side with the oregano. Toast for about 5 minutes, or until the baguette slices are crisp and lightly golden. Rub the toasts with the 2 remaining halved garlic cloves.

**5.** Ladle the fish soup into deep bowls and stir some of the *rouille* into each or place a dollop on top. Serve the soup with the garlicky croutons, the Parmesan cheese and the remaining *rouille* on the side. —*Pascal Rigo*

## Smoked Salmon and Celery Root Bisque

**TOTAL: 45 MIN**

6 SERVINGS ●

You can use hot- or cold-smoked salmon here (see p. 21)—just make sure the fish isn't too salty.

- 2 tablespoons unsalted butter
- 1 large onion, coarsely chopped
- 1 medium fennel bulb, fronds discarded, bulb halved, cored and coarsely chopped
- 1 medium celery root (12 ounces), peeled and cut into ½-inch pieces
- ½ pound hot- or cold-smoked salmon, cut into 1-inch pieces
- 1 cup Pinot Gris
- 3½ cups fish stock or 1¾ cups clam juice mixed with 1¾ cups water
- 1 cup heavy cream

Salt and freshly ground pepper

Lemon wedges, for serving

**1.** Melt the butter in a large saucepan. Add the onion, fennel and celery root and cook over moderate heat, stirring occasionally, until crisp-tender, about 10 minutes. Add the salmon and cook, stirring, for 1 minute. Add the wine and cook over high heat until reduced to ⅓ cup, 7 to 8 minutes. Add the fish stock and bring to a boil. Cover, reduce the heat to moderately low and simmer until the vegetables are tender, about 15 minutes.

**2.** Strain the broth into a bowl. Working in batches, puree the solids in a blender, adding just enough of the broth to make a smooth puree. Return the puree and the remaining broth to a clean saucepan. Stir in the cream and season with salt and pepper. Simmer over low heat for about 5 minutes. Ladle the bisque into bowls and serve with lemon wedges. —*Michael Allemeier*

**MAKE AHEAD** The soup can be refrigerated overnight.

# lemongrass

It looks a bit like scallions and smells a bit like lemon, but delicately flavored, gently aromatic lemongrass is extremely unique. Here, this Asian staple enhances two different, delicious kinds of soups.

## Lemongrass-Scented Noodle Soup with Shrimp

**TOTAL: 30 MIN**

4 SERVINGS ● ●

- ¼ pound Asian rice noodles
- 4 cups chicken stock or low-sodium broth
- 2 plump lemongrass stalks, inner bulbs thinly sliced, tops crushed
- 1 medium garlic clove, thinly sliced

Salt and freshly ground pepper

- 1 pound peeled and deveined medium shrimp
- 1 cup snow peas, halved crosswise
- ½ bunch watercress, tough stems discarded (2 cups)
- ¼ cup finely chopped cilantro
- 2 scallions, thinly sliced
- 2 tablespoons fresh lime juice

**1.** Soak the noodles in a large bowl of hot tap water until pliable, about 15 minutes. Meanwhile, in a large saucepan, combine the stock with the sliced and crushed lemongrass and the garlic. Cover and simmer over low heat for 20 minutes. Season with salt and pepper and discard the large lemongrass stalks.

**2.** Bring a large saucepan of water to a boil. Drain the noodles and cook them in the boiling water until tender, about 2 minutes. Drain and rinse under cool water.

**3.** Add the shrimp, snow peas and watercress to the lemongrass broth and cook until the shrimp are pink and the vegetables are crisp-tender, about 2 minutes.

Stir in the cilantro, scallions, lime juice and noodles and cook just until heated through. Serve at once. —*Grace Parisi*

## Chicken and Potato Soup with Lemongrass

**TOTAL: 30 MIN**

6 SERVINGS ● ●

- 6 cups chicken stock or low-sodium broth
- 1 stalk of fresh lemongrass, cut into 2-inch lengths and lightly crushed

Four ¼-inch-thick slices of fresh ginger, lightly crushed

- 1 small jalapeño, thinly sliced crosswise, with seeds
- 2 garlic cloves, thinly sliced
- 1 small onion, coarsely chopped
- 2 medium carrots, thinly sliced
- 2 celery ribs, thinly sliced

Salt and freshly ground pepper

- 2 pounds Yukon Gold potatoes, peeled and cut into 1½-inch cubes
- 2 cups shredded roasted chicken
- 2 tablespoons thinly sliced mint

In a soup pot, combine the stock with the lemongrass, ginger, jalapeño and garlic and bring to a boil. Add the onion, carrots and celery and season with salt and pepper. Cover and cook over moderate heat until the vegetables are nearly tender, about 5 minutes. Add the potatoes, cover and cook until all the vegetables are tender, about 15 minutes longer. Add the chicken and simmer just until warmed through. Remove the lemongrass and ginger and stir in the mint. Serve the soup in deep bowls. —*Maggie Pond*

### HOW TO TRIM THE STALK

**CUT** off the root and the upper two-thirds of the stalk. What's remaining contains the lemongrass bulb.

**PEEL** the outer leaves of the lemongrass stalk—usually just one or two layers— to reveal the bulb.

**MINCE, SLICE OR CRUSH** the bulb before adding it to a dish that will then be cooked.

# soups

### Sweet-and-Sour Meatball Soup

**TOTAL: 30 MIN**

**6 SERVINGS** ● ●

- ¼ cup extra-virgin olive oil
- 2 large onions, halved lengthwise and thinly sliced crosswise
- 2 tablespoons light brown sugar

Two 14½-ounce cans diced tomatoes

- 4 cups beef stock or low-sodium broth
- 2 tablespoons fresh lemon juice

Kosher salt and freshly ground pepper

- 1 pound ground pork
- 1 large egg white
- 1½ teaspoons cornstarch

Finely grated zest of 1 lemon

- 2 tablespoons chopped cilantro
- 2 scallions, finely chopped

**1.** In a medium soup pot, heat the olive oil. Add the onions, cover and cook over moderately high heat, stirring occasionally, until they are softened, 3 to 4 minutes. Uncover; cook until lightly browned, about 5 minutes longer. Add the brown sugar and cook for 1 minute. Add the tomatoes and their juices, the stock and lemon juice, season lightly with salt and pepper and bring to a boil. Simmer the soup over moderate heat for 10 minutes.

# health

**Hot borscht is an iconic Russian dish. It's also full of nutrients: Cabbage contributes** vitamins A and C and phytochemicals; **beets offer** betacyanin, **a pigment believed to be a cancer fighter; and potatoes have** vitamins, potassium and iron. **Some versions of borscht are loaded with fatty meat, but the recipe on this page uses lean brisket.**

**2.** Meanwhile, in a medium bowl, combine the pork with the egg white, cornstarch, lemon zest, 2 teaspoons of salt, 1 teaspoon of pepper and half of the chopped cilantro and scallions. Using lightly moistened hands, roll slightly rounded tablespoons of the meat mixture into balls.

**3.** Add the meatballs to the soup, cover and cook over moderate heat until cooked through, about 5 minutes. Stir in the remaining cilantro and scallions. Ladle the soup into deep bowls and serve right away. —*Maggie Pond*

**MAKE AHEAD** The soup can be refrigerated overnight.

### Hearty Goulash Soup

**ACTIVE: 20 MIN; TOTAL: 1 HR 30 MIN**

**4 SERVINGS** ●

- 3 tablespoons vegetable oil
- 2 small onions, finely chopped
- 3 large garlic cloves, minced
- ¼ cup Hungarian sweet paprika
- 1 tablespoon tomato paste
- 1 tablespoon ground caraway seeds
- 1 teaspoon dried marjoram
- ½ teaspoon dried thyme
- 1 bay leaf
- 3 pounds beef shin, bones removed, meat cut into 1-inch pieces
- 6 cups water
- 1 large Yukon Gold potato, peeled and cut into ⅓-inch dice
- 2 teaspoons fresh lemon juice

Kosher salt and freshly ground pepper

Heat the oil in a large skillet. Add the onions and garlic and cook over moderate heat, stirring frequently, until lightly browned, about 8 minutes. Add the paprika; cook for 2 minutes, stirring frequently. Stir in the tomato paste and cook for 1 minute. Stir in the caraway, marjoram, thyme and bay leaf. Add the meat and water and bring to a simmer. Cover the soup and cook until the meat is very tender, about 1 hour. Add

the potatoes and cook, uncovered, until they are tender, about 15 minutes. Add the lemon juice, season with salt and pepper and serve. —*Kurt Gutenbrunner*

**MAKE AHEAD** The soup can be refrigerated for up to 3 days.

### Winter Borscht with Brisket

**ACTIVE: 1 HR; TOTAL: 4 HR 45 MIN**

**10 SERVINGS** ● ●

- 3 pounds lean beef brisket, trimmed of any fat
- 4 quarts plus 2 cups water
- 3 onions, 2 halved, 1 finely chopped
- 3 carrots, 2 halved, 1 coarsely shredded
- 1 parsnip, halved
- 1 bay leaf
- ½ teaspoon black peppercorns

Kosher salt

- 2 large beets (1½ pounds total), scrubbed
- 1 tablespoon vegetable oil
- 1 thick slice of meaty bacon
- 1 large green bell pepper, cut into ½-inch pieces
- 2 cups chopped green cabbage
- 3 all-purpose potatoes, peeled and cut into 1½-inch chunks
- 1 cup chopped canned tomatoes
- 1 medium Granny Smith apple— peeled, cored and cut into ½-inch pieces

Freshly ground pepper

- 3 tablespoons distilled white vinegar

Pinch of sugar

- 3 garlic cloves, minced
- 2 tablespoons finely chopped flat-leaf parsley

Reduced-fat sour cream, chopped dill and sliced scallions, for serving

**1.** Cut the brisket into 4 pieces and put them in a large soup pot. Add the water and bring to a boil over high heat, skimming. Add the halved onions, halved carrots, parsnip, bay leaf, peppercorns and a generous pinch of salt. Reduce the heat to low, cover partially and simmer until the meat is just tender, about 3 hours. Using a slotted spoon, transfer the brisket to a cutting board and cut it into 1-inch pieces. Strain the broth into a bowl and discard the vegetables. Let the broth cool and skim off any fat.

2. Meanwhile, preheat the oven to 375°. Wrap the beets individually in foil and bake for 1 hour, or until tender. Let cool, then peel and coarsely grate them.

3. Wipe out the soup pot, add the vegetable oil and heat. Add the bacon and cook over moderate heat until crisp. Remove the bacon; reserve for another use. Add the chopped onion, shredded carrot and bell pepper and cook over moderate heat until just softened, about 7 minutes. Add the cabbage and cook, stirring occasionally, until softened, about 7 minutes longer. Add the reserved broth, the potatoes, tomatoes, apple and brisket and season with salt and pepper. Cover partially and simmer until the potatoes are barely tender, 15 minutes. Reduce the heat to moderately low, add the beets and cook until the potatoes are very tender, about 30 minutes longer. Stir in the vinegar and sugar and season with salt.

4. In a mortar, pound the garlic, parsley and 1 teaspoon of pepper to a paste; stir into the soup. Ladle the borscht into deep bowls and serve, passing the sour cream, dill and scallions at the table.

—*Anya von Bremzen*

**MAKE AHEAD** The borscht can be refrigerated for up to 3 days.

### Star Anise–Beef Soup

**ACTIVE: 1 HR 20 MIN; TOTAL: 3 HR 45 MIN, PLUS OVERNIGHT REFRIGERATING**

6 SERVINGS

SOUP

6　meaty pieces of beef shank, cut about 1 inch thick

2　tablespoons vegetable oil

2　large onions, halved

½　pound fresh ginger, sliced lengthwise ½ inch thick

3　star anise pods

2　cinnamon sticks, broken in half

1　teaspoon whole cloves

1　teaspoon crushed red pepper

5　pounds meaty oxtails

4½　quarts water

3　large stalks of lemongrass, cut into 4-inch lengths

1　head garlic, halved crosswise

1　pound medium rice noodles

1　pound sirloin steak, cut 1 inch thick

GARNISHES

¾　pound baby bok choy, halved lengthwise

6　asparagus spears, cut into 1-inch lengths

¼　pound snow peas

Salt and freshly ground pepper

1　pound bean sprouts

¼　cup julienned peeled fresh ginger

6　scallions, julienned

6　mint sprigs

6　basil sprigs

6　Thai chiles, thinly sliced

6　lime wedges

Soy sauce and Asian fish sauce

1. **MAKE THE SOUP:** Cut the meat off the shank bones. In a large saucepan, cover the bones with water and bring to a boil. Prepare a bowl of ice water. Transfer the bones to the ice bath to cool, then pat dry.

2. Heat 1 tablespoon of the oil in a large skillet. Add the onions, cut side down, and cook over moderately high heat until blackened on the bottoms, about 12 minutes; remove the onions to a plate. Heat the remaining 1 tablespoon of oil in the skillet. Spread the ginger slices in a single layer and cook over moderately high heat until blackened, about 12 minutes.

3. In a medium skillet, toast the star anise pods, cinnamon sticks, cloves and crushed red pepper over moderate heat for 2 minutes, shaking the skillet.

4. In a large stockpot, cover the shank meat and oxtails with the 4½ quarts of water and bring to a boil. Skim, then add the lemongrass, garlic, blackened onions and ginger and the toasted spices and simmer over moderately low heat, skimming occasionally, until the meats are tender, about 2 hours. Strain the broth; refrigerate the broth and the meats separately overnight or for up to 2 days.

5. Discard the fat from the cold broth. Bring the broth to a boil, lower the heat and keep hot. Thinly slice the meats, discarding any bones.

6. In a large bowl, soak the rice noodles in water until they are soft and pliable, about 30 minutes. Bring a large saucepan of water to a boil.

7. **MEANWHILE, PREPARE THE GARNISHES:** In a medium saucepan of boiling salted water, blanch the bok choy, asparagus and snow peas separately until crisp-tender; remove the vegetables to a platter. Add the shank bones to the saucepan and cook over moderate heat for 2 minutes. Drain and let cool slightly, then use a small spoon to scoop out the marrow.

8. Preheat a grill pan. Generously season the sirloin with salt and pepper and cook over high heat until rare, about 2 minutes per side. Transfer the sirloin to a carving board and let rest for 5 minutes, then thinly slice it.

9. Drain the rice noodles and add a handful to a long-handled strainer that will fit into the saucepan of boiling water. Lower it into the water and cook the noodles until barely tender, 30 seconds to 1 minute. Drain well and transfer the noodles to a large soup bowl. Add some of the shank and oxtail meats and cover with broth. Add a piece of marrow and slices of sirloin and serve, allowing the diner to garnish the soup with the remaining ingredients. Repeat for the rest of the diners. —*Jean-Georges Vongerichten*

FRESH PASTA WITH SPICY CORN AND ASPARAGUS, P. 78

# pasta

**PASTA WITH BORLOTTI BEANS**

**CAVATELLI WITH SPICY WINTER SQUASH**

## Pasta with Borlotti Beans, Olives and Cherry Tomatoes

**ACTIVE: 25 MIN; TOTAL: 2 HR 30 MIN, PLUS SOAKING**

**4 SERVINGS** ●

- 1 cup dried borlotti or cranberry beans (6 ounces), soaked overnight or quick-soaked and drained (see Note)

Salt

- ¼ cup extra-virgin olive oil, plus more for serving
- 2 garlic cloves, minced
- 1 tablespoon tomato paste
- 8 cherry tomatoes, halved

Pinch of dried oregano

- ½ pound tubetti, mezzi rigatoni or other pasta
- 12 pitted oil-cured black olives

Freshly grated Pecorino Romano cheese, for serving

**1.** In a saucepan, cover the beans with 2 inches of water and bring to a boil. Simmer over moderately low heat, stirring occasionally, until tender, 2 hours. Add water as necessary to keep the beans submerged in 1 inch of water. Remove from the heat, season with salt and drain, reserving the cooking liquid.

**2.** Heat the ¼ cup of olive oil in a large saucepan. Add the garlic and cook over moderate heat until golden, 2 minutes. Add the tomato paste and cook, stirring, for 1 minute. Add the cherry tomatoes and oregano and cook for 3 minutes. Add the beans and ¼ cup of their cooking liquid and simmer for 5 minutes. Add ¼ cup more of the bean cooking liquid and simmer for 3 minutes. Season with salt.

**3.** Meanwhile, in a large pot of boiling salted water, cook the pasta until al dente. Drain well.

**4.** Add the pasta to the beans along with another ½ cup of the bean cooking liquid. Simmer for 1 minute and add the olives. Add more cooking liquid if necessary to coat the pasta and beans with sauce. Ladle into bowls and serve, passing the Pecorino and olive oil at the table.
—*Christophe Hille*

**NOTE** To quick-soak beans, rinse them, then, in a saucepan, cover with water and boil for 2 minutes. Remove from the heat, cover and let stand for 1 hour; drain.

**WINE** Medium-bodied, round Pinot Blanc.

## Cavatelli with Spicy Winter Squash

**TOTAL: 45 MIN**

**8 SERVINGS** ● ●

Mario Batali, the chef at New York City's Babbo, likes to serve this pasta family-style at home. You can substitute pumpkin or hubbard squash—whichever looks more beautiful at your market—for the butternut. "Cook the squash until it is soft but not falling apart," Batali says. "You don't want al dente squash, but you don't want mush either."

¼ cup plus 2 tablespoons extra-virgin olive oil
6 large garlic cloves, very thinly sliced
1 large red onion, very thinly sliced
2 teaspoons crushed red pepper
2 pounds butternut squash— peeled, seeded and cut into ½-inch cubes
1 tablespoon finely chopped thyme
Salt and freshly ground pepper
1½ pounds cavatelli or small shells
¾ cup freshly grated caciocavallo, pecorino or Parmesan cheese, plus more for serving

1. Bring a large pot of salted water to a boil. In a large, deep skillet, heat the olive oil until shimmering. Add the garlic, onion, and crushed red pepper and cook the mixture over moderately high heat, stirring occasionally, until the garlic and onion are softened, about 5 minutes. Add the squash and thyme, season with salt and pepper and cook for 5 minutes, stirring occasionally. Cover the skillet and cook over moderately low heat, stirring occasionally, until the squash is tender when pierced with a fork but not mushy, about 5 minutes.
2. Meanwhile, add the cavatelli to the boiling water and cook until al dente. Drain well, reserving 1 cup of the pasta cooking water. Add the cavatelli to the squash mixture in the skillet, then stir in ½ cup of the pasta cooking water and toss gently to combine. Add the ¾ cup of caciocavallo, season with salt and pepper and stir gently; add a little more pasta water if necessary. Serve the pasta immediately, passing additional cheese at the table. —*Mario Batali*
**WINE** Dry, full-flavored Alsace Riesling.

## Penne all'Arrabbiata
**TOTAL: 30 MIN**
6 SERVINGS ● ●
1 pound penne
¼ cup plus 2 tablespoons extra-virgin olive oil
6 garlic cloves, minced
2 teaspoons crushed red pepper
One 28-ounce can crushed tomatoes
1 teaspoon dried oregano
Salt
2 tablespoons chopped flat-leaf parsley
Freshly grated pecorino cheese, for serving

1. In a large pot of boiling salted water, cook the penne until al dente.
2. Meanwhile, in a large, deep skillet, heat ¼ cup of the olive oil. Add the garlic and crushed red pepper and cook over moderate heat until golden and fragrant, about 3 minutes. Add the crushed tomatoes, oregano and a pinch of salt and bring to a boil. Simmer over moderate heat, stirring occasionally, until slightly reduced, about 8 minutes.
3. Drain the penne, reserving ⅓ cup of the pasta cooking water. Add the penne to the skillet and toss well. Add the reserved pasta cooking water, the remaining 2 tablespoons of olive oil and the parsley, season with salt and stir well. Transfer the pasta to shallow bowls and serve with the pecorino cheese.
—*Celestino Drago*
**WINE** Light, spicy Pinot Grigio.

## Roasted Tomatoes with Penne and Ricotta Salata
**ACTIVE: 25 MIN; TOTAL: 1 HR 15 MIN**
4 SERVINGS ●
You can use farmers' market "seconds"— tomatoes that are blemished, soft or split—for this garlic-infused recipe. Slow-roasting concentrates the sugars, making the tomatoes especially flavorful.

¼ cup plus 2 tablespoons extra-virgin olive oil
3 pounds ripe plum tomatoes, halved lengthwise
3 small onions, coarsely chopped
6 garlic cloves, coarsely chopped
Salt and freshly ground pepper
¾ pound penne or farfalle
1 cup coarsely shredded ricotta salata cheese (3 ounces)

1. Preheat the oven to 350°. Pour ¼ cup of the olive oil into a large roasting pan. Add the tomato halves and the chopped onions and garlic and toss to coat the vegetables with the olive oil. Season lightly with salt and pepper and roast for about 50 minutes, or until the tomatoes are soft and beginning to brown and the juices have begun to thicken.
2. In a large pot of boiling salted water, cook the penne until al dente; drain well. Add the cooked penne to the roasting pan, toss to coat the pasta with the sauce and season with salt and pepper. Transfer the pasta to a large serving bowl and drizzle with the remaining 2 tablespoons of olive oil. Sprinkle with the ricotta salata and serve immediately.
—*Barbara Spencer*
**MAKE AHEAD** The pasta can be refrigerated overnight. Drizzle with the olive oil and ricotta salata before serving.
**WINE** Tangy, crisp Vernaccia.

## Whole Wheat Spaghetti with Fresh Ricotta and Lemon Zest
**TOTAL: 20 MIN**
6 SERVINGS ●
1 pound whole wheat spaghetti
2 tablespoons unsalted butter
Finely grated zest of 2 lemons
1 cup heavy cream
Salt and freshly ground pepper
1 pound fresh ricotta cheese
¼ cup freshly grated Parmesan cheese

# pasta

1. In a large pot of boiling salted water, cook the spaghetti until al dente.

2. Meanwhile, in a large, deep skillet, melt the butter. Add the lemon zest and cook over moderate heat, stirring, for about 1 minute. Add the heavy cream and bring to a boil. Simmer over moderate heat for 3 minutes. Add a pinch each of salt and pepper and remove the skillet from the heat. Stir in the fresh ricotta.

3. Drain the pasta. Add it to the skillet and toss well. Add the Parmesan, season with salt and pepper and toss again. Transfer to bowls and serve.
—*Celestino Drago*

**WINE** Simple, fruity Chianti or Sangiovese.

## Fettuccine with Walnut-Parsley Pesto

**TOTAL: 30 MIN**
**4 SERVINGS** ●

¾ cup walnut halves (3 ounces)
¼ cup flat-leaf parsley leaves, plus 2 tablespoons coarsely chopped
½ cup freshly grated Parmesan cheese, plus shavings for garnish
½ pound fettuccine
1 garlic clove, smashed
¼ cup extra-virgin olive oil
Salt and freshly ground pepper
½ cup vegetable stock
1 tablespoon unsalted butter

1. Preheat the oven to 350°. Toast the walnuts in a pie plate for 7 minutes, or until they are golden; let cool. Coarsely chop ¼ cup of the walnuts and transfer to a bowl; add the 2 tablespoons of chopped parsley and half of the grated Parmesan.

2. In a large pot of boiling salted water, cook the pasta until al dente; drain. In a mini food processor, pulse the remaining ½ cup of walnuts with the ¼ cup of parsley leaves and the garlic until finely chopped. Add the remaining grated Parmesan cheese and the olive oil and process to a coarse puree. Season the pesto with salt and pepper.

3. Return the pasta to the pot. Add the vegetable stock and butter and simmer until the liquid is nearly absorbed, 1 to 2 minutes. Off the heat, add the pesto and toss until combined. Transfer the pasta to a large bowl, garnish with the walnut, parsley and Parmesan mixture and Parmesan shavings and serve.
—*Bill Telepan*

**WINE** Light, zesty, fruity Dolcetto.

## Tagliolini with Eggplant and Mint

**TOTAL: 30 MIN**
**6 SERVINGS** ● ●

1 pound tagliolini or linguine
¼ cup extra-virgin olive oil
1 small shallot, minced
1 large Japanese eggplant (about 6 ounces), cut into ¼-inch pieces (2 cups)
½ cup vegetable stock
1 cup chopped canned tomatoes, drained
2 tablespoons chopped mint
Salt and freshly ground pepper
1 tablespoon unsalted butter
¼ cup freshly grated Romano cheese, plus more for serving

1. In a large pot of boiling salted water, cook the tagliolini until al dente.

2. Meanwhile, in a large, deep skillet, heat the olive oil. Add the shallot and cook over moderately high heat until softened, about 1 minute. Add the eggplant pieces in an even layer and cook undisturbed until browned on the bottom, about 1 minute. Cook, stirring a few times, until tender, about 2 minutes more. Add the vegetable stock and simmer for 1 minute. Add the tomatoes and mint, season with salt and pepper and cook over low heat for 4 minutes.

3. Drain the tagliolini, reserving 1 cup of the cooking water. Add the pasta to the skillet along with the butter and ¼ cup of the Romano cheese and toss well. Add enough of the reserved pasta cooking water to moisten the pasta, then season with salt and pepper. Transfer the pasta to bowls and serve with additional Romano cheese. —*Celestino Drago*

**WINE** Tart, low-tannin Barbera.

## Penne with Zucchini and Basil

**TOTAL: 25 MIN**
**10 FIRST-COURSE SERVINGS** ●
Packed with summer squash and herbs, this pasta makes a terrific starter. It will serve eight as a main dish.

1½ pounds penne or gemelli
½ cup extra-virgin olive oil
1½ pounds small zucchini, halved lengthwise and sliced ½ inch thick
Salt and freshly ground pepper
4 tablespoons unsalted butter
¾ cup freshly grated Parmesan cheese (about 2 ounces)
¼ cup plus 2 tablespoons fresh basil leaves

1. In a large pot of boiling salted water, cook the pasta until al dente.

2. Meanwhile, heat ¼ cup of the olive oil in each of 2 large skillets. Add half of the zucchini to each skillet, season with salt and pepper and cook over high heat, stirring occasionally, until lightly browned, about 5 minutes.

3. Drain the penne, reserving 1 cup of the cooking water. Return the pasta to the pot and add the butter and zucchini along with any olive oil in the skillets. Add ½ cup of the reserved pasta cooking water and half of the Parmesan and season with salt and pepper. Cook over moderate heat, stirring, until the liquid is creamy and slightly thickened, 1 to 2 minutes. Add more of the pasta cooking water if the pasta is dry. Stir in half of the basil and transfer the pasta to a platter. Sprinkle with the remaining Parmesan and basil and serve immediately.
—*Marcella Giamundo*

**WINE** Light, dry Soave or similar white.

## Sheep's-Milk Ricotta Gnocchi with Mushrooms and Corn

**ACTIVE: 1 HR 15 MIN;**

**TOTAL: 3 HR 15 MIN**

4 SERVINGS

- 1 pound sheep's-milk ricotta cheese (see Note)
- ½ cup all-purpose flour
- ⅓ cup freshly grated Parmesan cheese
- 2 large egg yolks
- Kosher salt and freshly ground pepper
- ¾ cup fresh corn kernels (from 2 medium ears)
- 4 tablespoons unsalted butter
- ¼ cup plus 2 tablespoons extra-virgin olive oil
- 1 pound mixed mushrooms—such as chanterelles, oysters and shiitake—shiitake stemmed, mushrooms quartered if large
- ½ cup dry white wine
- 1 cup chicken stock or low-sodium broth
- 1 tablespoon cornstarch
- 1 tablespoon coarsely chopped tarragon

**1.** Line a large, rimmed baking sheet with wax paper. In a large bowl, blend the ricotta with the flour, Parmesan cheese, egg yolks, ¾ teaspoon of salt and ¼ teaspoon of pepper to form a soft dough. Spoon the gnocchi dough into a large, sturdy, resealable plastic bag. Cut off a ½-inch corner from the bag. Pipe the dough onto the prepared baking sheet in five 12-inch-long strips about ¾ inch wide. Cover with plastic wrap and freeze until firm, about 3 hours.

**2.** Meanwhile, in a small saucepan of boiling salted water, cook the corn until just tender, about 3 minutes. Drain and return the corn to the saucepan. Stir in 2 tablespoons of the butter.

**3.** In a very large skillet, heat 2 tablespoons of the olive oil until shimmering. Add the mushrooms, season with salt

**PENNE WITH ZUCCHINI AND BASIL**

**SHEEP'S-MILK RICOTTA GNOCCHI WITH MUSHROOMS**

# pasta

and pepper and cook over moderately high heat until browned on the bottom, about 5 minutes. Stir and cook until browned and tender, about 4 minutes longer. Transfer to a plate. Add the wine to the skillet and boil over moderately high heat until reduced by half, about 3 minutes. Add the chicken stock and boil until reduced to ¾ cup, about 4 minutes. Add the corn and set aside.

**4.** Preheat the oven to 275°. Let the gnocchi dough stand at room temperature for 5 minutes to soften. Cut the strips of dough into 1-inch lengths. Sprinkle with the cornstarch and toss gently to coat so the gnocchi don't stick together.

**5.** In a large nonstick skillet, heat 2 tablespoons of the olive oil until shimmering. Add half of the gnocchi and cook over high heat until browned on the bottom, about 1 minute. Reduce the heat to moderately high. Using a spatula, turn the gnocchi and brown the other side, 1 to 2 minutes. Transfer the gnocchi to a baking sheet; keep warm in the oven. Repeat with the remaining 2 tablespoons of olive oil and the gnocchi.

**6.** Reheat the corn in the skillet. Add the mushrooms, the chopped tarragon and the remaining 2 tablespoons of butter and season with salt and pepper. Transfer the gnocchi to plates, spoon the mushroom ragout around them and serve.
—*Melissa Perello*

**NOTE** Sheep's-milk ricotta is available at specialty food stores and by mail order from Old Chatham Sheepherding Company (blacksheepcheese.com or 888-743-3760). Alternatively, use cow's-milk ricotta and drain it overnight in a fine strainer, covered, in the refrigerator; discard the whey.

**MAKE AHEAD** The gnocchi strips can be frozen for up to 3 days. The ragout components can be cooked up to 2 hours ahead and kept at room temperature.

**WINE** Fruity, low-oak Chardonnay.

## Spinach and Ricotta Gnocchi
**TOTAL: 1 HR**
**8 SERVINGS**

This dish is also known as naked ravioli because the gnocchi are essentially buttery mounds of ravioli filling. Spinach helps keep the gnocchi together here, so be sure to squeeze the leaves completely dry.

- 6 **pounds fresh spinach, stems trimmed**
- 8 **large egg yolks**
- 2 **cups whole-milk ricotta cheese (1 pound), preferably fresh**
- 2 **cups freshly grated Parmesan cheese, plus more for sprinkling**
- ½ **cup all-purpose flour, plus more for dusting**
- 2 **teaspoons kosher salt**
- ½ **teaspoon freshly ground pepper**
- 1 **teaspoon finely grated lemon zest**
- 1 **teaspoon freshly grated nutmeg**
- 1 **stick (4 ounces) unsalted butter, melted**

**1.** Bring a large pot of water to a boil. Add one-third of the spinach and boil just until wilted. Using a slotted spoon, transfer the spinach to a colander and let cool under running water. Repeat with the remaining spinach. Squeeze the spinach as dry as possible.

**2.** Finely chop the cooked spinach and transfer it to a large bowl. Add the egg yolks, ricotta, 1½ cups of the Parmesan, ½ cup of the flour, and the salt, pepper, grated lemon zest and nutmeg. Stir to form a soft dough.

**3.** Divide the dough into 8 pieces. On a lightly floured surface, roll each piece of dough into a 1-inch-thick rope. Cut each rope into 1-inch pieces. Using floured hands, roll the pieces into balls, flatten them slightly and transfer the gnocchi to a generously floured, rimmed baking sheet.

**4.** Bring a large pot of salted water to a boil. Pour half of the melted butter into a large baking dish. Add one-quarter of the gnocchi to the boiling water, gently stir once and let the gnocchi rise to the surface. Simmer the gnocchi until tender and cooked through, 2 to 3 minutes. Using a slotted spoon, transfer the gnocchi to the buttered baking dish. Cover with foil and cook the remaining gnocchi in batches. Reserve ½ cup of the gnocchi cooking water.

**5.** In a large, deep skillet, combine the remaining 4 tablespoons of melted butter and ½ cup of Parmesan with the reserved gnocchi cooking water and simmer over moderate heat until slightly thickened, about 4 minutes. Pour the sauce over the gnocchi and toss to coat. Sprinkle with additional Parmesan and serve right away. —*Steven Wagner*

**MAKE AHEAD** The gnocchi can be prepared through Step 3 and refrigerated overnight.

**WINE** Light, zesty, fruity Dolcetto.

## Fresh Pasta with Spicy Corn and Asparagus
**TOTAL: 1 HR**
**4 SERVINGS**
PASTA

- 4 **large eggs**
- 2 **large egg yolks**
- 1 **teaspoon extra-virgin olive oil**

Salt

- 2½ **cups all-purpose flour, plus more for rolling**

VEGETABLES

- ¼ **cup extra-virgin olive oil**
- 1 **small red onion, finely chopped**
- 1 **large jalapeño, seeded and thinly sliced**
- 2 **cups fresh corn kernels (from 4 large ears)**
- 1 **pound pencil-thin asparagus, stalks sliced ¼ inch thick, tips left whole**

Salt and freshly ground pepper

- 6 **tablespoons freshly grated Pecorino Romano cheese, plus more for serving**

1. **MAKE THE PASTA:** In a glass measuring cup, mix the whole eggs with the egg yolks, olive oil and a pinch of salt. Put the 2½ cups of flour in a food processor. Drizzle the egg mixture over the flour and process in long pulses until the dough is evenly moistened and forms small clumps, about 2 minutes. Transfer the dough to a work surface and knead until smooth and silky, about 2 minutes. Shape into a ball, wrap in plastic and let stand at room temperature for 15 minutes or refrigerate overnight.

2. Cut the dough into quarters; work with 1 piece at a time and keep the rest covered. Flatten the dough slightly and run it through successively narrower settings on a pasta machine until you reach the last setting. Trim the ends and cut the pasta sheet into 12-inch lengths. Drape the pasta sheets over a drying rack and let dry for 10 minutes. Repeat with the remaining dough.

3. Lightly flour 2 pasta sheets and stack them on top of each other. Starting at a short end, roll up the sheets very loosely. Trim the edges and, using a large knife, cut the rolled dough into ¼-inch-wide strips. Unroll the strips, toss lightly with flour and transfer to a rimmed baking sheet lined with wax paper. Repeat the process with the remaining sheets of pasta. Toss the cut pasta occasionally to separate the strands.

4. Bring a large pot of salted water to a boil. Add the pasta and cook, stirring occasionally, until it is just barely al dente, 2 to 3 minutes. Drain the pasta, reserving 1½ cups of the cooking water.

5. **MEANWHILE, PREPARE THE VEGETABLES:** Heat the olive oil in a large, deep skillet until shimmering. Add the onion and jalapeño and cook over moderately high heat, stirring, until softened, about 2 minutes. Add the corn and asparagus and cook, stirring occasionally, until crisp-tender, about 3 minutes.

6. Add 1 cup of the reserved pasta cooking water and a generous pinch each of salt and pepper to the vegetables and bring to a boil over moderately high heat. Add the pasta and cook, stirring, until the liquid is nearly absorbed and the pasta is tender, about 2 minutes; if necessary, add a little more of the pasta cooking water. Add the 6 tablespoons of grated Pecorino and toss. Serve the pasta in shallow bowls, passing extra Pecorino at the table.
—*Scott Conant*

**MAKE AHEAD** The pasta can be prepared through Step 3 and refrigerated overnight or frozen for up to 1 month. To freeze, toss with cornmeal and store in a sturdy plastic bag.
**WINE** Light, soft Chenin Blanc.

## Orecchiette with Hazelnuts and Goat Cheese
**TOTAL: 30 MIN**
8 SERVINGS ●
- ½ cup fresh bread crumbs
- ½ cup hazelnuts, coarsely chopped
- 1 cup fresh goat cheese (½ pound), at room temperature
- ¼ cup extra-virgin olive oil
- ¼ cup finely chopped flat-leaf parsley
- 1½ teaspoons crushed red pepper
- 1½ pounds orecchiette
- Salt and freshly ground pepper

1. Preheat the oven to 350°. Spread the bread crumbs in a pie plate and toast for about 4 minutes, or until golden.

2. Bring a large pot of salted water to a boil. In a food processor, pulse the hazelnuts until finely chopped. Transfer to a very large serving bowl and stir in the goat cheese, olive oil, parsley and crushed red pepper.

3. Add the orecchiette to the boiling water and cook until al dente. Drain, reserving 1 cup of the pasta cooking water. Transfer the orecchiette to the serving bowl. Add the pasta cooking water, season with salt and pepper and toss well to coat the pasta with the sauce. Sprinkle the orecchiette with the toasted bread crumbs and serve right away.
—*Mario Batali*
**WINE** Round-textured Sémillon.

## Spaghetti with Browned Butter and Crispy Bread Crumbs
**TOTAL: 20 MIN**
6 SERVINGS ●
- 1½ pounds spaghetti
- 1 tablespoon extra-virgin olive oil
- ⅓ cup dry bread crumbs
- 1 teaspoon finely grated lemon zest
- Salt and freshly ground pepper
- 2 tablespoons chopped flat-leaf parsley
- 1½ sticks (6 ounces) unsalted butter
- 1 cup plus 2 tablespoons grated myzithra (see Note) or ricotta salata cheese
- 1 cup plus 2 tablespoons freshly grated Parmesan cheese

1. In a large pot of boiling salted water, cook the spaghetti until al dente.

2. Meanwhile, in a small skillet, heat the olive oil. Add the bread crumbs and cook over moderately high heat, stirring, until browned, about 2 minutes. Remove the toasted bread crumbs from the heat and add the lemon zest. Season with salt and pepper and let cool. Stir in the parsley.

3. In a small, heavy saucepan, melt the butter over moderate heat. Cook until foamy and dark brown, about 5 minutes. Remove from the heat.

4. Drain the pasta and return it to the pot. Add the browned butter and the two cheeses, season with salt and pepper and toss. Transfer to a platter, sprinkle with some of the bread crumbs and serve with the remaining dressing on the side.
—*Tom Douglas*
**NOTE** Myzithra is a Greek sheep's-milk cheese similar in texture to a dry ricotta.
**WINE** Fruity, low-oak Chardonnay.

# pasta

## Cold Noodles with Tofu in Peanut Sauce

**TOTAL: 30 MIN**

4 SERVINGS ● ●

 3 tablespoons Japanese mirin
 3 tablespoons rice vinegar
 3 tablespoons low-sodium
　 soy sauce
 ½ pound sliced (½ inch)
　 silken tofu
 ¾ pound lo mein noodles
 ¾ pound mung bean sprouts
 1 large bunch cilantro,
　 leaves only
 ¾ cup natural peanut butter
Chili-garlic sauce
Salt
Lime wedges and chopped peanuts,
　 for serving

1. Preheat the oven to 350°. In a baking dish, mix the mirin, vinegar and soy sauce. Add the tofu; let stand for 15 minutes, turning halfway through. Pour the marinade into a bowl. Bake the tofu for 10 minutes. Cut into ½-inch pieces.

2. Meanwhile, bring a large pot of salted water to a boil and fill a large bowl with ice water. Add the noodles to the pot and cook until al dente, 6 minutes. Drain the noodles, reserving ⅓ cup of cooking water. Immediately plunge the noodles into the ice water to cool; drain well. Transfer the noodles to a large bowl and add the bean sprouts and cilantro.

3. In a food processor, combine the peanut butter with 1 teaspoon of chili-garlic sauce. With the machine on, slowly add the ⅓ cup of reserved noodle cooking water. Pour in the reserved marinade, season with salt and process until combined. Pour the peanut sauce over the noodles and toss well. Transfer the noodles to bowls, top with the tofu and serve with the lime wedges, chopped peanuts and chili-garlic sauce.
*—Ilene Rosen*
**WINE** Tart, peppery Grüner Veltliner.

## Spaghetti with Shrimp and Spicy Tomato Sauce

**TOTAL: 20 MIN**

4 SERVINGS ● ●

 ¾ pound thin spaghetti
 ¼ cup extra-virgin olive oil
 6 garlic cloves, thinly sliced
 2 dried red chiles, crumbled
 1 pound cherry tomatoes,
　 chopped
Salt
 1 pound frozen deveined medium
　 shrimp—thawed, shelled and
　 halved lengthwise
 ¼ cup shredded basil leaves

In a large pot of boiling salted water, cook the spaghetti until al dente. Meanwhile, warm the oil in a medium saucepan. Add the garlic and chiles and cook over moderate heat until the garlic is golden. Add the tomatoes, season with salt and cook for 5 minutes. Add the shrimp and basil and cook for 2 minutes. Barely drain the pasta and return it to the pot. Add the sauce, toss and serve. *—Jane Sigal*
**WINE** Light, spicy Pinot Grigio.

## Gemelli with Shrimp and Green Peppercorns

**TOTAL: 30 MIN**

6 SERVINGS ● ●

 1 pound gemelli or fusilli
 1 tablespoon unsalted butter
 3 garlic cloves, minced
 1 small shallot, minced
 1 tablespoon brined green
　 peppercorns, drained
 ⅓ cup brandy
 1 cup bottled clam juice
 2 plum tomatoes, cut into
　 ½-inch dice
 1 pound shelled and deveined
　 medium shrimp
Salt
 3 tablespoons chopped
　 flat-leaf parsley
 2 tablespoons extra-virgin olive oil

1. In a large pot of boiling salted water, cook the gemelli until al dente.

2. Meanwhile, in a large, deep skillet, melt the butter. Add the garlic, shallot and peppercorns and cook over moderately high heat until the vegetables are golden, about 2 minutes. Add the brandy and carefully ignite it with a long match. When the flames die down, add the clam juice and simmer for 2 minutes. Add the tomatoes and simmer for 1 minute. Add the shrimp, season with salt and cook over moderate heat, stirring a few times, until the shrimp are just white throughout, about 2 minutes.

3. Drain the gemelli, add it to the shrimp and peppercorn sauce and toss well. Stir in the parsley and olive oil and season with salt. Spoon the pasta into bowls and serve. *—Celestino Drago*
**WINE** High-acid, savory Vermentino.

## Spicy Chinese Noodles with Shrimp

**TOTAL: 25 MIN**

4 SERVINGS ● ●

Salt
 1½ tablespoons tomato paste
 2 garlic cloves, very finely
　 chopped
 2 teaspoons minced fresh ginger
 2 teaspoons hot paprika
 ¼ teaspoon ground turmeric
 2 tablespoons water
 ¼ cup peanut oil
 1 small onion, minced
 1 pound shelled and deveined
　 large shrimp
 3 tablespoons Asian fish sauce
 1 tablespoon rice vinegar
 1 teaspoon Asian sesame oil
 2 scallions, white and light green
　 parts only, thinly sliced
 1 pound fresh Chinese egg
　 noodles, Japanese yakisoba
　 noodles or linguine
Lime wedges, for serving

GEMELLI WITH SHRIMP AND GREEN PEPPERCORNS

# pasta

1. Bring a large pot of salted water to a boil. In a small bowl, stir the tomato paste with the garlic, ginger, paprika, turmeric and water.

2. In a large skillet, heat the peanut oil. Add the onion and cook over moderately high heat, stirring occasionally, until it begins to brown, about 5 minutes. Add the tomato paste mixture and cook, stirring constantly, until fragrant, 1 to 2 minutes. Add the shrimp and cook until just opaque, about 3 minutes. Add the fish sauce, rice vinegar, sesame oil and half of the scallions. Remove from the heat.

# equipment

TIP

## STEAMERS

**Steaming is an easy, healthy way to cook food, and a** pasta pot fitted with a deep, perforated basket **is a great tool for the job. There's room at the bottom for only about an inch of water, so these pots are best for foods that cook in less than 30 minutes. Other steamer options include** shallow stainless steel baskets, **which hold less food but allow more room for water, so you can use them for ingredients that cook more slowly; you can also boil some ingredients in the water while steaming others in the basket above.** Foldable baskets **are inexpensive and can fit any size pot.** Bamboo steamers **that fit over woks don't cost much, but boiling water in a wok can ruin its seasoning.** Stacked oval metal steamers **are expensive, but they're the most versatile—they can hold everything from fish to Cornish hens.** —Stephanie Lyness

3. Boil the noodles for about 1 minute; drain and reserve 1 cup of the noodle cooking liquid. Add the noodles to the skillet and toss to coat. Stir in the reserved noodle liquid and cook, tossing, for 1 minute longer. Season with salt. Transfer the noodles to plates, garnish with the remaining scallions and serve with lime wedges. —Charmaine Solomon
**WINE** Full-bodied, fragrant Viognier.

## Fettuccine with Shrimp, Asparagus and Peas
**TOTAL: 30 MIN**
4 SERVINGS ●

- ¾  pound fettuccine
- 2  tablespoons pure olive oil
- 1  pound peeled and deveined large shrimp
- 2  garlic cloves, minced
- Salt and freshly ground pepper
- ½  pound pencil-thin asparagus, thinly sliced on the diagonal
- ½  cup dry white wine
- ¾  cup heavy cream
- 3  scallions, thinly sliced
- 1  cup frozen baby peas, thawed
- 2  tablespoons minced dill

1. In a large pot of boiling salted water, cook the fettuccine until al dente.

2. Meanwhile, in a large, deep skillet, heat the olive oil. Add the shrimp and garlic, season with salt and pepper and cook over moderately high heat, stirring occasionally, until the shrimp are not quite cooked through, about 2 minutes. Transfer to a plate. Add the asparagus to the skillet and cook over moderately high heat until crisp-tender, 2 minutes; transfer to the plate. Add the wine and cook until nearly evaporated. Whisk in the cream and bring to a boil.

3. Drain the fettuccine and reserve ½ cup of the cooking water. Add the pasta and reserved cooking water to the skillet. Add the scallions, peas, shrimp and asparagus, season with salt and pepper and

cook over moderately high heat, tossing, until creamy, about 2 minutes. Stir in the dill and serve. —Julie Ridlon
**WINE** Round, rich Sauvignon Blanc.

## Campofilone Pasta with Lobster and Tomato
**TOTAL: 30 MIN**
6 SERVINGS ●

The Italian hill town of Campofilone, overlooking the Adriatic, is known for its exquisite, thin egg pasta.

- **Four 8-ounce frozen lobster tails, thawed, or 1½ pounds large shrimp, shelled and deveined**
- ½  cup extra-virgin olive oil
- **Salt and freshly ground pepper**
- 2  large garlic cloves, thinly sliced
- 1  large fresh chile, thinly sliced
- 1  cup dry white wine
- 1  large tomato, seeded and diced
- 1  pound Campofilone maccheroncini or angel-hair pasta
- ½  cup coarsely shredded basil

1. Using kitchen scissors, cut down the center of the lobster tail shells; remove the meat from the shells. Halve the lobster tails lengthwise and remove the intestinal veins. Slice the lobster tails crosswise ½ inch thick and pat dry.

2. In a large, deep skillet, heat 2 tablespoons of the olive oil. Add the lobster to the pan, season with salt and pepper and cook over high heat, stirring occasionally, until lightly browned and almost cooked through, about 4 minutes. Transfer the lobster to a plate.

3. Add 1 tablespoon of the oil to the skillet. Add the garlic and chile and cook over high heat for 1 minute. Add the wine and bring to a boil, scraping up any browned bits from the bottom of the pan. Simmer until the wine has reduced to 1 tablespoon, about 6 minutes. Add the remaining 5 tablespoons of olive oil and the tomato to the skillet and cook, stirring, for 1 minute.

pasta

**4.** Meanwhile, cook the pasta in boiling salted water until al dente. Drain, reserving ½ cup of the cooking water. Add the pasta, lobster and basil to the skillet and toss; add a few tablespoons of the cooking water if the pasta seems dry. Season with salt and pepper, transfer to a large bowl and serve. —*Fabio Trabocchi*
**WINE** Light, dry Soave or similar white.

## Spaghetti with Curried Seafood Marinara
**TOTAL: 30 MIN**
6 SERVINGS ● ●
- 1 pound spaghetti
- ¼ cup extra-virgin olive oil
- 3 garlic cloves, minced
- 1 tablespoon curry powder
- ½ teaspoon crushed red pepper
- Salt
- ½ cup dry white wine
- 2 cups plain tomato sauce
- ½ pound shelled and deveined medium shrimp
- ½ pound squid, bodies cut into thin rings
- ½ pound sea scallops, quartered
- ½ cup chopped flat-leaf parsley

**1.** In a large pot of boiling salted water, cook the spaghetti until al dente.
**2.** Meanwhile, in a large, deep skillet, heat the olive oil. Add the garlic and cook over moderate heat until golden, 1 minute. Add the curry powder, crushed red pepper and a pinch of salt and cook, stirring, for 1 minute. Add the wine and cook over high heat until evaporated, 2 minutes. Add the tomato sauce and cook over high heat, stirring occasionally, for 4 minutes. Add the shrimp, squid and scallops and simmer, stirring, until they are just cooked through, about 3 minutes.
**3.** Drain the spaghetti, add it to the skillet and toss well. Season with salt and sprinkle with the parsley. Transfer to bowls and serve. —*Celestino Drago*
**WINE** Dry, medium-bodied Pinot Gris.

## Seafood Capellini with Saffron
**TOTAL: 30 MIN**
4 SERVINGS ●
- 6 tablespoons extra-virgin olive oil
- 1 pound shelled and deveined jumbo shrimp (8 shrimp)
- 1 pound monkfish or other firm white fish such as halibut, trimmed and cut into 8 pieces
- Kosher salt and freshly ground pepper
- One 14-ounce can diced tomatoes, drained
- 4 garlic cloves, very finely chopped
- 2 tablespoons very finely chopped flat-leaf parsley
- 1 serrano chile with seeds, very finely chopped
- 1 teaspoon hot paprika
- 2 cups chicken stock or low-sodium broth
- One 8-ounce bottle clam juice (1 cup)
- Pinch of saffron threads
- 6 ounces capellini, broken into 3-inch lengths
- Lemon wedges, for serving

**1.** In a large skillet, heat 3 tablespoons of the olive oil over moderately high heat. Season the shrimp and monkfish with salt and pepper and add to the skillet. Cook for 6 minutes, turning once, until barely opaque. Transfer to a plate.
**2.** In the same skillet, heat the remaining 3 tablespoons of olive oil over moderate heat. Add the diced tomatoes and cook for 3 minutes. Stir in the garlic, 1 tablespoon of the parsley, the serrano chile and the paprika. Add the chicken stock, clam juice and saffron, season with salt and bring to a boil. Add the capellini and cook, stirring occasionally, until the pasta is al dente and has absorbed most of the sauce, about 5 minutes. Return the shrimp and monkfish to the skillet along with any accumulated juices and toss well. Transfer the pasta to bowls and garnish with the remaining 1 tablespoon of parsley. Serve with the lemon wedges. —*Charmaine Solomon*
**WINE** Light, spicy Pinot Grigio.

## Midnight Pasta with Tuna, Pancetta and Spinach
**TOTAL: 25 MIN**
4 SERVINGS ●
This pasta is very adaptable. Canned clams or squid can replace the tuna, and the pancetta or bacon is optional, but the spinach, garlic and crushed red pepper are all essential.
- ¾ pound spaghetti or thin linguine
- ¼ cup plus 2 tablespoons extra-virgin olive oil
- 3 large garlic cloves, very thinly sliced
- 3 ounces thinly sliced pancetta or bacon, coarsely chopped (½ cup)
- ¾ teaspoon crushed red pepper
- ½ cup thawed frozen chopped spinach, squeezed dry
- One 6-ounce can imported oil-packed tuna, drained and flaked
- ¼ cup dry white wine
- Salt

**1.** In a large pot of boiling salted water, cook the spaghetti until al dente.
**2.** Meanwhile, in a large skillet, heat ¼ cup of the olive oil until shimmering. Add the garlic and cook over moderate heat until fragrant, about 30 seconds. Add the pancetta and crushed red pepper and cook, stirring occasionally, until the pancetta is golden and crisp, about 5 minutes. Add the spinach and tuna, breaking up the tuna with a wooden spoon. Add the white wine and cook until the liquid has nearly evaporated, about 1 minute.
**3.** Drain the spaghetti, reserving ½ cup of the cooking liquid. Add the pasta and reserved cooking liquid to the skillet and cook over moderate heat, tossing, until

● FAST ● HEALTHY ● MAKE AHEAD ● STAFF FAVORITE

83

**FARFALLE WITH CREAMY SMOKED SALMON**

**PASTA SHELLS WITH SWORDFISH**

the liquid is nearly absorbed, 1 minute. Drizzle with the remaining 2 tablespoons of olive oil, season with salt and serve immediately. —*Steven Wagner*
**WINE** Light, dry Soave or similar white.

### Farfalle with Creamy Smoked Salmon and Vodka Sauce

**TOTAL: 30 MIN**
**6 SERVINGS** ●

- 1 pound farfalle
- 2 tablespoons unsalted butter
- 1 small shallot, minced
- ¼ cup vodka
- 2¼ cups heavy cream
- 4 ounces thinly sliced smoked salmon, cut into thin strips

Salt and freshly ground pepper

- 3 large egg yolks
- 2 tablespoons minced chives

**1.** In a large pot of boiling salted water, cook the farfalle, stirring occasionally, until al dente.

**2.** Meanwhile, in a large, deep skillet, heat the butter until sizzling. Add the minced shallot and cook over moderate heat until it is golden, about 3 minutes. Add the vodka and cook until evaporated, about 1 minute. Add 2 cups of the heavy cream and simmer over moderately high heat, stirring often, until reduced by half, about 4 minutes. Stir in the smoked salmon, season with salt and pepper and remove the skillet from the heat.

**3.** In a small bowl, beat the egg yolks with the remaining ¼ cup of heavy cream until smooth.

**4.** Drain the farfalle. Add it to the skillet and stir to coat with the vodka cream. Add the egg yolk mixture and stir over low heat until the sauce is warmed through and creamy, about 30 seconds. Season with salt and pepper. Transfer the pasta to shallow bowls, scatter the chives on top and serve immediately.
—*Celestino Drago*
**WINE** Ripe, oaky Chardonnay.

### Pasta Shells with Swordfish

**TOTAL: 30 MIN**

6 SERVINGS ● ●

- 1 pound medium pasta shells, farfalle or penne
- ¼ cup extra-virgin olive oil
- 1½ pounds skinless swordfish steaks, sliced 1 inch thick and cut into 1-inch cubes
- Salt and freshly ground pepper
- 1 medium zucchini or yellow summer squash, halved lengthwise and sliced crosswise ¼ inch thick
- 1 pint grape tomatoes
- 4 garlic cloves, thinly sliced
- 6 scallions, white and light green parts only, chopped
- ¼ cup coarsely chopped mint leaves
- ¼ cup coarsely chopped parsley leaves
- ½ cup dry white wine

**1.** In a large pot of boiling salted water, cook the pasta shells, stirring often, until al dente. Drain the shells and return them to the pot.

**2.** Meanwhile, heat the olive oil in a large, deep skillet until shimmering. Add the cubed swordfish and season generously with salt and pepper. Cook over moderately high heat, stirring frequently, until the swordfish cubes are lightly browned all over, about 4 minutes. With a slotted spoon, transfer the swordfish to a large serving bowl.

**3.** Add the zucchini, tomatoes and garlic to the skillet and cook over moderately high heat for 3 minutes, stirring. Add the scallions and cook until the tomato skins pop, 2 minutes longer. Return the swordfish and any accumulated juices to the skillet and stir in the mint and parsley. Add the wine and pasta and season with salt and pepper. Transfer to the large bowl and serve. —*Rachael Ray*

**WINE** High-acid, savory Vermentino.

### Spaghetti with Creamy Pancetta Sauce

**TOTAL: 30 MIN**

6 SERVINGS ●

Chef Paul Bertolli of Berkeley's Oliveto uses *guanciale,* cured pork from a pig's cheek and jowl, to prepare this recipe, but pancetta is a fine substitute.

- 3 tablespoons extra-virgin olive oil
- ¾ pound thinly sliced pancetta or *guanciale,* cut into 1-inch pieces
- 1 medium onion, finely chopped
- 3 large plum tomatoes, chopped
- 1 tablespoon tomato paste or sun-dried tomato paste
- 1 small fresh red chile, seeded and minced
- 1 pound spaghetti
- ½ cup freshly grated Parmigiano-Reggiano cheese
- ½ cup freshly grated Pecorino Romano cheese

**1.** Heat the olive oil in a large, deep skillet. Add the pancetta and cook over moderately high heat, stirring often, until the fat is rendered and the meat begins to brown, about 4 minutes. Add the onion and cook over high heat until softened, about 2 minutes. Stir in the tomatoes, tomato paste and the chile and cook over moderate heat, stirring occasionally, until thickened, 3 minutes. Cover and remove from the heat.

**2.** In a large pot of boiling salted water, cook the spaghetti until al dente. Drain, reserving ½ cup of the cooking water. Add the spaghetti and the Parmigiano and Pecorino cheeses to the sauce and toss over moderate heat, adding small amounts of the reserved pasta cooking water until the sauce is thick and creamy. Transfer the pasta to a bowl and serve at once. —*Paul Bertolli*

**MAKE AHEAD** The recipe can be prepared through Step 1 early in the day and refrigerated.

**WINE** Intense, berry-flavored Zinfandel.

### Fettuccine with Mushrooms and Prosciutto

**TOTAL: 30 MIN**

6 SERVINGS ●

- 1 pound fettuccine
- ¼ cup extra-virgin olive oil
- ¼ cup very finely chopped onion
- 3 garlic cloves, very finely chopped
- 1 pound assorted mushrooms—such as shiitake, cremini and oyster—stems trimmed, mushrooms thinly sliced
- ¼ pound thinly sliced prosciutto, cut into thin strips
- Salt and freshly ground pepper
- ¾ cup mascarpone cheese
- ¼ cup freshly grated Parmesan cheese, plus more for serving
- ¼ cup very finely chopped flat-leaf parsley

**1.** In a large pot of boiling salted water, cook the fettuccine until al dente.

**2.** Meanwhile, in a large, deep skillet, heat the olive oil until shimmering. Add the chopped onion and garlic and cook over moderate heat until fragrant, about 2 minutes. Add the mushrooms and prosciutto in an even layer, season with salt and pepper and cook undisturbed over moderately high heat until browned on the bottom, about 3 minutes. Cook, stirring, until the mushrooms are tender, about 3 minutes longer.

**3.** Drain the fettuccine, reserving 1 cup of the pasta cooking water. Add the fettuccine to the skillet. Stir in the mascarpone and the reserved pasta cooking water and toss the pasta over low heat until the sauce is creamy. Stir in the ¼ cup of Parmesan cheese and season the fettuccine with salt and pepper. Transfer the pasta to shallow bowls, sprinkle with the chopped parsley and serve at once, with extra Parmesan cheese. —*Celestino Drago*

**WINE** Tart, low-tannin Barbera.

# pasta

## Tagliarini with Almond-Arugula Pesto and Meatballs

**TOTAL: 45 MIN**

6 SERVINGS ●

1½ pounds ground pork
½ pound ground lamb
½ medium red onion, very finely chopped
¼ cup dry red wine
1 tablespoon finely chopped parsley
1½ teaspoons grated lemon zest
1 teaspoon chopped thyme
½ teaspoon ground fennel seeds
¼ teaspoon crushed lavender
¼ teaspoon crushed red pepper
3 medium garlic cloves, very finely chopped
Salt and freshly ground pepper

A hand-cranked food mill is an excellent tool for pureeing homemade sauces, particularly tomato sauce.

**WHAT TO LOOK FOR** Choose a funnel-shaped model—stainless steel or plastic—with a sturdy handle, several interchangeable metal disks and small legs that secure the mill to bowls.

**HOW TO USE IT** Attach the finer disk for silky sauces, purees and baby food; the coarser one for applesauce, soups, guacamole and mashed potatoes. Add the ingredients to the mill, then turn the crank to rotate the curved blade over the disk, pressing the food through. Turn the crank backward to scrape up and redistribute the ingredients.

10 tablespoons extra-virgin olive oil, plus more for serving
1 bunch arugula (6 ounces)
½ cup unsalted roasted almonds, chopped
½ cup freshly grated Parmesan cheese, plus more for serving
1¼ pounds fresh tagliarini

1. In a large bowl, mix the pork and lamb with the onion, wine, parsley, zest, thyme, fennel, lavender and crushed red pepper. Add one-third of the garlic, 2 teaspoons of salt and ½ teaspoon of pepper. Roll the mixture into 1-inch meatballs.

2. In a very large skillet, heat 2 tablespoons of the oil. Add the meatballs and cook over moderately high heat, turning frequently, until browned, 5 minutes. Reduce the heat to moderate and cook for 5 minutes longer, or until no trace of pink remains. Transfer to a plate.

3. In a food processor, puree the arugula with the almonds, ½ cup of Parmesan and the remaining ½ cup of olive oil and the garlic. Scrape the pesto into a bowl; season with salt and pepper.

4. In a pot of boiling salted water, cook the pasta until al dente. Reserve 1 cup of the cooking water. Drain the pasta and transfer to a bowl. Toss with the pesto and ½ cup of the cooking water; add more water if the sauce is dry. Serve with the meatballs and more Parmesan and olive oil. —*Duskie Estes and John Stewart*
**WINE** Complex, savory Chianti Classico.

## Pappardelle with Red Wine and Meat Ragù

**TOTAL: 30 MIN**

6 SERVINGS ● ●

1 pound pappardelle
1 ounce dried porcini mushrooms
1 cup boiling water
¼ cup extra-virgin olive oil
2 ounces thinly sliced pancetta, finely chopped
2 medium celery ribs, minced

1 medium carrot, minced
1 small onion, minced
3 thyme sprigs
1 pound ground beef
1 pound ground turkey
Salt and freshly ground pepper
1 cup dry red wine
2 cups tomato puree
1 tablespoon unsalted butter
¼ cup freshly grated Parmesan cheese, plus more for serving

1. In a large pot of boiling salted water, cook the pappardelle until al dente.

2. Meanwhile, in a medium heatproof bowl, cover the porcini with the boiling water and let stand until softened, about 5 minutes. Lift the mushrooms from the water, taking care to leave any sediment behind in the bowl, and coarsely chop them. Reserve the soaking liquid.

3. In a large saucepan, heat the oil until shimmering. Add the porcini, pancetta, celery, carrot, onion and thyme sprigs and cook over moderately high heat, stirring often, until the vegetables start to brown, about 5 minutes. Add the ground beef and turkey, season with salt and pepper and cook, breaking up the meat with a wooden spoon, until no pink remains, about 5 minutes. Add the wine and boil over high heat until reduced by half, about 3 minutes. Add the tomato puree. Pour in the reserved mushroom soaking liquid, stopping before you reach the grit at the bottom of the bowl. Bring the ragù to a boil and simmer over moderate heat, stirring occasionally, until thickened and flavorful, about 12 minutes. Discard the thyme sprigs.

4. Drain the pasta and return it to the pot. Toss with the butter, stir in half of the ragù and toss with the ¼ cup of Parmesan. Season with salt and pepper, transfer to bowls, top with the remaining ragù and serve. Pass more Parmesan at the table. —*Celestino Drago*
**WINE** Complex, savory Chianti Classico.

PAPPARDELLE WITH RED WINE AND MEAT RAGÙ

MASCARPONE-STUFFED ROAST CHICKEN WITH SPRING HERB SALAD, P. 94

# poultry

CHICKEN WITH SPINACH, LEEK AND SAFFRON SAUCE

CHICKEN WITH RED ONIONS AND THYME

## Chicken Breasts with Spinach, Leek and Saffron Sauce

**TOTAL: 45 MIN**

6 SERVINGS

- ½ cup dry white wine, such as Chardonnay or a dry Riesling
- ⅛ teaspoon saffron threads
- 2 tablespoons extra-virgin olive oil

Six 6- to 7-ounce boneless chicken breast halves, with skin

Salt and freshly ground pepper

- 1 tablespoon unsalted butter
- 3 large leeks, white and tender green parts only, halved lengthwise and thinly sliced
- 1 large garlic clove, very finely chopped
- 1½ cups chicken stock or low-sodium broth
- 1 bay leaf
- ¼ cup plus 2 tablespoons heavy cream
- 4 cups packed torn curly spinach leaves
- 2 teaspoons Dijon mustard

**1.** In a glass measuring cup, warm the wine in a microwave oven. Lightly crumble the saffron into the wine. Heat the olive oil in a large, deep skillet until shimmering. Season the chicken breasts with salt and pepper and add them to the skillet, skin side down. Cook the chicken over moderately high heat for 2 minutes. Reduce the heat to moderate and cook until the skin is browned and crisp, about 4 minutes. Turn and cook for 3 minutes longer. Transfer to a plate.

**2.** Melt the butter in the skillet until sizzling. Add the leeks and cook over moderate heat, stirring, until softened, about 3 minutes. Add the garlic and cook over moderately low heat until the garlic is golden, about 3 minutes. Add the wine and saffron and simmer for 2 minutes. Add the chicken stock and bay leaf and bring to a simmer over moderately high heat. Return the chicken breasts to the skillet, skin side up, and simmer over moderately low heat until just cooked through, about 10 minutes. Transfer the chicken to a warmed platter.

**3.** Add the heavy cream to the skillet and simmer over moderately high heat until slightly thickened, about 4 minutes. Add the spinach and cook until wilted, about 1 minute. Remove from the heat and stir in the mustard; season the sauce with salt and pepper. Discard the bay leaf. Spoon the sauce onto plates, top with the chicken breasts and serve.

—*Marcia Kiesel*

**WINE** Ripe, oaky Chardonnay.

### Chicken Breasts with Red Onions and Thyme

**TOTAL: 25 MIN**

4 SERVINGS ● ●

The almost black gills of Portobello mushrooms would stain this sauce a dark, inky color, so we prefer to scrape them out.

- 2 tablespoons extra-virgin olive oil
- 4 skinless, boneless chicken breast halves

Salt and freshly ground pepper

- 2 large Portobello mushrooms, stemmed, black gills cut off, caps sliced ¼ inch thick
- 1 medium red onion, very thinly sliced
- 2 large garlic cloves, very thinly sliced
- ¼ cup white wine vinegar
- ½ cup chicken stock or low-sodium broth
- 1 teaspoon coarsely chopped thyme leaves

**1.** In a large skillet, heat the olive oil until shimmering. Season the chicken breasts with salt and pepper and add them to the skillet. Scatter the mushrooms, red onion and garlic around the chicken; cook over high heat until the chicken is browned on the bottom, about 3 minutes. Turn the breasts over, stir the mushrooms, onions and garlic and continue cooking until the chicken is browned on the second side, about 3 minutes longer.

**2.** Add the white wine vinegar, chicken stock and thyme to the skillet and simmer, scraping up the browned bits from the bottom of the pan. Reduce the heat to low and cook, turning the chicken once, until it is white throughout, about 7 minutes. Transfer the chicken to plates. Simmer the sauce over moderate heat until slightly reduced and flavorful, about 1 minute. Season the sauce with salt and pepper, pour it over the chicken breasts and serve. —*Kimball Jones*

**WINE** Light, dry Soave or similar white.

### Lemon Chicken with Potatoes and Tomatoes

**ACTIVE: 20 MIN; TOTAL: 2 HR**

4 SERVINGS ●

- ¼ cup fresh lemon juice, plus 1 peeled, seeded and diced lemon
- ¼ cup water
- 1 tablespoon Dijon mustard
- ¼ cup finely chopped parsley

Two 7-ounce skinless, boneless chicken breast halves

- ¾ pound Yukon Gold potatoes, peeled and cut into ¾-inch dice
- 2 tomatoes, cut into 1-inch dice
- 1 small sweet onion, such as Vidalia, cut into ½-inch dice
- 1 garlic clove, minced
- 2 tablespoons snipped chives
- 2 thyme sprigs
- 2 tablespoons extra-virgin olive oil

Salt and freshly ground pepper

**1.** In a glass baking dish, combine the lemon juice with the water, mustard and 2 tablespoons of the parsley. Add the chicken and turn to coat. Cover and let stand at room temperature for 1½ hours.

**2.** Meanwhile, preheat the oven to 400°. In a medium baking dish, toss the potatoes with the diced lemon, tomatoes, onion, garlic, chives, thyme, 1½ tablespoons of the olive oil and the remaining 2 tablespoons of parsley. Season with salt and pepper. Bake the potatoes for about 40 minutes, or until tender.

**3.** Preheat the broiler. Transfer the chicken breasts to a baking sheet and brush with the remaining ½ tablespoon of olive oil. Season with salt and pepper; broil 8 to 10 inches from the heat, turning once, until golden and cooked through, 12 to 14 minutes. Transfer to a cutting board and let rest for 5 minutes. Broil the potatoes for about 2 minutes, or just until golden. Thinly slice the chicken. Spread the potatoes on plates, top with the chicken and serve. —*Josiah Citrin*

**WINE** Round, supple, fruity Syrah.

### Chicken Piccata with Artichokes and Olives

**TOTAL: 30 MIN**

8 SERVINGS ● ●

- 1 cup fine dry bread crumbs
- 2 teaspoons salt
- ½ teaspoon freshly ground black pepper

Eight 6-ounce chicken cutlets, about ⅛ inch thick

- 4 tablespoons unsalted butter
- ¼ cup plus 2 tablespoons vegetable oil
- 16 pitted Calamata olives, drained and coarsely chopped
- 4 marinated artichoke hearts from a jar, drained and quartered
- ⅔ cup chicken stock or low-sodium broth
- ¼ cup fresh lemon juice
- 2 tablespoons drained capers
- 2 tablespoons coarsely chopped parsley leaves

**1.** In a large, shallow bowl, combine the bread crumbs with the salt and pepper. Dredge the chicken cutlets in the seasoned bread crumbs.

**2.** In each of 2 large skillets, melt half of the butter in half of the oil over moderately high heat. When the foam subsides, add the breaded chicken cutlets to the skillets and cook over moderately high heat, turning once, until golden brown on the outside and white throughout, about 2 minutes per side. Transfer the cutlets to a platter.

**3.** Wipe out one of the skillets and add the olives and artichoke hearts. Cook over moderately high heat, stirring, until heated through. Add the chicken stock, lemon juice and capers to the skillet and boil for 1 minute, stirring. Spoon the artichoke and olive sauce over the chicken, sprinkle with the parsley and serve right away. —*Anne Byrn*

**WINE** Round-textured Sémillon.

# poultry

## Sautéed Chicken with Fresh Herbs and Wilted Greens

**TOTAL: 25 MIN**

4 SERVINGS ● ●

Four 6-ounce skinless, boneless
    chicken breast halves

Salt and freshly ground pepper

  ¼  cup all-purpose flour

  3  tablespoons extra-virgin olive oil

Three 5-ounce bags baby spinach

  1  leek, halved lengthwise and thinly
     sliced crosswise

  2  garlic cloves, thinly sliced

  2  tablespoons minced parsley

  1  tablespoon minced tarragon

  2  tablespoons fresh lemon juice

  2  tablespoons dried currants

**1.** Lightly pound the chicken breast halves ½ inch thick, then season with salt and pepper and dust with the flour.

Heat 2 tablespoons of the olive oil in a very large skillet. Add the chicken and sauté over moderately high heat until cooked through, about 8 minutes. Transfer to a platter, cover and keep warm.

**2.** Wipe out the skillet. Add the spinach in batches and cook over moderately high heat, tossing, until wilted; transfer to a colander. Press to remove the liquid.

**3.** Wipe out the skillet; add the remaining 1 tablespoon of olive oil. Add the leek and garlic and cook over moderately high heat until softened, 2 minutes. Add the spinach, parsley and tarragon and toss. Add the lemon juice and currants; season with salt and pepper. Spread the spinach on plates, arrange the chicken on top and serve. —*Julie Ridlon*

**WINE** Ripe, oaky Chardonnay.

## Chicken, Tomato and Mozzarella Salad with Spicy Basil Dressing

**TOTAL: 30 MIN**

6 SERVINGS ● ●

This recipe calls for part-skim-milk mozzarella, not only because it's lower in fat but also because it melts more slowly and holds its shape better than the fresh whole-milk kind.

  ⅓  cup minced red onion

  3  tablespoons extra-virgin olive oil,
     plus more for brushing

  3  tablespoons red wine vinegar

  1  large garlic clove, minced

  1  jalapeño, seeded and minced

  ¼  cup chopped basil

Salt and freshly ground pepper

  2  pints cherry tomatoes

  6  ounces part-skim mozzarella
     cheese, cut into ¾-inch cubes

Six 5-ounce skinless, boneless
    chicken breast halves, pounded
    ¼ inch thick

**1.** Light a grill. In a small bowl, combine the onion with the 3 tablespoons of olive oil, the vinegar, garlic, jalapeño and basil. Season with salt and pepper.

**2.** Thread six 12-inch metal skewers with the tomatoes, alternating with the mozzarella after every 2 tomatoes. Brush the chicken with olive oil and season with salt and pepper.

**3.** Grill the chicken over a hot fire until just cooked through, about 4 minutes. Transfer to a platter. Grill the tomato and cheese skewers over a hot fire, turning once, until the cheese is lightly charred and just starting to melt, about 1 minute. Slide the tomatoes and cheese from the skewers onto the platter. Drizzle 2 tablespoons of the dressing over the chicken and pass the remaining dressing at the table. —*Marcia Kiesel*

**WINE** Light, spicy Pinot Grigio.

## Hoosier Chicken with Potato Chip Crust

**TOTAL: 30 MIN**

8 SERVINGS ●

This crispy chicken spiked with Chinese five-spice powder is named for the natives of chef Daniel Orr's home state, Indiana. It's perfect for picnics because it's good both hot and at room temperature. For a more refined dish, slice the chicken and serve it over a green salad.

  ½  cup mayonnaise

  2  teaspoons pure chile powder

  1  teaspoon five-spice powder

  1  teaspoon finely grated lemon zest

  1  teaspoon coarsely ground pepper

Kosher salt

2½  pounds thin chicken cutlets

One 5½-ounce bag plain, salted
    potato chips, finely crushed

  3  tablespoons unsalted butter

**1.** Preheat the oven to 225°. In a medium bowl, mix the mayonnaise with the chile powder, five-spice powder, lemon zest, pepper and a generous pinch of salt. Add the chicken and turn to coat.

**2.** Spread the potato chips on a sheet of wax paper. Coat the chicken with the crumbs, pressing to help them adhere.

---

## strategy

**TIP** | **USING RUBS**

Last-minute cooks love rubs like the one for the Crisp Chicken with Garlic on the next page because, unlike marinades, they work instantly: no need to wait for them to penetrate the food. But some rubs can be applied hours ahead. **WHOLE CHICKENS OR ROASTS** can be rubbed up to five hours before cooking; apply the rub thickly for a flavorful crust. **CHICKEN AND DUCK BREASTS AND PORK CHOPS** can be rubbed two hours in advance. **SEAFOOD** shouldn't be prepared more than an hour in advance, as acidic ingredients in the rub, like vinegar and tomatoes, can break down the delicate flesh; a light coating works best.

**3.** Melt 1 tablespoon of the butter in a large skillet. When the foam subsides, add one-third of the chicken cutlets and cook over moderately high heat, turning once, until browned and cooked through, about 5 minutes. Transfer the chicken to a platter and keep warm while you cook the remaining 2 batches. —*Daniel Orr*
**WINE** Light, soft Chenin Blanc.

## Crisp Chicken with Garlic
**TOTAL: 30 MIN**
4 SERVINGS ●

6 garlic cloves
1½ tablespoons cracked black peppercorns
2 teaspoons kosher salt, plus more for seasoning
1 cup cilantro leaves, plus 1 tablespoon chopped leaves for garnish
2 tablespoons fresh lime juice
1 teaspoon crushed red pepper
1 tablespoon extra-virgin olive oil, plus more for drizzling
4 boneless chicken breast halves (2½ pounds total), with skin
2 large tomatoes, cut into wedges
1 scallion, white and light green parts only, chopped
Pinch of sugar
Lime wedges, for serving

**1.** Preheat the broiler. In a mini food processor, pulse the garlic cloves with the cracked pepper and 2 teaspoons of salt until the garlic is minced. Add the 1 cup of cilantro, the lime juice, crushed red pepper and 1 tablespoon of olive oil and pulse until a chunky paste forms. Rub the paste under the skin and all over the chicken breasts. Transfer the chicken to a baking sheet and let stand at room temperature for 10 minutes.
**2.** Meanwhile, in a medium bowl, toss the tomatoes with the scallion and season with a generous pinch each of sugar and salt. Drizzle with olive oil and toss well.

**3.** Season the chicken all over with salt. Set a rack in the oven 5 inches from the heat source. Broil the chicken skin side down for 6 minutes, then turn and broil for 6 minutes longer, until the skin is crisp and the chicken is cooked through. Transfer the chicken to plates, garnish with the 1 tablespoon of cilantro and the lime wedges and serve with the tomato salad. —*Charmaine Solomon*
**SERVE WITH** Jasmine rice.
**WINE** Tart, low-tannin Barbera.

## Buttermilk-Roasted Chicken with Date Butter
**TOTAL: 25 MIN, PLUS 4 HR MARINATING**
4 SERVINGS ●

2 garlic cloves, crushed
1 shallot, thinly sliced
1 tablespoon thyme leaves
1 tablespoon rosemary leaves
2 cups buttermilk
Salt and freshly ground pepper
Four 6-ounce skinless, boneless chicken breast halves
2 tablespoons unsalted butter, softened
2 dates, pitted and finely chopped
3 tablespoons plus ½ teaspoon fresh lemon juice
1 tablespoon extra-virgin olive oil

**1.** In a food processor, coarsely puree the garlic, shallot, thyme and rosemary with ½ cup of the buttermilk. Blend in the remaining 1½ cups of buttermilk. Pour into a baking dish; season with salt and pepper. Add the chicken and turn to coat. Cover and refrigerate for at least 4 hours.
**2.** Preheat the oven to 400°. Blend the butter with the dates and lemon juice and season with salt and pepper.
**3.** Remove the chicken from the buttermilk and pat dry. Season with salt and pepper. In a large ovenproof nonstick skillet, heat the olive oil until shimmering. Add the chicken breasts and cook over moderately high heat until browned on the bottom,

about 3 minutes. Turn the breasts and roast them in the oven for about 10 minutes, or until just cooked through. Serve with the date butter. —*Jeff Orr*
**WINE** Fruity, low-oak Chardonnay.

## Roast Chickens with Black Pepper–Maple Glaze
**ACTIVE: 20 MIN; TOTAL: 2 HR 30 MIN**
6 SERVINGS ●

2 tablespoons unsalted butter
½ cup pure maple syrup
Coarsely ground pepper
2 medium onions, halved lengthwise and thinly sliced crosswise
2 teaspoons extra-virgin olive oil
Salt
Two 3½-pound organic chickens

**1.** Preheat the oven to 350°. In a small saucepan, melt the butter with the maple syrup and 2 teaspoons of ground pepper. Remove the glaze from the heat.
**2.** On a large, heavy-duty, rimmed baking sheet, toss the sliced onions with the olive oil. Season the onions with salt and pepper and spread in an even layer. Season the chickens inside and out with salt, then arrange them on top of the onions. Loosely tie the chicken legs together with kitchen string.
**3.** Roast the chickens for 45 minutes. Brush the chickens all over with half of the maple glaze and continue roasting for 1 hour longer. Increase the oven temperature to 425°. Generously brush the chickens with the remaining glaze and roast for 15 minutes longer, or until the cavity juices run clear and the chickens are richly browned.
**4.** Transfer the chickens to a platter and let rest for 10 minutes before carving. Pour the onions and pan juices into a large glass measuring cup and skim the fat from the surface. Season with salt and pepper and serve with the chickens. —*Maria Helm Sinskey*
**WINE** Complex, silky red Burgundy.

# poultry

## Roast Chickens with Lebanese Rice and Pomegranate Jus

**ACTIVE: 30 MIN; TOTAL: 1 HR 30 MIN**

**6 SERVINGS**

Extra-virgin olive oil
Two 3½-pound chickens
1½ teaspoons ground allspice
Kosher salt and freshly ground pepper
1 cup water
1½ cups (10 ounces) medium-grain rice
4 tablespoons unsalted butter
½ cup pine nuts
½ cup slivered almonds
½ pound lean ground lamb or beef
½ teaspoon ground cinnamon
3 cups chicken stock
½ tablespoon pomegranate molasses (see Note)

1. Preheat the oven to 350°. Lightly oil a large roasting pan and set the chickens in it. Rub the outside of each chicken with ½ teaspoon of the allspice and season the cavities with salt and pepper.
2. Roast the chickens for 30 minutes. Add the 1 cup of water to the roasting pan and roast for 40 minutes longer, or until an instant-read thermometer inserted in the thickest part of a thigh without touching the bone registers 165°. Transfer the chickens to a platter and cover loosely with foil.
3. Meanwhile, in a sieve, rinse the rice under cold water until the water runs clear. Drain well. Melt the butter in a medium saucepan. Add the pine nuts and almonds and cook over moderate heat, stirring, until golden, 3 minutes. Transfer to a plate.
4. Add the meat to the saucepan and cook, stirring and breaking it up with a wooden spoon, until no pink remains, about 3 minutes. Stir in the rice, cinnamon, 1½ teaspoons of salt, ¼ teaspoon of pepper, three-fourths of the nuts and the remaining ½ teaspoon of allspice. Add 2½ cups of the stock; bring to a boil. Cover and cook over low heat for 10 minutes. Stir, then cover and continue cooking until the stock has been absorbed and the rice is tender, about 5 minutes. Remove the rice from the heat and let stand, covered, for 10 minutes. Fluff with a fork, transfer to a bowl and sprinkle with the remaining nuts.
5. Meanwhile, pour the roasting pan juices into a small saucepan and skim off the fat. Set the roasting pan over 2 burners; heat until sizzling. Add the remaining ½ cup of chicken stock and cook over moderately high heat, scraping up any browned bits stuck to the bottom and sides of the pan with a wooden spoon. Strain into the saucepan and whisk in the pomegranate molasses. Season with salt and pepper and transfer to a warmed gravy boat.
6. Carve the chickens and serve with the rice and pomegranate jus. —*Anissa Helou*
**NOTE** Pomegranate molasses is available at specialty food stores and Middle Eastern markets.
**WINE** Bright, fruity rosé.

## Roast Chickens with Lemon and Orange

**ACTIVE: 20 MIN; TOTAL: 1 HR 30 MIN**

**6 SERVINGS**

Two 3½-pound chickens
Salt and freshly ground pepper
1 lemon, halved
1 orange, halved
8 garlic cloves
8 rosemary sprigs
8 thyme sprigs

1. Preheat the oven to 425°. Season the chickens with salt and pepper; stuff each with a lemon and orange half, 2 garlic cloves and 2 sprigs each of rosemary and thyme. Tie the legs together with kitchen string. Set the chickens in a roasting pan and tuck the remaining garlic and rosemary and thyme sprigs between the legs.
2. Roast the chickens for about 1¼ hours, or until an instant-read thermometer inserted in the thickest part of a thigh registers 165°. Let them rest for 10 minutes before carving. —*Steven Wagner*
**WINE** Light, fruity Beaujolais.

## Mascarpone-Stuffed Roast Chicken with Spring Herb Salad

**ACTIVE: 30 MIN; TOTAL: 1 HR 40 MIN**

**6 SERVINGS** ●

1 cup mascarpone cheese
½ cup flat-leaf parsley leaves, plus 1 tablespoon minced parsley
1 tablespoon minced thyme
1 tablespoon minced tarragon
1 teaspoon finely grated lemon zest
1 garlic clove, minced
Salt and freshly ground pepper
Two 3½-pound chickens
¼ cup plus 2 tablespoons hazelnut oil
¼ cup fresh orange juice
1 tablespoon snipped chives
1 tablespoon minced shallot
2 cups mâche or mesclun
½ cup basil leaves
½ cup celery leaves
¼ cup chervil leaves

1. Preheat the oven to 400°. In a small bowl, mix the mascarpone with the minced parsley, thyme, tarragon, lemon zest and garlic and season the mixture with salt and pepper. Starting at the neck of one of the chickens, gently loosen the chicken skin, working your hands toward the drumsticks; be sure to leave the skin nearest the cavity opening attached. Spread half of the mascarpone filling under the skin, working it toward the drumsticks. Season the cavity with salt and pepper. Repeat with the other chicken.
2. Put the chickens in a large roasting pan and season them all over with salt and pepper. Roast for 15 minutes. Lower the oven temperature to 350° and bake for 45 minutes longer, or until an instant-read thermometer inserted in a thigh registers 170°. Let the chickens stand for 20 minutes, then carve and transfer to a platter.
3. Meanwhile, in a bowl, stir the hazelnut oil with the orange juice, chives and shallot and season with salt and pepper.

ROAST CHICKENS WITH LEMON AND ORANGE

# poultry

**4.** In a large bowl, toss the mâche, basil, celery leaves, chervil and the remaining ½ cup of parsley leaves with half of the vinaigrette. Mound the salad over the chicken and serve, passing more vinaigrette on the side. —*Geoffrey Zakarian*
**WINE** Lively, assertive Sauvignon Blanc.

### Chicken with Almonds and Honey

**ACTIVE: 30 MIN; TOTAL: 2 HR 15 MIN**
**8 SERVINGS** ●

- ¼ cup vegetable oil
- 2 large onions, coarsely chopped
- 1½ teaspoons cinnamon
- 1 teaspoon ground ginger
- Four 8-ounce chicken breast halves, on the bone
- 4 whole chicken legs, split
- 1½ quarts water
- 1 tablespoon fresh lemon juice
- ½ teaspoon saffron threads, crumbled
- Salt and freshly ground pepper
- 1½ cups whole blanched almonds
- ¼ cup honey
- 1 tablespoon rose water (see Note)

**1.** Preheat the oven to 350°. Heat the oil in a large enameled cast-iron casserole. Add the onions, cover and cook over low heat, stirring occasionally, until softened, about 30 minutes.
**2.** Stir the cinnamon and ginger into the onions, then add the chicken pieces, stirring to coat with the flavorings. Add the water, lemon juice and saffron and season with salt and pepper. Bring to a boil, cover and simmer, moving the chicken pieces around for even cooking, until the breasts are just done, about 25 minutes. Transfer the breasts to a cutting board and cut them in half crosswise. Transfer to a platter and cover with foil. Continue cooking the drumsticks and thighs until done, about 5 minutes longer. Transfer to the platter. Boil the cooking liquid over high heat until reduced to about 3 cups, about 35 minutes.

**3.** In a food processor, pulse the almonds until coarsely chopped. Transfer to a bowl and stir in the honey and rose water.
**4.** Remove the skin from the chicken and transfer to a large, shallow baking dish. Pour the reduced sauce over the chicken and spread with the almond paste. Bake for about 20 minutes, or until the topping is browned. Serve hot. —*Nadia Roden*
**NOTE** Rose water is available at specialty food stores.
**MAKE AHEAD** The recipe can be prepared up to 1 day ahead. Spread the almond paste on the chicken just before baking.
**WINE** Spicy Alsace Gewürztraminer.

### Chicken Stuffed with Prosciutto, Spinach and Boursin

**TOTAL: 30 MIN**
**4 SERVINGS** ●

- One 5-ounce bag baby spinach
- Four 6- to 8-ounce thin chicken cutlets
- Salt and freshly ground pepper
- 1 teaspoon chopped dill
- 8 thin slices of prosciutto (about ¼ pound total)
- One 5-ounce package Boursin cheese, cut into 5 pieces
- ¼ cup all-purpose flour
- 2 tablespoons extra-virgin olive oil
- ½ cup dry white wine
- ½ cup chicken stock or low-sodium broth
- ½ teaspoon cornstarch dissolved in 1 tablespoon water

**1.** Preheat the oven to 425°. Heat a large, deep, ovenproof skillet until hot to the touch. Add the spinach and cook over high heat, tossing, until wilted, 1 minute. Transfer the spinach to a colander and let cool slightly. Press out as much of the liquid as possible.
**2.** Season the chicken cutlets with salt and pepper and sprinkle with the dill. Place 2 slices of prosciutto on each chicken cutlet. Top with the spinach and place 1 piece of Boursin on each cutlet.

Roll the cutlets up lengthwise and secure in 2 or 3 places with toothpicks. Season with salt and pepper and dust with flour, tapping off any excess.
**3.** Wipe out the skillet, add the olive oil and heat. Add the stuffed chicken and cook over high heat until golden on the bottom, about 4 minutes. Turn the cutlets and cook for 2 minutes longer. Add the wine and stock to the skillet, cover and bake in the oven for about 12 minutes, or until the chicken is cooked through. Transfer the cutlets to plates or a platter and remove the toothpicks. Cover with foil and keep warm.
**4.** Add the cornstarch mixture to the skillet and whisk over high heat until slightly thickened. Whisk in the remaining piece of Boursin and season with salt and pepper. Pour the sauce over the chicken and serve at once. —*Julie Ridlon*
**WINE** Rich, velvety Merlot.

### Lemon Confit Chicken with Calamata Olives

**ACTIVE: 30 MIN; TOTAL: 1 HR 30 MIN**
**4 SERVINGS**

- ¼ cup extra-virgin olive oil
- 1 medium onion, minced
- 4 large chicken breast halves, on the bone, with skin (about 3½ pounds total)
- Kosher salt and freshly ground pepper
- 2 cinnamon sticks
- ¾ cup minced flat-leaf parsley
- ½ cup minced cilantro, plus 12 cilantro sprigs
- 1 heaping teaspoon finely grated fresh ginger
- Pinch of saffron
- 1 cup dry white wine
- 1 cup chicken stock or low-sodium broth
- 1 cup Calamata olives, pitted
- 1 Moroccan preserved lemon from a jar, pulp discarded, peel finely diced (see Note)

1. In a large enameled cast-iron casserole, heat 2 tablespoons of the olive oil. Add the onion and cook over moderately high heat, stirring occasionally, until it is just starting to brown, about 5 minutes. Scrape into a bowl.

2. Season the chicken breasts with salt and pepper. Add the remaining 2 tablespoons of olive oil to the casserole and sear the chicken breasts in 2 batches until browned, about 3 minutes per side. Return all the chicken to the casserole.

3. Add the cinnamon sticks, flat-leaf parsley, cilantro, ginger, saffron, sautéed onion, wine and stock to the casserole and bring to a boil. Reduce the heat to moderate, cover and simmer for 30 minutes. Stir the olives and preserved lemon into the casserole and simmer until the chicken breasts are cooked through, about 15 minutes longer. Transfer the chicken to a warm platter and cover with foil.

4. Boil the cooking liquid in the casserole over high heat until reduced by half and slightly thickened, about 10 minutes. Discard the cinnamon sticks. Spoon the sauce over the chicken, garnish with the cilantro sprigs and serve. —*Marie Paillard*

**NOTE** Storebought preserved lemons imported from Morocco have a silken texture and a distinctive pungent flavor similar to that of homemade lemon confit ($18 for half a liter from Bella Cucina; 800-580-5674 or bellacucina.com).

**SERVE WITH** Rice pilaf or couscous, and butter-glazed baby carrots.

**WINE** Fruity, low-oak Chardonnay.

## Cider-Braised Chicken Legs with Onion-Raisin Sauce

**ACTIVE: 45 MIN; TOTAL: 3 HR**

20 SERVINGS ●

½ cup pure olive oil
20 whole chicken legs
Salt and freshly ground black pepper
4 large Spanish onions, halved crosswise and thinly sliced
20 sage leaves
6 bay leaves
2 cups mixed dark and golden raisins
1 teaspoon crushed red pepper
2 quarts plus 2 cups apple cider
1 cup cider vinegar
3 quarts chicken stock or low-sodium broth
½ cup coarsely chopped flat-leaf parsley

1. Preheat the oven to 400°. Heat ¼ cup of olive oil in each of 2 large skillets until shimmering. Season the chicken legs with salt and black pepper. Add 5 of the chicken legs to each skillet, skin side down, and cook over moderately high heat until the skin is crisp and browned, about 8 minutes. Turn and cook for 3 minutes longer. Transfer the chicken legs to baking sheets, skin side up. Repeat with the remaining chicken legs.

2. Add half of the onions to each skillet and cook over moderately high heat, stirring occasionally, until slightly softened, about 5 minutes. Divide the sage, bay leaves, raisins and crushed red pepper between the skillets and cook, stirring occasionally, until the onions are golden and starting to stick to the bottom of the skillet, about 5 minutes. Add 5 cups of cider to each skillet and simmer over moderately high heat until the cider is syrupy, about 25 minutes. Add ½ cup of vinegar to each pan and simmer for 2 minutes. Season lightly with salt and black pepper. Stir 6 cups of stock and ¼ cup of parsley into each skillet and season lightly with salt and black pepper.

3. Divide the onion-raisin sauce between 2 large roasting pans. Arrange the chicken legs in the sauce skin side up. Set the roasting pans on the upper and lower racks of the oven and reduce the heat to 350°. Roast the chicken until cooked through, about 1¼ hours; switch the pans top to bottom halfway through.

4. Transfer the chicken to 2 platters and keep warm. Set each roasting pan over high heat and boil until the sauce in each is reduced to about 5 cups and slightly thickened, about 10 minutes. Season with salt and pepper. Serve the chicken legs with the sauce. —*Morgan Brownlow*

**MAKE AHEAD** The braised chicken legs and sauce can be refrigerated separately overnight. Let both return to room temperature, then reheat the chicken legs in the onion-raisin sauce, skin side up, for 30 minutes in a 350° oven.

**SERVE WITH** Polenta or couscous, and sautéed spinach or Swiss chard.

**WINE** Soft, off-dry Riesling.

## Roasted Chicken Legs with Garlicky Potatoes and Peppers

**ACTIVE: 15 MIN; TOTAL: 1 HR 25 MIN**

6 SERVINGS

Bottled marinated peppers bring a rich flavor to this super-simple chicken dish. And they are an enormous time-saver because they have already been roasted, peeled, seeded, sliced and mixed with chopped garlic and herbs.

2 pounds Yukon Gold potatoes, peeled and sliced ¼ inch thick
Two 19-ounce jars roasted peppers marinated in oil with garlic and herbs, drained, peppers cut into large pieces, 6 tablespoons of the garlic-herb marinade reserved
3 tablespoons extra-virgin olive oil
1½ teaspoons thyme leaves
Salt and freshly ground black pepper
6 whole chicken legs (about 3½ pounds total)

1. Preheat the oven to 425°. Lightly oil a large roasting pan. Add the potatoes, peppers, 3 tablespoons of the reserved garlic-herb marinade, the olive oil and thyme to the roasting pan. Season with salt and ground pepper and toss well to coat the potatoes and peppers.

# poultry

2. Using a sharp knife, make 3 or 4 deep slashes in each chicken leg and set them on top of the vegetables. Rub the remaining 3 tablespoons of garlic-herb marinade all over the chicken and into the slashes. Season with salt and pepper.

3. Roast the chicken legs for 1 hour and 10 minutes, stirring the vegetables once or twice, or until the chicken is cooked through and the potatoes and peppers are tender and crispy in spots. Transfer to a platter and serve. —*Grace Parisi*
**WINE** Light, zesty, fruity Dolcetto.

## Basque Chicken and Chorizo Sauté
**TOTAL: 1 HR 15 MIN**
6 SERVINGS

- 4 ounces dry chorizo, sliced ¼ inch thick
- 2 tablespoons extra-virgin olive oil
- 6 whole chicken legs, split (3½ pounds total)
- Salt and freshly ground pepper
- 2 medium red bell peppers, cut into ½-inch-wide strips
- 2 medium red onions, thinly sliced
- 6 large garlic cloves, thinly sliced
- 2 large thyme sprigs
- 1 cup cherry tomatoes, halved
- ¾ cup dry sherry
- 2 teaspoons sweet paprika
- ¾ teaspoon crushed red pepper
- One 9-ounce package frozen artichoke hearts, thawed and pressed dry
- 2 tablespoons shredded basil
- Crusty French bread, for serving

1. Heat a large skillet. Add the chorizo and cook over moderate heat, stirring, until lightly browned and some of the fat is rendered, about 5 minutes. Using a slotted spoon, transfer the chorizo to a plate.

2. Heat the olive oil in the skillet. Season the chicken with salt and pepper and cook over moderately high heat, turning once, until well browned, 15 minutes. Add the chicken to the chorizo.

3. Add the peppers, onions, garlic and thyme to the skillet and cook over moderate heat until just barely softened, about 5 minutes. Add the cherry tomatoes, dry sherry, paprika and crushed red pepper and cook for 1 minute, scraping up any browned bits from the pan.

4. Return the chicken and chorizo to the skillet. Cover and simmer over moderately low heat, turning occasionally, until the chicken is cooked through, about 25 minutes. Add the artichokes, tucking them in between the chicken pieces. Raise the heat to moderate and cook uncovered until the sauce is slightly thickened, about 10 minutes. Transfer the chicken to a deep platter. Stir the basil into the sauce and spoon the sauce over the chicken. Serve with crusty bread. —*Daniel Boulud*
**WINE** Soft, earthy Rioja.

## Chicken with Leafy Greens and Lemon
**TOTAL: 45 MIN**
4 SERVINGS ● ●

- 4 whole chicken legs (2½ pounds total), skinned and split
- Salt and freshly ground pepper
- All-purpose flour, for dusting
- 2 tablespoons extra-virgin olive oil
- 1 medium onion, coarsely chopped
- ½ cup dry white wine
- 1 cup chicken stock
- 1½ pounds mixed leafy greens, thick stems discarded, leaves coarsely chopped
- 6 scallions, thinly sliced
- ¼ cup finely chopped parsley
- ¼ cup finely chopped dill
- 2½ tablespoons fresh lemon juice

1. Season the chicken with salt and pepper and dust lightly with flour. Heat the olive oil in a large, deep skillet. Add the chicken and cook over high heat, turning once, until lightly browned, about 8 minutes. Add the onion; cook over moderate heat, stirring occasionally, until softened,

about 4 minutes. Add the white wine and simmer until nearly evaporated, about 3 minutes. Add the stock, cover and cook over moderately low heat for 12 minutes. Using tongs, carefully transfer the chicken to a platter.

2. Boil the pan juices over moderately high heat until slightly reduced, about 12 minutes. Stir in the greens gradually, adding more as they wilt. Add the scallions and 3 tablespoons each of parsley and dill. Season with salt and pepper. Return the chicken to the skillet, cover and cook over moderate heat for 10 minutes. Stir in the lemon juice. Transfer the chicken and greens to a platter, sprinkle with the remaining parsley and dill and serve. —*Aglaia Kremezi*
**WINE** Fruity, low-oak Chardonnay.

## Asian-Style Grilled Chicken
**TOTAL: 30 MIN, PLUS 1 HR MARINATING**
4 SERVINGS

Using Asian fish sauce as a marinade for the chicken legs creates a salty, savory flavor that is surprisingly complex.

- ⅓ cup Asian fish sauce
- 2 whole chicken legs, split
- 4 chicken breast halves on the bone, each cut crosswise into 3 pieces
- Freshly ground black pepper

1. Put the fish sauce in a large bowl. Add the chicken and toss to coat. Generously season with freshly ground black pepper and toss again. Let the chicken marinate at room temperature for 1 hour or refrigerate it for up to 2 hours.

2. Light a grill and oil the grate. Grill the chicken over a medium-hot fire, turning often, until lightly charred in spots and cooked through, about 15 minutes for the breast pieces and 25 minutes for the legs and thighs.
—*Naomi Duguid and Jeffrey Alford*
**SERVE WITH** Steamed rice.
**WINE** Spicy New World Gewürztraminer.

BASQUE CHICKEN AND CHORIZO SAUTÉ

# poultry

### Tuscan Chicken Under a Brick
**ACTIVE: 15 MIN; TOTAL: 45 MIN,**
**PLUS 1 HR MARINATING**
**2 SERVINGS**

This recipe calls for a two-piece clay vessel called a *mattone*. Either part of the *mattone*—or both—can be replaced by a cast-iron skillet, as long as one fits inside the other.

One 2½-pound organic, free-range
    or kosher chicken
½  cup extra-virgin olive oil
2  tablespoons fresh lemon juice
1  tablespoon minced garlic
2  teaspoons chopped rosemary
¾  teaspoon crushed red pepper
Kosher salt and freshly ground pepper
Lemon wedges, for serving

**1.** Using poultry shears, cut along both sides of the backbone and remove it. Turn the chicken breast up and press down on the breastbone to flatten the chicken to an even thickness (Figure 1). Twist the wings up and tuck them under at the top of the breast. Slit the skin on either side of the lower breast to allow the legs to move freely, then pull up the legs so the ends of the drumsticks are next to the wings. Push a 12-inch bamboo skewer through the drumstick, wing, breast, wing and finally through the second drumstick (Figure 2).

**2.** In a small bowl, mix 2 tablespoons of the olive oil with the lemon juice, garlic, rosemary, crushed red pepper, 1 teaspoon of salt and ½ teaspoon of pepper. Put the chicken in a dish and rub all over with the marinade. Cover and refrigerate for at least 1 hour or overnight.

**3.** About 1 hour and 15 minutes before serving, preheat the *mattone* (if you have an electric stove, use a heat-diffusing pad): Pour 1 tablespoon of the olive oil into the bottom of the *mattone* and set it over very low heat; set the *mattone* lid flat side down on another burner over very low heat. Heat both parts for about 30 minutes, very gradually increasing the heat to moderately high.

**4.** Add the remaining 5 tablespoons of olive oil to the bottom of the *mattone*; when it sizzles, add the chicken, breast side down, to coat with hot oil. Using tongs, turn the chicken breast up. Using an oven mitt, immediately put the hot *mattone* lid on the chicken and firmly press down to flatten (Figure 3). Cook over moderately high heat for 15 minutes. Uncover and turn the chicken, then replace the lid and cook until the skin is browned and crisp and an instant-read thermometer inserted in a thigh registers 165°, about 12 minutes longer.

**5.** Transfer the cooked chicken to a cutting board and let stand for 10 minutes. Halve the chicken, season with salt and pepper and serve with lemon wedges.
—*Paula Wolfert*
**WINE** Simple, fruity Chianti or Sangiovese.

# technique

**TIP** **TUSCAN CHICKEN UNDER A BRICK (SEE RECIPE ABOVE)**

**1. FLATTENING**
Cut down both sides of the backbone and remove it. Turn the chicken over and press down with the heel of your hand to flatten the breast.

**2. SKEWERING**
To give the bird an even thickness, tuck the wings under the top of the breast and pull the drumsticks up to meet them; skewer to hold the pieces in place.

**3. COOKING**
Heat both pieces of the *mattone*. Turn the marinated chicken to coat with hot oil. Place it, breast up, in the pan, top with the hot lid, press down and cook.

### Soy-Marinated Chicken Thighs with Shiitake Mushrooms
**TOTAL: 1 HR 30 MIN, PLUS 1 HR MARINATING**
**4 SERVINGS** ●

½  cup low-sodium soy sauce
2  large garlic cloves, very
    finely chopped
1  tablespoon finely grated ginger
2  teaspoons hot sauce
½  cup water
8  skinless chicken thighs
2  tablespoons vegetable oil
1  pound shiitake mushrooms,
    stems discarded, caps sliced
    ¼ inch thick
Salt and freshly ground pepper
6  large scallions, white and tender
    green parts only, thinly sliced
2  teaspoons fresh lemon juice
1  teaspoon walnut or hazelnut oil

1. In a baking dish, combine the soy sauce, garlic, ginger and hot sauce. Stir in the water. Add the chicken thighs to the soy marinade and turn to coat well. Cover and refrigerate for 1 hour, turning a few more times to recoat with the marinade.

2. Preheat the oven to 350°. Bring the chicken to room temperature. Discard half of the marinade. Bake the chicken for 40 minutes, basting a few times.

3. Meanwhile, heat the oil in a large non-stick skillet until shimmering. Add the shiitake, season with salt and pepper and cook over moderately high heat for 4 minutes. Add the scallions; cook over moderate heat for 5 minutes. Stir in the lemon juice and walnut oil and serve with the soy-marinated chicken. —*Jeff Orr*

**WINE** Rich, velvety Merlot.

## Korean-Style Chicken Wraps

**TOTAL: 30 MIN**

6 SERVINGS ● ●

This Korean-inspired dish is great for people trying to cut down on carbohydrates because the meat is wrapped in lettuce instead of served on bread.

- ¼ cup hoisin sauce, plus more for serving
- ¼ cup low-sodium soy sauce
- 2 tablespoons honey
- 1 tablespoon grated fresh ginger
- 2 large garlic cloves, minced
- 1 teaspoon Asian chili-garlic sauce
- 1 teaspoon Asian sesame oil
- Salt and freshly ground pepper
- 3 pounds skinless, boneless chicken thighs, trimmed of visible fat
- Vegetable oil, for brushing
- 1 head green leaf lettuce, separated into leaves
- 1 small cucumber, peeled and cut into 2-inch matchsticks
- 3 scallions, cut into 2-inch matchsticks
- Lime wedges, for serving

1. Light a grill. In a medium bowl, combine the ¼ cup of hoisin sauce with the soy sauce, honey, ginger, garlic, chili-garlic sauce and sesame oil. Season the barbecue sauce with salt and pepper.

2. Brush the chicken with vegetable oil and season with salt and pepper. Grill the chicken over a hot fire, turning occasionally, until golden and almost cooked through, about 10 minutes. Brush with the barbecue sauce and grill, turning and brushing, until golden brown, about 3 minutes longer. Transfer the grilled chicken to a cutting board and let stand for 5 minutes, then cut it into ½-inch strips.

3. Arrange the chicken and lettuce on a serving platter. Allow diners to make their own wraps by dabbing a small amount of hoisin sauce on a lettuce leaf, topping it with cucumber, scallions, chicken and a squeeze of lime and rolling it up. —*Grace Parisi*

**WINE** Spicy New World Gewürztraminer.

## Chicken Skewers with Lemon-Mint Vinaigrette

**TOTAL: 30 MIN**

6 SERVINGS ● ● ●

- 1 tablespoon hot paprika
- 1½ teaspoons minced garlic
- ½ teaspoon dried oregano
- ½ teaspoon ground cumin
- ½ cup plus ⅓ cup extra-virgin olive oil
- Salt and freshly ground black pepper
- 2 tablespoons chopped parsley
- 2 tablespoons chopped fresh mint
- 2 tablespoons fresh lemon juice
- 2 teaspoons grated lemon zest
- ⅛ teaspoon cayenne pepper
- 2 pounds skinless, boneless chicken thighs, cut into 1½-inch pieces
- 1 large red onion, sliced crosswise ½ inch thick
- 8 cups loosely packed washed arugula or spinach
- Lemon wedges, for serving

1. Light a grill or preheat a grill pan. In a small bowl, mix the paprika with 1 teaspoon of the minced garlic, the dried oregano and the cumin. Whisk in ⅓ cup of the olive oil and season with salt and black pepper.

2. In another small bowl, combine the parsley, mint, lemon juice, lemon zest, cayenne and the remaining ½ teaspoon of garlic. Whisk in the remaining ½ cup of olive oil and season the vinaigrette with salt and black pepper.

3. Thread the chicken onto 6 skewers. Brush the chicken and the onion slices with the paprika oil and arrange on the grill. Cook the onions for about 4 minutes, turning once, until they are slightly softened. Grill the chicken for 12 minutes, turning the skewers occasionally, until the chicken is cooked through.

4. Arrange the arugula on a platter. Spread the onions and chicken on top, drizzle with the vinaigrette and serve with lemon. —*Tom Douglas*

**WINE** Tart, peppery Grüner Veltliner.

# superfast

**BONELESS CHICKEN THIGHS**    TIP

**STICKY ASIAN CHICKEN**
Brush chicken thighs with a mix of hoisin sauce, soy sauce and honey and roast until cooked through. Serve with steamed rice.

**INDIAN CHICKEN WITH RAITA**
Dust chicken thighs with Madras curry powder, season with salt and roast. Serve with yogurt mixed with diced cucumbers, cumin seed and salt.

**BUFFALO CHICKEN THIGHS**
Season chicken thighs with salt, roast, then brush with a mixture of hot sauce and butter. Serve with blue cheese dressing.

● FAST    ● HEALTHY    ● MAKE AHEAD    ● STAFF FAVORITE

# poultry

## Herb-and-Cheese-Filled Chicken Thighs

**ACTIVE: 30 MIN; TOTAL: 1 HR 15 MIN**

**8 SERVINGS** ●

1½ cups fresh bread crumbs
1½ cups freshly grated Parmesan cheese (4½ ounces)
 2 large eggs, lightly beaten
 ½ cup grated Provolone cheese (1½ ounces)
 ½ cup coarsely chopped basil leaves
 ¼ cup coarsely chopped flat-leaf parsley leaves
Finely grated zest of 2 lemons
 1 tablespoon finely chopped rosemary
Sixteen 5-ounce boneless chicken thighs, with skin
Salt and freshly ground black pepper

**1.** Preheat the oven to 450°. In a medium bowl, mix the fresh bread crumbs with the Parmesan, eggs, Provolone, basil, parsley, lemon zest and rosemary. Stir well to combine.

**2.** Set the chicken thighs skin side down on a work surface and season with salt and pepper. Mound ¼ cup of the herb-and-cheese filling on each thigh. Fold the sides of the thighs over the filling to enclose it and securely tie each chicken thigh in 2 or 3 places with kitchen string. Generously season the bundles with salt and pepper.

**3.** Arrange the stuffed chicken thighs on a large, rimmed baking sheet and roast for about 35 minutes, or until they are golden brown and crisp. Let the chicken rest for 10 minutes, then discard the strings, transfer to a platter and serve. —*Mario Batali*

**MAKE AHEAD** The uncooked, stuffed chicken thighs can be refrigerated overnight. Let them return to room temperature before proceeding.

**WINE** Rich, velvety Merlot.

## Chicken Salad with Poblano Vinaigrette

**TOTAL: 30 MIN**

**4 SERVINGS** ●

 1 large poblano, chopped
 1 large garlic clove, smashed
 1 scallion, cut into 1-inch lengths
 ¼ cup cilantro leaves
 ¼ cup fresh lime juice
Pinch of salt
Pinch of sugar
 ¼ cup plus 3 tablespoons vegetable oil
 2 ears of corn, shucked
 1 large roasted chicken breast, boned and sliced crosswise
 1 large bunch watercress, thick stems discarded
 1 cup mixed small tomatoes, quartered lengthwise
 1 small Hass avocado, cut into ½-inch pieces
Freshly ground pepper

**1.** Light a grill. In a mini food processor, combine the poblano, garlic, scallion, cilantro, lime juice, salt and sugar and puree. With the machine on, add 6 tablespoons of the oil in a thin stream.

**2.** Rub the ears of corn with the remaining 1 tablespoon of oil; grill until lightly charred. Cut the kernels off the cobs.

**3.** Arrange the chicken on plates and surround it with the watercress, grilled corn, tomatoes and avocado; season lightly with salt and pepper. Pass the poblano vinaigrette at the table. —*Grace Parisi*

**WINE** Dry, medium-bodied Pinot Gris.

## Garlicky Lemongrass Chicken

**TOTAL: 40 MIN**

**6 TO 8 SERVINGS** ●

This spicy lemongrass paste is also wonderful rubbed on pork tenderloin or any firm, white-fleshed fish, such as snapper, sea bass or halibut.

 5 plump lemongrass stalks, inner bulb only, coarsely chopped
 3 scallions, white and light green parts only, coarsely chopped
 1 large garlic clove, smashed
 1 large jalapeño, chopped
Pinch of sugar
 ¼ cup vegetable oil, plus more for brushing
Salt and freshly ground pepper
 4 pounds skinless, boneless chicken thighs and breasts

**1.** In a food processor, pulse the lemongrass until finely chopped. Add the scallions, garlic, jalapeño and sugar and pulse until finely chopped. With the machine on, add the ¼ cup of vegetable oil in a steady stream and process to a fine paste. Season the paste with salt and pepper.

**2.** Using a small knife, make ½-inch-deep slashes into the chicken and rub the lemongrass paste all over, working it into the slashes. Let the chicken marinate for 15 minutes at room temperature or refrigerate overnight.

**3.** Light a grill. Brush the chicken with oil, season with salt and pepper and grill over a medium-hot fire, turning occasionally, until browned and cooked through, about 15 minutes. —*Grace Parisi*

**WINE** Tangy, crisp Vernaccia.

## Spicy Poached Chicken Burgers

**TOTAL: 45 MIN**

**6 SERVINGS** ●

 ½ cup water
 ½ cup instant couscous
 2 pounds ground chicken
 2 tablespoons chopped mint, plus several whole mint leaves for garnish
 2 teaspoons ground cumin
 1 teaspoon finely grated lemon zest
 2 tablespoons pine nuts, lightly toasted and finely chopped
Kosher salt

HERB-AND-CHEESE-FILLED CHICKEN THIGHS

SPICY POACHED CHICKEN BURGER

2 Hass avocados

1 tablespoon fresh lemon juice

1 jalapeño, partially seeded and minced

1 small shallot, minced

2 cups chicken stock or low-sodium broth

2 tablespoons *harissa* (see Note) or Asian chili-garlic sauce

Freshly ground pepper

Six 6-inch pita breads, warmed

1. In a small saucepan, bring the water to a boil and stir in the couscous. Cover the saucepan, remove from the heat and let stand until the water has been absorbed, about 5 minutes. Fluff the couscous with a fork and let cool.

2. In a large bowl, gently mix the ground chicken with the couscous, chopped mint, ground cumin, grated lemon zest, pine nuts and 2 teaspoons of salt. With lightly oiled hands, pat the chicken-couscous mixture into 6 burgers. Cover the burgers tightly with plastic wrap and refrigerate until chilled.

3. Meanwhile, in a medium bowl, coarsely mash the avocados with a fork. Stir in the fresh lemon juice and the minced jalapeño and shallot. Season the avocado mash with salt.

4. Preheat the oven to 325°. In a very large, deep skillet, bring the chicken stock to a boil with the *harissa*. Season the burgers with salt and pepper. Gently set the burgers in the skillet and simmer over moderately low heat until they are cooked through, about 4 minutes per side. Transfer the poached burgers to a rimmed baking sheet, cover with foil and keep warm in the oven. Boil the poaching liquid over high heat until reduced to ½ cup, about 6 minutes.

5. Set the pitas on plates. Top with the chicken burgers and spoon some of the reduced sauce over them. Garnish with the avocado mash and mint leaves and serve. —*James Boyce*

NOTE *Harissa* is available at Middle Eastern markets and specialty shops.

MAKE AHEAD The uncooked burgers and the avocado mash (covered with plastic wrap pressed directly onto the surface) can be refrigerated overnight.

WINE Bright, citrusy Riesling.

## Garlicky Broccoli Rabe with Chicken Sausage and Peppers

TOTAL: 40 MIN

6 SERVINGS ●

F&W staffers especially like the different varieties of chicken sausage made by Bruce Aidells, available at many supermarkets and at aidells.com.

● FAST    ● HEALTHY    ● MAKE AHEAD    ● STAFF FAVORITE

103

# poultry

Salt

1 pound broccoli rabe, trimmed

2 tablespoons plus 1 teaspoon extra-virgin olive oil

1 medium red onion, finely chopped

1 yellow bell pepper, thinly sliced

4 garlic cloves, finely chopped

One 19-ounce can cannellini beans, rinsed and drained

1 cup chicken stock or low-sodium broth

¼ cup pitted black olives, chopped

Freshly ground pepper

Six 3-ounce hot Italian chicken sausages

1. Fill a large, deep skillet with water and bring to a boil. Add a large pinch of salt and the broccoli rabe, cover and cook over high heat until tender, about 8 minutes. Drain well.

2. Wipe out the skillet. Add the 2 tablespoons of olive oil and heat until shimmering. Add the onion and bell pepper and cook over moderately high heat, stirring occasionally, until softened and just starting to brown, about 8 minutes. Add the garlic and cook, stirring, until fragrant, about 1 minute. Add the broccoli rabe, beans, stock and olives and simmer over moderate heat for 5 minutes. Season with salt and pepper.

3. Meanwhile, heat the remaining 1 teaspoon of oil in a skillet. Add the sausages and cook over moderate heat, turning occasionally, until browned, about 10 minutes. Mound the broccoli rabe and beans on plates, top with the chicken sausages and serve. —*Victoria Abbott Riccardi*

WINE Complex, savory Chianti Classico.

## Arrowhead Farms Fried Chicken

TOTAL: 1 HR, PLUS 2 HR MARINATING

8 SERVINGS ●

Two 3½- to 4-pound chickens, each cut into 8 pieces

Kosher salt

4 large eggs, lightly beaten

1 quart buttermilk

1 cup mayonnaise

¾ cup amber ale

½ cup finely chopped basil

1 teaspoon dried oregano

1 tablespoon plus 1 teaspoon sweet paprika

4 cups all-purpose flour

Freshly ground pepper

2 quarts vegetable or peanut oil

1. Season the chicken generously with salt and let stand at room temperature for 20 minutes. Rinse and pat dry.

2. In a large bowl, whisk the eggs with the buttermilk, mayonnaise, ale, basil, oregano and 2 teaspoons of the paprika. Add the chicken and turn several times to coat. Refrigerate for 2 hours.

3. In another large bowl, combine the flour with the remaining 2 teaspoons of paprika and season generously with salt and pepper. Remove the chicken from the marinade, shaking off any excess. Dredge the chicken in the seasoned flour, pressing to help it adhere. Transfer the coated pieces to a wire rack.

4. In 2 large, deep skillets with tight-fitting lids, heat the oil until it registers 350° on a deep-frying thermometer. Add the chicken, cover tightly and cook over moderate heat until the chicken pieces are golden on the bottom, about 12 minutes. Turn the pieces, cover and cook over moderately low heat for 10 minutes. Uncover and cook over moderately high heat, turning once or twice, until the chicken is crisp and deep golden and an instant-read thermometer inserted in the thickest part of a leg and breast without touching the bone registers 165°, about 10 minutes longer. Drain on paper towel–covered wire racks and serve.
—*Mary Lynn Van Wyck*

MAKE AHEAD The fried chicken can be served at room temperature.

WINE Light, fruity Beaujolais.

## Creamy Chicken Stew

TOTAL: 30 MIN

4 SERVINGS ● ●

2 tablespoons vegetable oil

4 chicken drumsticks (1 pound total)

3 skinless, boneless chicken breast halves (1½ pound total), each cut into 4 pieces

Kosher salt and freshly ground pepper

½ pound small white mushrooms, quartered

1 large Yukon Gold potato (10 ounces), peeled and cut into ½-inch dice

1 large carrot, cut into ½-inch dice

1 medium onion, cut into ½-inch dice

2 garlic cloves

1 tablespoon unsalted butter

¼ cup all-purpose flour

1 cup dry white wine

2 cups chicken stock or low-sodium broth

4 thyme sprigs

1 bay leaf

½ cup heavy cream

1 tablespoon coarsely chopped flat-leaf parsley

1. Heat a large skillet. Add the vegetable oil and heat until wisps of smoke appear. Add the chicken drumsticks and breasts in a single layer, season with salt and pepper and cook over moderately high heat, turning once, until golden brown, about 7 minutes total; transfer the chicken to a plate. Add the mushrooms to the skillet and cook until lightly browned, about 3 minutes. Using a slotted spoon, transfer the mushrooms to a small bowl.

2. Add the potato, carrot, onion, garlic and butter to the skillet and cook until lightly browned, about 4 minutes. Stir in the flour. Pour in the wine and bring to a simmer, scraping up any browned bits

ARROWHEAD FARMS FRIED CHICKEN, WITH CORN PUDDING (P. 225) AND CUCUMBER SALAD (P. 44)

# poultry

from the bottom of the pan. Add the stock, thyme, bay leaf and chicken along with any accumulated juices and bring to a boil. Cover the skillet and simmer over moderately low heat until the potato and carrot are tender and the chicken drumsticks are cooked through, about 15 minutes. Discard the bay leaf and thyme. Stir in the cream and the reserved mushrooms and season with salt and pepper. Sprinkle with the parsley and serve.
—*Galen Zamarra*

**WINE** Medium-bodied, round Pinot Blanc.

## Spiced Turkey Tagine with Prunes
**ACTIVE: 45 MIN; TOTAL: 1 HR 15 MIN**
6 SERVINGS ● ● ●

  2  tablespoons extra-virgin olive oil
  1  red onion, coarsely chopped
  1  leek, white and very tender green parts only, chopped
  1  pound skinless, boneless turkey breast, cut into 1-inch pieces
  1  teaspoon cinnamon
  1  teaspoon ground cumin
  1  teaspoon ground ginger
  1  teaspoon dried basil
  ¼  teaspoon turmeric
Salt and freshly ground pepper
One 15-ounce can chickpeas, drained and rinsed
  1  cup pitted prunes (about 20)
  2  tomatoes, coarsely chopped
  1  large sweet potato (1 pound), peeled and cut into 1-inch pieces
  1  medium carrot, coarsely chopped
  6  pitted dates, chopped
  2  cups vegetable stock or low-sodium broth

**1.** Heat the olive oil in a large enameled cast-iron casserole. Add the onion and leek and cook over moderately high heat until lightly browned, about 6 minutes; push to the side. Add the turkey and half

of the cinnamon, cumin, ginger, basil and turmeric; season with salt and pepper. Cook until the turkey is lightly browned all over, about 4 minutes; transfer the turkey to a plate.
**2.** Add the remaining seasonings to the casserole and stir until aromatic, 30 seconds. Add the chickpeas, prunes, tomatoes, sweet potato, carrot, dates and stock; bring to a boil. Reduce the heat to low, cover and simmer for 15 minutes.
**3.** Return the turkey to the casserole and simmer until the turkey is cooked all the way through and the vegetables are tender, about 15 minutes. Season with salt and pepper and serve. —*Dana Jacobi*

**SERVE WITH** Couscous.

**WINE** Rich, earthy Pinot Noir.

## Tina's Turkey Chili
**ACTIVE: 30 MIN; TOTAL: 1 HR 30 MIN**
8 SERVINGS ●

  ½  cup extra-virgin olive oil
  1  bunch scallions, sliced ½ inch thick
  1  red bell pepper, finely diced
  1  large poblano, finely diced
  2  garlic cloves, minced
Salt and freshly ground pepper
  3  pounds ground turkey
  ⅓  cup pure ancho chile powder
  3  tablespoons ground cumin
One 28-ounce can tomato sauce (3 cups)
  3  cups water
  5  thyme sprigs
  2  canned chipotle chiles in adobo, stemmed and minced
  2  tablespoons stone-ground cornmeal
  2  imported bay leaves
  1  teaspoon dried oregano, crumbled
Two 15-ounce cans black beans or pink beans, drained (3 cups)
Shredded Cheddar cheese, chopped cilantro, sour cream and warm corn tortillas, for serving

**1.** Heat 1½ tablespoons of the olive oil in a large enameled cast-iron casserole. Add the scallions, bell pepper, poblano and garlic, season with salt and pepper and cook over moderately high heat, stirring, until softened and just beginning to brown, about 5 minutes. Scrape the vegetables onto a plate.
**2.** Add the remaining 2½ tablespoons of olive oil to the casserole. Add the turkey, season with salt and pepper and cook, stirring to break up the meat, until nearly cooked but still slightly pink, about 4 minutes. Add the ancho chile powder and cumin and cook until the liquid evaporates, about 5 minutes longer. Add the tomato sauce, water, thyme, chipotles, cornmeal, bay leaves, oregano and cooked vegetables and bring to a boil. Partially cover and cook over moderately low heat, stirring occasionally, until the sauce is slightly reduced and the meat is tender, about 45 minutes. Add the beans, season with salt and pepper and simmer 10 minutes longer. Serve in deep bowls, passing the cheese, cilantro, sour cream and tortillas on the side. —*Tina Ujlaki*

**MAKE AHEAD** The chili can be refrigerated for up to 2 days.

**WINE** Light, zesty, fruity Dolcetto.

## Turkey Burgers with Pesto Mayonnaise
**TOTAL: 30 MIN**
4 SERVINGS ● ●

  1½  teaspoons extra-virgin olive oil
  1  small onion, finely chopped
  1  garlic clove, minced
  2  tablespoons water
  1½  pounds ground turkey breast
  1½  tablespoons *panko* (Japanese bread crumbs)
Kosher salt and freshly ground black pepper
  4  whole wheat kaiser rolls, split in half

# miso

Miso isn't the prettiest ingredient in the pantry, but it's tremendously versatile. This Japanese paste of fermented soybeans and grains gives the gravy for the roast chicken here terrific richness and concentrated flavor.

## Crispy Roast Chicken and Shallots with Miso Gravy

ACTIVE: 25 MIN; TOTAL: 1 HR 15 MIN

6 SERVINGS ●

- 8 medium shallots, 7 halved lengthwise, 1 minced
- 2 tablespoons extra-virgin olive oil

Salt and freshly ground pepper

- ¼ cup white (*shiro*) or red (*aka*) miso
- 4 tablespoons unsalted butter, softened
- 2 tablespoons minced flat-leaf parsley
- 2 tablespoons very finely chopped chives
- 2 teaspoons finely grated fresh ginger
- 1 tablespoon all-purpose flour
- 4 pounds chicken breasts and whole legs on the bone, with skin
- 1 cup low-sodium chicken broth

1. Preheat the oven to 425°. In a large roasting pan, toss the halved shallots with the olive oil and season generously with salt and pepper.

2. In a medium bowl, mix the miso with the minced shallot and the butter, parsley, chives and ginger. Transfer 3 tablespoons of the shallot-miso butter to a bowl and stir in the flour to form a paste.

3. With your fingers, gently separate the chicken skin from the breasts and legs.

Work the remaining shallot-miso butter under the loosened skin, spreading it evenly. Season the chicken with salt and pepper and transfer to the roasting pan.

4. Roast the chicken in the center of the oven for 45 minutes, or until the skin is browned and the juices run clear when the meat is pierced with a knife. Transfer the chicken and shallots to a platter and cover loosely with foil.

5. Pour the pan juices into a saucepan and skim off the fat. Set the roasting pan over high heat. Add the chicken broth and cook, scraping up the browned bits from the bottom and sides of the roasting pan with a wooden spoon. Pour the deglazed drippings into the saucepan and bring to a boil. Whisk in the miso-flour paste and simmer until thickened, about 2 minutes. Transfer the miso gravy to a bowl and serve at once, with the chicken and shallots. —*Grace Parisi*

MAKE AHEAD The shallot-miso butter can be refrigerated overnight. Let soften before using.

WINE Ripe, oaky Chardonnay.

# poultry

4 oil-packed sun-dried tomatoes,
drained and chopped, plus
1 tablespoon oil from the jar
2 tablespoons mayonnaise
1 tablespoon prepared pesto
Red onion slices
1 bunch arugula, stems trimmed

**1.** Light a grill. In a small skillet, heat the olive oil until shimmering. Add the chopped onion and garlic and cook over moderate heat, stirring occasionally, until softened, about 5 minutes. Add the water and cook, stirring, until the onion is lightly browned, about 5 minutes longer. Scrape the onion and garlic into a medium bowl and let cool. Add the ground turkey, *panko*, 1 teaspoon of salt and ¼ teaspoon of pepper. Knead the mixture lightly and form it into 4 patties.
**2.** Grill the burgers over a hot fire, turning once, until lightly charred on the outside and cooked through, about 6 minutes per side. Brush the cut sides of the rolls with the sun-dried-tomato oil and grill until toasted, about 1 minute.

# health

**3.** In a small bowl, mix the mayonnaise with the pesto and sun-dried tomatoes. Spread the pesto mayo on the rolls and top with the burgers, red onion slices and arugula. Close the burgers and serve.
*—Elizabeth Mendez*
**WINE** Dry, mineral-flavored Chenin Blanc.

## Turkey-Date Meatballs with Lentils and Yogurt Sauce

**ACTIVE: 30 MIN; TOTAL: 2 HR**
4 SERVINGS ● ●
1 pound ground turkey
2 cups fresh bread crumbs
6 dates, pitted and finely chopped
2 large eggs, beaten
2 tablespoons sesame seeds
1 teaspoon Asian sesame oil
Salt and freshly ground pepper
1 cup French green lentils
2 large garlic cloves, crushed
and peeled
2 thyme sprigs
1 cinnamon stick
3 tablespoons extra-virgin
olive oil
1½ tablespoons sherry vinegar
1 cup plain low-fat yogurt
2 tablespoons fresh lemon juice
1 tablespoon chopped mint
1 teaspoon finely grated
lemon zest

**1.** In a large bowl, combine the ground turkey with the bread crumbs, dates, eggs, sesame seeds, sesame oil, 2 teaspoons of salt and ½ teaspoon of pepper. Cover and refrigerate for 1 hour.
**2.** Preheat the oven to 400°. Meanwhile, in a medium saucepan, cover the lentils, garlic, thyme and cinnamon stick with 2 inches of water; bring to a boil. Simmer over moderately low heat until the lentils are tender, about 25 minutes. Drain the lentils and transfer to a bowl; pick out and discard the seasonings. Stir the olive oil and vinegar into the lentils and season with salt and pepper.

**3.** Form the turkey mixture into 1-inch meatballs. Transfer the meatballs to a large, rimmed, lightly oiled baking sheet and bake for 20 minutes, or until browned on the bottoms and cooked through.
**4.** Meanwhile, blend the yogurt with the lemon juice, mint and lemon zest and season with salt and pepper. Serve the meatballs with the lentils and yogurt sauce.
*—Jeff Orr*
**WINE** Bright, fruity rosé.

## Turkey and Green Bean Stir-Fry with Peanuts

**TOTAL: 30 MIN**
4 SERVINGS ●
3 tablespoons vegetable oil
One 2-inch piece of peeled fresh
ginger, cut into fine matchsticks
4 large garlic cloves, thinly sliced
1 pound ground turkey
Salt and freshly ground pepper
3 tablespoons soy sauce
3 tablespoons Japanese mirin
1 pound green beans, trimmed
2 loosely packed cups basil leaves
(from 1 large bunch)
¼ cup plus 2 tablespoons roasted
salted peanuts, coarsely chopped

**1.** In a large skillet, heat 2 tablespoons of the oil until shimmering. Add the ginger and garlic; cook over moderate heat until fragrant, 30 seconds. Add the turkey and season with salt and pepper. Stir-fry, breaking up the meat, until it is nearly cooked, 4 minutes. Add the soy sauce and mirin and cook for 1 minute. Transfer to a bowl and wipe out the skillet.
**2.** Add the remaining 1 tablespoon of oil to the skillet; heat until shimmering. Add the beans and stir-fry over high heat until crisp-tender and blackened in spots, 5 minutes. Add the beans to the turkey and let cool slightly. Add the basil and toss. Transfer to plates, sprinkle with the peanuts and serve. *—Ilene Rosen*
**WINE** Tart, low-tannin Barbera.

## Turkey Breast Fajitas with Strawberry-Jalapeño Salsa

**TOTAL: 30 MIN**

**6 SERVINGS ● ●**

Butterflying a whole boneless turkey breast allows it to cook as quickly as an ordinary cutlet. Removing the turkey skin before applying the spice paste lets the flavor penetrate the meat more fully and helps reduce fat.

- 1 **tablespoon vegetable oil**
- 1 **tablespoon pure ancho chile powder**
- ½ **teaspoon ground cumin**
- ¼ **teaspoon cinnamon**
- ¼ **teaspoon cayenne pepper**

One 3½-pound skinless, boneless turkey breast, butterflied to a 1-inch thickness

Kosher salt

- 1 **medium red onion, very thinly sliced on a mandoline**
- 2 **small jalapeños, very thinly sliced**
- 5 **tablespoons sherry vinegar**
- 3 **tablespoons honey**
- 1 **quart strawberries, thinly sliced**
- 12 **corn tortillas**
- 1 **red bell pepper, thinly sliced**
- 2 **medium tomatoes, coarsely chopped**
- 1 **Hass avocado, cut into ½-inch dice**
- 1 **large bunch cilantro, separated into small sprigs**

**1.** Light a gas or charcoal grill. In a small bowl, combine the vegetable oil, chile powder, cumin, cinnamon and cayenne pepper until it forms a smooth paste. Rub the spice paste all over the butterflied turkey breast, then generously season the breast with salt.

**2.** In a medium bowl, toss the sliced red onion and jalapeños with the sherry vinegar. Add a pinch of salt to the salsa and let stand, tossing the salsa a few more times, for 15 minutes.

**TURKEY AND GREEN BEAN STIR-FRY**

**TURKEY BREAST FAJITAS**

HERB-ROASTED TURKEY WITH MAPLE GRAVY

**3.** Meanwhile, grill the turkey breast over a medium-hot fire until lightly charred and just cooked through, about 8 minutes per side. Transfer the turkey to a carving board.

**4.** Stir the honey into the salsa until dissolved, then fold in the strawberries and season with salt.

**5.** Heat the corn tortillas on the grill until they are warm, about 5 seconds per side. Transfer the tortillas to a cloth-lined basket and cover to keep warm. Thinly slice the turkey breast and transfer to a platter; serve with the tortillas, salsa, red bell pepper, tomatoes, avocado and cilantro sprigs. —*Marcia Kiesel*
**WINE** Bright, fruity rosé.

### Alsatian-Brined Turkey with Riesling Gravy

**ACTIVE: 30 MIN; TOTAL: 3 HR 30 MIN, PLUS 2 DAYS BRINING**
**12 SERVINGS** ● ●
   5  quarts plus 2 cups cold water
Kosher salt
   1  cup sugar
   ¼  cup yellow mustard seeds
   ¼  cup dried chopped onion
   2  tablespoons caraway seeds
   2  tablespoons black peppercorns, lightly crushed
   2  tablespoons juniper berries, lightly crushed
   6  bay leaves
One 18-pound turkey, neck and giblets reserved for another use
2½  cups Riesling
   1  large onion, quartered
   1  head garlic, cloves separated but not peeled
   3  tablespoons all-purpose flour
2½  cups Rich Turkey Stock (p. 112) or low-sodium chicken broth
Freshly ground pepper

**1.** In a large pot, bring 4 cups of the water to a boil. Add 1¼ cups of salt, the sugar, mustard seeds, dried onion, caraway seeds, peppercorns, juniper berries and bay leaves. Stir to dissolve the salt and sugar completely. Remove the pot from the heat.

**2.** Line a large stockpot with 2 very large and sturdy plastic bags. Put the turkey into the bags, neck first. Pour the warm brine over the turkey. Add 1½ cups of the Riesling and 4 quarts of the cold water. Seal the bags; press out as much air as possible. Refrigerate for 2 days.

**3.** Preheat the oven to 350°. Drain the brined turkey, scraping off the spices, then transfer it to a large roasting pan and let it return to room temperature. Discard the brine.

**4.** Add the quartered onion, the garlic and 1 cup of the water to the pan and roast the turkey for 1½ hours. Add the remaining 1 cup of water to the pan and roast for about 1½ hours longer, or until an instant-read thermometer inserted into an inner thigh registers 165°. Cover the breast loosely with foil during the last hour of roasting to prevent it from browning too quickly.

**5.** Transfer the turkey to a cutting board. Strain the pan juices into a measuring cup and skim off the fat; reserve 3 tablespoons of the fat. In a bowl, mix the reserved fat with the flour until a paste forms.

**6.** Set the roasting pan over 2 burners and heat until sizzling. Add the remaining 1 cup of Riesling and bring to a simmer over moderately high heat, scraping up any browned bits from the bottom and sides of the pan. Strain the wine into a medium saucepan and boil until reduced to ¼ cup, about 5 minutes. Add the stock and the reserved pan juices and bring to a boil. Whisk in the flour paste and simmer over moderate heat until the gravy thickens slightly and no floury taste remains, about 10 minutes. Season with salt and pepper. Carve the turkey and serve with the Riesling gravy on the side. —*Grace Parisi*
**WINE** Dry, full-flavored Alsace Riesling.

### Herb-Roasted Turkey with Maple Gravy

**ACTIVE: 30 MIN; TOTAL: 4 HR**
**10 SERVINGS** ● ●
One 18-pound turkey, neck and giblets reserved for another use
   1  head garlic, halved horizontally
   1  medium onion, quartered
  20  sage sprigs
  20  thyme sprigs
  20  parsley sprigs
Salt and freshly ground pepper
   3  cups Rich Turkey Stock (recipe follows)
   3  tablespoons unsalted butter
   3  tablespoons all-purpose flour
   3  tablespoons maple syrup

**1.** Preheat the oven to 350°. Rinse the turkey inside and out and pat dry. Trim the neck skin. Stuff with the garlic, onion and sage, thyme and parsley sprigs. Generously season inside and out with salt and pepper. Transfer to a large, oiled roasting pan and roast for about 3 hours, or until an instant-read thermometer inserted into an inner thigh without touching the bone registers 175°. Cover with foil if the skin begins to look very brown. Transfer the turkey to a cutting board and let rest for 30 minutes.

**2.** Meanwhile, pour the pan juices into a heatproof bowl and skim off the fat. Set the roasting pan over 2 burners on high heat until sizzling. Add 1 cup of the Rich Turkey Stock; bring to a boil, scraping up any browned bits stuck to the bottom of the pan; add to the pan juices in the bowl.

**3.** In a medium saucepan, melt the butter. Add the flour and cook over moderately high heat, stirring, for 1 minute. Add the pan juices and remaining 2 cups of stock and cook, whisking, until thickened, about 5 minutes. Stir in the maple syrup and season with salt and pepper. Strain into a gravy boat. Carve the turkey and serve with the gravy. —*Lee Hefter*
**WINE** Rich, earthy Pinot Noir.

# poultry

## RICH TURKEY STOCK

**ACTIVE: 20 MIN; TOTAL: 4 HR 30 MIN**

**MAKES ABOUT 3 QUARTS ● ●**

- 7 pounds turkey parts, such as wings, thighs and drumsticks
- 4 quarts water
- 1 large onion, thickly sliced
- 1 large carrot, thickly sliced
- 1 large celery rib, thickly sliced
- 2 garlic cloves, smashed
- 1 teaspoon kosher salt

Freshly ground pepper

**1.** Preheat the oven to 400°. In a large roasting pan, roast the turkey parts for 1½ hours, or until very well browned; transfer to a large pot.

**2.** Set the roasting pan over 2 burners. Add 4 cups of the water and bring to a boil, scraping up the browned bits from the pan. Add the liquid to the pot.

**3.** Add the onion, carrot, celery, garlic, salt and several pinches of pepper to the pot along with the remaining 3 quarts of water and bring to a boil. Reduce the heat to moderately low, cover partially and simmer for about 2½ hours. Strain the stock and skim the fat before using or freezing. —*L.H.*

**MAKE AHEAD** The stock can be refrigerated for 3 days or frozen for 1 month.

# health

**TIP** 

## TURKEY LEFTOVERS

**Thanksgiving wouldn't be Thanksgiving without turkey sandwiches the next day. But how long can you safely enjoy leftover turkey? The National Turkey Federation recommends keeping cooked turkey—carved from the bone, separated from the stuffing and stored between 35° and 40°— for** no more than four days.

## Paprika-Glazed Turkey

**ACTIVE: 45 MIN; TOTAL: 4 HR 45 MIN**

**12 SERVINGS ●**

- 1½ sticks (6 ounces) unsalted butter, softened
- 1 tablespoon sweet Hungarian paprika
- 1 tablespoon hot Hungarian paprika
- 1 tablespoon plus 2 teaspoons chopped thyme leaves

Salt and freshly ground pepper

One 18-pound turkey, at room temperature, neck and giblets reserved for another use

- 3 cups water
- 4 bay leaves
- 1 cup dry white wine
- ½ cup all-purpose flour
- 3 cups Rich Turkey Stock (recipe at left) or low-sodium chicken broth

**1.** Preheat the oven to 350°. In a medium bowl, blend the butter with the sweet and hot Hungarian paprikas and 1 tablespoon of the chopped thyme leaves. Season the paprika butter with salt and pepper. Refrigerate 6 tablespoons of the paprika butter for making the gravy. Using your fingers, carefully loosen the turkey breast skin. Spread 4 tablespoons of the remaining paprika butter under the skin, then rub it evenly over the breast. Rub 2 more tablespoons of the paprika butter all over the outside of the turkey.

**2.** Set the turkey in a large roasting pan and roast in the lower third of the oven for 45 minutes. Add 2 cups of the water and the bay leaves to the pan and roast the turkey for 1 hour longer. Add the white wine and the remaining 1 cup of water. Continue roasting the bird for 1 hour and 15 minutes, then loosely cover the breast with foil. Roast the turkey for 1 hour longer, or until an instant-read thermometer inserted into an inner thigh registers 165°.

**3.** Transfer the turkey to a carving board, cover loosely with aluminum foil and let rest for 20 minutes. Pour the pan juices into a large measuring cup. Skim off the fat, reserving 2 tablespoons.

**4.** Meanwhile, in a medium saucepan, melt 2 tablespoons of the reserved paprika butter in the 2 tablespoons of reserved fat. Stir in the flour and then whisk in the Rich Turkey Stock. Cook the gravy over moderately high heat, whisking frequently, until it is thickened and very smooth. Whisk in the pan juices and simmer the gravy over moderate heat, whisking from time to time, until no floury tastes remains, about 10 minutes. Remove from the heat and whisk in the remaining 2 teaspoons of thyme and the remaining 4 tablespoons of reserved paprika butter. Season with salt and pepper and transfer to a gravy boat. Carve the turkey and serve with the gravy.
—*Marcia Kiesel*

**MAKE AHEAD** The paprika butter can be formed into a log, wrapped in plastic and refrigerated for up to 3 days or frozen for up to 1 month.

**SERVE WITH** Pumpkin Seed Bread Salad (p. 255).

**WINE** Light, fruity Beaujolais.

## Shepherd's Pie with Parsnip Puree Topping

**ACTIVE: 25 MIN; TOTAL: 55 MIN**

**8 SERVINGS ●**

This recipe makes use of nearly all of the Thanksgiving leftovers—turkey, gravy *and* vegetables—and replaces the classic shepherd's pie topping with a delicious, slightly sweet mashed-parsnip crust.

- 2 pounds parsnips, peeled and thinly sliced
- ¾ cup milk
- ¾ cup heavy cream
- 2 tablespoons unsalted butter
- 1 teaspoon chopped thyme

Salt and freshly ground pepper

4 cups leftover cubed turkey
2 cups leftover gravy
2 cups leftover vegetables
½ cup fresh bread crumbs

1. Preheat the oven to 350°. In a medium saucepan, cover the parsnips with the milk and heavy cream and bring to a boil. Cover and simmer over moderately low heat until the parsnips are tender, about 15 minutes. Transfer the parsnips and their cooking liquid to a food processor. Add the butter and puree. Scrape the puree into a bowl, add the thyme and season with salt and pepper.

2. In another medium saucepan, combine the cubed turkey with the gravy and vegetables and bring to a simmer over moderate heat. Season with salt and pepper and transfer to a 9-by-13-inch baking dish. Spread the parsnip puree over the top. Sprinkle with the bread crumbs and bake for about 30 minutes, or until golden brown on top and bubbling underneath. Let stand for 10 minutes before serving. —Lee Hefter

**WINE** Complex, savory Chianti Classico.

### Turkey Leg Confit with Garlic Gravy

**ACTIVE: 1 HR; TOTAL: 5 HR, PLUS OVERNIGHT MARINATING**

12 SERVINGS ● ●

12 garlic cloves, peeled
¼ cup kosher salt
1½ tablespoons chopped thyme
Finely grated zest of 1 large lemon
1 tablespoon juniper berries
1 teaspoon black peppercorns, plus freshly ground pepper
Twelve 12-ounce turkey legs
6 cups duck fat (3 pounds), melted (see Note)
6 cups vegetable oil
4 cups Rich Turkey Stock (p. 112) or low-sodium chicken broth
¼ cup all-purpose flour
1½ teaspoons balsamic vinegar

1. In a food processor, chop 8 of the garlic cloves with the salt, thyme and lemon zest. Add the juniper berries and peppercorns, pulse until slightly cracked.

2. Preheat the oven to 325°. Arrange the turkey legs in a large roasting pan and rub all over with the seasoned salt. Let stand for 30 minutes. Pour the duck fat and vegetable oil over the turkey legs and add the remaining 4 garlic cloves to the pan.

3. Roast the turkey legs for about 2 hours, turning them every 30 minutes, until the meat is very tender and pulls away from the drumsticks. Transfer the legs to a large pot and carefully strain the fat over them, stopping when you reach the sediment and any caramelized pan juices. Reserve the garlic cloves. Let the turkey legs cool to room temperature, then refrigerate overnight or for up to 5 days.

4. While the turkey legs are cooling, return the garlic to the roasting pan and set the pan over 2 burners. Add 2 cups of the stock and bring to a simmer over moderately high heat, scraping up the browned bits on the bottom and sides of the pan and mashing the garlic into the juices. Strain the pan juices into a large measuring cup, let cool, then refrigerate for up to 5 days.

5. To serve the confited turkey legs, preheat the oven to 350°. Gently rewarm the turkey legs in the large pot over moderate heat just until the fat melts. Remove the legs from the fat and transfer them to a roasting pan; reserve 2 tablespoons of the fat. Roast the legs for 25 minutes, turning once or twice, or until golden and crisp in spots. Transfer the turkey legs to a platter, cover loosely with aluminum foil and keep warm.

6. Pour off any fat from the roasting pan and set the pan over 2 burners. Add the remaining 2 cups of stock and the reserved pan juices and bring to a boil, scraping up any browned bits stuck to the bottom of the pan. Pour the pan juices into a saucepan and bring back to a boil.

7. In a small bowl, blend the flour with the reserved 2 tablespoons of fat. Whisk the flour paste into the pan juices and simmer over moderate heat, stirring, until the gravy thickens and no floury taste remains, about 10 minutes. Stir in the balsamic vinegar and season lightly with pepper. Serve the turkey legs with the gravy. —Grace Parisi

**NOTE** Duck fat is available at some specialty markets. You can also mail-order it from D'Artagnan (800-327-8246 or dartagnan.com). The unique and decadent flavor imparted by this luxurious fat is worth the effort of finding it. Duck fat is also economical, as it can be strained and reused many times. Store it in the freezer for up to 1 year.

**WINE** Round, supple, fruity Syrah.

### Seared Duck with Fig Sauce

**ACTIVE: 30 MIN; TOTAL: 4 HR 45 MIN**

6 SERVINGS

Sonoma, California, is famed for both its duck farms and its Zinfandel producers. This recipe brings the two together: crisp-skinned duck breast in a lush Zinfandel-fig sauce. The combination is so appealing, you might be tempted to serve duck instead of turkey next Thanksgiving.

6 boneless Pekin duck breast halves, skin scored in a crosshatch pattern
6 tablespoons extra-virgin olive oil
5 tablespoons red wine vinegar
2 tablespoons honey
1 scallion, light and tender green parts only, very finely chopped
1 teaspoon very finely chopped oregano
1 teaspoon very finely chopped sage
3 large garlic cloves, very finely chopped
2 teaspoons very finely chopped thyme
Salt and freshly ground pepper

# poultry

Ground allspice

- 1 cup Zinfandel
- 1 cup low-sodium chicken broth
- 2 tablespoons minced onion
- 4 teaspoons sugar

One 2-inch strip of lemon zest

- 14 dried Mission figs, quartered

**1.** Arrange the duck breasts in a large baking dish, skin side up. In a bowl, whisk 2 tablespoons each of the olive oil and red wine vinegar with the honey, scallion, oregano, sage, two-thirds of the garlic, 1 teaspoon of the thyme, 1 teaspoon of salt, ½ teaspoon of pepper and ¼ teaspoon of allspice. Pour the marinade over the duck breasts and turn to coat. Cover and refrigerate for 4 hours, turning after 2 hours. Let stand at room temperature for 30 minutes before cooking.

**2.** Meanwhile, in a medium saucepan, combine the wine, broth and onion with the remaining garlic, the sugar, lemon zest, ½ teaspoon of the thyme and a pinch of allspice. Bring to a boil and add the figs. Reduce the heat to moderately low, cover and simmer until the figs are soft, about 25 minutes. Discard the zest.

**3.** Puree one-third of the fig mixture in a food processor, then return it to the saucepan. Stir in the remaining ½ teaspoon of thyme and 3 tablespoons of vinegar and season with salt; keep warm.

**4.** Remove the duck from the marinade; pat dry. Season lightly with salt. In each of 2 medium skillets, heat 2 tablespoons of the remaining olive oil. Add the duck to the skillets, skin side down, and cook over moderately high heat until golden brown, about 4 minutes. Turn, reduce the heat to moderate and cook until medium rare, about 3 minutes longer. Transfer to a cutting board and let stand for 5 minutes. Thinly slice the duck on the diagonal and serve with the fig sauce.
—*Leslie Kunde*

**SERVE WITH** Zucchini Cakes (p. 207).
**WINE** Intense, berry-flavored Zinfandel.

## Duck Two Ways with Chickpea Crêpes and Fennel Compote

**TOTAL: 3 HR**

**4 SERVINGS**

BRAISED DUCK LEGS AND FENNEL

- 4 duck legs, trimmed of excess fat
- 3 small fennel bulbs, cored and sliced lengthwise ⅓ inch thick, ½ cup coarsely chopped, plus the feathery fronds chopped
- 2 medium onions, 1 coarsely chopped, 1 thinly sliced
- 1 carrot, thinly sliced
- 1 thyme sprig
- 1 small rosemary sprig
- ½ cup dry white wine
- ½ cup fresh orange juice

Finely grated zest of 1 orange

- 1 cup chicken or beef stock

Salt and freshly ground pepper

- 1 tablespoon extra-virgin olive oil
- ¼ cup water
- 1 tablespoon Pernod or other anise-flavored liqueur
- 8 Chickpea Crêpes (recipe follows)

HONEY-GLAZED DUCK BREASTS

- 1 teaspoon fennel seeds
- 1 teaspoon coriander seeds
- ½ teaspoon cumin seeds
- ¼ cup honey
- ¼ teaspoon cayenne pepper

Four 8- to 10-ounce duck breasts, skin scored lightly in a crosshatch pattern

Salt and freshly ground pepper

**1. PREPARE THE BRAISED DUCK LEGS AND FENNEL:** Preheat the oven to 325°. Heat a large, deep, ovenproof skillet. Add the duck legs, skin side down, and cook over moderate heat, turning once, until the skin is browned and crisp, 15 minutes. Transfer the duck legs to a plate and pour all but 1 tablespoon of the fat into a heatproof bowl.

**2.** Heat the skillet. Add the coarsely chopped fennel and onion and the sliced carrot and cook over moderate heat until softened, 5 minutes. Stir in the thyme, rosemary and white wine and cook until nearly evaporated, 2 to 3 minutes.

**3.** Return the duck legs to the skillet, skin side up. Add the orange juice, half of the orange zest and the stock and bring to a boil. Cover the skillet tightly, transfer to the oven and bake for about 1½ hours, or until the duck is very tender and the liquid has reduced by half. Transfer the duck legs to a work surface and let them cool slightly. Raise the oven temperature to 400°.

**4.** Strain the sauce through a fine sieve into a small saucepan, pressing down on the solids. Skim the fat from the sauce. Discard the duck skin and coarsely shred the meat. Season with salt and pepper.

**5.** Heat the olive oil in the skillet. Add the sliced onion, cover and cook over moderately low heat until softened, 5 minutes. Add the sliced fennel, water and the remaining grated orange zest and season with salt and pepper. Cover and cook, stirring, until softened but not browned, about 15 minutes. Add the Pernod and cook, uncovered, until all of the liquid evaporates. Stir the fennel fronds into the fennel compote.

**6.** Lightly brush a baking sheet with some of the reserved duck fat. Arrange the Chickpea Crêpes on a work surface. Spoon the braised duck leg meat onto the crêpes and fold each one into quarters. Transfer the duck-filled crêpes to the baking sheet, brush lightly with duck fat and cover with foil.

**7. PREPARE THE HONEY-GLAZED DUCK BREASTS:** In a spice grinder, process the fennel, coriander and cumin seeds just until coarsely ground. Transfer to a small bowl and add the honey and cayenne. Set a large ovenproof skillet over moderate heat. Season the duck breasts with salt and pepper and add them to the skillet, skin side down. Cook, spooning off the rendered fat as it accumulates, until the skin is deeply golden and crisp, about 10 minutes. Turn the duck breasts and brush with the honey mixture. Roast in the upper third of the oven for 4 minutes, or until the duck is medium rare and the skin is lacquered. Transfer to a cutting board and let rest for 5 minutes, then thinly slice. Stir 1 tablespoon of the caramelized pan juices into the reserved sauce and reheat.

**8.** Heat the duck crêpes in the oven and rewarm the fennel compote. Set 2 duck crêpes on each of 4 large plates and top with a sliced duck breast. Spoon the fennel compote alongside. Drizzle the sauce over the duck breasts and serve at once. —*Bradford Thompson*

**MAKE AHEAD** The recipe can be prepared 1 day ahead through Step 6; refrigerate all of the components separately. **WINE** Rich, velvety Merlot.

### CHICKPEA CRÊPES
**ACTIVE: 15 MIN; TOTAL: 45 MIN**
MAKES 8 CRÊPES ●
- 1 cup chickpea flour (see Note)
- ⅓ cup all-purpose flour
- ¾ teaspoon salt
- 1¼ cups milk
- 1 tablespoon extra-virgin olive oil
- ¼ cup water
- Reserved duck fat or melted unsalted butter, for brushing

**1.** In a medium bowl, mix the chickpea flour with the all-purpose flour and salt. Whisk in the milk until smooth. Whisk in the olive oil and let the batter rest for 30 minutes. Whisk in the water.
**2.** Lightly brush a 7-inch crêpe pan with reserved duck fat and set it over moderately high heat. Pour 3 tablespoons of the crêpe batter into the pan and swirl to coat the bottom. Cook for 1 minute, or until brown around the edge. Flip the crêpe and cook for 20 seconds longer. Transfer to a large plate. Repeat with the remaining batter. —*B.T.*

**NOTE** Chickpea flour is available at ethnic food stores. At Indian groceries, it's called *besan*.
**MAKE AHEAD** The crêpes can be cooked up to 4 hours ahead; stack and let stand at room temperature.

### Duck Confit Potpie
**ACTIVE: 1 HR; TOTAL: 3 HR 30 MIN, PLUS 14 HR FOR CURING THE CONFIT**
6 SERVINGS ●
- 3 medium sweet potatoes, peeled and cut into ½-inch dice
- ½ pound cipollini onions, peeled and halved
- 8 large garlic cloves, peeled
- 5 thyme sprigs
- 1 large rosemary sprig
- ¼ cup extra-virgin olive oil
- Salt and freshly ground pepper
- Buttery Cornmeal Pastry (p. 249)
- 1 large egg beaten with 2 tablespoons water
- 1 large shallot, very finely chopped
- ½ pound kale, stems and inner ribs discarded, leaves coarsely chopped (2 packed cups)
- ¼ cup dry white wine
- 3 cups chicken stock or low-sodium broth
- 2 tablespoons all-purpose flour
- 3 cups shredded Three-Pepper Duck Confit (recipe follows; see Note)
- ¼ cup dried currants

**1.** Preheat the oven to 425°. On a large, rimmed baking sheet, toss the sweet potatoes with the onions, garlic, thyme, rosemary and 3 tablespoons of olive oil. Season with salt and pepper. Cover with foil and roast for 30 minutes, stirring once or twice, until the vegetables are tender and lightly browned on the bottom. Remove from the oven and set aside the garlic. Discard the herb sprigs. Reduce the oven temperature to 375°.

**2.** Line a baking sheet with parchment paper. On a lightly floured work surface, roll out the Buttery Cornmeal Pastry to a 14-inch round about ⅛ inch thick. Using a 5½-inch plate as a template, cut out 4 rounds as close together as possible. Roll out the scraps and cut out 2 more rounds. Set the rounds on the prepared baking sheet. Brush with the egg wash and freeze the pastry for 5 minutes. Bake the rounds for about 15 minutes, or until golden and crisp.

# health

**CUTTING BOARD SAFETY**    TIP

*Clostridium perfringens.* What *wouldn't* you do to avoid such a gruesome-sounding bacteria? To help prevent food-borne illnesses, Britain's Identibord has developed a line of color-coded, solid-beech cutting boards in three sizes to separate ingredients during prep. A set of six boards includes one with a red dot for raw meat and poultry and a blue-dotted one for raw fish. Green is for washed fruits and vegetables, while white is for bread and dairy products (from $160; 011-44-870-240-8117 or identibord.com).

DUCK WITH PORT-FRUIT CHUTNEY

DUCK CONFIT POTPIE, P. 115

**3.** Meanwhile, in a large, deep skillet, heat the remaining 1 tablespoon of olive oil. Add the shallot and cook over moderate heat until softened, about 3 minutes. Add the kale and cook, stirring, until it is wilted, about 2 minutes. Add the white wine and cook until nearly evaporated. Add 2½ cups of the chicken stock and bring to a simmer.

**4.** In a small bowl, whisk the flour into the remaining ½ cup of chicken stock, then whisk the mixture into the skillet. Simmer until it is slightly thickened, about 5 minutes. Mash the roasted garlic cloves and whisk them into the sauce. Add the roasted vegetables, duck confit and currants and cook until heated through; keep warm.

**5.** Ladle the duck filling into six 1-cup ramekins, cover with the pastry rounds and serve at once. —*Ashley Christensen*

**NOTE** Instead of making your own duck confit, you can use the meat from 5 confited duck legs, available from D'Artagnan (800-327-8246 or dartagnan.com).

**MAKE AHEAD** The potpie filling can be made 3 days ahead and refrigerated.

**WINE** Soft, earthy Rioja.

### THREE-PEPPER DUCK CONFIT

**ACTIVE: 25 MIN; TOTAL: 2 HR 45 MIN, PLUS 14 HR CURING**

**MAKES 3 CUPS** ●

You can ask your butcher to quarter the duck for you. Use any extra confit in a ragù for pasta or in duck quesadillas.

One 5-pound duck

  1  teaspoon whole white peppercorns

  1  teaspoon whole black peppercorns

  8  whole cloves

  ¼  teaspoon crushed red pepper

  1  cup kosher salt

  2  tablespoons rosemary leaves

  4  thyme sprigs

  1  large garlic clove

Finely grated zest of 1 orange

  3  pounds duck fat (1½ quarts), melted (see Note p. 113)

**1.** Using poultry shears, carefully remove the duck backbone and the wings at the second joint. Cut the duck into 2 breasts and 2 whole legs and trim off the excess fat. Set the duck pieces aside

**2.** In a small skillet, toast the white and black peppercorns, the cloves and the crushed red pepper over moderate heat until fragrant, about 2 minutes. Transfer the spice mixture to a food processor. Add the salt, rosemary, thyme, garlic and orange zest and process until finely ground, 2 minutes.

**3.** Transfer the salt mixture to a large bowl, add the duck and dredge well. Set the duck breasts and legs in a baking pan, skin side up. Sprinkle lightly with more of the salt mixture, cover with plastic wrap and refrigerate for 6 to 8 hours.

**4.** Preheat the oven to 275°. Rinse the duck pieces and arrange them in a deep baking dish just large enough to hold them. Pour the duck fat over the duck so it's completely submerged. Cook the duck for 2 hours and 15 minutes, turning occasionally, until fork-tender; the skin will separate from the meat when the duck is done. Let the duck cool in the fat, then refrigerate for 8 hours. —*A.C.*

**MAKE AHEAD** The duck confit can be refrigerated for up to 2 weeks.

## Seared Duck Breasts with Port-Fruit Chutney

**TOTAL: 25 MIN**

6 SERVINGS ● ●

- ¾ cup ruby port
- ⅓ cup dried figs, stemmed and chopped (2 ounces)
- 2 tablespoons light brown sugar
- 2 tablespoons balsamic vinegar
- 1 large rosemary sprig

Salt and freshly ground pepper

- 1½ cups fresh cranberries (6 ounces)
- ⅓ cup granulated sugar

Six 6-ounce boneless duck breasts

**1.** In a medium saucepan, combine the port with the chopped figs, brown sugar, balsamic vinegar and rosemary sprig and season with salt and pepper. Bring the mixture to a boil, then reduce the heat to low and simmer until slightly reduced, about 10 minutes.

**2.** Stir the cranberries and granulated sugar into the figs. Cook the port-fruit chutney over moderate heat, stirring occasionally, until the cranberries soften, 6 to 8 minutes. Discard the rosemary sprig and transfer the chutney to a bowl.

**3.** Meanwhile, warm a large, heavy skillet over moderate heat until the pan is very hot but not smoking. Season the duck breasts with salt and pepper and add them, skin side down, to the skillet. Cook until the skin is deeply browned and the fat is rendered, about 12 minutes. Discard the fat. Turn the duck breasts and cook for 5 to 7 minutes for medium. Transfer to a cutting board and let rest for 5 minutes.

**4.** Slice the duck breasts crosswise and serve with the warm port-fruit chutney. Remove the duck skin before eating.
—*Victoria Abbott Riccardi*

**WINE** Rich, earthy Pinot Noir.

## Cornish Hens with Shiitake and Watercress

**ACTIVE: 25 MIN; TOTAL: 1 HR 5 MIN**

4 SERVINGS ●

- ½ pound shiitake mushrooms, stems discarded, large caps quartered
- 6 cilantro sprigs, plus 2 tablespoons chopped cilantro
- 4 dried sliced porcini mushrooms
- 2 garlic cloves, smashed
- 2 bay leaves
- 2 tablespoons soy sauce
- 1 scallion, thinly sliced
- 1 teaspoon whole black peppercorns

Two 1½-pound Cornish hens, halved

- 2 bunches watercress, large stems discarded (about ¾ pound total)
- 2 teaspoons fresh lemon juice
- 1 teaspoon Asian sesame oil

**1.** Pour 1½ inches of water into a large, wide pot. Make 4 foil balls 2½ inches in diameter. Set a large cake rack on the foil balls in the pot. Bring the water to a boil.

**2.** Tear off two 18-inch-long sheets of extra-heavy-duty foil. Mound half of the shiitake caps, cilantro sprigs, porcini, garlic, bay leaves, soy sauce, scallion and peppercorns in the center of each piece of foil. Set 2 hen halves on top, fold up the foil edges and seal.

**3.** Carefully set the packages on the cake rack over the boiling water, cover and steam over moderate heat for 40 minutes. Transfer the packages to a large, rimmed platter.

**4.** Spread the watercress on a large heat-proof plate. Set the plate on the cake rack, cover and steam for 4 minutes. Open the packages carefully. Remove the skin from the hens and transfer them to warmed shallow bowls. Stir 1 teaspoon of the lemon juice and ½ teaspoon of the sesame oil into each package, then spoon the mushrooms and sauce into the bowls. Sprinkle the Cornish hens and mushrooms with the chopped cilantro and serve.
—*Stephanie Lyness*

**WINE** Tart, low-tannin Barbera.

## Roasted Quail with Corn Bread Stuffing and Port-Orange Sauce

**ACTIVE: 30 MIN; TOTAL: 1 HR 10 MIN**

4 SERVINGS

- 5 tablespoons unsalted butter
- 1 small onion, finely chopped
- 2 small celery ribs, finely chopped
- 1¼ teaspoons rubbed sage
- ½ cup finely chopped dates
- 4 cups crumbled Buttermilk Corn Bread (p. 249)
- 1 large egg, lightly beaten

Salt and freshly ground pepper

- 2 tablespoons plus 1 teaspoon vegetable oil, plus more for rubbing
- 1 small carrot, very finely chopped
- 1½ teaspoons tomato paste
- ½ cup ruby port
- 2 teaspoons finely grated orange zest
- ½ cup fresh orange juice
- 1 quart chicken stock or low-sodium broth
- 1 bay leaf
- 1 thyme sprig

# poultry

1 teaspoon whole black peppercorns
8 partially boned quail
¼ teaspoon finely ground fennel seeds

1. In a medium skillet, melt 2 tablespoons of the butter. Add half of the onion and half of the celery and cook over moderate heat until softened, about 5 minutes. Stir in 1 teaspoon of the sage, 2 tablespoons of the butter and the dates and remove the skillet from the heat.

2. In a large bowl, combine the corn bread with the contents of the skillet. Add the egg and blend well, then season with salt and pepper.

3. In a medium saucepan, heat 1 teaspoon of the oil until shimmering. Add the remaining onion and cook over high heat until browned, about 3 minutes. Add the carrot and the remaining celery and cook over moderate heat, stirring occasionally, until they are softened, about 3 minutes. Add the tomato paste and cook, stirring, until glossy, about 30 seconds. Add the port, orange zest and orange juice and boil over high heat until reduced by three-fourths, about 3 minutes. Add the stock, bay leaf, thyme sprig and peppercorns and bring to a boil, then simmer the sauce over moderate heat until reduced to ¾ cup, about 30 minutes. Strain the port-orange sauce into a small saucepan.

4. Preheat the oven to 350°. Scoop up ½ cup of the corn bread stuffing and squeeze to form it into a fat cylinder. Slide the cylinder into a quail and press to shape the quail around the stuffing. Pull the neck skin over the stuffing and secure it with a toothpick. Repeat with the remaining stuffing and quail.

5. In a small bowl, mix the ground fennel with 1 teaspoon of salt, ¼ teaspoon of pepper and the remaining ¼ teaspoon of sage. Rub the stuffed quail all over with vegetable oil and sprinkle all over with the spice mixture.

6. In a skillet, heat 1 tablespoon of the oil. Add 4 of the quail, breast side down, and cook over high heat until browned, about 4 minutes. Turn and cook for 2 minutes longer. Transfer the quail to a large, rimmed baking sheet. Repeat with the remaining 1 tablespoon of oil and 4 quail.

7. Roast the quail in the oven until an instant-read thermometer inserted in the center of the stuffing registers 155°, about 12 minutes.

8. Meanwhile, bring the port sauce to a boil. Off the heat, whisk in the remaining 1 tablespoon of butter and season with salt and pepper. Spoon the sauce onto plates, set 2 stuffed quail in the center of each and serve. —*Bob Isaacson*

**MAKE AHEAD** The corn bread stuffing and the sauce base can be refrigerated separately overnight.

**WINE** Complex, silky red Burgundy.

## Quail with Sweet Pea Oatmeal and Summer Vegetable Ragout
**TOTAL: 1 HR**
4 SERVINGS

1 cup shelled fresh or thawed frozen green peas
Salt and freshly ground pepper
½ cup steel-cut oats (not quick-cooking or old-fashioned oatmeal)
2 tablespoons unsalted butter, softened
¼ cup plus 1 tablespoon extra-virgin olive oil
1 large shallot, minced
1 large garlic clove, minced
1 small yellow squash, quartered lengthwise and thinly sliced
1 small zucchini, quartered lengthwise and thinly sliced
1½ cups grape tomatoes, halved
8 partially boned quail, rinsed and patted dry
¼ pound chanterelle mushrooms, thinly sliced
2 thyme sprigs

1. If using fresh peas, blanch them in a saucepan of boiling water until tender but still bright green, about 5 minutes; drain. In a blender, puree half of the blanched or thawed frozen peas with 2 tablespoons of water until smooth. Season the green pea puree with salt and pepper.

2. Rinse out the saucepan. Add 2½ cups of salted water and bring to a boil. Add the oats and cook over moderately low heat, stirring frequently, until al dente, about 25 minutes. Stir in the pea puree, butter and the remaining whole peas and season with salt and pepper.

3. Meanwhile, in a medium skillet, heat 1 tablespoon of the olive oil. Add the minced shallot and garlic and cook over moderately high heat until they are softened, about 1 minute. Add the yellow squash and zucchini and cook over moderate heat, stirring occasionally, just until tender, 6 to 7 minutes. Add the grape tomatoes and cook for 3 minutes, crushing them lightly. Season with salt and pepper and keep warm.

4. Heat 2 tablespoons of the olive oil in each of 2 large skillets until shimmering. Season the quail with salt and pepper and add 4 to each skillet, breast side down. Cook over moderately high heat until crisp, about 3 minutes. Turn and cook the quail for 1 minute longer. Transfer all the quail to 1 skillet, breast side up, and continue cooking the quail for 2 minutes longer, until the quail are cooked through and the skin is very crisp.

5. Meanwhile, heat the second skillet until almost smoking. Add the chanterelles and thyme sprigs and cook over high heat, tossing, until the mushrooms are browned, about 5 minutes; discard the thyme sprigs.

6. Rewarm the sweet pea oatmeal and mound on 4 plates. Arrange the vegetable ragout and the chanterelles around the oatmeal and top each serving with 2 quail. Serve right away. —*Graham Elliot Bowles*
**WINE** Rich, earthy Pinot Noir.

QUAIL WITH SWEET PEA OATMEAL AND SUMMER VEGETABLE RAGOUT

PECAN-CRUSTED BEEF TENDERLOIN WITH JUNIPER JUS, P. 125

# beef
# +lamb

GRILLED SKIRT STEAK WITH CHIMICHURRI SAUCE

SKIRT STEAK BURGERS WITH TOMATILLO-CORN RELISH

## Skirt Steak Burgers with Tomatillo-Corn Relish

**ACTIVE: 40 MIN; TOTAL: 1 HR 30 MIN**

**6 SERVINGS**

- 3 cups fresh corn kernels (from 5 ears)
- 5 tomatillos (¾ pound), husked and finely chopped
- 3 jalapeños, seeded and finely chopped
- 2 cups apple cider vinegar
- 1 large onion, finely chopped
- 1 red bell pepper, finely chopped
- ½ cup sugar
- 1 teaspoon yellow mustard seeds
- 1 teaspoon celery seeds
- ½ teaspoon coriander seeds
- Salt
- 3 pounds skirt steak, cut into ¼-inch dice and chilled
- Freshly ground pepper
- 3 ounces creamy blue cheese, such as Cabrales
- 6 sourdough rolls, split and lightly toasted

**1.** In a large saucepan, combine the corn, tomatillos, jalapeños, vinegar, onion, bell pepper, sugar and the mustard, celery and coriander seeds. Bring to a boil; simmer over moderate heat until thickened, 40 minutes. Let cool and season with salt.
**2.** Light a grill. Working in small batches, put a handful of diced skirt steak in a food processor and pulse about 4 times, until very finely chopped. Transfer to a bowl and repeat with the remaining skirt steak. Pat the mixture into 6 burgers.
**3.** Season the burgers with salt and pepper and grill over a hot fire until medium rare, about 3 minutes per side. About 1 minute before the burgers are done, place the blue cheese neatly on top of them. Set a burger on the bottom half of each roll, spoon some relish onto each, close the sandwiches and serve.
—*Guillermo Pernot*

**MAKE AHEAD** The cooked and cooled tomatillo-corn relish can be refrigerated for up to 1 week.

**WINE** Plummy, earthy Malbec.

## Sirloin Burgers with Wasabi Mayo and Ginger-Pickled Onions

**TOTAL: 45 MIN, PLUS 3 HR MARINATING**

**6 SERVINGS** ●

- One 6-ounce jar pickled ginger
- 1 large sweet onion, such as Vidalia, sliced ¼ inch thick
- 2¼ pounds ground aged sirloin or chuck
- 1 tablespoon wasabi powder
- 1 tablespoon boiling water

5 tablespoons mayonnaise

3 tablespoons white (*shiro*) miso

1 tablespoon honey

2 teaspoons soy sauce

1½ tablespoons unseasoned rice vinegar

1 teaspoon Asian sesame oil

Salt and freshly ground pepper

6 sesame seed–topped hamburger buns or hard rolls, lightly toasted

**1.** In a large glass or stainless-steel baking dish, spread ¼ cup of the pickled ginger in an even layer. Sprinkle the ginger with 2 tablespoons of the pickling juice from the jar. Lay the onion slices on top of the ginger in a single layer. Cover the onion slices with the remaining pickled ginger and pickling juice from the jar. Cover with plastic wrap and refrigerate for at least 3 hours or overnight.

**2.** Meanwhile, pat the ground sirloin into 6 burgers. Refrigerate the burgers, covered, until chilled.

**3.** In a small bowl, stir the wasabi powder into the boiling water. Whisk in the mayonnaise and refrigerate. In another small bowl, whisk the miso with the honey, soy sauce, rice vinegar and sesame oil.

**4.** Light a grill. Remove the onion slices from the pickling mixture. Generously season the sirloin burgers with salt and pepper. Grill the burgers over a hot fire for 3 to 4 minutes per side for medium rare. Spread the wasabi mayonnaise on both sides of the hamburger buns. Lay the pickled onion slices on the bottom buns and set the grilled burgers on top. Spoon the miso sauce over the burgers, close the sandwiches and serve.

—*Josh DeChellis*

**MAKE AHEAD** The ginger-pickled onions, wasabi mayonnaise and miso sauce can be refrigerated separately in airtight containers overnight.

**WINE** Rich, velvety Merlot.

## Pancetta-Beef Burgers with Horseradish Ketchup
**TOTAL: 40 MIN**
6 SERVINGS

These burgers stay incredibly moist even when they're well done. The secret? Ground pancetta mixed into the ground beef bastes the burgers from the inside while they cook on the grill.

1 pound pancetta, sliced ¼ inch thick

1 cup fresh ½-inch bread cubes

⅓ cup whole milk

2 pounds ground beef chuck

3 tablespoons minced garlic

1 tablespoon crushed red pepper

1 tablespoon chopped thyme

1 tablespoon chopped rosemary

Kosher salt and freshly ground black pepper

3 tablespoons red wine vinegar

3 tablespoons water

2 teaspoons sugar

¼ teaspoon cayenne pepper

1 red onion, thinly sliced

1 cup ketchup

3 tablespoons freshly grated horseradish or drained prepared horseradish

Boston lettuce leaves

6 crusty sourdough rolls or kaiser rolls, halved and toasted

**1.** Lay the pancetta slices in a single layer on a large baking sheet lined with plastic wrap and freeze until firm, about 25 minutes. Finely chop the pancetta and transfer to a food processor. Pulse until minced.

**2.** In a small bowl, soak the bread cubes in the milk for 5 minutes. In a large bowl, combine the ground chuck, minced garlic, crushed red pepper, thyme, rosemary and ½ teaspoon each of salt and black pepper. Add the ground pancetta and soaked bread and mix gently with your hands. Pat into 6 burgers, cover with plastic wrap and refrigerate.

**3.** In a saucepan, combine the vinegar, water, sugar, cayenne and a pinch of salt and boil to dissolve the sugar. Remove from the heat, add the onion and let cool.

**4.** Light a grill. In a small bowl, combine the ketchup and grated horseradish and season with salt. Grill the pancetta-beef burgers over a hot fire until they are just cooked through, about 4 minutes per side. Put a lettuce leaf on the bottom half of each sourdough roll and top each with a burger. Spoon the pickled red onions onto the burgers and cover with the horseradish ketchup. Close the sandwiches and serve. —*Koren Grieveson*

**MAKE AHEAD** The uncooked burgers, ketchup and pickled onions can be refrigerated separately overnight.

**WINE** Intense, berry-flavored Zinfandel.

## Grilled Skirt Steak with Chimichurri Sauce
**TOTAL: 25 MIN**
8 SERVINGS ● ●

This recipe was adapted from Mark Bittman's *The Minimalist Cooks Dinner*, published by Broadway Books.

2 cups chopped parsley

⅔ cup extra-virgin olive oil

6 tablespoons fresh lemon juice

2 tablespoons minced garlic

2 teaspoons crushed red pepper

Salt and freshly ground pepper

4 pounds skirt steak

**1.** Light a grill. In a bowl, mix the parsley, olive oil, lemon juice, garlic and crushed red pepper; season with salt and pepper.

**2.** Season the skirt steak with salt and pepper and grill over a hot fire until the meat is charred on the outside and rare within, 2 to 3 minutes per side. Transfer the meat to a carving board and let rest for 5 minutes. Thinly slice the steak across the grain. Serve right away, passing the chimichurri sauce at the table.

—*Mark Bittman*

**WINE** Plummy, earthy Malbec.

# beef + lamb

## Beef Tenderloin with Bacon and Creamed Leeks

**TOTAL: 45 MIN**

6 SERVINGS

The decadent creamed leeks with bacon would also be a delicious side to chops or roast chicken.

**One 2-pound trimmed and tied center-cut beef tenderloin (about 10 inches long)**

**3 tablespoons extra-virgin olive oil**

**Salt and freshly ground pepper**

**16 garlic cloves, peeled**

**8 thyme sprigs**

**1 cup chicken stock or low-sodium broth**

**6 slices of thick-cut bacon (6 ounces)**

**6 tablespoons unsalted butter**

**6 large leeks, halved lengthwise and cut crosswise into 1-inch pieces**

**1 cup crème fraîche or sour cream**

**1.** Preheat the oven to 425°. Rub the tenderloin all over with 1 tablespoon of the olive oil and season generously with salt and pepper.

**2.** In a medium roasting pan or enameled cast-iron baking dish, heat the remaining 2 tablespoons of olive oil until shimmering. Add the tenderloin to the pan and cook over moderately high heat until browned all over, about 7 minutes. Add the garlic cloves and thyme sprigs and cook for 1 minute longer. Add ½ cup of the chicken stock to the pan and transfer the meat to the oven. Roast the tenderloin for 5 minutes, then turn it over and add the remaining ½ cup of chicken stock. Cook the tenderloin for about 5 minutes longer, or until an instant-read thermometer inserted in the center registers 125°.

**3.** Meanwhile, in a large, deep skillet, cook the bacon over moderately high heat until browned and crisp, about 6 minutes. Transfer to paper towels to drain, then cut into 1-inch pieces.

**4.** Pour off all but 2 tablespoons of the bacon fat from the skillet. Add the butter and stir in the leeks. Cover the skillet with a sheet of wax paper and a tight-fitting lid and cook the leeks over moderate heat, stirring once or twice, until they are tender, about 8 minutes. Uncover the skillet, increase the heat to moderately high and cook the leeks until they are lightly browned, about 2 minutes. Add the crème fraîche, season with salt and pepper and cook over low heat until creamy and thickened, 5 to 6 minutes longer. Stir in the bacon.

**5.** Transfer the roast to a cutting board and let stand for 10 minutes. Remove the strings and cut into thick slices. Serve the tenderloin with the creamed leeks, roasted garlic and thyme sprigs.
—*Geoffrey Zakarian*

**WINE** Complex, silky red Burgundy.

## Beef Tenderloin Steaks with Fontina Fonduta

**TOTAL: 30 MIN**

6 SERVINGS ●

In Le Marche, a remote region of Italy, this dish is prepared with a strong-flavored cheese called Ambra di Talamello, which is made in the summer and *cave*-aged in hay and clay until November. Imported Fontina cheese is a fine substitute.

**Six 7-ounce beef tenderloin steaks**

**Extra-virgin olive oil**

**Salt and freshly ground pepper**

**3 tablespoons unsalted butter**

**¼ cup plus 2 tablespoons dry white wine**

**7 ounces imported Fontina cheese, cut into ¼-inch pieces (about 1½ cups)**

**1.** Light a grill. Brush the steaks with olive oil and season with salt and pepper. Grill over moderately high heat, turning occasionally, about 15 minutes for medium rare. Transfer the steaks to a platter and let stand for 5 minutes.

**2.** Meanwhile, in a small saucepan, melt the butter in the wine. Add the Fontina and cook over low heat, stirring, until the sauce is piping hot. Transfer the steaks to warmed plates, top with the Fontina sauce and serve. —*Fabio Trabocchi*

**WINE** Tannic, complex Cabernet.

## Seared Steaks with Porcini Mushroom Cream Sauce

**TOTAL: 20 MIN**

6 SERVINGS ●

In place of porcini preserved in oil, you can use fresh porcini or a mixture of other mushrooms like cremini and oyster.

**2 tablespoons extra-virgin olive oil**

**Six ½-pound New York strip steaks, cut 1 inch thick**

**Salt and freshly ground pepper**

**½ cup minced shallots**

**One 280-gram jar preserved sliced porcini mushrooms in oil, drained (see Note)**

**½ cup brandy**

**½ cup chicken stock**

**½ cup crème fraîche**

**¼ cup chopped chives**

**1.** Heat 2 large skillets until very hot. Add 1 tablespoon of olive oil to each pan and swirl. Season the steaks with salt and pepper; add 3 to each skillet. Cook over moderately high heat, turning once or twice, for about 8 minutes total for medium-rare meat. Transfer the steaks to a large platter and keep warm.

**2.** Pour out all but 1 tablespoon of the fat from each skillet. Add half of the shallots to each skillet and cook over moderate heat, stirring, until softened, about 2 minutes. Add half of the porcini to each skillet and cook, stirring occasionally, until golden, about 2 minutes. Add half of the brandy to each skillet and scrape up any browned bits stuck to the sides of the pans. Add half of the stock and crème fraîche to each skillet and simmer until slightly thickened, about 1 minute.

**3.** Scrape the sauce from one skillet into the other and add any accumulated juices from the steaks. Stir in the chives and season with salt and pepper. Spoon the sauce over the steaks and serve. —*Grace Parisi*
**NOTE** Jars of Trullo Funghi Porcini in olive oil are available by mail order from Grace's Marketplace (212-737-0600).
**WINE** Tannic, complex Cabernet.

## Grilled Flank Steak with Soy-Chile Glaze
**TOTAL: 25 MIN**
6 SERVINGS ● ●

1 tablespoon vegetable oil
1 tablespoon minced garlic
1 tablespoon grated fresh ginger
½ cup soy sauce
⅓ cup lightly packed dark
    brown sugar
½ teaspoon crushed red pepper
2¼ pounds flank steak
Salt and freshly ground pepper
Thinly sliced scallions
    and lime wedges

**1.** Light a grill or preheat a grill pan. In a small saucepan, heat the oil. Add the garlic and ginger and cook over moderately high heat, stirring occasionally, until the garlic begins to turn golden. Add the soy sauce, brown sugar and crushed red pepper and cook, stirring, until thickened and syrupy, about 3 minutes; let cool.
**2.** Season the flank steak with salt and pepper. Grill the steak over a hot fire for 5 minutes per side for medium-rare meat; during the last minute, brush all but 2 tablespoons of the soy-chile glaze over the steak. Transfer the grilled steak to a cutting board and let stand for about 5 minutes.
**3.** Thinly slice the steak and brush with the reserved 2 tablespoons of glaze. Transfer to a platter, sprinkle with scallions and serve with lime wedges.
—*Tom Douglas*
**WINE** Plummy, earthy Malbec.

## Peppercorn Beef with Gorgonzola Cheese
**TOTAL: 30 MIN**
4 SERVINGS ●

Four 5-ounce trimmed beef tenderloin
    steaks, about 2 inches thick
Salt
1 tablespoon crushed peppercorns
2 tablespoons vegetable oil
¾ cup balsamic vinegar
1 teaspoon sugar
¼ pound Gorgonzola, cut into pieces

**1.** Preheat the oven to 400°. Season the steaks with salt and pat the peppercorns all over them. In a large skillet, heat the oil. Add the steaks and cook over moderately high heat until browned, 4 minutes per side. Transfer to a rimmed baking sheet and roast in the oven for 12 minutes, or until an instant-read thermometer inserted in the center of each steak registers 130° for medium-rare meat.
**2.** Meanwhile, wipe out the skillet. Add the vinegar and sugar and boil over high heat until reduced to ⅓ cup, 3 minutes.
**3.** Top the steaks with the Gorgonzola and roast for 2 minutes longer, or until the cheese is just melted. Transfer the steaks to plates, drizzle with the balsamic reduction and serve. —*Jamie Samford*
**WINE** Intense, berry-flavored Zinfandel.

## Pecan-Crusted Beef Tenderloin with Juniper Jus
**ACTIVE: 30 MIN; TOTAL: 1 HR 45 MIN**
10 SERVINGS ●

Two 2½-pound well-trimmed center-
    cut beef tenderloins, not tied
Salt and freshly ground pepper
4 tablespoons unsalted butter
2 tablespoons extra-virgin olive oil
¼ cup ketchup
¼ cup Dijon mustard
4 large egg yolks
1 cup pecans, finely chopped
3 shallots, thinly sliced
1 garlic clove, thinly sliced
1 carrot, thinly sliced
1 tablespoon tomato paste
2 teaspoons dried juniper
    berries, crushed
1½ cups full-bodied red wine
1 cup beef demiglace (see Note)

**1.** Preheat the oven to 425°. Season the tenderloins with salt and pepper. In each of 2 large, deep skillets, melt 1 tablespoon of butter in 1 tablespoon of olive oil. Add the tenderloins and cook over high heat until browned all over, about 8 minutes. Transfer to a rack and let cool slightly.
**2.** In a bowl, combine the ketchup, mustard and egg yolks and brush the mixture all over the tenderloins. Transfer the meat to a roasting pan. Sprinkle with the pecans and press to help the nuts adhere. Roast in the middle of the oven for 25 minutes, or until an instant-read thermometer inserted in the thickest part of each tenderloin registers 125° for medium rare. Cover the meat loosely with foil if the coating browns too quickly. Transfer to a cutting board; let stand for 10 minutes.
**3.** Meanwhile, pour off the fat in one of the skillets. Add 1 tablespoon of the butter. Add the shallots, garlic and carrot and cook over moderate heat, stirring occasionally, until softened and just beginning to brown, 6 minutes. Add the tomato paste and juniper berries and cook, stirring, for 2 minutes. Add the wine and cook over moderate heat, scraping up any browned bits, until the sauce is slightly thickened and reduced to ½ cup, about 10 minutes. Add the demiglace and bring to a boil. Strain the sauce through a fine sieve into a saucepan, pressing hard on the solids. Season with salt and pepper and stir in the remaining 1 tablespoon of butter.
**4.** Carve the roasts and serve with the juniper jus on the side. —*Gabriel Kreuther*
**NOTE** Beef demiglace is available in the freezer section of large supermarkets and specialty food shops.
**WINE** Powerful, spicy Syrah.

# beef + lamb

## Meat Loaf Stuffed with Prosciutto and Spinach

ACTIVE: 45 MIN; TOTAL: 2 HR 10 MIN

8 SERVINGS ● ●

This luxurious yet easy take on meat loaf gets stuffed with spinach, prosciutto and cheese. Mild and tangy caciocavallo, made in Italy from cow's milk, is excellent, but provolone is a good substitute.

- 2 large carrots, each cut lengthwise into 6 slices
- 3 ounces spinach (4 cups), thick stems discarded
- 2 pounds lean ground beef
- 2 pounds ground pork
- 2½ cups fresh bread crumbs
- 6 ounces freshly grated pecorino cheese (2 cups)
- 6 large eggs, lightly beaten
- Kosher salt and freshly ground black pepper
- 3 tablespoons all-purpose flour
- 12 thin slices of prosciutto (about 4 ounces)
- ½ pound caciocavallo or provolone cheese, cut into twelve ⅛-inch-thick slices
- ¼ cup extra-virgin olive oil
- 4 rosemary sprigs
- 2 cups dry red wine
- 1 cup water

1. Preheat the oven to 400°. In a medium saucepan of boiling salted water, cook the carrots until tender, about 7 minutes. Using a slotted spoon, transfer to a plate. Add the spinach to the boiling water and cook just until wilted; drain well and add to the carrots.

2. In a large bowl, combine the beef with the pork, 2 cups of the bread crumbs, the pecorino, eggs, 1 teaspoon of salt and ½ teaspoon of pepper; mix well with your hands.

3. Line a work surface with a 15-inch-long sheet of plastic wrap. In a bowl, mix the flour with the remaining ½ cup of bread crumbs. Sprinkle half of the crumb mixture all over the plastic wrap. Transfer half of the meat loaf mixture to the plastic and press it into a 12-by-10-inch rectangle, about ½ inch thick. Lay half of the spinach leaves over the meat, leaving a 1-inch border on the short sides. Arrange half of the carrots over the spinach and top with half of the sliced prosciutto and cheese. Starting from the long end of the plastic wrap closest to you, tightly roll up the meat loaf, tucking in the filling and using the plastic wrap to guide you; discard the plastic. Repeat with another 15-inch sheet of plastic and the remaining bread crumb mixture, meat mixture, spinach, carrots, prosciutto and cheese. Drizzle each meat loaf with 2 tablespoons of olive oil.

# equipment

**TIP**   **KNIVES**

The F&W Test Kitchen tried out a selection of steel chefs' knives from around the world, many borrowed from New York City's Broadway Panhandler. Here's how they performed.

### Japanese
Lightweight knives that are renowned for keeping a razor-sharp edge longer than other types; especially useful for fine dicing and slicing.
**BRANDS** Global, Shun, Masamoto

### American
Versatile, well-balanced knives that are good for everything from mincing to heavy chopping; generally a good value.
**BRANDS** LamsonSharp, Dexter-Russell, Chicago Cutlery

### French
Relatively lightweight and narrow-bladed all-purpose knives. The collar that separates the blade from the handle is rounded, making it comfortable to grasp.
**BRANDS** Sabatier, Deglon

### German
Sturdy knives with wide blades that are great for "rock" chopping—rocking the knife back and forth on the cutting board.
**BRANDS** Wüsthof-Trident, Zwilling J.A. Henckels, Messermeister

**4.** Put the rosemary sprigs in the bottom of a broiler pan and pour in the red wine. Cover with the broiler pan grate. Set the meat loaves about 2 inches apart on the grate. Bake in the center of the oven for 40 minutes. Turn the broiler pan around and pour the water through the grate. Continue baking for about 35 minutes longer, or until an instant-read thermometer inserted in the center of each meat loaf registers 165°.

**5.** Transfer the meat loaves to a carving board and cover them loosely with foil. Discard any cheese from the bottom of the pan and strain the pan juices into a small saucepan. Boil the pan juices over high heat until slightly thickened and reduced to 1 cup, about 5 minutes. Pour the pan juices into a serving bowl and season with salt and pepper.

**6.** Using a serrated knife, slice the meat loaves 1 inch thick, transfer to a platter and serve, passing the pan juices at the table. —*Mario Batali*

**MAKE AHEAD** The unbaked meat loaves can be refrigerated overnight. Let return to room temperature before baking.

**WINE** Plummy, earthy Malbec.

## Cape Malay Meat Loaf

**ACTIVE: 25 MIN; TOTAL: 1 HR 15 MIN**

**8 SERVINGS** ●

An enduring culinary legacy of colonial South Africa, this meat loaf with its custardy topping, called *bobotie* in Afrikaans, combines dried fruits and Eastern spices. It is traditionally served with yellow rice sweetened with honey.

3 slices of white bread, crusts removed, bread cut into 1-inch dice
1½ cups milk
2 tablespoons vegetable oil
2 large white or yellow onions, finely chopped
1 large carrot, shredded
1 apple, peeled and shredded
1½ tablespoons curry powder
2 pounds ground lamb
¼ cup raisins
¼ cup mango chutney
1 tablespoon apricot jam
1 tablespoon white wine vinegar
Salt and freshly ground pepper
2 large eggs

**1.** Preheat the oven to 350°. Put the bread in a medium bowl, pour the milk over it and let stand until the bread is completely saturated with the milk, about 15 minutes.

**2.** In a large skillet, heat the oil until shimmering. Add the onions and cook over high heat for 2 minutes. Reduce the heat to moderately low and cook, stirring occasionally, until the onions are softened and browned, about 10 minutes. Add the carrot and apple and cook over moderate heat for 3 minutes. Add the curry powder and cook, stirring, until fragrant, about 4 minutes. Add the lamb and cook, stirring to break up the meat, until no pink remains, about 5 minutes. Stir in the raisins, chutney, jam and vinegar and cook for 1 minute.

**3.** Squeeze the milk from the bread cubes and add the bread to the lamb mixture; reserve the milk. Using a fork or the back of a wooden spoon, mash the bread into the lamb until blended. Season with salt and pepper. Transfer the lamb mixture to a 9-by-13-inch baking dish and smooth the surface.

**4.** In a medium bowl, whisk the eggs and the reserved milk and pour the mixture evenly over the lamb. Bake for about 35 minutes, or until the custard is set. Let the meat loaf rest for 10 minutes before serving.

—*Institute of Culinary Arts, South Africa*

**MAKE AHEAD** The recipe can be prepared through Step 3 and refrigerated overnight. Let return to room temperature before proceeding.

**WINE** Assertive, heady Grenache.

## Meat-Stuffed Poblanos with Cilantro-Lime Sauce

**TOTAL: 30 MIN**

**4 SERVINGS** ●

Canola oil
1 small onion, finely chopped
2 large garlic cloves, minced
½ pound ground pork
½ pound ground beef
1 teaspoon ground cumin
1 teaspoon ground coriander
¼ teaspoon dried oregano
Pinch of cayenne
Salt
¼ cup toasted sunflower seeds
¼ cup freshly grated Cotija or Pecorino Romano cheese
3 tablespoons raisins, chopped
4 large poblanos (1½ pounds)
½ cup shredded Cheddar cheese
¼ cup sour cream
2 tablespoons milk
1 tablespoon chopped cilantro
½ tablespoon fresh lime juice

**1.** Preheat the broiler. Position an oven rack 8 inches from the heat. In a large skillet, heat 1 tablespoon of oil. Add the onion and garlic; cook over high heat until softened. Add the pork, beef, cumin, coriander, oregano and cayenne and cook, stirring, until the meat is no longer pink, 7 minutes. Season with salt. Stir in the sunflower seeds, Cotija and raisins.

**2.** Rub the poblanos with oil and broil, turning occasionally, until charred all over, 7 minutes. Transfer to a plate, let cool slightly, then peel. Slit the chiles along one side. Using scissors, snip out the cores. Scoop out the seeds. Fill the chiles with the meat mixture, sprinkle with the Cheddar and broil until the cheese is golden. Transfer to plates.

**3.** In a bowl, blend the sour cream, milk, cilantro and lime juice. Season with salt, spoon over the poblanos and serve.

—*Grace Parisi*

**WINE** Intense, berry-flavored Zinfandel.

BEEF RIB EYE AND VEGETABLE STEW

## Beef Rib Eye and Vegetable Stew

TOTAL: 25 MIN

4 SERVINGS ●

- 2 tablespoons vegetable oil
- 2 pounds boneless beef rib eye, trimmed of visible fat and cut into 1-inch chunks

Salt and freshly ground pepper

- 1 tablespoon unsalted butter
- 2 carrots, cut into ¼-inch dice
- 2 garlic cloves, coarsely chopped
- 1 large Yukon Gold potato, cut into ¼-inch dice
- 1 large onion, cut into ¼-inch dice
- ¼ cup all-purpose flour
- 1 cup dry red wine
- 2 cups beef stock or canned low-sodium broth
- 4 thyme sprigs, plus thyme leaves for garnish
- 1 bay leaf
- 1 cup frozen peas

1. Heat a large skillet. Add the oil and heat until wisps of smoke appear. Add the meat, season generously with salt and pepper and brown on all sides over moderately high heat, about 4 minutes total. Using a slotted spoon, transfer the meat to a plate.

2. Melt the butter in the skillet. Add the carrots, garlic, potato and onion and cook until lightly colored, about 3 minutes. Stir in the flour. Add the wine and simmer, scraping up any browned bits from the bottom of the pan. Add the stock, thyme sprigs and bay leaf; bring to a boil. Cover and simmer over moderately low heat until the carrots and potato are fork-tender, about 6 minutes.

3. Add the peas and the meat along with any accumulated juices, cover and simmer until the meat is heated through and medium rare, about 3 minutes. Discard the bay leaf and thyme sprigs. Season with salt and pepper, garnish with thyme leaves and serve. —*Galen Zamarra*

WINE Rich, smoky-plummy Shiraz.

## Beef and Vegetable Daube with Celery Root Puree

ACTIVE: 1 HR; TOTAL: 3 HR, PLUS OVERNIGHT MARINATING

6 SERVINGS ●

Like most braised dishes, this stew is best served the day after it's made, when the flavors are richer.

- 2 cups red Meritage (a Bordeaux-style blend)
- 1¾ pounds beef chuck, cut into 1-inch pieces
- 2 garlic cloves, smashed
- 3 large carrots, 1 thinly sliced, 2 cut into ½-inch pieces
- 2 shallots, thinly sliced
- 2 thyme sprigs
- 2 bay leaves

Freshly ground pepper

- 2 tablespoons vegetable oil

Salt

- 2 celery ribs, cut into ½-inch pieces
- 2 parsnips, peeled and cut into ½-inch chunks
- 1 large onion, cut into ½-inch pieces
- 1 teaspoon drained green peppercorns in brine
- 1 rosemary sprig
- 4 plum tomatoes—peeled, seeded and cut into ½-inch pieces
- 4 cups rich veal stock or 2 cups veal demiglace mixed with 2 cups water
- 2 tablespoons unsalted butter, slightly softened
- 2 tablespoons all-purpose flour

Celery Root Puree, for serving (p. 220)

1. In a large, sturdy, resealable plastic bag, combine 1 cup of the wine with the meat, garlic, sliced carrot, shallots, thyme, bay leaves and 1 teaspoon of pepper. Seal the bag, pressing out any air, and refrigerate overnight.

2. Drain the meat from the marinade and pat dry with paper towels; reserve the thyme sprigs and bay leaves. In a large enameled cast-iron casserole, heat the oil until shimmering. Season the meat with salt and pepper. Add half of the meat to the casserole and cook over moderately high heat until browned all over, about 10 minutes; reduce the heat to moderate if the meat starts to brown too quickly. Using a slotted spoon, transfer the meat to a plate, then brown the remaining beef.

3. Return the first batch of meat to the casserole. Add the carrot chunks, celery, parsnips, onion, green peppercorns, rosemary and the reserved thyme and bay leaves. Cook, stirring frequently, until the vegetables are barely softened, about 7 minutes. Add the remaining 1 cup of wine and cook until reduced to about ⅓ cup, 10 minutes. Add the tomatoes and veal stock, stir to combine and season with salt and pepper; bring the mixture to a boil. Cover the daube and simmer over low heat until the meat is tender, about 2 hours.

4. Strain the daube in a colander set over a heatproof bowl; discard the thyme, rosemary and bay leaves. Return the braising liquid to the casserole and simmer over moderate heat until slightly reduced, about 10 minutes.

5. Meanwhile, in a small bowl, mix the butter with the flour until a paste forms. Whisk the paste into the simmering braising liquid and cook until thickened, about 5 minutes. Return the meat and vegetables to the casserole, season with salt and pepper and cook until heated through. Spoon the Celery Root Puree into deep bowls, ladle the beef on top and serve. —*Michael Allemeier*

MAKE AHEAD The daube can be refrigerated for up to 2 days. Let return to room temperature before reheating gently. The Celery Root Puree can be refrigerated overnight. Reheat gently.

WINE Tannic, complex Cabernet.

# beef + lamb

## Beef Stew with Belgian-Style Pale Ale

ACTIVE: 20 MIN; TOTAL: 2 HR 20 MIN

6 SERVINGS ●

For this earthy and satisfying beef stew, TV chef Jacques Pépin prefers to use flatiron steaks (also known by the butcher's term chicken steaks), a newly popular and surprisingly tender and inexpensive cut of beef that comes from the top blade near the shoulder.

- 2 tablespoons unsalted butter
- 2 tablespoons extra-virgin olive oil
- 3 pounds beef top blade, or flatiron, steaks (½ to ¾ inch thick), cut into 4-by-1-inch strips

Salt and freshly ground pepper

- 1 large onion, halved lengthwise and thickly sliced
- 3 tablespoons all-purpose flour

Two 12-ounce bottles Belgian-style pale ale

- 3 bay leaves
- ½ cup chicken stock
- 5 thyme sprigs
- 1½ cups baby carrots
- 1 cup frozen baby peas

1. In a large enameled cast-iron casserole, melt 1 tablespoon of the butter in 1 tablespoon of the olive oil. Season the meat with 1 teaspoon each of salt and pepper. Add half of the meat to the casserole and cook over high heat until lightly browned on the bottom, about 2 minutes. Turn the meat and brown the other side. Transfer to a large plate. Repeat with the remaining butter, olive oil and meat, reducing the heat if the meat browns too quickly.

2. Add the onion to the casserole and cook over moderately high heat, stirring with a wooden spoon, until lightly browned, about 4 minutes. Sprinkle the flour over the onion and stir well. Stir in the pale ale and bay leaves, scraping up any browned bits on the bottom of the pan. Add the chicken stock and thyme and return the beef to the casserole along with any accumulated juices. Bring the stew to a boil, skimming the surface occasionally. Cover and simmer over low heat, stirring occasionally, until the meat is tender, about 1 hour and 15 minutes.

3. Add the carrots, cover the pot and simmer until tender, about 15 minutes. Add the peas and simmer for 5 minutes. Season the stew with salt and pepper, discard the bay leaves and thyme sprigs and serve. —Jacques Pépin

MAKE AHEAD The beef stew can be prepared through Step 2 and refrigerated for up to 2 days. Reheat the beef stew gently before proceeding.

WINE Rich, velvety Merlot.

## Grandma Selma's Brisket

ACTIVE: 45 MIN; TOTAL: 4 HR 45 MIN, PLUS OVERNIGHT MARINATING

8 SERVINGS

- ⅓ cup light brown sugar
- 2 tablespoons kosher salt
- 1 teaspoon garlic powder
- 1 teaspoon cayenne pepper
- 1 teaspoon sweet paprika
- 1 teaspoon coarsely ground black pepper
- ½ teaspoon cinnamon
- ½ teaspoon unsweetened cocoa powder
- ½ teaspoon ground coriander
- ½ teaspoon freshly ground white pepper

One 5-pound beef brisket, trimmed

- 3 tablespoons vegetable oil
- 4 large onions, sliced ½ inch thick
- 2 pounds carrots, cut diagonally ⅛ inch thick
- 2 cups Coca-Cola

One 28-ounce can crushed tomatoes

- ¼ cup ketchup

1. In a bowl, mix the brown sugar, salt, garlic powder, cayenne, paprika, black pepper, cinnamon, cocoa, coriander and white pepper. Rub the mixture all over the brisket, set it in a baking dish and cover with foil. Refrigerate overnight.

2. Preheat the oven to 350°. In a large enameled cast-iron casserole, heat the oil. Add the brisket, fat side down, and brown well over moderately high heat, 6 minutes per side. Transfer to a plate.

3. Reduce the heat to moderate and add the onions. Stir well, cover and cook, stirring, until softened, about 15 minutes. Add the carrots, cover and cook, stirring, until the carrots begin to soften, 5 minutes. Transfer to a bowl.

4. Add the Coca-Cola, crushed tomatoes and ketchup to the pot and stir over moderate heat. Add the brisket and any juices and spread the onions and carrots around the meat. If needed, add enough water to half-submerge the brisket in liquid. Cover tightly and braise in the oven for 2½ hours.

5. Transfer the brisket to a cutting board, cover with foil and let stand for 30 minutes. Raise the oven temperature to 425°. Slice the meat across the grain ¼ inch thick, return to the casserole and spoon the sauce over the meat.

6. Return the pot to the oven and cook uncovered for 1 hour, or until the meat is fork-tender. Check every 20 minutes; if necessary, add water so the meat is half submerged. Remove from the oven. Let stand for 15 minutes, transfer the meat to a platter, spoon the onions, carrots and sauce over and serve. —Russ Pillar

WINE Rich, smoky-plummy Shiraz.

## Slow-Braised Lamb Shanks

ACTIVE: 1 HR; TOTAL: 5 HR, PLUS OVERNIGHT MARINATING

6 SERVINGS ●

- 3 tablespoons ground cumin
- 3 tablespoons ground coriander
- 2 tablespoons Madras curry powder
- 2 tablespoons minced rosemary
- 2 tablespoons minced thyme
- 2 tablespoons minced garlic

1 tablespoon coarsely ground
black pepper
½ cup extra-virgin olive oil
Kosher salt
6 lamb shanks (1 to 1¼ pounds
each), trimmed of excess fat
2 celery ribs, coarsely chopped
1 large onion, coarsely chopped
1 carrot, coarsely chopped
1 cup dry white wine
8 cups rich veal stock (see Note)

1. In a small bowl, combine the cumin, coriander, curry powder, rosemary, thyme, garlic and pepper. Stir in 6 tablespoons of the olive oil to make a paste and season generously with salt. Place the lamb shanks in a large roasting pan and rub with the spice paste. Cover with plastic wrap and refrigerate overnight.

2. Return the lamb to room temperature. Scrape off most of the spice paste from the shanks. In a large skillet, heat 1 tablespoon of the olive oil until shimmering. Add half of the lamb shanks and cook over moderately high heat until browned all over, about 10 minutes; transfer the shanks to a plate. Wipe out the skillet. Lower the heat to moderate and repeat with the remaining tablespoon of olive oil and lamb.

3. Preheat the oven to 350°. Add the celery, onion and carrot to the skillet and cook over moderate heat until barely softened, about 5 minutes. Add the wine and bring to a boil. Add the stock and bring to a boil. Wash the roasting pan and return the browned shanks to it. Pour the vegetable mixture over the shanks, cover with foil and roast for about 3½ hours, or until the lamb is very tender. Lower the oven temperature to 200°. Carefully transfer the shanks to a baking dish and cover tightly with foil; keep warm in the oven.

4. Strain the sauce into a medium saucepan. Skim off as much fat as possible. Boil the sauce over high heat until reduced to 4 cups, about 40 minutes; season with salt and pepper. Transfer the shanks to a platter, pour the sauce on top and serve. —Geoffrey Zakarian

NOTE You can buy rich veal stock in the freezer section of many supermarkets.

MAKE AHEAD The lamb shanks can be refrigerated in the sauce for up to 2 days.

WINE Deep, pungent, tannic Barolo.

## Lamb Braised in Milk with Garlic and Fennel

ACTIVE: 30 MIN; TOTAL: 1 HR 45 MIN
8 SERVINGS ● ●

3 garlic cloves, minced
1 cup chopped flat-leaf parsley
2 teaspoons fennel seeds
½ cup extra-virgin olive oil
4 pounds boneless lamb shoulder,
trimmed and cut into
2-inch pieces
Salt and freshly ground pepper
1 quart milk
1¼ cups heavy cream
2 rosemary sprigs

1. Using a chef's knife, chop the garlic with the parsley and fennel seeds to form a coarse paste. In a large enameled cast-iron casserole, heat the olive oil. Add the garlic paste and cook over moderate heat until fragrant, about 1 minute. Raise the heat to moderately high and add half of the lamb pieces. Cook, turning, until the meat is lightly browned all over. Transfer the lamb to a bowl and season with salt and pepper. Repeat with the remaining lamb.

2. Add ½ cup of the milk to the casserole and cook over high heat for 2 minutes, stirring to scrape up any browned bits from the bottom of the pan. Add the remaining 3½ cups of milk, the heavy cream, rosemary and the seared lamb and its juices. Bring to a simmer, then reduce the heat to low. Cover and cook, stirring occasionally, until the lamb is tender, about 1 hour and 15 minutes.

3. Using a slotted spoon, transfer the lamb to a bowl; discard the rosemary. Boil the milk mixture over high heat until reduced to 4 cups, about 10 minutes. Working in batches, puree the hot milk mixture in a blender. Return the sauce to the casserole, add the lamb and simmer over low heat until warmed through. Season with salt and pepper and serve. —Mario Batali

MAKE AHEAD The braised lamb can be refrigerated overnight in the pureed sauce. Reheat gently before serving.

SERVE WITH Roman-style artichokes (artichokes braised with olive oil and garlic) or roasted root vegetables.

WINE Deep, pungent, tannic Barolo.

## Braised Lamb with Giant White Beans

ACTIVE: 30 MIN; TOTAL: 3 HR 30 MIN,
PLUS OVERNIGHT SOAKING
6 SERVINGS

1 tablespoon extra-virgin olive oil
10 garlic cloves, 4 minced, 6 peeled
1 medium onion, finely chopped
1 medium carrot, finely chopped
1¼ pounds dried giant *haricots
blancs* or giant lima beans, soaked
overnight and drained
2 large thyme sprigs, plus
1 tablespoon chopped thyme
1 quart plus 1 cup chicken stock
1 quart water
One 6-ounce piece of slab bacon
Salt and freshly ground pepper
1 tablespoon minced parsley
One 4-pound boneless lamb shoulder
roast, trimmed of excess fat

1. Preheat the oven to 350°. Heat the olive oil in a large saucepan. Add the minced garlic, the onion and carrot and cook over moderately high heat, stirring occasionally, until lightly browned, about 5 minutes. Add the *haricots blancs*, thyme sprigs, 1 quart of the stock and the water and bring to a boil. Add the

● FAST ● HEALTHY ● MAKE AHEAD ● STAFF FAVORITE

GRILLED LAMB KEBAB

MOROCCAN-SPICED LAMB CHOPS

bacon and simmer over low heat, stirring occasionally, until the beans are very tender, about 2½ hours. Season with salt and pepper and stir in the parsley.

**2.** Meanwhile, rub the lamb all over with the chopped thyme, season with salt and roll into the shape of a roast; tie at 1-inch intervals with kitchen string.

**3.** Set the roast in a shallow 12-inch baking dish. Add the remaining 1 cup of stock and roast the lamb for 30 minutes. Add the remaining 6 garlic cloves, cover with foil and roast for 2½ hours, turning once, until the lamb is tender. Transfer the lamb to a carving board. Cover loosely with foil and let rest for 10 minutes.

**4.** Mash the garlic into the pan juices and season with salt. Carve the lamb into thick slices and serve with the pan sauce and the beans. —*Jean-Pierre Xiradakis*
**WINE** Tannic, complex Cabernet.

## Grilled Lamb Kebabs with Smoky Tomato Sauce
**TOTAL: 40 MIN, PLUS 2 HR MARINATING**
**6 SERVINGS**

- ¼ cup extra-virgin olive oil
- 4 large garlic cloves, minced
- 2 teaspoons Aleppo pepper (see Note) or 1 teaspoon crushed red pepper
- 2¼ pounds trimmed boneless leg of lamb, cut into 2-inch pieces
- 6 large firm, ripe tomatoes

Salt
- 2 green bell peppers, cut into 2-inch pieces

Freshly ground black pepper
- 2 tablespoons chopped parsley

**1.** In a large glass dish, combine the olive oil, garlic and Aleppo pepper. Add the lamb and turn to coat. Cover with plastic wrap; refrigerate for 2 hours.

**2.** Light a grill. Grill the tomatoes over a hot fire until charred. Let cool slightly, then peel, core, seed and coarsely chop. Transfer to a medium saucepan. Using a potato masher or large fork, crush the tomatoes until chunky. Season with salt.

**3.** Thread the lamb onto six 12-inch metal skewers, alternating the meat with pieces of bell pepper. Season the kebabs with salt and black pepper and grill over a medium-hot fire, turning once, until the lamb is medium rare, about 8 minutes.

**4.** Reheat the tomato sauce and spoon it onto plates. Set a kebab on each plate, sprinkle with the parsley and serve. Alternatively, remove the lamb from the skewers, heat in the tomato sauce and serve. —*Musa Dagdeviren*
**NOTE** Turkish Aleppo pepper is available at specialty and Middle Eastern markets.
**WINE** Intense, berry-flavored Zinfandel.

### Lemony Lamb Chops with Asparagus

**TOTAL: 30 MIN**

4 SERVINGS ●

- ¼ cup plus 1 tablespoon extra-virgin olive oil
- ¼ cup fresh lemon juice
- 8 lamb loin chops, cut about 1 inch thick (2¼ pounds)
- Salt and freshly ground pepper
- ½ pound pencil-thin asparagus, cut on the diagonal into ½-inch lengths
- Two 5-ounce bunches arugula, trimmed
- 2 ounces Parmesan cheese, thinly shaved (⅔ cup)

**1.** Preheat the oven to 400°. In a small bowl, combine ¼ cup of the olive oil with the lemon juice. Pour half of the mixture over the lamb chops and let stand for 10 minutes.

**2.** Heat a large skillet until hot to the touch. Add the remaining 1 tablespoon of olive oil. Drain the lamb chops and season with salt and pepper. Add the lamb chops to the skillet and cook over moderately high heat, turning once, until they are lightly browned, about 5 minutes. Transfer to a baking pan and roast for 7 minutes for medium meat. Transfer to plates and keep warm.

**3.** Pour off all but 1 tablespoon of the fat from the skillet. Add the asparagus and cook over moderately high heat until crisp-tender, about 2 minutes. Add the arugula and cook just until barely wilted, about 1 minute. Add the remaining lemon juice and olive oil mixture along with any accumulated juices from the lamb's baking pan and bring to a simmer. Season the vegetables with salt and pepper and transfer to the plates with the lamb chops. Scatter the Parmesan over the lamb and vegetables and serve.
—*Jamie Samford*
**WINE** Rich, velvety Merlot.

### Moroccan-Spiced Lamb Chops

**TOTAL: 15 MIN**

4 SERVINGS ● ●

- ½ teaspoon ground cumin
- ¼ teaspoon ground cardamom
- ¼ teaspoon ground allspice
- ¼ teaspoon freshly ground black pepper
- ¼ teaspoon ground ginger
- ¼ teaspoon cayenne pepper
- ¼ teaspoon cinnamon
- Kosher salt
- 3 garlic cloves, minced
- 8 lamb rib chops (2 pounds)
- 2 tablespoons vegetable oil
- 1 tablespoon chopped cilantro

**1.** In a small bowl, mix the spices with 1½ teaspoons of salt. Pat the garlic all over the lamb chops, then sprinkle them with the spice mixture.

**2.** In a large skillet, heat the vegetable oil. Add the chops and cook over moderately high heat, turning once, for about 6 minutes for medium rare. Transfer the chops to plates, garnish with the cilantro and serve. —*Charmaine Solomon*
**SERVE WITH** Couscous.
**WINE** Bright, fruity rosé.

### Lamb Chops with Mint-Cilantro Relish

**TOTAL: 45 MIN**

6 SERVINGS

- ⅔ cup chopped mint leaves
- ⅓ cup chopped cilantro leaves
- 1 garlic clove, minced
- ¾ teaspoon finely grated lemon zest
- 3 tablespoons extra-virgin olive oil
- Salt and freshly ground pepper
- 6 double-rib lamb chops (about 10 ounces each), trimmed
- 1 teaspoon fresh lemon juice

**1.** In a medium bowl, combine the mint, cilantro, garlic, lemon zest and 2 tablespoons of the olive oil and season with salt and pepper. Season the lamb chops

generously with salt and pepper and coat them with half of the herb mixture. Wrap the lamb in plastic and let stand at room temperature for 20 minutes. Stir the remaining 1 tablespoon of olive oil and the lemon juice into the remaining herb mixture.

**2.** Light a grill or preheat the broiler. Scrape the marinade off the lamb and grill the chops over a medium-hot fire or broil, turning, until an instant-read thermometer inserted in the center of one of the chops registers 125°, about 17 minutes for medium-rare meat. Transfer the lamb to plates, drizzle with the mint-cilantro relish and serve. —*Waldy Malouf*
**WINE** Tannic, full-bodied Barbaresco.

### Grilled Ouzo-and-Nutmeg Lamb Chops

**TOTAL: 25 MIN, PLUS 3 HR MARINATING**

6 SERVINGS

- 1½ cups ouzo
- ¼ cup extra-virgin olive oil
- 2 teaspoons freshly grated nutmeg
- 1 teaspoon cracked black peppercorns
- Salt and freshly ground black pepper
- 12 lamb loin chops

**1.** Pour the ouzo into a shallow dish just large enough to hold the lamb chops in a single layer; add the olive oil, nutmeg, peppercorns and a big pinch of salt. Turn the chops to coat. Let stand at cool room temperature for 3 hours, turning the chops every 30 minutes.

**2.** Light a gas or charcoal grill. Remove the chops from the marinade and season them with salt and pepper; reserve the marinade. Grill the chops over a medium-hot fire, basting with the marinade, until lightly charred outside and medium rare within, about 8 minutes per side.
—*Diane Kochilas*
**WINE** Deep, pungent, tannic Barolo.

---

# beef + lamb

## Lamb Steaks with Milk, Honey and Cumin Marinade

**TOTAL: 35 MIN, PLUS OVERNIGHT MARINATING**

**6 SERVINGS**

- 1 tablespoon plus 1 teaspoon cumin seeds, lightly toasted
- ¼ cup plus 2 tablespoons honey, warmed in the microwave
- 1 cup whole milk, warmed in the microwave
- 4 garlic cloves, minced
- ¼ cup plus 1 tablespoon extra-virgin olive oil

Kosher salt and freshly ground pepper

Six 7-ounce boneless lamb steaks cut from the leg, 1¼ inches thick

- 1 teaspoon fresh lemon juice
- ½ cup water

1. In a mortar, grind the cumin seeds to a coarse powder. Stir into the warm honey and transfer 1 tablespoon to a bowl.

2. In a baking dish, combine the remaining honey mixture with the milk. Stir in the garlic, 3 tablespoons of olive oil, 1 teaspoon of salt and ¼ teaspoon of pepper. Add the lamb and turn to coat well. Cover and refrigerate overnight.

3. Preheat the oven to 450°. Heat a large, heavy-duty, rimmed baking sheet in the oven. Remove the lamb from the marinade; season with salt and pepper. In a large skillet, heat the remaining 2 tablespoons of olive oil until almost smoking. Add the lamb and cook until browned on both sides. Transfer to the hot baking sheet and roast for 8 minutes for medium rare. Transfer to a warmed platter.

4. Stir the lemon juice into the reserved 1 tablespoon of honey mixture; lightly brush half on the steaks. Put the baking sheet on a burner over moderately high and heat until sizzling. Add the water and scrape up any browned bits from the bottom of the pan. Add any accumulated juices from the lamb; simmer for 2 minutes. Remove from the heat and stir in

the remaining honey–lemon juice mixture. Season with salt. Pour the sauce around the lamb and serve at once. —*Marcia Kiesel*

**WINE** Deep, pungent, tannic Barolo.

## Lamb Schnitzel with Aioli

**TOTAL: 35 MIN**

**6 SERVINGS**

- ¼ cup mayonnaise
- 1 tablespoon Dijon mustard
- 1 tablespoon white wine vinegar
- 1 large garlic clove, minced
- ½ cup plus 2 tablespoons vegetable oil

Salt

- ½ cup all-purpose flour
- 2 cups *panko* (Japanese bread crumbs) or coarse dry bread crumbs
- 2 large eggs
- 2 tablespoons water

Six ½-inch-thick boneless lamb leg steaks (1½ pounds total), pounded to ¼-inch thickness

Freshly ground pepper

- 2 tablespoons unsalted butter

1. In a medium bowl, whisk the mayonnaise with the mustard, vinegar and garlic. Gradually whisking in ½ cup of the oil. Season the aioli with salt.

2. Spread the flour and *panko* in 2 separate shallow bowls. In a third bowl, lightly beat the eggs with the water. Season the lamb with salt and pepper. Dredge the lamb in the flour, tapping off any excess. Dip the floured cutlets in the egg and then coat with the *panko*.

3. In each of 2 large skillets, melt 1 tablespoon of the butter in 1 tablespoon of the remaining oil. Add the cutlets and cook over high heat until golden, 3 minutes. Turn the cutlets and cook for 2 minutes. Serve with the aioli. —*Paul Condron*

**SERVE WITH** Green Beans with Onions and Capers (p. 215).

**WINE** Tannic, complex Cabernet.

## Coconut Lamb Curry

**TOTAL: 35 MIN**

**4 SERVINGS** ●

- 2 tablespoons vegetable oil
- 1 medium onion, coarsely chopped
- 2 garlic cloves, minced
- 1 tablespoon minced fresh ginger
- 1½ pounds lean ground lamb
- 1½ tablespoons curry powder
- 1 medium sweet potato (½ pound), peeled and cut into ½-inch dice

One 14-ounce can unsweetened coconut milk, stirred

- 1 cup chicken stock or low-sodium broth

Salt and freshly ground pepper

- ½ cup frozen baby peas, thawed
- ⅓ cup coarsely chopped cilantro

Hot sauce, for serving

In a large, deep skillet, heat the oil. Add the onion, garlic and ginger and cook over moderately high heat until barely softened, about 4 minutes. Add the lamb and cook over moderately high heat, breaking it up with a wooden spoon, until it starts to brown, about 10 minutes. Add the curry and sweet potato and cook for 2 minutes. Add the coconut milk and stock and season with salt and pepper. Cover partially and simmer over moderate heat until the sweet potato is tender, about 15 minutes. Add the peas and cook until heated through. Stir in the cilantro and serve with hot sauce. —*Grace Parisi*

**MAKE AHEAD** The curry can be refrigerated overnight; reheat before serving.

**SERVE WITH** Warm nan or white rice.

**WINE** Powerful, spicy Syrah.

## Citrus-Scented Lamb Stew

**ACTIVE: 45 MIN; TOTAL: 1 HR 45 MIN**

**6 SERVINGS** ●

- 4 tablespoons unsalted butter
- 1¼ pounds lean boneless lamb shoulder, cut into 1-inch pieces

Kosher salt and freshly ground pepper

- 3 medium carrots, thinly sliced

1 medium onion, finely chopped
½ teaspoon ground cinnamon
¼ teaspoon ground allspice
One 3-inch strip of lemon zest
One 3-inch strip of orange zest
One 28-ounce can diced Italian
    tomatoes, drained
¾ cup chicken stock
1 package (10 ounces) frozen baby
    peas (2 cups)

**1.** Melt the butter in a medium enameled cast-iron casserole. Season the lamb with salt and pepper. Add the meat to the casserole and cook over moderately high heat until browned all over, about 10 minutes. Using a slotted spoon, transfer the meat to a large plate.

**2.** Add the carrots and onion to the casserole and cook over moderate heat until just softened, about 10 minutes. Return the browned meat to the casserole. Add the cinnamon, allspice, lemon and orange zests and a generous pinch of pepper and cook, stirring, until fragrant. Add the tomatoes and stock and bring the stew to a boil.

**3.** Partially cover the stew and cook over moderate heat until the meat is just tender, 40 minutes. Stir in the peas and cook uncovered until the meat is very tender and the sauce thickens slightly, about 10 minutes. Discard the lemon and orange zests and serve. —*Anissa Helou*
**MAKE AHEAD** The stew can be refrigerated for up to 4 days.
**WINE** Powerful, spicy Syrah.

### Lamb Stew with Lemon
**ACTIVE: 30 MIN; TOTAL: 2 HR**
4 SERVINGS ●
¾ cup extra-virgin olive oil
1½ pounds lean boneless leg of lamb,
    cut into ¾-inch cubes
Salt and freshly ground pepper
1 medium onion, chopped
4 garlic cloves, thinly sliced
1¼ cups dry white wine

1 large rosemary sprig
3 large eggs, beaten
¼ cup heavy cream
1 cup freshly grated Parmesan
    cheese
3 tablespoons finely chopped
    flat-leaf parsley
1 teaspoon grated lemon zest

**1.** In an enameled cast-iron casserole, heat 2 tablespoons of the olive oil until shimmering. Season the cubes of lamb with salt and pepper and add half of the meat to the casserole in a single layer. Cook over moderately high heat, turning once or twice, until browned all over, about 7 minutes. Transfer the lamb to a plate and pour off the oil. Add 2 more tablespoons of olive oil to the casserole and repeat with the remaining lamb. Wipe out the casserole.

**2.** Add the remaining ½ cup of olive oil to the casserole. Add the onion and garlic and cook over moderate heat until the onion is softened.

**3.** Return the lamb and any accumulated juices to the casserole. Add the wine and rosemary and bring to a boil, scraping up any browned bits from the bottom of the casserole. Cover and simmer over moderately low heat until the lamb is tender, about 1¼ hours.

**4.** Uncover the casserole and simmer the stew until the liquid has nearly evaporated, about 20 minutes. Remove from the heat and discard the rosemary sprig.

**5.** Meanwhile, in a medium bowl, whisk the eggs with the heavy cream. Whisk in the Parmesan, finely chopped parsley and lemon zest.

**6.** Using a wooden spoon, stir the egg mixture into the lamb stew. Cook over low heat, stirring gently, until the eggs just begin to set and the sauce is thick and creamy, about 5 minutes. Transfer the stew to a bowl and serve.
—*Fabio Trabocchi*
**WINE** Tannic, full-bodied Barbaresco.

### Herb-Roasted Rack of Lamb with Smoky Cabernet Sauce
**TOTAL: 1 HR, PLUS 4 HR CHILLING**
4 SERVINGS
3 slices of thick-cut applewood-
    smoked bacon, cut crosswise
    into ½-inch-thick strips
1 small onion, chopped
1 medium carrot, chopped
1 celery rib, chopped
9 garlic cloves, 3 whole, 6 minced
1 plum tomato, chopped
10 black peppercorns
4 thyme sprigs
1 bay leaf
One 750-ml bottle
    Cabernet Sauvignon
1 cup ruby port
2 cups rich veal stock
Two 1½-pound racks of lamb, chine
    bone removed, bones frenched
2 tablespoons herbes de Provence
½ cup extra-virgin olive oil
Salt and freshly ground pepper
4 tablespoons unsalted butter
**Roquefort Bread Puddings
    (p. 251), for serving**

**1.** In a large saucepan, cook the bacon over moderate heat until crisp around the edges. Add the onion, carrot, celery and whole garlic cloves and cook until softened, about 10 minutes. Add the tomato, peppercorns, thyme, bay leaf, wine and port. Cook over moderate heat until reduced by half, about 15 minutes.

**2.** Strain the sauce into a medium saucepan and cook over moderate heat until reduced to 1 cup, about 10 minutes. Add the veal stock and reduce to ½ cup, about 20 minutes. Transfer the sauce to a saucepan and refrigerate for 4 hours.

**3.** Meanwhile, set the lamb fat side up in a medium roasting pan. Mix the minced garlic with the herbes de Provence and the olive oil and rub all over the lamb. Refrigerate for at least 30 minutes or for up to 3 hours.

● FAST    ● HEALTHY    ● MAKE AHEAD    ● STAFF FAVORITE

ROAST LEG OF LAMB WITH DRIED-CHERRY SAUCE

**4.** Preheat the oven to 425°. Season the lamb with salt and pepper and roast for 40 minutes, or until an instant-read thermometer inserted in the thickest part of the meat registers 140° for medium rare. Transfer the lamb to a carving board and let the meat rest for 10 minutes.

**5.** Meanwhile, skim the fat from the surface of the chilled Cabernet sauce. Bring to a gentle simmer over moderate heat, whisk in the butter 1 tablespoon at a time and season with salt and pepper.

**6.** Carve the racks into double chops and transfer to plates. Drizzle the sauce over the lamb and serve with the Roquefort Bread Puddings. —*John Vlandis*

**WINE** Tannic, complex Cabernet.

## Roast Leg of Lamb with Dried-Cherry Sauce

ACTIVE: 45 MIN; TOTAL: 2 HR 30 MIN

6 SERVINGS, PLUS LEFTOVERS

This recipe calls for verjus, the sour juice pressed from unripe grapes. You can buy verjus at specialty food stores, or substitute red wine vinegar.

One 5- to 5½-pound semiboneless leg of lamb, tied with kitchen string at 2-inch intervals
Salt and freshly ground pepper
1¾ pounds cipolline onions, peeled
12 large garlic cloves, peeled
3 large carrots, sliced ¾ inch thick
¼ cup Dijon mustard
1 tablespoon minced rosemary, plus 1 large sprig
1 tablespoon minced thyme
2 tablespoons sugar
3 tablespoons verjus or red wine vinegar
⅔ cup Syrah
1 cup veal demiglace (see Note)
¾ cup veal stock or low-sodium chicken broth
¼ cup dried cherries, coarsely chopped

**1.** Preheat the oven to 450°. Season the lamb with salt and pepper and transfer it to a medium roasting pan. Scatter the onions, garlic and carrots around the meat and roast for 15 minutes. Reduce the oven temperature to 325° and roast the lamb until an instant-read thermometer inserted in the thickest part of the meat registers 120°, about 1½ hours. Leave the oven on.

**2.** Spread the mustard all over the meat. In a small bowl, combine the minced rosemary with the thyme and 1½ teaspoons each of salt and pepper. Pat the herb mixture all over the lamb and roast for 10 minutes longer, or until an instant-read thermometer inserted in the thickest part of the meat registers 130°. Transfer the lamb to a cutting board and let rest for 20 minutes. Transfer the vegetables to a bowl and keep warm.

**3.** Meanwhile, heat a medium skillet until very hot. Sprinkle the sugar in the skillet and cook over moderate heat until caramelized, about 20 seconds. Add the verjus and cook for 10 seconds. Add the Syrah and cook, shaking the pan frequently, until the sugar dissolves and the wine is reduced by half, about 10 minutes. Stir in the demiglace, stock and rosemary sprig and simmer over moderate heat until reduced to 1 cup, about 15 minutes. Add the cherries and simmer over low heat just until softened, about 5 minutes. Season with salt and pepper. Discard the rosemary sprig and transfer the sauce to a warmed gravy boat.

**4.** Discard the kitchen string and slice the roast thickly. Transfer to a platter, arrange the vegetables around the lamb and serve with the dried-cherry sauce. —*Michael Allemeier*

**NOTE** Demiglace is available at specialty food stores and butcher shops.

**MAKE AHEAD** The dried-cherry sauce can be refrigerated for up to 2 days.

**WINE** Powerful, spicy Syrah.

## Lamb Meatballs in Sour-Cherry Sauce

ACTIVE: 30 MIN; TOTAL: 1 HR

8 SERVINGS ●

2 cups dried sour cherries (13 ounces)
2 cups warm water
2 pounds marbled boneless lamb shoulder, trimmed of silver skin and gristle, meat and fat finely ground
1¾ teaspoons cinnamon
1 teaspoon ground allspice
Kosher salt and freshly ground black pepper
¼ cup plus 1 tablespoon vegetable oil
2 medium onions, coarsely chopped
3 tablespoons fresh lemon juice
2 tablespoons flat-leaf parsley leaves (optional)
Mini pita breads, warmed

**1.** In a bowl, soak the dried cherries in the water until softened, about 30 minutes.

**2.** Meanwhile, in a large bowl, spread the lamb in an even layer. In a small bowl, combine the cinnamon, allspice, 2½ teaspoons of salt and ½ teaspoon of pepper. Sprinkle the spices over the lamb and knead them in. Form the spiced lamb mixture into ¾-inch meatballs; you should have about 60.

**3.** In a large skillet, heat 2 tablespoons of the oil until shimmering. Add the meatballs and cook over high heat, shaking the pan, until lightly browned outside and rare in the centers, about 4 minutes. Drain well.

**4.** In a large saucepan, heat the remaining 3 tablespoons of oil until shimmering. Add the onions; cook over moderately low heat, stirring occasionally, until softened and golden, about 12 minutes. Add the cherries and their soaking liquid and the lemon juice and simmer the sauce over moderate heat for 10 minutes. Add the

# beef + lamb

meatballs and any accumulated juices and simmer over low heat until they are slightly pink inside and the sauce has reduced slightly, 5 to 10 minutes. Season with salt and pepper, garnish with the parsley leaves and serve with pita breads.
—Nadia Roden

**MAKE AHEAD** The cooked meatballs can be refrigerated overnight in their sauce. Reheat gently.

**WINE** Bright, fruity rosé.

## Moroccan-Spiced Lamb-and-Rice Meatballs

**TOTAL: 1 HR**

**6 SERVINGS** ●

You may wonder whether the raw rice in the meatballs will cook fully by the time the lamb is done. It does. Any grains of rice that fall out of the meatballs give the saffron-infused broth a lovely richness.

# equipment

½ cup medium-grain rice, such as arborio

2 medium onions, 1 quartered, 1 thinly sliced

1 cup cilantro leaves, plus ¼ cup finely chopped cilantro

¼ cup mint leaves

1 teaspoon ground cumin

1 teaspoon sweet paprika

Scant ½ teaspoon ground allspice

Scant ½ teaspoon cayenne pepper

Scant ½ teaspoon ras el hanout (optional; see Note)

Kosher salt

1½ pounds lean ground lamb

4½ cups water

4 tablespoons unsalted butter

¼ cup chopped flat-leaf parsley

¼ teaspoon crushed red pepper

Pinch of saffron threads, crumbled

2 tablespoons fresh lemon juice

1. In a small bowl, soak the rice in water for 15 minutes. Drain in a fine-mesh sieve and rinse under cold water until the water runs clear. Drain well.

2. In a food processor, pulse the quartered onion with the cup of cilantro leaves and the mint, cumin, paprika, allspice, cayenne, ras el hanout and 1½ tablespoons of salt until pureed. Scrape the puree into a large bowl and mix in the ground lamb and rice.

3. Line a large baking sheet with plastic wrap. Using lightly moistened hands, roll rounded tablespoons of the meat mixture into 1½-inch balls and transfer them to the baking sheet.

4. Pour the 4½ cups of water into a large, deep skillet. Add the sliced onion, butter, parsley, crushed red pepper and saffron and bring to a boil. Remove from the heat and add the meatballs; they will not fit in a single layer. Cover with a tight-fitting lid and cook over moderately low heat until the meatballs are cooked and the rice is tender, about 20 minutes. Stir gently once or twice halfway through.

5. Using a slotted spoon, transfer the cooked meatballs to a large platter. Strain the cooking liquid into a heatproof bowl and skim off as much fat as possible. Return the cooking liquid to the skillet and boil over high heat until thickened, about 10 minutes.

6. Return the meatballs to the sauce and simmer over moderate heat until heated through, about 2 minutes. Stir in the chopped cilantro and the lemon juice, season with salt and serve.
—Anissa Helou

**NOTE** Ras el hanout, a Moroccan blend of up to 30 spices, including cinnamon, ginger, anise, nutmeg, peppercorns, cardamom and cloves, is available at Middle Eastern markets.

**MAKE AHEAD** The cooked meatballs can be refrigerated in their sauce overnight. Reheat gently before serving.

**SERVE WITH** Pita bread.

**WINE** Assertive, heady Grenache.

## Eggplants Stuffed with Tarragon Lamb

**TOTAL: 1 HR 20 MIN**

**8 FIRST-COURSE SERVINGS** ●

4 Japanese or Asian eggplants (about 10 ounces each), halved lengthwise

Salt

1 large Yukon Gold potato, peeled and cut into ½-inch dice

2 tablespoons extra-virgin olive oil

1 medium onion, very finely chopped

1 pound coarsely ground lamb

½ cup chicken stock or low-sodium broth

1 tablespoon finely chopped tarragon

Freshly ground pepper

¼ cup freshly grated Parmesan cheese

**1.** Preheat the oven to 400° and lightly oil a large, rimmed baking sheet. Arrange the halved eggplants cut side down on the baking sheet and bake for 20 minutes, or until they are softened but not falling apart.

**2.** Meanwhile, bring a small saucepan of salted water to a boil. Add the diced potato and cook until crisp-tender, about 5 minutes; drain. Heat 1 tablespoon of the olive oil in a large skillet until shimmering. Add the onion and cook over moderately high heat for about 5 minutes, stirring occasionally, until softened. Add the lamb and cook, stirring occasionally with a wooden spoon to break up the meat, until no liquid remains and the lamb is beginning to brown, about 10 minutes. Add the potato and stock and cook over moderate heat until the mixture is dry and the potato is tender, about 8 minutes.

**3.** Heat the remaining 1 tablespoon of olive oil in a large nonstick skillet. Add the eggplants cut side down and cook over high heat until browned, 1 to 2 minutes. Transfer to a work surface and let cool. Carefully scoop the flesh out of each eggplant, leaving a ¼-inch-thick shell. Chop the eggplant flesh. Add the eggplant and tarragon to the lamb mixture. Stir to combine and season generously with salt and pepper.

**4.** Lightly oil a large baking dish. Arrange the eggplant shells in the dish and fill with the lamb mixture, mounding slightly. Sprinkle with the Parmesan and bake for about 10 minutes, until the filling is heated through and the cheese is melted. Preheat the broiler and broil for about 1 minute, until lightly browned. Transfer the eggplants to a platter and serve.
—*Pascal Rigo*

**MAKE AHEAD** The stuffed eggplants can be refrigerated overnight; bring to room temperature before baking.

**WINE** Tannic, full-bodied Barbaresco.

## Moussaka with Yogurt Béchamel
**TOTAL: 1 HR 30 MIN**
**12 TO 16 SERVINGS** ● ●

- 2 tablespoons unsalted butter
- ⅓ cup all-purpose flour
- 1½ cups heavy cream
- 1½ cups whole milk
- 2½ large onions, 2 diced
- 1 bay leaf
- 2 whole cloves
- ½ cup plain whole milk yogurt
- Freshly grated nutmeg
- Salt and freshly ground black pepper
- ¼ cup dried currants
- 6 tablespoons extra-virgin olive oil, plus more for brushing
- 1 pound ground beef
- 1 pound ground lamb
- 3½ tablespoons *ras el hanout* (see Note)
- 2 tablespoons plus ½ teaspoon cinnamon
- 1 teaspoon crushed red pepper
- 6 garlic cloves, thinly sliced
- 2 cups dry red wine
- One 28-ounce can whole tomatoes, chopped, juices reserved
- 2 medium eggplants, peeled and sliced lengthwise ½ inch thick
- 2 green bell peppers, diced
- 2 cups grated Parmesan cheese

**1.** Melt the butter in a medium saucepan. Stir in the flour until a paste forms. Remove the pan from the heat and whisk in the cream. Set the saucepan over moderately high heat and whisk in the milk. Whisk constantly until the sauce starts to boil. Reduce the heat to moderate and whisk occasionally.

**2.** Add the onion half, bay leaf and cloves to the sauce and simmer over moderately low heat, whisking often, for 12 minutes. Remove from the heat, whisking occasionally until just warm. Strain into a bowl and whisk in the yogurt. Season with nutmeg, salt and pepper. Lay plastic wrap directly on the béchamel sauce.

**3.** Preheat the oven to 500°. Soak the currants in warm water. Set a colander over a large bowl.

**4.** In a large, deep skillet, heat 2 tablespoons of the oil. Add the beef and lamb and cook over moderately high heat, breaking up the meat, until it begins to brown, 5 minutes. Stir in ½ tablespoon of the *ras el hanout* and ½ teaspoon each of the cinnamon and the crushed red pepper. Season with salt and black pepper and scrape the meat into the colander to drain.

**5.** Heat 2 tablespoons of the oil in the skillet. Add the garlic and diced onions and cook over moderate heat, stirring occasionally, until softened, 6 minutes. Add the remaining 3 tablespoons of *ras el hanout*, 2 tablespoons of cinnamon and ½ teaspoon of crushed red pepper and stir until fragrant, 2 minutes. Add the wine and boil until reduced to 2 tablespoons, 6 minutes. Add the tomatoes, their juices and the meat; simmer over moderate heat for 5 minutes. Drain the currants and stir them in; simmer for 5 minutes. Season with salt and pepper.

**6.** Arrange the eggplant slices on 2 large, rimmed baking sheets. Brush both sides of the eggplant with olive oil, season with salt and pepper and bake on the upper and lower racks of the oven for 10 minutes, or until tender. Preheat the broiler. Broil the eggplant, one sheet at a time, for 1 minute, or until lightly charred. Reduce the oven temperature to 350°.

**7.** In a medium skillet, heat the remaining 2 tablespoons of oil. Add the diced bell peppers and cook over moderate heat, stirring occasionally, until softened, about 7 minutes.

**8.** Arrange the eggplant slices in a glass or ceramic 10-by-17-by-2-inch oval baking dish. Spread the bell peppers and meat filling over the eggplant. Spread the béchamel sauce over the meat and sprinkle the Parmesan on top. Bake the

# beef + lamb

moussaka for 30 minutes, or until bubbling. Preheat the broiler and broil in the center of the oven for about 2 minutes, or until browned. Let rest for 10 minutes, then serve. —*Jim Botsacos*

**NOTE** *Ras el hanout,* a heady Moroccan spice blend, is available at specialty and Middle Eastern markets.

**MAKE AHEAD** The baked moussaka can be refrigerated overnight.

**WINE** Simple, fruity Chianti or Sangiovese.

## Lamb and Two-Cheese Quesadillas

**TOTAL: 30 MIN**

4 SERVINGS ●

 2 tablespoons extra-virgin olive oil, plus more for brushing
 1 pound lean ground lamb
 1 tablespoon very finely chopped oregano
 3 garlic cloves, minced
Salt and freshly ground pepper
 1 cup whole milk yogurt
 3 scallions, thinly sliced
 1 medium seedless cucumber (about ¾ pound), peeled and coarsely shredded
Four 10-inch flour tortillas
 ¼ pound mozzarella, sliced
 ¼ pound feta cheese, crumbled (1 cup)

**1.** Preheat the oven to 225°. In a skillet, heat the 2 tablespoons of olive oil until nearly smoking. Add the lamb, oregano and two-thirds of the minced garlic, season with salt and pepper and cook over moderately high heat, stirring occasionally, until browned, 5 to 6 minutes. Spoon some of the fat out of the skillet.

**2.** Meanwhile, in a medium bowl, mix the yogurt with the remaining garlic and two-thirds of the scallions. Season with salt and pepper. Working over a colander set in the sink, squeeze the shredded cucumber until it is fairly dry, then fold the cucumber into the yogurt mixture.

**3.** Preheat a large cast-iron griddle. Brush the tortillas on one side with olive oil. Place 2 tortillas oiled side down on the griddle. Top each with one-fourth of the mozzarella, feta and lamb mixture and cook over moderate heat until the tortillas are lightly browned and the cheese has begun to melt. Fold in half and cook, flipping once, until the tortillas are browned and crisp and the cheese is melted, about 4 minutes. Transfer the quesadillas to a baking sheet and keep warm in the oven while you make the rest. Transfer the quesadillas to a platter, top with the cucumber-yogurt sauce and the remaining sliced scallion and serve immediately. —*Julie Ridlon*

**WINE** Rich, smoky-plummy Shiraz.

## Lamb Burgers with Cilantro-Yogurt Sauce

**TOTAL: 45 MIN**

6 SERVINGS ●

This spicy burger served with a cooling yogurt sauce is a take on lamb vindaloo, the classic Indian dish.

 ¼ cup plus 1 tablespoon fresh lemon juice
 4 jalapeños, seeded and minced
 2 cups cilantro leaves
 2 tablespoons minced peeled fresh ginger
 1 tablespoon sugar
 1 small red onion, ½ minced, ½ thinly sliced
Kosher salt
2½ pounds ground lamb
 6 medium scallions, white and tender green parts only, very finely chopped
 ½ cup very finely chopped mint leaves
 ½ cup freshly grated Parmigiano-Reggiano cheese
1½ teaspoons finely grated lemon zest
Freshly ground black pepper

 ¼ teaspoon cayenne pepper
 1 medium tomato, thinly sliced
 1 small cucumber—peeled, halved, seeded and thinly sliced
 ¾ cup plain yogurt
 6 hard rolls, split in half and lightly toasted

**1.** In a food processor, combine 3 tablespoons of the lemon juice with half of the minced jalapeños, the cilantro leaves, ginger, sugar, minced onion and ½ teaspoon of salt. Process until pureed. Transfer to a bowl and refrigerate.

**2.** Light a grill. In a large bowl, combine the ground lamb with the remaining minced jalapeños, the scallions, mint, cheese, lemon zest and 2 teaspoons of the lemon juice. Add 1 teaspoon of salt, ½ teaspoon of black pepper and the cayenne and mix gently with your hands. Pat the meat into 6 burgers.

**3.** In a medium bowl, toss the tomato, cucumber and sliced onion with the remaining 1 tablespoon plus 1 teaspoon of lemon juice. Season with salt and black pepper.

**4.** Grill the burgers over a hot fire until nicely charred on the outside and pink within, about 4 minutes per side. Fold the yogurt into the cilantro puree. Spread some of the yogurt sauce on the bottom half of each roll; top each with a burger, another dollop of yogurt sauce and some of the tomato-cucumber salad. Close the sandwiches and serve at once.
—*Suvir Saran*

**WINE** Assertive, heady Grenache.

## Moroccan Lamb Burgers with Mint-Yogurt Sauce

**TOTAL: 40 MIN**

4 SERVINGS

 1 cup plain whole milk yogurt
 ¼ cup chopped mint leaves
 1 garlic clove, minced
 1 tablespoon plus 1 teaspoon fresh lemon juice

Kosher salt and freshly ground pepper

- 2 tablespoons dried currants
- 2 tablespoons pine nuts
- 2 tablespoons coarsely chopped flat-leaf parsley
- 1 teaspoon finely grated lemon zest
- ½ teaspoon ground cumin
- ½ teaspoon ground coriander
- ½ teaspoon cinnamon
- 1¾ pounds ground lamb

Vegetable oil, for the grill

- 4 hamburger buns or kaiser rolls, split in half

**1.** In a small bowl, mix the yogurt with the mint leaves, garlic and 1 tablespoon of the lemon juice. Season the mint-yogurt sauce with salt and pepper, cover and refrigerate.

**2.** In a mini food processor, combine the dried currants, pine nuts, chopped parsley, lemon zest, cumin, coriander and cinnamon with the remaining 1 teaspoon of lemon juice and 1 teaspoon of salt. Process the ingredients until a coarse paste forms.

**3.** Scrape the currant–pine nut paste into a large bowl and add the ground lamb. Using your hands, gently mix the ground meat thoroughly to combine it with the seasonings and pat into 4 plump burgers. Set the burgers on a plate, cover them with plastic wrap and refrigerate for 15 minutes.

**4.** Light a grill. Lightly brush the grate with oil. Grill the burgers over a medium-hot fire for about 6 minutes per side for medium rare. Grill the buns, cut side down, until toasted. Set the burgers on the buns and serve with the mint-yogurt sauce. —*Sally James*

**MAKE AHEAD** The mint-yogurt sauce and the lamb burger patties can be refrigerated overnight. Let the burgers stand at room temperature for about 15 minutes before grilling them.

**WINE** Light, fruity Beaujolais.

**LAMB AND TWO-CHEESE QUESADILLAS**

**LAMB BURGERS WITH CILANTRO-YOGURT SAUCE**

ROAST BACON-WRAPPED PORK, P. 145

# pork
# +veal

ROAST PORK LOIN WITH ARMAGNAC-PRUNE SAUCE

HERBED PORK RIB ROAST

## Roast Pork Loin with Armagnac-Prune Sauce

**ACTIVE: 30 MIN; TOTAL: 3 HR**

6 TO 8 SERVINGS

½  cup Armagnac or brandy

18  large pitted prunes

10  garlic cloves, 6 peeled, 4 minced

2  teaspoons caraway seeds, crushed

Kosher salt

One 6½-pound pork loin roast on the bone, rack of rib bones removed in one piece and reserved

Freshly ground pepper

6  cups water

1  tablespoon unsalted butter

3  tablespoons all-purpose flour

**1.** Preheat the oven to 375°. In a medium saucepan, bring the Armagnac to a boil. Add the prunes and simmer over low heat for 3 minutes. Set aside.

**2.** In a bowl, combine the minced garlic, caraway seeds and 1 teaspoon of salt. Rub the mixture on the pork loin and let stand at room temperature for 1 hour.

**3.** Set the rack of rib bones in a roasting pan meaty side up and season with salt and pepper. Set the pork loin on the rack fat side down. Add the 6 peeled garlic cloves and pour in 2 cups of the water; roast for 30 minutes. Add 1 cup of water to the pan and roast for 30 minutes longer. Turn the pork loin fat side up and roast for 30 minutes longer, or until an instant-read thermometer inserted in the thickest part of the meat registers 145°. Transfer the pork to a carving board and cover loosely with foil for at least 10 minutes or up to 20 minutes.

**4.** In a heatproof bowl, blend the butter with the flour to make a paste. Turn the rib rack meaty side down. Set the pan over 2 burners on moderately high heat. Add the remaining 3 cups of water and simmer for 2 minutes, scraping up the browned bits from the bottom and sides of the pan. Reduce the heat to moderate and simmer for 10 minutes, stirring often and mashing the garlic cloves.

**5.** Whisk ½ cup of the pan juices into the butter paste. Remove the rib rack from the roasting pan. Whisk the dissolved butter paste into the pan juices and simmer, whisking often, for 5 minutes. Strain the sauce into a saucepan. Add the prunes and simmer over moderate heat for 5 minutes. Season with salt and pepper. Carve the pork loin into ¼-inch-thick slices and serve with the sauce.
—*Kurt Gutenbrunner*

**SERVE WITH** Green Cabbage and Apple Sauté (p. 216).

**WINE** Spicy Alsace Gewürztraminer.

## Herbed Pork Rib Roast

**ACTIVE: 10 MIN; TOTAL: 3 HR 15 MIN**

6 SERVINGS

This versatile cut of pork can be sliced into chops and cooked individually or roasted whole and carved at the table.

- 3 garlic cloves, minced
- 3 tablespoons extra-virgin olive oil
- 1 tablespoon chopped thyme
- 1 tablespoon chopped rosemary leaves

One 4-pound pork rib roast cut from the loin end, chine bone removed

Salt and freshly ground pepper

**1.** In a small bowl, blend the garlic with the olive oil and chopped thyme and rosemary leaves. Rub the herb paste all over the pork roast and let stand at room temperature for 2 hours or refrigerate overnight.

**2.** Preheat the oven to 500°. Set the pork in a small roasting pan and season generously with salt and pepper. Roast the pork for 15 minutes, then reduce the oven temperature to 325°. Continue roasting the pork for 40 minutes longer, or until an instant-read thermometer inserted in the thickest part of the meat registers 155°. Transfer the pork to a carving board and let stand for 10 minutes. Cut between the ribs, transfer the chops to a platter or plates and serve. —*Frank Stitt*

**SERVE WITH** Grits and grilled eggplant.
**WINE** Complex, silky red Burgundy.

## Roast Bacon-Wrapped Pork

**ACTIVE: 20 MIN; TOTAL: 1 HR 30 MIN**

8 SERVINGS

One 3-pound boneless pork loin
- 2 garlic cloves, thinly sliced

Salt and freshly ground pepper
- 4 ounces thinly sliced bacon or pancetta
- 6 long rosemary sprigs
- 6 long thyme sprigs

**1.** Preheat the oven to 350°. Using a knife, make 1-inch-deep slits all over the pork. Stuff each slit with a slice of garlic. Season the pork all over with salt and pepper and wrap with the bacon. Top with the herbs, tucking them under the bacon in several spots. Tie the roast at 1-inch intervals with kitchen string.

**2.** Transfer the pork to a roasting pan and roast for 1 hour, or until an instant-read thermometer inserted in the center of the loin registers 140°. Transfer to a cutting board, cover loosely with foil and let rest for 15 minutes. Discard the string and herb sprigs. Carve the loin into thick slices and serve. —*Steven Wagner*

**MAKE AHEAD** The pork can be prepared through Step 1 and refrigerated overnight. Let return to room temperature before roasting.

**WINE** Tannic, full-bodied Barbaresco.

## Pork Medallions with Tangerine-Chile Pan Sauce

**TOTAL: 20 MIN**

4 SERVINGS ●

- ½ cup fresh tangerine juice
- 1 tablespoon *sambal oelek* or other Asian-style chile sauce
- 1 tablespoon unsalted butter
- 1 tablespoon extra-virgin olive oil

Four 1¼-inch-thick boneless pork loin chops (2 pounds)

Kosher salt and freshly ground pepper

Four ¼-inch-thick tangerine slices, for garnish

**1.** In a small bowl, mix the tangerine juice and *sambal oelek*. In a large skillet, melt the butter in the olive oil over moderately high heat until sizzling. Season the pork chops with salt and freshly ground pepper and add them to the skillet. Cook the chops for 6 minutes per side, until browned and cooked through. Transfer the chops to a plate.

**2.** Add the tangerine slices to the skillet and cook over moderately high heat, turning them once, until browned, about 1 minute. Transfer to the plate. Add the tangerine juice to the hot skillet and bring to a boil, scraping up any browned bits. Simmer the glaze until it thickens, about 2 minutes. Return the pork and any accumulated juices to the skillet and turn the chops to coat them in the glaze. Transfer the pork and glaze to plates, garnish with the tangerine slices and serve. —*Charmaine Solomon*

**SERVE WITH** Cooked carrots.
**WINE** Light, fruity Beaujolais.

## Tandoori Pork with Gingered Mango Salad

**TOTAL: 30 MIN**

6 SERVINGS ● ●

For the first seven ingredients listed here, you can substitute a total of 1½ tablespoons of tandoori spice powder.

- 1 tablespoon ground coriander
- ½ teaspoon ground cumin
- ½ teaspoon ground fennel seeds
- ¼ teaspoon cayenne pepper
- ¼ teaspoon turmeric

Pinch of cinnamon

Pinch of ground cloves
- 1 large garlic clove, mashed
- 2½ teaspoons finely grated fresh ginger
- ¾ cup plain low-fat yogurt

Salt and freshly ground black pepper

Two ¾-pound pork tenderloins, each cut crosswise into 6 slices and pounded ½ inch thick
- 2 large mangoes, peeled and thinly sliced
- 1 large jalapeño, thinly sliced
- 2 tablespoons fresh lime juice
- 2 tablespoons extra-virgin olive oil

**1.** In a large bowl, combine the ground coriander, cumin, fennel, cayenne, turmeric, cinnamon and cloves with the garlic, 1½ teaspoons of the ginger and the yogurt. Season with salt and black pepper. Add the pork to the marinade and turn to coat. Let stand at room temperature for 10 minutes.

2. Meanwhile, in a medium bowl, toss the mangoes with the remaining 1 teaspoon of ginger and the jalapeño and lime juice. Season lightly with salt.

3. Light a grill. Lightly oil the grate with some of the olive oil. Remove the pork from the marinade and scrape off some of the excess. Brush the pork on both sides with the remaining olive oil and season lightly with salt. Grill the pork over a hot fire, turning occasionally, until it is nicely browned and cooked through, about 5 minutes. Transfer the pork to a platter and serve with the mango salad. —Grace Parisi

WINE Spicy Alsace Gewürztraminer.

### Cassoulet with Bacon, Andouille and Country Ribs

ACTIVE: 40 MIN; TOTAL: 3 HR, PLUS OVERNIGHT FOR SOAKING THE BEANS
6 TO 8 SERVINGS ●

This Southern-style dish is an easy version of the French country classic cassoulet, replacing the usual duck or goose confit with three varieties of pork—the South's favorite meat.

- 2 cups dried white beans, such as *haricots blancs* or Great Northerns, soaked overnight in cold water and drained
- 2 quarts plus 2 cups chicken stock or low-sodium broth
- 2 tablespoons unsalted butter
- 3 pounds meaty country-style pork loin ribs—fat trimmed, meat removed from the bones and cut into 1-inch pieces, rib bones reserved

Salt and freshly ground pepper
- ½ pound thick-cut applewood-smoked bacon, cut into 1-inch pieces
- ¾ pound andouille sausage, thickly sliced crosswise
- 1 large onion, finely chopped
- 2 medium carrots, finely diced
- 6 large garlic cloves, chopped
- 6 large plum tomatoes, seeded and chopped
- 1 tablespoon chopped thyme
- 1 bay leaf

1. In a large saucepan, cover the beans with the stock and bring to a boil. Reduce the heat to moderately low and simmer until the beans are tender, about 1 hour. Drain the beans, reserving the stock. Return the stock to the saucepan and boil over high heat until it is reduced to 4 cups, about 7 minutes.

2. Meanwhile, melt the butter in a large skillet. Working in 2 batches, season the rib meat with salt and pepper and cook over moderately high heat until browned all over, about 4 minutes per batch. Transfer to a platter. Add the bacon to the skillet and cook until the fat is rendered and the meat begins to crisp, about 5 minutes. Transfer the bacon to the platter. Add the andouille to the skillet and cook over moderately high heat until lightly browned, about 3 minutes. Transfer to the platter. Add the reserved rib bones to the skillet and cook over moderately high heat until lightly browned, about 2 minutes per side. Add to the platter.

3. Add the onion, carrots and garlic to the skillet and cook over moderate heat, stirring occasionally, until softened and golden, about 8 minutes. Add the chopped tomatoes, thyme and bay leaf and cook, stirring until the tomatoes release their juices, about 3 minutes. Return the rib meat, bacon and andouille to the skillet; stir until heated through.

4. Preheat the oven to 300°. Scrape the meat and vegetables into a large glass or ceramic baking dish. Nestle in the rib bones and top with the white beans and the reduced stock. Bake the cassoulet for 1 hour and 30 minutes, or until bubbling and the beans on top are crisp. Let stand for 15 minutes. Pick out the bay leaf and serve. —Bob Waggoner

MAKE AHEAD The baked cassoulet can be refrigerated for up to 4 days. Cover with aluminum foil and bring to room temperature before reheating in a 350° oven for about 40 minutes.

WINE Powerful, spicy Syrah.

### Pan-Roasted Pork with Apple Chutney and Pepper Relish

ACTIVE: 50 MIN; TOTAL: 1 HR 20 MIN
4 SERVINGS ● ●

Pork chops and applesauce are traditional partners. This recipe substitutes tenderloin and a tangy apple chutney.

- 3½ tablespoons extra-virgin olive oil
- 1 Granny Smith apple, cut into ¼-inch wedges
- ½ cup white wine vinegar
- ½ cup light brown sugar
- ½ tablespoon mustard seeds
- ¼ teaspoon whole allspice berries
- Pinch of cayenne pepper
- Salt and freshly ground pepper
- 2 jalapeños, seeded and finely chopped
- 1 large red bell pepper, cut into ¼-inch dice
- 1 large yellow bell pepper, cut into ¼-inch dice
- 1 small red onion, cut into ¼-inch dice
- 1 large garlic clove, minced
- ¼ cup minced, peeled fresh ginger
- Two ¾-pound pork tenderloins

1. In a medium skillet, heat ½ tablespoon of the olive oil. Add the apple and cook over high heat until browned on the bottom, about 3 minutes. Add the vinegar, brown sugar, mustard seeds, allspice and cayenne and simmer over moderate heat until thickened, about 5 minutes. Season with salt and pepper.

**2.** In a large skillet, heat 2 tablespoons of the olive oil. Add the jalapeños, red and yellow bell peppers, onion, garlic and ginger. Cover and cook over moderately low heat, stirring occasionally, until softened, about 10 minutes. Season with salt and pepper. Transfer the pepper relish to a bowl and wipe out the skillet.

**3.** In the same large skillet, heat the remaining 1 tablespoon of olive oil. Season the tenderloins with salt and pepper and add to the skillet. Cook them over moderate heat on four sides until lightly browned, about 3 minutes per side. Cover and cook, turning once, until an instant-read thermometer inserted in the center registers 145°, about 10 minutes. Transfer the tenderloins to a carving board, cover loosely with foil and let rest for 10 minutes. Slice the pork ⅓ inch thick and serve with the apple chutney and pepper relish. —*Kimball Jones*
**WINE** Soft, off-dry Riesling.

### Grilled Maple-Brined Pork Chops
**ACTIVE: 20 MIN; TOTAL: 2 HR, PLUS 8 HR BRINING**
6 SERVINGS
The sweet and tangy maple syrup and cider vinegar brine used on these double-cut pork chops enhances the natural juiciness of the meat.

- 2 **quarts water**
- ½ **cup kosher salt**
- ½ **cup light brown sugar**
- ½ **cup pure maple syrup**
- ¼ **cup cider vinegar**
- 1 **whole clove**
- 3 **bay leaves**
- 4 **whole allspice berries**
- 1 **tablespoon yellow mustard seeds**
- 4 **fresh sage leaves**
- 1 **tablespoon coarsely ground black pepper**
- 6 **double-cut, bone-in pork chops (about 1 pound each)**

**Olive oil, for brushing**

**PORK WITH APPLE CHUTNEY**

**MAPLE-BRINED PORK CHOPS**

**PORK AND CHICKPEA STEW**

**HONEY-GLAZED PORK SHOULDER**

1. In a large pot, combine the water, salt, brown sugar, maple syrup, vinegar, clove, bay leaves, allspice berries, mustard seeds, sage and pepper. Bring to a boil and remove from the heat. Let the brine cool to room temperature, then refrigerate for 1 hour. Add the pork chops to the brine and refrigerate for 7 to 8 hours, turning the chops after 4 hours. Remove the pork chops from the brine and pat dry.
2. Light a grill. Brush both sides of the chops with oil and grill over a medium-hot fire for 18 minutes per side, or until an instant-read thermometer inserted in the thickest part of the meat registers 155°. Transfer to plates and let rest for 5 minutes before serving. —*Melissa Kelly*
**MAKE AHEAD** The dry, brined chops can be refrigerated, uncooked, for 4 hours.
**SERVE WITH** Polenta and braised greens.
**WINE** Spicy New World Gewürztraminer.

**Pork and Chickpea Stew with Orange and Cumin**
**ACTIVE: 50 MIN; TOTAL: 1 HR 30 MIN**
**6 SERVINGS** ●
　2　**tablespoons extra-virgin olive oil**
　3　**pounds boneless trimmed pork shoulder, cut into 1½-inch pieces**
**Salt and freshly ground pepper**
　1　**medium onion, finely chopped**
　3　**large garlic cloves, minced**
　½　**cup fresh orange juice**
　1　**quart water**
　1　**bay leaf**
1½　**teaspoons cumin seeds, toasted**
　1　**cup canned chickpeas, drained**
1½　**teaspoons finely grated orange zest**
　2　**tablespoons chopped parsley leaves**

1. Heat the oil in a large enameled cast-iron casserole. Working in 3 batches, add the pork, season with salt and pepper and cook over moderately high heat until browned all over, about 9 minutes. Transfer the pork to a bowl.
2. Add the onion and two-thirds of the garlic to the casserole and cook over moderate heat, stirring occasionally, until softened, about 5 minutes. Add the fresh orange juice and simmer until reduced by half. Add the water and bay leaf and bring to a simmer. Return the pork to the casserole along with any accumulated juices and bring to a simmer. In a mortar, grind the toasted cumin seeds to a powder and stir into the stew. Simmer over low heat until the pork is tender, about 30 minutes.
3. Using a slotted spoon, transfer the pork to a bowl. Add the chickpeas to the

stew and cook over moderate heat for 10 minutes. Return the pork to the stew. Stir in the zest, the remaining garlic and the parsley and simmer for 1 minute. Season with salt and pepper. Discard the bay leaf and serve. —*Marcia Kiesel*
**MAKE AHEAD** The stew can be made through Step 2 and refrigerated for 2 days. Reheat, add the chickpeas and stir in the garlic, orange zest and parsley.
**SERVE WITH** White rice.
**WINE** Light, zesty, fruity Dolcetto.

## Stir-Fried Pork with Ginger and Basil

**TOTAL: 30 MIN**
6 SERVINGS ● ●
- ¼ cup chicken stock or low-sodium broth
- 2 tablespoons oyster sauce
- 1 tablespoon Asian fish sauce
- 3 tablespoons vegetable oil
- 3 Thai chiles or 2 jalapeños, minced
- 2 large garlic cloves, minced
- 1 tablespoon minced fresh ginger
- 1¾ pounds pork tenderloin, sliced crosswise ⅛ inch thick
- 1 pound Asian eggplants, cut into 1-inch dice
- 1 cup coarsely chopped basil
- 1 kaffir lime leaf, thinly sliced, or 1 teaspoon finely grated lime zest

Lime wedges, for serving

Heat a wok or skillet over moderately high heat for 5 minutes. In a small bowl, mix the stock with the oyster and fish sauces. Add the oil to the wok and swirl to coat. Add the chiles, garlic and ginger and cook for 30 seconds. Add the pork and stir-fry for 3 minutes. Add the eggplant and stir-fry until tender, about 5 minutes. Stir in the sauce mixture. Remove from the heat and stir in the basil and lime leaf. Transfer to plates and serve with lime wedges. —*Ian Chalermkittichai*
**SERVE WITH** White rice or rice noodles.
**WINE** Full-bodied, fragrant Viognier.

## Honey-Glazed Pork Shoulder with Braised Leeks

**ACTIVE: 45 MIN; TOTAL: 6 HR**
8 SERVINGS
**One 4-pound boneless pork shoulder, with skin**
- 3 tablespoons vegetable oil

**Salt and freshly ground pepper**
- 4 very large leeks (3 pounds), white and tender green parts coarsely chopped, dark greens cut into ¾-inch pieces
- 3 large shallots, thinly sliced
- 5 large garlic cloves, chopped
- 3 dried red chiles
- 2¼ cups chicken stock
- ⅓ cup soy sauce
- ¾ cup honey
- ¼ cup Chinese cooking wine
- 1½ teaspoons miso paste
- 2 teaspoons black rice vinegar

**1.** Preheat the oven to 250°. Score the pork skin in a crosshatch pattern. In a large ovenproof skillet, heat 1 tablespoon of the vegetable oil. Season the pork with salt and pepper and brown over moderately high heat, about 8 minutes. Transfer the pork to a plate.
**2.** Heat the remaining 2 tablespoons of oil in the skillet. Add the chopped leeks, shallots, garlic and chiles, cover and cook over moderate heat for 5 minutes. Return the pork to the skillet. Add 2 cups of the stock and bring to a boil. Pour the soy sauce over the pork and cover with foil. Roast in the oven, basting occasionally, for about 4 hours, or until an instant-read thermometer registers 190°.
**3.** Increase the oven temperature to 400°. Uncover the meat and brush it with 6 tablespoons of the honey. Roast for 15 minutes, or until glossy. Transfer to a rack set over a plate and brush with the remaining 6 tablespoons of honey.
**4.** Blanch the leek greens in boiling salted water for 3 minutes. Drain the greens and rinse in cold water, then drain again. In a large skillet, simmer the remaining ¼ cup of stock, the cooking wine and the miso for 3 minutes. Add the leek greens and cook over moderate heat for 8 minutes. Season with salt and pepper.
**5.** Strain the pork juices into a small saucepan and skim. Add the rice vinegar and boil until reduced to 1¼ cups, about 5 minutes. Slice the pork and serve with the leeks and pan sauce. —*Zak Pelaccio*
**WINE** Light, fruity Pinot Noir.

## Ground Pork Satay on Lemongrass Skewers

**TOTAL: 30 MIN**
4 SERVINGS ●
- 6 plump lemongrass stalks
- 2 pounds ground pork
- ¼ cup finely chopped cilantro
- 2 tablespoons soy sauce
- 1 tablespoon minced fresh ginger
- 1 large garlic clove, minced
- ½ teaspoon green curry paste

**Vegetable oil, for brushing**
**Salt and freshly ground pepper**
**Chopped peanuts, for sprinkling**
**Lime wedges, for serving**

**1.** Light a grill. Cut two-thirds off the tops of the lemongrass. Cut the tops crosswise into 5-inch lengths to make 16 skewers. Peel off any browned layers. Peel the bottom-third portions of 2 of the stalks to their inner bulbs and mince. Freeze the other 4 bulbs for another use.
**2.** In a large bowl, combine the ground pork with the minced lemongrass, chopped cilantro, soy sauce, ginger, garlic and curry paste.
**3.** Line a large baking sheet and a work surface with plastic wrap. On the work surface, using moistened hands, form scant ¼-cup mounds of the pork mixture into sixteen 3-by-2-inch rectangles. Lay the lemongrass skewers on the pork rectangles and pinch the meat all around the lemongrass skewers. Transfer the skewers to the baking sheet.

TUSCAN-STYLE SPARERIBS WITH BALSAMIC GLAZE

**4.** Brush the pork lightly with oil, season with salt and pepper and grill the skewers over a medium-hot fire, turning once or twice, until browned and just cooked through, about 7 minutes. Transfer the pork skewers to a large platter, sprinkle with the chopped peanuts and serve with lime wedges. —*Grace Parisi*
**WINE** Bright, fruity rosé.

## Tuscan-Style Spareribs with Balsamic Glaze

**ACTIVE: 20 MIN; TOTAL: 4 HR 30 MIN**
6 SERVINGS ●
Meat guru Bruce Aidells loves to barbecue spareribs, but his favorite way to prepare them is to season the ribs with a mix of herbs and spices and slow-roast them until tender and crisp. He finishes the ribs with a simple balsamic glaze.

- 2 tablespoons extra-virgin olive oil
- 2 tablespoons chopped rosemary
- 1½ tablespoons kosher salt
- 1½ tablespoons fennel seeds
- 2 teaspoons freshly ground black pepper
- 2 teaspoons chopped sage
- 2 teaspoons chopped thyme
- 2 teaspoons sweet paprika
- 1 teaspoon crushed red pepper
- 1 teaspoon ground coriander
- ½ teaspoon ground allspice
- 6 pounds pork spareribs
- 3 tablespoons balsamic vinegar, preferably one aged for at least 5 years

**1.** In a small bowl, combine the olive oil, rosemary, salt, fennel, black pepper, sage, thyme, paprika, crushed red pepper, coriander and allspice. Rub the spice paste all over the spareribs and let stand at room temperature for 2 hours or refrigerate overnight.
**2.** Preheat the oven to 325°. Arrange the ribs on a large, rimmed baking sheet or in a roasting pan, meaty side up. Roast the ribs for 2 hours, or until tender.

**3.** Preheat the broiler. Brush the meaty side of the ribs with the vinegar. Broil 6 inches from the heat until browned, about 2 minutes. Let stand for 5 minutes, cut apart and serve. —*Bruce Aidells*
**WINE** Complex, savory Chianti Classico.

## Sweet-and-Spicy Pork Ribs

**ACTIVE: 30 MIN; TOTAL: 3 HR, PLUS OVERNIGHT MARINATING**
8 SERVINGS ●
Soaking and slow-baking ribs in a spiced mix of honey, ketchup and mustard make them fragrant, sticky, sweet and succulent.

- ¼ cup extra-virgin olive oil
- 1 large onion, finely chopped
- 2 tablespoons minced garlic
- 2 teaspoons dried oregano
- 2 teaspoons ground black pepper
- 1 teaspoon sweet paprika
- 1 teaspoon cayenne pepper
- 1 teaspoon crushed red pepper
- 1 cinnamon stick
- 1 cup honey
- 1 cup ketchup
- ¾ cup Dijon mustard
- ¾ cup distilled white vinegar
- ½ cup veal demiglace (see Note)
- 2 large racks of meaty pork ribs (8 pounds), cut into individual ribs
- 1 cup water

**1.** In a large saucepan, heat the olive oil until shimmering. Add the onion and garlic and cook over moderately low heat until softened, about 7 minutes. Add the oregano, black pepper, paprika, cayenne, crushed red pepper and cinnamon stick and cook, stirring, until fragrant, 1 to 2 minutes. Add the honey, ketchup and mustard and cook over moderate heat until the sauce is slightly thickened, about 5 minutes. Add the vinegar and demiglace and cook until the sauce is thickened, about 10 minutes; let cool.
**2.** Put the ribs in 2 large resealable plastic bags. Add the sauce to the bags. Seal and refrigerate overnight.
**3.** Preheat the oven to 350°. Transfer the ribs and marinade to a large roasting pan and bake for 1½ hours. Add the water to the pan, turn the ribs and bake for about 1 hour longer, until the ribs are very tender and thickly glazed. Discard the cinnamon stick. Transfer the ribs to a large platter and serve. —*Pascal Rigo*
**NOTE** Veal demiglace is available at specialty food shops and in the freezer section of many large supermarkets.
**MAKE AHEAD** The cooked ribs can be refrigerated for up to 2 days and then reheated, covered, in the oven.
**WINE** Intense, berry-flavored Zinfandel.

# equipment

**GAS GRILL** | TIP

**TEC PATIO II** TEC invented the infrared gas grill, whose ceramic burners give off such intense heat that the cooking surface reaches a temperature twice that of conventional gas or charcoal grills. Steaks sear quickly yet stay rare (from $1,500; 800-331-0097 or tecgasgrills.com).

# pairing

All pork—salty ham, smoky bacon, succulent chops and roasts—has an underlying sweetness and lightness that pairs best with light- to medium-bodied wines with lots of fruit and low tannins.

**HAM, BACON OR SAUSAGES** The fruit and acidity of off-dry German Rieslings balance the smoke and salt in ham and bacon, while Rieslings from Alsace, France, have the weight to stand up to sausages. Try the 2002 Bassermann-Jordan Spätlese Pfalz Forster Jesuitengarten from Germany ($28) or the 2002 Hugel from Alsace ($16).

**SPICY PORK** The spice and light sweetness of Gewürztraminer will flatter similar flavors in spicy pork dishes. Try the 1999 Trimbach Cuvée des Seigneurs de Ribeaupierre ($30).

**HERBED PORK** A ripe and creamy Chardonnay with notes of apple, citrus and oak won't overwhelm the mild herbal flavors in roasts or braises. Try the 2002 Beringer Private Reserve ($27).

**ASIAN-SPICED PORK** The deep fruitiness, low tannins and hint of soy in a New World Pinot Noir give it a special affinity for pork with Asian spices. Try the 2002 Brick House Les Dijonnais ($42) from Oregon.

**ROAST SUCKLING PIG AND BARBECUED RIBS** Boldly flavored pork dishes with lots of crispy fat or tomato-based sauces require a spicy red with acidity and low tannins, like a medium-bodied Zinfandel. Try the 2001 Dry Creek Vineyard Old Vines ($18).
—*Elin McCoy*

### Tuscan Baby Back Ribs
**ACTIVE: 30 MIN; TOTAL: 3 HR, PLUS OVERNIGHT BRINING**
6 SERVINGS ● ●

- 2 quarts water
- ¼ cup plus 3 tablespoons kosher salt
- ⅓ cup sugar
- 2 tablespoons cracked black peppercorns
- 2 tablespoons ground fennel
- 1 tablespoon coriander seeds
- 2 teaspoons juniper berries, crushed
- 2 teaspoons dried marjoram, crumbled
- 4 bay leaves
- 1 head garlic, halved horizontally, plus 2 teaspoons minced garlic
- Two 2-pound racks of pork baby back ribs
- 4 large anchovy fillets, mashed
- 6 tablespoons fresh lemon juice
- ½ cup extra-virgin olive oil, plus more for brushing
- 2 tablespoons chopped parsley

**1.** In a medium saucepan, combine 2 cups of the water with the salt, sugar, peppercorns, fennel, coriander seeds, juniper berries, marjoram, bay leaves and the halved head of garlic. Bring the brine to a simmer, stirring, until the sugar dissolves. Arrange the racks of pork ribs in a single layer in a roasting pan just large enough to hold them. Add the brine and the remaining 6 cups of water. Cover the ribs and refrigerate for at least 8 hours and for up to 12 hours.

**2.** Preheat the oven to 325°. Drain and rinse the ribs and pat dry. Set the racks on a large, rimmed baking sheet in a single layer and cover with foil. Roast for about 2 hours, or until very tender.

**3.** In a large bowl, mash the anchovies and the 2 teaspoons of minced garlic, then stir in the fresh lemon juice. Add the ½ cup of olive oil and the parsley.

**4.** Light a grill. Brush the grate with oil and grill the racks over a medium-hot fire for 5 minutes, turning occasionally, until crisp and browned. Transfer the racks to a cutting board and cut in between the ribs. Toss the ribs in the dressing and pile on a platter. Serve hot, warm or at room temperature.
—*Jody Denton*

**MAKE AHEAD** The ribs can be grilled 4 hours ahead. Keep them at room temperature, covered.

**WINE** Complex, savory Chianti Classico.

### Standing Rib Roast of Pork with Tuscan Herb Sauce
**ACTIVE: 30 MIN; TOTAL: 3 HR, PLUS OVERNIGHT MARINATING**
8 SERVINGS

Ask the butcher for a roast with the chine and rib bones, as it will make for a more flavorful and better-looking dish. Also, to simplify serving, have the butcher cut through the chine bone between each rib.

- ½ cup finely chopped rosemary
- ⅔ cup plus 2 tablespoons extra-virgin olive oil
- Coarse sea salt and freshly ground pepper
- One 6-pound bone-in pork loin rib roast, with chine bone
- 2 cups coarsely chopped flat-leaf parsley
- ⅔ cup chopped mint leaves
- 4 large garlic cloves, very finely chopped
- 2 tablespoons fresh lemon juice

**1.** In a small bowl, mix the rosemary with 2 tablespoons of the olive oil and season generously with salt and pepper. Spread the rub all over the pork and into the space between the partially detached roast and the rib bones. Using kitchen string, tie up the roast to give it a nice shape. Transfer the pork to a roasting pan, cover with plastic wrap and refrigerate overnight.

**2.** Remove the pork roast from the refrigerator and let stand at room temperature for 1 hour before roasting. Preheat the oven to 400°. Roast the pork for about 1½ hours, or until an instant-read thermometer inserted in the thickest part registers 135° for medium. Let the pork roast stand for 20 minutes before carving into chops.

**3.** Meanwhile, in a food processor, combine the parsley with the mint, garlic and fresh lemon juice and pulse until finely chopped. With the machine on, slowly pour in the remaining ⅔ cup of olive oil until the sauce is smooth. Season the herb sauce with salt and pepper.

**4.** Untie the roast and carve it into chops. Transfer to a platter, top with some of the herb sauce and serve the remaining herb sauce on the side. —*Trevor Kaufman*
**MAKE AHEAD** The herb sauce can be refrigerated for up to 2 days.
**WINE** Tannic, complex Cabernet.

### Vietnamese Grilled Pork Meatball Sandwiches

**ACTIVE: 40 MIN; TOTAL: 1 HR 30 MIN**
**6 SERVINGS** ●

These pork grinders, topped with cilantro and pickled carrots and served on baguettes, are modeled on the classic French-Vietnamese sandwich *banh mi.*

- 2 tablespoons plus 1 teaspoon vegetable oil, plus more for brushing
- 2 large garlic cloves, minced
- 2 Thai chiles or 1 large jalapeño, minced
- 1 large shallot, thinly sliced
- 3 tablespoons rice wine or dry white wine
- One 16-ounce can plain tomato sauce
- 3½ tablespoons Asian fish sauce
- 1½ pounds ground pork
- ½ cup minced onion
- 4 canned water chestnuts, minced
- 3 tablespoons cornstarch
- 2 tablespoons chopped cilantro leaves, plus 12 large sprigs
- 1 tablespoon Korean-style kimchi (see Note)
- 2 teaspoons soy sauce
- 1½ teaspoons freshly ground pepper
- ½ teaspoon Asian sesame oil
- 1 large egg beaten with 2 tablespoons water
- Six 6-inch French bread rolls or pieces of baguette
- Quick Pickled Carrots (recipe follows)
- Hot sauce, for serving

**1.** Soak six 10-inch bamboo skewers in water for 20 minutes; drain.

**2.** Meanwhile, in a medium skillet, heat 2 tablespoons of the vegetable oil. Add the garlic, chiles and shallot and cook over moderate heat until softened, about 3 minutes. Add the rice wine and bring to a boil. Stir in the tomato sauce and simmer, stirring occasionally, until the sauce is thickened, about 10 minutes. Stir in 1 tablespoon of the fish sauce.

**3.** In a large bowl, gently mix the ground pork with the onion, water chestnuts, cornstarch, chopped cilantro, kimchi, soy sauce, pepper, sesame oil, beaten egg mixture and the remaining 1 teaspoon of vegetable oil and 2½ tablespoons of fish sauce. Using moistened hands, roll the mixture into 30 meatballs. Thread the meatballs onto the skewers and refrigerate until chilled.

**4.** Light a grill. Lightly brush the meatballs with vegetable oil and grill over a hot fire until well browned and cooked through, about 10 minutes.

**5.** Halve the rolls lengthwise without cutting all the way through. Halve the meatballs, stuff them into the rolls and spoon the tomato sauce over them. Top with the Quick Pickled Carrots and cilantro sprigs and serve with hot sauce. —*Charles Phan*
**NOTE** Kimchi, spicy pickled, fermented cabbage, is available at Asian markets and many supermarkets.

**MAKE AHEAD** The raw meatballs can be refrigerated overnight.
**WINE** Round, supple, fruity Syrah.

### QUICK PICKLED CARROTS

**ACTIVE: 10 MIN; TOTAL: 40 MIN**
**MAKES ABOUT 4 CUPS** ● ●

- ½ cup sugar
- ½ teaspoon salt
- ½ cup distilled white vinegar
- 3 large carrots, julienned on a mandoline or shredded

In a bowl, stir the sugar and salt into the vinegar until completely dissolved. Add the julienned carrots and cover with plastic wrap. Let the carrots marinate for at least 30 minutes at room temperature or refrigerate overnight. —*C.P.*

# ingredient

**MAIL-ORDER PORK** | **TIP**

**BACON** Flying Pigs Farm produces theirs from heritage pigs. It's succulent but not greasy (518-854-3844 or flyingpigsfarm.com). Nueske's peppery smoked bacon has been made by the Nueske family in Wisconsin since 1933 (800-392-2266 or nueskes.com). **HAM** Karl Ehmer's Old Country Ham is juicy, salty and subtly smoky (800-487-5275 or karlehmer.com). Snake River Farms, based in Idaho, cures its well-marbled meat from Kurobuta (a.k.a. Japanese black) pigs (snakeriverfarms.com). **SAUSAGE** Virginia-based Edwards' hickory-smoked sausages are a standout (800-222-4267), and Niman Ranch produces innovative sausages, like cranberry-orange (nimanranch.com).

**ASTURIAN PORK AND BEANS**

**SAUSAGE AND BROCCOLI RABE BURGER**

### Asturian Pork and Beans

**ACTIVE: 30 MIN; TOTAL: 2 HR 45 MIN,
PLUS OVERNIGHT FOR SOAKING THE
BEANS**

**6 SERVINGS** ●

This dish is called *fabada asturiana*
because it is regarded as the signature
dish of Asturias, Spain. Traditional versions use Asturian *fabes* (fava beans)
and blood sausage, which is replaced
here with a meaty ham hock.

- 1 **pound dried *fabes,* cannellini
  or other large white beans—
  picked over, rinsed and
  soaked overnight**
- 1 **large onion, peeled**
- 1 **head garlic**
- 1 **tablespoon smoked *pimentón*
  (Spanish paprika)**
- **Large pinch of saffron
  threads, crushed**
- 1 **meaty fresh ham hock
  (1 pound)**
- ½ **pound slab bacon, in one piece**
- 12 **cups cold water**
- ½ **pound semi-dry Spanish-style
  chorizos**
- **Salt and freshly ground pepper**

**1.** Drain the beans and transfer them to
a large enameled cast-iron casserole.
Add the onion, garlic, *pimentón,* crushed
saffron, ham hock, bacon and cold water
to the casserole and bring to a boil.
Reduce the heat to moderate and simmer the stew, tucking the ham hock under
the cooking liquid as necessary, until the
beans are almost tender, about 1 hour
and 30 minutes.

**2.** Add the chorizos to the stew and cook
until the meat and beans are tender and
the cooking liquid is thick and slightly
reduced, about 45 minutes longer.

**3.** Discard the onion and garlic and
transfer the meat to a bowl. Pull the meat
from the ham hock and cut it into large
pieces. Cut the bacon and chorizos into
pieces. Add the meat to the beans and
season lightly with salt and pepper.
—*José Andrés*

**MAKE AHEAD** The pork and beans can be
refrigerated for up to 1 week. Reheat and
season just before serving.
**WINE** Assertive, heady Grenache.

### Sausage and Broccoli Rabe Burgers

**TOTAL: 35 MIN**

**6 SERVINGS** ●

- ½ **pound thinly sliced pancetta**
- 1 **pound ground pork**
- ½ **pound ground veal**
- ½ **pound ground beef chuck**
- **Kosher salt**

½ teaspoon ground cinnamon

½ teaspoon ground allspice

¼ teaspoon ground cloves

¼ teaspoon freshly grated nutmeg

2 large bunches broccoli rabe (about 2½-pounds), large stems trimmed

2 tablespoons extra-virgin olive oil

2 medium garlic cloves, minced

¾ teaspoon crushed red pepper

Freshly ground pepper

6 ounces Italian Fontina cheese, cut into 6 slices

6 kaiser rolls, split and toasted

**1.** Lay the pancetta on a baking sheet lined with plastic wrap and freeze until firm. Finely chop the pancetta, transfer to a food processor and pulse until minced.

**2.** In a large bowl, combine the ground pork, veal and beef with the minced pancetta. In a small bowl, combine 1 teaspoon of salt with the cinnamon, allspice, cloves and nutmeg. Sprinkle the spices over the meat and mix thoroughly but gently with your hands. Pat the meat into 6 burgers and refrigerate.

**3.** Light a grill. In a pot of boiling salted water, cook the broccoli rabe until tender, about 2 minutes. Drain, lightly squeeze out any excess water and coarsely chop.

**4.** Heat the olive oil in a large skillet. Add the garlic and crushed red pepper and cook over moderate heat until fragrant, about 1 minute. Add the broccoli rabe and cook, stirring, until heated through. Season with salt and pepper.

**5.** Season the burgers with pepper and grill over a hot fire until cooked through, about 5 minutes per side. Melt the Fontina on the burgers about 1 minute before they are done. Spoon the broccoli rabe onto the bottom buns, then set the burgers on top. Close the sandwiches and serve at once. —*Marc Vetri*

**MAKE AHEAD** The uncooked burgers can be refrigerated overnight.

**WINE** Intense, berry-flavored Zinfandel.

## Sausage Burgers with Grilled Green Chiles

**TOTAL: 1 HR**

6 SERVINGS ●

2½ pounds ground pork

2 tablespoons minced garlic, plus 4 garlic cloves thinly sliced

2 tablespoons balsamic vinegar

1 teaspoon crushed red pepper

1 teaspoon chopped thyme

Kosher salt and freshly ground pepper

5 large fresh Anaheim chiles

1 large poblano chile

2 tablespoons extra-virgin olive oil

½ teaspoon chopped rosemary

6 ounces Gruyère or Italian Fontina cheese, cut into 6 slices about ¼ inch thick

6 ciabatta or kaiser rolls, split and lightly toasted

¼ cup plus 2 tablespoons whole-grain or Dijon mustard

2 cups arugula leaves

1 large Creole tomato (see Note) or beefsteak tomato, cut into 6 slices

**1.** In a large bowl, gently mix the ground pork with the minced garlic, balsamic vinegar, crushed red pepper, chopped thyme, 1 tablespoon of salt and 2 teaspoons of black pepper. Pat the meat into 6 burgers, cover them with plastic wrap and refrigerate.

**2.** Light a grill. Grill the Anaheim and poblano chiles over a hot fire, turning, until charred all over. Transfer to a bowl, cover with plastic wrap and let steam for 10 minutes. Peel, stem and seed the chiles, then cut them into long, thin strips. Transfer the chiles to a bowl and add the olive oil, rosemary and sliced garlic. Season with salt and pepper.

**3.** Grill the burgers over a hot fire until just cooked through, about 5 minutes per side. About 1 minute before the sausage burgers are done, place a slice of cheese on each one.

**4.** Spread the bottom half of each roll with 1 tablespoon of mustard. Top with the arugula and a tomato slice. Set the burgers on the tomato slices and cover with the marinated chiles. Close the sandwiches and serve. —*Donald Link*

**NOTE** Creole tomatoes are a large, juicy, bright red variety grown in the hot and humid Mississippi Delta region of Louisiana. They have a lower acid content and meatier texture than other tomatoes.

**MAKE AHEAD** The uncooked burgers can be refrigerated overnight.

**WINE** Plummy, earthy Malbec.

## equipment

**ELECTRIC GRILL**　　**TIP**

**GEORGE FOREMAN INDOOR/ OUTDOOR BBQ** The nonstick surface of this electric grill heats up quickly, creating a good crust and sear marks on burgers and salmon; the fat flows down a sloping grate, away from the food. Although this grill is larger than most indoor models, it can still sit on a kitchen counter. The appliance also comes with a detachable pedestal, so it's easy to use outdoors ($60; 888-889-0899 or esalton.com).

# pork + veal

### Chorizos Braised in Hard Cider

**ACTIVE: 15 MIN; TOTAL: 45 MIN**

**6 SERVINGS** ● ●

Hard cider is sweet apple cider that has been allowed to ferment. Hard ciders are generally sold at liquor stores, but those with a lower alcohol content may be available at some supermarkets.

- 6 **semi-dry Spanish-style chorizos (2 ounces each)**
- 2 **tablespoons extra-virgin olive oil**

**One 24-ounce bottle hard apple cider**

**Crusty bread, for serving**

**1.** Make four ½-inch-deep slashes on one side of each chorizo. In a medium, deep skillet, heat the olive oil until shimmering. Add the chorizos and cook over moderate heat, turning occasionally, until lightly browned, about 5 minutes.

**2.** Add the hard cider to the skillet and bring to a boil over high heat. Reduce the heat to moderate and cook, turning occasionally, until the chorizos are softened and the liquid is reduced to ⅔ cup, about 30 minutes. Transfer the chorizos and sauce to a shallow bowl and serve with hunks of crusty bread.

*—José Andrés*

**MAKE AHEAD** The chorizos can be cooked earlier in the day. Rewarm them over low heat in a covered skillet.

**WINE** Soft, earthy Rioja.

### Crispy Fresh Ham with Rum Sauce

**ACTIVE: 1 HR; TOTAL: 6 HR 45 MIN, PLUS OVERNIGHT MARINATING**

**8 TO 12 SERVINGS**

Fresh hams, or whole uncured pork legs or half legs, need to be special ordered from your butcher, but they are great for large parties and guarantee delicious leftovers.

- 3 **cups plus 2 tablespoons Sofrito (recipe follows)**
- 1 **cup plus 2 tablespoons vegetable oil**
- ¾ **cup dry white wine**
- ¼ **cup achiote (annatto) seeds**
- 2 **tablespoons dried oregano**
- 6 **large garlic cloves, 4 minced, 2 thinly sliced**

**Kosher salt**

**One 14-pound bone-in fresh ham from the shank end (half leg), skin removed, fat scored**

- 2 **medium red onions, thinly sliced**
- 2 **medium red bell peppers, thinly sliced**
- 2 **medium green bell peppers, thinly sliced**
- 1 **cup Spanish pimiento-stuffed olives, thickly sliced**
- 1 **cup white vinegar**
- 8 **bananas, sliced ½ inch thick**

**Freshly ground pepper**

- ½ **cup dark rum**
- ½ **cup water**

**1.** In a large bowl, mix 2 cups of the Sofrito with 1 cup of the vegetable oil, the white wine, achiote seeds, oregano, minced garlic and 1 tablespoon of salt; let the marinade stand for 30 minutes. Set the ham in a large roasting pan and rub it all over with the marinade. Refrigerate the ham overnight.

**2.** Preheat the oven to 400°. Add 1 inch of water to the roasting pan and roast the ham for 45 minutes. Reduce the oven temperature to 275° and roast the ham for 5 hours, or until an instant-read thermometer inserted in the thickest part of the meat registers 155°.

**3.** Meanwhile, in a very large skillet, heat the remaining 2 tablespoons of oil until shimmering. Add the onions, red and green bell peppers, olives, 2 tablespoons of the Sofrito and the thinly sliced garlic and cook over moderately low heat until the vegetables just begin to soften, about 6 minutes. Add the vinegar and simmer for 3 minutes. Stir in the bananas and season with salt and pepper.

**4.** Transfer the ham to a carving board and cover loosely with foil. Set the roasting pan over 2 burners and bring the pan juices to a boil. Add the rum and simmer for 2 minutes. Strain the pan juices into a bowl and skim off the fat. Pour the juices into a medium saucepan. Stir in the water and the remaining 1 cup of Sofrito and boil over moderate heat until reduced by half. Strain the sauce through a fine sieve, pressing on the solids. Season

# equipment

with salt and pepper. Carve the ham and serve with the rum sauce and the pepper-banana sauté. —*Linda Japngie*

**MAKE AHEAD** The pepper-banana sauté can be refrigerated overnight. Reheat gently before serving.

**WINE** Light, fruity Pinot Noir.

### SOFRITO

**ACTIVE: 25 MIN; TOTAL: 40 MIN**
**MAKES ABOUT 4 CUPS** ● ●

Spanish and Latin American cooks use aromatic sofritos—sautéed mixtures of herbs, peppers, garlic, onions, spices and tomatoes—to flavor many dishes. You can also stir them into omelets, soups and stews.

- ¼ cup extra-virgin olive oil
- 1 large onion, finely chopped
- 8 large garlic cloves, very finely chopped
- 4 green bell peppers, chopped
- 2 jalapeños, seeded and very finely chopped

Large pinch of cayenne pepper

- 2 medium tomatoes, seeded and chopped, or one 28-ounce can peeled tomatoes, drained and chopped

Salt and freshly ground black pepper

- ½ cup chopped cilantro

Heat the olive oil in a large skillet. Add the onion and cook over low heat until softened, about 4 minutes. Add the garlic, green bell peppers, jalapeños and cayenne pepper and cook, stirring occasionally, until the vegetables are softened, about 20 minutes. Add the tomatoes and cook over moderately high heat, stirring frequently, until the juices have evaporated, about 7 minutes. Season with salt and black pepper and stir in the cilantro. —*L.J.*

**MAKE AHEAD** The Sofrito can be stored in an airtight container and refrigerated for up to 1 week.

### Dulce de Leche–Glazed Ham

**ACTIVE: 25 MIN; TOTAL: 3 HR**
**12 SERVINGS** ● ●

- ½ cup dulce de leche (see Note)
- ¼ cup plus 2 tablespoons Dijon mustard
- 2 tablespoons whole-grain mustard
- 1 large garlic clove, minced
- ¼ teaspoon cayenne pepper
- 1¼ cups chicken stock or low-sodium broth

One 10-pound bone-in smoked ham

- 1 medium onion, thinly sliced

**1.** Preheat the oven to 375°. In a bowl, whisk the dulce de leche with the Dijon and whole-grain mustards, the garlic and the cayenne. Whisk in ¼ cup of the stock.

**2.** Trim the skin off the ham, leaving a ¼-inch-thick layer of fat. Score the fat in a shallow crosshatch pattern. Spread the onion slices in a large roasting pan. Set the ham on top and add ½ cup of the stock. Cover the ham directly with parchment paper; cover the roasting pan tightly with foil. Roast the ham for 1¼ hours.

**3.** Remove the foil and parchment. Brush the ham generously with all but ¼ cup of the dulce de leche glaze. Roast the ham for 1 hour longer, or until nicely glazed all over. Transfer the ham to a cutting board and let rest for at least 15 minutes.

**4.** Meanwhile, pour the pan drippings into a small saucepan and skim off as much of the fat as possible. Set the roasting pan over 2 burners. Add the remaining ½ cup of stock and cook, scraping up any browned bits from the bottom and sides of the pan. Pour the liquid into the saucepan. Whisk in the remaining ¼ cup of dulce de leche glaze and bring to a boil. Transfer to a warmed gravy boat. Thinly slice the ham and serve with the gravy. —*Grace Parisi*

**NOTE** Dulce de leche, a sauce made by boiling whole milk with sugar until it's caramel-like, is available at specialty food shops and Latin markets.

**MAKE AHEAD** The glazed ham can be baked 2 hours ahead and served at room temperature.

**WINE** Dry, rich Champagne.

### Braised Veal Chops with Honey and Red Grapes

**TOTAL: 30 MIN**
**6 SERVINGS** ● ●

The area around Ancona, capital of Le Marche, Italy, is known for its corbezzolo honey, which has a slightly bitter finish that's delicious in savory dishes like this braised veal.

- ½ cup extra-virgin olive oil
- 6 anchovy fillets, very finely chopped

Six ½-pound veal rib chops, cut about ¾ inch thick

Salt and freshly ground black pepper

- 1 cup dry white wine
- 6 sage leaves
- 3 whole cloves
- 2 bay leaves
- 1 cup chicken stock or low-sodium broth
- 1½ cups seedless red grapes
- 3 tablespoons honey

**1.** In a very large skillet, heat the olive oil. Add the anchovies and cook over moderately low heat, mashing the anchovies until pureed, about 3 minutes. Increase the heat to high.

# pairing

MEAT + SAKE                              **TIP**

Sake pairs nicely with lean meats like veal, lamb and the less fatty cuts of pork. Aged sakes, which are not graded, have rich flavors that stand up to meat. Try the sherrylike Narutotai Daikoshu or the amber-colored Yashiorino.

● FAST     ● HEALTHY     ● MAKE AHEAD     ● STAFF FAVORITE                                157

**2.** Season the veal chops with salt and pepper. Add them to the skillet and cook until browned, about 3 minutes per side. Transfer the chops to a platter.

**3.** Add the wine, sage, cloves and bay leaves to the skillet and cook over moderately high heat until the wine is reduced to 2 tablespoons, about 5 minutes. Add the stock and bring to a boil. Add the veal chops and their juices, cover and simmer over low heat until the chops are barely pink in the center, about 3 minutes per side. Return the chops to the platter and cover loosely with foil.

**4.** Add the grapes and honey to the skillet, cover and cook over moderate heat until the grapes are tender, about 4 minutes. Scatter the grapes over the chops. Boil the pan juices over high heat until reduced to 1 cup, about 5 minutes. Discard the cloves and bay leaves. Pour the sauce over the chops and serve.
—*Fabio Trabocchi*

**WINE** Tart, low-tannin Barbera.

### Lemon-Parmesan Veal Rolls with Arugula Salad
**TOTAL: 25 MIN**
**6 SERVINGS** ● ● ●
You can substitute thinly sliced sirloin or chicken breast cutlets for the veal in this fast and healthy dish.

- ¼ cup plus 2 tablespoons freshly grated Parmesan cheese
- 2 tablespoons chopped chives
- 2 tablespoons minced parsley
- 1 teaspoon finely grated lemon zest
- 1½ pounds thin veal cutlets, cut into pieces about 2-by-3 inches
- Salt and freshly ground pepper
- 2 tablespoons extra-virgin olive oil, plus more for brushing
- 2 tablespoons fresh lemon juice
- 2 bunches arugula, tough stems discarded (10 ounces)
- ¼ cup very thinly sliced sweet onion

**1.** Light a grill. In a small bowl, mix the Parmesan cheese with the chopped chives, parsley and lemon zest. Spread the veal pieces on a work surface and season them with salt and pepper. Sprinkle ¼ cup of the Parmesan mixture on the veal and roll the pieces up to form neat cylinders.

**2.** Thread the veal rolls onto pairs of parallel bamboo or metal skewers, leaving ¼ inch between each of the rolls. Lightly brush the rolls with olive oil and season with salt and pepper. Grill over a hot fire, turning the skewers once or twice, until the veal is lightly charred but still slightly pink in the center, about 6 minutes. Transfer the grilled veal rolls to a large serving platter.

**3.** Meanwhile, in a large bowl, combine the lemon juice with the 2 tablespoons of olive oil and season with salt and pepper. Add the arugula and sliced onion and toss well to coat. Mound the salad on the platter beside the veal skewers, sprinkle with the remaining Parmesan cheese mixture and serve immediately.
—*Grace Parisi*

**MAKE AHEAD** The veal skewers can be refrigerated overnight. Let them return to room temperature before grilling.

**WINE** Tart, low-tannin Barbera.

### Easter Veal Loin with Fennel–Lima Bean Puree
**ACTIVE: 40 MIN; TOTAL: 3 HR 15 MIN**
**6 SERVINGS**

- 1 pound dried large lima beans
- 2 garlic cloves, minced
- 2 medium fennel bulbs—halved, cored and finely chopped, plus 2 tablespoons minced fennel fronds
- ½ small onion, minced
- 1 teaspoon finely grated lemon zest
- One 4-pound boneless veal loin, tied at 2-inch intervals with kitchen string
- Salt and freshly ground black pepper
- ½ cup Dijon mustard blended with ½ cup crème fraîche
- 10 sage leaves
- 1½ teaspoons fennel seeds, lightly toasted and finely ground

**1.** In a large saucepan, cover the lima beans with 4 inches of water and bring to a boil. Simmer over low heat for 1 hour, then add water to cover by 2 inches. Add the garlic, chopped fennel bulb, minced onion and grated lemon zest. Boil over moderately high heat for 15 minutes, stirring often. Reduce the heat to low and simmer, stirring occasionally, until the lima beans and fennel become a thick and creamy puree, about 2 hours.

**2.** Meanwhile, preheat the oven to 450°. Season the veal loin all over with salt and pepper and place it fat side down on a rack set in a medium roasting pan. Spread half of the mustard cream over the veal and press half of the sage leaves on top. Put the veal loin in the oven, reduce the temperature to 300° and roast for 45 minutes. Carefully turn the veal fat side up; spread with the remaining mustard cream and top with the remaining sage leaves. Roast for 1 hour longer, or until an instant-read thermometer inserted in the thickest part of the meat registers 145°. Transfer the veal to a carving board and let it rest for about 10 minutes.

**3.** Stir the ground fennel seeds into the fennel-lima puree. Season with salt and pepper. Discard the kitchen string and slice the meat thickly. Transfer the veal to plates and spoon the fennel-lima puree alongside. Garnish with the fennel fronds.
—*Jim Clendenen*

**MAKE AHEAD** The fennel–lima bean puree can be refrigerated overnight. Reheat gently before serving.

**SERVE WITH** Sautéed wild mushrooms.

**WINE** Ripe, oaky Chardonnay.

EASTER VEAL LOIN WITH FENNEL—LIMA BEAN PUREE

SWEET-AND-SOUR SWORDFISH, P. 168

# fish

**SALMON WITH CUCUMBER AND FENNEL**

**SALMON ROLLS WITH CREOLE MUSTARD SPAETZLE**

### Salmon with Saffron-Braised Cucumber and Fennel

**TOTAL: 25 MIN**

4 SERVINGS ● ●

Buy round fennel bulbs—they tend to be less stringy than slimmer ones.

¼ cup plus 1 tablespoon extra-virgin olive oil

2 small fennel bulbs (1½ pounds)—halved, cored and cut into ½-inch dice

2 cucumbers—peeled, seeded and cut into ½-inch dice

¼ cup dry white wine

Pinch of saffron threads

1½ cups vegetable stock or low-sodium broth

1½ pounds skinless center-cut salmon fillet, cut into 1½-inch pieces

Salt and freshly ground pepper

1 tablespoon all-purpose flour

**1.** In a large saucepan, heat ¼ cup of the olive oil. Add the diced fennel and cook over moderate heat for 2 minutes. Add the diced cucumber and cook for 2 minutes. Add the wine and saffron and cook, stirring occasionally, until the wine has reduced by half, about 2 minutes. Add the vegetable stock and cook until the fennel is tender, 10 minutes.

**2.** Meanwhile, season the salmon pieces with salt and pepper and dust them lightly with the flour. In a large nonstick skillet, heat the remaining 1 tablespoon of olive oil. Add the salmon pieces and cook over moderately high heat until barely cooked through, about 3 minutes per side. Transfer the salmon pieces to the saucepan and cook for 1 minute. Season the salmon with salt and pepper and serve at once. —*Galen Zamarra*

**WINE** Dry, full-flavored Alsace Riesling.

### Salmon Rolls with Fennel and Creole Mustard Spaetzle

**ACTIVE: 1 HR 15 MIN; TOTAL: 1 HR 40 MIN**

4 SERVINGS

2 fennel bulbs, cut into 16 wedges

2 tablespoons extra-virgin olive oil

Salt and freshly ground pepper

2 tablespoons Pernod

1 cup heavy cream

4 whole star anise, crushed

1 teaspoon unsalted butter

2 tablespoons finely chopped shallot

1 large garlic clove, minced

1 teaspoon finely grated lemon zest

1 teaspoon finely grated orange zest

1½ tablespoons fine dry bread crumbs

2 tablespoons finely chopped flat-leaf parsley

Two 12-ounce skinless center-cut salmon fillets, butterflied (see Note)

Creole Mustard Spaetzle (recipe follows)

1. Preheat the oven to 425°. In a medium roasting pan, toss the fennel with the olive oil and season with salt and pepper. Roast the fennel for 30 minutes, turning halfway through, or until tender and browned.

2. Meanwhile, in a small saucepan, bring the Pernod to a boil. Add the heavy cream and star anise and simmer over moderate heat until reduced to ¾ cup, about 8 minutes. Strain the cream and season with salt and pepper.

3. Light a grill. In a small skillet, melt the butter. Add the shallot and garlic and cook over moderate heat, stirring, until softened, about 1 minute. Remove from the heat. Stir in the lemon and orange zests, the bread crumbs and the parsley and let cool.

4. Spread open the salmon fillets, season them with salt and pepper and sprinkle with the parsley mixture. Starting at the thinner end, roll each fillet into a log. Tie the logs at each end with kitchen string, then cut each log into 2 equal pieces; you should have 4 rolls secured with kitchen string.

5. Season the salmon rolls with salt and pepper and grill over a medium-hot fire for 6 minutes, turning once. Move the salmon rolls to indirect heat and continue grilling until just barely cooked through, about 3 minutes longer. Transfer to a plate and carefully remove the strings. Rewarm the fennel and the Pernod cream sauce.

6. Spoon the Creole Mustard Spaetzle onto 4 large plates. Set the salmon on the spaetzle, arrange the fennel wedges around it and spoon the sauce around the fish. Serve right away. —*Mat Wolf*

**NOTE** To butterfly the salmon, make a horizontal slice at the thinnest side of the fillet, cutting three-quarters of the way through toward the thicker side. Alternatively, have your fishmonger butterfly the fillets for you.

**WINE** Spicy Alsace Gewürztraminer.

## CREOLE MUSTARD SPAETZLE
**TOTAL: 30 MIN**
4 SERVINGS ● ● ●

- 3 large eggs, beaten
- ½ cup milk
- ½ cup Creole or other grainy mustard
- Salt and freshly ground pepper
- 1 cup all-purpose flour
- 2 tablespoons unsalted butter

1. In a medium bowl, whisk the eggs, milk, mustard and a generous pinch each of salt and pepper. Whisk in the flour; the batter will be stiff. Refrigerate for at least 10 minutes or for up to 4 hours.

2. Set a colander with large holes (at least ¼ inch) over a large pot of boiling salted water. Add the spaetzle batter and scrape it back and forth with a rubber spatula, pressing it through the holes into the boiling water. Stir the spaetzle once or twice to separate them and simmer until firm, 2 to 3 minutes. Drain in a clean colander.

3. In a large nonstick skillet, melt the butter. Add the spaetzle and cook over moderately high heat, tossing, until lightly golden, 5 minutes. Serve hot. —*M.W.*

**MAKE AHEAD** The spaetzle can be boiled 6 hours ahead. Sauté before serving.

## Grilled Salmon with Mustard Sauce
**TOTAL: 15 MIN**
4 SERVINGS ●

- 5 tablespoons extra-virgin olive oil
- 5 tablespoons minced tarragon
- Four 6-ounce salmon fillets, with skin
- Salt and freshly ground pepper
- ⅔ cup crème fraîche
- ¼ cup Dijon mustard
- 2 tablespoons drained prepared horseradish

1. Light a gas grill or preheat a cast-iron grill pan. In a bowl, mix 3 tablespoons of the olive oil with 3 tablespoons of the tarragon and rub it over the salmon. Let stand for 5 minutes, then season with salt and pepper and grill over medium-high heat, turning once, until crisp on the outside and just barely cooked through, about 8 minutes. Transfer to a plate.

2. Meanwhile, in a small bowl, combine the crème fraîche, mustard, horseradish and the remaining olive oil and tarragon. Season the sauce with salt and pepper, spoon over the salmon and serve. —*Jamie Samford*

**WINE** Subtle, complex white Burgundy.

## Asian Watercress Salad with Salmon
**TOTAL: 30 MIN**
4 SERVINGS ● ●

- 3 tablespoons plus 2 teaspoons vegetable oil
- 2 tablespoons sherry vinegar
- 1 teaspoon Thai red curry paste or Asian chili paste
- 1 teaspoon soy sauce
- 1 teaspoon Dijon mustard
- Salt and freshly ground pepper
- Four 6-ounce skinless salmon fillets
- 1 bunch watercress (6 ounces), large stems discarded
- ½ cup mung bean sprouts
- 1 tablespoon chopped mint
- 1 tablespoon chopped cilantro
- 1 tablespoon chopped peanuts

1. Preheat the oven to 400°. In a small bowl, whisk together 3 tablespoons of the oil with the sherry vinegar, curry paste, soy sauce and mustard and season with salt and pepper.

2. Set a large ovenproof skillet over high heat. Heat the remaining 2 teaspoons of oil in the skillet. Add the salmon fillets, skinned side up, season with salt and pepper and cook until browned on the bottom, about 3 minutes. Turn the fillets. Transfer the skillet to the oven and bake for about 5 minutes, or until just cooked through. Transfer the salmon to a platter and let cool to warm, then break it up into chunks.

# fish

**3.** Meanwhile, in a large bowl, toss the watercress with the bean sprouts, mint, cilantro and peanuts. Add 5 tablespoons of the dressing and toss to coat. Mound the salad on plates and top with the salmon. Dab the remaining dressing on the salmon and serve. —*Eric Ripert*
**WINE** Dry, fruity sparkling wine.

## Pan-Fried Salmon Burgers with Cabbage Slaw and Avocado Aioli

**ACTIVE: 1 HR; TOTAL: 3 HR**
**6 SERVINGS** ●

Don't be put off by the long list of ingredients: Everything is easy to assemble and can be made ahead. All you have to do is pan-fry the burgers just before serving.

1½ **pounds skinless center-cut salmon fillet, finely chopped**
½ **cup mayonnaise**
2 **tablespoons Asian fish sauce**
2 **tablespoons *sambal oelek* (see Note) or hot sauce**
2 **garlic cloves, minced**

# technique

**TIP** | **STEAMING IN FOIL**

**The easiest, most delicious way to steam fish is to cook it in foil. Here, a few flavoring tricks.**
**ADD CHOPPED HERBS, thinly sliced garlic, onions or tomatoes, which will steam while your main ingredient does; precook hard vegetables such as carrots before adding them to the pouch.**
**DRIZZLE OLIVE OIL or add a teaspoon of butter to lend a lot of flavor and only a little fat.**
**SPLASH ON WINE OR CITRUS JUICE; it will combine with any liquid the food gives off to make a simple and tasty sauce.**

1 **medium shallot, minced**
1 **tablespoon minced fresh ginger**
½ **teaspoon finely grated lemon zest**
½ **cup plus 2 tablespoons chopped cilantro**
½ **cup plus 1 tablespoon chopped mint**
**Kosher salt and freshly ground pepper**
1½ **cups Japanese *panko* or plain dry bread crumbs**
2 **tablespoons fresh lemon juice**
2 **tablespoons fresh lime juice**
2 **tablespoons unseasoned rice vinegar**
1 **teaspoon sugar**
½ **small green cabbage, shredded**
1 **small cucumber—peeled, halved lengthwise, seeded and julienned**
1 **small red onion, thinly sliced**
1 **small red bell pepper, thinly sliced**
¼ **cup sesame seeds**
¼ **cup vegetable oil**
**Avocado Aioli, for serving (recipe follows)**
6 **onion rolls, split and toasted**

**1.** In a food processor, pulse the salmon about 10 times, or until minced. Scrape the salmon into a bowl. Mix the mayonnaise with the fish sauce, *sambal oelek*, garlic, shallot, ginger, lemon zest, 2 tablespoons of the cilantro, 1 tablespoon of the mint, 1 teaspoon of salt and ½ teaspoon of pepper. Add the mixture to the salmon along with 1 cup of the *panko* and fold together with a rubber spatula. With lightly oiled hands, pat the salmon mixture into 6 burgers. Cover with plastic wrap and refrigerate for 2 hours.

**2.** Meanwhile, in a large bowl, combine the lemon and lime juice with the vinegar. Add the sugar; stir until dissolved. Add the cabbage, cucumber, onion, red pepper and the remaining ½ cup each of cilantro and mint and toss well.

**3.** In a shallow bowl, mix the remaining ½ cup of *panko* with the sesame seeds. Pat the mixture onto the salmon burgers.

**4.** In each of 2 medium nonstick skillets, heat 2 tablespoons of the oil until shimmering. Add 3 salmon burgers to each skillet and cook over moderately high heat, turning once, until well browned but barely cooked in the center, about 7 minutes.

**5.** Spread the aioli on the rolls. Add the burgers, top with the slaw, close and serve. —*Zov Karamardian*
**NOTE** *Sambal oelek,* an Indonesian chili-garlic sauce, is available at Asian markets and many supermarkets.
**MAKE AHEAD** The uncooked burgers and the slaw can be refrigerated overnight.
**WINE** Light, soft Chenin Blanc.

### AVOCADO AIOLI

**TOTAL: 10 MIN**
**MAKES ABOUT 3 CUPS** ● ● ●

3 **Hass avocados**
½ **cup sour cream**
3 **tablespoons chopped basil**
2 **tablespoons minced garlic**
2 **tablespoons fresh lemon juice**
2 **tablespoons fresh lime juice**
1 **seeded serrano chile or unseeded jalapeño, minced**
1 **small shallot, minced**
**Salt and freshly ground pepper**

In a medium bowl, coarsely mash the avocados with a fork. Fold in the sour cream, basil, garlic, lemon juice, lime juice, chile and shallot. Season with salt and pepper and serve. —*Z.K.*
**MAKE AHEAD** The aioli can be covered with plastic wrap pressed directly onto the surface and refrigerated overnight.

## Poached Salmon in a Fresh Herb and Spring Pea Broth

**ACTIVE: 20 MIN; TOTAL: 40 MIN**
**6 SERVINGS** ● ●

1 **bunch tarragon, 1 tablespoon chopped**
1 **bunch chives, 1 tablespoon chopped**
3 **cups water**

1 cup dry white wine

1 cup flat-leaf parsley leaves

3 medium scallions, white and tender green parts only, cut into thirds

2 celery ribs with leaves, cut into thirds

2 garlic cloves, smashed

2 thyme sprigs

1 teaspoon coriander seeds

½ teaspoon black peppercorns

One 1½-by-½-inch strip of lemon zest

Kosher salt

Six 6-ounce skinless center-cut salmon fillets

1 cup fresh shelled peas or frozen baby peas

¼ cup extra-virgin olive oil

**1.** In a medium saucepan, combine the unchopped tarragon and chives with the water, white wine, parsley leaves, scallions, celery, garlic, thyme, coriander seeds, black peppercorns, lemon zest and 1 teaspoon of salt. Bring to a boil, then reduce the heat to moderate and simmer the broth for 20 minutes. Strain the vegetable-herb broth into a very large skillet, then discard the solids.

**2.** Bring the vegetable-herb broth to a simmer. Season the salmon with salt and carefully add the fillets to the skillet, skinned side up. Bring the broth back to a simmer. Cover the skillet and reduce the heat to moderately low. Cook the salmon for 3 minutes, then turn the fillets and add the peas. Cover and cook until the peas are bright green and the salmon is barely cooked through, about 4 minutes.

**3.** Using a slotted spoon, transfer the salmon to bowls and scatter the peas on top. Whisk the olive oil into the broth. Pour the broth over the salmon, sprinkle with the chopped tarragon and chives and serve. —*Melissa Clark*

**MAKE AHEAD** The vegetable-herb broth can be refrigerated for up to 3 days.

**WINE** Dry, full-flavored Alsace Riesling.

**PAN-FRIED SALMON BURGER**

**SALMON IN A FRESH HERB AND SPRING PEA BROTH**

**SALMON WITH SCOTCH BONNET–HERB SAUCE AND ONION TOASTS**

## Salmon with Scotch Bonnet–Herb Sauce and Onion Toasts

**TOTAL: 45 MIN**

6 SERVINGS ●

½ cup plus 2 tablespoons
  extra-virgin olive oil

1 tablespoon Dijon mustard

Six 6- to 7-ounce center-cut salmon
  fillets, with skin

¾ cup Riesling

3 tablespoons mayonnaise

¼ cup minced chives

¼ cup chopped basil

3 tablespoons chopped cilantro

1 small Scotch bonnet chile,
  seeded and finely chopped

Salt and freshly ground pepper

2 tablespoons unsalted butter

1 large onion, thinly sliced

Twelve ¾-inch slices of sourdough
  baguette, lightly toasted

1. In a very large glass baking dish, blend 2 tablespoons of the olive oil with the mustard. Add the salmon fillets, turn to coat and refrigerate.

2. Preheat the oven to 500°. In a small saucepan, boil the Riesling over moderately high heat until reduced to ¼ cup, about 7 minutes. Remove from the heat and let cool.

3. In a medium bowl, whisk the mayonnaise with 6 tablespoons of the olive oil. Whisk in the wine reduction, chives, basil, cilantro and chile. Season the chile-herb sauce with salt and pepper.

4. Melt the butter in a medium skillet. Add the onion and cook over moderate heat until softened and starting to brown, about 8 minutes. Place the baguette toasts on a baking sheet and top with the onion. Bake in the upper third of the oven for 1 minute.

5. Meanwhile, in each of 2 medium skillets, heat 1 tablespoon of the remaining olive oil until shimmering. Season the salmon fillets all over with salt and pepper and add 3 fillets to each skillet, skin side down. Cook over high heat until the skin is browned and crisp, about 4 minutes. Turn the fillets and cook them over moderately high heat until they are an even pink throughout, about 5 minutes.

6. Spoon the chile-herb sauce onto plates. Top with the fillets and serve with the onion toasts. —Marcia Kiesel

**MAKE AHEAD** The salmon can marinate in the refrigerator overnight.

**WINE** Dry, full-flavored Alsace Riesling.

## Steamed Ginger Salmon with Stir-Fried Bok Choy

**ACTIVE: 20 MIN; TOTAL: 50 MIN**

4 SERVINGS ●

STEAMED SALMON

2 tablespoons Chinese cooking
  wine (Shao-Hsing) or dry sherry

2 tablespoons plus 1 teaspoon
  low-sodium soy sauce

2¼ teaspoons sugar

Four 5-ounce skinless center-cut
  salmon fillets

2½ tablespoons low-sodium
  chicken broth

1½ teaspoons rice vinegar

2 teaspoons finely grated fresh
  ginger plus ¼ cup finely
  julienned ginger

1 small garlic clove, smashed

1½ teaspoons Asian sesame oil

2 small scallions, thinly sliced

BOK CHOY

1½ tablespoons peanut oil

1 teaspoon Asian sesame oil

6 garlic cloves, sliced

1 teaspoon finely grated fresh ginger

¼ teaspoon Chinese chili paste

1½ pounds bok choy, sliced
  crosswise ½ inch thick

Salt

3 tablespoons low-sodium
  chicken broth

2 tablespoons Chinese cooking
  wine (Shao-Hsing) or dry sherry

1½ teaspoons low-sodium soy sauce

1. PREPARE THE SALMON: In a small bowl, combine the Chinese cooking wine with 1 tablespoon of the soy sauce and 1 teaspoon of the sugar. Put the salmon on a heatproof plate that will fit snugly into a steamer or deep skillet with a tight-fitting lid. Pour the soy mixture on top of the salmon, turn to coat and let stand for 30 minutes.

2. In a small bowl, combine the chicken broth with the rice vinegar, grated ginger, garlic, ½ teaspoon of the sesame oil and half of the scallions. Add the remaining 1 tablespoon plus 1 teaspoon of soy sauce and 1¼ teaspoons of sugar.

3. Pour off the marinade from the salmon and brush the fillets with the remaining 1 teaspoon of sesame oil. Scatter the julienned ginger on top of the fish, cover and steam until barely cooked through, about 8 minutes. Sprinkle the remaining scallions on top of the salmon and steam for 1 minute longer.

4. MEANWHILE, MAKE THE BOK CHOY: Heat a large wok or skillet until very hot. Add the peanut oil and sesame oil and heat until just smoking. Add the garlic, ginger and chili paste and stir-fry until lightly browned, about 30 seconds. Add the bok choy and a pinch of salt and stir-fry until crisp-tender, about 5 minutes. Add the chicken broth, cooking wine and soy sauce and cook, tossing to coat the bok choy, for 2 minutes longer.

5. Transfer the salmon and greens to plates and pass the sauce at the table. —Anya von Bremzen

**WINE** Dry, full-flavored Alsace Riesling.

## Chile-Rubbed Swordfish Kebabs with Cucumber Salad

**TOTAL: 20 MIN**

6 SERVINGS ● ● ●

A source of omega-3 fatty acids, swordfish is an extra-healthy choice, but the assertive spice rub here also works well on shrimp and pork tenderloin.

# fish

Vegetable oil, for the grill

1½ tablespoons pure ancho
chile powder

¾ teaspoon ground cumin

¾ teaspoon ground coriander

Scant ½ teaspoon caraway seeds

Scant ½ teaspoon cayenne pepper

3 large garlic cloves, smashed

¼ cup extra-virgin olive oil

Salt and freshly ground pepper

2 pounds skinless swordfish
steaks (¾ inch thick), cut
into 1-inch pieces

3 tablespoons fresh lime juice

¾ teaspoon sugar

4 kirby cucumbers, thinly sliced

½ small red onion, thinly sliced

1 small green chile, such as
serrano, thinly sliced

3 tablespoons finely chopped mint

**1.** Light a grill. Lightly oil the grate. In a medium bowl, combine the ancho powder, cumin, coriander, caraway seeds and cayenne pepper with the garlic and mash to a paste with the back of a spoon. Stir in the olive oil and season generously with salt and pepper. Add the swordfish and toss well to coat. Thread the swordfish chunks on twelve 8-inch bamboo skewers.
**2.** In another medium bowl, combine the lime juice with the sugar and stir until the sugar has dissolved. Add the cucumbers, red onion, green chile and mint. Season with salt and pepper.
**3.** Season the swordfish with salt and grill the skewers over a hot fire, turning occasionally, until lightly charred and just cooked through, about 4 minutes. Transfer the swordfish skewers to a platter and serve right away with the cucumber salad. —*Grace Parisi*

**MAKE AHEAD** The swordfish can marinate for up to 4 hours in the refrigerator. Let stand at room temperature for 15 minutes before grilling.

**WINE** Fruity, low-oak Chardonnay.

## Swordfish Steaks with Mint and Garlic

**TOTAL: 15 MIN**

**10 SERVINGS** ● ● ●

Rafaella Giamundo, a talented home cook in Sorrento, Italy, always prepares these fish steaks in plenty of olive oil to make enough pan juices for dipping bread.

4 pounds swordfish steaks, about
½ inch thick

Salt and freshly ground pepper

1 cup extra-virgin olive oil

8 garlic cloves, thinly sliced

½ cup white wine vinegar

½ packed cup mint leaves

Season the swordfish with salt and pepper. In each of 2 very large skillets, heat ½ cup of the olive oil until shimmering. Add the swordfish in a single layer along with the garlic and vinegar. Cover and cook over moderate heat until the fish is opaque throughout, about 5 minutes. Add the mint and cook until wilted. Using a slotted spatula, transfer the swordfish to a large platter. Pour half of the pan juices on top and serve immediately. Pass the remaining pan juices at the table. —*Rafaella Giamundo*

**WINE** Ripe, oaky Chardonnay.

## Sweet-and-Sour Swordfish

**ACTIVE: 20 MIN; TOTAL: 1 HR**

**8 SERVINGS** ●

¼ cup plus 2 tablespoons
extra-virgin olive oil

1 large Spanish onion, thinly sliced

3 orange bell peppers, thinly sliced

2 medium tomatoes, chopped

⅔ cup dry white wine

1 teaspoon dried oregano

½ cup raisins

¼ cup fresh lime juice

¼ cup light brown sugar

½ cup chopped flat-leaf parsley

Salt and freshly ground pepper

Eight ½-pound swordfish steaks,
cut 1 inch thick

**1.** In a large enameled cast-iron casserole, heat 2 tablespoons of the olive oil. Add the onion and cook over moderately low heat, stirring occasionally, until softened, about 10 minutes. Add the bell peppers, cover and cook for 10 minutes. Add the tomatoes and cook for 5 minutes. Add the wine and simmer for 5 minutes. Add the oregano, raisins, lime juice, brown sugar and parsley; cook for 3 minutes. Season with salt and pepper.
**2.** Heat 2 tablespoons of the remaining olive oil in each of 2 large skillets. Add 4 swordfish steaks to each skillet, season with salt and pepper and cook over moderately high heat until browned on the bottom, about 5 minutes. Turn and cook 3 to 4 minutes longer. Spoon the sauce onto plates, top with the swordfish steaks and serve. —*Sylvie Chantecaille*

**WINE** Dry, fruity sparkling wine.

## Braised Swordfish with Black Olives, Tomatoes and Marjoram

**TOTAL: 35 MIN**

**6 SERVINGS** ●

3 tablespoons extra-virgin olive oil

2 garlic cloves, thinly sliced

1 jalapeño, seeded and minced

Finely grated zest of 1 small orange

2 tablespoons dry vermouth

1 bay leaf

One 28-ounce can diced tomatoes,
with their juices

Salt

1 tablespoon marjoram, chopped

Sherry vinegar

Six 7-ounce swordfish steaks, cut
1 inch thick

⅓ cup Gaeta olives, pitted and
halved

**1.** In a medium skillet, heat 2 tablespoons of the oil. Add the garlic and jalapeño and cook over moderate heat until the garlic is golden, about 2 minutes. Add the orange zest, vermouth and bay leaf and boil over moderately high heat

SWORDFISH STEAK WITH MINT AND GARLIC

# fish

until the liquid has almost evaporated, about 1 minute. Add the tomatoes and their juices and a pinch of salt; simmer over moderate heat, stirring occasionally, until slightly thickened, 10 minutes. Stir in the marjoram. Season the sauce with salt and sherry vinegar.

**2.** In a large skillet, heat the remaining 1 tablespoon of olive oil until shimmering. Season the fish with salt and add to the skillet. Cook the fish over high heat until browned, about 4 minutes per side. Add the sauce, shaking the skillet to distribute it evenly. Cover and simmer the swordfish over low heat, turning once, until the steaks are just cooked through, about 4 minutes. Using a spatula, transfer the swordfish to plates. Stir the olive halves into the sauce and season with salt and sherry vinegar; discard the bay leaf. Spoon the sauce around the steaks and serve. —*Erica De Mane*

**WINE** Round, rich Sauvignon Blanc.

## Seared Tuna with Chimichurri Sauce and Greens

**TOTAL: 30 MIN**
**4 SERVINGS** ● ●

- ½ cup plus 2 tablespoons extra-virgin olive oil
- ½ cup chopped parsley
- ½ small red onion, minced
- 3 tablespoons red wine vinegar
- 2 tablespoons chopped basil
- 2 tablespoons chopped cilantro
- 2 garlic cloves, very finely chopped
- 1 teaspoon crushed red pepper
- 1½ teaspoons chopped thyme
- Salt and freshly ground black pepper
- Four 6-ounce tuna steaks
- 8 packed cups mesclun (5 ounces)

**1.** In a small bowl, combine ½ cup of the olive oil with the parsley, red onion, vinegar, basil, cilantro, garlic, crushed red pepper and ½ teaspoon of the thyme. Season this chimichurri sauce with salt and black pepper.

**2.** Season the tuna steaks with salt, pepper and the remaining 1 teaspoon of thyme. In each of 2 skillets, heat 1 tablespoon of the remaining olive oil until shimmering. Add 2 tuna steaks to each skillet and cook over high heat until browned on the outside but rare in the center, 1 to 2 minutes per side.

**3.** In a large bowl, toss the mesclun with half of the chimichurri sauce and mound it on plates. Thinly slice the tuna steaks and set on the plates. Pass the remaining chimichurri sauce at the table to dress the tuna. —*Eric Ripert*

**WINE** Lively, assertive Sauvignon Blanc.

## Sesame-Crusted Tuna Steaks

**TOTAL: 20 MIN**
**6 SERVINGS** ● ●

The thick crust of crunchy sesame seeds—fragrant and spicy with lemongrass, lime zest and hot pepper—makes this tuna a hearty main course.

- 3 tablespoons white sesame seeds
- 3 tablespoons black sesame seeds
- 1 tablespoon finely grated lime zest
- 1 tablespoon minced lemongrass (tender inner part only)
- 1 teaspoon sweet paprika
- 1 teaspoon Aleppo pepper flakes or ¼ teaspoon crushed red pepper
- 1 teaspoon freshly ground black pepper
- 1 teaspoon kosher salt
- Six 10-ounce tuna steaks, cut ½ inch thick
- ¼ cup vegetable oil, plus more for brushing
- Lime wedges and mayonnaise, for serving

**1.** In a small bowl, combine the white and black sesame seeds with the lime zest, lemongrass, paprika, Aleppo pepper flakes, black pepper and salt. Lightly brush the tuna with oil and sprinkle the sesame mixture all over it, pressing to help the crust adhere.

**2.** In each of 2 large nonstick skillets, heat 2 tablespoons of the vegetable oil until almost smoking. Add the crusted tuna steaks and cook over moderately high heat until slightly pink in the center, about 2 minutes per side. Transfer the crusted tuna steaks to plates and serve with lime wedges and mayonnaise. —*Geoffrey Zakarian*

**WINE** Light, fruity Pinot Noir.

## Vermentino-Braised Sea Bass

**TOTAL: 15 MIN**
**4 SERVINGS** ● ●

- Four 6-ounce sea bass fillets, with skin
- Salt and freshly ground pepper
- All-purpose flour, for dusting
- 3 tablespoons extra-virgin olive oil
- 1 cup dry white wine, such as Vermentino
- 2 bay leaves
- ¼ cup fish stock or bottled clam juice

**1.** Using a sharp knife, lightly score the skin of the sea bass fillets in a cross-hatch pattern. Season both sides of the sea bass fillets with salt and pepper, then dust very lightly with flour.

**2.** In a large skillet, heat 2 tablespoons of the olive oil until almost smoking. Add the sea bass fillets, skin side down, and cook over moderately high heat until browned and crisp, about 3 minutes. Carefully turn the sea bass fillets with a spatula. Pour the white wine into the skillet and add the bay leaves. Cook the fillets over moderate heat until just cooked through, about 2 minutes longer. Transfer the fillets to a warmed platter and cover loosely with aluminum foil.

**3.** Add the fish stock to the skillet and simmer over moderately high heat until slightly reduced, about 2 minutes. Season with salt and stir in the remaining tablespoon of olive oil. Discard the bay leaves. Spoon the sauce over the fish and serve. —*Valentina Argiolas*

**WINE** High-acid, savory Vermentino.

**SEARED TUNA WITH CHIMICHURRI SAUCE**

**SESAME-CRUSTED TUNA STEAKS**

## Salt-Baked Sea Bass with Warm Tomato Vinaigrette
**ACTIVE: 15 MIN; TOTAL: 35 MIN**
**2 SERVINGS** ●

Vegetable oil cooking spray
- 3 cups kosher salt
- 5 large egg whites, lightly beaten

One 2-pound sea bass, cleaned and scaled
- 4 garlic cloves, 3 smashed, 1 minced
- 2 flat-leaf parsley sprigs, plus 1 tablespoon chopped leaves
- 2 lemon slices, halved
- 2½ teaspoons extra-virgin olive oil

Pinch of saffron threads, crumbled
- 1 small shallot, minced
- ¾ cup cherry tomatoes, halved
- 2 tablespoons canned low-sodium chicken broth
- 1 tablespoon sherry vinegar

Freshly ground pepper

**1.** Preheat the oven to 425°. Line a baking sheet with parchment paper and coat with cooking spray. In a bowl, stir the salt with the egg whites. Set the fish on the prepared baking sheet and fill the cavity with the smashed garlic, parsley sprigs and lemon slices. Pat the salt mixture all over the fish to completely cover it. Bake the fish for 25 minutes.

**2.** Meanwhile, heat the oil in a small skillet. Add the saffron and cook over low heat for 5 minutes. Add the shallot and minced garlic and cook, stirring occasionally, until fragrant, about 2 minutes. Add the tomatoes and cook until slightly softened, about 3 minutes. Add the broth and cook just until the tomatoes begin to break down, about 3 minutes longer. Remove from the heat. Add the sherry vinegar and chopped parsley and season with pepper.

**3.** Using a wooden spoon, tap the salt on the fish to crack it; lift off the crust in large pieces and discard it. Carefully remove the fish skin and lift the fillets from the bones. Transfer the fillets to plates and top with the warm tomato vinaigrette. Serve right away.
—*Anya von Bremzen*
**WINE** Dry, medium-bodied Pinot Gris.

## Creole-Style Sea Bass Fillets
**TOTAL: 15 MIN**
**4 SERVINGS** ● ●

- 2 tablespoons all-purpose flour
- 1 tablespoon freshly ground black pepper
- 1½ teaspoons kosher salt
- 1½ teaspoons garlic powder
- 1½ teaspoons paprika
- 1 teaspoon dried oregano
- 1 teaspoon cayenne pepper

# fish

Four 6-ounce skinless sea bass or
other firm, white fish fillets

3   tablespoons extra-virgin olive oil

Lime wedges, for serving

1. In a wide, shallow bowl, combine the flour with the black pepper, salt, garlic powder, paprika, oregano and cayenne. Dredge each fish fillet in the spice mixture, tapping off any excess, and transfer them to a plate.

2. In a large skillet, heat the olive oil until shimmering. Add the fillets and cook over moderately high heat for 2 minutes per side, until crisp and cooked through. Transfer the fish to plates, garnish with lime wedges and serve.

—*Charmaine Solomon*

**SERVE WITH** Rice, black-eyed peas and greens or okra and tomatoes.

**WINE** Tart, peppery Grüner Veltliner.

## Sea Bass with Rice Noodles in Tomato-Pineapple Broth

**TOTAL: 30 MIN**
**4 SERVINGS** ● ●

6   ounces rice vermicelli

Hot water plus 2 cups room-
temperature water

2   teaspoons vegetable oil

2   garlic cloves, thinly sliced

2   teaspoons finely grated peeled
fresh ginger

1   teaspoon Sriracha sauce or Asian
chili paste

½   red bell pepper, thinly sliced

1   cup tomato juice

½   pound peeled fresh pineapple,
cut into 1-inch pieces (1 cup)

2   tablespoons Asian fish sauce

1   tablespoon fresh lime juice

Four 6-ounce skinless sea bass fillets

Salt and freshly ground pepper

2   scallions, thinly sliced

2   tablespoons chopped cilantro

2   tablespoons chopped mint

2   tablespoons chopped peanuts

1   small carrot, shredded

Lime wedges, for serving

1. In a large bowl, cover the rice vermicelli with the hot water. Let stand until softened, about 10 minutes, then drain.

2. Heat the oil in a medium saucepan. Add the garlic, ginger, Sriracha sauce and red bell pepper and cook over moderately high heat, stirring, until fragrant, about 2 minutes. Add the 2 cups water, tomato juice and pineapple and boil over moderately high heat for 10 minutes. Stir in the fish sauce and lime juice.

3. Bring a skillet of water to a simmer. Season the bass with salt and pepper, add to the skillet and poach over moderate heat until just cooked through, about 5 minutes. Transfer the fillets to a plate.

4. Bring the water back to a boil over high heat. Add the rice vermicelli and boil until al dente, about 1 minute. Drain the vermicelli and transfer to shallow bowls.

Top with the sea bass fillets and ladle the tomato-pineapple broth all around. Top with the scallions, cilantro, mint, peanuts and shredded carrot and serve right away, with lime wedges. —*Eric Ripert*

**WINE** Full-bodied, fragrant Viognier.

## Indian-Spiced Sea Bass with Spinach, Peas and Carrots

**TOTAL: 25 MIN**
**4 SERVINGS** ● ●

3   small carrots, sliced ¼ inch thick

1   shallot, minced

½   teaspoon sugar

6   tablespoons chicken stock or
low-sodium broth

2   tablespoons extra-virgin olive oil

½   pound sugar snap peas

¼   pound baby spinach (4 cups)

Salt and freshly ground pepper

½   teaspoon pink peppercorns,
finely ground

½   teaspoon ground coriander

½   teaspoon ground fennel

¼   teaspoon ground ginger

¼   teaspoon ground cumin

Pinch of cinnamon

Pinch of freshly grated nutmeg

Two 6-ounce sea bass fillets, with skin,
each halved crosswise

1. In a skillet, combine the carrots, shallot, sugar, ¼ cup of the stock and 1 tablespoon of the oil. Cover partially and simmer over moderate heat until the liquid evaporates and the carrots are tender. Add the sugar snaps and the remaining 2 tablespoons of stock and cook for 3 minutes. Add the spinach, cover and cook for 1 minute; season with salt and pepper.

2. Combine the spices. Season the bass with salt and the spices. Heat the remaining 1 tablespoon of olive oil in a nonstick skillet. Add the fish and cook over high heat, turning once, until cooked through. Serve the bass on the vegetables.

—*Josiah Citrin*

**WINE** Spicy New World Gewürztraminer.

## Striped Bass with Wild Mushrooms

**TOTAL: 25 MIN**

4 SERVINGS ● ●

- 2 cups chicken stock or low-sodium broth
- 3 large pieces of dried porcini mushrooms
- 2 tablespoons unsalted butter
- 2 tablespoons extra-virgin olive oil
- 1 large shallot, coarsely chopped
- 2 pounds mixed mushrooms—such as cremini, shiitake and white mushrooms—stems discarded, mushrooms cut into 1-inch pieces

Salt and freshly ground pepper

- 1 tablespoon prepared garlic paste
- ¼ cup dry sherry
- 1½ pounds skinless striped bass fillets, cut into 2-inch pieces
- 2 tablespoons chopped chives

Worcestershire sauce

Hot sauce

**1.** In a small saucepan, bring the chicken stock and dried porcini to a simmer over moderate heat. Remove the saucepan from the heat and let stand.

**2.** In a large skillet, melt the butter in 1 tablespoon of the olive oil. Add the chopped shallot and cook over moderate heat until softened, about 4 minutes. Add the mushrooms, season with salt and pepper and cook over moderately high heat until tender, about 6 minutes.

**3.** Remove the porcini pieces from the stock, coarsely chop them and add them to the fresh mushrooms along with the garlic paste. Add the sherry and cook until reduced by half, about 1 minute. Pour in the porcini stock, stopping before you reach the grit at the bottom, and simmer the mushroom stew until it is reduced by half, about 5 minutes.

**4.** In a large nonstick skillet, heat the remaining 1 tablespoon of oil. Add the fish, season with salt and pepper and cook over moderately high heat for 2 minutes per side. Add the fish to the mushroom stew and cook for 1 minute. Add 1 tablespoon of the chives and season with salt, pepper, Worcestershire sauce and hot sauce. Garnish with the remaining 1 tablespoon of chopped chives and serve at once. —*Galen Zamarra*

**WINE** Medium-bodied, round Pinot Blanc.

## Seared Cod with Spicy Mussel Aioli

**TOTAL: 30 MIN**

4 SERVINGS ● ● ●

- ⅓ cup dry white wine
- 2 dozen mussels
- ½ cup mayonnaise
- 2 garlic cloves, minced
- 2 tablespoons chopped parsley
- 2 teaspoons fresh lemon juice

Cayenne pepper

Salt and freshly ground black pepper

- 1 tablespoon vegetable oil

Four 6-ounce skinless cod fillets

- 1 roasted red bell pepper, cut into thin strips

**1.** Bring the wine to a boil in a medium saucepan. Add the mussels, cover and cook over high heat, shaking the pan a few times, until they open, about 3 minutes. Transfer to a bowl and discard any that do not open. Shell the mussels and reserve the meat. Rinse the saucepan. Pour the mussel liquid into the pan, stopping before you reach the grit at the bottom.

**2.** In a bowl, mix the mayonnaise with the garlic, parsley and lemon juice. Season with cayenne, salt and black pepper.

**3.** Heat the oil in a large skillet. Season the cod with salt and black pepper and cook over moderate heat until lightly browned, about 4 minutes per side.

**4.** Bring the mussel liquid to a boil and remove from the heat. Whisk in the mayonnaise mixture, then stir in the mussels. Transfer the cod to shallow bowls and spoon the mussels and sauce around it. Garnish with the red pepper strips and serve. —*Eric Ripert*

**WINE** Medium-bodied, round Pinot Blanc.

## Spanish Cod with Chickpeas and Sherry

**TOTAL: 30 MIN**

8 SERVINGS ● ●

This recipe was adapted from *The Minimalist Entertains,* Broadway Books.

- ¼ cup extra-virgin olive oil
- 3¾ pounds skinless cod fillets

Salt and freshly ground pepper

Two 19-ounce cans chickpeas, drained and rinsed

- 1 cup plus 1 tablespoon dry or semi-dry sherry, such as amontillado
- 2 tablespoons minced garlic
- ¼ cup chopped parsley

**1.** Preheat the oven to 325°. In a large nonstick skillet, heat 1 tablespoon of the olive oil until shimmering. Season the cod fillets with salt and pepper and add half of the fillets to the skillet. Cook over moderately high heat until browned on the bottom, about 4 minutes. Turn the fish and cook for 1 minute longer.

**2.** Transfer the cooked cod to a large, rimmed baking sheet. Repeat the process with 1 more tablespoon of olive oil, browning the remaining cod and adding it to the baking sheet. Bake the cod for about 6 minutes, or until just white throughout.

**3.** Meanwhile, set the skillet over high heat. Add the chickpeas and stir until warmed through. Add 1 cup of the sherry and boil until the pan is dry and the chickpeas begin to brown, about 5 minutes. Add the garlic and cook, stirring frequently, until fragrant, about 1 minute. Season with salt and pepper and stir in the remaining 1 tablespoon of sherry and 2 tablespoons of olive oil.

**4.** Spoon the chickpeas onto a large serving platter. Set the cod fillets on top and pour any accumulated cod juices over the fish. Sprinkle with the parsley and serve right away. —*Mark Bittman*

**WINE** Zesty Albariño or Vinho Verde.

MONKFISH AND CHORIZO KEBABS

RED SNAPPER WITH MUSSELS AND CHORIZO

### Steamed Cod with Crisp Vegetables

**ACTIVE: 20 MIN; TOTAL: 45 MIN**

**4 SERVINGS** ●

16  thin asparagus, halved crosswise
¼  pound snow peas
 1  small zucchini, quartered
     lengthwise and sliced ¼ inch thick
 1  small red bell pepper, thinly sliced
½  cup chopped mixed herbs
Kosher salt and freshly ground pepper
Four 6-ounce cod fillets
¼  cup dry white wine
 2  tablespoons unsalted butter

1. In a pot fitted with 2 stackable steamer baskets or in 2 pots each fitted with a steamer basket, bring 1 inch of water to a boil. Tear off four 15-inch-long sheets of foil. Mound one-fourth of the vegetables in the center of each sheet. Sprinkle with the herbs; season with salt and pepper. Set a cod fillet on each mound and sea-son with salt and pepper. Top each with 1 tablespoon of wine and ½ tablespoon of butter. Fold up the foil edges and seal.

2. Transfer the packages to the steamer baskets. Cover and steam for 15 minutes. Transfer the packages to a large, rimmed platter and let rest for 5 minutes. Open carefully, slide the contents onto plates and serve. *—Stephanie Lyness*

**WINE** Tart, peppery Grüner Veltliner.

### Roasted Fish with Charmoula, Tomatoes and Potatoes

**ACTIVE: 30 MIN; TOTAL: 1 HR 25 MIN**

**8 SERVINGS** ● ●

*Charmoula* is a heady blend of garlic, cilantro and cumin.

 4  pounds red potatoes, peeled and
     sliced ⅓ inch thick
¾  cup extra-virgin olive oil, plus
     more for drizzling
Salt
 2  pounds plum tomatoes, sliced
     ½ inch thick
 8  garlic cloves, halved
 1  fresh red chile, such as jalapeño,
     seeded and finely chopped
 1  cup finely chopped cilantro
¼  cup fresh lemon juice
 2  teaspoons ground cumin
 2  teaspoons sweet paprika
 3  pounds fish fillets, such as
     Spanish mackerel or cod, with skin

1. Preheat the oven to 475°. Oil the bottom of a large roasting pan. Arrange the potato slices in an overlapping layer in the pan; drizzle with olive oil and season with salt. Spread the tomato slices over the potatoes, drizzle with oil and season with salt. Bake in the lower third of the oven for 50 minutes, or until the potatoes are tender and crisp on the bottom.

**2.** Meanwhile, in a mortar, pound the garlic, a few cloves at a time, with a little salt until well mashed. Add the chile and pound to a paste. Blend in ¼ cup of the oil and transfer the paste to a medium bowl. Stir in the cilantro, lemon juice, cumin, paprika and the remaining ½ cup of oil. Season with salt. (Alternatively, blend all of the *charmoula* sauce ingredients in a mini food processor.)

**3.** Slash the skin side of the fish fillets 3 times. Transfer the fish fillets, skin side down, to a large, rimmed baking sheet and coat the fish with half of the *charmoula* sauce. Let marinate at room temperature for 30 minutes.

**4.** When the potatoes are tender, remove them from the oven and set the fish fillets, skin side down, on top. Season with salt. Bake in the upper third of the oven for about 12 minutes, or until the fish is just cooked through. Serve hot or at room temperature with the remaining *charmoula* on the side. —*Nadia Roden*

**MAKE AHEAD** The fish can be cooked up to 4 hours ahead.

**WINE** Round-textured Sémillon.

## Monkfish and Chorizo Kebabs

**TOTAL: 30 MIN**

4 SERVINGS ●

- ½ pound chorizo, cut into 16 slices
- 16 cherry tomatoes
- 1½ pounds trimmed monkfish or swordfish fillets, cut into 2-inch chunks
- ½ medium red onion, cut into 1-inch pieces
- 2 tablespoons extra-virgin olive oil, plus more for brushing

Salt and freshly ground pepper

- 2 tablespoons fresh lemon juice
- 2 tablespoons finely chopped cilantro
- 1 French baguette, halved lengthwise
- 1 large garlic clove
- 1 large tomato, halved

**1.** Light a grill. Alternately thread 4 slices of the chorizo, 4 of the cherry tomatoes, 3 or 4 chunks of the monkfish and 3 pieces of the red onion onto each of four 12-inch metal skewers. Brush the monkfish and chorizo kebabs with olive oil and season generously with salt and pepper.

**2.** Grill the kebabs over a medium-hot fire, turning once, until they are lightly charred and the fish is cooked through, about 4 minutes per side.

**3.** Meanwhile, in a small bowl, combine the 2 tablespoons of olive oil with the lemon juice and cilantro.

**4.** Transfer the kebabs to a platter and drizzle with the cilantro dressing. Grill the baguette halves, cut side down, until toasted, 20 seconds. Rub the toasted sides with the garlic and halved tomato. Halve the baguette pieces crosswise and serve with the kebabs. —*Eric Ripert*

**WINE** Dry, medium-bodied Pinot Gris.

## Red Snapper with Mussels, Potatoes and Chorizo

**TOTAL: 30 MIN**

4 SERVINGS ● ●

- ¼ cup dry white wine
- ¼ cup water
- 1 pound mussels, scrubbed and debearded
- 3 tablespoons extra-virgin olive oil
- 2 medium Yukon Gold potatoes, sliced ¼ inch thick
- 1 chorizo sausage (6 ounces), sliced ¼ inch thick
- ⅓ cup finely chopped onion
- 2 teaspoons chopped garlic

Salt and freshly ground pepper

Four 6-ounce red snapper fillets, with skin

- 1 tablespoon coarsely chopped flat-leaf parsley

**1.** Preheat the broiler. In a medium saucepan, pour the wine and water over the mussels and bring to a boil over high heat. Cover and steam for 3 minutes, or

until the mussels open. Drain, reserving the cooking liquid. (You should have 1 cup of liquid; if you don't, add water.) Discard any mussels that do not open.

**2.** In a large skillet, heat 2 tablespoons of the olive oil. Add the sliced potatoes and chorizo and cook over moderate heat, stirring occasionally, until the potatoes are lightly browned and tender, about 10 minutes. Add the chopped onion and garlic and cook, stirring, for 30 seconds.

**3.** Meanwhile, remove the top shells from the steamed mussels and discard; transfer the mussels in their half shells to a bowl. Carefully pour in the 1 cup of reserved mussel cooking liquid, stopping when you get to the grit at the bottom.

**4.** Add the mussels and their liquid to the skillet and bring to a boil. Simmer over moderately low heat for 2 minutes, or until the liquid thickens slightly. Season with salt and pepper.

**5.** Rub the red snapper fillets with the remaining 1 tablespoon of olive oil and season them generously with salt and pepper. Set the fillets skin side up on a large, rimmed baking sheet and broil them 4 inches from the heat until white throughout, 3 to 4 minutes.

**6.** Spoon the potatoes, chorizo and mussels into 4 soup plates. Top with the red snapper fillets, sprinkle with the parsley and serve immediately. —*Jacques Pépin*

**WINE** Dry, light, crisp Champagne.

## Roasted Whole Snapper with Tomato-Bread Salad

**TOTAL: 45 MIN**

8 SERVINGS ●

Mario Batali, the chef at New York City's Babbo, recommends using an electric carving knife to cut the roasted fish into bone-in steaks with mixed herbs and lemon slices in the center. You can also serve the fish in a more traditional way: Remove the skin and carefully lift the fillets off the bone.

# fish

## FISH

- ¼ cup plus 2 tablespoons extra-virgin olive oil
- One 5- to 6-pound fresh whole red snapper or sea bass, cleaned and scaled
- Sea salt and freshly ground black pepper
- 1 cup coarsely chopped mixed herbs, such as basil, thyme, flat-leaf parsley and fennel fronds
- 4 large lemons, 2 thinly sliced, 2 cut into wedges for serving
- 1 cup dry white wine, such as Chardonnay

## SALAD

- ⅔ cup extra-virgin olive oil
- ¼ cup red wine vinegar
- 1½ pounds assorted ripe tomatoes, cut into 1-inch cubes
- 2 small green or underripe tomatoes, cut into ¼-inch dice

## superfast

**TIP**  **FISH**

**BLACK BASS TARTARE** Finely dice uncooked black bass. Garnish with minced jalapeño, tomato, mint and cilantro. Drizzle with olive oil and plenty of lemon juice and serve right away, with toast.

**SHRIMP GAZPACHO** Cut 1 small onion, 1 peeled cucumber, 1 red bell pepper and 4 tomatoes into chunks. Puree in a blender, then season with olive oil, vinegar and hot sauce; top with sautéed shrimp and chopped parsley.

**THYME-RUBBED TUNA** Rub tuna steaks with thyme, sea salt, pepper and olive oil. Sear and serve with mesclun.

- 2 medium cucumbers—peeled, halved lengthwise, seeded and sliced crosswise ¼ inch thick
- 1 small zucchini or yellow summer squash, thinly sliced crosswise
- 1 medium red onion, very thinly sliced
- 6 squash blossoms (optional), torn into large pieces
- ¼ cup finely shredded basil
- 1 tablespoon marjoram leaves
- 3 cups diced day-old white bread (½-inch dice)

Salt and freshly ground pepper

**1. MAKE THE FISH:** Preheat the oven to 425°. Line a large roasting pan with foil. Add ¼ cup of the olive oil and tilt the pan to coat the bottom evenly. Generously season the fish inside and out with salt and pepper and set it in the roasting pan. Stuff the cavity with the chopped herbs and sliced lemons. Drizzle the fish with the remaining 2 tablespoons of olive oil and the white wine. Put the fish in the oven, increase the temperature to 475° and roast for about 35 minutes, or just until the fish flakes easily when tested with a fork and an instant-read thermometer inserted in the thickest part of the fish registers 130°. Remove the roasted fish from the oven and let rest in the pan for 10 minutes.

**2. MEANWHILE, MAKE THE SALAD:** In a large bowl, combine the olive oil and vinegar. Add the tomatoes, cucumbers, zucchini, red onion, squash blossoms, basil and marjoram and toss well. Add the diced bread to the salad, season with salt and pepper and toss again to coat the bread cubes with the dressing.

**3.** Carefully transfer the roasted fish to a work surface and fillet it. Serve, garnished with the lemon wedges, on warmed plates. Pass the tomato-bread salad at the table. —*Mario Batali*

**WINE** Dry, rich Champagne.

## Pan-Roasted Halibut with Jalapeño Vinaigrette

**TOTAL: 25 MIN**

**6 SERVINGS** ● ●

- 2 tablespoons apple cider vinegar
- 2 tablespoons very finely chopped red onion
- Kosher salt
- 1 tablespoon honey
- 1 tablespoon chopped cilantro leaves
- ½ teaspoon Dijon mustard
- ½ teaspoon very finely chopped garlic
- ½ cup plus 1 teaspoon extra-virgin olive oil
- 1 medium jalapeño
- Freshly ground pepper
- Six 5- to 6-ounce halibut fillets
- Avocado wedges or watercress, for serving

**1.** In a small bowl, combine the vinegar and onion with ½ teaspoon of salt. Let stand for 10 minutes, then whisk in the honey, cilantro, mustard, garlic and ¼ cup of the olive oil.

**2.** Meanwhile, in a small skillet, heat 1 teaspoon of the olive oil over high heat until just smoking. Add the jalapeño and cook, turning, until charred and blistered on all sides, about 2 minutes; let cool slightly. Slip off the charred skin, discard the stem and halve the jalapeño lengthwise. Scrape out the seeds and finely chop the jalapeño. Stir the chopped jalapeño into the vinaigrette and season with salt and pepper.

**3.** In a large nonstick skillet, heat the remaining ¼ cup of olive oil over moderately high heat. Season the halibut fillets with salt and pepper and cook, turning once, until they are opaque throughout, about 8 minutes. Transfer the halibut to a platter. Whisk the vinaigrette, spoon it over the fish and serve with avocado wedges or watercress. —*Tom Douglas*

**WINE** Soft, off-dry Riesling.

## Roasted Halibut with Green Olive Sauce

ACTIVE: 20 MIN; TOTAL: 1 HR

6 SERVINGS

- ¼ cup fresh lime juice
- 1 tablespoon extra-virgin olive oil

Six 7-ounce skinless halibut fillets

- 1 cup fish stock or bottled clam juice
- ½ cup dry white wine
- 1 medium shallot, minced
- 6 whole white peppercorns, plus freshly ground white pepper
- 1 bay leaf
- 1 cup heavy cream

Salt

- ½ cup green olives, such as Picholine, pitted and chopped
- 2 tablespoons cold unsalted butter
- 2 tablespoons chopped flat-leaf parsley

**1.** Preheat the oven to 450°. In a large, shallow dish, mix 2 tablespoons of the lime juice with the olive oil. Add the halibut fillets and turn to coat. Refrigerate for 15 minutes.

**2.** Meanwhile, in a medium skillet, combine the fish stock, wine, shallot, white peppercorns, bay leaf and the remaining 2 tablespoons of lime juice. Boil over high heat until reduced to ½ cup, about 6 minutes. Add the cream, bring to a boil and simmer over moderately low heat until reduced to ⅔ cup, about 10 minutes. Strain the sauce into a saucepan.

**3.** Season the halibut with salt and white pepper and transfer to a baking sheet. Bake in the upper third of the oven until just cooked through, about 10 minutes.

**4.** Add the olives to the cream sauce and bring to a boil. Pour in any accumulated fish juices. Remove from the heat and whisk in the butter. Stir in the parsley; season with salt and white pepper. Set the fillets on plates, spoon the sauce on top and serve. —*Barak Hirschowitz*

WINE Round, rich Sauvignon Blanc.

**HALIBUT WITH JALAPEÑO VINAIGRETTE**

**HALIBUT WITH GREEN OLIVE SAUCE**

# fish

## Halibut and Fall Harvest Sauté

**TOTAL: 30 MIN**

4 SERVINGS ●

- 3 tablespoons unsalted butter
- 1 large shallot, coarsely chopped
- 1 large garlic clove, coarsely chopped
- 6 ounces peeled butternut squash, cut into ½-inch dice (1½ cups)
- 1 medium parsnip, cut into ½-inch dice
- 1 small turnip, cut into ½-inch dice

Kosher salt and freshly ground pepper

- ½ cup dry white wine
- 4 thyme sprigs, plus thyme leaves for garnish
- 1 bay leaf
- 1¼ cups chicken stock or low-sodium broth
- 1 tablespoon extra-virgin olive oil
- 1½ pounds skinless halibut fillets, cut into 2-inch pieces
- 2 tablespoons all-purpose flour

1. In a large saucepan, melt 2 tablespoons of the butter. Add the shallot and garlic and cook over moderate heat until softened, about 3 minutes. Add the squash, parsnip and turnip and cook over moderately high heat until they begin to soften, about 5 minutes. Season with salt and pepper. Add the wine, thyme sprigs and bay leaf and cook until the wine reduces by half, about 2 minutes. Add the stock, cover and simmer until the vegetables are fork-tender, about 10 minutes.

2. Meanwhile, in a large nonstick skillet, heat the olive oil. Season the halibut pieces with salt and pepper and dust them lightly with the flour. Add the halibut to the hot skillet and cook over moderately high heat until light golden, about 2 minutes per side.

3. Add the halibut to the vegetables in the saucepan and simmer for 2 minutes. Using a slotted spoon, transfer the fish and vegetables from the pan to shallow bowls. Discard the thyme sprigs and the bay leaf. Swirl the remaining 1 tablespoon of butter into the broth. Season with salt and pepper and spoon over the sauté. Garnish with the thyme leaves and serve. —*Galen Zamarra*

**WINE** Subtle, complex white Burgundy.

## Matzo Meal–Crusted Trout

**TOTAL: 30 MIN, PLUS 24 HR FOR THE OIL**

8 SERVINGS ●

This trout is lovely at Passover. In place of bread crumbs—which, like all leavened products, are forbidden at Passover—the mild fish is coated with well-seasoned matzo meal.

- 1 large egg
- ¼ cup water

Kosher salt

- 1 cup matzo meal
- ½ teaspoon freshly ground black pepper
- ¼ teaspoon garlic powder

Eight 6-ounce rainbow trout fillets, with skin, rinsed and patted dry

- 6 tablespoons vegetable oil

Oregano Oil (recipe follows)

1. In a medium bowl, beat the egg and water with a pinch of salt. In a shallow baking dish, toss the matzo meal with the pepper, garlic powder and 1½ teaspoons of salt.

2. Dip the trout fillets in the beaten egg, then dredge in the matzo meal mixture; transfer to a baking sheet.

3. Heat 3 tablespoons of vegetable oil in each of 2 large nonstick skillets until shimmering. Add 4 fillets, skin side up, to each skillet and cook over moderately high heat until browned at the edges, about 5 minutes. Turn and cook until the skin is crisp and the fish is just opaque throughout, about 3 minutes. Transfer to a platter and sprinkle with salt. Serve with the Oregano Oil. —*Russ Pillar*

**WINE** Dry, mineral-flavored Chenin Blanc.

## OREGANO OIL

**TOTAL: 5 MIN, PLUS 24 HR STEEPING**

MAKES ⅔ CUP ● ●

You can use this fragrant oil to enhance roasted meats and vegetables and just about anything that you grill.

- 3 oregano sprigs, lightly crushed
- ⅔ cup extra-virgin olive oil

In a glass measuring cup, combine the oregano sprigs and olive oil. Cover and refrigerate for at least 1 and up to 2 days. Discard the sprigs before using. —*R.P.*

**MAKE AHEAD** The oil can be refrigerated for up to 1 week.

## Sautéed Trout Fillets with a Pumpkin Seed Crust

**TOTAL: 35 MIN**

4 SERVINGS

The nutty, crunchy pumpkin seeds, with the added kick of cayenne pepper, form a delicious crust on the trout fillets.

- ¼ cup plus 2 tablespoons vegetable oil
- 1 large garlic clove, very finely chopped
- ¼ cup dry white wine
- ¼ cup chicken stock or low-sodium broth
- 6 tablespoons unsalted butter, cut into tablespoons and chilled
- ¼ pound shiitake mushrooms, stems discarded, caps quartered
- 1 tablespoon sesame seeds

Salt and freshly ground pepper

- ½ cup shelled raw pumpkin seeds, finely chopped
- ⅛ teaspoon cayenne

Four 6-ounce trout fillets, with skin

- 2 scallions, white and tender green parts only, thinly sliced
- 1 medium tomato, very finely chopped
- 1 tablespoon finely chopped cilantro leaves
- 2 teaspoons fresh lime juice

**1.** In a medium skillet, heat 1 tablespoon of the oil until shimmering. Add the garlic and cook over moderately high heat until fragrant, about 30 seconds. Add the wine and boil until reduced by half, about 1 minute. Add the chicken stock and boil until reduced by half again, about 1 minute. Remove the skillet from the heat and whisk in the cold butter, 1 tablespoon at a time, until smooth.

**2.** In another medium skillet, heat 3 tablespoons of the oil. Add the shiitake caps and cook over moderate heat, stirring occasionally, until browned, about 5 minutes. Stir in the sesame seeds and cook, stirring frequently, until lightly browned, about 1 minute. Season the shiitake with salt and pepper and remove the skillet from the heat.

**3.** On a plate, toss the pumpkin seeds with ½ teaspoon of salt and the cayenne. Press the boned side of the trout fillets into the pumpkin seeds to coat.

**4.** In a large nonstick skillet, heat the remaining 2 tablespoons of oil until shimmering. Add the trout fillets, crusted side down, and cook over moderately high heat until browned, about 2 minutes. Turn the fillets and cook until the fish is white throughout and the skin is crisp, about 3 minutes. Transfer the fish to plates and keep warm.

**5.** Add the scallions, tomato, cilantro and lime juice to the sauce and rewarm over moderately high heat, stirring; do not let it boil. Spoon the sautéed shiitake and the sauce over the trout and serve. —*Bob Isaacson*
**WINE** Subtle, complex white Burgundy.

### Grilled Quick-Cured Trout with Mustard-Olive Dressing
**TOTAL: 20 MIN, PLUS 1 HR CURING**
6 SERVINGS ●
A light salt-and-honey brine gives the trout a clean, almost sweet and delicate flavor and shortens its grilling time.

1 quart cold water
Kosher salt
¼ cup honey
Twelve 4-ounce trout fillets, with skin
2 tablespoons chopped
Calamata olives
2 tablespoons Dijon mustard
2 tablespoons white wine vinegar
2 tablespoons extra-virgin olive oil,
plus more for brushing
Freshly ground pepper
6 cups lightly packed baby greens

**1.** In a very large bowl, combine the water with 1 cup of salt and the honey; stir to dissolve the salt. Add the trout and refrigerate for 1 hour.

**2.** Meanwhile, in a small bowl, whisk the chopped olives with the mustard, vinegar and the 2 tablespoons of olive oil. Season the dressing with salt and pepper.

**3.** Light a grill. Drain the trout and pat dry. Brush the trout on both sides with olive oil and grill over a hot fire, skin side down, until lightly charred and crisp, about 3 minutes. Turn and grill until just cooked through, 1 to 2 minutes longer.

**4.** Transfer the trout to plates. In a large bowl, toss the greens with 1 tablespoon of the dressing. Add the salad to the plates; pass the remaining dressing at the table for the trout. —*Marcia Kiesel*
**WINE** Bright, citrusy Riesling.

### Pan-Fried Pompano with Tomato-Caraway Glaze
**TOTAL: 35 MIN**
6 SERVINGS ●
Dot grilled chicken or shrimp with this slightly spicy and tomato-y butter, or toss it with steamed or grilled vegetables or spaghetti.

2 tablespoons extra-virgin olive oil
2 medium tomatoes—peeled, seeded and chopped
1½ teaspoons hot paprika
1 teaspoon sweet paprika
2 small garlic cloves, minced

1 tablespoon plus 1 teaspoon chopped thyme, preferably lemon thyme
1 teaspoon chopped caraway seeds
1 stick plus 4 tablespoons (6 ounces) unsalted butter, softened
Salt
Six 6-ounce pompano or Spanish mackerel fillets, with skin
Freshly ground pepper

**1.** Preheat the oven to 500°. Heat the olive oil in a medium skillet. Add the tomatoes and cook over moderately high heat for 2 minutes. Reduce the heat to moderate and cook, stirring and mashing the tomatoes with a fork until a thick

## equipment
**KNIFE SHARPENER**　**TIP**

**CHANTRY RETRO** This Art Deco chrome sharpener was created by British butchers in 1929 and redesigned in 1960 ($49 from Broadway Panhandler; 866-266-5927 or broadwaypanhandler.com).

# fish

puree forms, about 15 minutes. Add the hot and sweet paprikas and cook, stirring, for 1 minute. Scrape the tomato puree into a bowl and let cool. Stir in the garlic, thyme and caraway seeds. Fold in the butter and season with salt.

**2.** Lightly oil a large, rimmed baking sheet and arrange the pompano fillets on it, skin side down. Season with salt and pepper. Spread the tomato butter over the fillets, leaving a ½-inch border all around. Roast the fish in the top third of the oven for 6 minutes, or until golden brown and just cooked through. Transfer the fillets to plates and serve.

—*Marcia Kiesel*

**MAKE AHEAD** The butter can be refrigerated overnight. Bring to room temperature before using.

**WINE** Flinty, high-acid Chablis.

### Grilled Whole Fish with Curried Yogurt Marinade

**ACTIVE: 30 MIN; TOTAL: 1 HR 35 MIN**

4 SERVINGS ●

1½ cups plain whole milk yogurt
½ cup coarsely chopped
    cilantro leaves
2 tablespoons fresh lime juice
1 tablespoon curry powder
½ teaspoon ground ginger
1 tablespoon extra-virgin
    olive oil
Four 1¼-pound whole sea bass or
    pompano, scaled and gutted
Salt and freshly ground pepper

**1.** In a medium bowl, mix the whole milk yogurt with the chopped cilantro, lime juice, curry powder, ground ginger and olive oil until combined.

**2.** Make 3 crosswise slashes on both sides of each whole fish, carefully cutting down to the bone. Transfer the fish to a large, rimmed baking sheet and coat them all over with the curried yogurt marinade. Cover and refrigerate the fish for 1 to 2 hours.

**3.** Light a grill. Oil the grate. Remove the fish from the marinade, leaving on a light coating; reserve the marinade. Season the fish with salt and pepper and grill over a medium-hot fire, basting with the marinade, until lightly charred and just cooked through, about 10 minutes per side. Serve right away.

—*Marie van der Merwe*

**WINE** Dry, mineral-flavored Chenin Blanc.

### Grilled Dorado with Walnut and Parsley Pesto

**TOTAL: 35 MIN**

6 SERVINGS

½ cup plus 1 tablespoon extra-virgin
    olive oil, plus more for brushing
½ medium Spanish onion,
    thinly sliced
1 cup packed flat-leaf parsley leaves
1 cup walnuts, lightly toasted
Kosher salt and freshly ground
    black pepper
Six 6- to 7-ounce dorado, pompano,
    Spanish mackerel or sea bass
    fillets, with skin
⅓ cup Picholine or green Greek or
    Spanish olives, pitted and
    coarsely chopped
1 tablespoon minced preserved
    lemon (optional, see Note)

**1.** Light a gas or charcoal grill. In a medium skillet, heat 1 tablespoon of the olive oil until shimmering. Add the thinly sliced onion and cook over moderate heat, stirring occasionally, until golden brown, about 8 minutes.

**2.** In a food processor, puree the parsley leaves with ¼ cup of the olive oil and scrape the puree into a medium bowl. Add the walnuts and onion to the food processor bowl and process to a coarse paste. With the machine on, slowly add the remaining ¼ cup of olive oil. Scrape the walnut paste into the bowl of parsley puree, stir to combine and season with salt and pepper.

**3.** Brush the dorado fillets with olive oil and season with salt and pepper. Grill the fish over a hot fire, skin side down, until the skin is crisp, about 2 minutes. Turn the fillets and grill until just cooked through, about 3 minutes longer. Transfer the fillets to plates. Spread the walnut-parsley pesto over the fish. Top with the olives and preserved lemon and serve.

—*John Villa*

**NOTE** Preserved lemons are available at speciality and Middle Eastern markets.

**SERVE WITH** Roasted shallots, fingerling potatoes and sautéed spinach.

**WINE** Lively, assertive Sauvignon Blanc.

### Grilled Calamari with Parsley

**TOTAL: 20 MIN**

10 SERVINGS ● ●

½ cup plus 2 tablespoons
    extra-virgin olive oil
½ cup finely chopped flat-leaf
    parsley
3 garlic cloves, minced
Salt and freshly ground pepper
2 pounds cleaned small squid
    (see Note)

**1.** Light a gas or charcoal grill. In a small bowl, combine ½ cup of the olive oil with the parsley, garlic and a generous pinch each of salt and pepper.

**2.** In a large bowl, toss the squid with the remaining 2 tablespoons of olive oil and season generously with salt and pepper. Double-skewer the squid bodies and grill until cooked through and charred in spots, about 3 minutes. Baste the cooked squid with half of the parsley mixture, then grill the squid for 1 minute longer. Mound the squid on a platter, drizzle with the remaining parsley mixture and serve immediately. —*Marcella Giamundo*

**NOTE** When shopping for squid, look for small ones—they're super-tender and cook very quickly. The bodies should be about 3 inches long.

**WINE** High-acid, savory Vermentino.

**GRILLED CALAMARI WITH PARSLEY**

SHRIMP AND BROCCOLI WITH HONEY-WALNUT CARAMEL SAUCE, P. 184

# shellfish

SPICY SHRIMP WITH GARLIC-ALMOND SAUCE

SAUTÉED SHRIMP WITH OLIVES AND ANCHOVIES, P. 189

### Spicy Shrimp with Garlic-Almond Sauce

**ACTIVE: 25 MIN; TOTAL: 1 HR**

**4 SERVINGS** ● ●

Almonds are a great source of vitamin E. One handful provides half of the recommended dietary allowance for adults.

- 8 garlic cloves, peeled
- 2 jalapeños, preferably red, halved and seeded
- 1 large tomato, halved
- ½ cup whole blanched almonds
- ¼ cup extra-virgin olive oil
- 2 tablespoons Cabernet or red wine vinegar

Salt and freshly ground black pepper

Cayenne pepper

- 1½ pounds large shrimp, shelled and deveined
- 1 teaspoon ancho chile powder
- ¼ cup dry white wine

**1.** Preheat the oven to 350°. Spread the garlic, jalapeños and tomato halves on a rimmed baking sheet and bake for about 30 minutes, or until the garlic is golden brown and just tender. Spread the almonds in a pie plate and bake for 7 minutes, or until golden brown. Let the almonds cool and coarsely chop them.

**2.** In a food processor, coarsely puree the garlic with the jalapeños, tomato and almonds. With the machine on, gradually add 3 tablespoons of the olive oil, and then the wine vinegar. Scrape the sauce into a bowl and season with salt, black pepper and cayenne.

**3.** In a large skillet, heat the remaining 1 tablespoon of olive oil. Season the shrimp with salt and pepper and toss with the ancho chile powder. Add the shrimp to the skillet and cook them over moderately high heat until barely white throughout,

about 1 minute per side. Add the white wine and simmer, shaking the skillet, until the shrimp are cooked, about 30 seconds longer. Using a slotted spoon, transfer the shrimp to a serving platter. Simmer the pan juices until thickened, about 30 seconds, then pour them over the shrimp and toss to coat evenly. Serve the shrimp with the garlic-almond sauce on the side.
—*Kimball Jones*

**WINE** Bright, citrusy Riesling.

### Shrimp and Broccoli with Honey-Walnut Caramel Sauce

**TOTAL: 40 MIN**

**6 FIRST-COURSE SERVINGS** ●

Using walnuts that have been bottled in honey is a quick way to add a sweet, nutty flavor and a pleasing crunch to shrimp and broccoli without having to toast, cool and candy walnuts.

3 tablespoons vegetable oil

1 cup walnuts packed in honey, lightly drained, plus 1 tablespoon of honey from the jar

6 large garlic cloves, thinly sliced

Freshly ground pepper

½ cup soy sauce

1½ tablespoons fresh lemon juice

1 pound broccoli florets, cut into 1-inch pieces

1½ pounds large shrimp, shelled and deveined

4 Thai chiles or ½ habanero, sliced

**1.** In a saucepan, heat 1 tablespoon of the oil. Add the walnuts and cook over moderate heat, stirring frequently, until browned, about 4 minutes. Transfer the walnuts to a plate with a slotted spoon.

**2.** Add another tablespoon of the oil to the saucepan. Add the garlic, season with pepper and cook over low heat, stirring occasionally, until golden, 4 minutes. Add the 1 tablespoon of reserved honey; cook over moderate heat, stirring, until deeply browned, 1 minute. Add the soy sauce and simmer until slightly reduced, about 4 minutes. Stir in the lemon juice and remove the garlic-caramel sauce from the heat.

**3.** In a large skillet, heat the remaining 1 tablespoon of oil. Add the broccoli, cover and cook over moderate heat for 3 minutes. Uncover, add the shrimp and chiles and cook, stirring a few times, just until the shrimp are pink and curled. Stir in the garlic-caramel sauce, sprinkle the walnuts on top and serve. —*Marcia Kiesel*
**WINE** Bright, citrusy Riesling.

### Winter Shrimp Salad with Fennel and Ruby Grapefruit

**ACTIVE: 30 MIN; TOTAL: 1 HR 30 MIN, PLUS 8 HR CHILLING**

6 SERVINGS ●

For this dish, wild Pacific Northwest spot prawns would be delicious, but large shrimp are a good substitute.

One 1-inch piece of peeled fresh ginger, thinly sliced

1 medium carrot, thinly sliced

1 leek, white and tender green parts only, halved lengthwise and thinly sliced crosswise

1 medium fennel bulb, tops chopped, bulb halved lengthwise and very thinly sliced on a mandoline

4 cups water

⅔ cup Pinot Blanc

Kosher salt

1¼ pounds large shrimp, shelled and deveined

1 Ruby Red grapefruit

⅓ cup fresh Ruby Red grapefruit juice

2 tablespoons extra-virgin olive oil

2 tablespoons vegetable oil

Pinch of sugar

Freshly ground pepper

4 ounces spinach leaves, large stems discarded (about 4 cups loosely packed)

**1.** In a large saucepan, combine the ginger, carrot, leek, fennel tops, water, wine and 1 tablespoon of salt and bring to a boil. Cover partially and simmer over low heat for 20 minutes.

**2.** Add the shrimp to the broth in the saucepan, cover and remove from the heat. Let stand at room temperature for 20 minutes. Refrigerate overnight.

**3.** Mince 2 teaspoons of the grapefruit zest; set aside. Using a sharp knife, peel the grapefruit; be sure to remove all of the bitter white pith. Working over a bowl, cut in between the membranes to release the grapefruit sections.

**4.** In a medium bowl, whisk the reserved zest and the grapefruit juice with the olive oil, vegetable oil and sugar. Season with salt and pepper. Add the sliced fennel, toss well to coat and let the citrus dressing stand at room temperature for 15 minutes.

**5.** Remove the shrimp from the cooking broth and pat dry. Arrange the spinach in the center of 6 plates. Using a slotted spoon, remove the fennel slices from the dressing and mound them over the spinach. Add the shrimp and grapefruit sections to the dressing in the bowl, toss and then arrange around the salad. Drizzle with any remaining dressing and serve. —*Michael Allemeier*
**MAKE AHEAD** The dressing and the shrimp can be refrigerated overnight; leave the shrimp in their cooking liquid.
**WINE** Medium-bodied, round Pinot Blanc.

### Spicy Orange Shrimp Seviche

**TOTAL: 35 MIN, PLUS 8 HR MARINATING**

8 FIRST-COURSE SERVINGS ● ● ●

1 pound large shrimp

½ cup ketchup

¾ cup fresh orange juice

¼ cup fresh lime juice

3 tablespoons fresh lemon juice

2 large garlic cloves, minced

1 jalapeño, seeded and thinly sliced

½ teaspoon dried oregano, crumbled

½ teaspoon freshly ground pepper

Large pinch of ground cumin

Small pinch of ground cinnamon

Small pinch of ground cloves

Salt

Hot sauce

1 medium red onion, thinly sliced

1 medium tomato, seeded and cut into ½-inch dice

½ cup chopped cilantro, plus leaves for garnish

1 Belgian endive, leaves separated

**1.** Fill a medium bowl with ice water. Bring a large saucepan of salted water to a boil. Add the shrimp and immediately remove the pan from the heat. Let the shrimp sit in the hot water for 2 minutes, then drain and cool in the ice water. Drain the shrimp, then peel and devein them; pat dry.

# shellfish

**2.** In a large bowl, whisk the ketchup with the orange juice. Add the lime and lemon juices, garlic, jalapeño, oregano, freshly ground pepper, cumin, cinnamon and cloves. Whisk to combine and season generously with salt and hot sauce.

**3.** Add the cooked shrimp, red onion, diced tomato and chopped cilantro to the sauce mixture. Cover and refrigerate for at least 8 hours or overnight; stir the shrimp once or twice.

**4.** Spoon the shrimp and sauce into martini glasses or onto small plates, garnish with the endive and cilantro leaves and serve. —*Terry Zarikian*

**MAKE AHEAD** The recipe can be prepared through Step 3, covered tightly, and refrigerated overnight.

**WINE** Lively, assertive Sauvignon Blanc.

## Spicy King Prawns
**TOTAL: 30 MIN**
**8 SERVINGS ● ● ●**

- ½ cup extra-virgin olive oil
- 8 garlic cloves, very finely chopped
- 1 tablespoon plus 1 teaspoon sweet paprika
- 1 tablespoon ground cumin
- 1½ teaspoons ground ginger
- ½ teaspoon cayenne pepper
- 3 pounds large shrimp, shelled and deveined

Salt
- 1 cup coarsely chopped cilantro or flat-leaf parsley

Heat the olive oil in a very large skillet. Add the garlic, paprika, cumin, ginger and cayenne and cook over moderate heat until fragrant, about 1½ minutes. Add the shrimp and cook, stirring often, until they turn pink, 2 to 4 minutes. Season with salt. Sprinkle with the cilantro and toss gently to combine. Transfer to a platter and serve at once. —*Nadia Roden*

**WINE** Dry, crisp sparkling wine.

## Grilled Shrimp and Corn Wraps
**TOTAL: 30 MIN**
**4 SERVINGS ● ●**

- 1 pound peeled and deveined large shrimp
- 3 tablespoons extra-virgin olive oil

Salt and freshly ground pepper
- 1 cup fresh corn kernels (from 2 large ears)
- 1 celery rib, finely chopped
- 1 tablespoon fresh lemon juice
- 1 garlic clove, minced
- ⅓ cup mayonnaise
- ½ teaspoon hot paprika
- ⅛ teaspoon cayenne pepper
- 1½ cups shredded napa cabbage

Four 10-inch flour tortillas

**1.** Light a grill or heat a grill pan. In a medium bowl, toss the shrimp with 2 tablespoons of the olive oil and season with salt and pepper. Grill, turning once, until the shrimp are pink and curled, about 5 minutes. Transfer to a plate.

**2.** Heat the remaining 1 tablespoon of olive oil in a medium skillet. Add the corn and cook over moderately high heat until crisp-tender, about 2 minutes. Transfer to a bowl and let cool. Add the celery, lemon juice, garlic, mayonnaise, paprika and cayenne and season with salt and pepper. Stir in the shredded cabbage.

**3.** Quickly warm the tortillas on the grill. Spread the tortillas on a work surface and mound the corn slaw in the center of each. Top with the shrimp. Roll up the wraps, cut in half and serve.
—*Annie Miler*

**WINE** Light, soft Chenin Blanc.

## Grilled Shrimp and Chayote Salad with Chili-Garlic Dressing
**TOTAL: 30 MIN**
**6 SERVINGS ● ● ●**

Chayote, a type of squash widely used in Latin American cooking, is perfect for grilling because it stays crisp and turns sweet when charred.

- ½ cup fresh orange juice
- 1 tablespoon plus 2 teaspoons low-sodium soy sauce
- 2 teaspoons Asian chili-garlic sauce
- 1 teaspoon Asian sesame oil
- 1 large red onion, sliced crosswise ¼ inch thick
- 6 Portobello mushroom caps, cleaned with a damp paper towel
- 1 large chayote (¾ pound)— halved lengthwise, pitted and cut lengthwise into 24 slices
- 2 pounds shelled and deveined medium shrimp
- ¼ cup pure olive oil, for brushing

Salt and freshly ground pepper

**1.** Light a grill. In a small bowl, combine the orange juice, soy sauce, chili-garlic sauce and sesame oil.

**2.** Insert a toothpick through each onion slice to the center to hold it together. Arrange the onion slices, Portobello caps and chayote slices on 2 large, rimmed baking sheets. Thread the shrimp onto six 12-inch metal skewers. Brush the vegetables and shrimp with the olive oil and season with salt and pepper.

**3.** Grill the onion and chayote over a medium-hot fire until they are lightly charred, about 2 minutes per side. Grill the Portobellos until tender and lightly charred, 4 minutes per side. Return the vegetables to the baking sheets. Grill the shrimp until just cooked through, about 1 minute per side.

**4.** Thickly slice the Portobellos. Remove the toothpicks from the onion slices and separate into rings. Drizzle 3 tablespoons of the chili-garlic dressing over the Portobello slices, onion rings and chayote. Toss until evenly coated. Mound the vegetable salad on plates and top with the shrimp skewers. Drizzle with the remaining dressing and serve.
—*Marcia Kiesel*

**WINE** Ripe, oaky Chardonnay.

## Indian-Style Shrimp and Rice Pilaf

**TOTAL: 25 MIN**

4 SERVINGS ● ●

1½  cups water

1  tablespoon kosher salt

1  bay leaf

1¼  cups basmati rice (½ pound)

2  tablespoons vegetable oil

1  small onion, very finely chopped

¼  cup slivered almonds

¼  cup shelled unsalted whole pistachios

1  teaspoon ground coriander

1  teaspoon turmeric

¾  pound shelled and deveined medium shrimp, cut into ½-inch pieces

4  pitted prunes, cut into ½-inch dice

½  teaspoon finely grated orange zest

Salt and freshly ground pepper

2  tablespoons coarsely chopped fresh dill

1  tablespoon fresh lemon juice

**1.** In a medium saucepan, combine the water with the salt and bay leaf and bring to a boil. Add the rice, cover and cook over low heat until the water is absorbed and the rice is tender, about 20 minutes. Discard the bay leaf.

**2.** Meanwhile, heat the vegetable oil in a large, deep skillet. Add the onion, slivered almonds, pistachios, ground coriander and turmeric and cook over moderate heat until the onion is softened, about 4 minutes.

**3.** Add the shrimp, prunes and orange zest to the skillet and season with salt and pepper. Cook, stirring, until the shrimp are opaque, about 3 minutes. Add the rice and cook, stirring, to heat through. Add the dill and lemon juice and season with salt and pepper. Spoon onto plates and serve. *—Eric Ripert*

**WINE** Dry, crisp sparkling wine.

**GRILLED SHRIMP AND CORN WRAPS**

**INDIAN-STYLE SHRIMP AND RICE PILAF**

**VERY SOFT POLENTA WITH ROCK SHRIMP RAGOUT**

### Shrimp and Lemon Skewers with Feta-Dill Sauce

**TOTAL: 30 MIN**

6 SERVINGS ● ● ●

Squeeze the charred lemons over the shrimp before serving for a tangy, smoky hit of flavor. You may want to make extra feta sauce to have with lean lamb steaks or chicken skewers.

½ cup plain low-fat yogurt
1 scallion, white and light green parts only, thinly sliced
4 large garlic cloves, very finely chopped
2½ tablespoons finely chopped fresh dill
½ cup crumbled feta cheese (2 ounces)
Salt and freshly ground pepper
¼ cup extra-virgin olive oil
2 pounds shelled and deveined large shrimp
2 lemons, halved lengthwise and cut into 12 wedges

**1.** Light a grill. In a medium bowl, mix the yogurt with the scallion, one-quarter of the garlic and ½ tablespoon of the dill. Stir in the feta, mashing it slightly. Season with salt and pepper.

**2.** In a large bowl, combine the remaining chopped garlic and 2 tablespoons of dill with the olive oil. Add the shrimp and lemon wedges, season with salt and pepper and toss to coat. Thread 4 shrimp and 2 lemon wedges onto each of 12 long skewers (if using bamboo skewers, soak them in water for 30 minutes to keep them from burning on the grill).

**3.** Season the skewers with salt and pepper and grill the over a medium-hot fire, turning occasionally, until the shrimp are charred in spots and cooked through, about 5 minutes. Transfer the shrimp and lemon skewers to a large platter and serve at once, with the feta-dill sauce. —*Grace Parisi*

**WINE** Light, soft Chenin Blanc.

### Very Soft Polenta with Rock Shrimp Ragout

**TOTAL: 25 MIN**

8 SERVINGS ● ●

Chef Mario Batali of New York City's Babbo created this variation on a classic Italian specialty from the coastal villages outside of Trieste, where the fresh seafood is among the most prized in the world. The polenta that accompanies the shrimp must be very soft, almost saucelike. "Thick, lumpy polenta is criminal in that part of Italy, and justly so," Batali says.

5¼ cups water
1 tablespoon sugar
1 cup quick-cooking polenta (6 ounces)
¼ cup plus 2 tablespoons extra-virgin olive oil
Salt
4 scallions, thinly sliced
½ teaspoon crushed red pepper
3 tablespoons tomato paste
½ cup dry white wine
1½ pounds shelled rock shrimp
¼ cup coarsely chopped flat-leaf parsley
1 tablespoon fresh lemon juice
1½ teaspoons finely grated lemon zest
Freshly ground pepper

**1.** In a medium saucepan, bring 5 cups of the water to a boil with the sugar. Whisk in the polenta in a thin stream. Cook over low heat, stirring constantly, until thickened, about 5 minutes. Remove from the heat. Stir in 3 tablespoons of the olive oil and season with salt. Press a piece of parchment paper or wax paper directly onto the surface of the polenta and keep warm.

**2.** In a large, deep skillet, heat the remaining 3 tablespoons of oil. Add the scallions and crushed red pepper and cook over moderate heat for 1 minute. Add the tomato paste and cook, stirring, until slightly darkened, about 3 minutes.

Add the wine and the remaining ¼ cup of water and simmer over moderately high heat for 1 minute. Add the shrimp and simmer, stirring, until just cooked through, about 2 minutes. Stir in the parsley, lemon juice and lemon zest and season with salt and pepper. Remove from the heat.

**3.** Rewarm the polenta over moderately high heat, whisking constantly. Spoon a pool of polenta in the center of 8 shallow bowls. Spoon the shrimp and sauce over and around the polenta and serve right away. —*Mario Batali*

**WINE** Light, spicy Pinot Grigio.

### Sautéed Shrimp with Green Olives, Scallions and Anchovies

**TOTAL: 25 MIN**

6 SERVINGS ● ●

¼ cup extra-virgin olive oil
4 large scallions, white and tender green parts only, thinly sliced
3 large garlic cloves, very thinly sliced
6 large anchovy fillets, finely chopped
18 green Greek olives, pitted and coarsely chopped
1¾ pounds shelled and deveined medium shrimp
¼ cup dry white wine, such as Verdejo, Albariño or Sauvignon Blanc
1 tablespoon unsalted butter
1 tablespoon fresh lemon juice
Salt and freshly ground pepper

**1.** Heat the olive oil in a large skillet until shimmering. Add the scallions and garlic and cook over moderate heat until they are softened, about 3 minutes. Add the anchovies and cook, mashing them with a fork, for 2 minutes. Add the olives and stir for 1 minute to heat through. Add the shrimp and cook, turning once or twice, until they start to curl, about 2 minutes. Add the white wine and simmer, stirring

# shellfish

constantly, until the shrimp are just cooked, about 1 minute longer.

2. Remove the skillet from the heat. Stir in the butter and lemon juice and season with salt and pepper. Transfer the shrimp to plates and serve. —*Marcia Kiesel*

**SERVE WITH** Orzo with toasted almonds.
**WINE** Round, rich Sauvignon Blanc.

## Grilled Yucatán Shrimp

**TOTAL: 45 MIN**

6 SERVINGS ●

- 2 tablespoons achiote powder (see Note)
- 2 large garlic cloves, minced
- ⅓ cup fresh orange juice
- 1 tablespoon fresh lemon juice
- 1 tablespoon ancho chile powder
- ¼ teaspoon cayenne pepper

Salt

- ¼ cup extra-virgin olive oil
- 2 pounds shelled and deveined large shrimp
- ½ cup cilantro leaves, minced

Summer Vegetable Rice (p. 237) and lemons, for serving

1. Light a grill. In a large bowl, blend the achiote, garlic, orange and lemon juices, chile powder, cayenne and ¼ teaspoon of salt. Whisk in the oil. Add the shrimp and toss. Refrigerate for 30 minutes.

2. Thread the shrimp onto six 12-inch skewers. Season with salt; reserve the marinade. Grill the shrimp over a hot fire, basting with the marinade, until barely cooked through, 2 minutes per side. Transfer to plates, sprinkle with the cilantro and serve with Summer Vegetable Rice and lemon wedges.
—*Dolores Cakebread*

**NOTE** Achiote powder, available at Latin markets and some supermarkets, is ground from achiote (annatto) seeds. Virtually flavorless, it is used in Latin cooking to give dishes a bright reddish-orange color.

**WINE** Lively, assertive Sauvignon Blanc.

## Pan-Fried Shrimp with Lemon and Ouzo

**ACTIVE: 10 MIN; TOTAL: 2 HR 10 MIN**

6 SERVINGS ● ●

- ½ cup ouzo
- ¼ cup fresh lemon juice
- ½ teaspoon cayenne pepper
- 1½ pounds large shrimp, shelled
- 3 tablespoons extra-virgin olive oil

Salt

1. In a large, shallow dish, combine the ouzo, lemon juice and cayenne. Add the shrimp and toss to coat thoroughly with the marinade. Cover and refrigerate for at least 1½ hours or for up to 2 hours.

2. Dry the shrimp. In a large skillet, heat 1½ tablespoons of the oil until shimmering. Add half of the shrimp and cook over high heat, stirring, until golden and just cooked, 2 minutes. Season with salt and transfer to a platter. Repeat with the remaining oil and shrimp. Serve hot or warm. —*Diane Kochilas*

**WINE** Full-bodied, fragrant Viognier.

## Sautéed Shrimp and Tarragon with Parsnip Puree

**TOTAL: 30 MIN**

4 FIRST-COURSE SERVINGS ●

- 1 pound parsnips, peeled and thinly sliced
- 2 cups milk
- 1 cup water

Salt

Freshly ground pepper

- 3 tablespoons unsalted butter
- 12 large shrimp—shelled, deveined and halved lengthwise
- 1 tablespoon coarsely chopped tarragon

Lemon wedges, for serving

1. In a medium saucepan, cover the parsnips with the milk and water, add a generous pinch of salt and bring to a boil. Simmer over moderately low heat until the parsnips are just tender, about 10 minutes; drain, reserving ¼ cup of the

cooking liquid. Transfer the parsnips and the reserved cooking liquid to a food processor and puree. Return the puree to the saucepan, season with salt and pepper and keep warm.

2. In a large skillet, melt the butter. Add the shrimp, season with salt and pepper and cook over moderate heat, stirring, until the shrimp are pink and just white throughout, about 3 minutes. Stir in the tarragon. Spoon the parsnip puree onto plates, top with the shrimp and drizzle with the butter. Serve with lemon wedges.
—*Mohammad Islam*

**WINE** Flinty, high-acid Chablis.

## Curried Shrimp and Carrot Bouillabaisse

**TOTAL: 30 MIN**

4 SERVINGS ● ●

- 2 tablespoons extra-virgin olive oil
- 2 pounds shelled and deveined large shrimp

Kosher salt and freshly ground pepper

- 2½ teaspoons curry powder
- 1 tablespoon unsalted butter
- 1 large shallot, coarsely chopped
- 1 large garlic clove, coarsely chopped
- 1 pound medium carrots, sliced on the diagonal ¼ inch thick
- 2 teaspoons caraway seeds
- 2 teaspoons coriander seeds
- 2 teaspoons mustard seeds
- 1 bay leaf
- ½ cup dry white wine
- 2 cups fresh carrot juice
- 1 tablespoon chopped cilantro (optional)

1. In a large skillet, heat 1 tablespoon of the olive oil until shimmering. Add the shrimp and season with salt, pepper and 1½ teaspoons of the curry powder. Cook over moderately high heat for 3 minutes, stirring frequently. Transfer the shrimp to a bowl.

2. In the same skillet, melt the butter in the remaining 1 tablespoon of olive oil over moderately low heat. Add the shallot, garlic and the remaining 1 teaspoon of curry; cook for 3 minutes. Increase the heat to moderate, add the carrots and cook, stirring occasionally, until they begin to soften, about 5 minutes.

3. Wrap the caraway, coriander and mustard seeds and the bay leaf in cheesecloth, tie with kitchen string and add to the pan. Add the wine and simmer, scraping up any browned bits, until reduced by half, 2 minutes. Add the carrot juice, cover and simmer until the carrots are tender, 10 minutes. Add the shrimp; simmer 2 minutes. Season with salt and pepper. Discard the spices. Garnish with cilantro and serve. —Galen Zamarra

**WINE** Dry, mineral-flavored Chenin Blanc.

### Sea Scallops with Spinach and Grape Tomatoes

**TOTAL: 25 MIN**

4 SERVINGS ● ●

  1  cup grape tomatoes, halved
  ¼  cup extra-virgin olive oil
  1  tablespoon fresh lemon juice
Salt and freshly ground pepper
1½  pounds sea scallops
Two 10-ounce bags spinach, large
     stems removed
  2  tablespoons minced chives

1. In a saucepan fitted with a steamer basket, bring 1 inch of water to a boil. Add the tomatoes, cover and steam over moderately high heat for 1 minute. In a shallow bowl, mix 3 tablespoons of the oil with the lemon juice. Add the tomatoes, season with salt and pepper and stir.

2. Spread the scallops in the steamer basket. Drizzle them with the remaining 1 tablespoon of olive oil and season with salt and pepper. Cover and steam over moderately high heat until just cooked, about 5 minutes. Transfer the scallops to a shallow bowl and keep warm.

3. Add half of the spinach to the steamer, cover and steam for 2 minutes; stir. Add the remaining spinach, sprinkle with ½ teaspoon of salt and toss well. Cover and steam for 2 minutes.

4. Mound the spinach on plates. Top with the scallops, any accumulated juices and the tomato vinaigrette. Sprinkle with the chives and serve. —Stephanie Lyness

**WINE** Light, spicy Pinot Grigio.

### Sautéed Sea Scallops and Mâche Salad with Moutarde Violette

**TOTAL: 25 MIN**

4 FIRST-COURSE SERVINGS ● ●

*Moutarde violette,* a tangy purple mustard flavored with grapes and spices, can be found at zingermans.com (see box at right). It's lovely in vinaigrettes, but also perfect with cold cuts, grilled sausages or in a pan sauce for sautéed fish or chicken.

  ¼  cup plus 1 tablespoon *moutarde violette* or slightly sweet whole-grain mustard
  ¼  cup extra-virgin olive oil
  1  tablespoon walnut oil
  1  tablespoon fresh lemon juice
Salt and freshly ground pepper
  1  large egg
  1  cup fine dry bread crumbs
1¼  pounds large sea scallops (about 12), rinsed and patted dry
  4  cups mâche (1 ounce) or young arugula
  1  cup walnuts, toasted

1. Preheat the oven to 275°. In a bowl, blend 1 tablespoon of the *moutarde violette* with 1 tablespoon of the olive oil, the walnut oil and the lemon juice; season with salt and pepper.

2. In another bowl, beat the egg with the remaining ¼ cup of *moutarde violette.* Put the bread crumbs in a shallow bowl. Season the scallops with salt and pepper. Dip each scallop in the egg mixture and then in the bread crumbs, pressing to help the crumbs adhere.

# web sites

**PAULA WOLFERT'S FAVORITES**    **TIP**

Cookbook author Paula Wolfert, whose sautéed sea scallop recipe is featured at left, uses a variety of online sources to buy imported or hard-to-find ingredients and tools.
**BIENMANGER.COM** Artisanal French cakes, confections and sweets.
**DARTAGNAN.COM** Wide selection of poultry, including guinea hens, quail and a variety of ducks; duck confit; sausages; pâtés; foie gras and cured meats.
**FANTES.COM** Cookware and utensils, including wood-handled ceramic Kyocera knives and German Rumtopf pots for putting up fruit confit.
**FORMAGGIOKITCHEN.COM** Preserves, oils, charcuterie and condiments, like the apple-based Mostarda di Mantova, and cheeses, like Pecorino di Pienza Gran Riserva.
**KALUSTYANS.COM** Spices, bulgur in all sizes, beans and legumes, orange- and rose-flower waters, nuts, dried fruits, pomegranate molasses, *basturma* (Middle Eastern spice-cured beef) and mulberry syrup.
**SEASONEDPIONEERS.COM** Delicious spices and spice mixtures, including Moroccan *ras el hanout* and Tunisian *tabil.*
**SPANISHTABLE.COM** and **TIENDA.COM** Spanish specialties, including piquillo peppers, chorizo, assorted rices, lentils, oils and vinegars, plus ceramics.
**SUNNYLANDMILLS.COM** Grano (durum wheat) and other grains.
**ZINGERMANS.COM** Condiments, cheeses, honeys, breads, olives, oils, balsamic vinegars and dried maras Turkish red pepper.

● FAST    ● HEALTHY    ● MAKE AHEAD    ● STAFF FAVORITE      

# shellfish

3. Set a rack over a baking sheet. In a large skillet, heat the remaining 3 tablespoons of olive oil over high heat. Add the scallops and cook undisturbed until browned, 30 seconds per side. Transfer the scallops to the rack and bake for 8 to 10 minutes, or until cooked through.

4. In a large bowl, toss the mâche with the walnuts. Add 2 tablespoons of the vinaigrette and toss well. Mound the salad on plates and top with the scallops. Drizzle on the remaining vinaigrette and serve. —Paula Wolfert

**WINE** Round, rich Sauvignon Blanc.

### Scallops with Orzo, Tomatoes and Ginger
**TOTAL: 30 MIN**
4 SERVINGS ● ●

1 cup orzo or other tiny pasta
One 1-inch piece of fresh ginger, peeled and coarsely chopped
1 large stalk of fresh lemongrass, tender inner core of bottom third only, coarsely chopped
¼ cup vegetable oil
1¼ pounds tomatoes, chopped
3 tablespoons chopped basil
1 tablespoon fresh lemon juice
Salt and freshly ground pepper
1½ pounds large sea scallops

1. In a saucepan of boiling salted water, cook the orzo, stirring occasionally, until al dente, about 5 minutes. Drain.

2. Meanwhile, in a mini processor, mince the ginger with the lemongrass. Heat 2 tablespoons of the oil in a medium skillet until shimmering. Add the ginger and lemongrass and cook over moderately high heat until fragrant, about 2 minutes. Add the tomatoes and cook, stirring, for 1 minute. Add 2 tablespoons of the basil and the lemon juice and season with salt and pepper.

3. In a large skillet, heat the remaining 2 tablespoons of oil until shimmering. Add the scallops, season with salt and pepper and cook over high heat until browned on the bottom, about 2 minutes. Turn and cook for 1 minute longer.

4. Mound the orzo in shallow bowls and top with the tomatoes and scallops. Sprinkle with the remaining 1 tablespoon of basil and serve. —Eric Ripert

**WINE** Round-textured Sémillon.

### Scallops, Corn and Basil Steamed in Foil
**TOTAL: 25 MIN**
6 SERVINGS ● ● ●

Foil pouches, or hobo packs, are fabulous for grilling seafood and sliced or cubed meat because the food steams in its own juices.

¾ cup dry white wine
2 medium shallots, thinly sliced
2 tablespoons unsalted butter, cut into 6 pieces
2 tablespoons extra-virgin olive oil
2¼ pounds sea scallops
36 cherry tomatoes, halved
3 cups baby spinach (2 ounces)
1 cup fresh or frozen corn kernels
¾ cup chopped basil
Salt and freshly ground pepper

1. Light a grill. Cut six 18-by-20-inch pieces of heavy-duty aluminum foil. In the center of each piece of aluminum foil, combine 2 tablespoons of the white wine with one-sixth of the sliced shallots, 1 piece of butter and 1 teaspoon of olive oil. Top with the scallops, followed by the tomatoes, spinach, corn and basil. Season with salt and pepper. Bring the sides of the foil together and fold to form neat rectangles. Grill the foil packs over a medium-hot fire until steam inflates them and you hear the juices bubbling, about 10 minutes.

2. Carefully open the foil packs to let the steam escape, then transfer the contents to shallow soup bowls and serve immediately. —Marcia Kiesel

**WINE** Dry, mineral-flavored Chenin Blanc.

### Four Pea Salad with Scallops
**TOTAL: 30 MIN**
4 SERVINGS ● ●

There is an unexpected, playful finishing touch to this bright-flavored dish: a topping of spicy, crunchy, crushed wasabi peas.

¾ cup packed mint leaves
2 tablespoons fresh lemon juice
½ cup vegetable oil
Salt and freshly ground pepper
¼ pound snow peas, trimmed
¼ pound sugar snap peas, trimmed
½ pound pea shoots or 2 bunches watercress, thick stems removed (4 packed cups)
1½ pounds sea scallops
¼ cup wasabi peas, lightly crushed

1. In a blender, puree the mint leaves, lemon juice and 6 tablespoons of the oil. Season with salt and pepper.

2. Bring a saucepan of salted water to a boil and fill a medium bowl with ice water. Add the snow peas and sugar snap peas to the boiling water and cook until crisp-tender, about 1½ minutes. Drain the peas and transfer to the ice water to cool. Drain from the ice water and pat dry. Transfer to a large bowl and add the pea shoots.

3. In a large skillet, heat the remaining 2 tablespoons of oil until almost smoking. Season the scallops with salt and pepper and cook over high heat until deeply browned, 3 minutes. Using a spatula, flip the scallops and cook until they are white throughout, 1 minute longer. Transfer the scallops to a plate.

4. Add all but 1 tablespoon of the dressing to the peas, season with salt and pepper and toss to coat. Transfer the salad to plates. Add the scallops and the remaining dressing to the bowl and toss. Arrange the scallops on top of the salad and sprinkle with the crushed wasabi peas. —Ilene Rosen

**WINE** Soft, off-dry Riesling.

**SCALLOPS WITH ORZO, TOMATOES AND GINGER**

**SPICE-CRUSTED SCALLOPS WITH CAPERS**

## Spice-Crusted Scallops with Crisp Capers

**TOTAL: 40 MIN**

**4 SERVINGS** ●

- ⅓ cup strained fresh orange juice
- 1 hard-cooked large egg yolk
- 1 tablespoon rice vinegar
- ½ teaspoon Dijon mustard
- ⅓ cup plus 2 tablespoons extra-virgin olive oil

Kosher salt and freshly ground pepper

- ¼ cup canola oil
- ¼ cup capers, preferably nonpareil, rinsed and patted dry
- 1 medium pink grapefruit
- 1 tablespoon ground coriander
- 1 tablespoon ground cumin
- 16 large sea scallops (about 1¼ pounds)

Mint leaves and tarragon leaves, for garnish

**1.** In a small skillet, simmer the orange juice over moderate heat until reduced to about 2 tablespoons, 6 to 7 minutes. Transfer the thickened juice to a blender. Add the hard-cooked egg yolk, rice vinegar and mustard and process until smooth. With the machine on, add ⅓ cup of the olive oil in a thin stream and process until emulsified. Season the sauce with salt and pepper and transfer to a small heatproof bowl. Set the bowl over a small saucepan of barely simmering water and keep the sauce warm; do not let it boil.

**2.** Wipe out the skillet. Add the canola oil and heat until shimmering. Add the capers and cook over moderately high heat until they open slightly and begin to brown, about 4 minutes. Using a slotted spoon, transfer the capers to a paper towel–lined plate to drain.

**3.** Using a sharp knife, peel the grapefruit, removing the bitter white pith. Over a bowl, cut between the membranes to yield the grapefruit segments.

**4.** In a bowl, combine the ground coriander and cumin. Season the scallops with salt and pepper and dip half of each scallop into the spice mixture to coat it. In a large skillet, heat the remaining 2 tablespoons of oil until almost smoking. Add the scallops in a single layer and cook over high heat until golden, about 3 minutes. Turn the scallops; cook for 1 minute longer. Remove from the heat.

**5.** Spoon 2 tablespoons of the warm sauce onto each of 4 plates. Arrange the scallops on the sauce and place the grapefruit segments around them. Scatter the capers and herbs over the scallops and serve. —*Rob Evans*

**WINE** Zesty Albariño or Vinho Verde.

● FAST     ● HEALTHY     ● MAKE AHEAD     ● STAFF FAVORITE

CLAMS WITH SPICY SAUSAGE

SAKE-STEAMED CLAMS, P. 196

## Seared Scallops with Braised Collard Greens and Cider Sauce

**ACTIVE: 45 MIN; TOTAL: 2 HR 30 MIN**

**8 FIRST-COURSE SERVINGS**

Collard greens are commonly known as the homey, Southern partner to black-eyed peas. Here, they take a decidedly elegant turn when topped with delicate scallops and a hint of cider. Be sure to include some of their flavorful broth with each serving.

- 2 tablespoons vegetable oil
- 4 thick slices of bacon, thinly sliced crosswise
- 1 onion, halved and thinly sliced
- 1½ pounds collard greens, stems and ribs discarded, leaves cut into 1-inch ribbons
- 1 cup dry white wine
- 4 cups chicken stock or low-sodium broth
- Salt and freshly ground pepper
- 3 tablespoons cider vinegar
- 5 tablespoons unsalted butter
- 16 very large diver scallops or 2 pounds large sea scallops
- 2 tablespoons all-purpose flour
- ⅔ cup apple cider

**1.** In a large pot, heat 1 tablespoon of the vegetable oil. Add the bacon and cook over moderate heat until browned, about 5 minutes. Add the onion and cook, stirring occasionally, until softened, about 5 minutes. Add the collard greens and cook, stirring, for 2 minutes. Add the wine and cook, stirring, until the collards are wilted, about 5 minutes longer.

**2.** Add all but ⅓ cup of the stock to the collards and bring to a simmer. Season with salt and pepper and cook over moderately low heat until tender, 1½ hours. Add 2 tablespoons of the cider vinegar and 2 tablespoons of the butter and simmer for 10 minutes; keep warm.

**3.** Season the scallops with salt and pepper and sprinkle with the flour, tapping off the excess. In a large skillet, melt

1 tablespoon of the butter in the remaining 1 tablespoon of oil. Add the scallops and cook over high heat until golden on the bottom, about 4 minutes. Turn and cook the scallops until lightly browned and cooked through, 1 to 2 minutes longer. Transfer the scallops to a large plate and keep warm.

**4.** Return the skillet to high heat. Add the apple cider and the remaining ⅓ cup of chicken stock and 1 tablespoon of vinegar and cook, scraping up any browned bits, until slightly reduced, 5 minutes. Reduce the heat to moderate, add the remaining 2 tablespoons of butter and shake the pan until the butter is incorporated. Strain into a bowl.

**5.** Using a slotted spoon, mound the collards on 8 plates. Top each serving with 2 scallops and sauce and serve. —*Ashley Christensen*

**MAKE AHEAD** The collard greens can be prepared and refrigerated, covered, for up to 2 days.

**WINE** Fruity, low-oak Chardonnay.

## Celery Root Remoulade with Scallops and Caviar

**ACTIVE: 30 MIN; TOTAL: 1 HR 30 MIN**

4 FIRST-COURSE SERVINGS

- ½ cup mayonnaise
- 2 tablespoons Dijon mustard
- 1 tablespoon fresh lemon juice
- 2 tablespoons chopped parsley
- 1 pound celery root—quartered, peeled and cut on a mandoline into thin julienne strips
- Salt and freshly ground black pepper
- Four 2-ounce sea scallops
- Pinch of cayenne pepper
- 1 tablespoon melted butter
- Osetra caviar, for garnish

**1.** In a medium bowl, combine the mayonnaise, mustard, lemon juice and parsley. Fold in the celery root and season with salt and black pepper. Cover and refrigerate for at least 1 hour or overnight.

**2.** Preheat the broiler. Cut each scallop crosswise into 3 slices. On a medium, rimmed baking sheet, arrange each scallop like a clover leaf, overlapping the slices slightly in the middle. Add the cayenne to the melted butter and brush the scallops with the seasoned butter. Season with salt and black pepper. Broil the scallops for about 1 minute, until barely cooked but heated through.

**3.** Mound the celery root remoulade on plates. Using a spatula, transfer the scallops along with any pan juices to the remoulade. Garnish with caviar and serve. —*Jean-Georges Vongerichten*

**WINE** Flinty, high-acid Chablis.

## Clams with Spicy Sausage

**TOTAL: 25 MIN**

4 SERVINGS ● ●

- ¼ cup extra-virgin olive oil
- 3 garlic cloves, thinly sliced
- 1 medium onion, thinly sliced
- 1 teaspoon finely grated lemon zest
- 1½ teaspoons curry powder
- ¼ pound andouille sausage, thinly sliced
- 1 cup chicken stock
- 4 dozen littleneck clams, scrubbed
- ¼ cup chopped cilantro
- Lemon wedges, for serving

**1.** Heat the olive oil in a large saucepan. Add the garlic, onion, lemon zest and curry powder and cook over moderate heat, stirring occasionally, for 5 minutes. Add the andouille and cook over moderately high heat for 2 minutes. Add the stock and bring to a boil. Add the clams, cover and cook, shaking the pan a few times, until they open, 5 minutes. Discard any clams that do not open.

**2.** Using a slotted spoon, spoon the clams into shallow bowls. Stir the cilantro into the broth, then pour over the clams. Serve with lemon wedges.—*Eric Ripert*

**WINE** Fruity, low-oak Chardonnay.

## Sardinian Clams with Fregola

**TOTAL: 40 MIN**

4 SERVINGS ● ●

*Fregola,* sometimes referred to as *fregula,* is a lumpy, pebble-shaped pasta from Sardinia that is formed by hand and then lightly toasted until golden. It comes in small, medium and large grains and is available at specialty markets or by mail-order from Formaggio Kitchen (888-212-3224 or formaggiokitchen.com) or from chefshop.com.

- ⅓ cup extra-virgin olive oil
- 2 garlic cloves, minced
- 4 large plum tomatoes, chopped (about 2 cups)
- 1½ cups water
- ½ cup *fregola*
- 2 dozen littleneck clams, rinsed and scrubbed
- Salt and freshly ground pepper
- 2 tablespoons coarsely chopped flat-leaf parsley

**1.** Heat the olive oil in a large skillet until shimmering. Add the garlic and cook over moderately high heat until fragrant, about 30 seconds. Add the chopped tomatoes and cook until softened, about 3 minutes. Add the water and bring to a boil. Stir in the *fregola,* cover and cook over moderately low heat, stirring occasionally, until the pasta is tender, about 17 minutes.

# pairing

**SHELLFISH + SAKE**    TIP

For briny shellfish like clams, choose a crisp sake like **Moriko Junmai Daiginjo, which has a minerally quality. The tangy flavor** of **Wakatake Daiginjo also works with grilled vegetables and hard-to-pair foods, like asparagus.**

# shellfish

**2.** Add the clams to the skillet in a single layer. Cover and cook over moderately high heat until the clams open, about 4 minutes. Discard any clams that do not open. Season the *fregola* with salt and pepper. Spoon the *fregola,* clams and broth into shallow bowls. Sprinkle with the parsley and serve at once.
—*Valentina Argiolas*

**WINE** High-acid, savory Vermentino.

### Sake-Steamed Clams
**ACTIVE: 10 MIN; TOTAL: 1 HR 15 MIN**

**4 SERVINGS** ●

You can use a cooking sake, or *ryori,* for steaming the clams. One good brand is Shochikubai.

Salt
- 2 pounds Manila clams or cockles, scrubbed
- 1 cup sake
- 1 cup water
- 2 teaspoons unsalted butter, cut into 4 pieces
- 2 scallions, white and light green parts only, thinly sliced

Pinch of *togarashi* spice blend (optional; see Note)

**1.** Fill a medium bowl with cold water and add 1 tablespoon of salt. Add the clams and let stand for 1 hour. Drain the clams and rinse them well.

**2.** In a large, deep skillet, combine the sake with the water and bring to a boil. Add the clams, cover the skillet tightly and cook, shaking the pan occasionally, until the clams open, about 4 minutes. Discard any that do not open.

**3.** Spoon the steamed clams and the broth into 4 bowls. Top each with a piece of butter, garnish with the scallions and *togarashi* and serve at once.
—*Nobuo Fukuda*

**NOTE** *Togarashi* is a Japanese blend of cayenne, sesame seeds and seaweed. It is available at Asian markets.

**WINE** Flinty, high-acid Chablis.

### Mussels in Sailor's Sauce
**TOTAL: 20 MIN**

**4 SERVINGS** ● ●

Mussels are a staple in the cooking of Galicia, a rugged coastal region in north-western Spain. The unusual name for this dish refers to the fast, fresh sauces (which usually contained onions and tomatoes) that the wives of fishermen would prepare from their husbands' catch of the day.

- ¼ cup extra-virgin olive oil
- 1 small onion, chopped
- 2 medium garlic cloves, finely chopped
- 1 jalapeño, finely chopped
- 1 large tomato—peeled, seeded and coarsely chopped
- ½ teaspoon dried oregano, lightly crumbled

Large pinch of Spanish saffron, lightly crumbled
- ½ teaspoon all-purpose flour
- ½ cup dry white wine, such as Albariño
- 2 pounds mussels, scrubbed and debearded
- ½ cup fish stock or bottled clam juice
- 2 tablespoons finely chopped flat-leaf parsley
- 1½ teaspoons fresh lemon juice

Crusty country bread, for serving

In a large, heavy saucepan, heat the olive oil. Add the onion, garlic and jalapeño and cook over moderately high heat, stirring, until softened, about 3 minutes. Add the tomato, oregano and saffron and cook for 1 minute, stirring. Sprinkle the flour over the vegetables and stir it in. Add the wine and mussels, cover the pan and cook, stirring, for 1 minute. Add the fish stock, parsley and lemon juice and cook over high heat, stirring, until the mussels open, about 5 minutes. Discard any mussels that do not open. Transfer the mus-

sels and their sauce to deep bowls. Serve at once with crusty bread to soak up the sauce. —*Marisol Bueno*

**WINE** Zesty Albariño or Vinho Verde.

### Mussel and Fingerling Potato Salad
**ACTIVE: 30 MIN; TOTAL: 1 HR 20 MIN**

**8 SERVINGS** ● ● ●

With this recipe, Paris-born fragrance and cosmetics entrepreneur Sylvie Chantecaille honors one of her favorite restaurants—Chez Hortense in Lège-Cap-Ferret near Bordeaux, which she says serves the best mussels in the world.

- 3 pounds small fingerling potatoes

Salt
- ¼ cup extra-virgin olive oil
- 8 garlic cloves, thinly sliced
- 8 thyme sprigs
- 1 large onion, thinly sliced
- 1 cup dry rosé wine
- 5 tablespoons fresh lemon juice
- 6 pounds mussels, scrubbed and debearded
- ¾ cup mayonnaise
- 1 tablespoon Dijon mustard
- 2 tablespoons chopped capers
- 2 tablespoons chopped cornichons
- 2 tablespoons chopped parsley
- 2 tablespoons chopped chives

Freshly ground pepper

**1.** In a large saucepan, cover the potatoes with water, add a large pinch of salt, bring to a boil and simmer over moderately high heat until the potatoes are tender, about 20 minutes. Drain and let cool, then slice the potatoes ¼ inch thick and transfer to a bowl.

**2.** Heat the olive oil in a large pot. Add the garlic, thyme sprigs and onion and cook over moderately low heat until softened, about 12 minutes. Add the rosé and 2 tablespoons of the lemon juice and bring to a boil over high heat. Add the mussels, cover and cook, shaking the pan a few times, until the mussels open,

MUSSELS IN SAILOR'S SAUCE

# shellfish

about 7 minutes. Discard any mussels that do not open. Set a colander over a large bowl. Pour the mussels into the colander, and when cool enough to handle, shell them. Add the mussels to the potatoes and cover with plastic wrap.

**3.** Slowly pour the mussel juices back into the pot, stopping before you reach the grit at the bottom. Bring to a boil over high heat and cook until reduced to ⅓ cup, about 12 minutes. Let cool.

**4.** In a medium bowl, whisk the mayonnaise with the remaining 3 tablespoons of lemon juice and the mustard. Stir in the capers, cornichons, parsley, chives and the reduced mussel juices. Season with salt and pepper. Fold into the potatoes and mussels. Serve the salad at room temperature or slightly chilled. —*Sylvie Chantecaille*
**WINE** Bright, fruity rosé.

## Mussels with Tomatoes and Feta
**TOTAL: 30 MIN**
6 SERVINGS ● ●

 3 tablespoons extra-virgin
  olive oil
 2 garlic cloves, thinly sliced
 1 small onion, thinly sliced
 1 small green bell pepper,
  finely chopped
 1 pound plum tomatoes, peeled
  and chopped
 1 teaspoon dried Greek oregano,
  crumbled
 ¼ teaspoon cayenne pepper
 2 tablespoons ouzo
 3 pounds mussels, scrubbed
  and debearded
 ¼ cup plus 2 tablespoons
  crumbled feta cheese
 1 tablespoon unsalted butter
Crusty bread, for serving

**1.** In a large pot, heat the olive oil. Add the garlic, onion, bell pepper, tomatoes, oregano and cayenne; cook over moderately high heat, stirring occasionally,

until softened, about 4 minutes. Add the ouzo and boil for 1 minute. Add the mussels, cover and cook until the mussels open, about 5 minutes.

**2.** Transfer the mussels to 6 bowls. Return the pot to high heat and stir in the feta and butter. Pour the broth over the mussels and serve with crusty bread.
—*Diane Kochilas*
**WINE** Lively, assertive Sauvignon Blanc.

## Chile-Steamed Mussels with Green Olive Crostini
**TOTAL: 25 MIN**
8 SERVINGS ● ● ●

 ¼ cup extra-virgin olive oil
 6 garlic cloves, thinly sliced
 1 medium red onion,
  finely chopped
 1 red bell pepper, finely chopped
 2 jalapeños, seeded and
  thinly sliced
 1 habanero, seeded and
  thinly sliced
 2 cups dry white wine
 1 cup tomato sauce
Salt and freshly ground pepper
 4 pounds black mussels, scrubbed
  and debearded
 4 scallions, thinly sliced
Green Olive Crostini, for serving
  (recipe follows)

In a large pot, heat the olive oil. Add the garlic, onion, bell pepper, jalapeños and habanero. Cook over moderately high heat, stirring occasionally, until the onion is golden, about 5 minutes. Add the wine; boil over high heat for 1 minute. Add the tomato sauce, season with salt and pepper and bring to a boil. Add the mussels, cover and cook, shaking the pot a few times until the mussels open, about 5 minutes; discard any that don't open. Divide the mussels and broth among 8 bowls, sprinkle with scallions and serve with Green Olive Crostini. —*Mario Batali*
**WINE** Dry, crisp sparkling wine.

**GREEN OLIVE CROSTINI**
**TOTAL: 15 MIN**
MAKES 8 CROSTINI ● ●

 4 garlic cloves, peeled and smashed
 2½ cups large green pitted olives,
  such as Sicilia (¾ pound)
 2 tablespoons capers, rinsed
  and drained
 ½ cup extra-virgin olive oil
 8 large slices of crusty bread

**1.** Preheat the oven to 400°. In a food processor, process the garlic, olives, capers and olive oil to a coarse paste.

**2.** Toast the bread on the oven rack for 6 minutes, or until crisp and browned. Spread the olive paste thickly over the toasts and serve. —*M.B.*

**MAKE AHEAD** The olive paste can be refrigerated for 2 days. Let return to room temperature before using.

## Pan-Fried Asian-Style Crab Burgers
**ACTIVE: 40 MIN; TOTAL: 1 HR 15 MIN**
6 SERVINGS ●

In this recipe, Dungeness crab is blended with Korean kimchi and *panko* (Japanese bread crumbs) to transform American crab cakes into Asian-style burgers.

 2 large eggs
 ¼ cup mascarpone, at room
  temperature
 1½ cups kimchi, drained and
  chopped, plus 2 tablespoons of
  the pickling juice (see Note)
 3 garlic cloves, minced
Kosher salt
 2 teaspoons very finely grated
  peeled fresh ginger
 1½ pounds Dungeness or lump
  crabmeat, picked over
 1 cup Japanese *panko* or plain dry
  bread crumbs
 1¼ cups mayonnaise
 1 tablespoon fresh lime juice
 1 tablespoon *sambal oelek* (see
  Note) or other hot sauce

1 teaspoon Dijon mustard
1 teaspoon finely grated lime zest
Freshly ground pepper
2 Belgian endives, halved crosswise and cut lengthwise into thin strips
1 medium carrot, julienned on a mandoline or shredded
Vegetable oil, for frying
12 slices of brioche or 6 split brioche or Portuguese rolls, lightly toasted

1. In a large bowl, beat the eggs. Stir in the mascarpone until blended, then add ½ cup of the drained kimchi, two-thirds of the minced garlic, ½ teaspoon of salt and the ginger. Fold in the crabmeat and ½ cup of the *panko*. Pat the crabmeat mixture into 6 burgers, cover with plastic wrap and refrigerate until chilled and firm, about 30 minutes.

2. Meanwhile, in a small bowl, mix the mayonnaise with the lime juice, *sambal oelek*, mustard, grated lime zest and the remaining garlic. Season the mixture with salt and pepper. In a large bowl, toss the endives with the carrot, the remaining 1 cup of kimchi and the 2 tablespoons of pickling juice.

3. Spread the remaining *panko* on a plate and coat the burgers. In a very large non-stick skillet, heat ¼ inch of oil. Add the burgers and cook over moderately high heat, turning once, until browned, 7 minutes. Drain on paper towels.

4. Spread the mayonnaise mixture on the toasted brioche. Set the crab burgers on the brioche toast and top with the kimchi slaw. Close the crab burger sandwiches and serve. —*Shawn McClain*

NOTE Kimchi (spicy pickled and fermented cabbage) and *sambal oelek,* an Indonesian chili-garlic sauce, are both available at Asian markets and specialty shops.

MAKE AHEAD The uncooked crab burgers, spicy mayonnaise and kimchi slaw can be refrigerated separately overnight.
WINE Dry, mineral-flavored Chenin Blanc.

## Warm Lobster Salad with Gazpacho Consommé

ACTIVE: 45 MIN; TOTAL: 1 HR 15 MIN, PLUS 4 HR DRAINING
4 SERVINGS ● ●

CONSOMMÉ
2 pounds tomatoes, chopped
2 medium red bell peppers, chopped
1 medium cucumber, peeled and chopped
1 medium red onion, coarsely chopped
1 large garlic clove, coarsely chopped
¼ cup basil leaves
¼ cup sherry vinegar
2 dashes of Tabasco
1 tablespoon kosher salt

LOBSTER SALAD
Two 1½-pound live lobsters
4 thick asparagus spears
¼ pound thin green beans
2 tablespoons late-harvest Riesling or other sweet white dessert wine
1 tablespoon fresh lemon juice
1 tablespoon extra-virgin olive oil
Salt and freshly ground pepper
4 scallions, white and tender green parts only, thinly sliced
3 celery ribs, peeled and very thinly sliced, plus ¼ cup celery leaves
2 cups mixed baby greens, preferably micro greens

1. MAKE THE CONSOMMÉ: In a food processor, puree the tomatoes, bell peppers, cucumber, red onion, garlic, basil, vinegar, Tabasco and salt. Line a colander with a double layer of dampened cheesecloth and then with a layer of dampened coffee filters. Set the colander over a deep bowl. Pour the puree into the colander and refrigerate for at least 4 hours or overnight. You should have about 3 cups of clear liquid in the bowl. Discard the puree.

2. MEANWHILE, MAKE THE LOBSTER SALAD: In a large pot of boiling salted water, cook the lobsters just until they turn bright red, 8 minutes. Using tongs, carefully transfer the lobsters to a bowl and let cool.

3. Twist off the lobster claws and remove the meat in one piece. Twist off the tails. Using scissors, cut down the soft undersides of the lobsters and remove the tail meat in one piece. Split the tail meat lengthwise; remove and discard the dark intestinal veins. Put all of the lobster meat on a large, rimmed baking sheet and set aside.

4. Preheat the oven to 350°. In a medium saucepan of boiling salted water, cook the asparagus spears and beans until barely tender, about 3 minutes. Drain and let cool. Thinly slice the asparagus and beans on a diagonal.

5. In a small bowl, whisk the Riesling with the lemon juice and olive oil and season with salt and pepper. Brush the lobster

# health

**BENEFITS OF STEAMING**   **TIP**

**One health benefit of steaming mussels and lobster (as well as vegetables) is obvious: You don't need to add any fat to the pan. Steaming is also one of the best ways to** preserve vitamins B and C in food. **These water-soluble vitamins are destroyed by slow-cooking methods like braising and get washed away by boiling. A recent study in the** Journal of the Science of Food and Agriculture **found that steaming** best preserves flavonoids, **compounds that may help protect against disease.** —*Stephanie Lyness*

meat with 2 tablespoons of the Riesling dressing and bake for about 3 minutes, or until just heated through.

6. Arrange the asparagus, beans, scallions and sliced celery in the center of 4 shallow bowls, mounding the vegetables slightly. Carefully pour about ¾ cup of the consommé around the vegetables in each bowl. In a small bowl, toss the baby greens and celery leaves with the remaining Riesling dressing. Set the warmed lobster on the vegetables, top with the dressed greens and serve.
—*Dominique Filoni*
**WINE** Full-bodied, fragrant Viognier.

## Lobster with Pinot Noir Sauce, Salsify Puree and Frizzled Leeks

**ACTIVE: 3 HR**
**8 SERVINGS ●**

Eight 1¼-pound live lobsters
    (see Note)
 1  tablespoon extra-virgin olive oil
 1  large shallot, finely chopped
 2  large garlic cloves, smashed
1½  cups Pinot Noir
1½  cups veal demiglace
 ¼  cup ruby port
Salt and freshly ground pepper

# technique

**TO EXTRACT COOKED MEAT FROM A CLAW,** break open the claw using crackers or by tapping it with the back of a knife. Pull out the meat and inspect it for any bits of shell.

**TO EXTRACT MEAT FROM THE TAIL,** break off the fins from the narrow end of the tail. Using your finger or a fork, push the meat out through the wide end of the tail.

 1  lemon half, plus 2 tablespoons fresh lemon juice
 1  pound salsify
 1  stick (4 ounces) unsalted butter
 ½  cup heavy cream
Pinch of sugar
 6  tablespoons grapeseed oil
 2  medium leeks, white and tender green parts only, cut into 2-inch julienne
 2  vanilla beans, split lengthwise, seeds scraped

1. **COOK THE LOBSTERS:** Fill the sink with ice water. Set a rack in a very large stockpot, add 5 inches of water and bring to a boil. Add 4 of the lobsters, cover and steam until bright red, about 11 minutes. Using tongs, transfer the lobsters to the ice water. Repeat with the remaining lobsters; add water to the pot if necessary.

2. Drain the lobsters and pat dry. Twist off the tails, claws and knuckles. Crack the shells and remove the meat. Slit the tails and pull out the intestinal veins. Using sturdy shears, cut the shells of 2 of the lobsters into 2-inch pieces; discard the remaining lobster shells.

3. **MAKE THE SAUCE:** In a large saucepan, heat the olive oil until shimmering. Add the shallot and cook over moderate heat until just beginning to brown. Add the garlic cloves and cook until fragrant. Add the lobster shells and cook, stirring, until beginning to brown in spots, about 8 minutes. Add the wine and cook over moderately high heat until nearly evaporated, about 15 minutes. Add the veal demiglace and cook over moderate heat until slightly reduced, about 5 minutes. Strain the sauce through a fine sieve into a medium saucepan, pressing hard on the shells to extract as much sauce as possible. Add the port, season with salt and pepper and simmer over moderately low heat for 5 minutes. Cover the Pinot Noir sauce and keep warm.

4. **PREPARE THE SALSIFY:** Fill a bowl with water. Squeeze the lemon half into the water and add it to the bowl. Peel the salsify, cut it into 1-inch lengths and add it to the water.

5. In a large saucepan, combine 1 cup of water with the lemon juice, 6 tablespoons of the butter and a pinch of salt. Drain the salsify, then add it to the pan and bring to a boil. Cover and simmer over moderate heat until the salsify is tender and the liquid is reduced to a glaze, about 15 minutes. Add the cream and sugar and simmer for 1 minute.

6. Transfer the salsify mixture to a food processor and puree until very smooth. Season with salt and pepper. Return the puree to the saucepan and keep warm.

7. **PREPARE THE LEEKS:** In a medium saucepan, heat ¼ cup of the grapeseed oil until shimmering. Add the leeks and fry over moderate heat, stirring, until golden and crisp, 3 to 4 minutes. Using a slotted spoon, transfer the leeks to paper towels. Sprinkle lightly with salt.

8. **MAKE THE VANILLA OIL:** In a small bowl, stir the vanilla seeds into the remaining 2 tablespoons of grapeseed oil.

9. In a large skillet, melt the remaining 2 tablespoons of butter over moderately low heat. Add the lobster meat and cook until warmed through. Slice the tails crosswise into medallions. Mound the salsify puree in the center of 8 warmed dinner plates and arrange 2 claws and 1 tail around each mound. Spoon the Pinot Noir sauce around the lobster and top with the leeks. Dot the plates with the vanilla oil and serve. —*Hubert Keller*
**NOTE** To save time, you can buy cracked, steamed lobsters for this dish.
**MAKE AHEAD** The salsify puree can be chilled overnight. The lobsters, sauce, leeks and oil can be prepared through Step 8 early in the day. Chill the lobster. Reheat everything just before serving.
**WINE** Light, fruity Pinot Noir.

LOBSTER WITH PINOT NOIR SAUCE, SALSIFY PUREE AND FRIZZLED LEEKS

ZUCCHINI PAPPARDELLE WITH TOMATOES AND FETA, P. 206

vegetables

10

GRILLED EGGPLANTS WITH YOGURT SAUCE

ZUCCHINI MUSAKKA

### Eggplant Salad with Cumin and Fresh Herbs

**ACTIVE: 40 MIN; TOTAL: 1 HR 30 MIN**

**8 SERVINGS** ● ●

Two 1-pound eggplants

3 tablespoons extra-virgin olive oil

1½ pounds plum tomatoes, peeled and coarsely chopped

4 garlic cloves, chopped

Salt

¼ cup coarsely chopped flat-leaf parsley

¼ cup coarsely chopped cilantro

3 tablespoons fresh lemon juice

1 teaspoon ground cumin

1 teaspoon sweet paprika

Pinch of cayenne pepper

Assorted olives, for garnish

**1.** Preheat the oven to 500°. Put the eggplants on a large, rimmed baking sheet and prick them in a few places with a knife. Bake in the upper third of the oven for about 1 hour, or until blackened and soft. Scoop the flesh out of the skins, discard most of the seeds and finely chop the flesh. Drain in a colander, pressing to extract as much moisture as possible.

**2.** Meanwhile, heat the oil in a medium skillet. Add the chopped plum tomatoes, the garlic and a pinch of salt. Cook over moderate heat, stirring occasionally, until thick and saucy, about 15 minutes.

**3.** In a large bowl, combine the eggplant, tomato sauce, parsley, cilantro, lemon juice, cumin, paprika and cayenne and season with salt. Spread the eggplant salad on a large serving plate. Scatter the olives on top and serve.

*—Nadia Roden*

**MAKE AHEAD** The salad can be refrigerated overnight. Bring to room temperature before serving.

### Eggplant Tempura Fans

**TOTAL: 45 MIN**

**6 SERVINGS**

8 thin 3-ounce Japanese or Asian eggplants, or four 6-ounce eggplants, halved lengthwise

Vegetable oil, for frying

1⅓ cups all-purpose flour

2 large egg yolks

1⅓ cups ice water

Salt

Lemon wedges, for serving

**1.** Preheat the oven to 325°. Set a large wire rack over a large, rimmed baking sheet. On a cutting board, using a paring knife and starting just below the stem, cut each eggplant half lengthwise into ¼-inch slices attached at the stem. Press down on the eggplant halves to fan the slices out.

**2.** In a large, deep skillet, heat ½ inch of vegetable oil to 350°, or until shimmering. In a medium bowl, whisk the flour with the egg yolks and half of the ice water until almost smooth, then whisk in the remaining ice water.

**3.** Working in 3 batches, dip the eggplants in the batter and add them to the skillet. Fry the eggplants over high heat until nicely browned, about 3 minutes. Turn and cook until browned on the second side, 3 minutes longer. Reduce the heat if the eggplants brown too quickly. Transfer the eggplant tempura to the rack and season with salt; keep warm in the oven while you fry the rest. Serve at once, with lemon wedges.

—*Jacques Pépin*

## Grilled Eggplants with Cumin-Yogurt Sauce

**TOTAL: 30 MIN**

4 SERVINGS ● ● ●

- ¼ cup extra-virgin olive oil
- 2 tablespoons fresh lemon juice
- 1 tablespoon soy sauce
- 1 teaspoon curry powder
- ½ teaspoon crushed red pepper
- Four 6-ounce Japanese eggplants, halved lengthwise
- 1½ cups plain yogurt
- ½ cup coarsely chopped basil
- 1½ teaspoons ground cumin
- 1 garlic clove, minced
- ½ teaspoon finely grated lemon zest
- Salt and freshly ground black pepper

**1.** Light a grill. In a small bowl, combine the olive oil with the lemon juice, soy sauce, curry powder and crushed red pepper. Put the eggplant on a rimmed baking sheet, cut side up, and coat generously with the marinade. Let stand at room temperature for 15 minutes.

**2.** Meanwhile, in a small bowl, mix the yogurt with the basil, cumin, garlic and lemon zest. Season the yogurt sauce with salt and pepper.

**3.** Grill the eggplants over a medium fire until they are lightly charred and tender, about 4 minutes per side. Serve the grilled eggplants with the yogurt sauce.

—*Mohammad Islam*

**MAKE AHEAD** The eggplants can be kept at room temperature for 4 hours. Refrigerate the cumin-yogurt sauce.

## Zucchini Musakka with Chickpeas and Spiced Lamb

**ACTIVE: 25 MIN; TOTAL: 50 MIN**

6 SERVINGS ● ●

The zucchini is soaked in a saltwater bath, so it stays green and crisp even after it's cooked.

- 2 quarts water
- Kosher salt
- 4 medium zucchini, halved lengthwise and sliced crosswise ¼ inch thick
- 2 tablespoons extra-virgin olive oil
- ¼ pound ground lamb
- 4 medium garlic cloves, minced
- 1 medium onion, finely chopped
- 3 tomatoes, finely chopped
- 2 tablespoons tomato paste blended with ¼ cup water
- 1½ tablespoons Turkish sweet red pepper paste (see Note) or mild chile sauce
- ¾ cup canned chickpeas, drained
- Freshly ground pepper
- 1 tablespoon chopped parsley
- 1 tablespoon chopped mint leaves

**1.** In a very large bowl, combine the water and 3 tablespoons of salt and stir until dissolved. Add the zucchini slices and let soak for 25 minutes. Drain.

**2.** In a large, deep skillet, heat the olive oil until shimmering. Add the lamb and cook over moderate heat, stirring often, until no pink remains, 3 minutes. Add the garlic and onion and cook, stirring occasionally, until the onion is softened, about 4 minutes. Add the tomatoes, diluted tomato paste and the red pepper paste

and simmer for 1 minute. Add the zucchini and cook over moderately high heat, stirring, until just tender, about 5 minutes. Stir in the chickpeas and cook for 1 minute. Season with salt and pepper. Transfer to a bowl and let cool slightly. Sprinkle with the parsley and mint and serve warm or at room temperature.

—*Musa Dagdeviren*

**NOTE** Turkish sweet red pepper paste is available at Middle Eastern markets.

## Rice-and-Dill-Stuffed Zucchini

**ACTIVE: 45 MIN; TOTAL: 2 HR**

4 MAIN-COURSE SERVINGS ● ●

Baking the zucchini with the optional brined grape leaves will give the dish a tangy flavor.

- ½ cup medium-grain rice, such as Spanish or arborio
- 2 cups warm water
- 6 medium zucchini (about 2¼ pounds total), ends trimmed
- ¼ cup extra-virgin olive oil
- 1 large sweet onion, coarsely chopped
- 1 medium fennel bulb, cored and coarsely chopped
- 1 teaspoon Aleppo pepper (see Note) or pinch of crushed red pepper
- 1 cup drained canned diced tomatoes
- ⅓ cup roasted, salted almonds, finely chopped (1½ ounces)
- ¼ cup finely chopped dill
- ¼ cup finely chopped parsley
- 1 tablespoon finely chopped mint leaves
- Salt and freshly ground pepper
- 12 brined grape leaves (optional), drained and rinsed
- ½ cup chicken stock

**1.** In a medium bowl, soak the rice in the warm water for 20 minutes, then drain. Halve each zucchini crosswise, making 12 cylinders about 4 inches long. Using a melon baller or small spoon, scoop out the flesh from the zucchini cylinders to form cups with a ¼-inch-thick shell. Coarsely chop the zucchini flesh and reserve ¾ cup. Save the remaining flesh for another use.

**2.** In a large skillet, heat 2 tablespoons of the olive oil. Add the onion, fennel and reserved ¾ cup chopped zucchini and cook over moderately high heat, stirring occasionally, until lightly browned, about 10 minutes. Add the Aleppo and cook for 1 minute. Stir in half of the diced tomatoes, the drained rice, almonds, dill, parsley, mint and 1½ teaspoons of salt and season with pepper.

# health

**TIP** **THE RAINBOW DIET**

**Bright-colored fruits and vegetables are certainly pretty; now researchers are saying in popular books like** *The Color Code,* **by James Joseph and Daniel Nadeau, that eating a rainbow of hues is the best way to get a range of nutrients. That's because antioxidants and other healthful compounds are often also natural pigments, and different colors correspond to different varieties.**
**RED tomatoes and watermelon contain lycopene, which can help in the prevention of strokes.**
**ORANGE-YELLOW winter squash and sweet potatoes have beta-carotene, which protects the eyes.**
**PURPLE Concord grapes offer flavonoids, which help to lower "bad" cholesterol.**
**GREEN broccoli has sulforaphane, found to fight cancer.**
*—Victoria Abbott Riccardi*

**3.** Using a small spoon, fill the zucchini cups with the rice mixture, mounding it. Transfer the cups to a small cast-iron casserole or large saucepan. Tuck the grape leaves in between the zucchini cups to keep them upright. Spoon the remaining tomatoes on top and pour the stock all around. Drizzle with the remaining 2 tablespoons of olive oil.

**4.** Cover and bake for 1 hour and 5 minutes, or until the zucchini and rice are tender. Let the zucchini cool for 15 minutes and discard the grape leaves. Serve the stuffed zucchini warm or at room temperature. *—Aglaia Kremezi*

**NOTE** Aleppo pepper is a mildly hot, coarsely ground red chile with a complex, fruity flavor. It can be mail-ordered from Penzeys Spices (800-741-7787 or penzeys.com).

**MAKE AHEAD** The cooked stuffed zucchini can be refrigerated for up to 2 days.

## Zucchini Gratin with Gruyère Cheese
**TOTAL: 25 MIN**
4 SERVINGS ●
- 2 pounds small zucchini, shredded on the large holes of a box grater
- Salt
- 3 tablespoons unsalted butter
- 1 small shallot, minced
- ½ cup heavy cream
- 1½ ounces Gruyère cheese, shredded (½ cup)

**1.** Preheat the broiler. Put the shredded zucchini in a large colander and toss with ½ teaspoon of salt. Let stand for 5 minutes, then squeeze as much liquid out of the zucchini as possible.

**2.** In a large nonstick skillet, heat the butter until sizzling. Add the shallot and cook over moderate heat until the shallot is softened, about 3 minutes. Add the zucchini and cook over high heat, tossing, until just softened, about 2 minutes. Add the cream and simmer until thickened,

about 1 minute. Remove from the heat and season with salt. Transfer to a shallow baking dish. Scatter the Gruyère on top of the zucchini and broil 4 inches from the heat for 1 minute, or until the cheese topping is golden brown. Serve right away.
*—Jamie Samford*

## Zucchini Pappardelle with Tomatoes and Feta
**TOTAL: 30 MIN**
4 SERVINGS ● ● ●
- 3 tablespoons extra-virgin olive oil
- 2 tablespoons fresh lemon juice
- 1 teaspoon Dijon mustard
- ½ teaspoon honey
- ½ teaspoon finely grated lemon zest
- Salt and freshly ground black pepper
- Four ½-pound zucchini, or 2 zucchini and 2 yellow squash
- 1 garlic clove, minced
- 1 teaspoon coarsely chopped thyme
- ½ teaspoon coarsely chopped rosemary
- ¼ teaspoon crushed red pepper
- 20 cherry or grape tomatoes, halved
- 6 ounces feta cheese, preferably French, cut into small dice
- 3 ounces pitted Calamata olives, chopped (½ cup)

**1.** Preheat the broiler. In a small bowl, mix 2 tablespoons of the olive oil with the lemon juice, mustard, honey and lemon zest and season the dressing with salt and pepper.

**2.** Using a mandoline, slice the zucchini lengthwise into ⅛-inch-thick "pappardelle," turning the zucchini and slicing on four sides only until the seeds in the central portion are reached; discard the zucchini centers.

**3.** In a small bowl, combine the garlic with the thyme, rosemary, crushed red pepper and the remaining 1 tablespoon of olive oil. Spread the zucchini slices on a large, rimmed baking sheet and brush them with the garlic and herb oil. Broil for about 3 minutes, or until the zucchini is browned on top.

**4.** Spread the halved cherry tomatoes on another baking sheet and broil for about 1 minute, or until they are lightly browned on top.

**5.** Add the tomatoes to the zucchini and drizzle with the mustard dressing. Toss the vegetables well and transfer to plates or a platter. Top with the feta and olives and serve. —*Mohammad Islam*

## Zucchini Cakes
**TOTAL: 20 MIN**
6 SERVINGS ● ●

- 2 medium zucchini, coarsely shredded and squeezed dry
- 1 small onion, minced
- 1 garlic clove, minced
- ½ cup freshly grated Parmesan cheese
- 2 large eggs, lightly beaten
- 1 tablespoon vegetable oil
- 1 cup all-purpose flour
- 1½ teaspoons baking powder
- ½ teaspoon salt
- ¼ cup plus 2 tablespoons olive oil

**1.** In a large bowl, combine the zucchini with the onion, garlic, cheese, eggs and vegetable oil. Stir in the flour, baking powder and salt.

**2.** In each of 2 large skillets, heat 3 tablespoons of the olive oil until shimmering. Add just slightly heaping 2-tablespoon mounds of batter to the skillets 3 inches apart. Spread each pancake to a 2½-inch round and cook over moderately high heat until golden around the edges and bubbling in the centers, about 3 minutes. Flip the pancakes and cook until golden on the bottoms, about 2 minutes longer. Serve hot. —*Leslie Kunde*

**MAKE AHEAD** The pancakes can be cooked early in the day; drain on paper towels and reheat in a warm oven.

## Fried Zucchini Blossoms
**TOTAL: 30 MIN**
6 SERVINGS ● ●

In Greece, zucchini flowers, similar in flavor to the vegetable, are often added to vegetable stews or to grated zucchini and cheese in savory pies. The petals should be closed when you buy them.

- 18 baby zucchini with blossoms attached
- 4½ ounces feta cheese, cut into 18 pieces
- 4 large eggs
- 1½ cups fine dry bread crumbs
- ⅔ cup extra-virgin olive oil
- Salt
- Lemon wedges, for serving

**1.** Gently open each zucchini blossom and nip off the stamen. Place a piece of feta cheese inside each blossom and twist lightly to close.

**2.** Beat the eggs in a bowl. Spread the bread crumbs in a shallow bowl. Dip each zucchini in the beaten eggs, then dredge in the bread crumbs.

**3.** Set a large rack over a large, rimmed baking sheet. In each of 2 large skillets, heat ⅓ cup of the olive oil until shimmering. Carefully lay half of the zucchini in each skillet and fry over moderately high heat until crisp and golden, about 1½ minutes per side. Transfer to the rack to drain. Sprinkle with salt and serve with lemon wedges. —*Diane Kochilas*

## Braised Artichoke Hearts with Parsley
**ACTIVE: 25 MIN; TOTAL: 50 MIN**
4 SERVINGS ● ●

- 1 large lemon, halved
- 4 large artichokes
- 3 tablespoons extra-virgin olive oil
- 1 small onion, minced
- Salt
- 2 tablespoons chopped flat-leaf parsley
- 2 cups water

**1.** Squeeze the lemon halves over a medium bowl of water and reserve them. Working with 1 artichoke at a time, snap off the outer leaves. Using a sharp knife, trim the stem to ½ inch and cut off the top two-thirds of the leaves. Peel the bottom and the stem. Using a spoon or a melon baller, scoop out the furry choke. Rub the artichoke heart with a lemon half and add the artichoke to the bowl of acidulated water. Repeat the process with the remaining artichokes and drop the lemon halves into the water.

**2.** Heat the oil in a medium saucepan. Add the onion and cook over moderate heat until softened, about 4 minutes. Drain and quarter the artichokes; add them to the pan. Season with salt and cook, stirring, for about 2 minutes. Stir in 1 tablespoon of the parsley, add the water and bring to a boil. Reduce the heat to moderately low and simmer until the artichokes are tender and most of the water has evaporated, 25 minutes. Transfer the artichokes and their cooking liquid to a bowl; season with salt. Sprinkle with the remaining tablespoon of parsley and serve. —*Valentina Argiolas*

**MAKE AHEAD** The artichokes can be refrigerated in their cooking liquid for up to 2 days. Reheat gently.

## Braised Artichokes with Red and White Pearl Onions
**TOTAL: 1 HR 15 MIN**
12 SERVINGS ● ●

- ½ lemon, plus four 3-inch strips of zest
- 6 large artichokes
- ¼ cup plus 2 tablespoons extra-virgin olive oil
- 6 large garlic cloves, thinly sliced
- 4 oregano sprigs
- 3 bay leaves
- 1 cup plus 2 tablespoons water
- 1 tablespoon fresh lemon juice

# vegetables

Salt and freshly ground pepper

3 pounds mixed red and white
   pearl onions

3 tablespoons unsalted butter

8 small sage leaves

3 tablespoons sherry vinegar

**1.** Squeeze the lemon half over a bowl of water and drop it in. Working with 1 artichoke at a time, snap off the dark green outer leaves. Using a sharp knife, cut off the top two-thirds of the leaves and trim the stem to ½ inch. Peel the bottom and stem. Using a teaspoon, scrape out the hairy choke. Drop the artichoke heart into the lemon water. Repeat with the remaining artichokes.

**2.** Heat the olive oil in a large skillet. Drain the artichoke hearts and pat dry. Halve the hearts crosswise and slice ⅓ inch thick. Add the artichokes, garlic, oregano, bay leaves and lemon zest to the skillet and cook over moderately high heat, stirring, until the herbs are fragrant, about 2 minutes. Add 1 cup of the water. Reduce the heat to moderate, cover and cook until the artichokes are tender, about 10 minutes. Discard the lemon zest, oregano sprigs and bay leaves. Stir in the lemon juice and season with salt and pepper. Transfer the artichokes and their liquid to a large bowl. Wipe out the skillet.

**3.** Bring a large pot of water to a boil. Add the pearl onions and cook over moderately high heat until tender, about 10 minutes. Drain, and when cool enough to handle, cut off the root ends and peel.

**4.** Melt the butter in the large skillet. Add the boiled pearl onions and sage leaves, season with salt and pepper and cook over moderate heat until the onions are browned on the bottoms, about 10 minutes. Add the sherry vinegar and cook for 1 minute. Stir in the remaining 2 tablespoons of water. Remove from the heat. Season with salt and pepper. Add the onions to the artichokes and serve.
—*Marcia Kiesel*

**MAKE AHEAD** The recipe can be prepared 5 days ahead and refrigerated. Reheat gently and season lightly with vinegar and salt and pepper.

## Artichokes Simmered with Green Beans and Bacon
**TOTAL: 30 MIN**
4 SERVINGS ●

1 tablespoon extra-virgin olive oil,
   plus more for drizzling

4 strips of bacon, sliced crosswise
   ½ inch thick

1 medium onion, halved and
   thinly sliced

1 medium carrot, sliced
   ¼ inch thick

2 garlic cloves, very thinly sliced

2 cups water

1 cup dry white wine

Juice of 1 lemon

1 teaspoon thyme leaves

1 bay leaf

4 ounces thin green beans

Two 9-ounce packages frozen
   quartered artichoke hearts,
   thawed and drained

Kosher salt and freshly ground pepper

1 tablespoon coarsely chopped
   flat-leaf parsley

**1.** In a medium saucepan, heat the 1 tablespoon of olive oil. Add the bacon and cook over moderate heat until the fat is rendered, about 3 minutes. Add the onion, carrot and garlic and cook, stirring occasionally, until the vegetables are slightly softened, about 4 minutes. Add the water, wine, lemon juice, thyme leaves and bay leaf, cover and simmer until the onion and carrot are tender, about 10 minutes.

**2.** Add the green beans and artichokes, cover and cook until tender, about 3 minutes. Season with salt and pepper. Discard the bay leaf. Add the parsley and transfer to bowls. Serve with a drizzle of olive oil. —*Galen Zamarra*

## Chestnut and Artichoke Roast
**ACTIVE: 30 MIN; TOTAL: 1 HR**
6 SERVINGS ● ● ●

1½ large lemons, 1 halved
   lengthwise and thinly sliced

6 artichokes (each ¾ pound)

1½ cups vacuum-packed whole
   chestnuts (9 ounces)

3 garlic cloves, thickly sliced

½ cup low-sodium chicken broth

¼ cup extra-virgin olive oil

3 thyme sprigs

Salt and freshly ground pepper

**1.** Preheat the oven to 350°. Squeeze the lemon half over a bowl of cold water and drop it in. Working with 1 artichoke at a time, snap off the dark green outer leaves. Cut off the top two-thirds of the leaves and trim the stem to ½ inch. Peel the bottom and stem. Using a teaspoon, scrape out the hairy choke. Drop the artichoke into the lemon water. Repeat with the remaining artichokes.

**2.** Drain the artichoke hearts and cut them into 1-inch wedges. In a roasting pan, toss the wedges with the chestnuts, garlic, lemon slices, chicken broth, olive oil and thyme. Season with salt and pepper. Cover with foil and roast for 25 minutes, or until the artichokes are tender. Remove the foil and roast for 15 minutes, or until the artichokes are golden and the pan juices are evaporated.
—*Grace Parisi*

## Creamed Cipollini Onions and Mushrooms
**TOTAL: 1 HR 15 MIN**
10 SERVINGS ●

1 pound cipollini onions

4 tablespoons unsalted butter

½ cup plus 2 tablespoons
   extra-virgin olive oil

2 garlic cloves, minced

Salt and freshly ground pepper

1 pound chanterelles,
   large ones halved

CREAMED CIPOLLINI ONIONS AND MUSHROOMS

BRUSSELS SPROUTS WITH BACON

MUSHROOMS À LA GRECQUE

1 pound shiitake mushrooms, stems discarded, caps halved

1 pound oyster mushrooms, large ones halved

½ cup chicken stock or low-sodium broth

¾ cup heavy cream

1. In a medium saucepan of boiling water, cook the onions over moderate heat until just tender, about 8 minutes. Drain and peel.

2. In a large skillet, melt the butter in ¼ cup of the olive oil. Add the peeled onions and cook over moderate heat until browned, about 4 minutes per side. Add the minced garlic and cook, stirring, until fragrant, about 3 minutes. Season with salt and pepper.

3. In each of 2 large skillets, heat 2 tablespoons of the olive oil until shimmering. Add the chanterelles to one skillet and

the shiitake to the other, season with salt and pepper and cook over moderate heat until the mushrooms release their liquid, about 4 minutes. Continue cooking until the chanterelles are tender and the shiitake are browned, stirring occasionally, about 5 minutes longer. Transfer the mushrooms to a bowl.

4. In one of the skillets, cook the oyster mushrooms in the remaining 2 tablespoons of olive oil. Add the chicken stock and heavy cream and bring to a boil. Stir in the onions, chanterelles and shiitake and simmer over moderately low heat, stirring gently, until heated through, about 4 minutes. Season with salt and pepper and serve. —*Lee Hefter*

**MAKE AHEAD** The creamed onions and mushrooms can be refrigerated, tightly covered, for up to 2 days. Gently reheat before serving.

### Stuffed Onions

ACTIVE: 45 MIN; TOTAL: 3 HR

8 SERVINGS ● ●

Two 1-pound white onions, peeled

6 large Swiss chard leaves, ribs discarded

1 teaspoon unsalted butter, plus more for the baking dish

3 ounces thickly sliced prosciutto, cut into ¼-inch dice

1½ tablespoons finely chopped shallots

½ pound peasant bread, crusts trimmed, bread cut into ½-inch dice (1½ cups)

⅓ cup milk

2 large eggs, beaten

2 tablespoons coarsely chopped flat-leaf parsley

2 tablespoons finely chopped chives

1 tablespoon all-purpose flour

¾ teaspoon kosher salt

½ teaspoon freshly ground pepper

Pinch of freshly grated nutmeg

2 chicken livers, trimmed and finely chopped

1 cup chicken stock or low-sodium broth

¼ cup crème fraîche

Aged balsamic vinegar (optional)

**1.** Bring a large saucepan of salted water to a boil. Using a sharp knife, make a lengthwise slit in each onion from stem end to root end, cutting about halfway through the onions. Add the onions to the saucepan and boil over moderately high heat for 12 minutes. Using a slotted spoon, transfer the onions to a bowl of cold water and let cool. Pat the onions thoroughly dry.

**2.** Cut off the root end and peel off and discard the thick outer layer of each onion. Carefully peel off the next 4 layers of each onion; take care not to crack or break the layers. Remove and discard the thin, filmy membrane between the onion layers. Reserve the remaining onions for another use.

**3.** Bring the water in the saucepan back to a boil. Add the Swiss chard leaves and cook until wilted but still bright green, about 2 minutes. Drain and cool under cold water. Squeeze the leaves completely dry and coarsely chop them.

**4.** In a small skillet, heat the 1 teaspoon of butter. Add the prosciutto and shallots and cook over moderate heat until most of the fat has rendered and the shallots soften, about 2 minutes. Scrape the prosciutto mixture into a food processor and let cool, then pulse until finely chopped; transfer to a small plate.

**5.** In a medium bowl, sprinkle the bread with the milk and knead until moistened. Squeeze out as much milk as possible; discard the milk. Return the bread to the bowl, add the eggs and mash with a fork

until blended. Add the prosciutto mixture, Swiss chard, parsley, chives, flour, salt, pepper and nutmeg and mix well. Stir in the chicken livers and 2 tablespoons of the chicken stock.

**6.** Preheat the oven to 300°. Generously butter a 2-quart shallow baking dish. Spoon ⅛ of the stuffing into the rounded cup of an onion layer and spread it evenly. Roll up the onion layer and set it in the baking dish, seam side down. Repeat with the remaining onion layers and stuffing, laying them side by side.

**7.** Pour ½ cup of the chicken stock over the onions. Cover the dish with foil and bake the stuffed onions for 1 hour. Turn the onions and spread with 2 tablespoons of the crème fraîche. Bake uncovered for 30 minutes, basting occasionally with the pan juices. Turn the onions again and top them with the remaining 2 tablespoons of crème fraîche. Pour the remaining stock around the onions and bake for 35 to 40 minutes, until they are very tender and golden and the pan juices are thick. Remove from the oven and let stand for 10 to 15 minutes. Lightly drizzle the onions with balsamic vinegar before serving. —*Michel Bras*

**MAKE AHEAD** The cooked onions can be refrigerated for 2 days. Cover with foil and reheat gently.

## Brussels Sprouts with Chestnuts and Bacon

**TOTAL: 25 MIN**

10 SERVINGS ●

3 pounds brussels sprouts, halved lengthwise

6 slices of thick-cut bacon, cut into ¼-inch dice (6 ounces)

4 tablespoons unsalted butter

20 vacuum-packed peeled whole chestnuts, thinly sliced

Salt and freshly ground pepper

½ cup Rich Turkey Stock (p. 112)

**1.** Bring a large pot of salted water to a boil over high heat. Add the brussels sprouts and cook until just tender, about 7 minutes. Drain well.

**2.** Meanwhile, in a large skillet, cook the bacon over moderate heat until crisp, about 5 minutes. Add the butter. When the foam subsides, add the brussels sprouts and cook over moderate heat, until lightly browned, about 5 minutes. Add the chestnuts; season with salt and pepper. Add the Rich Turkey Stock, simmer until heated and serve. —*Lee Hefter*

## Mushrooms à la Grecque

**ACTIVE: 45 MIN; TOTAL: 1 HR 10 MIN**

4 SERVINGS ●

¾ cup golden raisins

4 cups small cauliflower florets

4 scallions, white and tender green parts only, halved crosswise

⅓ cup plus 2 tablespoons extra-virgin olive oil

1½ teaspoons coriander seeds, tied up in cheesecloth

1 medium onion, finely chopped

1½ cups dry white wine

Bouquet garni (6 parsley stems, 2 leafy celery tops and 2 thyme sprigs tied with kitchen string)

2 teaspoons ground coriander

Salt

1½ pounds small mushrooms

1 tablespoon fresh lemon juice

Freshly ground pepper

4 plum tomatoes, cut into ¼-inch dice

2 tablespoons tomato paste

2 tablespoons small mint leaves

2 tablespoons chives, cut into 1-inch lengths

**1.** In a saucepan of boiling water, blanch the raisins for 2 minutes. Using a slotted spoon, transfer the raisins to a plate; let cool. Blanch the cauliflower florets until crisp-tender, about 2 minutes; transfer them to another plate. Blanch the scallions for 1 minute; add to the cauliflower.

# v.egetables

**2.** In a large skillet, heat ⅓ cup of the olive oil with the coriander seeds in the cheesecloth. Add the onion, cover and cook over moderate heat until softened, 4 minutes. Add the wine, bouquet garni and ground coriander; season with salt. Cover and cook for 5 minutes. Add the mushrooms and lemon juice, season with salt and pepper and simmer over moderately high heat, stirring, until the mushrooms are just tender, about 5 minutes. Transfer the mushrooms to a bowl.

**3.** Add the plum tomatoes, tomato paste and raisins to the skillet and simmer over moderately high heat until the sauce is thickened, about 8 minutes; discard the bouquet garni and coriander seeds. Add the mushrooms to the sauce and bring to a boil, then season with salt and pepper. Let cool.

**4.** Pat the cauliflower and scallions dry and transfer to a medium bowl. Add the remaining 2 tablespoons of olive oil, generously season with salt and pepper and toss. Spoon the mushrooms and the sauce onto plates and top with the cauliflower and scallions. Garnish with the mint leaves and chives and serve.

—*Jean-Georges Vongerichten*

## Asparagus Glazed with White Truffle Fondue

**TOTAL: 15 MIN**

6 SERVINGS ●

Truffle fondue (truffle-infused cheeses mixed with butter) quickly turns asparagus into a superluxe starter or side dish. One of our favorite brands is Urbani (urbanitruffles.com).

- 2 **tablespoons (1 ounce) unsalted butter**
- 2 **tablespoons minced shallots**
- 1 **pound pencil-thin asparagus**
- **Salt and freshly ground pepper**
- ¼ **cup white truffle fondue (from a 3.5-ounce jar)**
- 1 **teaspoon minced tarragon**

**1.** Preheat the broiler and position an oven rack 8 inches from the heat. Melt the butter in a large skillet. Add the minced shallots and cook over moderately high heat until barely softened, about 1 minute. Add the asparagus, season with salt and pepper and cook over moderate heat, stirring occasionally, until crisp-tender and lightly browned in spots, about 5 minutes.

**2.** Transfer the asparagus to a medium gratin dish and spread the truffle fondue over them. Broil until golden and bubbling, shifting the dish for even browning, about 1 minute. Sprinkle with the tarragon and serve. —*Grace Parisi*

## Asparagus and Potato Salad with Riesling-Tarragon Vinaigrette

**TOTAL: 40 MIN**

6 SERVINGS ●

- 2 **pounds thin asparagus**
- 1 **pound medium Yukon Gold potatoes, scrubbed but not peeled**
- 1 **teaspoon coriander seeds, crushed**
- ¼ **cup tarragon leaves**
- ¼ **cup flat-leaf parsley leaves**
- 2 **tablespoons snipped chives**
- ¼ **cup Riesling or other off-dry white wine**
- 1½ **tablespoons white wine vinegar**
- 1 **teaspoon Dijon mustard**
- ½ **cup plus 1 tablespoon extra-virgin olive oil**
- **Salt and freshly ground pepper**

**1.** Bring a large pot of salted water to a boil. Fill a bowl with ice water. Add the asparagus to the boiling water and cook until crisp-tender, 2 to 3 minutes. Using tongs, transfer the asparagus to the ice water to cool. Drain and pat dry.

**2.** Add the scrubbed potatoes to the boiling water and cook over moderate heat until just tender, about 30 minutes. Drain and let cool slightly.

**3.** Meanwhile, in a mini food processor, pulse the coriander seeds until coarsely ground. Add the tarragon, parsley and chives and process until finely chopped. Add the Riesling, vinegar and mustard and process until smooth. With the machine on, add the olive oil in a steady stream and process until emulsified. Season with salt and pepper.

**4.** Peel and thickly slice the potatoes and transfer them to a bowl. Add ¼ cup of the dressing, season with salt and pepper and toss gently. Arrange the asparagus on 6 plates and drizzle with some of the dressing. Mound the potatoes on top, drizzle with the remaining dressing and serve. —*David Bouley*

## Green Bean Ragout with Tomatoes and Mint

**TOTAL: 40 MIN**

6 SERVINGS ● ●

- ½ **cup extra-virgin olive oil**
- 2 **medium red onions, finely chopped**
- 3 **large garlic cloves, minced**
- 2½ **pounds green beans**
- 1¼ **cups drained oil-packed sun-dried tomatoes, thinly sliced**
- 2 **plum tomatoes, chopped**
- 1½ **cups water**
- **Salt and freshly ground pepper**
- ½ **cup finely shredded mint leaves**
- **Pinch of sugar**
- 2 **tablespoons red wine vinegar**

In a soup pot, heat the oil. Add the onions and cook over moderately high heat until softened, 5 minutes. Add the garlic and cook for 1 minute. Add the green beans and stir to coat with oil. Stir in the sun-dried and plum tomatoes and the water; bring to a boil. Season with salt and pepper, cover and simmer until the beans are tender, about 15 minutes. Add the mint and sugar and cook for 1 minute, then stir in the vinegar. Serve warm or at room temperature. —*Diane Kochilas*

**ASPARAGUS GLAZED WITH WHITE TRUFFLE FONDUE**

TINY PEPPERS IN CHERRY TOMATO SAUCE

## Tiny Peppers in Cherry Tomato Sauce

**TOTAL: 35 MIN**

10 SERVINGS ● ●

These peppers are so intensely flavored, they're almost more a condiment than a side dish.

- ¼ cup plus 2 tablespoons extra-virgin olive oil
- 1½ pounds miniature bell peppers (see Note), stems removed, or 3 pounds regular bell peppers, cut into 1-inch strips
- 2 garlic cloves, minced
- ½ teaspoon crushed red pepper
- 1 pint cherry or grape tomatoes, halved
- 1½ teaspoons dried oregano, crumbled

Salt and freshly ground pepper
- ¼ cup finely chopped basil

**1.** In a large skillet, heat 3 tablespoons of the olive oil until shimmering. Add the bell peppers and cook over moderate heat, stirring occasionally, until softened, about 12 minutes. Transfer the peppers and any olive oil to a bowl.

**2.** Add the remaining 3 tablespoons of olive oil to the skillet along with the garlic and crushed red pepper and cook over moderate heat until fragrant, about 20 seconds. Add the tomatoes, cover and cook, stirring and crushing the tomatoes occasionally, until they are slightly softened, 5 minutes. Return the bell peppers to the skillet. Add the oregano and season with salt and pepper. Cover and cook over moderately low heat until the sauce is slightly thickened, 2 to 3 minutes. Stir in the chopped basil and serve warm or at room temperature.
—*Rafaella Giamundo*

**NOTE** Miniature bell peppers (no bigger than 2 inches) are available at specialty food shops and large supermarkets.

**MAKE AHEAD** The peppers can be refrigerated for up to 2 days.

## Roasted Peppers with Preserved Lemon and Capers

**TOTAL: 20 MIN, PLUS OVERNIGHT MARINATING**

8 SERVINGS ● ●

- 4 red bell peppers
- 4 yellow bell peppers
- ¼ cup plus 2 tablespoons extra-virgin olive oil
- ¼ cup drained small capers
- ½ small preserved lemon (see Note), flesh discarded, rind julienned

Salt

**1.** Preheat the broiler. Roast the bell peppers directly over a gas flame or under the broiler, turning, until charred all over. Transfer the peppers to a large bowl, cover with plastic wrap and let stand for 10 minutes. Peel the peppers, discarding the cores and seeds. Cut the peppers into ⅔-inch strips.

**2.** In a large bowl, mix the pepper strips with the olive oil, capers and preserved lemon and season lightly with salt. Cover and refrigerate overnight. Serve lightly chilled or at room temperature.
—*Nadia Roden*

**NOTE** Preserved lemons are available at specialty food stores and by mail order from Kalustyan's (800-352-3451).

**MAKE AHEAD** The prepared peppers can be refrigerated for up to 5 days.

## Green Beans with Onions and Capers

**TOTAL: 25 MIN**

6 SERVINGS ● ●

Salt
- 1½ pounds green beans
- 2 tablespoons unsalted butter
- 1 small red onion, thinly sliced
- 2 anchovies, coarsely chopped
- 1 tablespoon drained capers

Freshly ground pepper

**1.** In a large pot of boiling salted water, cook the green beans until tender, about 5 minutes. Drain well.

**2.** Melt the butter in a large skillet. Add the onion and cook over moderate heat until softened, 5 minutes. Add the anchovies and capers; cook for 1 minute, stirring. Add the beans, season with pepper and cook for 2 minutes, stirring occasionally. Serve at once. —*Paul Condron*

## Green Beans in Cherry Tomato Sauce

**TOTAL: 30 MIN**

10 SERVINGS ● ● ●

- 2 pounds green beans
- ½ cup extra-virgin olive oil
- 3 large garlic cloves, minced
- ¾ teaspoon crushed red pepper
- 2 pounds cherry tomatoes, halved

Salt

**1.** Bring a large pot of salted water to a boil. Add the beans and cook over high heat until crisp-tender, 8 minutes. Drain.

**2.** Meanwhile, in a large, deep skillet, heat the olive oil. Add the garlic and crushed red pepper and cook over moderate heat until fragrant, about 20 seconds. Add the tomatoes, cover and cook until softened, about 5 minutes. Add the green beans, season with salt and simmer over moderate heat until tender, 4 to 5 minutes. Serve the beans warm or at room temperature. —*Rafaella Giamundo*

**MAKE AHEAD** The beans can be refrigerated for up to 2 days.

# pantry

**PRESERVED LEMONS**　　　**TIP**

Moroccan preserved lemons have been immersed in a salt-and-lemon-juice mixture for about 30 days. This renders them silky, sour-sweet and entirely edible—rind and all—with none of the bitterness of raw citrus.

# vegetables

## Smoky Sautéed Bacon and Leeks

**TOTAL: 25 MIN**

6 SERVINGS ●

½ pound thickly sliced applewood-smoked or other smoked bacon, cut crosswise into ½-inch pieces

2 tablespoons unsalted butter

2 pounds leeks, white and tender green parts only, sliced crosswise ¾ inch thick

Kosher salt and freshly ground black pepper

1. Heat a large cast-iron skillet. Add the bacon and cook over moderate heat until it is crisp around the edges, about 6 minutes. Transfer the bacon pieces to a paper towel–lined plate and carefully wipe out the hot skillet.

2. Melt the butter in the skillet over high heat until sizzling and starting to brown. Reduce the heat to moderate, add the sliced leeks and cook, stirring occasionally, until tender, 6 to 8 minutes. Return the bacon to the skillet and toss with the leeks. Season with salt and pepper, transfer to a bowl and serve.
—*Maria Helm Sinskey*

## Green Cabbage and Apple Sauté

**ACTIVE: 30 MIN; TOTAL: 2 HR**

6 SERVINGS ● ● ●

One 3-pound head green cabbage— halved, cored and coarsely shredded (12 cups)

1 cup dry Riesling or other dry white wine

2 tablespoons fresh lemon juice

1½ tablespoons sugar

¼ cup extra-virgin olive oil

1 large yellow or white onion, very thinly sliced

2 Granny Smith apples—peeled, halved, cored and sliced ⅛ inch thick

Salt and freshly ground black pepper

1. In a large bowl, toss the cabbage with the wine, lemon juice and sugar. Let marinate for 1 hour, tossing often.

2. In a large, deep skillet, heat the olive oil until shimmering. Add the onion and cook over moderate heat until golden, about 8 minutes. Add the cabbage and its marinade and cook over moderately high heat, tossing, until the cabbage is wilted, about 5 minutes. Cover and cook over moderately low heat, stirring occasionally, until tender, about 20 minutes. Add the apples and toss well. Cover and cook, stirring occasionally, until the apples are just tender, about 10 minutes. Season with salt and pepper and serve.
—*Kurt Gutenbrunner*

**MAKE AHEAD** The cabbage and apples can be refrigerated overnight.

## Savoy Cabbage and Pancetta

**TOTAL: 25 MIN**

4 SERVINGS ● ●

In this side dish, sherry vinegar adds a tangy taste to the cabbage and cuts through the richness of the pancetta.

1 tablespoon vegetable oil

3 ounces thinly sliced pancetta, finely chopped (½ cup)

1 medium onion, thinly sliced

One 1½-pound head Savoy cabbage, finely shredded

2 teaspoons sherry vinegar

Salt and freshly ground pepper

1. In a large skillet, heat the oil until shimmering. Add the chopped pancetta and cook over moderate heat until crisp and browned, about 8 minutes. Transfer the pancetta to a plate.

2. Add the sliced onion to the skillet and cook over moderate heat, stirring occasionally, until softened. Add the shredded cabbage and the pancetta and cook, stirring, until the cabbage is crisp-tender, about 4 minutes. Remove from the heat. Stir in the vinegar, season with salt and pepper and serve. —*Bob Isaacson*

## Spicy Carrots with Peperoncini

**TOTAL: 30 MIN**

4 SERVINGS ● ●

¼ cup extra-virgin olive oil

1 medium onion, halved and thinly sliced

4 large garlic cloves, thinly sliced

2 celery ribs, thinly sliced

8 oil-packed sun-dried tomato halves, drained and cut into thin strips

8 peperoncini (pickled chile peppers) from a jar—drained, stemmed, seeded and thinly sliced

2 tablespoons unsalted butter

1½ pounds carrots, peeled and cut into ¾-inch pieces

Salt

1 cup vegetable stock

Freshly ground pepper

1. In a large, deep skillet, heat the olive oil until shimmering. Add the onion, garlic and celery, cover the skillet and cook over moderately high heat, stirring occasionally, until the vegetables are almost softened, about 5 minutes. Add the sun-dried tomatoes and peperoncini and cook, stirring occasionally, until the vegetables are softened, about 3 minutes longer. Scrape the vegetables into a medium bowl and wipe out the skillet.

2. Melt the butter in the skillet. Add the carrots and season with salt. Cover the skillet and cook over moderate heat, stirring occasionally, until the carrots are barely tender, about 6 minutes. Add the stock, partially cover the skillet and cook over moderately high heat, stirring occasionally, until the carrots are tender and the liquid has reduced to a glaze, about 10 minutes longer. Stir the peperoncini mixture into the carrots and cook just until heated through, about 1 minute longer. Season the carrots and peperoncini with salt and pepper, transfer to a bowl and serve. —*Bill Telepan*

### Roasted Carrots and Fennel with Tomato and Olive Pesto

**ACTIVE: 25 MIN; TOTAL: 1 HR**

**6 SERVINGS** ●

- 1 medium onion, sliced ¼ inch thick and separated into rings
- 4 large carrots, sliced on the diagonal ½ inch thick
- 1 large fennel bulb—halved, cored and cut into ½ inch wedges
- 3 tablespoons extra-virgin olive oil

Salt and freshly ground pepper

- ¼ cup tomato-olive pesto (see Note)
- 2 tablespoons pitted oil-cured black olives, halved (optional)

**1.** Preheat the oven to 425°. In a large baking dish, toss the onion with the carrots, fennel and 2 tablespoons of the olive oil. Season with salt and pepper, toss again and roast for 20 minutes, or until crisp-tender and golden in spots.

**2.** In a small bowl, stir the tomato-olive pesto with the remaining 1 tablespoon of olive oil. Add the pesto to the vegetables and toss to coat. If using olives, scatter them on top. Bake the carrots and fennel for 10 minutes longer, or until tender and browned. Transfer to a bowl; serve hot or at room temperature. —*Grace Parisi*

**NOTE** Saclà makes a delicious olive and tomato pesto. It's available at specialty food shops and by mail from My Brands (888-281-6400 or mybrandsinc.com).

**VARIATION** Serve tossed with pasta or as a side dish for pan-seared salmon, steak or pork.

### Sautéed Turnips and Carrots with Rosemary-Ginger Honey

**TOTAL: 40 MIN**

**6 SERVINGS** ● ● ●

This savory dish is wonderful with meaty fish like mahimahi or swordfish or with grilled or pan-fried chicken breasts. It was inspired by a recipe from Rosemary Barron's cookbook *Flavors of Greece.*

- 3 tablespoons dried currants
- ⅓ cup hot water
- 3 tablespoons honey
- 1½ teaspoons minced fresh ginger
- 1½ teaspoons minced rosemary
- 2¼ pounds white turnips, peeled and cut into ½-inch wedges
- 3 medium carrots, cut into 1½-by-¼-inch sticks
- ¼ cup extra-virgin olive oil
- 3 Italian frying peppers, cut into 1-inch pieces

Salt and freshly ground pepper

- 1 tablespoon red wine vinegar

**1.** In a small bowl, soak the currants in the hot water. In a small saucepan, combine the honey, ginger and rosemary and simmer over low heat for 3 minutes. Remove from the heat.

**2.** In a large saucepan of boiling salted water, cook the turnips until just tender, about 5 minutes. Using a slotted spoon, transfer to a shallow dish. Add the carrots to the boiling water and cook until tender, about 5 minutes. Drain.

**3.** Heat the olive oil in a large skillet until shimmering. Add the turnip wedges in an even layer and cook over moderately high heat for 1 minute. Reduce the heat to moderate and cook, undisturbed, until lightly browned on the bottoms, about 4 minutes. Stir in the carrots and peppers and season with salt and pepper. Cover the vegetables and cook, stirring occasionally, until the peppers are tender, about 3 minutes.

**4.** Add the currants and their soaking liquid to the vegetables and cook until the liquid has thickened, about 2 minutes. Add the honey mixture, stir and simmer for 1 minute. Season with salt and pepper, add the vinegar and transfer to a bowl. Serve hot or warm. —*Marcia Kiesel*

**MAKE AHEAD** The recipe can be made through Step 3 and refrigerated, covered, overnight. Reheat before proceeding.

### Carrots with Sausage and Rosemary

**TOTAL: 30 MIN**

**12 SERVINGS** ● ●

- 3 pounds carrots, sliced crosswise ¼ inch thick
- 2 tablespoons extra-virgin olive oil
- ¾ pound sweet Italian sausage, removed from the casings
- 1 medium onion, finely chopped
- 1 tablespoon plus 1 teaspoon chopped rosemary
- 1 tablespoon tomato paste mixed with ½ cup water

Salt and freshly ground pepper

- ¼ cup chopped flat-leaf parsley

**1.** In a large pot of boiling salted water, cook the carrots over moderately high heat until tender, about 7 minutes. Drain.

**2.** In a large skillet, heat the oil. Add the sausage meat and cook over moderate heat, breaking up the meat with a wooden spoon, until no pink remains, 4 minutes. Add the onion and rosemary and cook over moderately low heat, stirring occasionally, until the onion is softened, 6 minutes. Stir in the carrots and cook until heated through. Stir in the diluted tomato paste; season with salt and pepper. Stir in the parsley, transfer to a bowl and serve. —*Marcia Kiesel*

**MAKE AHEAD** The carrots and sausage can be refrigerated overnight.

# superfast

**CREAMY CARROTS** | **TIP**

**Grate peeled carrots in a food processor fitted with a shredding disk, then sauté in butter until tender. Mix in a few tablespoons of cream, purée and season with salt and pepper. Top with chopped parsley or caramelized shallots.**

**BABY PEAS WITH BACON AND CRISPY LEEKS**

**CARROTS WITH SAUSAGE AND ROSEMARY, P. 217**

## Spring Peas with New Potatoes, Herbs and Watercress

**TOTAL: 45 MIN**

6 SERVINGS ●

- 1 quart water
- ½ pound small new potatoes
- Salt
- 4 cups shelled early spring peas or two 10-ounce packages frozen baby peas
- 2 tablespoons unsalted butter
- 2 tablespoons extra-virgin olive oil
- 1 medium leek, white and tender green parts only, thinly sliced crosswise
- 2 tablespoons chopped mint
- 2 tablespoons chopped chives
- 1 teaspoon fresh lemon juice
- Freshly ground pepper
- 2 medium bunches watercress, large stems discarded, leaves coarsely chopped (2 cups)

**1.** Bring the water to a boil in a medium saucepan. Add the potatoes and a pinch of salt. Cook over moderately high heat until fork-tender, about 20 minutes. With a slotted spoon, transfer the potatoes to a plate and let cool, then halve or quarter any large potatoes.

**2.** Add 1 teaspoon of salt to the potato water and bring to a boil. Add the peas and cook over moderately high heat until tender, about 5 minutes. Meanwhile, in a large skillet, melt the butter in the olive oil. Add the leek and cook over low heat, stirring occasionally, until tender, about 5 minutes. Reserve ½ cup of the potato cooking water, then drain the peas and add them to the skillet.

**3.** Add the potatoes and the reserved cooking water to the skillet and bring to a simmer over moderate heat, stirring. Add the mint, chives and lemon juice and season with salt and pepper. Remove the skillet from the heat and stir in the watercress. Transfer the vegetables to a warmed bowl and serve. —*Marcia Kiesel*

### Baby Peas with Bacon and Crispy Leeks

**TOTAL: 30 MIN**

**12 SERVINGS** ● ●

    3  large leeks, white and tender
       green parts only, sliced
       crosswise ¼ inch thick and
       separated into rings
Vegetable oil, for frying
Salt and freshly ground pepper
    6  slices of thick-cut bacon
    4  thyme sprigs
    1  cup Rich Turkey Stock (p. 112)
       or low-sodium chicken broth
    ¾  cup heavy cream
Three 10-ounce boxes frozen baby
       peas, thawed
    1  teaspoon cornstarch mixed
       with 1 tablespoon water

**1.** Wash the leeks well and pat dry. In a large saucepan, heat ½ inch of oil until shimmering. Add all but ½ cup of the leeks and cook over moderate heat, stirring occasionally, until they are golden brown, 10 to 12 minutes. Using a slotted spoon, transfer the leeks to a paper towel–lined plate and season with salt and pepper. Discard the oil.

**2.** In a large, deep skillet, cook the bacon over moderately high heat, turning once, until golden, about 5 minutes. Drain the bacon on paper towels and crumble.

**3.** Add the remaining ½ cup of leeks and the thyme to the fat in the skillet and cook over moderately low heat until the leeks are softened, about 8 minutes. Add ½ cup of the Rich Turkey Stock and cook over moderate heat until the liquid is reduced by half, about 7 minutes. Add the heavy cream and cook over moderately high heat until reduced by half, about 5 minutes. Stir in the peas, crumbled bacon and the remaining ½ cup of stock and bring to a boil. Discard the thyme sprigs. Season with salt and pepper. Add the cornstarch mixture, stir and cook until the sauce is slightly thickened, 3 to 4 minutes. Transfer the peas to a bowl and top with the crispy leeks just before serving. —*Grace Parisi*

**MAKE AHEAD** The crispy leeks can be stored overnight in an airtight container. Recrisp in a 350° oven.

### Caramelized Cauliflower with Pancetta and Spinach

**TOTAL: 30 MIN**

**4 SERVINGS** ● ●

    3  tablespoons extra-virgin olive oil
    ¼  pound thinly sliced pancetta,
       finely chopped
    1  small cauliflower (1¼ pounds),
       cored and cut into small florets
    1  small onion, finely chopped
    1  tablespoon coarsely chopped dill
    1  bay leaf
    1  tablespoon fresh lemon juice
Salt and freshly ground pepper
    5  ounces baby spinach

**1.** In a large skillet, heat 1 tablespoon of the olive oil until shimmering. Add the chopped pancetta and cook over moderate heat until the fat has been rendered, about 4 minutes. Stir in the cauliflower, onion, dill and bay leaf. Cover and cook, stirring occasionally, until the cauliflower is tender and browned, about 15 minutes. Discard the bay leaf.

**2.** In a large bowl, mix the lemon juice with the remaining 2 tablespoons of olive oil. Season with salt and pepper. Add the cauliflower mixture and spinach, toss and serve. —*Mohammad Islam*

### Cauliflower with Pine Nut Crumble

**TOTAL: 30 MIN**

**4 SERVINGS** ●

    1  tablespoon dried currants
    2  tablespoons water
    1  tablespoon pine nuts
    1  anchovy fillet (optional)
    5  tablespoons unsalted butter
    1  small head cauliflower (1½
       pounds), cut into 1½-inch florets
    ½  cup vegetable stock
Salt and freshly ground pepper
    ¼  cup fine dry bread crumbs
    ¼  cup minced onion
    1  large garlic clove, minced
    1  tablespoon dry white wine

**1.** Place the currants in a small microwavable bowl and cover with the water. Microwave on high for 1 minute, then drain. Transfer the currants to a mini food processor, add the pine nuts and anchovy and pulse to a paste.

**2.** In a large skillet, melt 2 tablespoons of the butter. Add the cauliflower and cook over moderate heat, stirring once, until golden in spots, about 7 minutes. Add the vegetable stock and season with salt and pepper. Cover and cook until the cauliflower is nearly tender, about 3 minutes. Uncover and cook until the liquid is nearly evaporated and the cauliflower is tender, about 2 minutes longer.

# health

**THE POWER OF FROZEN PEAS**   **TIP**

Almost any injury—from sprained ligaments to strained muscles—that's red or swollen should be iced. But ice packs can be awkward. What's the alternative? "A large bag of frozen peas or corn contours well to the body," says Bill Pesanelli, a physical therapist and the director of the clinical centers at Boston University. "Plus, it's reusable and inexpensive." Apply the frozen bag of vegetables for 10 minutes every two hours directly on the injury, or use a wet paper towel as a buffer. Along with icing, any injured part of the body should also be elevated, if possible.

● FAST   ● HEALTHY   ● MAKE AHEAD   ● STAFF FAVORITE

3. Meanwhile, in a skillet, heat 1 tablespoon of the butter until sizzling. Add the bread crumbs and toast, stirring often, until golden, about 2 minutes. Transfer to a plate. Melt the remaining 2 tablespoons of butter in the same skillet. Add the onion and garlic and cook over moderately low heat, stirring occasionally, until softened, about 5 minutes. Add the white wine. Stir in the currant paste and transfer to a bowl.

4. Transfer the cauliflower to a bowl. Stir the bread crumbs into the currant mixture, spoon over the cauliflower and serve at once. —*Bill Telepan*

### Celery Root Puree

ACTIVE: 15 MIN; TOTAL: 45 MIN
6 SERVINGS ●

- 2 celery roots (1 pound each), peeled and cut into ½-inch pieces
- 2 cups heavy cream
- 1 cup water

Salt and freshly ground pepper

1. In a large saucepan, combine the celery roots with the cream and water and bring to a boil. Cover and simmer over moderately low heat until tender, about 30 minutes. Uncover and cook over high heat until the cream is thickened and reduced by half, about 8 minutes.

2. Transfer the contents of the pan to a food processor and puree until smooth. Season with salt and pepper, return to the saucepan and cook over moderate heat, stirring constantly, until warmed. Serve at once. —*Michael Allemeier*

MAKE AHEAD The Celery Root Puree can be refrigerated overnight. Reheat gently.

### Celery Root and Green Apple Puree

ACTIVE: 30 MIN; TOTAL: 1 HR 15 MIN
10 SERVINGS ●

- 2 sticks (½ pound) unsalted butter
- 3 large celery roots (4½ pound total)—halved, peeled and coarsely chopped

Salt and freshly ground pepper

- 8 Granny Smith or other tart apples, peeled and coarsely chopped
- ¾ cup verjus or dry white wine
- 1 star anise pod
- 2 tablespoons sugar
- 2 cups baby spinach leaves

1. Melt the butter in a large, deep skillet. Add the celery root and cook over moderately low heat, stirring occasionally, until starting to soften, about 10 minutes. Season with salt and pepper. Add the apples, verjus, star anise pod and sugar. Cover and cook the mixture over low heat, stirring occasionally, until the celery root and apples are very tender, about 30 minutes.

2. Discard the star anise pod. In a food processor, working in batches, puree the celery root and apples with the raw spinach. Season with salt and pepper. Transfer to a bowl and serve hot. —*Lee Hefter*

MAKE AHEAD The celery root and apple puree can be refrigerated overnight. Rewarm the puree over moderate heat, stirring frequently.

### Celery Root–Leek Gratin

ACTIVE: 40 MIN; TOTAL: 1 HR 30 MIN
20 SERVINGS ●

- 1 lemon, halved
- 6½ pounds celery root
- 4 tablespoons unsalted butter
- 4 medium leeks, white and tender green parts only, thinly sliced crosswise
- 1 tablespoon chopped thyme
- ¼ teaspoon crushed red pepper
- 1 cup dry white wine
- 6 cups heavy cream
- 2 cups freshly grated Parmesan cheese (about 6 ounces)
- 2 tablespoons chopped flat-leaf parsley

Salt and freshly ground pepper

1. Preheat the oven to 400°. Bring a large pot of salted water to a boil. Squeeze the lemon into a large bowl of water. Peel the celery root and cut it into ½-inch dice, adding it to the bowl of water as you go.

2. Drain the celery root and add it to the boiling water. Boil until tender, 7 minutes. Drain well and wipe out the pot.

3. In the same large pot, melt the butter. Add the leeks, thyme and crushed red pepper and cook over moderate heat, stirring occasionally, until the leeks are softened, about 7 minutes. Add the wine and simmer over moderately high heat, stirring, until almost evaporated, 4 minutes. Add the celery root and cream and simmer for 1 minute. Stir in 1 cup of the Parmesan and the parsley. Season with salt and pepper. Transfer the mixture to two 10-by-15-inch baking dishes.

4. Evenly sprinkle the remaining 1 cup of Parmesan over the gratins and bake for 25 minutes, or until bubbling around the edges and golden on top. Let cool somewhat before serving. —*Morgan Brownlow*

MAKE AHEAD The gratins can be prepared through Step 3 and refrigerated overnight. Let return to room temperature before proceeding.

### Rich and Creamy Salsify Gratin

ACTIVE: 1 HR; TOTAL: 1 HR 30 MIN
10 SERVINGS ● ●

Salsify is a root vegetable that's shaped like a skinny parsnip with black skin and white flesh. It tastes a little like artichoke and is in season June through February.

- 3 pounds salsify
- 2 tablespoons unsalted butter
- 2 tablespoons all-purpose flour
- 1 quart half-and-half

Salt and freshly ground pepper
Freshly grated nutmeg

- ¼ pound Monterey Jack cheese, shredded
- ¼ pound Gruyère cheese, shredded

# mushrooms

There are many kinds of mushrooms—smooth and ridged, farmed and wild, pretty and pretty ugly. Sautéed or roasted, though, most will work beautifully in the quick and delicious recipes here.

### Wild Mushrooms with Miso, Fresh Herbs and Madeira

**TOTAL: 20 MIN**

6 SERVINGS ● ●

- 3 tablespoons unsalted butter
- 3 tablespoons extra-virgin olive oil
- 1 pound shiitake mushrooms, stems discarded, caps thickly sliced
- ½ pound oyster mushrooms, sliced
- 1 large shallot, minced
- ¼ cup Madeira
- 3 tablespoons white (*shiro*) or red (*aka*) miso
- ½ cup low-sodium chicken broth
- 2 tablespoons minced flat-leaf parsley
- 1 teaspoon chopped thyme leaves

Salt and freshly ground pepper

1. In a large skillet, melt 2 tablespoons of the butter in the oil. Add the shiitake and oyster mushrooms and cook over high heat, stirring occasionally, until lightly browned, about 6 minutes. Scrape the mushrooms to one side of the skillet.

2. Melt the remaining 1 tablespoon of butter on the other side of the skillet. Add the shallot and cook, stirring occasionally, just until softened, 1 to 2 minutes. Stir the shallot into the mushrooms and cook for 2 minutes longer.

3. In a bowl, whisk the Madeira with the miso. Add to the skillet and cook over moderately high heat for 1 minute, scraping up the browned bits from the bottom of the skillet. Add the broth, parsley and thyme and simmer until the sauce is slightly reduced, 2 minutes. Season the mushrooms with salt and pepper. Transfer to a bowl and serve. —*Grace Parisi*

**SERVE WITH** Roast chicken, grilled steak or pork or veal chops.

### Wild Mushroom Ragout

**TOTAL: 35 MIN**

6 SERVINGS

- 1 tablespoon unsalted butter
- 2 tablespoons extra-virgin olive oil
- 1 large shallot, minced
- 1½ pounds mixed wild mushrooms, such as chanterelles, oysters and shiitake, thickly sliced
- 2 tablespoons brandy or Cognac
- ¾ cup low-sodium chicken broth
- 1 cup heavy cream

Salt and freshly ground pepper

- 2 tablespoons snipped chives

In a large, deep skillet, melt the butter in the olive oil. Add the shallot and cook over moderately high heat until softened, about 3 minutes. Add the mushrooms and cook, tossing, until browned, about 15 minutes. Add the brandy; simmer until evaporated. Add the broth and cook, stirring frequently, until reduced by half. Add the cream and cook until slightly reduced, about 12 minutes. Season with salt and pepper and stir in the chives. —*Grace Parisi*

**SERVE WITH** Pasta, polenta or grilled steak, pork or lamb.

### Bacon-Wrapped Enoki

**ACTIVE: 10 MIN; TOTAL: 30 MIN**

MAKES 2 DOZEN

HORS D'OEUVRES ●

- 12 slices of bacon, halved crosswise
- Two 4-ounce packages enoki mushrooms, trimmed and split into 24 bundles
- 3 scallions, quartered lengthwise and cut into 3-inch lengths

Freshly ground pepper

1. Preheat the oven to 425°. Line a large, rimmed baking sheet with parchment paper and arrange the bacon slices on it 3 inches apart. Set the mushrooms on the bacon slices. Top with the scallions and season with pepper. Roll up into tight cylinders and secure with toothpicks.

2. Roast the enoki bundles for 18 minutes, or until the bacon is browned and crisp. Drain the bundles on paper towels, remove the toothpicks and serve right away. —*Grace Parisi*

# vegetables

1. Fill a large bowl with water. Peel the salsify and trim the ends. Transfer the salsify to the water as you peel it. Using a mandoline or the slicing blade in a food processor, slice the salsify ¼ inch thick. Return it to the water to keep it white.

2. In a large soup pot, melt the butter. Add the flour and cook over moderate heat for 2 minutes, whisking constantly. Add the half-and-half and bring to a boil, whisking constantly. Cook, whisking, for about 3 minutes, or until slightly thickened. Season with salt, pepper and nutmeg. Drain the salsify and pat it completely dry. Add the salsify to the thickened half-and-half and cook over moderate heat, stirring occasionally, until it is tender, 25 to 30 minutes.

3. Preheat the oven to 400° and position a rack in the upper third. Pour the salsify mixture into a 9-by-13-inch baking dish and sprinkle with the cheeses. Bake for about 20 minutes, until the cheese is melted and the gratin is bubbling. Preheat the broiler and broil the gratin for about 5 minutes, or until the cheese is golden and crusty. Let the gratin cool for 10 minutes before serving.
—*Gabriel Kreuther*

**MAKE AHEAD** The unbaked gratin can be refrigerated for up to 2 days.

## tool

**TIP** | **PEPPER MILL**

This 5-inch-tall mill from MoMA Design Store can be used one-handed ($24; 800-447-MOMA or momastore.org).

## Garlicky Potato and Baby Spinach Gratin
**TOTAL: 30 MIN**
**4 SERVINGS** ● ●

- 1 cup heavy cream
- ¼ cup plus 2 tablespoons freshly grated Parmesan cheese
- 1 teaspoon kosher salt
- ¼ teaspoon freshly ground pepper
- Pinch of freshly grated nutmeg
- 1 tablespoon unsalted butter
- 3 ounces baby spinach
- 1 garlic clove, minced
- One ½-pound baking potato, peeled and sliced on a mandoline ¹⁄₁₆ inch thick

1. Preheat the oven to 425° and butter an 8-by-12-inch baking dish. In a glass measuring cup, combine the cream with ¼ cup of the Parmesan and the salt, pepper and nutmeg.

2. In a medium skillet, melt the butter. Add the baby spinach and minced garlic and cook over moderately high heat, tossing, until the spinach is wilted, about 1 minute.

3. Spread the potato slices in the baking dish and cover with the spinach. Pour the cream over the top and shake the dish to distribute evenly. Sprinkle the remaining 2 tablespoons of Parmesan over the top and bake for about 20 minutes, or until the gratin is browned and bubbling and the potatoes are tender. Let the gratin rest for 5 minutes before serving.
—*Mohammad Islam*

## Spicy Broccoli Rabe
**TOTAL: 30 MIN**
**8 SERVINGS** ● ●

- 3 pounds broccoli rabe, thick stems discarded
- ½ cup extra-virgin olive oil
- 4 garlic cloves, minced
- 4 anchovies, minced
- 1½ teaspoons crushed red pepper
- Salt and freshly ground pepper

1. In a pot of boiling salted water, cook the broccoli rabe until crisp-tender, about 4 minutes; drain well.

2. In a large skillet, heat the olive oil until shimmering. Add the garlic, anchovies and crushed red pepper and cook over high heat until the garlic is lightly browned and fragrant, 1 to 2 minutes. Add the broccoli rabe, season with salt and pepper and cook, tossing, until tender, 5 to 6 minutes. Transfer to a bowl and serve. —*Steven Wagner*

## Coconut-Creamed Spinach
**TOTAL: 25 MIN**
**4 SERVINGS** ● ●

- Two 10-ounce bags spinach, thick stems discarded, rinsed
- 2 tablespoons unsalted butter
- 4 large shiitake mushrooms, stems discarded, caps thickly sliced
- 2 medium shallots, very thinly sliced
- 1½ teaspoons minced fresh ginger
- 1 large jalapeño, seeded and very finely chopped
- One 14-ounce can unsweetened coconut milk, stirred
- Salt and freshly ground pepper
- 1 tablespoon fresh lime juice

1. Heat a large skillet until hot to the touch. Add the spinach in handfuls and cook over high heat, tossing, until just wilted, about 1 minute. Transfer to a colander; let cool slightly. Press out as much liquid as possible. Wipe out the skillet with a paper towel.

2. Melt the butter in the skillet. Add the mushrooms and shallots and cook over moderately high heat until golden, about 3 minutes. Add the ginger and jalapeño and cook until fragrant. Add the spinach and coconut milk and season with salt and pepper. Simmer over moderate heat until slightly thickened, about 3 minutes. Stir in the lime juice and serve.
—*Grace Parisi*

## Curried Kaleslaw

TOTAL: 25 MIN, PLUS 4 HR CHILLING

6 SERVINGS ● ●

- 1 small red onion, halved lengthwise and thinly sliced crosswise
- 12 Tuscan kale leaves, finely shredded
- ½ small head green cabbage, finely shredded
- 2 medium red bell peppers, thinly sliced
- ¼ cup extra-virgin olive oil
- 1 garlic clove, minced
- 1 teaspoon mild curry powder
- 2 tablespoons cider vinegar
- 2 tablespoons fresh lemon juice

Salt and freshly ground pepper

1. In a colander, rinse the onion in cold water for 1 minute. Drain and pat dry.
2. In a large bowl, toss the kale with the cabbage, bell peppers and onion.
3. Heat the olive oil in a small skillet. Add the garlic and cook over moderate heat until softened, about 1 minute. Add the curry powder and cook until fragrant, about 1 minute; be careful not to burn it. Whisk in the vinegar and lemon juice and remove from the heat. Season the dressing with salt and pepper and pour it over the vegetables. Toss well. Cover the slaw and refrigerate for at least 4 hours or overnight. Season with salt and pepper and serve chilled. —Dana Jacobi

## Curried Mixed Vegetables

TOTAL: 30 MIN

4 SERVINGS ● ●

- 2 large carrots, cut into ¼-inch dice
- 1 medium Yukon Gold potato, peeled and cut into ¼-inch dice
- 1 medium zucchini, cut into ¼-inch dice
- 2 medium onions, cut into ¼-inch dice
- 2 long red chiles, seeded and minced
- 2 tablespoons ground coriander
- 1 teaspoon ground turmeric
- 3 tablespoons vegetable oil
- 2 teaspoons minced fresh ginger
- 2 medium tomatoes, diced
- ½ cup cilantro, coarsely chopped
- 1 cup shelled frozen edamame
- 1 cup plain nonfat Greek yogurt
- 1 tablespoon fresh lemon juice

Kosher salt

- 4 whole-wheat pocketless pitas, warmed

1. In a medium bowl, toss the diced carrots, potato, zucchini and onions with the chiles, ground coriander and ground turmeric.
2. In a large saucepan, heat the vegetable oil until shimmering. Add the ginger and cook over moderate heat until golden, about 1 minute. Add the seasoned vegetables and cook over moderately high heat until they just start to brown around the edges, about 4 minutes. Add the tomatoes and half of the cilantro, cover and cook until the vegetables are tender, about 10 minutes. Stir in the edamame and cook for 2 minutes longer. Remove from the heat. Stir in the yogurt and lemon juice and season with salt. Transfer the vegetables to bowls, garnish with the remaining cilantro and serve with the warmed pitas.
—Charmaine Solomon

## Warm Bok Choy with Soy Dressing

TOTAL: 10 MIN

4 SERVINGS ● ●

- 2 tablespoons soy sauce
- 2 tablespoons rice vinegar
- ¾ teaspoon Asian sesame oil
- 1¼ pounds baby bok choy

1. In a small bowl, combine the soy sauce, vinegar and sesame oil.
2. In a large saucepan of boiling water, cook the bok choy for 1 minute. Drain and transfer to a platter. Drizzle with the dressing, toss gently and serve.
—Naomi Duguid and Jeffrey Alford

## Roasted Endives with Prosciutto

ACTIVE: 30 MIN; TOTAL: 1 HR 30 MIN

10 SERVINGS ●

- 10 medium Belgian endives (about 3½ pounds total), halved lengthwise
- ½ pound thinly sliced prosciutto, cut into 2-inch pieces
- 4 tablespoons unsalted butter, cut into small pieces

Freshly ground pepper

1. Preheat the oven to 425° and position a rack in the lower third of the oven. Working with 1 endive half at a time, gently tuck pieces of prosciutto between the leaves. Continue until all of the endives are filled.
2. In a large roasting pan, arrange the endives cut side down in a single layer, overlapping them slightly. Scatter the butter on top and season with freshly ground pepper. Roast the endives for about 1 hour, until tender, turning them

# health

**FROZEN VEGETABLES**    **TIP**

**From the moment they're harvested, vegetables start losing nutrients. Freezing drastically slows the decline, so frozen vegetables often retain more vitamins than fresh produce that has been shipped across the country, then refrigerated for days. Frozen spinach and peas both have more vitamin A than fresh, even after cooking. And research from the University of Illinois at Urbana-Champaign has shown that even after four months, frozen green beans have twice the vitamin C of fresh beans stored for only six days.**

# vegetables

once or twice. Spoon off any liquid in the roasting pan and continue to roast the endives for 15 to 20 minutes longer, turning occasionally, until golden and lightly caramelized. Transfer the endives to a platter and serve. —*Gabriel Kreuther*
**MAKE AHEAD** The roasted endives can be refrigerated overnight.

## Butternut Squash–Polenta Gratin
**ACTIVE: 30 MIN; TOTAL: 2 HR 10 MIN**
**12 SERVINGS** ●
One 1½-pound butternut squash
2 tablespoons extra-virgin olive oil, plus more for drizzling
Salt and freshly ground pepper
2 quarts plus 2 cups water
2 cups instant polenta (12 ounces)
1 stick (4 ounces) unsalted butter
1⅓ cups freshly grated Parmesan cheese (4 ounces)

# health

**Corn is not just another carbohydrate. Even though it's a grain, it provides the benefits of a vegetable: Not only is it a good source of fiber, vitamin C, potassium, magnesium and phosphorous, it's also rich in disease-fighting antioxidants. Recent studies by Rui Hai Liu, a food scientist at Cornell University, have shown that corn contains more antioxidants than wheat, oats or rice, and that the antioxidants in corn can survive longer in the digestive system than those of some fruits and vegetables, potentially offering greater protection against some cancers.**

**1.** Preheat the oven to 375°. Lightly butter a 15-by-10-inch ceramic baking dish. Cut off the bulb end of the squash and halve it lengthwise. Scoop out the seeds. Drizzle the halves with olive oil and season with salt and pepper. Set the squash halves cut sides down on a medium, rimmed baking sheet and bake in the lower third of the oven for 30 minutes, or until tender but not collapsing. Scrape the squash flesh into a medium bowl and mash with a fork.
**2.** Meanwhile, peel the squash neck and halve it lengthwise. Using a sharp knife or a mandoline, slice the squash crosswise ⅛ inch thick. Lightly oil 2 large, rimmed baking sheets and arrange the squash slices on them in a single layer. Cover the baking sheets with foil and bake the squash in the upper third of the oven for 12 minutes, or until tender. Reduce the oven temperature to 350°.
**3.** In a large saucepan, bring the water to a boil. Add the 2 tablespoons of olive oil, then slowly add the polenta, whisking constantly until smooth. Reduce the heat to low and whisk until thickened, about 5 minutes. Whisk in the mashed squash. Stir in 6 tablespoons of the butter and 1 cup of the Parmesan and season with salt and pepper. Spread the polenta in the prepared baking dish and arrange the baked squash slices on top in an overlapping pattern.
**4.** Cut the remaining 2 tablespoons of butter into small pieces and evenly scatter them over the gratin. Sprinkle the remaining ⅓ cup of cheese over the top and bake in the upper third of the oven for 1 hour, or until bubbling and golden. Let stand for 15 minutes before serving. —*Marcia Kiesel*
**MAKE AHEAD** The recipe can be prepared through Step 3 and refrigerated, tightly covered, for up to 5 days. Bring the gratin to room temperature before baking it.

## Chipotle-Spiked Winter Squash and Black Bean Salad
**TOTAL: 25 MIN**
**6 SERVINGS** ● ●
1½ pounds butternut squash, peeled and cut into ½-inch dice
3 tablespoons balsamic vinegar
1½ tablespoons Dijon mustard
1 tablespoon pure maple syrup
1 chipotle chile in adobo sauce— drained, seeded and minced
2 tablespoons olive oil
Salt and freshly ground pepper
1 bunch watercress, tough stems removed (5 ounces)
One 15-ounce can black beans, rinsed and drained
3 scallions, thinly sliced
**1.** Spread the butternut squash in a steamer insert and set in a pot above boiling water. Cover and steam until tender, about 10 minutes. Let cool.
**2.** Whisk the vinegar with the mustard, maple syrup and chile. Gradually whisk in the oil. Season with salt and pepper.
**3.** In a large bowl, combine the watercress with the squash, black beans and scallions. Add the dressing and gently toss to coat. Season with salt and pepper and serve. —*Victoria Abbott Riccardi*

## Grilled Corn with Chiles, Cheese and Lime
**TOTAL: 30 MIN, PLUS 2 HR SOAKING**
**8 SERVINGS** ●
6 cups water
½ cup confectioners' sugar
Kosher salt
8 ears of fresh corn, husked
1 lime, halved
½ cup grated Cotija (see Note) or Pecorino Romano cheese
3 scallions, thinly sliced
1 fresh hot red chile or jalapeño, seeded and thinly sliced
1 teaspoon pure chile powder
Freshly ground pepper

1. In a large bowl, mix the water with the sugar and ¼ cup of salt. Add the corn and let soak for 2 hours or overnight, turning occasionally.

2. Light a grill. Drain the corn and grill over high heat until lightly browned in spots and tender, 6 to 8 minutes.

3. Transfer the corn to a large bowl and squeeze the lime all over. Add the cheese, scallions, fresh chile and chile powder and toss until evenly coated. Season with salt and pepper and toss again. Transfer the corn to a platter, scrape any cheese mixture on top and serve.

—*Daniel Orr*

**NOTE** Cotija is a salty and pungent aged cheese from Mexico that is sold in small rounds and used for grating. It is available at specialty food markets, Mexican markets and some grocery stores.

### Red Apple Inn Corn Pudding

ACTIVE: 25 MIN; TOTAL: 1 HR

8 SERVINGS ●

- 6 tablespoons unsalted butter
- ½ cup all-purpose flour
- 1½ teaspoons sugar
- 1 teaspoon salt
- 1¾ cups whole milk
- 4 cups fresh corn kernels (from 8 medium ears of corn)
- 3 large eggs

Freshly ground pepper

1. Preheat the oven to 375°. In a medium saucepan, melt 5 tablespoons of the butter until sizzling. Add the flour, sugar and salt and cook over moderately high heat for about 1 minute, whisking constantly. Gradually whisk in the milk and cook over moderately high heat, whisking, until the sauce thickens, about 5 minutes.

2. In a large nonstick skillet, melt the remaining 1 tablespoon of butter until sizzling. Add the corn kernels and cook over moderately high heat, stirring occasionally, until the corn is crisp-tender, about 4 minutes.

GRILLED CORN WITH CHILES, CHEESE AND LIME

CHIPOTLE-SPIKED WINTER SQUASH

# vegetables

**3.** In a medium bowl, beat the eggs. Gradually whisk in the hot white sauce. Add the corn, stir to combine and season with pepper.

**4.** Lightly grease a 9-inch cast-iron skillet and warm it on the stovetop. Pour in the corn-pudding batter, carefully transfer the hot skillet to the oven and bake for about 30 minutes, or until the pudding is cooked through and golden on top. Let the corn pudding cool for about 10 minutes before serving.

—*Mary Lynn Van Wyck*

**MAKE AHEAD** The corn pudding can be baked earlier in the day and reheated in a 325° oven.

## Buttery Root Vegetable Ragout
**TOTAL: 30 MIN**

4 SERVINGS ●

- 4 tablespoons unsalted butter
- 1 large white onion, coarsely chopped
- 2 large garlic cloves, very finely chopped
- ½ small butternut squash, peeled and cut into ½-inch pieces (1½ cups)

# ingredient

Roasted corn can add smoky-sweet flavor to corn bread, puddings, summer salads and other recipes. And you don't need an outdoor grill. Simply place shucked ears directly on the burners of a gas or electric stove, turn with tongs until blackened in spots, cool, then cut the kernels from the cob. Expect to hear crackling and popping as the corn roasts.

- 2 medium carrots, sliced ½ inch thick
- 1 small parsnip, sliced ½ inch thick
- 1 medium Yukon Gold potato, peeled and cut into ½-inch pieces
- 2 cups shredded Savoy cabbage
- 1½ cups vegetable stock
- ¼ cup dry white wine
- Salt and freshly ground pepper
- 1 tablespoon chopped flat-leaf parsley
- 1 tablespoon snipped chives
- Couscous, for serving

In a large, deep skillet, melt 2 tablespoons of the butter. Add the onion and garlic and cook over moderately high heat for 30 seconds. Add the squash, carrots, parsnip and potato, cover and cook, stirring frequently, until the vegetables are barely softened, 7 to 8 minutes. Add the cabbage, stock and wine and season with salt and pepper. Cover and cook, stirring occasionally, until the vegetables are tender, about 10 minutes longer. Stir in the remaining 2 tablespoons of butter along with the parsley and chives. Spoon the vegetable ragout over couscous and serve. —*Bill Telepan*

## Roasted Parsnips with Horseradish-Herb Butter
**ACTIVE: 30 MIN; TOTAL: 1 HR 30 MIN**

12 SERVINGS ●

- 4½ pounds parsnips, peeled and cut into 2-by-½-inch sticks
- ¼ cup extra-virgin olive oil
- Salt and freshly ground pepper
- 1 cup Rich Turkey Stock (p. 112) or low-sodium chicken broth
- 1 stick (4 ounces) unsalted butter, softened
- ¼ cup freshly grated horseradish or drained bottled horseradish
- 1½ tablespoons finely chopped flat-leaf parsley
- 1½ tablespoons minced chives
- 1 small garlic clove, minced

**1.** Preheat the oven to 400°. In a large roasting pan, toss the parsnips with the olive oil and season with salt and pepper. Add the Rich Turkey Stock, cover the pan with aluminum foil and roast, stirring the parsnips once or twice, until they are tender and the stock has evaporated, about 1 hour.

**2.** Meanwhile, in a medium bowl, mix the softened butter with the horseradish, parsley, chives and garlic and season with salt and pepper. Toss the warm roasted parsnips with the horseradish-herb butter and serve immediately.

—*Grace Parisi*

**MAKE AHEAD** The horseradish-herb butter can be wrapped in plastic and frozen for up to 2 weeks; bring to room temperature before using. The roasted parsnips can be refrigerated for up to 2 days. Reheat the parsnips in a 325° oven and toss with the butter.

## Okra in Tomato Sauce
**TOTAL 45 MIN**

8 SERVINGS ● ●

- ¼ cup plus 2 tablespoons extra-virgin olive oil
- 2 large onions, thinly sliced
- 4 garlic cloves, minced
- 2 pounds small okra (see Note), trimmed
- One 28-ounce can whole tomatoes, drained and chopped
- 3 tablespoons fresh lemon juice
- 1 teaspoon sugar
- Salt and freshly ground pepper
- ¼ cup coarsely chopped flat-leaf parsley

Heat the oil in a large enameled cast-iron casserole. Add the onions and cook over moderately high heat, stirring occasionally, until golden, about 6 minutes. Add the garlic and cook until fragrant, about 3 minutes. Add the okra and cook over moderate heat, stirring, until well coated with the flavorings, about 5 minutes. Add

the tomatoes, lemon juice and sugar and season with salt and pepper. Simmer over moderately low heat, stirring occasionally, until the okra is tender and the sauce is thickened, 15 to 20 minutes. Stir in the parsley and season with salt. Serve hot, warm or at room temperature.
—*Nadia Roden*

**NOTE** You can use small frozen okra in this recipe.

**MAKE AHEAD** The prepared okra can be refrigerated overnight. Reheat gently.

## Okra and Tomato Stew with Cilantro

**TOTAL: 35 MIN**

**6 SERVINGS** ● ●

A whole universe of simple Lebanese vegetarian dishes, referred to as *bi zeit* in Arabic, are cooked in and primarily flavored by olive oil. In this version, the sautéed cilantro and garlic and the slightly sticky texture of the okra add complexity.

⅓ cup vegetable oil
1½ pounds fresh or thawed frozen okra, patted dry
2 tablespoons extra-virgin olive oil
1 medium onion, thinly sliced
5 large garlic cloves, minced
½ cup coarsely chopped cilantro leaves
One 28-ounce can peeled Italian tomatoes, chopped, juices reserved
Salt and freshly ground pepper

**1.** In a large skillet, heat the vegetable oil until shimmering. Add the okra and cook over moderate heat, stirring, until bright green and crisp-tender, about 4 minutes. Transfer the okra to a plate with a slotted spoon; discard the oil.

**2.** Add the olive oil to the skillet and heat until shimmering. Add the onion and cook over moderate heat until softened and golden, about 8 minutes. Add the

garlic and cilantro and cook, stirring, until fragrant, about 1 minute. Add the tomatoes and their juices and bring to a simmer, then cook until slightly thickened, about 3 minutes.

**3.** Return the okra to the skillet and season with salt and pepper. Cover and simmer over low heat until the okra is tender and the sauce is thickened, 20 minutes. Serve warm or at room temperature.
—*Anissa Helou*

**MAKE AHEAD** The okra and tomato stew can be refrigerated overnight. Reheat gently before serving.

## Green-Tomato Pickle

**ACTIVE: 30 MIN; TOTAL: 2 HR 45 MIN, PLUS 2 HR DRAINING**

**MAKES ABOUT 2 PINTS** ● ●

2 pounds green tomatoes, cored and thinly sliced
1½ tablespoons salt
2 cups plus 2 tablespoons cider vinegar
¾ cup water
2 cups granulated sugar
½ cup lightly packed dark brown sugar
1 tablespoon pickling spice, tied in a cheesecloth bundle
1 small bay leaf
½ medium green bell pepper, thinly sliced
1 medium sweet onion, very thinly sliced

**1.** In a colander set in the sink, toss the tomatoes with the salt and let stand at room temperature until almost all of their liquid has been released, at least 2 hours or overnight. Drain and rinse the tomato slices, then pat dry.

**2.** In a large saucepan, combine the vinegar, water, granulated sugar, brown sugar, pickling spice bundle and bay leaf and bring to a boil. Reduce the heat to moderate and simmer until reduced by one-third, about 30 minutes.

**3.** Add the tomatoes, bell pepper and onion and cook over moderate heat until the liquid is reduced to a thick syrup, about 2 hours. Discard the pickling spice bundle and the bay leaf.

**4.** Pour the pickled green-tomato mixture into 2 hot sterilized 1-pint jars, stopping ¼ inch from the tops. Wipe the glass rims and seal the jars. Let cool and refrigerate. Alternatively, process the pickle: Set the jars in a water bath, bring to a boil and boil for 15 minutes. Remove the jars from the water bath and let cool completely. —*Mary Lynn Van Wyck*

**MAKE AHEAD** The unprocessed pickle can be refrigerated for up to 3 months. The processed pickle can be stored at room temperature for up to 1 year.

# equipment

**NEW AGA STOVE**          **TIP**

**AGA, the British company known for its gas-powered radiant-heat cookers, now manufactures a model that combines a radiant stovetop with electric ovens. Stoves come in 14 colors ($9,800; 866-424-2487 or aga-kitchen.com).**

CRISP HERB-ROASTED FINGERLINGS WITH SCALLIONS, P. 231

# potatoes, grains +more

11

OVEN FRIES WITH GARLIC AND PARSLEY

CRANBERRY BEAN STEW WITH POTATOES AND PEPPERS

### Oven Fries with Garlic and Parsley

**ACTIVE: 30 MIN; TOTAL: 1 HR 15 MIN**

4 SERVINGS ●

- 2 pounds baking potatoes, scrubbed and cut into ⅓-inch-wide fries
- ¼ cup extra-virgin olive oil
- Salt
- 2 large garlic cloves, minced
- 1 tablespoon finely chopped parsley
- Freshly ground pepper

**1.** Preheat the oven to 475°. Prepare a large bowl of ice water. Add the potatoes and let soak for 15 minutes. Drain well and pat dry.

**2.** In a large bowl, toss the potatoes with the olive oil and season with salt. Spread the potatoes on a large nonstick rimmed baking sheet in a single layer. Bake for about 20 minutes, or until the potatoes are golden on the bottom. Turn and bake for about 25 minutes longer, turning occasionally, until golden and crisp. Transfer the fries to a platter, sprinkle with the garlic, parsley and pepper and serve at once. —*Elizabeth Mendez*

### Cranberry Bean Stew with Potatoes and Bell Peppers

**ACTIVE: 25 MIN; TOTAL: 1 HR 30 MIN, PLUS OVERNIGHT SOAKING**

4 SERVINGS ● ●

- 1½ cups dried cranberry beans (½ pound), soaked overnight and drained
- ¼ cup extra-virgin olive oil
- 1 large sweet onion, coarsely chopped
- 1 large red bell pepper, cut into ½-inch strips
- 1 sweet Italian chicken sausage, casing removed
- 2 cups drained canned diced tomatoes
- 2 cups chicken stock
- 4 thyme sprigs
- Pinch of crushed red pepper
- Salt and freshly ground black pepper
- 2 medium Yukon Gold potatoes, peeled and cut into ½-inch dice
- 2 tablespoons finely chopped parsley

**1.** In a saucepan, cover the cranberry beans with 3 inches of cold water and bring to a boil. Cook over moderate heat until barely tender, 30 minutes. Drain.

**2.** Heat the olive oil in a large saucepan. Add the onion and bell pepper and cook over moderate heat until softened, about 7 minutes. Add the sausage and cook for 4 minutes, crumbling it with a spoon. Add the beans, tomatoes, stock, thyme and crushed red pepper and season with salt and black pepper. Cover partially and simmer over moderate heat until the beans are tender, about 20 minutes. Add the potatoes, cover partially and cook until tender, about 15 minutes longer. Remove the thyme sprigs. Stir in the parsley and serve. —*Aglaia Kremezi*

## Potato Salad with Bacon and Tomatoes

**TOTAL: 30 MIN**

4 SERVINGS ●

- ¾ pound sliced bacon
- 1½ pounds Yukon Gold potatoes, peeled and cut into ¾-inch cubes
- ¼ cup cider vinegar
- 2 teaspoons Dijon mustard
- ½ cup extra-virgin olive oil

Salt and freshly ground pepper

- 1 pint cherry tomatoes, halved
- 1 heart of romaine lettuce, thickly sliced (4 cups)
- 2 scallions, thinly sliced

**1.** Preheat the oven to 425°. Spread the bacon in a single layer on a large, rimmed baking sheet. Top with another baking sheet and bake for 10 minutes, or until just barely cooked. Remove the top sheet and bake the bacon until browned, 8 minutes longer. Transfer to paper towels to drain, then cut into 1-inch pieces.

**2.** Meanwhile, in a large saucepan of boiling salted water, cook the potatoes until tender, about 12 minutes. Drain and transfer to a bowl; let cool slightly.

**3.** In a small bowl, whisk the vinegar with the mustard. Whisk in the olive oil and season with salt and pepper. Add half of the dressing to the potatoes along with the bacon and half of the tomatoes; season with salt and pepper. In another bowl, toss the lettuce, scallions and remaining tomatoes with the remaining dressing and season with salt and pepper. Transfer the greens to 4 plates, top with the potato salad and serve. —*Ilene Rosen*

## Ikarian Potato Salad with Purslane

**TOTAL: 30 MIN**

6 SERVINGS ● ● ●

The bane of many gardeners, purslane is a hardy weed that is delicious both raw and cooked. It turns up at farmers' markets in summer months and is characterized by red stems and slightly succulent green leaves that have a tangy flavor.

Salt

- 3 medium Yukon Gold potatoes, peeled and sliced ⅓ inch thick
- ½ cup extra-virgin olive oil
- 3 tablespoons red wine vinegar
- 1 pound plum tomatoes, coarsely chopped
- ¼ pound purslane or arugula, torn
- 1 large cucumber—peeled, halved, seeded and cut into half-moons
- 1 medium red onion, thinly sliced
- 1 jalapeño, seeded and very finely chopped
- ½ cup chopped parsley
- ½ cup chopped mint

**1.** Bring a medium saucepan of salted water to a boil. Add the potatoes and cook until tender, about 12 minutes. Drain and let cool.

**2.** In a small bowl, combine the olive oil and vinegar and season with salt. Break the potato slices into quarters and spread on the bottom of a large, shallow bowl. Season with salt and drizzle with 3 tablespoons of the dressing. Layer the tomatoes over the potatoes, followed by the purslane, cucumber, onion, jalapeño, parsley and mint. Just before serving, pour the remaining dressing over the salad and toss well. —*Diane Kochilas*

## Crisp Herb-Roasted Fingerlings with Scallions

**ACTIVE: 25 MIN; TOTAL: 1 HR 10 MIN**

8 SERVINGS ● ●

After roasting the potatoes, you'll have leftover herb-scented olive oil; use it for sautéing meat or chicken.

- 2 pounds fingerling potatoes, halved lengthwise
- 1 head of garlic, cloves peeled
- 2 cups extra-virgin olive oil

Kosher salt and freshly ground pepper

- 12 thyme sprigs
- 8 rosemary sprigs
- 1 bunch scallions, thinly sliced

**1.** Preheat the oven to 375°. In a large roasting pan, toss the potatoes, garlic cloves and olive oil; season with salt and pepper. Using kitchen string, tie the thyme and rosemary sprigs into a bundle and add it to the pan. Roast the potatoes for 40 minutes, or until tender and just beginning to brown. Let cool slightly. Drain the potatoes and garlic, reserving the oil; discard the herb bundle.

**2.** Set the garlic cloves aside. Return the potatoes to the roasting pan, cut side down, and drizzle with 2 tablespoons of the reserved oil. Roast for 15 minutes longer, until golden and crisp. Add the scallions and roast for 1 minute. Add the reserved garlic cloves and toss. Transfer to a platter and serve. —*Pascal Rigo*

## Grilled Potatoes with Garlic Aioli

**ACTIVE: 20 MIN; TOTAL: 1 HR 20 MIN**

6 SERVINGS ●

- 3 pounds medium red potatoes
- 2 tablespoons mayonnaise
- 1½ tablespoons fresh lemon juice
- 2 large garlic cloves, smashed
- ½ tablespoon Dijon mustard
- ¾ cup extra-virgin olive oil
- ¼ cup vegetable oil

Salt and freshly ground pepper

- 1 tablespoon thyme leaves

**1.** In a large saucepan, cover the potatoes with cold water and bring to a boil. Cook over moderate heat until tender, 30 minutes. Drain and let cool for 20 minutes. Cut the potatoes in half.

**2.** Meanwhile, in a food processor, blend the mayonnaise, lemon juice, garlic and mustard. With the machine running, add

# potatoes, grains + more

½ cup of the olive oil and the vegetable oil in a thin stream and blend until emulsified. Season the aioli with salt and pepper and refrigerate until chilled.

3. Light a grill. Toss the potatoes with the thyme and the remaining ¼ cup of olive oil and season with salt and pepper. Grill over a hot fire for about 10 minutes, turning occasionally, until browned and sizzling. Transfer the potatoes to a platter and serve with the aioli. —*Jody Denton*

**MAKE AHEAD** The aioli can be refrigerated for 3 days. The potatoes can be boiled 6 hours ahead; grill before serving.

## Hobo Potatoes with Fennel and Herbs

ACTIVE: 20 MIN; TOTAL: 1 HR
8 SERVINGS ●

- 3 pounds fingerling potatoes, sliced ¼ inch thick
- 1 Spanish onion, thinly sliced
- 3 large garlic cloves, minced
- 1 fennel bulb, thinly sliced
- ½ lemon, thinly sliced and seeded
- ¼ cup plus 2 tablespoons extra-virgin olive oil
- 1 tablespoon kosher salt
- 1 teaspoon freshly ground pepper
- 2 thyme sprigs
- 2 rosemary sprigs
- 2 bay leaves

1. Light a grill. In a large bowl, toss all of the ingredients. Tear off four 20-inch-long sheets of extra-heavy-duty aluminum foil. Arrange 2 double-layered sheets side by side. Mound half of the potatoes on half of each sheet, making sure there's a thyme sprig, a rosemary sprig and a bay leaf in each mound. Fold the foil over and crimp the edges tightly to seal.

2. Set the packages on the grill and cook over moderate heat, shaking occasionally, until the potatoes are tender, about 40 minutes. Using tongs, carefully transfer the packages to a platter. Open, spoon into a bowl and serve. —*Daniel Orr*

## Crispy Potato-Leek Rösti

TOTAL: 45 MIN
6 SERVINGS ● ●

This rösti is terrific alongside scrambled eggs at breakfast. It also is marvelous topped with smoked salmon, sour cream and chives.

- 3½ tablespoons unsalted butter
- 3 medium leeks, white and tender green parts only, halved lengthwise and thinly sliced crosswise
- 1¼ pounds unpeeled Yukon Gold potatoes, scrubbed and coarsely shredded

Kosher salt

- 1 tablespoon extra-virgin olive oil

1. In a 10-inch nonstick skillet, melt the butter. Add the leeks and cook over moderate heat until softened, about 7 minutes. Scrape the leeks into a large bowl and toss them with the shredded potatoes and 1 teaspoon of salt. Wipe the skillet out with a paper towel.

2. Heat the olive oil in the skillet. Add the potato-leek mixture, pressing it into a cake with a spatula. Cook the rösti over moderate heat, pressing down on it occasionally with the spatula, until the bottom is nicely browned, 10 to 12 minutes; reduce the heat to low if the rösti seems to be browning too quickly. Slide the rösti out onto a plate, then carefully flip it back into the pan with the browned side up. Press down with the spatula and cook it over moderate heat, lowering the heat if necessary, until tender throughout and well browned on the bottom, about 12 minutes longer.

3. Slide the potato-leek rösti onto a cutting board and cut it into strips or wedges. Season with salt and serve immediately. —*Melissa Clark*

**MAKE AHEAD** The rösti can be kept at room temperature for up to 2 hours. Recrisp on a baking sheet in a 400° oven.

## Roasted Brussels Sprout and Potato Gratin

ACTIVE: 45 MIN; TOTAL: 2 HR
8 SERVINGS ● ●

- 2 tablespoons unsalted butter
- 2 tablespoons vegetable oil
- 1½ pounds brussels sprouts, thinly sliced crosswise
- 1 large shallot, minced
- ¼ cup dry white wine
- 2 cups heavy cream

Salt and freshly ground pepper

- 3 pounds baking potatoes, peeled and thinly sliced on a mandoline
- ½ cup freshly grated Parmesan cheese (about 2 ounces)

1. In a large, deep skillet, melt the butter in the oil. Add the brussels sprouts and shallot and cook over moderate heat, stirring, until softened, about 8 minutes. Add the white wine and cook until evaporated, 1 minute. Add the heavy cream, season with salt and pepper and bring to a simmer. Let cool to room temperature.

2. Preheat the oven to 325°. Generously butter a 1½-quart shallow baking dish. Arrange one-sixth of the potato slices evenly over the bottom of the dish and season with salt and pepper. Using a slotted spoon, spread a thin layer of the brussels sprouts over the potatoes and top with 1 tablespoon of the Parmesan cheese. Repeat the layering process, using all of the potatoes and brussels sprouts and all but 2 tablespoons of the Parmesan and ending with a layer of potatoes. Pour the cream over the potatoes and sprinkle with the remaining 2 tablespoons of Parmesan. Cover with buttered foil and bake for 45 minutes.

3. Uncover and bake the gratin for 30 minutes longer, or until the potatoes are tender and the top is golden brown. Let sit for 15 minutes before serving. —*Ashley Christensen*

**MAKE AHEAD** The gratin can be refrigerated overnight. Reheat before serving.

## Mashed Yukon Golds with Chives

**ACTIVE: 25 MIN; TOTAL: 50 MIN**

10 SERVINGS ●

5 pounds large Yukon Gold potatoes, peeled and cut into 2-inch chunks

Salt

1 cup heavy cream, warmed

1 stick (4 ounces) unsalted butter, at room temperature

½ cup buttermilk, warmed

¼ cup snipped chives

Freshly ground pepper

1. In a large pot, cover the potatoes with water and bring to a boil. Salt the water and cook the potatoes over moderately high heat until tender, about 25 minutes. Drain the potatoes and return them to the pot. Shake the pot over moderately high heat for 1 minute to dry out the potatoes.

2. Pass the potatoes through a ricer into another pot. Add the cream, butter and buttermilk to the potatoes and stir well. Fold in the chives and season with salt and pepper. Serve hot. —*Lee Hefter*

**MAKE AHEAD** The potatoes can be kept warm in the pan for up to 30 minutes. Fold in the chives just before serving.

## Red Skin Potato Mash

**ACTIVE: 15 MIN; TOTAL: 40 MIN**

12 SERVINGS ●

6 pounds red potatoes, scrubbed and cut into 2-inch chunks

Salt

2 sticks (½ pound) unsalted butter, softened

2 cups warmed milk

2 scallions, thinly sliced

Freshly ground pepper

1. Put the potatoes in a large pot and cover with water. Cover the pot and bring to a boil. Add a large pinch of salt and boil, uncovered, over moderately high heat, until fork-tender, about 25 minutes. Drain and return to the pot.

2. Shake the pot over moderately high heat to dry the potatoes. Off the heat, lightly mash the potatoes. Add the softened butter and warm milk and mash until incorporated. Stir in the scallions, season with salt and pepper and serve. —*Marcia Kiesel*

**MAKE AHEAD** The mashed potatoes can be made early in the day. Cover and keep warm, then reheat gently, adding more warm milk if the potatoes seem stiff.

## Fresh Corn and Blue Potato Hash

**ACTIVE: 10 MIN; TOTAL: 30 MIN**

4 SERVINGS ● ●

This fast and healthy hash takes advantage of two Native American ingredients: Peruvian blue potatoes and corn.

1 pound small blue potatoes or other small, slightly waxy potatoes

Salt

1 cup fresh corn kernels (from 2 ears)

1½ tablespoons vegetable oil

Freshly ground pepper

3 cups baby spinach leaves (2 ounces)

¾ cup shredded Manchego cheese (1½ ounces)

1. In a medium saucepan, cover the potatoes with water and bring to a boil. Add a large pinch of salt and boil over moderately high heat until just tender, about 15 minutes. Drain the potatoes and let cool, then quarter them.

2. Meanwhile, in a small saucepan of boiling salted water, cook the corn until crisp-tender, about 3 minutes. Drain and pat dry with paper towels.

3. In a large skillet, heat the oil until shimmering. Add the quartered potatoes and cook over moderately high heat until browned on the bottom, about 5 minutes. Add the corn and cook until lightly toasted, about 3 minutes. Season the hash with salt and pepper. Add the spinach and cook, tossing, until wilted, about 1 minute. Remove from the heat. Sprinkle the Manchego over the potatoes and stir twice, then transfer to a platter and serve. —*Bob Isaacson*

## Pan-Fried Potato Samosas

**ACTIVE: 40 MIN; TOTAL: 1 HR**

MAKES ABOUT 3 DOZEN SAMOSAS ●

These easy mini samosas are sautéed rather than deep-fried. Use gyoza wrappers, sold in the freezer section of many supermarkets.

3 medium Yukon Gold potatoes (1¼ pounds)

2 tablespoons unsalted butter

2 teaspoons black mustard seeds

1 small onion, finely chopped

1 tablespoon minced peeled fresh ginger

1 garlic clove, minced

2 teaspoons ground coriander

1 small serrano or jalapeño chile, seeded and minced

½ teaspoon dried mango powder (see Note)

½ teaspoon garam masala

2 tablespoons finely chopped cilantro

Salt and freshly ground pepper

Cornstarch, for dusting

36 to 40 gyoza wrappers

2 tablespoons canola oil

½ cup water

Tamarind-Date Dipping Sauce (recipe follows)

1. Put the potatoes in a medium saucepan, cover with cold water and bring to a boil. Simmer the potatoes over moderate heat until tender, about 25 minutes. Drain and let cool slightly. Peel the potatoes and cut them into ½-inch dice.

2. Melt the butter in a small saucepan. Skim off the foam, then slowly pour the clear melted butter into a large nonstick skillet set over moderately high heat,

# potatoes, grains + more

stopping when you reach the milky residue. Add the mustard seeds and cook until they begin to pop, 30 seconds. Add the onion, ginger, garlic and coriander and cook over moderate heat until the onion is softened, about 5 minutes. Add the chile, dried mango powder, garam masala and potatoes and cook for 5 minutes, stirring and mashing the samosa filling gently. Remove the skillet from the heat, stir in the cilantro and season with salt and pepper.

**3.** Line a baking sheet with wax paper and dust it lightly with cornstarch. Working with 3 gyoza wrappers at a time and keeping the rest covered with plastic wrap, brush the edges with water. Spoon 2 teaspoons of the potato filling into the center of each wrapper. Fold the wrappers in half over the filling, pressing out any air bubbles and sealing the edges. Gently press the samosas so they stand upright with the seam on top, then transfer to the prepared baking sheet. Repeat with the remaining wrappers and filling.

**4.** Heat 1 tablespoon of the oil in a large nonstick skillet. Add half of the samosas and cook over moderately high heat until sizzling and slightly browned. Add ¼ cup of water, cover and steam until the gyoza wrappers are tender, about 2 minutes. Uncover and cook until the water is evaporated and the samosas are golden on the bottom, about 1½ minutes longer. Transfer to a plate and repeat with the remaining oil, samosas and water. Serve with the tamarind sauce.
—*Akasha Richmond*

**NOTE** Dried mango powder, also called *amchoor,* is available at Kalustyan's (800-352-3451 or kalustyans.com) and at most Indian markets.

**MAKE AHEAD** The samosas can be refrigerated overnight or frozen in a single layer, then transferred to an airtight container and frozen for up to 1 month. There's no need to thaw before cooking.

## TAMARIND-DATE DIPPING SAUCE
**TOTAL: 15 MIN**
**MAKES 1½ CUPS** ● ● ●
Serve this sweet and tangy sauce with spicy samosas or with pappadams, the Indian fried-lentil wafers.

- 1 cup pitted dates, chopped (5 ounces)
- 1 cup hot water
- ¼ cup honey
- 2 tablespoons seedless tamarind concentrate

Pinch of cayenne pepper

In a small saucepan, combine the dates with the water, honey, tamarind and cayenne and simmer for 5 minutes. Transfer the mixture to a food processor and puree until smooth. Serve warm.
—*A.R.*

**MAKE AHEAD** The sauce can be refrigerated for up to 2 weeks. Gently rewarm before serving.

## Supercrispy Potato Latkes
**TOTAL: 45 MIN**
**MAKES ABOUT 9 LATKES** ●

- 2 pounds baking potatoes—peeled, halved and very thinly sliced or shredded
- 1 medium onion, coarsely grated
- 6 tablespoons all-purpose flour
- 2 large eggs, beaten

Salt and freshly ground pepper

- ½ cup vegetable oil

In a bowl, mix the potatoes, onion, flour and eggs; season well with salt and pepper. In a skillet, heat ¼ cup of the oil until shimmering. Drop about ½ cup of the latke mixure into the skillet and spread it slightly. Repeat to make 2 more latkes. Cook over moderately high heat until browned on the bottom, 7 minutes. Turn and cook until browned, 4 minutes. Transfer to a paper towel. Make 6 more latkes, using the remaining oil and potato mixture. Season with salt and pepper and serve hot. —*Kate Heddings*

## Bulgur, Pomegranate and Walnut Salad
**ACTIVE: 20 MIN; TOTAL: 1 HR**
**4 SERVINGS** ●

- ¾ cup walnut halves (2½ ounces)
- ⅓ cup drained oil-packed sun-dried tomatoes, chopped, plus 1 tablespoon oil from the jar
- 1 cup medium bulgur (6 ounces)
- 1 cup canned chickpeas, rinsed
- ½ teaspoon Aleppo pepper flakes or pure ancho chile powder
- 1¾ cups boiling water
- 1 pound grape tomatoes, halved
- ½ cup pomegranate seeds
- ⅓ cup coarsely chopped dill
- ⅓ cup coarsely chopped mint
- 2 tablespoons fresh lemon juice

Salt and freshly ground pepper

- 1 tablespoon pomegranate molasses (see Note) dissolved in 2 teaspoons cold water

**1.** Preheat the oven to 350°. Toast the walnuts in a pie plate for about 8 minutes, or until golden and fragrant. Let cool slightly, then coarsely chop.

**2.** Heat the sun-dried tomato oil in a large saucepan. Add the sun-dried tomatoes and cook over moderately high heat for 1 minute. Add the bulgur and stir to coat with the oil. Add the chickpeas, Aleppo pepper and boiling water and bring to a simmer. Reduce the heat to low, cover and cook without stirring for 20 minutes. Remove from the heat and let stand covered and undisturbed until cooled slightly, about 30 minutes.

**3.** Using 2 forks, fluff the bulgur. Add the tomatoes, pomegranate seeds, dill, mint and lemon juice and season with salt and pepper. Transfer to a platter. Drizzle the diluted pomegranate molasses over the salad and scatter the walnuts on top. Serve warm. —*Engin Akin*

**NOTE** Pomegranate molasses is available at specialty food stores and Middle Eastern markets.

BULGUR, POMEGRANATE AND WALNUT SALAD

# potatoes, grains + more

## Kasha and Noodles with Caramelized Onions

**TOTAL: 1 HR**

**8 SERVINGS** ●

Nutty kasha, or buckwheat groats, is a classic Russian dish. Adding noodles to the kasha lightens the dense grain; cremini mushrooms create a more complex flavor.

- ½ pound egg noodles
- 3 tablespoons vegetable oil
- 2 medium onions, finely chopped
- 1 pound cremini or white button mushrooms, sliced ⅛ inch thick

Kosher salt and freshly ground pepper

- 1 cup kasha (7 ounces)
- 1 large egg, lightly beaten
- 2 cups chicken stock

1. In a large pot of boiling salted water, cook the noodles until al dente. Drain and rinse under cold water; drain again.

2. In a nonstick skillet, heat the oil. Add the onions and stir; cover and cook over moderate heat, stirring, until softened, about 10 minutes. Uncover and cook over moderately high heat, stirring frequently, until golden, about 8 minutes.

3. Add the sliced mushrooms and cook, stirring, until softened and any liquid in the skillet has evaporated, about 6 minutes. Season with salt and pepper and transfer the mushrooms to a bowl.

4. In another bowl, stir the kasha with the egg. Add this mixture to the skillet and cook over moderate heat, stirring to break up any clumps, until lightly browned, about 4 minutes. Add the stock and bring to a boil. Reduce the heat to low; simmer until the stock is absorbed and the kasha is tender, 10 minutes. Fold in the noodles and season with salt and pepper. Stir into the onion mixture and serve hot. —*Russ Pillar*

## Yellow Lentil Dal

**TOTAL: 45 MIN**

**4 SERVINGS** ● ●

More than tandoori chicken or spicy vindaloos, dal defines Indian cooking, often constituting the main daily source of protein, especially for vegetarians. A generic Hindi word for dried legumes, *dal* has come to signify a whole universe of dishes simmered with spices and served with chapati in the north and rice in the south.

- 1 cup split yellow lentils or *toor* dal (about 7 ounces)
- 4 cups chicken stock or low-sodium broth
- 2 tablespoons minced fresh ginger
- ½ teaspoon turmeric
- 1 large zucchini, cut into 1-inch pieces

Salt

- 1 tablespoon vegetable oil
- 1½ teaspoons black mustard seeds
- 1 small onion, halved and thinly sliced
- 2 garlic cloves, minced
- 2 tablespoons thinly sliced seeded serrano chile
- 2 teaspoons ground cumin
- 10 fresh curry leaves or 2 bay leaves
- 1 large tomato, seeded and coarsely chopped
- 1 tablespoon fresh lemon juice

1. In a large saucepan, combine the lentils with 3 cups of the stock, the ginger and the turmeric and bring to a boil. Cover partially and cook over moderate heat, stirring occasionally, until the lentils are just tender, about 20 minutes.

2. Transfer 1 cup of the lentils to a food processor or blender and puree until smooth. Return the puree to the saucepan, add the remaining 1 cup of stock and the zucchini and bring to a simmer. Season with salt, cover and cook over moderately low heat, stirring, until the zucchini is tender, about 15 minutes.

3. Meanwhile, in a medium skillet, heat the oil until shimmering. Add the mustard seeds and cook over moderate heat, shaking the pan, until they begin to pop, about 30 seconds. Add the onion and cook, stirring occasionally, until softened, about 7 minutes. Add the garlic and serrano chile and cook for 1 minute. Add the cumin and curry leaves and cook until fragrant, about 1 minute. Add the tomato and cook, stirring, until softened, 7 minutes. Stir the tomato mixture into the dal and simmer for 5 minutes. Stir in the lemon juice and season with salt. —*Anya von Bremzen*

**MAKE AHEAD** The dal can be refrigerated overnight. Reheat before serving, stirring in a little water.

**SERVE WITH** Fragrant Basmati Rice (recipe follows).

## equipment

# potatoes, grains + more

## Fragrant Basmati Rice

**ACTIVE: 5 MIN; TOTAL: 40 MIN**
4 SERVINGS ●
- 1 cup basmati rice (7 ounces)
- 2 teaspoons vegetable oil
- 4 cardamom pods, lightly smashed
- 1 small cinnamon stick
- 2 bay leaves
- 1½ cups water
- Salt

1. In a sieve, rinse the basmati rice under cold running water until the water runs clear, about 2 minutes. Drain the rice until dry, shaking the sieve occasionally, about 5 minutes.

2. Heat the oil in a medium saucepan. Add the cardamom, cinnamon stick and bay leaves and cook until fragrant, about 30 seconds. Add the rice and cook, stirring, until opaque, about 2 minutes. Add the water and a generous pinch of salt and bring to a boil. Cover and cook over low heat until the water is absorbed and the rice is tender, about 18 minutes. Remove the rice from the heat and let stand, covered, for 10 minutes. Fluff with a fork, discard the spices and serve.
—*Anya von Bremzen*

## Summer Vegetable Rice

**TOTAL: 20 MIN**
6 SERVINGS ● ●
- 1½ cups long-grain white rice (10 ounces)
- 3 tablespoons extra-virgin olive oil
- 1 medium yellow squash or zucchini, cut into half-moons
- 1 cup yellow cherry tomatoes, halved
- 2 large scallions, thinly sliced
- Salt and freshly ground pepper
- 2 tablespoons chopped flat-leaf parsley

1. In a saucepan of salted water, boil the rice until tender, 15 minutes. Drain well.
2. Meanwhile, in a skillet, heat the oil. Add the squash, tomatoes and scallions, season with salt and pepper and sauté over moderately high heat, tossing, until lightly cooked, about 2 minutes. Add the parsley and rice and toss. Season with salt and pepper. —*Dolores Cakebread*

## Caribbean Rice and Beans

**ACTIVE: 10 MIN; TOTAL: 35 MIN**
4 TO 6 SERVINGS
- 1 tablespoon vegetable oil
- 1 medium onion, coarsely chopped
- 1 large jalapeño, seeded and minced
- 1½ cups long-grain white rice (10 ounces)
- One 14-ounce can unsweetened coconut milk, stirred
- ⅔ cup water
- 1½ teaspoons kosher salt
- One 15-ounce can kidney beans, drained and rinsed
- Hot sauce, for serving

1. In a large saucepan, heat the oil until shimmering. Add the onion and jalapeño and cook over moderate heat until they are barely softened, about 5 minutes. Stir in the rice. Add the coconut milk, water and salt and bring to a boil. Stir in the beans, cover and simmer over low heat until the liquid is absorbed and the rice is tender, about 20 minutes.

2. Remove the saucepan from the heat and fluff the rice with a fork. Cover the saucepan with a kitchen towel and the lid and let stand for 5 minutes. Serve with hot sauce. —*Grace Parisi*

## Rice with Fresh Herbs

**ACTIVE: 20 MIN; TOTAL: 45 MIN**
8 SERVINGS ●
- 3 cups basmati rice (21 ounces), rinsed
- 3 cups chopped mixed herbs, such as flat-leaf parsley, cilantro, chives, dill and tarragon
- 9 medium scallions, finely chopped
- 1 stick (4 ounces) unsalted butter, cut into small pieces
- Salt

1. Bring a large saucepan of salted water to a boil. Add the rice and boil, stirring occasionally, until slightly undercooked, about 10 minutes. Stir in the herbs and scallions and drain in a strainer; the herbs will cling to the rice.

2. Return the saucepan to the burner. Add half of the butter; melt over moderately low heat. Add the rice and the remaining 4 tablespoons of butter, stir and season with salt. Cover and cook for 15 minutes, fluff and serve. —*Nadia Roden*

**MAKE AHEAD** The finished rice can stand, covered, for 30 minutes; fluff, then serve.

## Wild Rice with Chestnuts and Dried Cranberries

**ACTIVE: 20 MIN; TOTAL: 2 HR**
8 SERVINGS
- 2 cups wild rice (14 ounces), rinsed
- 4 tablespoons unsalted butter
- 1½ cups vacuum-packed chestnuts (9 ounces), coarsely chopped
- 3 large scallions, thinly sliced
- 1½ cups low-sodium chicken broth
- ¾ cup dried cranberries
- 2 tablespoons chopped flat-leaf parsley
- Salt and freshly ground pepper

1. In a large saucepan, cover the rice with 2 inches of water and bring to a boil. Boil for 5 minutes, then remove from the heat and let stand for 1 hour. Drain and rinse.
2. In a saucepan of boiling salted water, cook the rice until the grains are tender and many have split, about 30 minutes. Drain well. Wipe out the saucepan.
3. Melt the butter in the saucepan. Add the rice, chestnuts and all but 2 tablespoons of the scallions and cook over moderate heat for 2 minutes. Add the broth and cranberries and cook, stirring occasionally, until the liquid is absorbed, about 15 minutes. Stir in the parsley and reserved scallions and season with salt and pepper. Transfer to a bowl and serve.
—*Grace Parisi*

# potatoes, grains + more

## Creamy Polenta with Wild Mushroom Ragout

**TOTAL: 40 MIN**

6 SERVINGS

If you don't want to buy four different herbs for the polenta, use just one or two, keeping the overall amount the same.

RAGOUT

- 2 tablespoons unsalted butter
- 2 tablespoons extra-virgin olive oil
- 4 shallots, finely chopped
- 2 garlic cloves, minced
- ¼ pound chanterelle mushrooms, cleaned and halved
- ½ pound oyster mushrooms, trimmed and halved
- ¼ pound shiitake mushrooms, stems discarded, caps thickly sliced

Salt and freshly ground pepper

- 1 cup rich chicken stock (see Note)
- 2 large thyme sprigs

POLENTA

- 2 cups whole milk
- 2 cups chicken stock or low-sodium broth
- 2 tablespoons unsalted butter
- 1 cup instant polenta
- ½ cup heavy cream
- 1 tablespoon mascarpone cheese
- ½ teaspoon chopped rosemary
- ½ teaspoon chopped thyme
- ½ teaspoon chopped flat-leaf parsley
- ½ teaspoon chopped marjoram
- 1 tablespoon freshly grated Parmesan cheese, plus more for serving

Salt and freshly ground pepper

**1. MAKE THE RAGOUT:** In a large, deep skillet, melt 1 tablespoon of the butter in 1 tablespoon of the olive oil. Add half of the shallots and garlic and all of the chanterelles and oyster mushrooms and cook over moderately high heat, stirring occasionally, until softened and golden, about 6 minutes. Scrape the mushrooms onto a plate.

**2.** In the same skillet, melt the remaining 1 tablespoon of butter in the remaining 1 tablespoon of olive oil. Add the remaining shallots and garlic along with the shiitake mushrooms; cook over moderately high heat, stirring occasionally, until softened and golden, about 6 minutes. Return all of the mushrooms to the skillet, season with salt and pepper and cook for 1 minute, stirring. Add the rich chicken stock and thyme sprigs to the skillet and simmer for 5 minutes. Discard the thyme sprigs.

**3. MAKE THE POLENTA:** In a large saucepan, combine the milk, chicken stock and butter and bring to a boil. Whisk in the polenta and cook over moderate heat, stirring constantly with a wooden spoon, until thick, about 8 minutes. Remove from the heat and stir in the heavy cream, mascarpone, chopped herbs and Parmesan cheese. Season with salt and pepper.

**4.** Spoon the polenta onto plates or into shallow bowls, top with the mushroom ragout and serve right away, passing more grated Parmesan at the table.
—*Geoffrey Zakarian*

**NOTE** Rich chicken stock is sold in the freezer section of many supermarkets.

## Caramelized Onion and Polenta Tart

**TOTAL: 30 MIN**

4 SERVINGS ●

- ½ pound thawed puff pastry

All-purpose flour, for dusting

- 1 large egg, lightly beaten
- 2 tablespoons unsalted butter
- 2 medium onions, thinly sliced
- 2 cups milk
- ⅓ cup instant polenta

Salt and freshly ground pepper

- 2 ounces Fontina cheese, coarsely shredded (½ cup)
- 1 teaspoon finely chopped thyme, plus more for garnish

**1.** Preheat the oven to 475° and line a baking sheet with parchment paper. On a lightly floured surface, roll out the puff pastry to a 12-inch square about ⅛ inch thick. Trim the edges to form a neat square. Cut a ½-inch-wide strip from each of the four sides of the pastry. Brush the pastry square lightly with the beaten egg, then arrange the strips along the edges to form a raised rim. Using a fork, prick the bottom of the crust all over. Bake the tart shell for 15 minutes, or until it is golden and the rim has risen; use a fork to flatten any bubbles.

**2.** Meanwhile, melt the butter in a large, deep skillet. Add the onions, cover and cook over high heat, stirring frequently, until softened and browned, 10 minutes; add a few tablespoons of water if necessary. Remove the onions from the heat.

**3.** In a medium saucepan, bring the milk to a boil. Add the polenta and whisk until smooth. Cook over moderate heat, stirring, until thickened, about 5 minutes. Season with salt and pepper and stir in the onions, Fontina and 1 teaspoon of thyme. Spread the polenta in the crust and bake for 5 minutes, or until the top is lightly browned. Sprinkle with thyme and serve. —*Bill Telepan*

**SERVE WITH** A crisp green salad.

## Indian Rice and Lentils with Raita

**TOTAL: 30 MIN**

4 SERVINGS ● ●

- 3 tablespoons vegetable oil
- 2 medium onions, thinly sliced
- 5 whole black peppercorns
- 5 cardamom pods
- 5 whole cloves
- 2 dried red chiles
- 1 cinnamon stick
- 1 cup jasmine rice or other long-grain rice (7 ounces), rinsed
- 1 cup red lentils, rinsed
- 3½ cups hot water

Kosher salt

CREAMY POLENTA WITH WILD MUSHROOM RAGOUT

EGGPLANT AND LENTIL STEW WITH POMEGRANATE MOLASSES

1 medium cucumber—peeled, seeded and thinly sliced

1 cup plain, nonfat Greek yogurt

2 jalapeños, seeded and very finely chopped

1 small garlic clove, very finely chopped

Freshly ground pepper

**1.** In a medium saucepan, heat the vegetable oil. Add the onions and cook over high heat, stirring occasionally, until they are golden brown, about 10 minutes. Transfer half of the onions to a plate.

**2.** Add the black peppercorns, cardamom pods, cloves, chiles and cinnamon stick to the onions in the saucepan and cook over moderately high heat for 1 minute, stirring. Stir in the rice, red lentils, water and 2 teaspoons of salt and bring to a boil. Reduce the heat to moderately low, cover and simmer for 15 minutes, until the water is absorbed and the rice and lentils are tender.

**3.** Meanwhile, in a medium bowl, toss the cucumber with the yogurt, jalapeños and garlic and season the raita with salt and pepper.

**4.** Gently fluff the rice and lentils with a fork and discard the whole spices. Transfer the rice to a platter, garnish with the reserved onions and serve with the cucumber raita. —*Charmaine Solomon*

## Warm Lentils with Radishes

**TOTAL: 30 MIN**

4 SERVINGS ● ●

1 cup French green lentils (7 ounces)

Salt

2 tablespoons extra-virgin olive oil

1 small shallot, thinly sliced

1 tablespoon sherry vinegar

Freshly ground pepper

½ cup thinly sliced radishes

2 tablespoons chopped flat-leaf parsley

**1.** In a medium saucepan, cover the lentils with 2 inches of water and bring to a boil. Add ½ teaspoon of salt. Simmer the lentils over low heat, stirring occasionally, until tender, about 25 minutes. Drain and transfer to a bowl.

**2.** Heat the olive oil in the saucepan. Add the shallot and cook over moderate heat until softened, about 3 minutes. Stir in the lentils and remove from the heat. Add the vinegar and season with salt and pepper. Stir in the radishes and parsley, transfer to bowls and serve.
—*Jamie Samford*

## Eggplant and Lentil Stew with Pomegranate Molasses

**ACTIVE: 30 MIN; TOTAL: 3 HR**

6 SERVINGS ● ● ●

This stew is best when made ahead and allowed to mellow for at least a few hours, or, even better, overnight.

One 1½-pound long, narrow Asian or Japanese eggplant

Salt

½ cup lentils

⅔ cup extra-virgin olive oil

1 medium onion, finely chopped

4 medium garlic cloves, very finely chopped

2 medium tomatoes, chopped

2 long green chiles, such as Anaheims—stemmed, seeded and coarsely chopped

2 tablespoons coarsely chopped mint leaves

1 tablespoon tomato paste

¼ teaspoon crushed red pepper

¼ cup pomegranate molasses (see Note)

**1.** Partially peel the eggplant so it has lengthwise stripes, then cut it lengthwise into 4 slices. Score each slice on one side in a crosshatch pattern. Cut each slice crosswise into 3 pieces and set on a rimmed baking sheet. Sprinkle with salt. Let stand for 1 hour.

**2.** Meanwhile, in a small saucepan, cover the lentils with 2 inches of water and bring to a boil. Reduce the heat and simmer until tender, about 15 minutes; drain.

**3.** Coat an enameled cast-iron casserole with 1 tablespoon of the oil. In a bowl, toss the onion with the garlic, tomatoes, green chiles, mint, tomato paste, crushed red pepper and 2 teaspoons of salt.

**4.** Rinse the eggplant and pat the slices dry. Spread ½ cup of the vegetable mixture in the casserole and top with half of the eggplant. Cover with half of the lentils and half of the remaining vegetable mixture. Top with the remaining eggplant, lentils and vegetables. Pour the remaining olive oil around the side and over the vegetables, then drizzle with the pomegranate molasses.

**5.** Bring the stew to a boil. Cover and cook over low heat until the eggplant is very tender, about 1½ hours. Serve hot, warm or at room temperature.
—*Musa Dagdeviren*

**NOTE** Pomegranate molasses is available at specialty food stores and Middle Eastern markets.

**MAKE AHEAD** The eggplant and lentil stew can be refrigerated for up to 2 days.

# health

**MIDDLE EASTERN FLAVORS** **TIP**

The flavorful spices used in Middle Eastern cooking come with health benefits too. In traditional holistic medicine, cumin is valued for its ability to aid digestion, turmeric is prized for its anti-inflammatory and blood-purifying properties and mustard seeds are believed to heal the bronchial system. Lentils contain protein and soluble fiber, which is good for the heart.

● FAST   ● HEALTHY   ● MAKE AHEAD   ● STAFF FAVORITE

# potatoes, grains + more

## Tangy Mung Bean Salad

**ACTIVE: 25 MIN; TOTAL: 1 HR**

6 SERVINGS ● ● ●

- ½ pound dried mung beans (see Note)
- ¼ cup plus 2 tablespoons extra-virgin olive oil
- ¼ cup fresh lemon juice
- 2 medium garlic cloves, minced
- 1 tablespoon plus ½ teaspoon pomegranate molasses (see Note)
- ½ teaspoon crushed red pepper

# health

## EAT BEANS, LIVE LONGER

Dried beans aren't just hearty—they're also good for your heart. According to a 2002 report by James Anderson and Amy Major of the Metabolic Research Group at the University of Kentucky, dried beans—such as mung beans, cannellini beans and chickpeas—can reduce cholesterol levels and prevent heart disease because of their high levels of soluble fiber. Their high-fiber content can also help lower blood pressure and reduce the risk of hypertension, and their low glycemic index (a ranking of carbohydrates and their effect on blood sugar levels) has been shown to reduce the risk of diabetes. Eating dried beans can also help you lose weight, because they stimulate hormones that decrease hunger. A recent Australian study even found a positive correlation between eating dried beans and longevity.

- Salt
- 8 scallions, thinly sliced
- 2 red bell peppers, cut into ¼-inch dice
- 1 cup finely chopped flat-leaf parsley
- ½ cup finely chopped mint leaves
- 2 tablespoons chopped dill

**1.** In a saucepan of boiling water, add the mung beans and bring back to a boil. Simmer over moderate heat, stirring occasionally, until the beans are tender, about 30 minutes. Drain the mung beans and let cool.

**2.** In a large bowl, mix the olive oil with the lemon juice, minced garlic, pomegranate molasses and crushed red pepper; season with salt. Add the drained mung beans, sliced scallions, red bell peppers, parsley, mint and dill and toss well. Season with salt. Serve the salad at room temperature or slightly chilled.

*—Musa Dagdeviren*

**NOTE** Mung beans are available at Middle Eastern and Asian markets. Pomegranate molasses is available at specialty food stores and Middle Eastern markets.

## Smoky Black-Eyed Peas

**ACTIVE: 1 HR; TOTAL: 3 HR**

8 SERVINGS ● ●

Although black-eyed peas are the quintessential Southern bean, any fresh shell bean, such as limas, purple hull peas or pigeon peas, can be substituted here.

- 1 meaty smoked ham hock
- 1 medium onion, coarsely chopped
- 1 jalapeño, seeded and finely chopped
- 3 quarts water
- 3 pounds fresh black-eyed peas, shelled (about 6 cups), or three 10-ounce packages frozen shelled black-eyed peas
- Salt and freshly ground pepper

**1.** Cut some of the meat from the ham hock into large chunks. In a large saucepan, combine the ham hock and meat with the onion, jalapeño and water and bring to a boil. Reduce the heat to moderately low and simmer until the meat is tender, about 2 hours.

**2.** Add the black-eyed peas to the ham broth and cook over moderate heat, stirring occasionally, until the black-eyed peas are tender, about 45 minutes. Drain the black-eyed peas in a colander. Cut the meat into ½-inch pieces; discard the bone. Transfer the meat and black-eyed peas to a serving bowl, season with salt and pepper and serve.

*—Mary Lynn Van Wyck*

**MAKE AHEAD** The black-eyed peas can be refrigerated for up to 2 days. Let them return to room temperature and reheat gently before serving.

**SERVE WITH** Green-Tomato Pickle (p. 227) or any pickled relish.

## Seven-Vegetable Couscous

**ACTIVE: 1 HR 30 MIN;**

**TOTAL: 3 HR 30 MIN**

8 SERVINGS ● ●

In Morocco, couscous is the traditional ending of a meal, served to ensure that no one leaves the table hungry. There are dozens of variations; this classic preparation calls for carrots, chickpeas, zucchini, turnips and butternut squash, all great sources of vitamins, minerals, fiber and phytochemicals. Together with the semolina couscous (a low-fat complex carbohydrate) and lean chicken, these ingredients combine to create a completely nutritionally balanced meal.

- 3 tablespoons unsalted butter
- 1 tablespoon extra-virgin olive oil
- 1 large onion, thinly sliced
- 2 pounds skinless chicken thighs
- 2 pounds veal shanks, cut 1½ inches thick
- 3 quarts plus 3½ cups water

2 large tomatoes—peeled, seeded and quartered

1½ teaspoons ground ginger

2 small cinnamon sticks

1 teaspoon sweet paprika

Large pinch of cayenne pepper

Large pinch of saffron threads, crumbled

10 cilantro sprigs and 10 flat-leaf parsley sprigs, tied in cheesecloth

Salt and freshly ground black pepper

3 medium carrots, cut into 2-inch pieces

3 medium turnips, peeled and quartered

1 fennel bulb, cored and cut lengthwise into thick wedges

1 pound peeled butternut squash, cut into 3-inch chunks

2 large zucchini, halved lengthwise and cut into 2-inch pieces

Two 15-ounce cans chickpeas, drained and rinsed

2 cups instant couscous (14 ounces)

*Harissa* or other hot sauce, for serving

**1.** In a large soup pot, melt 2 tablespoons of the butter in the olive oil. Add the onion and cook over moderately high heat, stirring, until the onions are softened, about 7 minutes. Using a slotted spoon, transfer the onion to a bowl, add the chicken and veal to the pot in a single layer and cook until the meat is browned on the bottom, about 5 minutes. Turn the meat and cook, stirring occasionally, until browned, about 5 minutes longer.

**2.** Add 2½ quarts of water, the cooked onion, the tomatoes, ginger, cinnamon sticks, paprika, cayenne, saffron and herb bundle to the pot and bring to a boil, skimming. Season generously with salt and black pepper. Cover partially and simmer over moderately low heat until the chicken is just cooked through, about 35 minutes; transfer the chicken to a plate. Continue cooking the veal, partially covered, until tender, about 1¼ hours longer. Add the veal to the chicken. Discard the herb bundle and cinnamon sticks and refrigerate the broth until chilled; skim off any fat from the surface.

**3.** Return the broth to a simmer. Add the carrots, turnips, fennel and squash, cover partially and cook over moderate heat for 15 minutes. Add the zucchini and cook, partially covered, until all the vegetables are tender, about 15 minutes longer; remove the vegetables with a slotted spoon as they're ready. Return the chicken and veal to the pot along with the vegetables. Add the chickpeas, season with salt and black pepper and cook until heated through.

**4.** Meanwhile, melt the remaining 1 tablespoon of butter in a large saucepan. Add the couscous and cook over moderately high heat, stirring constantly, until nutty and lightly toasted, about 5 minutes. Add 5½ cups of water and a generous pinch of salt and bring to a boil. Cover the saucepan, remove from the heat and let the couscous stand for 5 minutes. Using 2 forks, fluff the couscous and mound it in 8 large bowls. Spoon the meat, vegetables and broth over the couscous and serve, passing the *harissa* on the side. *—Anya von Bremzen*

**MAKE AHEAD** The recipe can be prepared through Step 3 and refrigerated for up to 2 days. Rewarm before serving.

## Couscous with Red Lentils and Easy Preserved Lemons

**TOTAL: 30 MIN**

4 SERVINGS ● ●

2¾ cups water, plus more for boiling the lentils

⅓ cup sugar

Salt and freshly ground pepper

1 large lemon, very thinly sliced

¼ cup plus 2 tablespoons extra-virgin olive oil

½ cup couscous

1 cup red lentils

5 ounces arugula, leaves torn

1 tablespoon fresh lemon juice

½ cup toasted shelled unsalted pistachios, coarsely chopped

**1.** In a small saucepan, boil 2 cups of water. Add the sugar, 1½ teaspoons of salt and ½ teaspoon of pepper; stir until the salt dissolves. Add the lemon slices and cook over moderately high heat until softened, 15 minutes. Transfer the lemon slices to a plate. Boil the liquid until reduced to ⅓ cup, 3 minutes; let cool. Whisk in ¼ cup of the olive oil.

**2.** Meanwhile, in another small saucepan, bring ¾ cup of water to a boil. Add ½ teaspoon of salt and the couscous; stir to combine. Remove the pan from the heat, cover and let stand for 5 minutes. Fluff the couscous with a fork.

**3.** Bring a medium saucepan of water to a boil; add the lentils and cook over moderately high heat until tender but not mushy, 6 minutes. Drain, transfer to a bowl and add the couscous.

**4.** Stir all but 1 tablespoon of the lemon oil into the couscous and season with salt and pepper. In a large bowl, toss the arugula with the lemon juice and the remaining 2 tablespoons of olive oil; season with salt and pepper. Transfer the arugula to plates, mound the couscous on top and drizzle with the remaining lemon oil. Top with the lemon slices and pistachios and serve. *—Ilene Rosen*

## Israeli Couscous with Peas and Mint

**TOTAL: 20 MIN**

4 SERVINGS ●

Like North African couscous, Israeli couscous is made from semolina wheat. But that's where the similarity ends. Israeli couscous tastes like pasta—in the shape of toasty, buttery, deliciously chewy tapioca-size pearls.

# potatoes, grains + more

1½ cups Israeli couscous
(8 ounces)
4 tablespoons unsalted butter
1 tablespoon very finely
chopped garlic
¾ cup frozen baby peas, thawed
Salt and freshly ground pepper
2 tablespoons finely chopped
mint leaves

1. Bring a medium saucepan of salted water to a boil. Add the couscous and cook until al dente, about 4 minutes. Drain the couscous, reserving 1½ cups of the couscous cooking liquid; wipe out the saucepan.
2. Melt 2 tablespoons of the butter in the saucepan. Add the garlic and cook over moderate heat until softened, 1 minute. Add the peas and toss to coat. Add the couscous, the remaining 2 tablespoons of butter and 1 cup of the couscous cooking liquid and simmer, stirring occasionally, until the couscous and the peas are tender and coated in a creamy sauce, 3 to 4 minutes. Season the couscous and peas with salt and pepper and stir in the mint. Stir in some of the remaining cooking liquid if the couscous seems dry. Transfer to a bowl and serve.
—*Jamie Samford*

## Porcini Risotto with Serrano Ham
**TOTAL: 45 MIN**
4 SERVINGS
1 cup dried porcini mushrooms
1½ cups boiling water
½ cup mascarpone cheese
½ cup freshly grated
Parmesan cheese
1 garlic clove, minced
7 cups chicken stock
2 tablespoons extra-virgin
olive oil
4 large scallions, white and
tender green parts only,
very finely chopped
3 slices of lean bacon, finely diced

½ teaspoon finely chopped fresh
rosemary
2 cups arborio rice
(14 ounces)
½ cup dry white wine
Salt and freshly ground pepper
1 tablespoon unsalted butter
½ pound thinly sliced Serrano
ham, cut into strips
2 tablespoons chopped
flat-leaf parsley

1. In a large heatproof measuring cup, soak the porcini mushrooms in the boiling water until softened, about 15 minutes. Reserve the mushrooms and their soaking liquid separately. In a small bowl, combine the mascarpone cheese with ¼ cup of the Parmesan and the minced clove of garlic.
2. Meanwhile, in a medium saucepan, bring the chicken stock to a boil. Cover the stock and keep at a gentle simmer over low heat.
3. Heat the olive oil in a large saucepan. Add the scallions, bacon and rosemary and cook over moderate heat, stirring, for 5 minutes. Stir in the arborio rice until coated with the oil. Add the wine and boil until almost evaporated, about 2 minutes. Pour in the mushroom soaking liquid, stopping when you reach the grit at the bottom of the measuring cup. Add 1 cup of the stock and cook over moderate heat, stirring constantly, until absorbed. Continue adding stock, 1 cup at a time, stirring until absorbed. The risotto is done when it is creamy and the rice is al dente, about 25 minutes total cooking time. Stir in the mascarpone mixture and the porcini. Season the risotto with salt and pepper.
4. Melt the butter in a medium skillet. Add the ham; toss over moderate heat until warm. Spoon the risotto into shallow bowls, top with the ham, sprinkle with the parsley and serve with the remaining ¼ cup of Parmesan. —*Iñigo Pérez*

## Tomato and Mint Pesto Risotto
**TOTAL: 40 MIN**
6 TO 8 SERVINGS ●
PESTO
3 garlic cloves, quartered
2 cups mint leaves
½ cup flat-leaf parsley leaves
½ cup extra-virgin olive oil
1 tablespoon fresh lemon juice
Salt and freshly ground pepper
RISOTTO
7 cups light chicken stock or
low-sodium broth
3 tablespoons extra-virgin
olive oil
½ small onion, finely chopped
1 garlic clove, thinly sliced
2 cups arborio or vialone nano
rice (14 ounces)
1 cup dry white wine
1¼ pounds tomatoes, cut into
½-inch dice
¼ cup freshly grated
Parmesan cheese
Salt and freshly ground pepper

1. MAKE THE PESTO: In a blender, combine the garlic, mint, parsley, olive oil and lemon juice and puree until smooth. Scrape into a bowl and season with salt and pepper.
2. MAKE THE RISOTTO: In a medium saucepan, bring the chicken stock to a boil. Cover and keep hot over low heat. In a large saucepan, heat the olive oil. Add the onion and garlic and cook over moderate heat until softened, 3 minutes. Add the rice and cook over moderately high heat, stirring, for 2 minutes. Add the white wine and boil, stirring, until almost evaporated. Add enough hot stock to just cover the rice and cook over moderate heat, stirring constantly, until it has been absorbed. Continue adding stock, 1 cup at a time, stirring the rice constantly until all of the stock is absorbed and the rice is just tender and very creamy, about 20 minutes.

**3.** Stir the tomatoes into the risotto and cook until heated through. Remove from the heat and stir in the mint pesto and the Parmesan. Season with salt and pepper, spoon into bowls and serve right away. —*Tom Fundaro*

**MAKE AHEAD** The pesto can be refrigerated for up to 2 days.

### Corn and Pea Risotto
**TOTAL: 40 MIN, PLUS 40 MIN**
**IF MAKING CORN BROTH**
**4 SERVINGS** ●

3½ cups Corn Broth (see below)
   or chicken broth
  2 tablespoons extra-virgin olive oil
  1 small onion, finely chopped
  1 cup arborio rice (7 ounces)
½ cup dry white wine
  1 cup fresh corn kernels
    (from 2 ears)
  1 cup shelled peas
¼ cup freshly grated Parmesan
Salt and freshly ground pepper
  2 tablespoons shredded basil

In a saucepan, bring the Corn Broth to a simmer and keep hot. Heat the olive oil in another saucepan. Add the onion and cook over moderate heat, stirring occasionally, until softened, about 5 minutes. Add the rice and cook, stirring, for 2 minutes. Add the wine and cook, stirring constantly, until absorbed, about 5 minutes. Add ½ cup of the hot broth and cook, stirring, until absorbed. Continue adding the remaining broth, ½ cup at a time, and cook the rice, stirring constantly, until al dente, about 20 minutes. Add the corn and peas and cook until tender, about 2 minutes. Stir in the Parmesan and season with salt and pepper. Spoon the risotto into bowls, garnish with the basil and serve. —*Lucia Watson*

**CORN BROTH** To make 1 quart of broth, simmer 6 cobs with 1 small chopped onion, herb sprigs and 2 quarts of cold water for 40 minutes, then strain.

**COUSCOUS WITH LENTILS AND PRESERVED LEMONS, P. 243**

**CORN AND PEA RISOTTO**

GRILLED CHEESE AND CHORIZO SANDWICHES, P. 259

# breads, pizzas + sandwiches

## 12

**ROBIN'S WHOLE WHEAT BREAD**　　　　　　　**CLINTON STREET BISCUITS**

### Robin's Whole Wheat Bread

**ACTIVE: 25 MIN; TOTAL: 2 HR 20 MIN,
PLUS OVERNIGHT RISING**

MAKES THREE 9-BY-5-INCH
LOAVES ●

Cookbook author Naomi Duguid named
these moist, tender loaves for her mother,
Robin, whose baking during Duguid's
childhood inspired the recipe.

　1　quart warm water
　2　cups milk, warmed
　2　tablespoons honey
　1　teaspoon active dry yeast
　3　cups whole wheat flour
　10　cups all-purpose flour
　2　tablespoons plus 1 teaspoon
　　　table salt
　2　tablespoons extra-virgin
　　　olive oil
　1　cup roasted unsalted
　　　sunflower seeds

**1.** In a large bowl, combine the warm
water and milk. Stir in the honey until
dissolved. Sprinkle the yeast on top and
let stand until foamy, about 5 minutes.
Using a wooden spoon, stir in the whole
wheat flour and 3 cups of the all-purpose
flour. Stir in the salt and olive oil, then
5 cups more of the all-purpose flour.

**2.** Using a dough scraper, scrape the
dough out onto a generously floured
work surface. Using the scraper, lift and
fold the wet dough while incorporating
the remaining 2 cups of all-purpose flour.
Knead lightly for a few minutes until a
smooth, slightly sticky dough forms.
Transfer the dough to a very large oiled
bowl. Cover with plastic wrap and let rise
overnight at room temperature.

**3.** Butter three 9-by-5-inch metal loaf
pans. Punch down the dough and sprinkle it all over with the sunflower seeds.

Scrape the dough out onto a generously
floured work surface and knead it lightly,
working in the seeds. Cut the dough into
3 equal pieces. Press each piece into a
rectangle about 8 by 10 inches. Starting
at a long end, roll up the dough, tucking
in the sides neatly. Transfer the dough to
one of the prepared loaf pans, seams
down. Repeat with the remaining dough.
Cover loosely with plastic wrap and let
rise in a warm, draft-free spot until the
top of the dough is just below the rim of
the pans, about 1 hour.

**4.** Preheat the oven to 400°. Position a
rack in the lower third of the oven.
Lightly sprinkle the tops of the loaves
with water and bake for 10 minutes. Turn
the heat down to 375° and bake the
loaves for 20 minutes. Rotate the pans
and bake for 25 minutes longer, or until
the loaves sound hollow when turned out

of the pans and tapped on the bottoms. (If necessary, bake the loaves for another 10 minutes.) Turn the loaves out of the pans and let them cool on a wire rack. Serve the bread warm or at room temperature. —*Naomi Duguid and Jeffrey Alford*
**MAKE AHEAD** The loaves can be frozen for up to 1 month. Let cool completely before freezing.

## Auntie Buck's Light and Buttery Dinner Rolls
**ACTIVE: 30 MIN; TOTAL: 3 HR 20 MIN, PLUS OVERNIGHT RISING**
**MAKES 16 ROLLS** ●

- 1 stick (4 ounces) unsalted butter, softened, plus 2 tablespoons melted
- ⅓ cup plus a pinch of sugar
- ½ cup boiling water
- 1 teaspoon salt
- 4 teaspoons active dry yeast (about 1½ envelopes)
- ½ cup warm water
- 1 large egg, lightly beaten
- 3 cups all-purpose flour
- 1½ teaspoons sesame seeds

1. In a large bowl, combine the softened butter with the ⅓ cup of sugar, the boiling water and the salt. Stir until the butter is melted. In a small bowl, combine the yeast with the warm water and the pinch of sugar. Let stand until foamy, about 5 minutes.
2. Add the yeast to the butter-sugar mixture. Beat in the egg until smooth. Stir in the flour with a wooden spoon until a dough forms. Gather the dough into a ball in the center of the bowl, cover with plastic wrap and refrigerate overnight.
3. Let the dough stand at room temperature for 2 hours. On a well-floured surface, roll out or pat the dough about ½ inch thick. Using a 2¾-inch round biscuit cutter, stamp out about 14 rounds as close together as possible. Gather and re-roll the scraps to cut out 2 more rounds.

4. Lightly butter an 8-by-11-inch glass baking dish. Fold the dough rounds in half and arrange the rolls in the prepared baking dish in 2 rows of 8. Brush the rolls with the melted butter and sprinkle with the sesame seeds. Let stand until slightly risen, about 30 minutes.
5. Preheat the oven to 425°. Bake the rolls in the center of the oven for 20 minutes, or until they are risen and the tops and bottoms are golden. Turn the rolls out into a basket and serve piping hot. —*Mary Lynn Van Wyck*
**MAKE AHEAD** The baked rolls can be kept at room temperature for 1 day or frozen for up to 1 month. Reheat in a 325° oven before serving.

## Clinton Street Biscuits
**TOTAL: 25 MIN**
**MAKES 12 BISCUITS** ● ●

- 1 cup all-purpose flour, plus more for dusting
- 1 cup cake or pastry flour
- 2 teaspoons baking powder
- ½ teaspoon baking soda
- 1 teaspoon sugar
- 1 teaspoon salt
- 3 tablespoons cold unsalted butter, cut into small cubes
- 3 tablespoons cold shortening
- ¾ cup plus 2 tablespoons buttermilk

1. Preheat the oven to 425°. Into a medium bowl, sift the flours with the baking powder, baking soda, sugar and salt. Using a pastry blender or 2 knives, cut in the butter and shortening until the mixture resembles coarse meal. Make a well in the center and add the buttermilk. Stir just until a dough forms. Turn the dough out onto a lightly floured surface and knead 2 or 3 times.
2. Pat or roll out the dough ¾ inch thick. Using a lightly floured 2½-inch round biscuit cutter, stamp out 12 biscuits. Dust the top of each biscuit with flour.

3. Transfer the biscuits to a greased baking sheet. Bake for 15 minutes, or until the tops are lightly browned; serve. —*Neil Kleinberg*

## Buttermilk Corn Bread
**TOTAL: 30 MIN**
**MAKES ONE 8-INCH SQUARE** ● ● ●

- 2½ tablespoons vegetable oil
- 2½ cups fine stone-ground cornmeal
- 1 teaspoon salt
- 1 teaspoon baking powder
- ½ teaspoon baking soda
- 2 cups buttermilk
- 2 large eggs, lightly beaten
- 2 tablespoons honey

1. Preheat the oven to 400°. Grease an 8-inch-square baking pan with ½ tablespoon of the oil. In a bowl, whisk the cornmeal, salt, baking powder and baking soda. In another bowl, whisk the buttermilk with the eggs, honey and the remaining 2 tablespoons of oil. Stir the buttermilk mixture into the dry ingredients just until blended.
2. Scrape the batter into the prepared pan and bake until the corn bread is golden brown and springy to the touch, about 20 minutes. Turn out onto a rack to cool completely. —*Bob Isaacson*
**MAKE AHEAD** The corn bread can be wrapped in plastic and refrigerated for up to 3 days or frozen for up to 2 weeks.

## Buttery Cornmeal Pastry
**ACTIVE: 10 MIN; TOTAL: 40 MIN**
**MAKES ONE 10-INCH TART SHELL** ● ●

- 1 cup all-purpose flour
- ¼ cup plus 2 tablespoons fine white cornmeal
- ½ teaspoon salt
- 1 stick (4 ounces) cold unsalted butter, cut into ½-inch cubes
- ¼ cup ice water

# breads, pizzas + sandwiches

In a food processor, pulse the flour with the cornmeal and salt. Add the butter and pulse until it is the size of small peas. Sprinkle with the ice water and pulse just until the pastry is evenly moistened. Transfer to a lightly floured board and pat into a disk. Wrap and refrigerate the pastry for 30 minutes.
—*Ashley Christensen*

**MAKE AHEAD** The pastry can be refrigerated overnight or frozen for 1 month. The recipe can easily be doubled.

### Parmesan-Prosciutto Biscotti

ACTIVE: 15 MIN; TOTAL: 1 HR 45 MIN
MAKES 16 LARGE BISCOTTI ●

- 8  tablespoons (4 ounces) unsalted butter, at room temperature
- 3  large eggs, at room temperature
- 1½ cups all-purpose flour
- 1  cup freshly grated Parmesan cheese
- 2  ounces thinly sliced prosciutto, coarsely chopped
- 2  teaspoons coarsely ground black pepper
- 1  teaspoon kosher salt

1. Preheat the oven to 350°. Line a large baking sheet with parchment paper.
2. In a large bowl, using an electric mixer, beat the butter at medium-high speed for 1 minute, or until light and fluffy. Add the eggs 1 at a time, beating thoroughly between additions. Add the flour, grated Parmesan, chopped prosciutto and the pepper and salt and beat at medium speed until the dough just comes together. Do not overmix.
3. Scrape the dough out onto the prepared baking sheet. Using moistened hands, pat it into a 12-by-2½-inch log. Bake the dough in the center of the oven for 25 minutes, or until the top is light golden. Remove from the oven, transfer to a wire rack and let cool for 10 minutes. Reduce the oven temperature to 275°.

4. Using a serrated knife, cut the log crosswise on the diagonal ½ inch thick. Arrange the biscotti on the baking sheet cut side up. Bake for 20 minutes, or until the biscotti are golden and dry to the touch. Turn the biscotti over and bake for 15 minutes longer, or until golden and cooked through. Transfer the baking sheet to a wire rack and let the biscotti cool completely.
—*Alisa Barry*

**MAKE AHEAD** The biscotti can be stored at room temperature in an airtight container for up to 1 week.

### Bread Stuffing with Apple, Raisins and Marmalade

ACTIVE: 30 MIN; TOTAL: 1 HR
10 SERVINGS
With chopped meat, raisins and walnuts, this stuffing is practically a main course.

One 1-pound baguette, crusts trimmed, bread cut into 1-inch cubes
- 4  ounces shelled walnut halves (1 cup)
- 4  tablespoons unsalted butter
- 3  celery ribs, finely chopped
- 1  medium onion, finely chopped
- 1  pound lean ground beef
- 1  tablespoon finely chopped sage
- 1  tablespoon finely chopped thyme
- ¼  cup orange marmalade
- ¼  cup golden raisins
- 1  McIntosh apple, peeled and finely diced
Salt and freshly ground pepper
- 2  large eggs, beaten
- 1  cup Rich Turkey Stock (p. 112)

1. Preheat the oven to 350°. In a food processor, pulse the bread until coarsely shredded. Spread on a large, rimmed baking sheet and toast for about 10 minutes, or until lightly browned. Meanwhile, spread the walnuts in a pie plate and toast in the oven for about 5 minutes, or until fragrant and lightly browned. Let the nuts cool, then coarsely chop them.

2. Melt the butter in a large, deep skillet. Add the celery and onion and cook over moderately high heat until softened, about 5 minutes. Add the beef and cook, breaking up the meat with a wooden spoon, until no pink remains, about 6 minutes. Add the sage and thyme.
3. Transfer the meat to a large bowl and add the marmalade, raisins, apple, and the toasted bread and walnuts. Toss well and season generously with salt and pepper. Let cool slightly, then stir in the eggs and Rich Turkey Stock.
4. Butter a 2-quart shallow baking dish and spread the stuffing in it. Bake for about 30 minutes, or until the stuffing is heated through and the top is browned and crisp. —*Lee Hefter*

**MAKE AHEAD** The stuffing can be prepared through Step 2 and refrigerated for 2 days. Return to room temperature before baking.

### Artichoke Bread Pudding

ACTIVE: 20 MIN; TOTAL: 1 HR 35 MIN
6 TO 8 SERVINGS ●

One 1-pound loaf sourdough bread, sliced ½ inch thick
- 1  large garlic clove, halved
One 1¼-pound jar marinated artichokes, drained and thinly sliced, oil reserved
Salt and freshly ground pepper
- ¾  pound Manchego cheese, rind removed, cheese thinly sliced
- 1  quart whole milk
- 6  large eggs, lightly beaten

1. Preheat the oven to 425°. Toast the bread directly on the oven racks until dry and lightly golden, about 3 minutes. Rub one side of each slice of toast with the cut sides of the garlic clove. Lower the oven temperature to 375°.
2. Brush the bottom of a 9-by-13-inch baking dish with 1 tablespoon of the reserved artichoke oil and arrange one-

third of the toast in a single layer. Top with half of the artichokes. Season lightly with salt and pepper and top with one-third of the cheese. Repeat with another layer of toast, artichokes and cheese and season with salt and pepper. Top with the remaining toast and cheese.

3. In a bowl, mix the milk with the eggs. Season with salt and pepper. Pour the custard over the bread; cover with plastic wrap. Lay a few cans on the plastic to keep the bread submerged. Let soak until most of the custard is absorbed, about 15 minutes. Remove the plastic.

4. Place a sheet of oiled parchment paper on top of the pudding and cover with foil. Bake in the center of the oven for 30 minutes. Remove the foil and parchment; bake for 15 minutes longer, or until the top is golden. Let the pudding cool for 15 minutes before cutting into squares and serving. —*Grace Parisi*

**MAKE AHEAD** The pudding can be prepared through Step 3 and refrigerated overnight. Let stand at room temperature for 30 minutes before proceeding.

### Choucroute Bread Pudding

**ACTIVE: 45 MIN; TOTAL: 2 HR**

12 SERVINGS ● ●

One 1½-pound loaf sourdough bread
    or 2 baguettes, cut into ¾-inch
    cubes (12 cups)
  1  meaty ham hock
    (about 2 pounds)
  3  thyme sprigs plus
    1 tablespoon chopped thyme
  2  garlic cloves
  1  bay leaf
  6  cups water
  ½  pound meaty slab bacon,
    cut into ½-inch dice
  ½  pound andouille sausage, halved
    lengthwise and sliced crosswise
    ½ inch thick
  1  large onion, thinly sliced
  1  cup dry white wine

1½  cups drained sauerkraut,
    squeezed dry
  ¾  teaspoon caraway seeds
  4  tablespoons unsalted butter
  3  cups Rich Turkey Stock (p. 112)
    or low-sodium chicken broth
Salt and freshly ground pepper
  4  large eggs, lightly beaten

1. Preheat the oven to 300°. Spread the bread on a large, rimmed baking sheet and bake for 10 minutes, or until slightly crisp. Let cool; transfer to a large bowl.

2. In a large saucepan, combine the ham hock, thyme sprigs, garlic, bay leaf and water and bring to a boil. Cover and simmer over moderately low heat until the hock meat is very tender, about 1¼ hours. Remove the hock from the saucepan; pull off and coarsely shred the meat and discard the fat. Strain the broth and skim off the fat. You should have about 2 cups of the ham broth.

3. Meanwhile, in a large, deep skillet, cook the bacon and andouille over moderately high heat, stirring occasionally, until browned, about 10 minutes. Transfer the meat to a plate. Pour off all but 2 tablespoons of the fat in the skillet, add the onion and chopped thyme and cook over moderate heat, stirring occasionally, until the onion is softened, about 10 minutes. Add the wine and cook until almost evaporated, about 10 minutes.

4. Preheat the oven to 350°. Return the bacon and sausage to the skillet. Add the shredded hock meat, sauerkraut and caraway seeds and cook over moderate heat for 5 minutes, stirring often. Add 1 cup of the ham broth and simmer for 5 minutes. Stir in the butter until melted. Add the mixture in the skillet to the bread cubes and toss. Add the remaining 1 cup of ham broth and the Rich Turkey Stock and toss. Season with salt and pepper and let cool, then stir in the eggs. Butter a shallow 3-quart baking dish. Spread the stuffing in the dish. Cover with buttered foil.

5. Bake the pudding for 30 minutes, then remove the foil; bake for 30 minutes longer, or until the center is cooked through and the top is brown and crisp. —*Grace Parisi*
**MAKE AHEAD** The baked bread pudding can be refrigerated for up 2 days. Bring the bread pudding to room temperature and reheat before serving.

### Roquefort Bread Puddings

**ACTIVE: 25 MIN; TOTAL: 1 HR 30 MIN**

4 SERVINGS ●

  1  tablespoon unsalted butter
  3  medium garlic cloves, mashed
    to a paste
  ¾  cup heavy cream
  4  ounces Roquefort cheese,
    crumbled (½ cup)
  2  large eggs
  ¼  cup thinly sliced scallions, plus
    more for garnish
  ½  teaspoon salt
  ¼  teaspoon freshly ground pepper
  ½  pound sourdough bread,
    crusts removed, bread cut
    into 1-inch cubes

# ingredient

**STORING EGGS**     **TIP**

The bread puddings on these pages all use eggs. Because eggs absorb aromas and lose moisture through their shells, store them in the protective, closed carton in which you buy them, never in the open-air "egg holder" in the refrigerator door. Not only is the door the warmest part of the refrigerator, it's also the most jostled. For fried and scrambled eggs, omelets and frittatas, use the freshest eggs possible. Save older ones—up to 5 weeks—for baked goods.

# breads, pizzas + sandwiches

**1.** Preheat the oven to 325°. Generously butter four 4-ounce ramekins. Set the ramekins in a small roasting pan.

**2.** Melt the butter in a small saucepan. Add the garlic paste and cook over moderate heat, stirring, until just golden. Stir in the cream and Roquefort and bring to a boil. Remove from the heat.

**3.** In a large bowl, gradually whisk the Roquefort cream into the eggs. Whisk in the ¼ cup of scallions and the salt and pepper. Stir in the bread cubes and let stand until the cream is absorbed, about 30 minutes.

**4.** Spoon the bread pudding mixture into the ramekins. Add enough water to the roasting pan to reach halfway up the sides of the ramekins and bake the bread puddings in the center of the oven for 25 minutes, or until they are set and golden. Transfer the ramekins to a wire rack and let cool slightly. Run a knife around the bread puddings, then turn them out onto plates. Garnish with the remaining scallions and serve. —*John Vlandis*

## Tomato Bread Pudding

**ACTIVE: 30 MIN; TOTAL: 2 HR**

**6 SERVINGS** ● ●

There's no custard in this bread pudding, so it's more like a hot, tangy bread salad.

- 8 large ripe tomatoes (about 3 pounds)
- 1 cup tomato juice (optional; see Note)
- 3 garlic cloves, very finely chopped

Kosher salt and freshly ground pepper

- ¼ cup plus 2 tablespoons extra-virgin olive oil

One 12-ounce baguette, sliced on the diagonal ¾ inch thick

- 5 tablespoons minced flat-leaf parsley
- 5 tablespoons finely chopped basil

**1.** Bring a large saucepan of water to a boil and fill a large bowl with ice water. Using a sharp knife, make a shallow X in the bottom of each tomato. Plunge the tomatoes into the boiling water for 10 seconds, then immediately transfer them to the ice water. Peel and core the tomatoes and halve them horizontally. Set a strainer over a medium bowl and scoop the seeds and pulp from the tomatoes into it. Press the pulp to extract as much of the juice as possible; there should be 1 cup. If not, add enough of the tomato juice to make 1 cup.

**2.** Arrange the tomatoes cut side up on a large plate, sprinkle with the garlic and season with salt and pepper. Drizzle with 2 tablespoons of the olive oil and let stand for 30 minutes. Add any juices that accumulate on the plate to the strained tomato juice.

**3.** Preheat a cast-iron grill pan or the broiler. Brush the baguette slices on both sides with the remaining ¼ cup of olive oil and grill until golden, about 1 minute per side. Transfer the toasts to a large plate. Add the tomatoes, cut side down, to the grill and cook just until lightly charred, about 1 minute. Return the tomatoes to the plate and flatten slightly with a spatula.

**4.** Preheat the oven to 350°. Lightly oil a shallow 8-by-11-inch baking dish and arrange half of the tomatoes on the bottom. Sprinkle the tomatoes with 2 tablespoons each of parsley and basil and season with salt and pepper. Top with half of the toasts; repeat with the remaining tomatoes, 2 tablespoons each of parsley and basil and the remaining toasts. Pour the tomato juice over the toasts. Lightly oil a sheet of parchment paper and place it directly on the toasts. Cover the bread pudding with foil, pressing slightly to compact it.

**5.** Bake the bread pudding in the center of the oven for about 45 minutes, or until the liquid is absorbed and the tomatoes are very soft. Remove the foil and parchment and bake about 10 minutes longer, or until crisp. Let the pudding stand for 15 minutes, sprinkle with the remaining 1 tablespoon each of parsley and basil and serve. —*Geoffrey Zakarian*

**NOTE** Use the tomato juice if the tomatoes yield less than 1 cup of fresh juice.

**MAKE AHEAD** The bread pudding can be baked up to 8 hours ahead. Reheat and sprinkle with the herbs before serving.

## Garlicky Cherry Tomato and Bread Gratin

**ACTIVE: 20 MIN; TOTAL: 55 MIN**

**6 SERVINGS** ● ● ●

One 5-ounce piece of day-old French baguette with crust, cut into 1-inch cubes (5 cups)

- 1½ pounds small cherry tomatoes
- ⅓ cup extra-virgin olive oil
- 3 medium garlic cloves, thinly sliced
- ½ cup chopped flat-leaf parsley
- ½ cup plus 2 tablespoons freshly grated Parmesan cheese
- ½ teaspoon kosher salt
- ¼ teaspoon freshly ground pepper

Preheat the oven to 375°. Lightly oil a 10-inch ceramic quiche dish. In a large bowl, toss the bread cubes with the tomatoes, olive oil, garlic, parsley, Parmesan and salt and pepper. Scrape the mixture into the baking dish and bake in the center of the oven for 35 minutes, or until the bread cubes are browned and crisp and the tomatoes are very tender. Serve the gratin warm or at room temperature. —*Jacques Pépin*

## Gaucho Pizzas

**ACTIVE: 1 HR; TOTAL: 2 HR 30 MIN**

**4 SERVINGS**

- ¼ cup extra-virgin olive oil, plus more for drizzling
- 1 garlic clove, minced
- 1 pound tomatoes—peeled, seeded and coarsely chopped
- 1 bay leaf
- 1 teaspoon chopped thyme

½ teaspoon chopped rosemary

Salt and freshly ground pepper

One 8-bone rack of lamb or 1 bone-in
    2-pound loin roast, meat cut off
    the bone in 1 piece (see Note)

All-purpose flour, for rolling out

Crispy Pizza Dough (recipe follows),
    or 1 pound frozen pizza dough,
    thawed and cut into 4 pieces

4 scallions, white and light green
    parts only, thinly sliced

½ small onion, thinly sliced

4 ounces fresh goat cheese

One 4-ounce bunch arugula, large
    stems discarded

**1.** Heat 1 tablespoon of the olive oil in a medium skillet. Add the garlic and cook over moderate heat, stirring occasionally, for 1 minute. Add the tomatoes and bay leaf and cook over moderate heat until the sauce thickens, about 10 minutes. Stir in the thyme and rosemary and season with salt and pepper. Discard the bay leaf.

**2.** Meanwhile, heat 1 tablespoon of the oil in another medium skillet. Season the lamb roast with salt and pepper and sear over high heat, turning occasionally, until well browned all over but very rare inside, 5 to 8 minutes. Transfer the lamb to a cutting board and let stand for at least 20 minutes or up to 45 minutes. Thinly slice the lamb.

**3.** Preheat the oven to 500°. Position racks in the upper and lower thirds of the oven. Lightly oil 2 large baking sheets. On a lightly floured surface, roll or stretch out the Crispy Pizza Dough into four 8-inch rounds. Transfer the dough rounds to the prepared baking sheets. Lightly brush the dough with the remaining 2 tablespoons of olive oil and spread the tomato sauce over the pizza crusts in a thin layer to within ½ inch of the edges. Bake the pizza crusts for 8 minutes, or until they are golden brown and almost cooked through.

**GARLICKY TOMATO AND BREAD GRATIN**

**GAUCHO PIZZA**

# breads, pizzas + sandwiches

**4.** Arrange the sliced lamb in a single layer over the pizza crusts. Scatter the scallions and onion on top and season with salt and pepper. Spoon small dollops of the goat cheese all over the pizzas and drizzle lightly with olive oil.

**5.** Slide the pizzas directly onto the oven racks and bake for 1 to 2 minutes, or until the lamb is medium rare and the crusts are crisp. Transfer the lamb pizzas to plates. Mound the arugula on top, drizzle lightly with more olive oil and serve immediately. —*Martin Molteni*

**NOTE** Ask your butcher to bone the lamb rack or loin roast for you.

### CRISPY PIZZA DOUGH
**ACTIVE: 15 MIN; TOTAL: 1 HR 45 MIN**
**MAKES 1 POUND DOUGH ●**
- ¾ cup plus 2 tablespoons warm water
- 1 envelope active dry yeast
- 1 teaspoon sugar
- 2 cups all-purpose flour, plus more for dusting
- ½ teaspoon salt

Extra-virgin olive oil

**1.** In a large bowl, mix the water with the yeast and the sugar and let stand until the mixture is foamy, about 5 minutes. Add the 2 cups of flour and the salt and stir until a raggy dough forms. Scrape the dough out onto a lightly floured work surface and knead until smooth and elastic, about 5 minutes.

**2.** Lightly oil the bowl and return the dough to it; turn the dough to coat it with olive oil. Cover with plastic wrap and let stand in a warm, draft-free spot until doubled in bulk, about 1½ hours. Punch down the dough and divide it into 4 balls. —*M.M.*

**MAKE AHEAD** The balls of dough can be wrapped in plastic and refrigerated overnight or frozen for up to 1 month. Let the dough return to room temperature before rolling out.

### Ham and Cheese Pizza Rustica
**ACTIVE: 30 MIN; TOTAL: 1 HR 45 MIN, PLUS 1 HR COOLING**
**MAKES ONE 10-INCH PIE ●**
PASTRY
- 2⅔ cups all-purpose flour
- 3 tablespoons sugar
- ¾ teaspoon salt
- ¾ cup chilled solid vegetable shortening, divided into 3 pieces
- 2 large eggs, lightly beaten
- 3 tablespoons milk

FILLING
- 6 large eggs, lightly beaten
- 1 pound salted mozzarella, cut into ½-inch dice
- ½ pound ricotta
- ½ pound glazed smoked ham, sliced ½ inch thick and cut into ½-inch dice

Salt and freshly ground pepper
- 1 egg lightly beaten with 1 tablespoon milk

**1. MAKE THE PASTRY:** In a food processor, combine the flour, sugar and salt and pulse several times. Add the shortening and pulse until the mixture resembles coarse meal. Add the eggs and milk and pulse until the dough is evenly moistened. Turn the dough out onto a lightly floured work surface and knead a few times until smooth. Form the dough into 2 disks, one slightly larger than the other. Wrap the disks of dough in plastic and refrigerate them for 30 minutes or for up to 3 days.

**2. MAKE THE FILLING:** In a large bowl, mix the eggs with the mozzarella, ricotta, ham, 1 teaspoon of salt and ½ teaspoon of pepper.

**3.** Preheat the oven to 375°. Between sheets of plastic wrap or on a lightly floured work surface, roll out the larger disk of dough to a 13-inch round and line a 10-by-1½-inch pie plate with it. Patch any cracks. Spoon in the filling. Roll out the remaining dough to an 11-inch round.

Brush the pastry rim with water and set the round on top. Press the edges together to seal. Trim the overhanging dough and crimp decoratively. Make 3 small slashes in the top crust and brush lightly with the egg wash. Bake the *pizza rustica* for 40 to 45 minutes, or until golden on top. Cover with foil if the crust browns too quickly. Let cool for 1 hour before serving. —*Marcella Giamundo*

**MAKE AHEAD** The baked pie can be refrigerated for up to 2 days and reheated before serving.

### Spinach and Artichoke Pizzas
**ACTIVE: 30 MIN; TOTAL: 1 HR 20 MIN**
**4 SERVINGS ●**
To quickly thaw 1 pound of frozen pizza dough, brush with olive oil, cover with plastic wrap and microwave at 100 percent power in 20-second bursts just until softened but not heated. Cut the dough into 4 pieces and microwave in 10-second bursts until it reaches room temperature.

Whole wheat flour, for dusting
- 1 pound frozen pizza dough, thawed and quartered
- 3 tablespoons extra-virgin olive oil
- 2 large red onions, thinly sliced

Two 9-ounce packages frozen artichoke hearts, thawed
- ¼ teaspoon minced rosemary

Salt and freshly ground pepper

Two 10-ounce packages frozen chopped spinach, thawed and squeezed dry
- ½ cup shredded Fontina cheese
- ¼ cup freshly grated pecorino cheese

**1.** Set a pizza stone on the bottom of the oven. Preheat the oven to 500°. Lightly dust a baking sheet with flour. Shape each piece of pizza dough into a disk, transfer to the baking sheet and dust with flour. Cover the disks loosely with plastic wrap and let rise at room temperature for 25 minutes.

2. In a large skillet, heat 2 tablespoons of the olive oil until shimmering. Add the onions, cover and cook over moderate heat, stirring occasionally, until lightly browned, 10 minutes; transfer to a bowl. Add the artichoke hearts and rosemary to the skillet and heat through. Season with salt and pepper. Add to the onions.

3. Heat the remaining 1 tablespoon of olive oil in the skillet. Add the spinach and cook over moderate heat, stirring, until heated through, about 2 minutes. Season with salt and pepper.

4. For each pizza, on a floured surface, roll 1 disk of dough into a 9-inch round. Flour a pizza peel and slide the dough onto it. Spread one-fourth of the spinach and artichoke hearts on the dough, top with one-fourth of the Fontina and 1 tablespoon of the pecorino and bake on the stone for about 6 minutes, or until crisp and bubbling. —*Marcia Kiesel*

### Grilled Radicchio and Cheese Calzones

**TOTAL: 30 MIN**

MAKES 8 CALZONES ● ● ●

¼ cup plus 2 tablespoons extra-virgin olive oil, plus more for brushing

2 pounds frozen pizza dough, thawed and cut into 8 pieces

¾ cup part-skim ricotta

1 ounce Parmesan cheese, freshly grated (¼ cup)

**Salt and freshly ground pepper**

**Vegetable oil, for the grill**

4 large heads radicchio, each cut into 8 wedges

3 large garlic cloves, minced

½ pound part-skim mozzarella, cut into 8 slices

1. Brush several large baking sheets with olive oil. On a lightly floured work surface, roll out 1 piece of dough to an 8-inch round about ¼ inch thick. Repeat with the remaining dough. Transfer the dough rounds to the prepared baking sheets.

2. In a small bowl, combine the ricotta with the Parmesan cheese. Season the mixture generously with salt and pepper.

3. Light a grill. Lightly oil the grate. Arrange the radicchio wedges on a large baking sheet and drizzle with 3 tablespoons of the olive oil. Sprinkle the garlic over the radicchio and season with salt and pepper. Grill the radicchio wedges over a hot fire, turning them occasionally, until wilted and charred in spots, about 3 minutes. Return the radicchio to the baking sheet. Clean the grill grate with a wire brush or a crumpled piece of aluminum foil and tongs.

4. Have all the ingredients near the grill. Brush the dough rounds with some of the remaining olive oil. Grill 2 or 3 rounds at a time just until the bottoms are set and lightly charred, about 1 minute. Quickly flip the rounds and top each one with a slice of mozzarella, one-eighth of the radicchio and one-eighth of the ricotta mixture in the center; season with salt. Immediately fold the dough over the filling to loosely form calzones. Using a spatula, transfer the barely cooked calzones to a large baking sheet. Repeat with the remaining dough rounds and filling.

5. Brush the calzones with the remaining olive oil. Grill the calzones over a low fire, turning frequently, until they are golden and charred in spots and the cheese is melted, 3 to 4 minutes longer. Transfer to a large platter and serve. —*Grace Parisi*

### Pumpkin Seed Bread Salad

**ACTIVE: 30 MIN; TOTAL: 50 MIN**

12 SERVINGS ● ●

**One 1½-pound loaf crusty country Italian bread, crust removed**

¼ cup extra-virgin olive oil

**Salt and freshly ground pepper**

4 tablespoons (2 ounces) unsalted butter

4 medium garlic cloves, thinly sliced

8 scallions, thinly sliced

4 small celery ribs, thinly sliced

¾ cup salted shelled pumpkin seeds, lightly toasted

1 cup coarsely chopped celery leaves

¼ cup medium-dry sherry, such as Amontillado

1. Preheat the oven to 400°. Slice the bread 1 inch thick. Using your fingers, pull the bread into coarse shreds. Spread the shreds of bread on 2 large, rimmed baking sheets. Drizzle with the olive oil and season with salt and pepper. Toss the bread to coat thoroughly with the olive oil. Bake the bread on the upper and lower oven racks for about 20 minutes, shifting the baking sheets between the racks halfway through, or until the shreds are golden brown and lightly crisp. Let the toasted bread cool.

2. Melt the butter in a medium skillet. Add the sliced garlic and cook over moderately low heat, stirring once or twice, until fragrant and golden brown, about 3 minutes. Add the sliced scallions and sliced celery ribs and cook over moderately low heat, stirring once or twice, until the scallions are softened but the sliced celery is still slightly crisp, about 6 minutes.

3. Just before serving the bread salad, transfer the toasted bread to a very large bowl. Add the toasted pumpkin seeds and the chopped celery leaves. Reheat the scallion mixture over moderately high heat until sizzling. Stir in the sherry and simmer for 30 seconds. Scrape the scallion mixture over the toasted bread in the bowl and toss until thoroughly combined. Season with salt and pepper and serve at once. —*Marcia Kiesel*

**MAKE AHEAD** The bread salad can be prepared through Step 2 early in the day and stored at room temperature. Reheat the scallion mixture and toss with the toasted bread just before serving.

# breads, pizzas + sandwiches

## Smoked Trout and Bacon Pitas

**TOTAL: 30 MIN**

**MAKES 4 PITAS** ●●

- 10 ounces thick-cut bacon (about 10 slices), cut into 1-inch pieces
- ¼ cup mayonnaise
- ¼ cup sour cream
- 2 tablespoons grainy mustard
- Salt and freshly ground pepper
- 6 ounces skinless smoked trout fillets, flaked
- ½ pound cherry tomatoes (1½ cups), halved
- 4 ounces frisée, torn (4 cups)
- 2 scallions, thinly sliced
- Four 7-inch pita breads

1. In a large skillet, cook the bacon over moderately high heat until browned and crisp, about 8 minutes. Drain the bacon on paper towels.

2. In a bowl, mix the mayonnaise with the sour cream and mustard and season with salt and pepper. Add the bacon, smoked trout, cherry tomatoes, frisée and scallions and toss to coat. Spoon the salad into the pita breads and serve.
—Annie Miler

## ingredient

**TIP** **FRYING BACON**

It's easiest to cut bacon into pieces (as called for in the Smoked Trout and Bacon Pita recipe above) if it's chilled. Let the bacon come to room temperature before cooking it. Use a cold, heavy, preferably cast-iron skillet large enough to hold the bacon in a single layer. Fry with low to medium-low heat to ensure even cooking and cut down on shrinking and curling—not to mention sputtering hot grease.

## BLTs on Toasted Brioche with Aioli and Basil

**TOTAL: 40 MIN**

**MAKES 6 SANDWICHES** ●

Instead of preparing the mayonnaise yourself, you can substitute ¾ cup of store-bought mayonnaise; if you use this homemade version, you'll have leftovers.

- 24 thick slices of applewood-smoked bacon (1¾ pounds)
- 2 large egg yolks
- 1 cup plus 2 tablespoons extra-virgin olive oil
- 2 tablespoons fresh lemon juice
- 1 large garlic clove, pounded to a paste in a mortar or minced
- Salt and freshly ground black pepper
- Cayenne pepper
- 3 tomatoes, sliced ¼ inch thick
- ⅓ cup thinly sliced basil, preferably opal
- Twelve ½-inch-thick slices of brioche
- 4 tablespoons unsalted butter, softened
- 12 small Boston lettuce leaves

1. Preheat the oven to 450°. Arrange the bacon slices on 2 large, rimmed baking sheets and bake for about 15 minutes, or until browned. Drain on paper towels.

2. In a medium bowl, whisk the egg yolks. Very gradually whisk in 1 cup of the olive oil; start with small drizzles, then whisk in a thin stream until the mayonnaise is very thick. Whisk in the lemon juice and garlic paste and season the aioli with salt, black pepper and cayenne.

3. Spread the tomato slices on a large plate. Season with salt and pepper and sprinkle with the thinly sliced basil and the remaining 2 tablespoons of olive oil.

4. Heat a large cast-iron skillet. Spread each slice of brioche with 1 teaspoon of butter and set 2 slices in the skillet, buttered side down. Toast over high heat until browned and crisp. Turn and toast the other side. Repeat with the remaining slices of brioche.

5. Set the brioche toasts on a work surface, buttered side up. Spread each toast with 1 tablespoon of the mayonnaise. Top 6 of the toast slices with 2 lettuce leaves, 2 tomato slices and 4 bacon strips and close the sandwiches. Carefully cut the sandwiches in half and serve.
—Suzanne Goin

**MAKE AHEAD** The aioli can be refrigerated, tightly covered, for up to 2 days.

## Roast Beef with Braised-Celery-and-Chile Relish on Ciabatta

**ACTIVE: 30 MIN; TOTAL: 1 HR**

**MAKES 20 SANDWICH HALVES** ●

Using mortadella—the smooth-textured, subtly spicy *salume*, or cured pork, from Bologna, Italy—instead of roast beef makes this already delicious sandwich deluxe.

- 5 tablespoons extra-virgin olive oil
- 1½ pounds celery ribs, cut crosswise into 4-inch lengths
- Salt
- 1 cup water
- ½ cup dry white vermouth
- 1 bay leaf
- 4 whole pickled jalapeños and 4 cherry peppers from jars, chopped, plus 2 tablespoons pickling liquid
- Freshly ground pepper
- 20 slices (¼ inch thick) of ciabatta cut from 1 oval loaf
- 2 large garlic cloves, halved
- 1¼ pounds thinly sliced roast beef or mortadella

1. In a large, deep skillet, heat 1 tablespoon of the olive oil until shimmering. Add the celery pieces, season with salt and cook over high heat, stirring a few times, until the celery begins to brown, about 4 minutes. Add the water, dry white vermouth and bay leaf. Cover the skillet and cook the mixture over moderately low heat, stirring occasionally, until the celery is tender, about 20 minutes.

2. Drain the celery and let cool slightly, then slice the ribs on the diagonal ⅛ inch thick. Transfer to a bowl. Stir in the chiles and their pickling liquid and the remaining 4 tablespoons of olive oil. Season the relish with salt and pepper.

3. Preheat the oven to 450°. Place the bread directly on 2 oven racks and bake until lightly toasted, 3 minutes. While still warm, rub the garlic on one side of each slice. Lay the bread on a work surface, garlic-rubbed side up. Top half of the slices with the roast beef and the celery-chile relish. Close the sandwiches, cut them in half and serve. —*Tommy Habetz*

**MAKE AHEAD** The celery-chile relish can be refrigerated overnight. The assembled sandwiches can be kept at room temperature for up to 2 hours.

### Grilled Skirt Steak and Gorgonzola Sandwiches

**TOTAL: 30 MIN**

**MAKES 4 SANDWICHES** ●

- 2 tablespoons extra-virgin olive oil
- 1 tablespoon Dijon mustard
- 1 large garlic clove, minced
- ½ teaspoon crushed red pepper

Salt and freshly ground black pepper

- 1¼ pounds skirt steak
- 1 large ripe tomato, thinly sliced
- 1 tablespoon balsamic vinegar
- ⅓ cup crumbled Gorgonzola dolce cheese
- 3 tablespoons mayonnaise
- 1 baguette, cut into four 6-inch lengths and split
- 1 bunch watercress (6 ounces), tough stems trimmed

1. Light a grill or preheat the broiler. In a small bowl, combine 1 tablespoon of the olive oil with the mustard, garlic and crushed red pepper. Season with salt and black pepper. Put the steak in a shallow baking dish and spread the mustard mixture all over it. Grill the steak over high heat, turning once, until charred and

medium rare, about 4 minutes per side. Transfer the meat to a cutting board and let rest.

2. Meanwhile, spread the tomato slices on a platter, drizzle with the balsamic vinegar and the remaining 1 tablespoon of olive oil and season with salt and black pepper. In a small bowl, mash the Gorgonzola with the mayonnaise. Spread the Gorgonzola mixture on the cut sides of the baguette lengths and grill, cheese side up, until the bread is toasted and the cheese is melted, about 1 minute, being careful not to burn the bread.

3. Cut the steak into 4-inch lengths, then thinly slice it across the grain. Pile the meat on the baguettes and spoon the accumulated meat juices over the top. Top with the tomato slices and watercress, close the sandwiches and serve. —*Annie Miler*

### Grilled Chicken Sandwiches with Remoulade and Shaved Lemon

**TOTAL: 30 MIN**

**MAKES 4 SANDWICHES** ● ● ●

- 4 thin chicken cutlets (1¼ pounds total)
- ½ cup fresh orange juice
- 3 tablespoons extra-virgin olive oil

Salt and freshly ground pepper

- 8 slices cut from 1 round loaf semolina bread
- ⅓ cup mayonnaise
- 1 tablespoon very finely chopped parsley leaves
- 1 tablespoon finely chopped cornichons
- 2 teaspoons Dijon mustard
- 1 scallion, finely chopped
- 1 small garlic clove, minced
- 1 teaspoon capers, drained and chopped
- ½ lemon, sliced paper-thin, plus 1 teaspoon lemon juice
- 1 bunch watercress (6 ounces), large stems discarded

1. Light a grill or preheat the broiler. In a medium bowl, toss the chicken with the orange juice and 2 tablespoons of the olive oil and season with salt and pepper. Let stand for 10 minutes.

2. Meanwhile, brush both sides of the bread slices with the remaining 1 tablespoon of oil and grill until toasted, turning once. In a bowl, mix the mayonnaise with the parsley, cornichons, mustard, scallion, garlic, capers and lemon juice.

3. Grill the chicken over high heat until lightly charred and cooked through, about 6 minutes. Spread the remoulade on the toast. Top with the chicken, a few slices of lemon and the watercress. Close the sandwiches, cut in half and serve. —*Annie Miler*

### Indian-Spiced Chicken Salad Sandwiches

**TOTAL: 25 MIN**

**MAKES 6 SANDWICHES** ● ● ●

Vegetable oil, for the grill

Four 8-ounce skinless, boneless chicken cutlets

- 1 tablespoon extra-virgin olive oil, plus more for brushing
- 2 teaspoons mild curry powder

Salt and freshly ground pepper

- 6 whole wheat pita breads, top thirds trimmed off
- ¾ cup plain low-fat yogurt, preferably Greek-style
- 1 tablespoon honey
- 1 large carrot, shredded
- 2 tablespoons chopped cilantro
- 1 scallion, thinly sliced
- 2 tablespoons dried currants
- 3 tablespoons roasted and salted shelled sunflower seeds
- 6 cups lightly packed mesclun
- 1 cup alfalfa sprouts (2 ounces)

1. Light a grill. Lightly oil the grate. Rub the chicken cutlets with the 1 tablespoon of olive oil and the curry powder. Season with salt and pepper. Grill the chicken over

a medium-hot fire, turning occasionally, until lightly charred and cooked through, about 8 minutes. Transfer to a work surface and let stand for 5 minutes.

**2.** Lightly brush the pita breads with olive oil and grill, turning, just until heated through but not crisp, about 1 minute.

**3.** In a large bowl, combine the yogurt with the honey, carrot, cilantro, scallion, currants and ½ tablespoon of the sunflower seeds. Cut the chicken into ¾-inch pieces and add them to the bowl. Season with salt and pepper and toss.

**4.** Fill each pita with 1 cup of mesclun and 1 cup of the chicken salad. Tuck the alfalfa sprouts in the side, sprinkle with the remaining 2½ tablespoons of sunflower seeds and serve. —*Grace Parisi*

**MAKE AHEAD** The chicken salad can be refrigerated for up to 4 hours.

## Smoked Oyster Po'Boys

**TOTAL: 25 MIN**

**MAKES 6 SANDWICHES** ● ●

There is nothing more satisfying than a traditional Southern oyster po'boy sandwich—until you consider the time and effort it takes to shuck the fresh oysters and then deep-fry them. This simple variation, using smoked oysters sold in tins at the supermarket, is ready in a fraction of the time.

# equipment

**ROWENTA TL-90** Jasper Morrison, who has made chairs for Vitra and Cappellini, designed this toaster. A motor quietly raises and lowers the bread and an optical sensor turns the heat off before the toast burns ($135; 781-396-0600 or rowentausa-morrison.com).

¼ cup extra-virgin olive oil
¼ cup fresh lemon juice
1 large garlic clove, very finely chopped
1 tablespoon hot sauce or 2 tablespoons minced jalapeño
Salt and freshly ground pepper
3 inner celery ribs, thinly sliced on the diagonal
Two 3¾-ounce cans smoked oysters, drained
Two 6-ounce bunches watercress, thick stems discarded
One 1-pound baguette, halved lengthwise

**1.** In a medium bowl, combine the olive oil with the lemon juice, garlic and hot sauce and season with salt and pepper. Add the celery and oysters and toss. Add the watercress and toss again. Season with salt and pepper.

**2.** Mound the salad on the bottom half of the baguette, close the sandwich and press to flatten slightly, tucking in any greens. Cut the baguette into 6 sandwiches and serve right away. —*Grace Parisi*

## Salmon Niçoise Sandwiches

**ACTIVE: 30 MIN; TOTAL: 1 HR**

**MAKES 6 SANDWICHES** ● ● ●

This is a West Coast version of *pan bagnat,* the Provençal sandwich that's traditionally made with tuna. The flavors are best when the sandwiches are allowed to sit for 20 or 30 minutes before serving.

1½ pounds skinless center-cut salmon fillet
⅓ cup extra-virgin olive oil, plus more for brushing
Salt and freshly ground pepper
1 seedless cucumber—peeled, halved and thinly sliced
1 yellow bell pepper, thinly sliced
½ cup thinly sliced celery, plus 2 tablespoons celery leaves
3 scallions, thinly sliced

½ cup Niçoise or Calamata olives (3 ounces), pitted and chopped
¼ cup fresh lemon juice
1 pint grape tomatoes, halved
3 hard-cooked eggs, chopped
½ cup torn basil leaves
2 medium baguettes, split

**1.** Light a grill. Lightly brush the salmon with oil and season generously with salt and pepper. Grill over a hot fire for about 10 minutes, or until browned on the outside and medium rare inside. Transfer the salmon to a platter, cover loosely with foil and let cool for 20 minutes. Break up the fish into large chunks.

**2.** In a large bowl, toss the cucumber, bell pepper, sliced celery, celery leaves, scallions and olives. Add the ⅓ cup of olive oil and the lemon juice and toss. Add the tomatoes, eggs, basil and salmon, season with salt and pepper and toss gently. Mound the salmon salad on the baguettes; let stand for 20 minutes, then cut into 6 sandwiches.

—*Jody Denton*

**MAKE AHEAD** The sandwiches can be wrapped and kept at room temperature for up to 2 hours.

## Seared Pork and Pickled Eggplant Panini

**ACTIVE: 45 MIN; TOTAL: 1 HR**

**MAKES 6 SANDWICHES** ●

¼ cup plus 3 tablespoons extra-virgin olive oil
1 Italian eggplant (about ¾ pound), sliced crosswise ⅛ inch thick
Salt and freshly ground pepper
2 tablespoons sherry vinegar
1 tablespoon minced chives
1 tablespoon chopped flat-leaf parsley
1 teaspoon minced tarragon leaves
1 garlic clove, finely chopped
Two ¾-pound pork tenderloins, sliced on the diagonal ½ inch thick, slices pounded ¼ inch thick

1 stick (4 ounces) unsalted
butter, softened

1 oval loaf Italian country bread, cut
into twelve ¼-inch-thick slices

¾ pound Taleggio cheese, rind
removed, cheese cut into 12 slices

1. In a large skillet, heat 2 tablespoons of the olive oil until shimmering. Add half of the eggplant slices in a single layer and fry over moderately high heat until golden brown, about 2 minutes per side. Transfer the fried eggplant to a rimmed platter lined with paper towels and season with salt and pepper. Repeat the process with 2 more tablespoons of olive oil and the remaining eggplant slices. Discard the paper towels.

2. In a small bowl, mix the sherry vinegar with the chives, parsley, tarragon, garlic and 1 tablespoon of the olive oil. Season the marinade with salt and pepper, pour over the fried eggplant and turn to coat the slices. Let stand at room temperature for at least 10 minutes.

3. In a large skillet, heat 1 tablespoon of the olive oil. Season the pork with salt and pepper. Add half of the pork slices to the skillet and cook over high heat until golden and no longer pink in the center, about 1 minute per side. Transfer the pork to a plate. Repeat with the remaining tablespoon of olive oil and the remaining pork.

4. Set 2 large cast-iron skillets over moderately high heat for about 5 minutes, or until very hot. Spread 2 teaspoons of butter on one side of each slice of bread. Lay 6 slices on a work surface, buttered side down. Top each of the slices with one-sixth of the pork and pickled eggplant and 2 slices of cheese. Close the sandwiches with the remaining bread slices, buttered side up.

5. Place a sandwich in each cast-iron skillet and set a second heavy skillet directly on top of the sandwich. Set a large, heavy can in each skillet to weigh the sandwich down. Cook the panini over moderately high heat for 3 minutes. Flip each sandwich and cook for about 3 minutes longer, or until browned and crisp all over. Transfer the panini to a cutting board. Repeat with the remaining panini, reducing the heat to moderate. Cut the grilled panini in half, transfer to a platter and serve. —*Barbara Lynch*

**MAKE AHEAD** The pickled eggplant can be stored overnight at room temperature in an airtight container.

## Grilled Cheese and Chorizo Sandwiches

**TOTAL: 30 MIN**

**MAKES 4 SANDWICHES** ● ●

3 chorizo sausages
(6 ounces total), thinly sliced
on the diagonal

2 tablespoons unsalted
butter, softened

8 slices of sourdough bread, cut
from a pullman loaf

6 ounces Pepper Jack cheese,
thinly sliced

2 tablespoons drained and sliced
pickled jalapeños

6 ounces Havarti cheese,
thinly sliced

1. In a large skillet, cook the chorizo over moderately high heat, stirring occasionally, until lightly browned, about 3 minutes. Drain the chorizo on paper towels and wipe out the skillet.

2. Butter the bread on one side and turn 4 slices buttered side down on a work surface. Top with Pepper Jack, chorizo, pickled jalapeños and Havarti. Close the sandwiches with the remaining bread slices, buttered side up.

3. Preheat 2 large skillets. Add the sandwiches and cook over moderate heat, turning them once, until the bread is golden and crisp, about 8 minutes. Cut the sandwiches in half and serve.
—*Annie Miler*

## Mini Vietnamese Pork and Pickle Sandwiches

**TOTAL: 45 MIN**

**MAKES 4 DOZEN CANAPÉS** ● ●

5 tablespoons Asian fish sauce

2 tablespoons honey

Juice of 1 lime

½ teaspoon crushed red pepper

1 daikon radish (1 pound), peeled,
then julienned

1 large carrot, peeled, then julienned

1 tablespoon vegetable oil

½ pound ground pork

¼ pound sweet Italian sausage,
casings removed

1 teaspoon minced peeled ginger

1 teaspoon freshly ground pepper

¾ teaspoon ground coriander

¼ teaspoon ground fennel seeds

2 garlic cloves, minced

½ cup mayonnaise

Salt

2 baguettes, halved lengthwise

1 medium kirby cucumber,
thinly sliced crosswise (1 cup)

20 cilantro sprigs

Sriracha or other Asian chili sauce

# equipment

**PANINI PRESS**                    TIP

**BREVILLE This two-in-one model
adjusts to make thick or thin panini
using minimal butter or oil ($60;
866-273-8455 or breville.com).**

# breads, pizzas + sandwiches

**1.** Preheat the oven to 350°. In a large bowl, whisk 4 tablespoons of the fish sauce with the honey, lime juice and crushed red pepper. Add the julienned daikon and carrot and toss the pickle well, then refrigerate.

**2.** In a medium ovenproof skillet, heat the oil until shimmering. Add the pork and cook over moderate heat, breaking up the meat with a wooden spoon, until it is pale, about 4 minutes. Crumble in the sausage and cook, breaking it up, until no trace of pink remains, about 3 minutes. Stir in the ginger, pepper, coriander, fennel, half of the garlic, and the remaining 1 tablespoon of fish sauce and bake for 10 minutes.

**3.** Mix the mayonnaise with the remaining garlic and season with salt.

**4.** Bake the baguettes until just crisp, about 4 minutes.

**5.** Spread the cut sides of the baguette bottoms with the garlic mayonnaise and spread the pork mixture on top, pressing to help it adhere. Layer the cucumber slices on top. Gently squeeze the daikon-carrot pickle and scatter 2 cups of it over

## ingredient

### KEEPING HERBS FRESH

The grilled eggplant sandwich on this page is topped with parsley and basil. Store these leafy herbs and delicate greens like watercress root end down in a glass or jar of water—as you would flowers. This is also a great way to resuscitate herbs that are slightly wilted. If your house is cool, keep them on the counter; if not, refrigerate them, but be sure your refrigerator is set at 32° or higher; freezing destroys leafy herbs and lettuces.

the cucumber. Top with the cilantro sprigs and squiggles of the Sriracha sauce. Close the sandwiches and, using a heavy knife, cut them into 1½-inch lengths. Arrange the sandwiches on a platter and serve.
—*Zak Pelaccio*

**MAKE AHEAD** The daikon-carrot pickle, pork mixture and garlic mayonnaise can be refrigerated separately for up to 3 days. Gently reheat the pork before assembling the sandwiches.

### Date, Goat Cheese and Pancetta on Walnut-Raisin Bread

**TOTAL: 30 MIN**

**MAKES 40 MINI SANDWICHES** ● ● ●

- 10 thin slices of pancetta
- 1 tablespoon extra-virgin olive oil
- 1 medium red onion, very thinly sliced
- 5 Medjool dates, pitted and chopped
- ¼ cup balsamic vinegar
- 1 tablespoon sherry vinegar
- 10 ounces fresh goat cheese, at room temperature (1¼ cups)
- Freshly ground pepper
- 20 slices of walnut-raisin bread from 1 round or rectangular loaf

**1.** Preheat the oven to 375°. Spread the pancetta slices on a medium, rimmed baking sheet and bake for about 7 minutes, or until it is slightly crisp and browned. Remove from the oven and let cool.

**2.** Meanwhile, in a medium saucepan, heat the olive oil until shimmering. Add the onion and cook over moderately high heat, stirring, until golden, about 4 minutes. Add the chopped dates and the balsamic and sherry vinegars and cook over low heat until the dates are softened and the liquid is syrupy, about 4 minutes. Transfer the date mixture to a bowl and let cool. Stir in the goat cheese and season with a generous pinch of pepper.

**3.** Spread a slightly rounded tablespoon of the goat cheese–date mixture on one side of each slice of bread. Press the pancetta onto half of the slices. Close the sandwiches and cut into quarters.
—*Tommy Habetz*

**MAKE AHEAD** The sandwiches can be covered with a dish towel and kept at room temperature for up to 2 hours.

### Grilled Eggplant and Fresh Herb Salad Subs with Parmesan

**TOTAL: 30 MIN**

**MAKES 4 SUBS** ● ●

- 1½ pounds small eggplants, peeled and halved lengthwise
- ½ cup extra-virgin olive oil, plus more for brushing
- Salt and freshly ground pepper
- 4 crusty rolls, split
- 3 tablespoons red wine vinegar
- 1 garlic clove, minced
- ½ cup finely chopped celery, plus ⅓ cup celery leaves
- ½ cup flat-leaf parsley leaves
- ⅓ cup snipped chives
- ⅓ cup basil leaves, torn
- ¾ cup shaved Parmesan cheese (about 2 ounces)

**1.** Light a grill or preheat the broiler. Brush the eggplants with olive oil and season with salt and pepper. Grill over moderately high heat, turning occasionally, until charred and softened, about 15 minutes. Transfer to a cutting board and coarsely chop. Brush the cut sides of the rolls with olive oil and grill on both sides until lightly toasted, about 1 minute.

**2.** Meanwhile, in a large bowl, whisk the ½ cup of olive oil with the vinegar and garlic. Season with salt and pepper. Add the eggplant, celery, celery leaves, parsley, chives and basil and toss to coat. Mound the salad on the toasted rolls and top with the Parmesan. Close the sandwiches, cut them in half and serve.
—*Annie Miler*

DATE, GOAT CHEESE AND PANCETTA ON WALNUT-RAISIN BREAD

**HAM AND ARTICHOKE PANINI**

**ROASTED PEPPER AND HUMMUS SANDWICHES**

### Ham and Artichoke Panini

**TOTAL: 30 MIN**

**MAKES 4 PANINI ●**

- 4 extra-thick pocketless pita breads, split horizontally
- 6 ounces thinly sliced provolone cheese
- 6 ounces thinly sliced ham
- 2 ounces thinly sliced pepperoni
- ⅓ cup pitted Calamata olives, coarsely chopped
- One 7-ounce jar marinated artichokes, drained
- 12 basil leaves
- 6 ounces fresh mozzarella cheese, sliced
- 1 tablespoon extra-virgin olive oil

**1.** Arrange the pita rounds cut side up on a work surface. Cover 4 of the pita halves with the provolone. Arrange the ham, pepperoni, olives and artichokes each on its own quadrant of the 4 provolone-topped panini halves. Scatter the basil leaves and mozzarella on top and close with the remaining 4 pita rounds. Brush the tops of the panini with 1 teaspoon of the olive oil.

**2.** Heat 1 teaspoon of the remaining olive oil in each of 2 large skillets until shimmering. Add 2 pita panini to each and press down with a smaller skillet. Cook over moderate heat, turning once, until the cheese is melted and the panini are golden and crisp, about 10 minutes. Cut into quarters and serve warm.
—*Annie Miler*

### Open-Faced Roasted Pepper and Hummus Sandwiches

**TOTAL: 30 MIN**

**MAKES 8 SANDWICHES ● ●**

- 3 red bell peppers, halved and cored
- 8 slices of multigrain bread
- 5 tablespoons extra-virgin olive oil
- 2 large garlic cloves, thinly sliced
- ½ teaspoon crushed red pepper

Salt and freshly ground black pepper

¾ cup prepared hummus

1 bunch arugula (4 ounces), stemmed

2 medium tomatoes, thinly sliced

**1.** Preheat the broiler. Arrange the bell pepper halves in a broiler pan, skin side up, and flatten them with the heel of your hand. Broil the peppers until the skin is blackened, about 5 minutes. Transfer them to a plate, cover with plastic wrap and let stand for 5 minutes. Peel the roasted peppers and cut the flesh into ½-inch strips. Keep the broiler on.

**2.** Brush the bread on both sides with 1 tablespoon of the olive oil. Broil, turning once, until toasted.

**3.** In a medium skillet, heat the remaining ¼ cup of olive oil. Add the garlic and crushed red pepper and cook over moderate heat, stirring occasionally, until fragrant, about 2 minutes. Add the roasted pepper strips, season with salt and black pepper and cook, stirring occasionally, for 4 minutes. Remove the skillet from the heat and drain the roasted pepper oil into a small bowl.

**4.** Spread the hummus on the slices of toast and top with the roasted pepper strips, arugula and tomato slices. Season the open-faced sandwiches with salt and black pepper, drizzle with the reserved roasted pepper oil and serve.
—*Annie Miler*

### Summer Squash Sandwiches with Pecorino Butter

**TOTAL: 35 MIN**

**MAKES 6 SANDWICHES** ●

⅓ cup freshly grated pecorino cheese

1 stick (4 ounces) unsalted butter, softened

One 1-pound round or oval loaf semolina or Italian bread, cut into 18 slices

1½ tablespoons extra-virgin olive oil

1 tablespoon fresh lemon juice

1 garlic clove, minced

¼ cup Gaeta olives, pitted and finely chopped

¼ cup chopped basil

1 medium zucchini, coarsely chopped

Salt and freshly ground pepper

3 medium tomatoes, each cut into 4 crosswise slices

½ small head frisée, torn into bite-size pieces

**1.** Preheat the oven to 400°. In a bowl, stir the cheese into the butter and spread on one side of each slice of bread.

**2.** In a medium bowl, combine the oil, lemon juice, garlic, olives and basil. In a food processor, pulse the zucchini until finely chopped. Fold the zucchini into the oil and lemon juice mixture and season with salt and pepper. Season the tomatoes with salt and pepper.

**3.** Arrange the bread on 2 large baking sheets, buttered side up. Bake the bread for 4 minutes, or until lightly toasted.

**4.** Set 6 slices of toast buttered side up on a work surface. Top each with the frisée and the zucchini relish. Cover with another slice of bread, buttered side up, and top with 2 slices of tomato and the remaining bread, buttered side down. Cut the sandwiches in half with a serrated knife and serve. —*Marcia Kiesel*

### Egg Salad with Capers and Spinach on Toasted Brioche

**TOTAL: 30 MIN**

**MAKES 20 SANDWICH HALVES** ●
For an even more elegant version of this sandwich, replace the chopped capers with 2 teaspoons of white truffle oil.

16 large eggs

2 medium shallots, 1 minced, 1 thinly sliced

1 tablespoon Champagne vinegar or white wine vinegar

⅔ cup mayonnaise

3 tablespoons whole-grain mustard

1 large celery rib, finely chopped

2½ tablespoons brined capers, patted dry and finely chopped

2 tablespoons minced chives

1 teaspoon fresh lemon juice

Salt and freshly ground pepper

1 tablespoon extra-virgin olive oil

Two 10-ounce bags washed curly spinach, tough stems discarded

20 slices of brioche cut from 1 rectangular loaf, lightly toasted

**1.** In a large saucepan, cover the eggs with cold water and bring to a rapid boil over moderately high heat. Cover and remove the saucepan from the heat; let stand for 12 minutes.

**2.** Meanwhile, in a small bowl, combine the minced shallot with the vinegar and let soak for 10 minutes. Drain well and discard the vinegar.

**3.** Drain and rinse the hard-boiled eggs under cold water, shaking the pan vigorously to crack the shells. Let the eggs cool completely. Peel the eggs and pat them dry, then coarsely chop.

**4.** In a large bowl, combine the mayonnaise, mustard, celery, capers, chives, lemon juice and vinegar-infused minced shallot. Add the eggs and mix gently with a wooden spoon. Season the egg salad with salt and pepper and refrigerate.

**5.** In a large skillet, heat the oil. Add the sliced shallot and cook over high heat, stirring, until golden, 2 to 3 minutes. Add the spinach and cook, stirring, until wilted, 2 to 3 minutes. Drain the spinach and press out the water. Coarsely chop the spinach and transfer it to a bowl. Season with salt and pepper and refrigerate until chilled.

**6.** Arrange the toasted brioche slices on a work surface. Spoon the egg salad on half of the slices and top with the spinach. Close the sandwiches and cut in half. Serve right away. —*Tommy Habetz*

**MAKE AHEAD** The egg salad and spinach can be refrigerated, separately, overnight.

MIX-AND-MATCH GRANOLA, P. 277

# breakfast +brunch

13

SPINACH AND GOAT CHEESE FRITTATA     SHIRRED EGGS WITH SWISS CHARD

### Spinach and Goat Cheese Frittata

**TOTAL: 20 MIN**

4 SERVINGS ● ●

- 3 tablespoons extra-virgin olive oil
- 6 thin slices of pancetta (about 3 ounces)
- 1 small leek, white and tender green parts only, halved lengthwise and cut crosswise into ½-inch pieces
- 1 cup baby spinach
- 8 large eggs, beaten

Salt and freshly ground pepper

- 3 ounces fresh goat cheese, crumbled (½ cup)

**1.** Preheat the oven to 400°. Heat the olive oil in a 12-inch nonstick ovenproof skillet. Add the pancetta to the skillet and cook over moderately high heat until it is crisp and brown, about 3 minutes. Transfer the pancetta to a plate and let cool, then crumble it.

**2.** Add the leek to the skillet and cook over moderately low heat, stirring, until softened and lightly browned, 2 minutes. Add the spinach and cook until wilted, about 1 minute. Using a slotted spoon, transfer the leek and spinach to the plate with the pancetta.

**3.** Season the beaten eggs with salt and pepper, add them to the skillet and cook for about 1 minute. Scatter the reserved pancetta, leek and spinach and the crumbled goat cheese over the eggs and bake for about 4 minutes, or until the frittata is set. Slide onto a cutting board, cut into wedges and serve at once.
—*Julie Ridlon*

**MAKE AHEAD** The frittata can be refrigerated for up to 1 day. Serve it warm or at room temperature.

### Shirred Eggs with Mushrooms and Swiss Chard

**TOTAL: 30 MIN**

4 SERVINGS ●

- 1 tablespoon unsalted butter, plus more for the ramekins
- 1 cup thinly sliced white or cremini mushrooms
- 3 large Swiss chard leaves, stems and ribs removed, leaves shredded
- ¼ cup vegetable stock

Salt and freshly ground pepper

- 8 large eggs
- ¼ cup heavy cream
- 2 tablespoons freshly grated Parmesan cheese

**1.** Preheat the oven to 400° and lightly butter four ½-cup ramekins. In a medium skillet, melt the 1 tablespoon of butter. Add the mushrooms and cook over high heat, stirring occasionally, until tender and just beginning to brown, 4 minutes. Add the Swiss chard leaves and stock and cook over moderate heat, stirring, until wilted, 2 to 3 minutes; season with salt and pepper.

2. Spoon the cooked mushrooms and chard into the ramekins. Crack 2 eggs into each ramekin. Add 1 tablespoon of the cream to each and sprinkle each with ½ tablespoon of the Parmesan cheese. Bake for about 13 minutes, or until the egg whites are just set. Serve right away.
—Bill Telepan

### Deviled Crab Omelets

TOTAL: 20 MIN

4 SERVINGS ●

- 3 tablespoons unsalted butter
- 6 scallions, white and light green parts only, thinly sliced
- 2 long red chiles—halved lengthwise, seeded and thinly sliced crosswise
- 2 teaspoons fresh lemon juice
- ½ teaspoon finely grated lemon zest

Salt and freshly ground pepper
- ½ pound jumbo lump crabmeat, picked over
- 1 dozen large eggs
- 1 tablespoon finely chopped dill
- 1 tablespoon finely chopped cilantro

1. In a small skillet, melt 1 tablespoon of the butter over moderate heat. Add the scallions and chiles and cook until softened, about 5 minutes. Add the lemon juice and zest and season with salt and pepper. Transfer the mixture to a small bowl and gently mix in the crabmeat.

2. Crack the eggs into a medium bowl and lightly beat them. Whisk in the dill and season with salt and pepper.

3. In two 8-inch nonstick skillets or omelet pans, melt the remaining 2 tablespoons of butter over moderate heat. Pour half of the egg mixture into each pan. Cook, tilting the pans and drawing in the edges of the omelets with a spatula as they set to allow the uncooked eggs to seep underneath and cook, about 5 minutes. Spoon the crab mixture over half of each omelet. Fold the omelets over, then slide them onto plates. Cut each omelet in half, sprinkle with the chopped cilantro and serve at once.
—Charmaine Solomon

### Poached Eggs with Pancetta and Tossed Mesclun

TOTAL: 20 MIN

4 SERVINGS ● ●

- 8 large eggs
- 1 tablespoon extra-virgin olive oil
- 4 ounces thickly sliced pancetta, cut into ¼-inch dice
- 1 large shallot, minced
- 2 tablespoons white wine vinegar
- 2 tablespoons chopped tarragon leaves
- 2 scallions, thinly sliced
- 6 ounces mesclun (10 cups)

Salt and freshly ground pepper
Toast points or steamed, sliced new potatoes, for serving

1. Bring a large, deep skillet filled with 2 inches of water to a simmer. Crack each egg into a cup and gently slide it into the water. Cook until the whites are solid but the yolks are still soft, 5 minutes. Using a slotted spoon, transfer the eggs to a paper towel–lined plate to drain.

2. Meanwhile, in a large skillet, heat the olive oil until shimmering. Add the pancetta and cook over moderately high heat until crisp and brown, about 3 minutes. Add the minced shallot and cook until softened, 2 minutes. Remove from the heat and add the vinegar, tarragon and scallions.

3. In a large bowl, toss the mesclun with the dressing; season with salt and pepper. Transfer the salad to plates, top with the eggs and serve with toast points.
—Julie Ridlon

### Sautéed Corn and Shiitake Frittata with Parmesan

TOTAL: 30 MIN

4 SERVINGS ● ●

- 8 large eggs
- 1 tablespoon chopped cilantro
- 2 tablespoons plus 1 teaspoon extra-virgin olive oil
- 1 cup fresh corn kernels (from 2 ears)
- ¼ pound shiitake mushrooms, stems discarded, caps sliced ¼ inch thick

Salt and freshly ground black pepper
- 2 tablespoons freshly grated Parmesan cheese

1. Preheat the oven to 350°. Crack the eggs into a medium bowl and beat well, then beat in the cilantro.

2. In an 8-inch nonstick ovenproof skillet, heat 1 teaspoon of the olive oil. Add the corn and sauté for 2 minutes. Add the shiitake, season with salt and pepper and cook over moderate heat, stirring, until the vegetables are softened but not browned, about 5 minutes.

3. Add the remaining 2 tablespoons of olive oil to the skillet and heat. Add salt and pepper to the eggs and pour them into the skillet. Stir lightly to combine the

# technique

**PREPPING THE PAN**    **TIP**

**The best way to keep eggs, particularly delicate omelets, from sticking to the pan is to make sure the metal surface is perfectly clean. If you're using a steel or cast-iron skillet, scrub it with a cloth or paper towel and a handful of kosher salt until smooth, then wipe the pan clean and proceed.**

● FAST    ● HEALTHY    ● MAKE AHEAD    ● STAFF FAVORITE

# breakfast + brunch

ingredients, then transfer to the oven. Bake for 6 to 7 minutes, or until just set. Shake the skillet over high heat to loosen the frittata, then slide it onto a plate. Sprinkle with the Parmesan and serve. —*Mohammad Islam*

**MAKE AHEAD** The frittata can be refrigerated for up to 1 day. Serve it warm or at room temperature.

## Herb and Onion Frittata
**ACTIVE: 25 MIN; TOTAL: 1 HR**
8 SERVINGS ●
  1 dozen large eggs
  1 cup loosely packed chopped herbs, such as flat-leaf parsley, basil and tarragon
  ½ cup whole milk
Salt and freshly ground pepper
  4 tablespoons unsalted butter
  1 medium onion, finely chopped
  2 tablespoons extra-dry vermouth
  1 small tomato, thinly sliced

**1.** Preheat the oven to 350°. In a large bowl, whisk the eggs with the herbs and milk and season with salt and pepper.
**2.** In a medium nonstick ovenproof skillet, melt 2 tablespoons of the butter over moderate heat. Add the onion and cook, stirring occasionally, until softened, about 6 minutes. Add the vermouth, increase the heat to high and cook until evaporated, about 1 minute. Reduce the heat to moderate and add the remaining 2 tablespoons of butter. Pour in the egg and herb mixture. Neatly arrange the tomato slices on top of the eggs in a single layer. Cook undisturbed until the edge just begins to set, about 4 minutes.
**3.** Transfer the skillet to the oven and bake the frittata for 30 minutes, or until set in the center. Let the frittata stand for 5 minutes, then slide it onto a large plate and serve. —*Alexandra and Eliot Angle*

**MAKE AHEAD** The frittata can be refrigerated for up to 1 day. Serve it warm or at room temperature.

## Crusty Potato Frittatas with Romesco Sauce
**ACTIVE: 30 MIN; TOTAL: 1 HR**
20 SERVINGS ● ●
  4 pounds small red potatoes, or Yukon Gold potatoes, scrubbed and cut into ½-inch dice
  2 large rosemary sprigs, cut into 1-inch lengths
  ¾ cup extra-virgin olive oil
Salt and freshly ground black pepper
  2 dozen large eggs
Romesco Sauce (recipe follows) and thickly sliced dry-cured chorizo, for serving

**1.** Preheat the oven to 400°. On 2 large, rimmed baking sheets, toss the potatoes with the rosemary and ½ cup of the oil. Season with salt and pepper and roast for 35 minutes, turning twice, until tender and browned. Discard the rosemary sprigs. Reduce the oven temperature to 350°.
**2.** Crack half of the eggs into a medium bowl. Season with 1½ teaspoons of salt and ½ teaspoon of pepper and beat well. Pour 2 tablespoons of the olive oil into a 10-inch cast-iron skillet. Add half of the potatoes and cook over moderately high heat until they are warmed through. Pour the beaten eggs over the potatoes and cook for 2 to 3 minutes, or until set and golden around the edge.
**3.** Transfer the skillet to the oven and bake the frittata for 15 minutes, or until it is just set in the center. Let cool slightly, then turn out onto a plate. Invert the frittata again onto another plate so that it is right side up. Repeat with the remaining olive oil, eggs and potatoes to make a second frittata. Serve in wedges with the Romesco Sauce and chorizo. —*Naomi Hebberoy*

**MAKE AHEAD** The frittatas can be loosely covered with aluminum foil and stored at room temperature for up to 2 hours.

**SERVE WITH** Baby arugula and very thinly sliced lemon tossed with Parmesan shavings and extra-virgin olive oil.

## ROMESCO SAUCE
**TOTAL: 25 MIN**
MAKES ABOUT 4 CUPS ● ●
For an especially silky version of this classic Spanish sauce, use salted, fried marcona almonds, which are generally available at cheese shops and specialty food stores, in place of the roasted, blanched almonds.
  4 ancho chiles (1½ ounces), stems discarded
  1 cup boiling water
  1 cup plus 2 tablespoons extra-virgin olive oil
One 1-inch-thick slice of country bread, cut into 1-inch cubes (about 1 cup)
  8 garlic cloves, smashed
  1 cup roasted, blanched, unsalted almonds
  1 teaspoon ground coriander
  1 teaspoon ground cumin
  2 large plum tomatoes—halved, seeded and very coarsely chopped
One 7-ounce jar piquillo peppers, drained, or 1 cup drained roasted red bell peppers from a jar tossed with ½ teaspoon cayenne pepper
Kosher salt

**1.** Put the ancho chiles in a small heatproof bowl. Carefully add the boiling water and let stand until the chiles are softened, about 15 minutes.
**2.** Meanwhile, heat 2 tablespoons of the oil in a small skillet until shimmering. Add the bread cubes and cook over moderately high heat, stirring occasionally, until the bread is well browned, about 5 minutes. Using a slotted spoon, transfer the toasted bread cubes from the skillet to a plate and let them cool.
**3.** Drain the ancho chiles, reserving ½ cup of the soaking liquid. Using a sharp paring knife, slit the chiles and remove the seeds. Transfer the chiles to a mini food

processor, add the reserved soaking liquid and process until pureed. Strain the puree through a fine sieve set over a bowl.

**4.** In the food processor, combine the garlic with the almonds, coriander and cumin. Add the bread cubes and process until finely chopped. Add the ancho chile puree, tomatoes and piquillo peppers and process until smooth. With the machine on, slowly add the remaining 1 cup of olive oil and process until smooth. Season the Romesco Sauce with salt and scrape into a bowl. —N.H.

**MAKE AHEAD** The Romesco Sauce can be refrigerated for up to 1 week.

### Fresh Corn Muffins

**TOTAL: 35 MIN**
**MAKES 12 MUFFINS** ● ● ●

- 6 tablespoons canola oil
- ½ cup fresh corn kernels (from 1 ear)
- 2 jalapeños, seeded and finely chopped

Salt

- 1 cup yellow cornmeal
- 1 cup all-purpose flour
- ¼ cup sugar
- 1 tablespoon baking powder
- 1 cup buttermilk
- 1 large egg, lightly beaten

**1.** Preheat the oven to 375° and line a 12-cup muffin pan with paper liners. Heat 1 teaspoon of the oil in a medium skillet. Add the corn and jalapeños, season with salt and cook over moderately high heat until crisp-tender, 2 to 3 minutes. Scrape onto a plate to cool slightly.

**2.** In a bowl, whisk the cornmeal with the flour, sugar, baking powder and ¼ teaspoon of salt. Add the buttermilk, egg and the remaining oil and stir until blended. Quickly stir in the corn mixture and pour the batter into the muffin cups.

**3.** Bake the muffins for 16 minutes, or until a toothpick inserted in the center of one comes out clean. Serve warm or at room temperature. —Lucia Watson

**HERB AND ONION FRITTATA**

**FRESH CORN MUFFINS**

ORANGE-ROSEMARY SCONES

## Crispy Cornmeal-Gruyère Muffins

**ACTIVE: 15 MIN; TOTAL: 45 MIN**

**MAKES 2 DOZEN MUFFINS ● ●**

- 2 cups stone-ground yellow cornmeal
- 2 cups all-purpose flour
- 2 tablespoons plus 2 teaspoons baking powder
- 2 tablespoons sugar
- 1½ teaspoons salt
- ¼ teaspoon freshly ground pepper
- ¼ teaspoon ground cumin
- 2 sticks (½ pound) unsalted butter, softened
- 2 large eggs
- 2 cups whole milk
- 3 cups coarsely shredded Gruyère cheese (9 ounces)

**1.** Preheat the oven to 400° and line two 12-cup muffin tins with paper baking cups. In a medium bowl, whisk the cornmeal with the flour, baking powder, sugar, salt, pepper and cumin.

**2.** In a large bowl, using an electric mixer, beat the butter at high speed until light and fluffy. Beat in the eggs 1 at a time. At low speed, beat in half of the milk, followed by half of the dry ingredients. With a rubber spatula, fold in the cheese and the remaining milk and dry ingredients.

**3.** Spoon the batter into the baking cups; fill to within ¼ inch of the rims. Bake the muffins for 30 minutes, or until golden. Transfer to a rack to cool. —*Marcia Kiesel*

**MAKE AHEAD** The muffins can be frozen for up to 2 weeks.

## Orange-Rosemary Scones

**TOTAL: 45 MIN**

**MAKES 15 SCONES ● ●**

- 2 cups unbleached all-purpose flour
- ¼ cup sugar
- 1 tablespoon baking powder
- 1 teaspoon baking soda

Pinch of salt

- 1 cup plain yogurt
- ¼ cup fresh orange juice

- 4 tablespoons unsalted butter, melted
- 2 teaspoons grated orange zest
- 2 teaspoons minced rosemary
- ½ cup shelled roasted pistachios, coarsely chopped

Fig chutney and plain yogurt, for serving

**1.** Preheat the oven to 375° and position 2 racks in the upper and lower thirds of the oven. Line 2 large baking sheets with parchment paper.

**2.** In a medium bowl, combine the flour with the sugar, baking powder, baking soda and salt. In a small bowl, combine the yogurt with the orange juice, melted butter, orange zest and rosemary. Add the yogurt mixture to the dry ingredients and stir just until evenly moistened. Fold in the pistachios.

**3.** Using a ¼-cup measure, scoop the dough onto the prepared baking sheets. Bake the scones for about 16 minutes, or until golden on top. Serve warm or at room temperature with the fig chutney and yogurt. —*Akasha Richmond*

**MAKE AHEAD** The scones can be stored in an airtight container for up to 2 days. Rewarm in a 325° oven.

## Sour Cream–Pecan Scones

**ACTIVE: 15 MIN; TOTAL: 45 MIN**

**MAKES 2 DOZEN SCONES ●**

- 4 ounces pecan halves (1 cup)
- 3 cups all-purpose flour
- 1½ tablespoons sugar
- 1½ tablespoons baking powder
- 1½ teaspoons chopped thyme leaves
- 1 teaspoon kosher salt
- ½ teaspoon freshly ground pepper
- 1½ sticks (6 ounces) cold unsalted butter, cut into ½-inch pieces
- ¾ cup sour cream
- 1 large egg
- 1 large egg yolk
- ¼ cup whole milk, plus more for brushing

Coarse sea salt, for sprinkling

**1.** Preheat the oven to 350°. Spread the pecans on a rimmed baking sheet and bake for 6 minutes, or until fragrant and lightly toasted. Let cool, then coarsely chop them. Increase the oven temperature to 375°.

**2.** In a large bowl, whisk the flour with the sugar, baking powder, thyme, kosher salt and pepper. Using a pastry blender or 2 knives, cut in the butter until the mixture resembles small peas. Add the toasted pecans and toss to distribute them evenly. Make a well in the center of the dry ingredients.

**3.** In a small bowl, whisk the sour cream with the whole egg, egg yolk and ¼ cup of milk. Add the wet ingredients to the well in the dry ingredients and stir with a wooden spoon until moistened. Turn the dough out onto a lightly floured work surface and knead 2 or 3 times, or just until it comes together.

**4.** On a lightly floured work surface, roll out the dough into a 12-by-8-inch rectangle. Cut the dough into 24 two-inch squares and transfer them to a large

# strategy

**RECIPE RIFFS**  **TIP**

When you find a scone, muffin or biscuit recipe you like, experiment with different flavor variations. In the summer, for example, try replacing the orange zest and rosemary in the Orange-Rosemary Scones (at left) with lemon zest, ginger and blueberries. If you want the crunch of cornmeal but not the cheese and spices in the Crispy Cornmeal-Gruyère Muffins (at left), trade the savory ingredients for something sweet, like dried cherries.

● FAST  ● HEALTHY  ● MAKE AHEAD  ● STAFF FAVORITE

# breakfast + brunch

baking sheet. Lightly brush the tops of the scones with milk and sprinkle with sea salt. Bake the scones in the center of the oven for about 22 minutes, or until the tops and bottoms are golden. Let cool slightly before serving.
—Grace Parisi

**MAKE AHEAD** The baked scones can be frozen for up to 2 weeks. Thaw and reheat before serving.

# equipment

## Roasted Winter Squash and Onion Turnovers
**ACTIVE: 1 HR 15 MIN;**
**TOTAL: 3 HR 30 MIN**
MAKES ABOUT FORTY-TWO
4-INCH TURNOVERS ● ●
The filling for these turnovers also makes a terrific side dish on its own.

**One 3-pound butternut or buttercup squash, halved lengthwise and seeded**
**Salt and freshly ground pepper**
**1 medium sweet onion, sliced ½ inch thick**
**1½ cups shredded Gruyère cheese (5 ounces)**
**1 teaspoon finely chopped thyme leaves**
**All-purpose flour, for rolling out the pastry**
**Flaky Turnover Pastry (recipe follows; see Note)**
**2 large egg yolks lightly beaten with 2 tablespoons whole milk**

**1.** Preheat the oven to 400°. Lightly butter 2 large, rimmed baking sheets. Season the butternut squash halves with salt and pepper and place them cut side down on one of the baking sheets. Cover the baking sheet with aluminum foil. Spread the onion slices on the other baking sheet in a single layer. Season them with salt and pepper.

**2.** Roast the squash in the lower third of the oven for 1 hour, or until tender. Let cool, then scoop the flesh into a large skillet and mash until smooth.

**3.** Meanwhile, roast the onion slices in the middle of the oven for 30 minutes, turning once, until tender and golden. Let cool, then coarsely chop.

**4.** Cook the mashed squash over high heat, stirring constantly, until any excess moisture is evaporated, 5 minutes. Remove the squash from the heat and stir in the chopped onions, the Gruyère and the thyme. Generously season with salt and

pepper. Transfer the squash and onion filling to a bowl and let cool slightly. Refrigerate until chilled.

**5.** On a lightly floured work surface, roll out 1 disk of the Flaky Turnover Pastry ⅛ inch thick. Using a 4-inch round biscuit cutter, stamp out biscuits as close together as possible. Stack the pastry scraps and refrigerate. Repeat with the second disk of pastry. When all the scraps are thoroughly chilled, press them together, reroll and stamp out more rounds. Discard the remaining scraps.

**6.** Preheat the oven to 375°. Working in batches, brush 10 of the pastry rounds with some of the egg wash. Spoon about 1 tablespoon of the squash and onion filling onto the center of each round, fold into a half-moon and press to seal. Using a fork dipped in flour, crimp the edges. Transfer the turnovers to large, rimmed baking sheets, brush with the rest of the egg wash and bake for 22 minutes, or until golden all over. Let the turnovers cool slightly, transfer to a platter, then serve.
—Naomi Hebberoy

**NOTE** This amazingly flaky pastry is well worth the effort, but if you prefer, you can substitute store-bought puff pastry for the turnovers. If you do, cut the puff pastry sheets into 4-inch squares and make triangular turnovers.

**MAKE AHEAD** The unbaked turnovers can be frozen for up 2 weeks. Bake directly from the freezer.

## FLAKY TURNOVER PASTRY
**ACTIVE: 10 MIN; TOTAL: 1 HR**
MAKES ENOUGH PASTRY FOR
42 TURNOVERS ●
**5 cups all-purpose flour**
**1 tablespoon kosher salt**
**4 sticks (1 pound) unsalted butter, cut into tablespoons**
**¾ cup ice water**
**1 large egg**
**1 tablespoon cider vinegar**

**1.** In a food processor, pulse the flour with the salt. Add the butter and pulse until it is the size of large peas. Transfer the mixture to a large bowl and make a well in the center.

**2.** In a small bowl, lightly beat the ice water with the egg and vinegar. Add the liquid to the well and stir it into the butter-flour mixture. Using your hands, gather the dough and knead it in the bowl several times, until evenly moistened. Divide the pastry in half and flatten into 2 disks. Wrap with plastic and chill until firm. —*N.H.*

**MAKE AHEAD** The turnover pastry can be tightly wrapped in plastic and refrigerated overnight or frozen for up to 1 month.

### Zucchini Bread French Toast with Maple-Bourbon Butter

**ACTIVE: 45 MIN; TOTAL: 2 HR**

**8 SERVINGS**

To prepare this extravagant recipe more quickly, use store-bought zucchini bread. Or substitute a different kind of quick bread, such as banana-walnut, carrot or cranberry-orange.

- 1 **cup heavy cream**
- ½ **cup milk**
- 2 **large eggs, lightly beaten**
- 2 **teaspoons pure vanilla extract**
- ½ **cup confectioners' sugar**
- **Zucchini Bread (recipe follows) or other sweet quick bread, ends trimmed, bread cut into 8 slices**
- 1 **stick plus 2 tablespoons (5 ounces) unsalted butter**
- ½ **cup pure maple syrup**
- ¼ **cup bourbon**
- **Pinch of salt**

**1.** In a medium bowl, whisk the heavy cream, milk, eggs, vanilla extract and confectioners' sugar until blended. Transfer to a 9-by-13-inch glass or ceramic baking dish. Add the Zucchini Bread slices and let soak at room temperature, turning once, until the slices are saturated, about 10 minutes.

**2.** Meanwhile, in a medium saucepan, combine 1 stick of the butter with the maple syrup, bourbon and salt and bring to a simmer, whisking constantly, until slightly thickened, about 5 minutes.

**3.** Melt 1 tablespoon of the butter in each of 2 large nonstick skillets. Drain the zucchini bread. Add the slices to the skillets and cook over moderate heat, turning once, until golden and firm to the touch, about 15 minutes.

**4.** Arrange the French toast on 8 plates and spoon the hot maple-bourbon butter on top, passing more bourbon butter at the table. —*Ashley Christensen*

### ZUCCHINI BREAD

**ACTIVE 25 MIN; TOTAL: 1 HR 15 MIN**

**MAKES ONE 8½-BY-4½ INCH LOAF** ●

- 1½ **cups all-purpose flour**
- 1 **teaspoon cinnamon**
- ½ **teaspoon salt**
- ½ **teaspoon baking soda**
- ⅛ **teaspoon baking powder**
- ½ **cup canola oil**
- 2 **large eggs, lightly beaten**
- 1 **cup sugar**
- 1½ **teaspoons pure vanilla extract**
- 1 **pound zucchini, coarsely shredded**

**1.** Preheat the oven to 375°. Butter an 8½-by-4½-inch loaf pan and coat it with sugar. In a bowl, whisk the flour, cinnamon, salt and baking soda and powder.

**2.** In a medium bowl, whisk the canola oil with the eggs, sugar and vanilla. Add the shredded zucchini. Stir the zucchini batter into the dry ingredients.

**3.** Pour the batter into the prepared loaf pan and bake for about 50 minutes, or until a toothpick inserted into the center comes out clean. Let the loaf cool in the pan for 5 minutes, then turn it out onto a wire rack to cool completely. —*A.C.*

**MAKE AHEAD** The Zucchini Bread can be frozen for up to 2 months or refrigerated for up to 5 days.

### Nectarine and Cream Cheese Monte Cristos

**TOTAL: 30 MIN**

**MAKES 4 MONTE CRISTOS** ●

Monte Cristos are sandwiches that are dipped in beaten egg and cooked to a crispy brown, like French toast. This one can be eaten for breakfast or dessert.

- 3 **tablespoons unsalted butter**
- 4 **nectarines, cut into ½-inch wedges**
- 3 **tablespoons light brown sugar**
- 4 **large eggs**
- ½ **cup milk**
- **Pinch of cinnamon**
- 6 **ounces cream cheese, softened**
- 8 **slices of firm-textured bread**
- **Confectioners' sugar and fresh berries, for serving**

**1.** In a medium skillet, melt 2 tablespoons of the butter. Add the nectarine wedges and cook over moderately high heat, stirring occasionally, until softened, 2 to 3 minutes. Add the brown sugar and cook, swirling the pan, just until dissolved, about 1 minute. Transfer the nectarines to a plate.

**2.** In a 9-by-13-inch baking dish, whisk the eggs with the milk and cinnamon. Spread the cream cheese on the bread. Spoon the nectarines on half of the slices and close the sandwiches, pressing lightly. Soak the sandwiches in the egg mixture, turning to coat.

**3.** Melt ½ tablespoon of the remaining butter on a nonstick griddle or in a large skillet. Add the sandwiches to the skillet and cook over moderately high heat until browned on the bottoms, about 5 minutes. Transfer the sandwiches to a plate. Melt the remaining ½ tablespoon of the butter on the griddle. Invert the sandwiches onto the griddle and cook over moderate heat until browned on the bottoms and cooked through, about 5 minutes. Transfer the sandwiches to plates, sift confectioners' sugar on top, garnish with berries and serve. —*Annie Miler*

# breakfast + brunch

## Oatmeal Pancakes

TOTAL: 30 MIN, PLUS 4 HR SOAKING

4 SERVINGS

2 cups buttermilk
1 cup rolled oats, not instant or quick-cooking
2 large eggs, beaten
½ cup whole wheat flour
1 teaspoon baking soda
1 teaspoon baking powder
Pinch of salt
3 tablespoons unsalted butter, melted, plus more for the griddle and for serving
Maple syrup and applesauce, for serving

1. In a bowl, combine the buttermilk with the oats and refrigerate until very soft, at least 4 hours and up to 8. Add the eggs and whisk until combined. Add the flour, baking soda, baking powder and salt. Fold in the melted butter.

2. Heat a large griddle. Brush it with melted butter and ladle in about 2 table-spoons of the batter for each pancake, gently spreading them to 3-inch rounds. Cook over moderate heat until bubbles appear on the surface, 2 to 3 minutes. Flip and cook until the undersides are done, 1 to 2 minutes longer. Transfer the cooked pancakes to warmed plates and repeat with the remaining batter, brushing the griddle with more butter as necessary. Serve the pancakes with butter, maple syrup and applesauce.
—Tina Ujlaki

## Blueberry Corn Cakes with Maple Syrup

TOTAL: 25 MIN

MAKES 12 PANCAKES ● ●

The cornmeal crunch of these pancakes is so addictive you'll eat many more of them than you mean to.

⅔ cup all-purpose flour
⅔ cup fine stone-ground cornmeal
2 tablespoons sugar
1½ teaspoons baking powder
1½ teaspoons baking soda
½ teaspoon salt
1 cup buttermilk
1 large egg, separated
1 cup blueberries
2 tablespoons vegetable oil
Softened unsalted butter and warm pure maple syrup, for serving

1. In a medium bowl, whisk together the flour, cornmeal, sugar, baking powder, baking soda and salt. In a small bowl, whisk the buttermilk with the egg yolk. In a medium bowl, beat the egg white until firm peaks form. Add the buttermilk mixture to the dry ingredients and stir gently until evenly moistened; there will still be some lumps. Fold in the beaten egg white and then the blueberries.

2. Heat a large cast-iron skillet. Add 1 tablespoon of the oil, and when it is hot, spoon ¼ cup of the batter into the skillet for each pancake. Cook over moderate heat until the bottoms are browned and bubbles appear on the surface, 3 to 4 minutes. Flip and cook until browned on the second side, about 2 minutes longer. Keep the pancakes warm in a low oven while you continue with the remaining oil and batter. Serve the pancakes with butter and maple syrup. —Bob Isaacson

## Lemon–Poppy Seed Cake

ACTIVE: 20 MIN; TOTAL: 1 HR 50 MIN

MAKES ONE 8-INCH CAKE ●

⅔ cup sugar
8 large egg yolks
1 large whole egg
1½ tablespoons grated lemon zest
½ cup all-purpose flour
½ cup cornstarch
2 sticks (½ pound) unsalted butter, melted
½ cup poppy seeds

# taste test

F&W tasted almost 30 supermarket and mail-order pancake mixes; we selected these three as our favorites.

| PRODUCT | COMMENT | INTERESTING BITE |
| --- | --- | --- |
| **Robby's Pancake Mix** | "Moist, sweet—in a word, yummy." | Robby's was created in 1962 by the owners of a small pancake house in Clearwater, Florida. |
| **Aunt Jemima Buttermilk Complete** | "Light and fluffy—like a classic pancake." | Aunt Jemima is one of *Advertising Age*'s top 10 ad icons of the 20th century. |
| **Arrowhead Mills Multigrain** | "Hearty wheat flavor, great grainy texture." | The company is named for the Indian arrowheads found on its west Texas property in 1960. |

BLUEBERRY CORN CAKES WITH MAPLE SYRUP

**1.** Preheat the oven to 325°. Butter and flour an 8-inch fluted Bundt or tube pan, tapping out the excess flour. Butter the dull side of a 10-inch piece of foil.

**2.** In the bowl of an electric mixer fitted with the whisk, beat the sugar with the egg yolks and whole egg at medium-high speed until the mixture is pale yellow and very fluffy, about 8 minutes. Beat in the lemon zest. Sift the flour and cornstarch over the egg mixture and fold in with a rubber spatula. Using the electric mixer at medium speed, beat in the melted butter until just incorporated, then beat in the poppy seeds.

**3.** Pour the batter into the prepared pan and cover tightly with the buttered foil. Bake for 45 minutes, or until the cake pulls away from the side of the pan and a cake tester inserted in the center of the cake comes out clean. Carefully remove the foil and let the cake cool in the pan on a wire rack for 15 minutes. Invert the cake onto the rack and let cool completely before serving, at least 30 minutes.

—*Kurt Gutenbrunner*

**MAKE AHEAD** The Lemon–Poppy Seed Cake can be tightly wrapped in plastic and foil and left at room temperature for up to 3 days.

# ingredient

**TIP** | **FREEZING FRUIT**

**When using fresh berries in a batter, it's a good idea to freeze them for at least 1 hour before mixing them in. This helps prevent the delicate fruit from breaking during stirring, which will streak or even entirely tint a batter. Blueberry juice, for instance, turns muffins and pancakes a greenish gray.**

## Asparagus and Smoked Salmon Tart

**ACTIVE: 25 MIN; TOTAL: 3 HR 15 MIN**

**8 SERVINGS** ●

PASTRY

1¼ cups all-purpose flour

Pinch of kosher salt

1 stick (4 ounces) unsalted butter, cut into small pieces and chilled

5 tablespoons ice water

FILLING

¾ pound thin asparagus

1 cup heavy cream

2 large egg yolks

1 large egg

½ teaspoon salt

¼ teaspoon freshly ground black pepper

¼ pound thinly sliced smoked salmon or smoked salmon trout, cut into ½-inch strips

**1. MAKE THE PASTRY:** In a large bowl, mix the flour and salt together. Using a pastry blender or 2 knives, cut in the butter pieces until the mixture resembles coarse meal. Sprinkle on the ice water and toss with a fork to moisten evenly. Pat the dough into a disk, cover with plastic wrap and refrigerate until firm, about 1 hour.

**2.** Preheat the oven to 350°. On a lightly floured surface, roll the pastry out to a 13-inch round about ⅛ inch thick. Fold the pastry round in half and transfer it to an 11-inch fluted tart pan with a removable bottom. Unfold the pastry and gently press it into the tart pan without stretching the dough. Trim off any overhanging pastry and refrigerate the shell for 30 minutes.

**3.** Line the pastry shell with foil and fill with pie weights. Bake for about 40 minutes, or until the edge starts to brown. Remove the foil and weights and bake until golden brown, about 10 minutes longer. Turn the oven down to 325°.

**4. MAKE THE FILLING:** In a medium saucepan of boiling salted water, cook the asparagus until it is crisp-tender, about 3 minutes. Drain well and pat dry. Let cool slightly, then cut the asparagus into 1-inch lengths.

**5.** In a medium bowl, whisk the heavy cream with the egg yolks and whole egg and season with the salt and pepper. Scatter the asparagus and the smoked salmon strips in the pastry shell. Carefully pour the custard over the asparagus and salmon and bake for about 30 minutes, or until the custard is set. Transfer the tart to a rack and let cool slightly before unmolding and serving.

—*Barak Hirschowitz*

**MAKE AHEAD** The tart can be prepared up to 8 hours ahead. Reheat or serve at room temperature

## Buttermilk Ham and Cheese Biscuits

**TOTAL: 35 MIN**

**MAKES 16 BISCUITS** ● ●

1 cup all-purpose flour

1 cup cake flour

3 tablespoons sugar

1 tablespoon baking powder

½ teaspoon salt

¼ teaspoon freshly ground black pepper

1 stick (4 ounces) cold unsalted butter, cut into ½-inch pieces

⅓ cup shredded Gruyère or Swiss cheese

⅓ cup finely diced smoked ham

½ cup buttermilk, plus more for brushing

2 large eggs, beaten

**1.** Preheat the oven to 400°. In a medium bowl, combine the all-purpose and cake flours with the sugar, baking powder, salt and pepper. Cut in the butter until it's the size of large peas. Stir in the shredded Gruyère and diced ham and make a well in the center of the mixture.

**2.** In a bowl, combine the buttermilk and the beaten eggs. Pour the liquid into the well of dry ingredients and quickly stir until just moistened. Turn the dough out onto a lightly floured work surface and gently knead 2 or 3 times, just until it holds together.

**3.** Pat the dough into a 10-inch round about ¾ inch thick. Using a 2¼-inch round cookie cutter or an upside-down juice glass, stamp out biscuits as close together as possible. Gently press the scraps together, press flat or re-roll to about ¾ inch thick and stamp out more biscuits. Transfer the biscuits to a baking sheet and brush the tops with buttermilk. Bake for 15 minutes, or until they are golden and risen. Serve hot.
—*Lee Hefter*

**MAKE AHEAD** The baked buttermilk biscuits can be frozen in an airtight container for up to 2 weeks. Do not thaw before reheating.

### Crêpes with Smoked Trout and Caviar

**TOTAL: 1 HR**

4 SERVINGS ●

⅔ cup all-purpose flour

Kosher salt

⅛ teaspoon sugar

1 cup milk

2 large eggs

¾ cup crème fraîche or
   sour cream

3 tablespoons drained prepared
   horseradish

2 tablespoons finely chopped
   dill, plus 4 dill sprigs
   for garnish

Freshly ground pepper

2 tablespoons unsalted butter

1 red onion, halved and very
   thinly sliced

1 Golden Delicious or other sweet,
   crisp apple, halved and thinly
   sliced (1 cup)

1 smoked trout fillet (7 ounces),
   skinned, flesh flaked into
   ½-inch pieces

4 teaspoons American caviar

**1.** In a medium bowl, combine the flour with ¼ teaspoon of salt and the sugar. Whisk in the milk and eggs until the batter is smooth. Let rest at room temperature for 15 minutes.

**2.** In a small bowl, mix the crème fraîche with the horseradish and chopped dill and season with salt and pepper.

**3.** Strain the crêpe batter through a fine sieve set over a small bowl. Heat a 6-inch crêpe pan or nonstick skillet. Add ½ teaspoon of the butter. When the butter stops foaming, add 2 tablespoons of batter, quickly tilting the pan to coat the bottom evenly. Cook over moderately high heat until the edge of the crêpe is lightly browned, about 1 minute. Flip the crêpe and cook until it is lightly colored on the second side, about 30 seconds. Transfer the crêpe to a plate. Repeat the process with the remaining butter and batter, adjusting the heat as necessary so that the crêpes do not burn. Stack the crêpes on top of one another as they're done; you should have 12.

**4.** Spread each crêpe with 1 tablespoon of the horseradish–crème fraîche. Place 3 red onion slices, 2 apple slices and 1 heaping tablespoon of trout at the edge of each crêpe and loosely roll them up. Transfer the filled crêpes to 4 plates. Garnish each plate with a dollop of the remaining horseradish–crème fraîche, 1 teaspoon of caviar and a dill sprig and serve. —*Kurt Gutenbrunner*

**MAKE AHEAD** The crêpes can be frozen for up to 3 weeks. Let them cool completely, then layer with sheets of wax paper between them. Wrap tightly in plastic, then in foil. Let the crêpes return to room temperature before filling. The horseradish–crème fraîche can be made up to 2 days ahead.

### Mix-and-Match Granola

**ACTIVE: 15 MIN; TOTAL: 1 HR 15 MIN**

MAKES ABOUT 9 CUPS ● ●

The healthy ingredients in this granola belie its decadent flavor.

1 cup mixed nuts, such as
   almonds, pecans, walnuts,
   shelled pistachios and
   cashews

⅔ cup mild vegetable oil, such
   as peanut or canola

⅔ cup clover honey

4 cups rolled oats

¾ cup wheat germ

¾ cup wheat bran

¼ cup nonfat powdered milk

1 cup mixed dried fruit, such
   as raisins, dried cranberries
   and dried cherries

¼ cup toasted seeds, such as
   sunflower seeds or flax seeds

**1.** Preheat the oven to 350°. Spread the mixed nuts on a medium, rimmed baking sheet. Bake for 10 minutes, or until lightly toasted. Transfer the nuts to a plate and let cool completely. Reduce the oven temperature to 325°.

**2.** In a medium saucepan, warm the oil and honey over moderately low heat, stirring frequently, until the honey melts, about 2 minutes.

**3.** In a large bowl, toss the rolled oats, wheat germ, wheat bran and powdered milk. Pour the oil and honey mixture on top and stir until thoroughly coated.

**4.** Spread the oat clusters on a large, rimmed baking sheet. Bake the granola in the center of the oven for 20 minutes, or until golden brown, stirring halfway through. Transfer the baking sheet to a wire rack and let cool completely.

**5.** Add the nuts, dried fruit and toasted seeds to the oat clusters and toss.
—*Alisa Barry*

**MAKE AHEAD** The granola can be stored at room temperature in an airtight container for up to 3 weeks.

● FAST    ● HEALTHY    ● MAKE AHEAD    ● STAFF FAVORITE

FRESH RASPBERRY TART, P. 286

**GEORGIA PECAN PIE**

**BUTTERSCOTCH MOUSSE PIE**

## Georgia Pecan Pie

**ACTIVE: 30 MIN; TOTAL: 4 HR**

**MAKES ONE 9-INCH PIE ● ●**

PASTRY

- 1 cup all-purpose flour
- ½ teaspoon salt
- ½ teaspoon sugar
- 1 stick (4 ounces) cold unsalted butter, cut into ½-inch pieces
- ¼ cup ice water

FILLING

- 3 large eggs
- 1 cup sugar
- ¼ teaspoon salt
- ½ cup light corn syrup
- ½ cup dark corn syrup
- 4 tablespoons unsalted butter, melted
- 1 tablespoon pure vanilla extract
- 1¼ cups pecan halves (5 ounces)

**1. MAKE THE PASTRY:** In a food processor, pulse the flour with the salt and sugar. Add the butter and pulse several times until it's the size of small peas. Sprinkle on the ice water and pulse just until the crumbs are evenly moistened. Turn the pastry onto a work surface and gather it into a ball. Flatten into a disk, wrap in plastic and refrigerate for at least 30 minutes.

**2.** Preheat the oven to 350°. Position a rack in the bottom third of the oven. On a lightly floured surface, roll out the pastry to a 13-inch round. Ease the pastry into a 9-inch pie plate and trim the overhang to ½ inch. Fold the overhang under itself; crimp decoratively. Refrigerate until firm.

**3. MEANWHILE, MAKE THE FILLING:** In a medium bowl, whisk the eggs with the sugar and salt. Whisk in the light and dark corn syrups, the butter and the vanilla until well combined. Arrange the pecans in a decorative pattern in the pie shell. Carefully pour the filling over the nuts. Cover the rim of the pie with foil strips and bake the pie for 50 minutes, or until the crust is golden and the filling is puffed but still slightly jiggly. Remove the foil strips and let the pie cool completely before serving. —*Lee Hefter*

**MAKE AHEAD** The pie can be made 1 day ahead and kept at room temperature.

## Butterscotch Mousse Pie

**ACTIVE: 45 MIN; TOTAL: 3 HR, PLUS 3 HR CHILLING**

**MAKES ONE 9-INCH PIE ●**

FILLING

- ⅔ cup packed dark brown sugar
- 2 tablespoons cornstarch

**Pinch of salt**

- 1½ cups half-and-half

# pies +fruit desserts

14

2 large egg yolks

3 tablespoons unsalted butter, cut into tablespoons

2 teaspoons pure vanilla extract

CRUST

Fine dry bread crumbs, for dusting

4 large eggs, separated

½ cup packed dark brown sugar

2 tablespoons all-purpose flour

1 teaspoon pure vanilla extract

Pinch of salt

TOPPING

1 cup heavy cream

1½ tablespoons confectioners' sugar

1 teaspoon pure vanilla extract

Cinnamon, for sprinkling

**1. MAKE THE FILLING:** In a medium bowl, whisk the brown sugar with the cornstarch, salt and ½ cup of the half-and-half. Strain the half-and-half mixture through a fine sieve into a medium saucepan using a rubber spatula to press out any lumps of sugar. Whisk in the remaining 1 cup of half-and-half and the egg yolks. Cook the half-and-half mixture over moderate heat, stirring constantly with a heatproof rubber spatula, until it is thick and bubbling, about 7 minutes. Off the heat, whisk in the butter and vanilla. Scrape the butterscotch pudding into a bowl and press a piece of plastic wrap directly onto the surface. Refrigerate until chilled, at least 3 hours or overnight.

**2. MEANWHILE, MAKE THE CRUST:** Preheat the oven to 350°. Butter a 9-inch glass pie plate and dust it with bread crumbs, tapping out any excess. In a medium bowl, using an electric mixer, beat the yolks at high speed until they are thick and pale yellow, about 3 minutes. At medium speed, gradually beat in 6 tablespoons of the brown sugar, then beat at high speed until the mixture is very thick, about 5 minutes longer. Beat in the flour and vanilla.

**3.** In a large bowl, using clean beaters, beat the egg whites with the salt until soft peaks form. Sprinkle in the remaining 2 tablespoons of brown sugar and beat at high speed until the whites are stiff and glossy, about 2 minutes. Using a rubber spatula, gently fold one-fourth of the egg whites into the yolk mixture, then fold the mixture into the remaining whites until no streaks remain. Spread the mixture in the bread crumb–dusted pie plate and smooth the top. Bake for about 20 minutes, or until the soufflé has risen and then fallen slightly and is golden and springy to the touch. Turn off the oven; leave the crust in for 5 minutes. Transfer the crust to a rack to cool completely, about 30 minutes.

**4.** Fill the baked crust with the pudding. Refrigerate the pie for at least 3 hours or overnight.

**5. MAKE THE TOPPING:** Just before serving, in a bowl, beat the heavy cream with the confectioners' sugar and vanilla extract until firm. Spoon the whipped cream over the pie and dust with cinnamon. Cut into wedges and serve.

—*Greg Patent*

**MAKE AHEAD** The recipe can be prepared through Step 4 and refrigerated overnight.

## Sweet Potato Chiffon Pie

**TOTAL: 1 HR 30 MIN, PLUS 8 HR CHILLING**

**MAKES ONE 9-INCH PIE ●**

CRUST

18 graham crackers (1 packet)

¼ cup granulated sugar

½ teaspoon cinnamon

4 tablespoons unsalted butter, melted

FILLING

2 pounds sweet potatoes

1 envelope unflavored gelatin

¼ cup water

½ cup half-and-half

3 large eggs, separated

½ cup plus 2 tablespoons granulated sugar

2½ teaspoons pure vanilla extract

¾ teaspoon pumpkin pie spice

½ teaspoon salt

1 cup heavy cream

1½ tablespoons confectioners' sugar

Cinnamon, for dusting

**1. MAKE THE CRUST:** Preheat the oven to 350°. In a food processor, pulse the graham crackers with the granulated sugar and cinnamon until finely ground. Add the butter and pulse until the crumbs are evenly moistened. Press the graham cracker crumbs into the bottom and up the side of a lightly buttered 9-inch glass pie plate. Bake for 10 minutes, until the crust is lightly browned. Transfer the crust to a rack to cool completely. Leave the oven on.

**2. MEANWHILE, MAKE THE FILLING:** Poke the sweet potatoes all over with a fork and microwave at high power for about 5 minutes, until just barely tender. Transfer the potatoes to the oven and bake for about 10 minutes, until they are tender; let cool. Scoop the flesh into a food processor and puree until smooth.

**3.** In a small bowl, sprinkle the gelatin over the ¼ cup of water and let stand until softened. In a medium saucepan, heat the half-and-half just until small bubbles appear around the edge; cover and keep warm.

**4.** Meanwhile, in a medium heatproof bowl, using an electric mixer, beat the egg yolks at high speed until thick, about 3 minutes. Add ¼ cup of the granulated sugar and beat until the mixture is very thick, about 5 minutes. At low speed, gradually beat in the warm half-and-half. Fill the now-empty saucepan with 1 inch of water and bring to a simmer. Set the bowl with the yolks in it over the simmering water and cook, stirring constantly,

**LATTICE-TOPPED APPLE PIE**

until the mixture is thickened and an instant-read thermometer inserted in the yolks registers 170°, about 9 minutes. Add the softened gelatin to the custard and cook for 1 minute, stirring until dissolved. Remove the bowl from the pan. Stir in the pureed sweet potatoes, 2 teaspoons of the vanilla, the pumpkin pie spice and the salt.

**5.** Put the egg whites and the remaining ¼ cup plus 2 tablespoons of granulated sugar in a medium heatproof bowl. Set the bowl over the simmering water and cook, stirring, until an instant-read thermometer inserted in the whites registers 160°. Remove the bowl from the pan and, using clean beaters, beat the egg whites at high speed until stiff and glossy. Using a large rubber spatula, gently fold the egg whites into the custard until no streaks remain. Pour as much of the custard into the pie crust as will fit (there will be some left over) and refrigerate until the top is just set, about 15 minutes. Spoon the remaining custard on top and refrigerate the pie until very cold and firm, at least 8 hours.

**6.** In a medium bowl, using an electric mixer, beat the heavy cream with the confectioners' sugar and the remaining ½ teaspoon of vanilla at medium-high speed until firm. Spoon the whipped cream over the pie, dust with cinnamon and serve. —*Greg Patent*

**MAKE AHEAD** The sweet potato pie can be prepared through Step 5 and refrigerated, covered, for up to 2 days.

## Lattice-Topped Apple Pie

**ACTIVE: 1 HR; TOTAL: 3 HR**

**MAKES ONE 9-INCH PIE** ●

It's nice to use an assortment of slightly tart apples in this dense, fruit-packed pie. Some varieties to look for are Greening, Idared, Macoun, Cortland, Winesap, Braeburn, Jonamac, Granny Smith and Northern Spy.

**PASTRY**

1¼ **cups all-purpose flour, plus more for rolling**

⅓ **cup cake flour**

2 **tablespoons sugar**

¼ **teaspoon salt**

4 **ounces cream cheese, chilled**

1 **stick (4 ounces) unsalted butter, cut into ½-inch pieces**

1 **tablespoon ice water**

1 **large egg yolk**

1 **teaspoon cider vinegar**

**FILLING**

4 **pounds large apples (about 8)— peeled, cored and cut into eighths**

**Finely grated zest and juice of 1 lemon**

¾ **cup sugar, plus more for sprinkling**

¾ **teaspoon cinnamon**

¼ **teaspoon salt**

**Pinch of ground mace**

1 **stick (4 ounces) unsalted butter**

½ **cup apple cider**

**1. MAKE THE PASTRY:** In a large bowl, stir the all-purpose flour with the cake flour, sugar and salt. Add the cream cheese and use your fingertips to break up the cheese into the mixture until it resembles coarse meal. Cut in the butter with a pastry blender or 2 knives until pea-size clumps form.

**2.** In a small bowl, mix the ice water with the yolk and cider vinegar. Gradually add the ice water mixture to the flour mixture, stirring with a fork. Turn the pastry out onto a lightly floured surface and press it into a 10-inch log. Starting at the far end of the log, use the heel of your hand to quickly smear the pastry away from you, a little bit at a time. Use a pastry scraper to gather up the pastry and repeat the smearing process one more time. Gather the pastry together. Cut off one-third of the pastry and pat each piece into a disk. Wrap each disk in plastic and refrigerate for at least 30 minutes or up to 2 days.

**3. MEANWHILE, MAKE THE FILLING:** In a large bowl, toss the apples with the lemon zest and juice, ¾ cup sugar, cinnamon, salt and mace. In 2 large skillets, melt the butter. Add the apples and any accumulated juices and spread them in each skillet in a single layer. Cook the apples over moderate heat for 5 minutes, stirring occasionally, until lightly browned in spots. Add ¼ cup of the apple cider to each skillet, cover and cook, shaking the pans occasionally, until the apples are tender, about 5 minutes. Remove the lids and let the apples cool. If the juices are not thick and syrupy, simmer uncovered for 2 to 3 minutes longer. Let cool completely.

**4.** On a lightly floured surface, roll out the large pastry disk to a 12-inch round. Ease the pastry into a 9-inch glass pie plate. Trim the overhang to ½ inch and refrigerate. Roll out the smaller pastry disk to a rough 12-by-8-inch rectangle; trim the edges. Using a pastry or pizza cutter and a ruler as a guide, cut eight 12-by-1-inch strips. Line a baking sheet with parchment or wax paper. Weave the strips into a lattice on the baking sheet and brush the lattice with water. Sprinkle with sugar and freeze just until firm, about 10 minutes.

**5.** Preheat the oven to 375°. Fill the pie shell with the cooled apples and their juices and flatten them slightly with a spatula. Brush the rim of the pie shell with water and slide the lattice on top. Press the edges together to seal. Trim any overhanging lattice. Fold the rim over onto itself and crimp decoratively. Bake the pie for about 1 hour, until the crust is golden all over and the filling is bubbling. Cover the rim with strips of foil if it becomes too brown. Transfer the pie to a rack and let cool. —*Greg Patent*

**MAKE AHEAD** The pie can be made 1 day ahead and kept at room temperature. Rewarm before serving.

# pies + fruit desserts

## Pumpkin Meringue Puff Pie

ACTIVE: 30 MIN; TOTAL: 4 HR, PLUS
4 HR COOLING

MAKES ONE 9-INCH PIE ●

To keep the crust crunchy, pour in the filling while the pastry is piping hot. Then, as soon as the pie comes out of the oven, top it with the fluffy meringue; this will keep the meringue airy.

PASTRY

1¼ cups all-purpose flour
1 teaspoon granulated sugar
1 teaspoon salt
1 stick (4 ounces) unsalted butter, cut into ½-inch pieces and chilled
¼ cup ice water

FILLING

One 15-ounce can solid-pack pumpkin (about 2 cups)
¾ cup granulated sugar
1 teaspoon cinnamon
1 teaspoon ground ginger
⅛ teaspoon freshly grated nutmeg
⅛ teaspoon salt
4 large eggs
1⅓ cups heavy cream
1 teaspoon pure vanilla extract

MERINGUE

4 large egg whites, at room temperature
Pinch of cream of tartar
½ cup superfine sugar
1 teaspoon pure vanilla extract
Sugared Maple Leaves (see Note)

**1.** MAKE THE PASTRY: In a food processor, pulse the flour, granulated sugar and salt. Add the butter and pulse until it resembles small peas. Sprinkle the water over the pastry and pulse until moist crumbs form. Turn the pastry out onto a work surface; knead it with the heel of your hand 2 or 3 times. Flatten into a disk, wrap in plastic and refrigerate until chilled, at least 30 minutes. Let stand at room temperature for 15 minutes before rolling out the pastry.

**2.** On a lightly floured surface, roll the pastry out to a 13-inch round. Transfer the pastry to a 9-inch glass pie plate. Trim the overhang to 1 inch, then fold it under and crimp it decoratively. Using a fork, prick the bottom several times. Freeze the pastry until firm, about 1 hour or for up to 3 days.

**3.** Preheat the oven to 425°. Line the pastry with parchment and fill with pie weights or dried beans. Bake in the lower third of the oven for 30 minutes, or until the rim is lightly browned and the bottom is just set. Remove the parchment and pie weights. Bake for 5 minutes longer, until cooked through and lightly browned. Cover the rim with foil if it begins to darken too much. Lower the oven to 350°.

**4.** MEANWHILE, MAKE THE FILLING: In a large bowl, whisk the pumpkin, granulated sugar, cinnamon, ginger, nutmeg and salt. Whisk in the eggs, 1 at a time. Whisk in the cream and vanilla.

**5.** Pour the filling into the hot crust. Cover the rim with foil. Bake for 45 minutes, or until the custard is firm around the rim and slightly jiggly in the center. Transfer the pie to a baking sheet. Leave the oven on.

**6.** MAKE THE MERINGUE: In a bowl, beat the egg whites at medium speed until frothy. Add the cream of tartar and beat until soft peaks form. Slowly beat in the superfine sugar. Add the vanilla. Increase the speed to medium-high and beat until stiff and glossy, about 2 minutes longer.

**7.** Scoop the meringue onto the warm pie, spreading and swirling it decoratively; be sure the meringue touches the crust all around. Bake the pie on the middle rack of the oven for 10 minutes, or until the meringue is lightly browned. Transfer the pie to a wire rack to cool completely, at least 4 hours. Decorate with Sugared Maple Leaves and serve.
—*Peggy Cullen*

NOTE To make Sugared Maple Leaves, prepare an extra batch of the pastry in Step 1. On a sugared work surface, roll out the pastry ⅛ inch thick, sprinkling generously with sugar as you roll. Stamp out leaf shapes. Bake on parchment-lined baking sheets for 10 minutes; let cool.
MAKE AHEAD The pie can be refrigerated, uncovered, overnight. Garnish with the leaf cookies just before serving.

## Frozen Chocolate-Chestnut Pie

ACTIVE: 45 MIN; TOTAL: 4 HR

MAKES ONE 9-INCH PIE ● ●

24 chocolate wafer cookies, crumbled
¼ cup toasted blanched hazelnuts
1 tablespoon sugar
4 tablespoons unsalted butter
5 ounces bittersweet chocolate, finely chopped (1 scant cup)
1 cup plus 2 tablespoons heavy cream
1 can (500 grams) sweetened chestnut puree with vanilla
Pinch of salt
½ teaspoon unflavored gelatin
1 tablespoon cold water

**1.** Preheat the oven to 350°. In a food processor, combine the chocolate cookie crumbs with the hazelnuts and sugar and pulse until fine crumbs form. Add the butter and process until incorporated. Press the nut-crumb mixture evenly over the bottom and up the side of a 9-inch glass pie plate. Bake the crust for 8 minutes, or until set. Using a flat-bottomed glass, lightly tamp down the crust and transfer it to a rack to cool.

**2.** Put ⅔ cup of the chocolate in a large bowl. Put the remaining chocolate in a small bowl. In a small saucepan, heat the cream until bubbles appear around the edge of the pan. Spoon 2 tablespoons of the hot cream into the small bowl of chocolate; stir in 2 tablespoons of the chestnut puree. Set the ganache aside.

PUMPKIN MERINGUE PUFF PIE TOPPED WITH SUGARED MAPLE LEAVES

# pies + fruit desserts

**3.** Pour the remaining 1 cup of hot cream into the large bowl to melt the chocolate. Whisk in ⅔ cup of the chestnut puree and the salt. Refrigerate the mousse mixture until very cold, about 2 hours.

**4.** Using an electric mixer, beat the mousse until soft peaks form. In a glass bowl, sprinkle the gelatin over the water and let soften. Microwave for 8 seconds on high to melt the gelatin. Beat the gelatin into the mousse. Stir the remaining plain chestnut puree and spread it in the cookie crust. Spread the mousse on top and freeze until firm.

**5.** Rewarm the ganache in the microwave for 10 seconds, then spread it over the frozen mousse. Freeze until just set. Refrigerate the pie for 10 minutes before cutting and serving. —*Grace Parisi*

**MAKE AHEAD** The pie can be wrapped in plastic and frozen for up to 1 week.

## Fresh Raspberry Tart

**ACTIVE: 1 HR; TOTAL: 3 HR 30 MIN**

**6 SERVINGS**

To make sure the pastry stays crisp and flaky, arrange the raspberries on top no more than 30 minutes before serving. The jam not only sets the berries in place, it also gives them a beautiful shine and intensifies their flavor.

**PUFF PASTRY**

- **3 cups chilled all-purpose flour, plus more for rolling**
- **½ teaspoon salt**
- **3 sticks (¾ pound) unsalted butter, thinly sliced and chilled**
- **¼ teaspoon fresh lemon juice**
- **About 1 cup cold water**

**TART**

- **1 large egg yolk mixed with 1 tablespoon water**
- **¼ cup plus 3 tablespoons seedless raspberry jam**
- **1½ pints fresh raspberries**
- **Vanilla ice cream, whipped cream or crème fraîche (optional), for serving**

**1.** MAKE THE PUFF PASTRY: In a chilled bowl, whisk the 3 cups of flour with the salt. Scatter the butter over the flour. Add the lemon juice and 1 cup of cold water and stir with a wooden spoon just until the flour is moistened; add 1 to 2 tablespoons more water if needed. The butter will still be very visible.

**2.** Gather up the dough and turn it out onto a floured surface. Spread it with the heel of your hand into a rough 8-by-12-inch rectangle. Brush any flour off the surface of the dough. Using a pastry scraper, fold the dough in thirds (as you would fold a letter) to make a rough 8-by-4-inch rectangle.

**3.** Lightly flour the dough and pound it with a rolling pin to flatten it slightly. Roll out the dough to an 8-by-20-inch rectangle. Brush off any excess flour. Using the pastry scraper, fold in the bottom end and the top end so they meet in the center without overlapping, then fold the rectangle in half where they meet; this is called a "double fold." Roll out the dough to an 8-by-20-inch rectangle 2 more times, flouring as necessary and doing a double fold each time. Wrap the dough in plastic and refrigerate it for 1 hour, or until well chilled.

**4.** MAKE THE TART: Cut the dough into 3 equal pieces. Wrap 2 pieces in plastic and refrigerate or freeze for later use. On a lightly floured surface, roll out the dough to an 8-by-18-inch rectangle a scant ⅛ inch thick. Transfer to a parchment-lined baking sheet and freeze for 5 minutes, or until firm. Use a ruler and a very sharp knife or pastry wheel to trim the edges of the dough, forming it into a neat 7½-by-17-inch rectangle.

# technique

**TIP** **MAKING A PUFF PASTRY SHELL**

**1. FOLD THE EDGES**
To create the sides for the tart shell, fold in the chilled dough neatly, then press it firmly to seal. The sides will puff up when baked, creating a rim to hold in the filling.

**2. TRIM THE FOLDS**
To ensure that the rim rises nicely, use a very sharp knife or pastry cutter and firm pressure to trim the edges slightly. If the layers twist as they're cut, the rim won't rise evenly.

**3. PRICK THE SHELL**
To prevent the bottom of the tart shell from rising, prick it all over with the tines of a fork. Check during baking, and if the bottom puffs up, press it down with the back of the fork.

**5.** Brush 2 inches all around the edges of the rectangle with water, then fold in 1¼ inches of the edge all around the tart (Figure 1). Press lightly to seal. Using the ruler and knife, trim the edges all around so the 2 layers of dough can be seen on all 4 sides (Figure 2). Using a fork, prick the bottom of the dough to prevent it from rising (Figure 3). Brush the rim with the egg wash and, using a knife, score it with shallow crosshatched lines for decoration. Freeze the tart shell for 1 hour.

**6.** Preheat the oven to 400°. Position a rack in the lower third of the oven. Bake until the tart shell is golden and the rim well risen, about 35 minutes; if the bottom puffs during baking, press it down with the back of a fork.

**7.** While the shell is still warm, spread ¼ cup of the raspberry jam over the bottom in an even layer. Set aside ¾ pint of the best-looking berries. Spread the remaining raspberries in the tart shell in an even layer and lightly crush them with a fork. Transfer the tart on the parchment paper to a rack to cool.

**8.** In a small saucepan, melt the remaining 3 tablespoons of raspberry jam. Spoon half of it over the crushed berries. Arrange the remaining whole raspberries in neat rows on top and carefully brush with the remaining melted jam. Let the tart cool, then cut into strips and serve with vanilla ice cream, whipped cream or crème fraîche. —*Jacques Pépin*
**MAKE AHEAD** The dough can be made through Step 5 and refrigerated for up to 2 days or frozen for up to 4 months.

## Lattice-Topped Blackberry Tart
**ACTIVE: 35 MIN; TOTAL: 4 HR 30 MIN**
**MAKES ONE 9-INCH TART ● ●**
Don't let a fear of weaving together the lattice top keep you from making this sugar-crusted summer tart. Simply lay the strips of pastry over one another in a crisscross pattern.

PASTRY
2 cups all-purpose flour
¼ cup granulated sugar
Pinch of salt
1½ sticks (6 ounces) cold unsalted butter, cut into ½-inch pieces
2 large egg yolks mixed with 3 tablespoons water

FILLING
5 cups blackberries (1½ pounds)
¾ cup granulated sugar
¼ cup all-purpose flour
2 tablespoons unsalted butter, cut into small pieces
1 large egg yolk mixed with 1 tablespoon water
2 tablespoons turbinado sugar

WHIPPED CRÈME FRAÎCHE
½ cup heavy cream
1 tablespoon granulated sugar
½ cup crème fraîche
¼ teaspoon pure vanilla extract

**1. MAKE THE PASTRY:** In a food processor, pulse the flour, granulated sugar and salt. Add the butter and pulse until the mixture resembles small peas. Sprinkle the egg yolk–water mixture on top and pulse until the pastry comes together in large clumps. Turn the pastry out onto a work surface, knead 2 or 3 times and pat into a disk. Wrap in plastic and refrigerate just until chilled. Let the pastry stand at room temperature for 10 minutes before rolling it out.

**2.** On a lightly floured work surface, roll out two-thirds of the pastry to an 11½-inch round. Roll the pastry around the rolling pin and transfer it to a 9-inch fluted tart pan 1 inch deep with a removable bottom. Press into the pan, folding in the overhanging dough to reinforce the sides. Trim the overhang and knead the scraps into the remaining dough.

**3.** On a floured work surface, roll out the remaining pastry to a 9½-inch round. Using a pastry wheel, cut the round into ¾-inch-wide strips.

**4. MAKE THE FILLING:** Preheat the oven to 350°. In a bowl, toss the blackberries, granulated sugar and flour; spoon the berries into the tart shell. Scatter the butter on top. Arrange the pastry strips over the berries in a lattice pattern, pressing the ends onto the pastry rim. Trim any excess pastry. Brush the lattice with the egg yolk mixture; sprinkle with the turbinado sugar.

**5.** Bake the tart on a sheet of foil or a baking sheet in the bottom third of the oven for 1 hour, or until the pastry is golden and the juices are bubbling. Transfer to a wire rack to cool for at least 3 hours.

**6. WHIP THE CRÈME FRAÎCHE:** In a small bowl, beat the cream and granulated sugar to soft peaks. Add the crème fraîche and vanilla and beat until firm peaks form. Cut the tart into wedges and serve with the whipped crème fraîche.
—*Jody Denton*
**MAKE AHEAD** The recipe can be prepared through Step 5 and stored overnight at room temperature.

## Lemon-Coconut Tart with Brown-Sugar Cream
**ACTIVE: 30 MIN; TOTAL: 4 HR**
**MAKES ONE 9-INCH TART ●**
Pastry chef Karen Barker recommends stirring the cream of coconut in the can before adding it to the filling.

CRUST
1⅓ cups crushed graham cracker crumbs (10 squares)
¼ cup plus 2 tablespoons sweetened shredded coconut
1½ tablespoons granulated sugar
6 tablespoons unsalted butter, melted

FILLING
4 large egg yolks
One 14-ounce can sweetened condensed milk
1½ teaspoons finely grated lemon zest

# pies + fruit desserts

1 teaspoon pure vanilla extract

¼ teaspoon cream of tartar

¼ teaspoon salt

½ cup fresh lemon juice

½ cup cream of coconut, such as
   Coco Lopez

TOPPING AND ACCOMPANIMENTS

⅔ cup sweetened shredded
   coconut

2 pints strawberries, hulled
   and sliced

¼ cup light brown sugar

1½ cups cold heavy cream

**1. MAKE THE CRUST:** Preheat the oven to 350°. Lightly butter a 9-inch glass pie plate. In a medium bowl, mix the graham cracker crumbs, coconut and granulated sugar with the butter until evenly moistened. Press the crumbs over the bottom and up the side of the pie plate in an even layer. Bake the crust in the center of the oven for 8 minutes, or until lightly golden and barely set.

**2. MAKE THE FILLING:** In a medium bowl, whisk the egg yolks with the condensed milk, lemon zest, vanilla, cream of tartar and salt. Slowly whisk in the lemon juice and cream of coconut until smooth. Pour the filling into the crust and bake the tart for 20 minutes, or until the filling is just set but still slightly jiggly in the center. Transfer the tart to a wire rack to cool, then refrigerate until well chilled, about 3 hours.

**3. MEANWHILE, MAKE THE TOPPING AND ACCOMPANIMENTS:** Spread ⅓ cup of the shredded coconut on a baking sheet and toast in the oven for about 3 minutes, or until golden. Transfer the toasted coconut to a plate and stir in the remaining ⅓ cup of coconut.

**4.** Just before serving, in a medium bowl, toss the strawberries with 2 tablespoons of the brown sugar and let stand until juicy, about 10 minutes. In a large bowl, whip the heavy cream with the remaining 2 tablespoons of brown sugar until firm.

Spread some of the brown-sugar cream over the tart and sprinkle the toasted coconut on top. Serve with the strawberries and the remaining brown-sugar cream. —*Karen Barker*

**MAKE AHEAD** The lemon-coconut tart can be prepared through Step 2 up to 3 days ahead.

## Prune Custard Tart

ACTIVE: 30 MIN; TOTAL: 4 HR

MAKES ONE 11-INCH TART ●

1 cup tap water

¾ cup plus 3 tablespoons
   granulated sugar

1 pound pitted prunes

1¼ cups all-purpose flour

Pinch of salt

1 stick (4 ounces) cold unsalted
   butter, cut into pieces

5 tablespoons ice water

2 cups milk

1 tablespoon cinnamon,
   plus more for dusting

4 large eggs

1 cup heavy cream

1 tablespoon confectioners'
   sugar

**1.** In a medium saucepan, combine the tap water with ¼ cup of the granulated sugar and bring to a boil. Stir to make sure all of the sugar has dissolved. Remove the pan from the heat, add the prunes and let stand until plumped, at least 4 hours or overnight. Drain the prunes, pressing out the liquid, then finely chop them.

**2.** In a food processor, pulse the flour and salt with 1 tablespoon of the granulated sugar. Add the butter and pulse just until it is the size of peas. Remove the lid from the food processor, evenly sprinkle the ice water over the dry ingredients and pulse just until the pastry is evenly moistened. Turn the pastry out onto a work surface and gather it into a ball. Flatten the pastry into a disk, wrap it in plastic and refrigerate for at least 30 minutes, or until firm.

**3.** Preheat the oven to 375°. On a floured surface, roll out the pastry to a 13-inch round. Transfer the pastry to an 11-inch fluted tart pan with a removable bottom. Trim the overhang and refrigerate until chilled, about 20 minutes.

**4.** Line the pastry with foil and fill it with pie weights or dried beans. Bake in the lower third of the oven for about 40 minutes, until the crust is set. Remove the foil and weights and bake for about 15 minutes longer, just until the crust is golden and cooked through. Transfer the baked crust to a rack to cool. Reduce the oven temperature to 325°.

**5.** In a small saucepan, combine the milk with the cinnamon and bring to a simmer, whisking constantly. In a medium bowl, whisk the eggs with the remaining ½ cup plus 2 tablespoons of granulated sugar. Gradually whisk in the warm cinnamon milk. Pour the custard into the crust and bake for 45 to 50 minutes, until just set. Transfer the tart pan to a rack to cool completely, then refrigerate for 2 hours, until completely chilled.

**6.** In a medium bowl, beat the heavy cream with the confectioners' sugar until firm peaks form. Spread the chopped prunes all over the top of the tart, then spoon the whipped cream on top. Dust lightly with cinnamon, cut the tart into wedges and serve. —*Gabriel Kreuther*

## Chocolate-Caramel Hazelnut Tart

ACTIVE: 1 HR; TOTAL: 2 HR 30 MIN

MAKES ONE 9-INCH TART ● ●

PASTRY

½ cup confectioners' sugar

5 tablespoons unsalted butter,
   softened

½ vanilla bean, seeds scraped

1 large egg yolk mixed with
   1 tablespoon water

¾ cup plus 2 tablespoons
   all-purpose flour

Pinch of salt

FILLING AND TOPPING

- 1 cup heavy cream
- ½ vanilla bean, split lengthwise, seeds scraped

Pinch of baking soda

- 1 cup granulated sugar
- 1 tablespoon light corn syrup
- 5 tablespoons unsalted butter
- 2 tablespoons water
- 1 cup blanched raw hazelnuts
- 5 ounces bittersweet chocolate, finely chopped (1 cup)

Sweetened whipped cream, for serving

**1. MAKE THE PASTRY:** In a food processor, pulse the confectioners' sugar with the butter and vanilla bean seeds until smooth. Add the egg yolk and water and process until blended. Add the flour and salt and pulse until the pastry just comes together. Pat the pastry into a disk, wrap in plastic and refrigerate until just firm enough to roll out, about 20 minutes.

**2.** Preheat the oven to 350°. Roll out the dough between 2 sheets of plastic wrap to an 11-inch round. Peel off the top sheet of plastic. Invert the dough over a 9-inch fluted tart pan with a removable bottom. Discard the plastic and fit the pastry into the pan. Trim the overhang to ½ inch, fold in to reinforce the sides and patch any holes. Prick the bottom of the tart shell with a fork and refrigerate until chilled, about 30 minutes.

**3.** Line the pastry shell with foil and fill with pie weights or dried beans. Bake for 25 minutes, or until the pastry is set and the edges are golden. Carefully remove the foil and weights. Cover the rim of the tart with foil strips and bake for about 5 minutes, or until the pastry is golden and cooked through. Transfer to a rack and let cool.

**4. MEANWHILE, MAKE THE FILLING AND TOPPING:** In a small saucepan, gently warm ¼ cup of the heavy cream with the vanilla bean seeds and baking soda. In a medium saucepan, cook ½ cup of the granulated sugar with the light corn syrup over moderate heat until a deep amber caramel forms, about 8 minutes. Remove the pan from the heat and stir in 4 tablespoons of the butter. Slowly stir in the vanilla cream in a thin stream. Cook the caramel over moderate heat until slightly thickened, about 3 minutes. Pour the hot caramel into the pastry shell and refrigerate until set, about 30 minutes.

**5.** In another medium saucepan, simmer the remaining ½ cup of sugar with the water over high heat, stirring just until the sugar dissolves, about 2 minutes. Add the hazelnuts and cook over moderate heat, stirring frequently, until the hazelnuts are toasted and caramelized, about 10 minutes. The sugar will get very hard and crystallized after about 5 minutes, then it will melt and caramelize and the nuts will toast. Reduce the heat if the caramel darkens before the nuts are toasted. Stir in the remaining 1 tablespoon of butter. Pour the caramelized nuts onto a sheet of parchment paper and let them cool completely. Transfer the nuts to a plastic bag and crush them lightly with a rolling pin.

**6.** In a small saucepan, heat the remaining ¾ cup of cream until bubbles appear around the edge. Remove the saucepan from the heat, add the chocolate and let stand (without stirring) until melted, about 5 minutes. Whisk the chocolate until smooth, then pour it over the caramel in the tart shell. Jiggle the pan to spread the chocolate in a smooth layer. Sprinkle the crushed, caramelized hazelnuts on top and refrigerate until set, about 15 minutes.

**7.** Remove the tart pan and transfer the tart to a serving plate. Cut the tart into wedges and serve with whipped cream. —*Dimitri Fayard*

**MAKE AHEAD** The finished tart can be refrigerated for up to 3 days.

## Maple-Pear Kuchen

**TOTAL: 1 HR**

**12 SERVINGS** ●

*Kuchen* is German for "cake." Here, a thin layer of tender, almond-flavored cake is the tasty base for pears poached in pure maple syrup.

- 3½ pounds ripe but firm Bartlett or Anjou pears—peeled, halved, cored and quartered lengthwise

Finely grated zest and fresh juice of 1 lemon

- 1 cup pure maple syrup
- 1⅓ cups all-purpose flour
- 1½ teaspoons baking powder
- ½ teaspoon salt
- 10 tablespoons (5 ounces) unsalted butter, 4 tablespoons melted
- ½ cup plus 2 tablespoons sugar
- ½ teaspoon pure almond extract
- 1 large egg
- ⅓ cup milk
- ½ cup dried sour cherries (3 ounces)
- ½ teaspoon freshly grated nutmeg

**1.** In a large, deep skillet, toss the pears with the lemon juice. Arrange them in a single layer, add the maple syrup and bring to a boil. Cover and cook over moderate heat until the pears are almost tender, 10 minutes. Turn the pears and cook,

# equipment

**NONSTICK ROLLING PIN** | **TIP**

A silicone coating keeps dough from sticking to the rolling pin; contoured handles make for a comfortable grip ($50; 800-243-0852 or surlatable.com).

# technique

These tips are from Greg Patent, author of *Baking in America*.

**MEASURE DRY INGREDIENTS** over a sheet of wax paper to simplify cleanup. When you're finished, fold the paper and pour the spilled ingredient back into its original container.

**USE A GLASS PIE PLATE** instead of an aluminum one; it will allow you to see how the bottom of the crust is browning while it's baking.

**SAVE UNUSED SHOWER CAPS** from hotel rooms. They are perfect for covering bowls of rising dough.

**CHOOSE WHIPPING CREAM THAT'S PASTEURIZED,** not ultrapasteurized, which is more commonly found in stores but takes significantly longer to whip.

**BUY PRECUT PARCHMENT PAPER** in half sheets and round sheets from places like The Baker's Catalogue to help save time ($4 for 24 round sheets, $15 for 100 half sheets; 800-827-6836 or bakerscatalogue.com).

**STAND A PASTRY BAG UPRIGHT** in a large measuring cup or heavy drinking glass to make filling the bag easier.

**USE AN OFFSET SPATULA** with a long blade to help spread icing in an even layer.

**TAP DOUGH FIRMLY** with a rolling pin if it's too hard and cold to work with after refrigeration.

**KEEP TWO PASTRY SCRAPERS** on hand. Using them together makes it easier to lift and move large sheet cakes and pieces of dough.

**BAKE PIES ON THE BOTTOM RACK** of the oven for the first 15 minutes to ensure a crisp bottom crust.

uncovered, until tender but not mushy, about 10 minutes longer, depending on the ripeness of the pears. Using a slotted spoon, transfer the pears to a work surface and cut each piece in half lengthwise. Boil the maple glaze until reduced to ¾ cup, 2 to 3 minutes; let cool.

**2.** Preheat the oven to 400° and butter a 9-by-13-inch baking pan. On a sheet of wax paper, sift the flour with the baking powder and salt. In a medium bowl, using an electric mixer, beat the 6 tablespoons of solid butter until creamy. Add ¼ cup plus 2 tablespoons of the sugar and beat at medium speed until light and fluffy, 3 minutes. Beat in the almond extract and lemon zest. Beat in the egg until blended, then add the flour mixture in 3 batches, alternating with the milk.

**3.** Drop tablespoonfuls of the batter evenly over the bottom of the baking pan. Using an offset spatula, spread the batter in a thin, even layer. Arrange the pears on the batter in 3 lengthwise rows as close together as possible. Scatter the dried sour cherries over the pears. Brush the fruit with the 4 tablespoons of melted butter. In a small bowl, combine the nutmeg with the remaining ¼ cup of sugar. Sprinkle the sugar over the fruit and bake for 45 minutes, until the edges of the kuchen are browned and the pears are golden. Transfer the pan to a rack to cool. Cut the kuchen into squares, drizzle with the maple glaze and serve.
—*Greg Patent*

**MAKE AHEAD** The kuchen can be stored at room temperature for up to 2 days.

## Caramel Lady Apples
**TOTAL: 1 HR 30 MIN**
**MAKES 2 DOZEN CARAMEL APPLES** ●

Lady apples are tiny—only about 2 inches in diameter. Choose apples with sturdy stems to make dipping easier, or use clean twigs or wooden skewers as handles.

24   lady apples (about 3 pounds)
1   cup heavy cream
1¼   cups sugar
2   tablespoons water
¼   teaspoon fresh lemon juice
¾   cup light corn syrup
¼   teaspoon salt
4   tablespoons unsalted butter, cut into tablespoons
1   teaspoon pure vanilla extract

**1.** Line a large baking sheet with parchment paper or a silicone mat. If the lady-apple stems aren't sturdy, insert wooden skewers or twigs into the tops.

**2.** In a small saucepan, bring the cream just to a boil. Remove from the heat. In a large saucepan, combine ½ cup of the sugar with the water and lemon juice. Using a wet pastry brush, wash down the side of the saucepan. Bring to a simmer over moderate heat without stirring and cook until the syrup begins to color around the edge, about 4 minutes. Swirl the pan, then simmer until the caramel turns a light amber color, 2 to 3 minutes longer. Off the heat, using a long-handled wooden spoon, stir in the hot cream.

**3.** Return the caramel to the heat and stir in the corn syrup, salt and the remaining ¾ cup sugar. Add the butter and bring to a boil over moderately high heat. Wash down the side of the saucepan with a wet pastry brush. Insert a candy thermometer in the caramel and cook over moderate heat until the thermometer registers 242°, 6 to 7 minutes. Remove from the heat. Stir in the vanilla. Let the caramel stand for 5 minutes to cool slightly.

**4.** Working quickly, dip the apples into the caramel, letting any excess drip back into the pan. Set the apples on the prepared baking sheet. If the caramel in the saucepan becomes too thick, rewarm it over low heat. Let the caramel apples cool for 1 hour before serving. —*Peggy Cullen*
**MAKE AHEAD** The caramel apples can be made up to 4 hours ahead.

### Apple Crisp with Sweet Ginger and Macadamia Nuts

**ACTIVE: 30 MIN; TOTAL: 2 HR**

**8 SERVINGS** ● ●

To make chopping macadamia nuts easier, put them in a resealable plastic bag and break them up using a rolling pin.

- 1¼ cups all-purpose flour
- ½ cup packed dark brown sugar
- 1 teaspoon ground ginger
- 1 teaspoon cinnamon
- Salt
- 1 stick (4 ounces) cold unsalted butter, cut into 8 pieces
- ¾ cup macadamia nuts, finely chopped
- 3½ pounds large Granny Smith apples (about 7)—peeled, cored and thinly sliced
- ⅓ cup finely chopped crystallized ginger (2 ounces)
- ½ cup granulated sugar
- Finely grated zest and juice of 1 lime
- Vanilla ice cream, for serving

**1.** Preheat the oven to 400° and position a rack in the lower third. In a food processor, pulse the flour with the dark brown sugar, ground ginger, cinnamon and ¼ teaspoon of salt. Add the butter to the dry ingredients and pulse until the butter is the size of small peas. Add the chopped macadamia nuts and pulse twice, just until combined.

**2.** In a large bowl, toss the apples with the crystallized ginger, granulated sugar, lime zest, lime juice and a pinch of salt. Spread the apples in a shallow 3-quart glass or ceramic baking dish. Sprinkle the topping over the apples and press gently. Bake the crisp for 50 minutes, until the juices are bubbling and the top is golden. Let cool for at least 30 minutes before serving with vanilla ice cream. —*Greg Patent*

**MAKE AHEAD** The baked apple crisp can be refrigerated overnight. Rewarm in the oven before serving.

### Apple Skillet Cake

**TOTAL: 30 MIN**

**4 SERVINGS** ●

- 3 tablespoons unsalted butter
- 2 medium McIntosh apples— peeled, cored and cut into 10 wedges each
- 3 tablespoons granulated sugar
- 1 cup cottage cheese
- ¾ cup sour cream
- ¾ cup all-purpose flour
- 3 large eggs
- 1 teaspoon pure vanilla extract
- 1 tablespoon confectioners' sugar, for dusting
- Pure maple syrup, for serving (optional)

**1.** In a 10-inch ovenproof nonstick skillet, melt the butter over moderate heat. Arrange the apple wedges in a single layer in the skillet and sprinkle them with 1 tablespoon of the granulated sugar. Cook over moderate heat until the apple wedges are softened and lightly colored, about 8 minutes. Remove the skillet from the heat.

**2.** Preheat the broiler. Place a rack in the oven about 8 inches from the heat. In a food processor, combine the remaining 2 tablespoons of granulated sugar with the cottage cheese, sour cream, flour, eggs and vanilla. Process for 3 seconds. Scrape down the bowl and process the batter for 3 seconds more.

**3.** Pour the batter directly over the apples in the skillet. Cover the skillet with a lid or aluminum foil and cook over moderate heat until the edge of the cake is set and the center begins to bubble, about 7 minutes. Uncover and broil the cake, turning the skillet as necessary for even browning, about 4 minutes. Dust the top of the cake with the confectioners' sugar and cut it into wedges. Serve the apple cake warm directly from the skillet, with maple syrup if desired. —*Jacques Pépin*

### Phyllo Apple-Plum Strudel

**ACTIVE: 25 MIN; TOTAL: 1 HR**

**4 SERVINGS**

Nectarines make a delicious substitute for the plums here.

- 1 stick (4 ounces) unsalted butter, 6 tablespoons melted
- 1 Gala apple—peeled, cored and cut into ¼-inch wedges
- 2 large red plums, cut into ¼-inch wedges
- 2 tablespoons raisins
- 2 tablespoons light brown sugar
- ½ teaspoon cinnamon
- Pinch of allspice
- Pinch of ground cloves
- 1 tablespoon dark rum
- 8 sheets of phyllo dough
- Vanilla ice cream, for serving

**1.** Preheat the oven to 375°. In a large skillet, melt 1 tablespoon of the solid butter. Add the apple wedges and cook over moderate heat, stirring frequently, until the apples are golden, about 3 minutes. Scrape the apples into a large bowl.

**2.** Add the remaining 1 tablespoon of solid butter to the skillet. Add the plums and cook over moderate heat, stirring, until just tender, about 3 minutes. Pour off and discard any juices.

**3.** Return the apples to the skillet. Add the raisins, brown sugar, cinnamon, allspice and cloves; stir over moderately high heat to melt the sugar. Add the rum, stir and return to the bowl; let cool.

**4.** Place a sheet of phyllo dough on a work surface with a long edge in front of you and brush the phyllo with some of the melted butter. Continue layering with the remaining 7 sheets of phyllo dough, buttering between each sheet. Spoon the apple-plum filling in a strip that is parallel to and about 2 inches from the long edge of the stacked phyllo sheets. Lift the long edge up and over the fruit filling, then roll up the strudel, pushing in the sides as you go.

PEACH AND BERRY CROUSTADES

**5.** Transfer the apple-plum strudel, seam side down, to a medium, rimmed baking sheet and brush it with the remaining melted butter. Using a serrated knife, make 4 diagonal cuts in the top to allow steam to escape as the strudel bakes. Bake until the phyllo is golden brown and the filling is starting to bubble, about 35 minutes. Let the strudel cool slightly, then slice and serve with vanilla ice cream. —*Bob Isaacson*

**MAKE AHEAD** The apple-plum filling can be refrigerated overnight.

### Peach and Berry Croustades

**ACTIVE: 1 HR; TOTAL: 3 HR**

**MAKES 6 CROUSTADES** ● ●

CRUST

    2  sticks (½ pound) cold unsalted
       butter, cut into tablespoons
1¾  cups all-purpose flour
  ½  teaspoon salt
  ¼  cup cold water

FILLING

Vegetable oil cooking spray
    4  large peaches—halved, pitted
       and sliced ¼ inch thick
  ½  cup plus 3 tablespoons
       granulated sugar
    2  tablespoons cornstarch
    1  teaspoon cinnamon
Salt
  ½  cup raspberries
  ½  cup blackberries
All-purpose flour, for dusting
    4  tablespoons unsalted butter,
       cut into 6 pieces
    1  large egg, lightly beaten
Confectioners' sugar, for dusting

**1. MAKE THE CRUST:** In a food processor, pulse the cold butter with the flour and salt until it resembles coarse meal. Add the water and pulse just until a dough forms. Gather the dough, divide it into 6 pieces and flatten each piece into a disk. Wrap the dough in plastic and refrigerate for 30 minutes.

**2. MAKE THE FILLING:** Preheat the oven to 375°. Spray 2 baking sheets with cooking spray. In a medium bowl, toss the peaches with ½ cup of the granulated sugar, the cornstarch and the cinnamon; add a pinch of salt. Fold in the berries.

**3.** On a lightly floured work surface, roll out each disk of dough to a 6-inch round about ⅛ inch thick. Transfer 3 to each baking sheet. Spread the fruit on the rounds and fold 1 inch of dough over the fruit to form a rim. Top the fruit with a piece of butter; refrigerate for 30 minutes.

**4.** Brush the crusts with the beaten egg and sprinkle with the remaining 3 tablespoons of granulated sugar. Bake the croustades for about 50 minutes, or until the crusts are golden. Rotate the baking sheets halfway through baking. Transfer to racks to cool. Dust with confectioners' sugar and serve. —*Shelly Register*

**MAKE AHEAD** The croustades can be kept at room temperature overnight.

**SERVE WITH** Whipped cream.

### Ricotta and Prosecco-Poached Pear Crostatas

**ACTIVE: 45 MIN; TOTAL: 4 HR**

**MAKES TWO 10-INCH CROSTATAS** ●

    2  cups sugar
    1  bottle (750 ml) Prosecco or other
       sparkling white wine
1½  cups water
    1  vanilla bean, split, seeds scraped
Four 1-inch strips of lemon zest
  ½  of a 3-inch cinnamon stick
    3  whole cloves
    4  large, firm, ripe Bartlett pears—
       peeled, halved and cored
    1  pound ricotta cheese
    2  large egg yolks
    1  teaspoon salt
  ½  teaspoon freshly ground pepper
    1  tablespoon whole milk
All-purpose flour, for rolling out pastry
Crème Fraîche Pastry (recipe follows)
Honey, for drizzling

**1.** In a large saucepan, combine the sugar, Prosecco, water, vanilla bean and seeds, lemon zest, cinnamon stick half and cloves and bring to a boil. Add the pears and cover with a small lid to keep the pears submerged. Reduce the heat to moderate and simmer until the pears are tender but not mushy, about 20 minutes. Using a slotted spoon, transfer the pears to a cutting board. Let cool, then thinly slice them lengthwise. Reserve the poaching liquid in the refrigerator for poaching other fruit.

**2.** In a medium bowl, using a fork, blend the ricotta with 1 of the egg yolks and the salt and pepper. In another bowl, beat the remaining egg yolk with the milk.

**3.** On a well-floured work surface, roll out 1 disk of Crème Fraîche Pastry to a 13-inch round. Brush off any excess flour and transfer the round to a baking sheet lined with parchment paper.

**4.** Spread half of the ricotta mixture on the pastry, leaving a 2-inch border all around. Arrange half of the pear slices over the ricotta filling in a slightly overlapping circular pattern. Fold the edges of the pastry over the pears, crimping and pressing as you go; brush the pastry rim with half of the egg wash. Repeat with the remaining pastry, ricotta, pears and egg wash. Freeze the crostatas until firm, about 1 hour.

**5.** Preheat the oven to 375°. Bake the pear crostatas on the middle and lower racks of the oven for 40 minutes, or until deeply golden and cooked through. Shift the baking sheets from top to bottom and front to back halfway through baking for even browning. Let cool. Drizzle the crostatas with honey, cut into wedges and serve at room temperature.
—*Tommy Habetz and Naomi Hebberoy*

**MAKE AHEAD** The crostatas can be prepared through Step 3 and kept frozen, wrapped well, for up to 2 weeks. Bake directly from the freezer.

● **FAST**   ● **HEALTHY**   ● **MAKE AHEAD**   ● **STAFF FAVORITE**

# pies + fruit desserts

**CRÈME FRAÎCHE PASTRY**
ACTIVE: 10 MIN; TOTAL: 40 MIN
MAKES ENOUGH PASTRY FOR
TWO 10-INCH CROSTATAS ●

- 2 cups all-purpose flour
- 2 teaspoons kosher salt
- 2 teaspoons baking powder
- 2 sticks (½ pound) unsalted butter, cut into tablespoons
- 1 cup crème fraîche

1. In a food processor, combine the flour, salt and baking powder and pulse to blend. Add the butter and pulse until it is in ½-inch chunks. Add the crème fraîche and pulse just until evenly moistened.
2. Transfer the soft, crumbly mixture to a sheet of plastic wrap. Press the crumbs together, pat into 2 disks, wrap them and refrigerate until chilled. —*T.H. and N.H.*
**MAKE AHEAD** The pastry can be refrigerated for 1 day or frozen for up to 1 month.

## Eli's Golden Apple Turnovers
ACTIVE: 45 MIN; TOTAL: 1 HR 30 MIN
MAKES 12 TURNOVERS ●

- 1½ cups granulated sugar
- ½ cup water
- 1 stick (4 ounces) unsalted butter, softened
- 1 tablespoon fresh lemon juice
- 6 Gala apples—peeled, cored and quartered
- Two 1-pound sheets of all-butter puff pastry, thawed if frozen
- Coarse sugar, for sprinkling

1. In a very large, deep skillet, cook the granulated sugar, water, butter and lemon juice over high heat until a pale amber caramel forms, 15 minutes. Add the apples and cook over moderate heat, turning occasionally, until very soft but not falling apart, 30 minutes. Transfer the apples to a plate and let cool. Pour the caramel into a small bowl; let cool.
2. Preheat the oven to 375°. Line 2 baking sheets with parchment paper. On a lightly floured surface, roll out each sheet of puff pastry to a 10-by-15-inch rectangle. Cut each sheet into six 5-inch squares. For each turnover, lightly brush the edge of a pastry square with water. Place 2 cooled apple quarters in the middle and spoon a scant 1 tablespoon of the caramel on top. Fold the pastry over to form triangles and press the edges to seal. Transfer to the baking sheets.
3. Brush the turnovers with water and sprinkle with coarse sugar. Place the baking sheets in the oven and lower the temperature to 325°. Bake the turnovers for about 35 minutes, until golden and puffed. Let cool, then serve. —*Eli Zabar*
**MAKE AHEAD** The turnovers can be stored in an airtight container for 1 day.

## Blackberry Cobbler
ACTIVE: 45 MIN; TOTAL: 2 HR 15 MIN
8 SERVINGS ●
PASTRY

- 1½ cups all-purpose flour
- ½ teaspoon sugar
- ½ teaspoon salt
- 4 tablespoons cold solid vegetable shortening
- 4 tablespoons cold unsalted butter, cut into ½-inch pieces
- ¼ cup ice water

FILLING

- Six ½-pint baskets large blackberries
- 1¼ cups sugar
- 1 tablespoon fresh lemon juice
- ½ teaspoon freshly grated nutmeg
- ⅓ cup all-purpose flour
- 4 tablespoons unsalted butter, melted

1. **MAKE THE PASTRY:** In a food processor, pulse the flour, sugar and salt until combined. Add the vegetable shortening and pulse 5 or 6 times, until the mixture resembles small peas. Add the cold butter and pulse 5 or 6 times, until the mixture resembles larger peas. Add the ice water and pulse 5 or 6 times, just until the pastry is evenly moistened.
2. Transfer the pastry to a lightly floured surface and knead just until it comes together. Flatten the pastry into a 6-inch disk, wrap in plastic and refrigerate until firm, at least 30 minutes.
3. **MEANWHILE, MAKE THE FILLING:** Preheat the oven to 375°. In a very large bowl, toss the blackberries with the sugar, lemon juice, nutmeg and flour. Let stand at room temperature, stirring gently once or twice, until slightly juicy, about 15 minutes. Fold in the melted butter. Transfer the fruit to a round 2-quart glass or ceramic baking dish.
4. **ASSEMBLE THE COBBLER:** On a lightly floured surface, roll the pastry out to a ¼-inch thickness that is slightly larger than the baking dish. Drape the pastry over the berries. Trim the overhang to ½ inch and fold it under itself, pressing the pastry onto the rim of the dish. Crimp the edge decoratively and make 3 slashes in the center of the pastry.
5. Bake the cobbler for 1 hour, or until the filling is bubbling and the pastry is golden. Cover the edges with foil if the crust browns too quickly. Let cool for about 20 minutes before serving.
—*Ben Hussman*
**MAKE AHEAD** The pastry can be frozen for up to 1 month. The cobbler can be made early in the day and kept at room temperature.
**SERVE WITH** Vanilla ice cream.

## Apple and Mixed Berry Crumble
ACTIVE: 25 MIN; TOTAL: 1 HR 30 MIN
MAKES TWO 9-INCH CRUMBLES

- 2 Granny Smith apples—peeled, cored, halved lengthwise and sliced paper-thin
- ¼ cup fresh lemon juice
- 2 tablespoons granulated sugar
- ¾ teaspoon cinnamon
- 1 pint blueberries (3 cups)
- 1 pint raspberries (3 cups)
- 2 cups quick-cooking oats

2 cups lightly packed light
brown sugar

1 cup all-purpose flour

1 teaspoon finely grated fresh ginger

½ teaspoon salt

2 sticks plus 6 tablespoons
(11 ounces) unsalted butter,
cut into small pieces

Heavy cream, for serving

**1.** Preheat the oven to 375°. In a medium bowl, toss the apples with the lemon juice, granulated sugar and ¼ teaspoon of the cinnamon. Spread the apples in two 9-inch glass pie plates and top with the blueberries and raspberries.

**2.** In another medium bowl, toss the oats with the light brown sugar, flour, ginger, salt and the remaining ½ teaspoon of cinnamon. Using your fingers, mix in the butter until crumbly.

**3.** Spread the topping over the berries. Set the pie plates on a baking sheet and bake for 35 minutes, or until the berries are bubbling and the topping is golden brown. Transfer to a wire rack and let cool for 30 minutes. Serve the apple and berry crumbles with heavy cream.
—*Alexandra and Eliot Angle*

### Gramma's Buttermilk Biscuits with Berries and Ice Cream

ACTIVE: 25 MIN; TOTAL: 1 HR 30 MIN

8 SERVINGS

2 cups all-purpose flour

1 tablespoon baking powder

¼ teaspoon baking soda

½ teaspoon salt

3 tablespoons granulated sugar

1 stick (4 ounces) cold unsalted
butter, cut into ½-inch pieces

1 cup cold buttermilk, plus more
for brushing

1 tablespoon coarse sugar

2 pints strawberries (1 pound),
thickly sliced

½ pint raspberries

Vanilla ice cream, for serving

**BLACKBERRY COBBLER**

**GRAMMA'S BISCUITS WITH BERRIES AND ICE CREAM**

# pies + fruit desserts

**1.** Preheat the oven to 400°. In a large bowl, whisk the flour with the baking powder, baking soda, salt and 1 tablespoon of the granulated sugar. Using 2 knives or a pastry blender, cut in the butter until it is the size of small peas. Make a well in the center and add the buttermilk. Using a wooden spoon, stir until a crumbly dough forms.

**2.** Transfer the dough to a lightly floured surface and knead 2 or 3 times, just until evenly moistened. Pat the dough ½ inch thick. Using a 2¾-inch round biscuit cutter, stamp out as many rounds as close together as possible. Gather the scraps, pat flat and cut out 1 or 2 more biscuits.

**3.** Transfer the biscuits to a large baking sheet. Brush the tops lightly with buttermilk and sprinkle with the coarse sugar. Bake for 10 minutes. Reduce the heat to 350° and bake for 20 minutes longer, or until the biscuits are golden and cooked through. Let cool.

**4.** In a medium bowl, toss the berries with the remaining 2 tablespoons of granulated sugar and let stand for 5 minutes. Split the biscuits horizontally and transfer the bottom halves to plates. Top with scoops of ice cream and the berries. Replace the biscuit tops and serve right away. *—Daniel Orr*

### Strawberry-Rhubarb Galette

**ACTIVE: 30 MIN; TOTAL: 2 HR 10 MIN**

**6 SERVINGS** ● ●

Tender-Flaky Pastry (recipe follows)
- 1 pint strawberries, thickly sliced
- 1 pound very red fresh rhubarb stalks, cut crosswise ½ inch thick (see Note), or frozen sliced rhubarb
- ¾ cup sugar
- 2 tablespoons all-purpose flour
- 2 teaspoons fresh lemon juice
- 1 teaspoon pure vanilla extract
- 2 tablespoons whole milk
- 4 tablespoons cold unsalted butter, cut into small pieces

**1.** Preheat the oven to 400°. Line a large, rimmed baking sheet with parchment paper. On a lightly floured surface, roll the Tender-Flaky Pastry out to a 16-inch round ⅛ inch thick. Transfer to the parchment-lined baking sheet; the pastry will hang over the edges. Refrigerate the pastry for 10 minutes.

**2.** In a large bowl, toss the strawberries with the rhubarb, sugar, flour, lemon juice and vanilla extract. Spread on the pastry to within 2 inches of the edge. Fold the edge over the filling, pleating it at 2 inch intervals. Lightly brush the dough with the milk.

**3.** Dot the filling with the pieces of butter. Bake the galette in the center of the oven for 1 hour, or until the strawberries and rhubarb are bubbling and the pastry is golden brown. Let the galette cool slightly before cutting into wedges. *—Maria Helm Sinskey*

**NOTE** If using fresh rhubarb, trim every bit of the leaves—they are toxic. If using frozen sliced rhubarb, thaw it slightly.

**SERVE WITH** Whipped cream.

### TENDER-FLAKY PASTRY

**ACTIVE: 10 MIN; TOTAL: 40 MIN**

**MAKES ONE 12-INCH GALETTE CRUST** ● ●

- 1¼ cups all-purpose flour
- ¾ teaspoon kosher salt
- 1¼ sticks (5 ounces) cold unsalted butter, cut into 1-inch pieces
- 5 tablespoons ice water

**1.** In a medium bowl, using a fork, blend the flour and salt; scatter the butter on top. Using a pastry blender, cut the butter into the flour until it is the size of small peas. Sprinkle on the water and toss with the fork.

**2.** Using your hands, press the flour mixture together to form a dough. Pat into a 6-inch disk, wrap it in plastic and refrigerate for at least 30 minutes or overnight. *—M. H. S.*

### Strawberry and Sweet Wine Gelées with Candied Pistachios

**ACTIVE: 40 MIN; TOTAL: 1 HR, PLUS 6 HR CHILLING**

**6 SERVINGS** ● ●

- 3 pints strawberries, 2 pints coarsely chopped, 1 pint thinly sliced
- ½ cup sugar
- 1 cup water
- ¾ cup sweet dessert wine, such as late-harvest Riesling
- 1 tablespoon unflavored granulated gelatin
- ¼ cup unsalted shelled whole pistachios
- 1 teaspoon pure maple syrup

**1.** In a medium saucepan, combine the chopped strawberries with the sugar and coarsely mash with a potato masher. Let the berries stand until they release their liquid, about 20 minutes. Meanwhile, prepare an ice water bath and set a medium bowl in it.

**2.** Add the 1 cup of water to the crushed strawberries and bring to a boil, then simmer over moderate heat until the strawberries are softened, about 5 minutes. Stir in the dessert wine, then strain the sweetened strawberry juice through a fine sieve set over the bowl in the ice bath, pressing lightly on the solids. Stir occasionally until chilled, about 5 minutes. Wipe out the saucepan and return the strawberry liquid to it. Sprinkle the gelatin over the strawberry liquid and let stand for 5 minutes.

**3.** Set six ½-cup ramekins on a rimmed baking sheet. Spoon the sliced strawberries into the ramekins. Cook the strawberry liquid over moderate heat just until it is very warm but not simmering or boiling and the gelatin has completely dissolved, about 2 minutes. Ladle the liquid over the sliced strawberries in the ramekins and refrigerate until firm, at least 6 hours or overnight.

**4.** Meanwhile, preheat the oven to 400°. On a small, lightly oiled, rimmed baking sheet, toss the pistachios with the maple syrup until coated. Spread the pistachios in an even layer and bake for 3 minutes, or until glossy. Let cool completely, then coarsely chop the nuts.

**5.** To unmold the gelées, run a thin knife around the inside of the ramekins. Dip each ramekin in a bowl of boiling water for 5 seconds, then invert the ramekins onto plates to release the gelées. Sprinkle the strawberry gelées with the candied pistachios and serve.
—*Marcia Kiesel*

**MAKE AHEAD** The candied pistachios can be stored in an airtight container for up to 5 days. The gelées can be refrigerated for up to 2 days in their ramekins. Unmold the gelées just before serving.

## Rice Pudding with Strawberries
**TOTAL: 30 MIN**
6 SERVINGS ● ●
- ¾ cup arborio rice (5½ ounces)
- 3 cups milk
- Pinch of salt
- ½ vanilla bean, split lengthwise
- ½ cup sugar
- 1 pint strawberries, thickly sliced

**1.** In a strainer, rinse the rice under cold water for 1 minute. Transfer to a large saucepan and add the milk and salt. Scrape the seeds from the vanilla bean into the saucepan, add the vanilla bean and bring to a simmer. Cook over moderately low heat, stirring occasionally, until the rice is tender, about 20 minutes. Remove the rice from the heat and stir in the sugar.

**2.** Transfer the rice pudding to a large bowl set in a larger bowl of ice water and stir until cool, about 5 minutes. Discard the vanilla bean. Spoon half of the strawberries into 6 glasses. Add the cooled rice pudding, top with the remaining strawberries and serve. —*Gale Gand*

## Strawberry and Mascarpone Trifles with Riesling Syrup
**TOTAL: 25 MIN**
6 SERVINGS ● ●
- 1 cup dry Riesling
- ½ cup plus 1 tablespoon sugar
- ½ vanilla bean, split, seeds scraped
- 1 pound strawberries, hulled and sliced
- ½ cup mascarpone cheese
- ¼ cup heavy cream
- Six ½-inch-thick slices of pound cake, each slice cut into 4 triangles

**1.** In a small, heavy saucepan, combine the Riesling with ½ cup of the sugar and the vanilla bean and seeds. Bring to a boil over high heat, stirring, until the sugar dissolves. Continue to boil, undisturbed, until reduced to ½ cup, about 8 minutes. Let cool slightly.

**2.** Put the strawberries in a bowl and strain the syrup over them. Save the vanilla bean for another use.

**3.** In a medium bowl, using an electric mixer, whip the mascarpone with the cream and the remaining 1 tablespoon of sugar until soft peaks form. Place 2 cake triangles in each of 6 dessert bowls and top with half of the strawberries. Repeat with the remaining cake and strawberries. Spoon any remaining syrup over each bowl, dollop on the mascarpone cream and serve. —*Tom Douglas*

**MAKE AHEAD** The trifles can be refrigerated overnight.

## Blood Orange and Chocolate Trifles
**ACTIVE: 25 MIN; TOTAL: 3 HR 25 MIN**
6 SERVINGS ● ●
Look for bittersweet chocolate that has at least 70 percent cocoa. It has a deeper flavor than chocolate with less cocoa.
- 1½ cups part-skim ricotta cheese
- ¼ cup honey
- 4 small blood oranges

- 2 tablespoons Cointreau or Triple Sec
- 2 ounces bittersweet chocolate, coarsely grated
- Cinnamon, for sprinkling

**1.** In a small bowl, blend the ricotta with the honey and refrigerate.

**2.** Using a small, sharp knife, peel the blood oranges, removing all of the bitter white pith. Working over a bowl, cut in between the membranes to release the orange sections into the bowl; pour off the juice and reserve for another use. Add the Cointreau to the orange sections and toss to coat.

**3.** Line up 6 Champagne flutes or other tall, stemmed glasses on the counter. Add 4 orange sections to each glass. Spoon 2 tablespoons of the sweetened ricotta on top, then sprinkle on some of the grated chocolate. Repeat the layering of orange sections, ricotta and chocolate once. Top each trifle with a couple of orange sections, sprinkle with cinnamon and serve. —*Dana Jacobi*

**MAKE AHEAD** The trifles can be refrigerated for up to 4 hours. Sprinkle with cinnamon just before serving.

## Oranges in Citrus Syrup
**ACTIVE: 25 MIN; TOTAL: 2 HR 25 MIN**
8 SERVINGS ● ●
The oranges here have a slightly exotic flavor from being marinated in orange-flower syrup.
- 2 cups fresh orange juice
- ⅔ cup sugar
- 1½ tablespoons finely grated orange zest, plus strips for garnish
- 1½ tablespoons orange-flower water
- 8 navel oranges
- Cape gooseberries, for garnish (optional)

**1.** In a medium saucepan, combine the orange juice with the sugar and orange zest. Bring to a boil, stirring, until the sugar is dissolved. Let cool to room temperature. Stir in the orange-flower water.

# pies + fruit desserts

**2.** Meanwhile, using a sharp knife, peel the oranges, removing all of the bitter white pith. Cut the oranges crosswise into ⅓-inch-thick slices and transfer to a large, shallow serving bowl. Pour the syrup over the oranges and refrigerate until chilled, about 2 hours. Garnish with the orange zest strips and cape gooseberries and serve cold. —*Nadia Roden*

**MAKE AHEAD** The oranges can be refrigerated for up to 2 days.

## Muscat-Poached Peaches with Lemon Verbena

**ACTIVE: 10 MIN; TOTAL: 45 MIN**

8 SERVINGS ● ●

- 1 bottle Muscat wine, such as Moscato d'Asti
- Two 3-inch-long strips of lemon zest, julienned
- 8 peaches, halved and pitted
- Leaves from 2 sprigs of lemon verbena, crushed

In a medium saucepan, combine the wine and lemon zest and bring to a boil. Add the peaches and simmer over low heat until tender, about 5 minutes. Transfer to a large glass baking dish. Add the lemon verbena leaves and let cool to room temperature, then refrigerate until lightly chilled. Serve the peaches in the wine. —*Sylvie Chantecaille*

**MAKE AHEAD** The peaches can be refrigerated for up to 1 day.

## Lemon Panna Cottas with Peach Compote and Ginger Syrup

**ACTIVE: 1 HR; TOTAL: 4 HR**

6 SERVINGS ●

LEMON PANNA COTTAS

- 1 envelope unflavored gelatin (2¼ teaspoons)
- 1 cup whole milk
- 2 cups heavy cream
- ⅓ cup sugar
- Finely grated zest of 2 lemons
- 1 teaspoon pure vanilla extract

PEACH COMPOTE

- 1 cup water
- ⅔ cup late-harvest Riesling
- ½ cup sugar
- 1 vanilla bean, split lengthwise, seeds scraped and reserved
- 2½ ounces dried peaches, finely diced (½ cup)

GINGER SYRUP

- 1 cup water
- ½ cup sugar
- One 2-inch piece of fresh ginger, peeled and thickly sliced
- Juice and grated zest of 1 lemon
- Thin wafer cookies or tuiles, for serving

**1. MAKE THE LEMON PANNA COTTAS:** In a small skillet, sprinkle the gelatin over the milk and let stand for 5 minutes. Cook the gelatin over low heat just until dissolved, about 1 minute.

**2.** In a medium saucepan, combine the cream, sugar, lemon zest and vanilla and simmer over moderate heat just until the sugar dissolves. Remove from the heat and let cool for 10 minutes.

**3.** Stir the melted gelatin into the cream mixture until completely smooth. Strain the liquid into a large glass measuring cup and pour into six ½-cup ramekins. Refrigerate until firm, at least 3 hours.

**4. MEANWHILE, MAKE THE PEACH COMPOTE:** In a small saucepan, combine the water, late-harvest Riesling, sugar and vanilla bean and seeds. Add the peaches and bring to a boil, then simmer over moderate heat for 15 minutes. Let cool, then refrigerate for at least 2½ hours or overnight.

**5. MEANWHILE, MAKE THE GINGER SYRUP:** In a small saucepan, combine the water, sugar, ginger and lemon juice and zest and bring to a boil. Simmer over moderately low heat for 30 minutes. Remove from the heat and let stand for 1 hour, then strain and refrigerate until the ginger syrup is chilled.

**6.** Fill a medium skillet halfway with water and bring to a simmer. Remove from the heat. Dip each ramekin in the hot water for 10 seconds. Invert a plate over the ramekin, turn it over and gently tap the ramekin to unmold the panna cotta. Drain the peach compote and spoon onto the plates next to the panna cottas. Drizzle the ginger syrup around the panna cottas and serve with cookies. —*Michael Allemeier*

**MAKE AHEAD** The recipe can be prepared through Step 5 and refrigerated for up to 2 days.

## Lemon Curd Bread Pudding

**ACTIVE: 1 HR; TOTAL: 3 HR 15 MIN, PLUS OVERNIGHT CHILLING**

10 SERVINGS ●

- Vegetable oil cooking spray
- One 1¼-pound loaf brioche, crusts removed, bread sliced ½ inch thick
- 1 quart whole milk
- ¾ cup sugar
- 4 large eggs
- 1½ teaspoons minced lemon zest
- 3 tablespoons fresh lemon juice
- Lemon Curd (recipe follows)
- 1 cup heavy cream

**1.** Preheat the oven to 350°. Line the bottom and sides of a 12-by-16-inch jelly-roll pan with aluminum foil and coat with cooking spray. Arrange the brioche slices in the prepared pan, fitting them in a snug single layer.

**2.** In a medium, heavy saucepan, combine the milk with ¼ cup plus 2 tablespoons of the sugar and bring to a simmer. In a medium bowl, whisk the eggs with the remaining ¼ cup plus 2 tablespoons sugar. Slowly whisk 1 cup of the hot milk into the sugared eggs, then whisk in the remaining hot milk until thoroughly blended. Add the lemon zest and slowly whisk in the lemon juice. Pour the custard mixture evenly over the brioche and soak for 10 minutes.

MUSCAT-POACHED PEACHES WITH LEMON VERBENA

# pies + fruit desserts

**3.** Bake the brioche on the middle rack of the oven for 30 minutes, turning the pan halfway through baking. Transfer the pan to a wire rack and let the bread pudding cool to room temperature, about 1 hour. Refrigerate the pudding until chilled, about 1 hour longer.

**4.** Line a 10-by-5-inch loaf pan with plastic wrap, allowing 3 inches of overhang. Lightly coat the inside of the plastic wrap with cooking spray.

**5.** Trim ½ inch off the edges of the bread pudding. Cut the bread pudding into three 5-by-11-inch strips. Gently press 1 strip of the bread pudding into the loaf pan. Spread ¾ cup of the Lemon Curd evenly over the bread pudding. Repeat to form a second layer of pudding and curd. Press the last piece of bread pudding on top. Cover with overhanging plastic wrap and refrigerate overnight.

**6.** In a medium bowl, beat the heavy cream until stiff. Fold in the remaining ½ cup of Lemon Curd. Uncover the chilled bread pudding and turn it out onto a serving plate; remove the plastic wrap. Using a hot knife, slice the bread pudding ¾ inch thick, top with a dollop of the lemon whipped cream and serve. —*Lee Hefter*

## LEMON CURD

**ACTIVE: 30 MIN; TOTAL: 1 HR 30 MIN**

**MAKES 2 CUPS** ●

- ⅔ cup sugar
- 2 tablespoons finely grated lemon zest (4 lemons)
- 2 tablespoons finely grated lime zest (6 limes)
- 4 large eggs
- 3 large egg yolks
- ¼ cup plus 2 tablespoons fresh orange juice
- ¼ cup plus 2 tablespoons fresh lime juice
- 6 tablespoons unsalted butter, cut into pieces and softened

**1.** In a food processor, combine the sugar with the lemon zest and lime zest. Pulse about 10 times, until the sugar becomes light green.

**2.** In a medium heatproof bowl, whisk the eggs with the egg yolks, citrus sugar and orange and lime juices. Set the bowl over but not in a pan of simmering water and cook, stirring constantly with a wooden spoon, until the mixture is thickened, about 10 minutes.

**3.** Remove the bowl from the heat and whisk in the butter a few pieces at a time until fully incorporated. Press the curd through a fine strainer set over a small bowl to remove any zest or scrambled egg. Press a piece of plastic wrap directly on top of the curd and refrigerate until chilled, at least 1 hour. —*L.H.*

**MAKE AHEAD** The Lemon Curd can be refrigerated, tightly covered with plastic wrap, for up to 1 day.

## Neapolitan Lemon Granita

**ACTIVE: 15 MIN; TOTAL: 4 HR**

**10 SERVINGS** ● ●

- 3 cups water
- 1½ cups sugar
- 1 cup fresh lemon juice

**1.** In a small saucepan, combine 1 cup of the water with the sugar and bring to a boil, stirring occasionally to dissolve the sugar. Let the syrup cool, then add the remaining 2 cups of water and the fresh lemon juice.

**2.** Pour the lemon syrup into a 9-by-13-inch glass baking dish and freeze until slushy, about 2 hours. Using a fork, scrape the ice crystals into the center and freeze again. Repeat the scraping every 30 minutes or so until the entire mixture has turned into ice flakes, about 2 hours more. Spoon the granita into small glasses and serve.
—*Marcella Giamundo*

**MAKE AHEAD** The granita can be frozen for up to 5 days. Stir before serving.

## White Grapefruit and Star Anise Granita

**ACTIVE: 20 MIN; TOTAL: 4 HR 20 MIN**

**8 SERVINGS** ● ●

White grapefruits are tangier than pink ones, so they make this granita an especially good palate cleanser. If you'd like a sweeter granita, use only 3 cups of white grapefruit juice.

- ⅔ cup water
- ½ cup sugar
- 8 whole star anise pods
- 1 teaspoon finely grated grapefruit zest
- 5 cups fresh white grapefruit juice (from 9 medium grapefruits)

**1.** In a medium saucepan, combine the water with the sugar, star anise and grapefruit zest. Bring to a boil, then simmer over low heat for 5 minutes. Remove from the heat and let cool to room temperature, about 1 hour.

**2.** Remove the star anise and reserve. Stir in the grapefruit juice. Pour into a 9-by-13-inch baking dish and freeze for 1 hour, or until set around the edges. Using a fork, scrape the ice crystals into the center and freeze again. Repeat the scraping every 30 minutes until the entire mixture has turned into ice flakes, about 2 hours. Spoon into glasses, garnish with the reserved star anise pods and serve. —*Nadia Roden*

**MAKE AHEAD** The granita can be frozen, covered, for 5 days. Stir before serving.

## Strawberry Granita

**ACTIVE: 20 MIN; TOTAL: 3 HR**

**6 SERVINGS** ● ●

- 4 pints strawberries, hulled
- 1 cup water
- ½ cup sugar
- 1½ tablespoons fresh lime juice

**1.** Place the strawberries in a blender or food processor and puree until smooth. Pass the strawberry puree through a fine sieve into a medium bowl.

**2.** In a small saucepan, combine the water with the sugar and cook over moderate heat, stirring, just until the sugar has dissolved. Let the sugar syrup cool. Add the sugar syrup to the strawberry puree along with the lime juice. Transfer the granita mixture to a large, shallow nonreactive roasting pan and freeze just until ice crystals begin to form around the edge of the pan, about 30 minutes. Using a fork, scrape the ice crystals into the center of the roasting pan. Continue to freeze the granita for about 2 hours, scraping the ice crystals into the center every 30 minutes, until the granita is fluffy and icy. Transfer the granita to bowls or small glasses and serve.
—*Geoffrey Zakarian*

**MAKE AHEAD** The Strawberry Granita can be made up to 2 days ahead. Let stand at room temperature for 15 minutes, then scrape until fluffy and icy before serving.

## Pineapple Shortcakes with Dulce de Leche Whipped Cream

**TOTAL: 45 MIN**

8 SERVINGS

SHORTCAKES

- 2 cups all-purpose flour
- 1 tablespoon baking powder
- 2 tablespoons sugar
- ¼ teaspoon salt
- 6 tablespoons cold unsalted butter, cut into ½-inch pieces
- ½ cup plus 1 tablespoon heavy cream
- 1 large egg, lightly beaten
- 1 tablespoon dulce de leche

FILLING

- 2 cups heavy cream, chilled
- ¾ cup dulce de leche
- 2 tablespoons unsalted butter
- One 3½- to 4-pound pineapple— peeled, cored and cut into ½-inch-thick rings
- ¼ cup canned pineapple juice

**1. MAKE THE SHORTCAKES:** Preheat the oven to 375°. Line a large baking sheet with parchment paper. In a medium bowl, combine the flour with the baking powder, sugar and salt. Using a pastry blender or 2 knives, cut in the butter until it is the size of small peas. Make a well in the center of the dry ingredients.

**2.** In a small bowl, whisk ½ cup of the heavy cream with the lightly beaten egg and pour into the well in the dry ingredients. Stir until a shaggy dough forms. Turn the dough out onto a lightly floured surface and knead 2 or 3 times, or just until the dough comes together.

**3.** Roll out the shortcake dough ¾ inch thick. Using a 2½-inch biscuit cutter, stamp out 6 rounds as close together as possible. Pat the scraps together, re-roll and cut out 2 more rounds. Transfer the shortcakes to the prepared baking sheet.

**4.** In a small bowl, whisk the remaining 1 tablespoon of cream with the dulce de leche. Brush the tops of the shortcakes with the glaze and bake for 18 minutes, or until risen and golden. Transfer the shortcakes to a rack to cool.

**5. MAKE THE FILLING:** Fill a very large bowl with ice. In another large bowl, combine the heavy cream with ½ cup of the dulce de leche. Set the bowl over the ice and beat the cream until soft peaks form. Refrigerate the cream.

**6.** In a large skillet, heat the butter until sizzling. Add the pineapple rings in a single layer and cook over high heat, turning once, until lightly browned, about 5 minutes. Add the remaining ¼ cup of dulce de leche and the pineapple juice and cook until bubbling, turning the pineapple to coat, 2 to 3 minutes longer.

**7.** Split the shortcakes horizontally and set the bottom halves on plates. Spoon the pineapple rings and sauce over the cakes. Top with the whipped cream, then the shortcake tops, and serve.
—*Grace Parisi*

## Dulce de Leche Roasted Banana Split

**TOTAL: 15 MIN**

8 SERVINGS ●

- 4 tablespoons unsalted butter
- 16 firm, ripe baby bananas (about 3 pounds)
- ½ cup dulce de leche
- 2 vanilla beans, split lengthwise, seeds scraped
- Two 3-inch cinnamon sticks, broken in half
- ½ cup dark rum
- Vanilla ice cream, for serving

**1.** Preheat the oven to 450°. Melt the butter in a very large, ovenproof skillet. Add the bananas and cook over high heat until lightly browned, 2 to 3 minutes. Add the dulce de leche, vanilla beans and seeds and cinnamon sticks and cook over moderate heat just until the dulce de leche is melted.

**2.** Carefully add the rum to the skillet and stir gently just until combined. Transfer the skillet to the oven and bake for 5 minutes, or just until the bananas are tender and bubbling. Carefully pick out the cinnamon sticks and vanilla beans. Serve the bananas and sauce over vanilla ice cream.
—*Grace Parisi*

## Mango Sticky Rice

**ACTIVE: 25 MIN; TOTAL: 1 HR, PLUS OVERNIGHT SOAKING**

6 SERVINGS

When cooled, sticky rice, also known as sweet or glutinous rice, holds together without any gumminess.

- 1½ cups sticky rice (¾ pound)
- 2¼ cups unsweetened coconut milk
- ¼ cup plus 2 tablespoons sugar
- Salt
- 1 tablespoon vegetable oil
- ½ cup unsweetened puffed rice
- Banana leaves, for serving (optional)
- 2 mangoes, peeled and cut into 3-inch sticks

# pies + fruit desserts

1. Soak the sticky rice overnight in water to cover; drain.

2. Line a bamboo steamer with dampened cheesecloth. Spread the rice on the cheesecloth in an even layer, then set the steamer in a wok over boiling water. Cover and steam the rice until tender, about 15 minutes; transfer to a bowl.

3. Meanwhile, in a small saucepan, simmer 1¼ cups of the coconut milk with ¼ cup of the sugar, stirring to dissolve the sugar. Stir the coconut milk into the rice and season with salt; keep warm.

4. In a small saucepan, simmer the remaining 1 cup of coconut milk over moderately high heat until reduced by half, about 15 minutes.

5. In a medium skillet, cook the remaining 2 tablespoons of sugar with the oil over moderate heat until caramelized, about 2 minutes. Add the puffed rice and stir until coated, then transfer to a plate to cool. Spread a piece of rinsed and dried banana leaf on each plate. Mound the sticky rice on the banana leaves, pour some of the reduced coconut milk over the top and garnish with the caramelized puffed rice. Pile the mango sticks next to the rice and serve.
—*Jean-Georges Vongerichten*

### Yogurt with Sautéed Dried Fruits and Nuts
TOTAL: 15 MIN, PLUS 2 HR DRAINING
6 SERVINGS ●

- 3 cups plain whole goat's- or cow's-milk yogurt, drained for 2 hours
- 5 tablespoons unsalted butter
- ½ cup walnuts
- 3 tablespoons dried mulberries or sour cherries
- 3 tablespoons raisins
- 1 tablespoon hazelnuts
- 1 tablespoon blanched almonds, very coarsely chopped
- 1 tablespoon pine nuts

- 3 tablespoons tahini, at room temperature
- 3 tablespoons grape molasses (see Note) or unsulfured molasses
- Pinch of cinnamon
- 1 tablespoon chopped pistachios

1. Spoon half of the yogurt into 6 heatproof glasses. In a skillet, melt 3 tablespoons of the butter. Add the walnuts, mulberries, raisins, hazelnuts, almonds and pine nuts; sauté over moderately high heat, shaking the pan, until the butter is sizzling and beginning to brown around the edge of the pan. Stir in the tahini and 2 tablespoons of the grape molasses. Spoon the mixture into the glasses; top with the remaining yogurt.

2. Melt the remaining butter in the skillet. Stir in the remaining molasses and the cinnamon; drizzle over the yogurt. Sprinkle on the pistachios and serve.
—*Musa Dagdeviren*

NOTE Grape molasses is available at Middle Eastern markets.

### Mango-Raspberry Baked Alaskas
ACTIVE: 25 MIN; TOTAL: 4 HR
4 SERVINGS ●

- 1 cup unsweetened frozen raspberries, thawed
- 3 tablespoons sugar
- 4 store-bought dry ladyfingers, halved crosswise
- 1 cup mango sorbet, slightly softened (see Note)
- 2 large egg whites
- Pinch of salt

1. In a food processor, puree the raspberries with 1 tablespoon of the sugar. Using a rubber spatula, pass the puree through a fine strainer into a small bowl. Dip each ladyfinger half in the raspberry puree and turn to coat thoroughly. Lay 2 halves side by side on the bottom of each of four ¾-cup ramekins. Spoon the remaining puree over the ladyfingers and let stand for 10 minutes to soften.

2. Spoon ¼ cup of the mango sorbet into each ramekin and spread it over the ladyfingers in an even layer. Cover the ramekins with plastic wrap and freeze until firm, about 30 minutes.

3. In a medium bowl, beat the egg whites and salt at high speed until soft peaks form. Sprinkle 1 tablespoon of the sugar over the whites and beat until incorporated. Sprinkle the remaining 1 tablespoon of sugar over the whites and beat until firm and glossy. Spoon the whites on top of the sorbet, making decorative swirls. Freeze until firm, about 3 hours.

4. Preheat the broiler. Set the ramekins on a baking sheet; broil about 5 inches from the heat until the meringues are evenly browned. Serve immediately.
—*Marcia Kiesel*

NOTE The F&W Test Kitchen especially likes Ciao Bella mango sorbet (800-435-2863 or ciaobellagelato.com).

### Date and Fig Pastilla
ACTIVE: 20 MIN; TOTAL: 1 HR, PLUS OVERNIGHT MACERATING
8 SERVINGS ● ●

*Pastilla* (also known as *b'steeya*) is a traditional Moroccan dish in which phyllo dough is wrapped around a spiced pigeon-and-almond filling and baked. This is a playful dessert version of that classic.

- ¼ cup plus 2 tablespoons finely chopped dried Black Mission figs
- ¼ cup plus 2 tablespoons finely chopped dates
- ¼ cup finely chopped toasted almonds
- 2 tablespoons honey
- ¼ teaspoon pure vanilla extract
- Pinch of salt
- ¼ cup very hot tap water
- 4 sheets of phyllo dough
- 4 tablespoons unsalted butter, melted
- Confectioners' sugar, for dusting
- Crème fraîche, for serving

1. In a medium bowl, combine the figs, dates, almonds, honey, vanilla and salt. Stir in the hot water. Cover with plastic wrap and let stand overnight.

2. Preheat the oven to 400°. Line a large baking sheet with parchment paper. On a work surface, spread 1 sheet of phyllo dough with the long side facing you. Starting from the edges and working in, brush the phyllo with melted butter. Top with 3 more phyllo sheets, buttering each one. Spoon the fruit-and-nut filling along the bottom half of the phyllo dough and roll up the phyllo as tightly as possible, tucking in the ends as you roll, to form a neat, slightly flattened log.

3. Transfer the *pastilla* to the baking sheet, seam side down. Brush with butter and bake for about 35 minutes, or until golden. Let the *pastilla* cool, then transfer to a platter and dust generously with confectioners' sugar. Cut into wide slices and serve with crème fraîche.
—*Pascal Rigo*

**MAKE AHEAD** The *pastilla* can be made up to 1 day ahead and kept at room temperature overnight.

### Apricot Pavlova with Chamomile Cream

**ACTIVE: 1 HR 30 MIN; TOTAL: 4 HR**
**4 SERVINGS**

- ½ cup superfine sugar
- 4 large egg whites
- ½ cup large mint leaves
- 3 tablespoons granulated sugar
- ¾ cup plus 1 tablespoon confectioners' sugar
- 12 apricots (see Note)
- ⅔ cup honey
- 1 Thai chile or serrano chile, seeded and minced
- 2½ tablespoons unsalted butter
- 2 tablespoons water
- ½ teaspoon pure vanilla extract
- 1 cup heavy cream
- 2 chamomile tea bags

**YOGURT WITH SAUTÉED DRIED FRUITS AND NUTS**

**MANGO-RASPBERRY BAKED ALASKA**

# pies + fruit desserts

**1.** Preheat the oven to 450°, then turn it off. Meanwhile, line a baking sheet with a silicone liner or with parchment paper. Spread the superfine sugar on a small plate. In a medium bowl, whisk 2 of the egg whites until very frothy. Using a pastry brush, brush a mint leaf with some of the egg white, then dredge it in the superfine sugar. Repeat with the remaining mint leaves. Transfer the sugared mint leaves to the baking sheet. Put them in the oven and let them dry out for about 40 minutes; the leaves should not color, but they should be brittle-dry. Let cool, then transfer to a food processor and grind to a powder.

**2.** Transfer 3 tablespoons of the mint powder to a medium bowl and stir in the granulated sugar. Reserve the remaining mint powder in a small bowl to use for sprinkling.

**3.** Preheat the oven to 250° and line 2 baking sheets with parchment paper. In a bowl, using an electric mixer, beat the remaining 2 egg whites at medium speed until frothy. Increase the speed to medium-high and continue to beat the whites until soft peaks form. Beat in the mint sugar, 1 tablespoon at a time, and beat until the meringue is stiff and glossy. Sift ¾ cup of the confectioners' sugar over the meringue, then fold it in with a rubber spatula. Spoon 2 tablespoons of the meringue onto a baking sheet and spread it into a 4-inch oval a scant ⅓ inch thick. Repeat with the remaining meringue to form 9 more ovals. Bake for about 12 minutes, or until they are firm and dry. Turn off the oven, open the door slightly and let the meringues cool in the oven for 1 hour.

**4.** Preheat the oven to 400°. Prepare a large bowl of ice water. In a small saucepan of boiling water, blanch the apricots for 10 seconds, them immediately transfer them to the ice water. Peel the apricots, then halve and pit them.

**5.** In a small roasting pan, toss the apricots with the honey and chile. Roast the apricots for about 10 minutes, or until they are soft but not mushy. Using a slotted spoon, transfer the apricots to a plate to cool. Whisk the butter and water into the honey in the roasting pan, then strain the sauce into a small bowl. Stir in the vanilla.

**6.** In a small saucepan, heat ½ cup of the cream until bubbles appear around the edge. Remove the pan from the heat, add the tea bags and let steep until cool. Discard the tea bags and chill the cream. Transfer the chamomile cream to a medium bowl. Add the remaining ½ cup of cream and 1 tablespoon of confectioners' sugar and beat with an electric mixer until firm.

**7.** Place 1 meringue on each of 4 plates. Top the meringues with a dollop of the chamomile whipped cream and 3 apricot halves. Top with another meringue, more whipped cream and 3 more apricot halves. (You will have 2 extra meringues in case of breakage.) Drizzle 2 teaspoons of the spiced honey sauce all around the meringues, sprinkle with the remaining mint powder and serve at once. —*Johnny Iuzzini*

**NOTE** You can also use frozen unsweetened apricot halves for this recipe. They're available at most supermarkets.

**MAKE AHEAD** The meringues can be stored in an airtight container overnight. The apricots and honey sauce can be refrigerated overnight. Bring to room temperature before serving.

## Apricot and Almond Soufflés
**ACTIVE: 15 MIN; TOTAL: 40 MIN**
6 SERVINGS ●

- 1 tablespoon unsalted butter, softened
- ¼ cup granulated sugar, plus more for dusting
- ¾ cup sliced almonds (3 ounces)

- 1¼ cups fresh orange juice
- 2 tablespoons fresh lemon juice
- 1 cup dried apricot halves (6 ounces)
- 1 tablespoon orange liqueur
- 1½ teaspoons finely grated orange zest
- 5 large egg whites, at room temperature

Pinch of salt

Pinch of cream of tartar

- ¼ cup superfine sugar

Nonfat plain yogurt, for serving

**1.** Preheat the oven to 375°. Butter six 1-cup ramekins and dust with granulated sugar, tapping out any excess. Set the ramekins on a medium, rimmed baking sheet. Spread the sliced almonds in a pie plate and toast for 8 minutes, or until they are golden and fragrant. Let cool slightly, then lightly crush the almonds. Leave the oven on.

**2.** Meanwhile, in a medium saucepan, combine the orange and lemon juices, dried apricots, orange liqueur, the ¼ cup of granulated sugar and the orange zest and bring to a boil. Simmer over moderate heat until the apricots are softened and the liquid is slightly reduced, about 20 minutes. Let cool, then puree the mixture in a food processor.

**3.** In a large bowl, beat the egg whites with the salt and cream of tartar until very soft peaks form. Add the superfine sugar and beat until soft, glossy peaks form. Pour the apricot puree down the side of the bowl and fold it into the whites with a rubber spatula. Fold in all but 1 tablespoon of the almonds. Spoon the soufflé mixture into the ramekins and smooth the tops. Run your fingertip around the inside rim so the soufflés rise up straight. Sprinkle with the reserved almonds. Bake the soufflés for 15 minutes, or until they are risen and golden. Serve right away, passing yogurt alongside. —*Anya von Bremzen*

APRICOT AND ALMOND SOUFFLÉ

TRIPLE-LAYER CHOCOLATE MACAROON CAKE, P. 315

# cakes, cookies +more

15

SEMOLINA CAKE WITH FIG COMPOTE

CHOCOLATE SPIDER CAKE WITH CARAMEL MOUSSE

### Semolina Cakes with Fig Compote

ACTIVE: 30 MIN; TOTAL: 2 HR

MAKES TWO 9-INCH CAKES ● CAKES

2½ cups all-purpose flour

1½ cups semolina (see Note)

2 cups sugar

2 tablespoons baking powder

1½ teaspoons kosher salt

8 large egg whites

2 cups whole milk

Finely grated zest of 2 oranges

2 teaspoons pure vanilla extract

2 sticks (½ pound) unsalted butter, melted

FIG COMPOTE

1 pound dried Black Mission figs, stems trimmed

2 cups full-bodied red wine

½ cup fresh orange juice

Four 3-inch strips of orange zest, removed with a vegetable peeler

½ vanilla bean, split lengthwise, seeds scraped

½ cup honey

Sweetened whipped cream, for serving

**1.** MAKE THE CAKES: Preheat the oven to 325°. Butter the bottoms and sides of two 9-inch round cake pans and line the bottoms with buttered parchment paper. In a large bowl, whisk the flour with the semolina, sugar, baking powder and salt. In a small bowl, whisk the egg whites with the milk, grated orange zest and vanilla extract. Add the liquid ingredients to the semolina mixture and, using an electric mixer, beat at low speed until combined. Beat in the melted butter.

**2.** Pour the batter into the prepared cake pans and bake for 35 minutes, or until the cake tops are golden brown and lightly cracked and a toothpick inserted in the center of each cake comes out clean. Let the cakes cool in the pans for 10 minutes, then turn them out onto wire racks to cool completely. Invert the cakes onto plates.

**3.** MEANWHILE, MAKE THE COMPOTE: In a medium saucepan, bring the figs, wine, orange juice and zest, vanilla bean and seeds and honey to a boil. Simmer over moderately low heat until the figs are plumped and the liquid is slightly reduced, 1 hour. Using a slotted spoon, transfer the figs to a cutting board, slice in half, then return them to the syrup.

**4.** Peel the parchment paper off the cakes and invert them onto plates. Cut into wedges; serve with the fig compote and whipped cream. —*Marion Hoezel*

NOTE Semolina, coarsely ground durum wheat, is available in specialty markets.

**MAKE AHEAD** The cakes can be wrapped tightly in plastic and stored at room temperature for up to 2 days. The compote can be refrigerated for up to 1 week.

## Chocolate Spider Cake with Caramel-Coffee Mousse

**ACTIVE: 1 HR 30 MIN; TOTAL: 4 HR 30 MIN, PLUS 3 HR CHILLING**

**12 SERVINGS** ● ●

This dessert is close to perfect: moist, chocolaty cake layered with a silky caramel-coffee mousse and glazed with bittersweet chocolate ganache. The decorative spider web on top of the cake makes it ideal for a Halloween party.

**CARAMEL**

- 1 cup sugar
- ¼ cup water
- ¼ teaspoon fresh lemon juice
- 2 cups heavy cream
- 1 teaspoon pure vanilla extract

**CAKE**

- ¼ cup plus 2 tablespoons unsweetened cocoa powder (not Dutch-process)
- ¼ cup plus 2 tablespoons boiling water
- ¼ cup plus 2 tablespoons milk
- 1 cup plus 2 tablespoons cake flour
- ¾ teaspoon baking soda
- ¼ teaspoon baking powder
- ¼ teaspoon salt
- 6 tablespoons unsalted butter, softened
- 1 cup sugar
- 1 large egg, at room temperature
- 1 large egg yolk, at room temperature

**MOUSSE**

- 2½ teaspoons instant coffee (3 single-serving packets)
- 3 tablespoons cold water
- 1 envelope unflavored gelatin (about 2 teaspoons)
- Caramel (see above)
- ¼ cup crème fraîche

**GLAZE**

- 1 cup heavy cream
- ½ pound bittersweet chocolate, finely chopped
- ¼ cup confectioners' sugar
- 1½ teaspoons milk

**1. MAKE THE CARAMEL:** In a medium saucepan, combine the sugar with the water and lemon juice and bring to a boil over moderately high heat. Using a wet pastry brush, wipe down the side of the saucepan. Simmer the syrup undisturbed until it begins to brown around the edge, 4 to 5 minutes. Swirl the pan, then simmer until the caramel turns a medium-dark amber, about 3 minutes longer. Remove from the heat. Carefully add ½ cup of the cream in a steady stream. Stir with a long-handled wooden spoon to combine, then add the remaining 1½ cups of cream. Stir in the vanilla. Transfer to a bowl and refrigerate until very cold, at least 3 hours or overnight.

**2. MEANWHILE, MAKE THE CAKE:** Preheat the oven to 350°. Butter the bottoms only of three 9-inch round cake pans and line them with parchment paper. In a bowl, whisk the cocoa with the boiling water until a paste forms. Whisk in the milk until smooth; let cool.

**3.** Onto a sheet of wax paper, sift the cake flour with the baking soda, baking powder and salt. In a large bowl, using an electric mixer, beat the butter with the sugar at medium speed until light and fluffy. Add the egg and egg yolk and beat until creamy. Add the dry ingredients in 2 batches, alternating with the cocoa mixture; beat until smooth.

**4.** Divide the batter evenly among the 3 pans (the layers will be shallow) and smooth the tops. Bake for 12 to 14 minutes, or until the tops spring back when lightly pressed. Let the cakes cool in the pans for 15 minutes, then run a knife around the edges. Turn out onto a rack to cool completely. Peel off the parchment.

**5. MAKE THE MOUSSE:** In a microwave-safe bowl, dissolve the instant coffee in the cold water. Sprinkle on the gelatin and let stand until softened, about 5 minutes. Using an electric mixer, beat the caramel with the crème fraîche just until soft peaks form. Working quickly, microwave the coffee-gelatin mixture at 10-second intervals just until the gelatin is completely dissolved and hot to the touch. Quickly whisk the hot gelatin into the caramel.

**6. ASSEMBLE THE CAKE:** Line a 9-inch round springform pan with plastic wrap, leaving at least 4 inches of overhang all around. Place 1 of the cake layers flat side down in the bottom of the springform pan. Spoon half of the mousse over the cake in the pan and top with another cake layer. Press lightly. Add the remaining mousse and top with the final cake layer, flat side up. Fold the overhanging plastic wrap over the cake and refrigerate for at least 3 hours or overnight.

**7. MAKE THE GLAZE:** In a medium saucepan, heat the cream just until small bubbles appear around the edge. Remove from the heat. Add the chocolate and let stand for 5 minutes. Stir until smooth. Let the glaze cool for about 1 hour, until thick but pourable. In a small bowl, stir the confectioners' sugar with the milk and transfer to a pastry bag fitted with a tiny, plain tip.

**8.** Unwrap the top of the cake and invert it onto a serving plate. Slide wide strips of wax paper under the bottom edge of the cake all around to catch drips. Remove the side and bottom of the pan and unwrap the cake. Smooth the side of the cake with an offset spatula. Pour ¾ cup of the chocolate glaze over the cake and spread it all around, filling in any gaps. Refrigerate for about 5 minutes, until set. Pour the remaining glaze on the cake and spread it all around; do not spread once the glaze is smooth.

# cakes, cookies + more

**9.** Starting from the center and working quickly out toward the edge, pipe a continuous spiral of white glaze over the top of the cake. Using a toothpick or wooden skewer, run the tip gently through the glaze from the edge to the center to create a web pattern. Refrigerate the cake for about 15 minutes to set the glaze. Let the cake stand at room temperature for 30 minutes. Gently remove the wax-paper strips, cut the cake into wedges and serve. —*Peggy Cullen*

**MAKE AHEAD** The cake can be refrigerated for up to 2 days.

### Pecan-Spice Cake with Caramel Frosting

**ACTIVE: 1 HR; TOTAL: 4 HR**

**8 SERVINGS** ●

Like many southern desserts, this rich cake doesn't skimp on the sugar. It gets an extra hit of sweetness from the jam in the batter.

- 2 cups all-purpose flour
- 1 teaspoon baking soda
- 1 teaspoon salt
- 1 teaspoon cinnamon
- ½ teaspoon ground allspice
- 1½ sticks unsalted butter, softened
- 1 cup sugar
- 3 large eggs, separated
- ½ cup buttermilk
- 1 cup strawberry jam (12 ounces)
- ½ cup finely chopped pecans, plus
  ½ cup pecan halves for garnish

**Caramel Frosting (recipe follows)**

**1.** Preheat the oven to 350°. Butter and lightly flour two 8-inch round cake pans. In a medium bowl, whisk the flour, baking soda, salt, cinnamon and allspice.

**2.** In a large bowl, using an electric mixer, beat the butter until creamy. Add the sugar and beat until fluffy. Add the egg yolks and beat until blended, then beat in the buttermilk. At low speed, beat in the dry ingredients. Beat in the jam and the chopped pecans until combined.

**3.** In a clean stainless steel bowl, using clean beaters, beat the egg whites at medium speed until frothy. Increase the speed to high and beat until stiff peaks form. Using a rubber spatula, fold the beaten egg whites into the cake batter.

**4.** Pour the batter into the prepared pans and smooth the surfaces. Bake in the center of the oven for 30 minutes, or until a toothpick inserted in the centers comes out clean. Let the cakes cool in the pans for 10 minutes, then turn them out onto a wire rack to cool completely.

**5.** Set 1 cake on a plate and spread with a thin layer of Caramel Frosting. Top with the second cake and spread with the remaining frosting. Garnish the cake with the pecan halves.

—*Mary Lynn Van Wyck*

**MAKE AHEAD** The frosted cake can be stored at room temperature in an airtight container for up to 2 days.

### CARAMEL FROSTING

**TOTAL: 40 MIN**

**MAKES ABOUT 2 CUPS**

- 2 large eggs, lightly beaten
- 2 tablespoons unsalted butter
- 3 cups sugar
- ¾ cup whole milk
- ½ teaspoon salt

**1.** In a large bowl, beat the eggs and butter with 2½ cups of the sugar until moistened. Beat in the milk and salt.

**2.** In a large saucepan, cook the remaining ½ cup sugar over moderately high heat, without stirring, until an amber caramel forms, about 7 minutes. Gradually pour the caramel into the egg mixture, stirring constantly; bits of the frosting will harden but will melt again later.

**3.** Scrape the frosting into the saucepan and cook over moderate heat, stirring frequently, until the temperature reaches 230° on a candy thermometer, about 20 minutes. The frosting should be thick and dark amber.

**4.** Transfer the frosting to a large heat-proof bowl. Using an electric mixer, beat the frosting at medium-high speed until thickened, pale and smooth but still warm and spreadable, about 8 minutes; the frosting should resemble creamy peanut butter. Use the frosting right away; if it hardens, rewarm it over low heat, stirring, just until spreadable.

—*Mary Lynn Van Wyck*

### Salted Caramel Cheesecakes

**ACTIVE: 30 MIN; TOTAL: 1 HR 30 MIN, PLUS 3 HR CHILLING**

**6 SERVINGS** ● ●

**CHEESECAKES**

- ½ pound cream cheese, at room temperature
- ½ cup sugar
- 3 large eggs, at room temperature
- ½ cup sour cream

**CARAMEL**

- 6 tablespoons light corn syrup
- ½ cup plus 2 tablespoons sugar
- 3 tablespoons unsalted butter
- ½ cup heavy cream

**Fleur de sel**

**1. MAKE THE CHEESECAKES:** Preheat the oven to 325°. In a large bowl, beat the cream cheese and sugar at medium speed until smooth. Beat in the eggs 1 at a time, then beat in the sour cream. Pour the batter into six 5-ounce ramekins.

**2.** Set the ramekins in a small pan and set the pan in the center of the oven. Add enough hot water to the pan to reach halfway up the sides of the ramekins. Bake the cheesecakes for 10 minutes, until set at the edges but still quite jiggly in the centers. Turn off the oven and leave the cheesecakes in for 1 hour. Transfer the ramekins to a rack and let cool completely.

**3. MEANWHILE, MAKE THE CARAMEL:** In a heavy, medium saucepan, heat the corn syrup. Stir in the sugar and cook over moderately high heat, undisturbed, until a deep amber caramel forms, about 9 minutes. Off the heat, carefully stir in the butter with a long-handled wooden spoon. Stir in the cream in a thin stream. Transfer the caramel to a heatproof pitcher and let cool. Stir in ¾ teaspoon of fleur de sel.

**4.** Pour 1½ tablespoons of the caramel over each cheesecake and swirl to coat the tops. If the caramel is too thick, warm it in a microwave oven at 10-second intervals. Refrigerate the cheesecakes until chilled, at least 3 hours. Sprinkle with fleur de sel just before serving.
—*Michael Moorhouse*

**MAKE AHEAD** The cheesecakes can be refrigerated for up to 2 days.

### Crème Caramel Loaf
**ACTIVE: 20 MIN; TOTAL: 1 HR 30 MIN, PLUS 4 HR CHILLING**
**8 SERVINGS ●**

- 1 **cup sugar**
- 1 **tablespoon water**
- 1½ **cups milk**
- ½ **cup heavy cream**
- 4 **large eggs**
- 4 **large egg yolks**

**1.** Preheat the oven to 325°. In a medium skillet, combine ½ cup of the sugar with the water and cook over high heat until deep amber, about 4 minutes; swirl the pan occasionally. Immediately pour the caramel into an 8-by-4½-by-3-inch metal loaf pan, turning to evenly coat the bottom. Let the caramel harden.

**2.** In a bowl, whisk the remaining ½ cup of sugar, the milk, cream, eggs and egg yolks. Pour the custard into the prepared pan, set in a small baking dish and add enough water to the dish to reach halfway up the sides of the pan. Bake for 50 minutes, or until set around the edges but still slightly soft in the center. Remove the pan from the water bath and let cool to room temperature; refrigerate until chilled, at least 4 hours.

**PECAN-SPICE CAKE WITH CARAMEL FROSTING**

**SALTED CARAMEL CHEESECAKE**

# cakes, cookies + more

**3.** Run a thin knife around the edges of the custard. Invert a rectangular plate or platter over the pan and flip, tapping to loosen and unmold the custard. Spoon any remaining caramel from the pan on top. Cut into slices and serve.
*—Alessandro Lunardi*

**MAKE AHEAD** The crème caramel can be refrigerated overnight before unmolding.

## Cider–Caramelized Apple Pound Cake

**ACTIVE: 1 HR; TOTAL: 2 HR 30 MIN**

**12 SERVINGS** ●

CAKE

- 2 cups clear apple cider or unsweetened apple juice
- 3 cups granulated sugar
- 3 sticks plus 2 tablespoons unsalted butter, softened
- 1½ pounds large Granny Smith apples (about 3)—peeled, cored and thinly sliced
- 3 cups sifted cake flour
- 1½ teaspoons cinnamon
- 1 teaspoon freshly grated nutmeg
- ½ teaspoon ground mace
- ½ teaspoon salt
- ¼ teaspoon baking soda
- 2 teaspoons pure vanilla extract
- 6 large eggs
- ¾ cup sour cream

GLAZE

- 4 tablespoons unsalted butter
- ½ cup packed dark brown sugar
- ½ cup heavy cream
- 1 cup confectioners' sugar
- 2 teaspoons pure vanilla extract
- ¼ cup chopped toasted pecans

**1. MAKE THE CAKE:** In a large saucepan, boil the apple cider over high heat, swirling the pan occasionally, until reduced to ½ cup, about 15 minutes. Add 1 cup of the granulated sugar and cook over moderately high heat until a dark amber caramel forms, about 5 minutes. Off the heat, swirl in 2 tablespoons of the butter until melted. Add the apples and cook over moderately high heat, stirring occasionally, until the apples are softened and have absorbed a lot of the syrup, about 8 minutes. Pour the apples into a heatproof bowl and let cool.

**2.** Preheat the oven to 350° and position a rack in the lower third. Butter and flour a 12-cup bundt pan. Sift the cake flour, cinnamon, nutmeg, mace, salt and baking soda onto a sheet of wax paper. In a large bowl, using an electric mixer, beat the remaining 3 sticks of butter until creamy. Add the remaining 2 cups of granulated sugar and the vanilla and beat at medium-high speed until fluffy, about 5 minutes. Add the eggs 1 at a time, beating well between additions. Add the dry ingredients in 3 batches, alternating with the sour cream; beat just until combined. Stir ½ cup of the batter into the apples, then stir the apple mixture into the remaining batter.

**3.** Pour the batter into the prepared bundt pan and smooth the top. Bake for about 1 hour and 10 minutes, or until the top is golden and cracked and a skewer inserted in the center comes out with a few moist crumbs attached. Transfer the cake to a rack and let cool for 20 minutes, then turn it out onto the rack to cool completely.

**4. MAKE THE GLAZE:** In a saucepan, melt the butter. Add the brown sugar and cook over moderate heat, stirring, until thick and smooth. Gradually stir in the cream and bring to a boil. Cook over moderate heat, stirring occasionally, until thick and bubbling, 3 minutes. Let cool completely, then stir in the confectioners' sugar and vanilla extract.

**5.** Set the cake on a plate and drizzle the glaze all over it. Sprinkle with the pecans, cut into wedges and serve. *—Greg Patent*

**MAKE AHEAD** The cake can be kept in an airtight container at room temperature overnight or refrigerated for up to 1 week.

## Breton Butter Cake

**ACTIVE: 30 MIN; TOTAL: 3 HR**

**6 SERVINGS** ● ●

- 1 pound frozen bread or pizza dough, thawed
- 1 stick (4 ounces) chilled salted butter, cut into 16 slices, plus 1 tablespoon melted salted butter
- ¾ cup plus 2 tablespoons sugar

**1.** On a lightly floured work surface, roll out the dough to a rough 8-by-12-inch rectangle. Cover with plastic wrap and let rest for 25 minutes. Lightly flour the rolling pin and roll out the dough to a 14-by-18-inch rectangle. Cover with plastic wrap and let the dough rest again for 25 minutes.

**2.** Butter a 9-inch cast-iron skillet. Flour the work surface. Roll out the dough as thinly as possible, keeping a rectangular shape. Scatter 5 slices of the butter over two-thirds of the dough and sprinkle with ¼ cup of the sugar. Fold the bare dough into the center and fold in the opposite side, like folding a letter. Dust with flour and roll out again as thinly as possible, retaining the rectangular shape. Top with another 5 slices of butter and ¼ cup of sugar, folding, dusting with flour and rolling out the dough again as before. Repeat the process one last time, using the remaining 6 slices of butter and ¼ cup of the sugar, folding and rolling it out as thinly as possible.

**3.** Fold in the corners of the dough to make a slightly round shape and transfer it to the prepared skillet. With a sharp knife, make six 2-inch-long cuts all the way through the dough in a starburst pattern. Cover the dough with plastic wrap and let rise for 45 minutes. Place a baking stone or baking sheet in the lower third of the oven and preheat to 450°.

**4.** Brush the dough with the melted butter and sprinkle with the remaining 2 tablespoons of sugar. Put the skillet on the stone in the oven and bake for

25 minutes, until richly browned on top. With a spatula, transfer the cake to a large, round plate and let rest for 30 minutes. Cut into wedges and serve.

—*Naomi Duguid and Jeffrey Alford*

**MAKE AHEAD** The cake can be kept at room temperature overnight, but it's best eaten the day it's made.

## Citrus Chiffon Cake

**ACTIVE: 25 MIN; TOTAL: 2 HR**

**10 TO 12 SERVINGS** ● ●

2½  cups cake flour
1½  cups granulated sugar
 1   teaspoon baking powder
 ½   teaspoon salt
 ⅓   cup vegetable oil
 5   large egg yolks, at room
     temperature
Finely grated zest of 1 lemon
Finely grated zest of 1 orange
Finely grated zest of 1 lime
 1   teaspoon pure lemon extract
 1   teaspoon pure orange extract
 1   teaspoon pure vanilla extract
 ¾   cup fresh grapefruit juice
 8   large egg whites, at room
     temperature
 ½   teaspoon cream of tartar
Confectioners' sugar, nonfat frozen
     yogurt and orange segments,
     for serving

**1.** Preheat the oven to 325° and position a rack in the lower third. In a bowl, whisk the cake flour with 1 cup of the granulated sugar, the baking powder and salt. Make a well in the center and add the oil, egg yolks, zests, extracts and grapefruit juice. Slowly whisk the liquids into the flour mixture, then whisk vigorously until smooth, about 30 seconds.

**2.** In a bowl, using an electric mixer, beat the egg whites at medium speed until frothy. Add the cream of tartar and beat until very soft peaks form. Gradually add the remaining ½ cup of granulated sugar and beat until glossy but not stiff, about

1 minute. Fold one-fourth of the beaten whites into the batter, then fold in the rest. Scrape the batter into an ungreased 10-by-4-inch angel food cake pan (not nonstick) with a removable bottom.

**3.** Bake the cake for 50 minutes, or until a toothpick inserted in the center comes out clean. Invert the cake onto the neck of a wine bottle; let cool. Run a knife around the inside of the pan and remove the outer ring. Run the knife around the tube and along the bottom and remove the tube. Cut the cake into wedges and sift with confectioners' sugar. Serve with the frozen yogurt and oranges.

—*Greg Patent*

**MAKE AHEAD** The cake can be made up to 2 days ahead.

## Guinness Ginger Cake

**ACTIVE: 30 MIN; TOTAL: 1 HR 30 MIN**

**8 SERVINGS** ●

Seeds from 6 cardamom pods
One 1½-inch cinnamon stick
 3   whole black peppercorns
 1   whole clove
 1   cup stout, such as Guinness
 1   cup unsulfured molasses
1½  teaspoons baking soda
 3   large eggs
 ½   cup granulated sugar
 ½   cup packed dark brown sugar
 ¾   cup vegetable oil
 2   cups all-purpose flour
 2   tablespoons ground ginger
1½  teaspoons baking powder
 ¼   teaspoon freshly grated nutmeg
Pinch of salt
 1   tablespoon grated fresh ginger
Sweetened whipped cream, for serving

**1.** Preheat the oven to 350°. Butter and flour a 10-cup Bundt pan. In a small skillet, cook the cardamom seeds, cinnamon stick, peppercorns and clove over moderate heat until fragrant, about 1 minute. Transfer the spices to a spice grinder and let cool, then finely grind.

**2.** In a large saucepan, bring the stout and molasses to a boil. Remove from the heat and stir in the baking soda; it will bubble vigorously. Let cool.

**3.** In a bowl, whisk the eggs and granulated sugar and brown sugar. Whisk in the oil and then the stout mixture.

**4.** In a large bowl, whisk the flour with the ground ginger, baking powder, nutmeg, salt and freshly ground spices. Add the molasses mixture in 2 batches. Stir in the fresh ginger. Pour the batter into the prepared pan and bake for 45 minutes, or until the top is springy when lightly pressed. Transfer the pan to a rack to cool completely, then unmold the cake. Serve with whipped cream.

—*Claudia Fleming*

**MAKE AHEAD** The cake can be made up to 2 days ahead.

## Lemon Ricotta Cheesecake

**ACTIVE: 1 HR; TOTAL: 2 HR 15 MIN,**

**PLUS 2 HR CHILLING**

**10 SERVINGS** ●

**PASTRY**

2⅔  cups all-purpose flour
 3   tablespoons sugar
 ¾   teaspoon salt
 ¾   cup cold solid vegetable
     shortening, divided into 3 pieces
 2   large eggs, lightly beaten
 3   tablespoons milk
**FILLING**
1½  pounds ricotta (3 cups)
 1   cup sugar
 3   large eggs
 1   tablespoon grated lemon zest
1½  tablespoons anise liqueur
 2   teaspoons pure vanilla extract
 1   egg lightly beaten with
     1 tablespoon water

**1. MAKE THE PASTRY:** In a food processor, combine the flour, sugar and salt and pulse several times. Add the shortening and pulse until the mixture resembles coarse meal. Add the eggs and milk

# cakes, cookies + more

and pulse until lightly moistened. Turn the dough out onto a lightly floured work surface and knead a few times until smooth. Form the dough into 2 disks, one slightly larger than the other. Wrap the disks in plastic and refrigerate for 30 minutes or for up to 3 days.

**2.** MAKE THE FILLING: In a food processor, combine the ricotta, sugar, eggs, lemon zest, anise liqueur and vanilla and process until smooth.

**3.** Preheat the oven to 375°. On a lightly floured work surface or between sheets of plastic, roll out the larger disk of dough to a 13-inch round. Line a 10-by-1½-inch pie plate with it. Patch any cracks. Spoon in the filling. Roll out the remaining disk of dough to an 11-inch round. Brush the pastry pie rim with water and set the round on top. Press the edges together to seal. Trim the overhanging dough and crimp decoratively. Make 3 small slashes in the top and brush with the egg wash. Bake for 40 to 45 minutes, or until the pastry is golden; cover with foil if it browns too quickly. Let cool on a rack to room temperature, then refrigerate until chilled, about 2 hours. —*Rafaella Giamundo*

**MAKE AHEAD** The cheesecake can be refrigerated for up to 3 days.

# health

**BENEFITS OF CHOCOLATE**

**Eat chocolate and live longer? Using a test developed by Tufts University's USDA Human Nutrition Research Center on Aging, researchers at Penn State University found that chocolate— the darker the better—contains more anti-aging antioxidants than any other food. —*Dana Jacobi***

## Lemon Cheesecake with Olive Oil

**ACTIVE: 30 MIN; TOTAL: 2 HR, PLUS 2 HR CHILLING**

**8 TO 10 SERVINGS** ●

CRUST

- 1 **cup graham cracker crumbs**
- 2 **tablespoons sugar**
- 4 **tablespoons unsalted butter, melted**

FILLING

- 19 **ounces cream cheese, softened**
- ½ **cup plus 3 tablespoons sugar**
- 3 **large eggs, separated**

**Finely grated zest of 1 lemon**

- 2 **tablespoons extra-virgin olive oil**

**1.** MAKE THE CRUST: Preheat the oven to 325°. Butter the side only of a 9-inch springform pan. In a bowl, stir the graham cracker crumbs with the sugar and butter until moistened. Press the crumbs into the bottom of the springform pan in an even layer.

**2.** MAKE THE FILLING: In a large bowl, using an electric mixer, beat the cream cheese with ½ cup of the sugar until smooth. Add the egg yolks, lemon zest and olive oil and beat until smooth.

**3.** In another bowl, beat the egg whites at medium speed until frothy. Increase the speed to high and beat until firm peaks form. Slowly add the remaining 3 tablespoons of sugar and beat until the whites are stiff and glossy. Beat one-fourth of the whites into the cream cheese mixture, then fold in the rest until no streaks remain. Scrape the filling into the pan and smooth the surface.

**4.** Bake the cheesecake in the center of the oven for 45 minutes, or until the top is golden and lightly cracked. Transfer to a rack to cool completely, then refrigerate until chilled, at least 2 hours.

**5.** Remove the ring and transfer the cheesecake to a plate. Cut into wedges and serve. —*Pascal Rigo*

**MAKE AHEAD** The cheesecake can be refrigerated for up to 3 days.

## Cappuccino Cheesecakes

**TOTAL: 45 MIN, PLUS 3 HR CHILLING**

**6 SERVINGS** ●

**Vegetable oil**

- 1½ **cups graham cracker crumbs (5 ounces)**
- 4 **tablespoons unsalted butter, melted**
- ¼ **teaspoon cinnamon**
- 1½ **teaspoons unflavored gelatin**
- ½ **cup strong brewed coffee, at room temperature**
- 8 **ounces crème fraîche**
- ⅔ **cup sour cream**
- 6 **ounces cream cheese, softened**
- 3 **large egg whites**
- ¾ **cup sugar**

**Unsweetened cocoa powder, for dusting**

**1.** Preheat the oven to 350°. Line a rimmed baking sheet with parchment paper. Lightly oil six 3-inch flan rings that are at least 2 inches tall (see Note) and space evenly on the baking sheet.

**2.** In a medium bowl, mix the graham cracker crumbs with the melted butter and cinnamon. Spoon the crumbs into the flan rings and press to form an even layer of crust. Bake for 8 minutes, or until set. Let cool completely.

**3.** In a small saucepan, sprinkle the gelatin over the coffee and let stand until softened, 5 minutes. Warm the coffee over moderate heat to melt the gelatin, about 2 minutes. Let cool to tepid.

**4.** In a large bowl, combine the crème fraîche, sour cream and cream cheese and beat until smooth. Fold in the coffee gelatin. In another bowl, using clean beaters, beat the egg whites until soft peaks form. Gradually beat in the sugar and continue beating until the whites are firm and glossy, then fold them into the cream cheese mixture. Spoon the mixture into the flan rings. Cover and refrigerate the cheesecakes until firm, at least 3 hours or overnight.

**5.** To unmold, push the cheesecakes up through the flan rings and set them on plates. Sift cocoa over the cheesecakes and serve. —*Chris Erasmus*

**NOTE** Cleaned 8-ounce cans with the tops and bottoms removed can be used in place of flan rings.

## Nono's Mocha Praline Cake
**ACTIVE: 30 MIN; TOTAL: 1 HR 30 MIN**
**8 SERVINGS ●**
- 1 cup shelled hazelnuts
- ¼ cup plus 2 tablespoons superfine sugar
- 2 tablespoons instant espresso
- 2 tablespoons warm water
- 2½ cups heavy cream
- 3 cups strong brewed coffee
- 48 dry ladyfingers from two 7-ounce packages

**1.** Preheat the oven to 350°. Lightly oil a baking sheet. On another rimmed baking sheet, toast the hazelnuts for 8 minutes, or until fragrant and golden brown. Let them cool, then rub the hazelnuts in a kitchen towel to remove the skins.

**2.** In a medium skillet, sprinkle the hazelnuts with ¼ cup of the sugar. Cook over moderate heat, without stirring, until the sugar melts and browns, about 2 minutes. Stir to coat the hazelnuts with the caramel, then scrape them out onto the oiled baking sheet. Let the nuts cool and harden, then break them into pieces. Reserve 10 whole hazelnuts for garnish. Transfer the rest to a food processor and grind to a coarse powder.

**3.** In a small bowl, dissolve the instant espresso in the water. In a large, stainless steel bowl, beat the heavy cream until thickened. Add the remaining 2 tablespoons of sugar and the dissolved espresso and beat until soft peaks form. Refrigerate 1 cup of the whipped cream.

**4.** Put the coffee in a large shallow bowl. Moisten 12 of the ladyfingers in the coffee, lightly dipping each side. Arrange the ladyfingers side by side on the bottom of a 9-inch springform pan. Break a few of them if necessary to completely cover the bottom of the pan. Spread one-fourth of the espresso whipped cream over the ladyfingers and sprinkle with one-fourth of the hazelnut praline. Repeat with the remaining ladyfingers, whipped cream and praline. Refrigerate the cake until firm, about 1 hour.

**5.** Warm a thin knife under hot water and run it around the inside of the ring of the springform pan. Remove the ring. Using an offset spatula, spread the reserved 1 cup of espresso whipped cream around the top and side of the cake. Garnish with the reserved whole hazelnuts. Cut the cake into wedges and serve.
—*Nadia Roden*

**MAKE AHEAD** The cake can be frozen, tightly wrapped, for up to 2 days. Serve softened or partially thawed.

## Triple-Layer Chocolate Macaroon Cake
**ACTIVE: 35 MIN; TOTAL: 3 HR 15 MIN**
**8 SERVINGS ● ●**
- Vegetable oil spray
- 1⅔ cups heavy cream
- 10½ ounces bittersweet chocolate, coarsely chopped
- 3½ ounces milk chocolate, coarsely chopped
- 4 large eggs
- 1½ cups sugar
- 4⅔ cups dried unsweetened finely grated coconut (10 ounces)
- Chocolate curls, for garnish

**1.** Preheat the oven to 350°. Spray an 11-by-17-inch jelly-roll pan with vegetable oil and line the bottom with parchment paper; spray the paper.

**2.** In a small saucepan, bring the heavy cream to a boil. Remove from the heat, add the chocolates and let stand for 5 minutes, then whisk until smooth. Pour 1 cup of the chocolate ganache into a measuring cup and set aside at room temperature; scrape the rest into a bowl. Cover the bowl with plastic wrap and refrigerate the ganache until firm, at least 3 hours.

**3.** Meanwhile, in a medium saucepan, bring 1 inch of water to a bare simmer. Using an electric mixer, beat the eggs and sugar in a large bowl at medium speed until blended. Set the bowl over the simmering water and whisk until the eggs are warm to the touch. Remove from the heat and beat at high speed until the egg mixture has tripled in volume, about 5 minutes. Fold in 3⅔ cups of the grated coconut. Spread the batter in the prepared jelly-roll pan in an even layer. Bake for about 25 minutes, or until golden and firm to the touch. Let the cake cool for 15 minutes.

**4.** Run a knife around the edge of the cake; invert it onto a baking sheet and peel off the parchment. Slide the cake onto a work surface. Using a serrated knife, trim the edges and cut the cake into 3 rectangles of equal size. Stack the layers and trim off any uneven sides with the knife.

**5.** Set 1 cake layer right side up on a wire rack and spread with half of the chilled ganache. Cover with a second cake layer and the remaining chilled ganache. Top with the third cake layer, smooth side up; press down gently. Pour half of the reserved ganache on top and spread it evenly, letting it drip slightly down the sides. Pour on the remaining ganache and smooth the top and sides. Carefully transfer the cake to a cake plate and refrigerate for 15 minutes, then firmly press the remaining coconut onto the sides of the cake. Garnish with chocolate curls and serve, or, for best results, refrigerate the cake overnight.
—*François Payard*

**MAKE AHEAD** The cake can be refrigerated for up to 4 days.

# cakes, cookies + more

### Rum-Mocha Walnut Layer Cake
**ACTIVE: 45 MIN; TOTAL: 1 HR 30 MIN, PLUS 4 HR CHILLING**
**10 SERVINGS ●**
CAKE

**Fine dry bread crumbs, for dusting**
- 2   cups walnut halves (7 ounces)
- ¼   cup unsweetened cocoa powder (not Dutch-process)
- ½   cup cake flour
- 1   teaspoon instant espresso powder
- 8   large eggs, separated
- 1   cup sugar
- 2   teaspoons pure vanilla extract
- ¼   teaspoon salt

FILLING
- 6   large egg yolks
- ½   cup sugar

**Pinch of salt**
- 2   tablespoons instant espresso powder dissolved in ½ cup hot water
- 1   pound unsalted butter, softened
- 3   tablespoons coffee liqueur
- 1   tablespoon pure vanilla extract
- ½   cup dark rum, for brushing
- 1½  cups finely chopped walnuts (5 ounces), plus walnut halves for garnish

**1. MAKE THE CAKE:** Preheat the oven to 350°. Butter two 9-inch round cake pans and line the bottoms with parchment paper. Butter the parchment and dust with bread crumbs, tapping out any excess. In a food processor, pulse the walnuts until finely chopped. Add the cocoa powder, cake flour and espresso powder and pulse until the walnuts are finely ground. Transfer to a bowl.

**2.** In a large bowl, using an electric mixer, beat the egg yolks at medium speed until thick and pale, 3 minutes. Beat in ⅔ cup of the sugar; increase the speed to high and beat until thick, about 5 minutes. Beat in the vanilla. In a medium bowl, using clean beaters, beat the egg whites

and salt at medium speed until soft peaks form. Gradually add the remaining ⅓ cup of sugar and beat at high speed until the whites are stiff and glossy. Fold the egg whites and ground walnuts into the yolk mixture in 3 batches; fold just until no streaks remain.

**3.** Divide the batter between the prepared pans; smooth the tops. Bake for about 20 minutes, until the cakes are golden and springy. Transfer to a rack for 10 minutes, then invert the cakes and cool completely. Peel off the parchment; turn the cakes right side up.

**4. MAKE THE FILLING:** Fill a medium bowl with ice water. In a medium heatproof bowl, whisk the egg yolks, sugar and salt. Gradually whisk in the dissolved espresso. Place the bowl over a saucepan of barely simmering water and cook, stirring with a spatula, until the yolks are thick enough to coat the spatula and an instant-read thermometer inserted into the mixture registers 175°, about 10 minutes. Set the bowl in the ice bath and cool, stirring occasionally.

**5.** In a large bowl, using an electric mixer, beat the butter at medium speed until smooth. Beat in the yolk mixture in 4 batches, beating well between additions. Beat in the liqueur and vanilla.

**6.** Using a serrated knife, split each cake in half horizontally. Set a top layer, cut side up, on a cake plate; brush it with 2 tablespoons of the rum and spread with ½ cup of the filling. Top with a bottom cake layer; brush with 2 more tablespoons of rum and spread with another ½ cup of filling. Repeat with the remaining top cake layer, ending with the bottom layer, cut side down. Brush the top of the cake with the remaining 2 tablespoons of rum and spread the sides of the cake with a thin layer of filling. Spread the remaining filling on the top. Press the chopped walnuts around the side of the cake. Refrigerate the cake for

at least 4 hours or overnight. Let the cake stand at room temperature for 15 minutes, then scatter the walnut halves on top before serving. —*Greg Patent*
**MAKE AHEAD** The cake can be refrigerated for up to 4 days.

### Molten Chocolate Cakes
**TOTAL: 25 MIN**
**6 SERVINGS ● ●**
- 2   sticks (½ pound) unsalted butter, plus more for the ramekins
- 1   tablespoon plus 1 teaspoon cake flour, plus more for dusting
- ½   pound bittersweet chocolate, chopped
- ½   cup granulated sugar
- 4   large whole eggs
- 4   large egg yolks

**Unsweetened cocoa and confectioners' sugar, for dusting**

**1.** Preheat the oven to 350°. Butter six 4-ounce ramekins and dust with flour.
**2.** In the top of a double boiler, melt the butter with the chocolate. Remove from the heat; whisk in the granulated sugar, eggs and egg yolks. Whisk in the flour.
**3.** Scrape the batter into the ramekins and bake for 10 minutes, or until the sides of the cakes are set but the centers are still slightly loose. Let the cakes cool for 1 minute, then run a thin knife around the sides and invert them onto plates. Dust the cakes with cocoa and confectioners' sugar and serve. —*Margot Janse*
**SERVE WITH** Hazelnut Tuiles (p. 332) and ice cream.

### Chocolate-Pecan Brownie Cake with Glossy Chocolate Glaze
**ACTIVE: 30 MIN; TOTAL: 3 HR, PLUS 4 HR COOLING**
**MAKES ONE 9-INCH CAKE ●**
Closer to a dense Sacher torte than to a brownie, this nut-studded cake is great for a dinner party. And it freezes well, so you can make it in advance.

RUM-MOCHA WALNUT LAYER CAKE

# cakes, cookies + more

**CHOCOLATE-PECAN CAKE**

- 3 cups pecan halves (10 ounces)
- 5 large eggs
- 1 cup granulated sugar
- 1 cup confectioners' sugar
- 2½ sticks (10 ounces) unsalted butter
- 6 ounces bittersweet chocolate, chopped
- 1 tablespoon pure vanilla extract
- 1 cup all-purpose flour, sifted

**CHOCOLATE GANACHE**

- ¾ cup heavy cream
- 6 ounces bittersweet chocolate, chopped
- 1 tablespoon Grand Marnier (optional)

1. **MAKE THE CHOCOLATE-PECAN CAKE:** Preheat the oven to 375°. Butter a 9-inch round springform pan. Line the bottom of the pan with parchment paper and butter the paper. Spread the pecans on a large, rimmed baking sheet and bake for 8 minutes, or until lightly toasted. Transfer to a plate and let cool, then coarsely chop. Leave the oven on.

2. In a large saucepan, bring 2 inches of water to a simmer over low heat. In a large stainless steel bowl, whisk the eggs with the granulated and confectioners' sugars. Set the bowl over the simmering water and whisk the egg mixture constantly until it is warm to the touch, about 3 minutes. Remove from the heat.

3. Put the butter and chocolate in a medium stainless steel bowl and set over the simmering water until just melted, about 3 minutes. Add the vanilla, stir well and remove from the heat.

4. Using a handheld electric mixer, beat the egg mixture at high speed until pale yellow and doubled in volume, about 5 minutes. Add the flour all at once and gently fold it in with a whisk. Using a rubber spatula, fold in the melted chocolate and the pecans. Pour the batter into the prepared pan and set it on a baking sheet. Bake for 20 minutes. Reduce the oven temperature to 350° and continue to bake the cake for about 50 minutes longer, or until the cake is set and an instant-read thermometer inserted in the center registers 200°.

5. Transfer the cake to a wire rack and let cool to room temperature in the pan, about 4 hours. Remove the side of the springform pan and pierce any bubbles that formed on the surface of the cake.

6. **MAKE THE CHOCOLATE GANACHE:** In a small saucepan, bring the cream to a boil. Put the chocolate in a medium bowl, pour the hot cream over it and let stand for 5 minutes, or until the chocolate is melted. Add the Grand Marnier and whisk until smooth. Set aside, whisking occasionally, until shiny and just warm to the touch, 1½ to 2 hours.

7. Invert the cake onto a plate and peel off the parchment paper. Turn the cake over onto a rack set over a baking sheet. Pour ⅓ cup of the ganache over the top of the cake and spread it evenly with an offset spatula. Refrigerate the cake on the rack until set, about 20 minutes. Slowly pour the remaining ganache over the cake, spreading it over the top and around the sides. Refrigerate the cake until the ganache is set, about 20 minutes. Cut the cake into wedges with a hot knife, wiping the blade between cuts.
—*Jean-Claude Szurdak*

# taste test

**TIP** — **EASTER CHOCOLATE**

To find the best chocolate Easter eggs, the F&W staff tasted 20 different brands of milk and dark, solid and filled, imported and domestic, haute and camp and selected these four as our favorites.

| PRODUCT | COMMENT | INTERESTING BITE |
|---|---|---|
| **Lindt Dark Chocolate Truffle Egg** | "Slightly bitter shell; lovely creamy filling." | Rodolphe Lindt invented a process to make chocolate melt in the mouth. |
| **Godiva Solid Milk Chocolate Egg** | "The chocolate is creamy and complex, with a subtle nuttiness." | Godiva.com's hundreds of chocolate recipes range from breads to martinis. |
| **Reese's Peanut Butter Egg** | "The salty, chunky peanut butter is key here." | The original peanut butter cups, which debuted in the 1920s, cost 1 cent. |
| **Russell Stover Marshmallow Egg** | "Good balance of sugary marshmallow and chocolate." | Russell Stover makes over 100 million pounds of boxed chocolate each year. |

**MAKE AHEAD** The unglazed cake can be wrapped in plastic and stored at room temperature overnight. The glazed cake can be refrigerated for up to 2 days or wrapped in foil and frozen for up to 1 month. Bring the cake to room temperature before serving.

## Earl Grey Devil's Food Cakes with Cherries

**TOTAL: 3 HR**

**8 SERVINGS** ●

¾ cup plus 2 tablespoons heavy cream

3½ ounces bittersweet chocolate, finely chopped

4 tablespoons cold unsalted butter, plus 1½ tablespoons melted

1 pound sweet cherries, pitted and halved

¾ cup plus 3 tablespoons granulated sugar

1 tablespoon lemon juice

½ cup all-purpose flour

6 tablespoons unsweetened cocoa powder

¾ teaspoon baking soda

¼ teaspoon baking powder

1 large egg

1 large egg yolk

6 tablespoons buttermilk

¼ cup plus 2 tablespoons warm brewed Earl Grey tea

Toasted pistachios, for garnish

**1.** In a medium nonreactive saucepan, scald the cream. Off the heat, add the chocolate and let stand for 5 minutes; whisk until smooth. Add the cold butter and blend with an immersion blender until smooth. Refrigerate until firm, about 2 hours.

**2.** In a medium nonreactive saucepan, combine the cherries with 3 tablespoons of the sugar and the lemon juice and let stand for 30 minutes. Boil the mixture for 5 minutes, then cool.

**3.** Preheat the oven to 375°. Butter and flour 8 muffin cups. In a large bowl, whisk the remaining ¾ cup of sugar with the flour, cocoa, baking soda and baking powder. In another bowl, whisk the egg with the egg yolk, buttermilk, Earl Grey tea and melted butter; whisk into the dry ingredients.

**4.** Pour the batter into the cups and bake for 15 minutes. Let cool slightly, then invert the cakes on a rack; let cool. Set the cakes upside down on plates and top with chocolate ganache. Spoon on the cherries, sprinkle with nuts and serve. —*Nick Morgenstern*

**MAKE AHEAD** The cakes can be made up to 1 day ahead and kept, tightly covered, at room temperature. The ganache and cherries can be refrigerated, separately, for up to 1 day.

## Chocolate-Buttermilk Layer Cake with Vanilla Buttercream

**ACTIVE: 45 MIN; TOTAL: 1 HR 50 MIN, PLUS 3 HR 30 MIN COOLING AND CHILLING**

**MAKES TWO 9-INCH CAKES** ●

This simple recipe makes two moist chocolate-buttermilk cakes. Stash the second one in the freezer for another day when you need a quick homemade dessert.

CAKES

2⅓ cups all-purpose flour

1½ cups unsweetened cocoa powder

1 tablespoon baking powder

1 tablespoon baking soda

1¼ teaspoons salt

3 cups sugar

5 large eggs

1 tablespoon pure vanilla extract

1½ cups buttermilk

1½ sticks (6 ounces) unsalted butter, melted

1½ cups strong brewed coffee, cooled

FILLING AND FROSTING

Vanilla Buttercream (recipe follows)

Two 1.4-ounce Skor bars, finely crushed

Cornstarch, for rolling

1½ pounds prepared fondant

Colored fondant and diluted food coloring, for decorating

**1. MAKE THE CAKES:** Preheat the oven to 350°. Butter and flour two 9-inch round cake pans. In a large bowl, sift the flour with the cocoa, baking powder, baking soda and salt. Stir in the sugar.

**2.** In a medium bowl, mix the eggs with the vanilla until blended, then whisk in the buttermilk, melted butter and coffee. Whisk the liquid ingredients into the flour mixture. Scrape the batter into the prepared pans and bake for 1 hour, or until a tester inserted in the center of each cake comes out clean. Transfer the cakes to a rack and let cool for about 30 minutes. Run a knife around the edge of each cake, invert onto the rack and let cool completely, about 2 hours.

**3. FILL AND FROST THE CAKE:** Set 1 of the cakes on a cake circle. Using a serrated knife, cut the cake in half horizontally; set the top aside. Spread a ⅓-inch-thick layer of Vanilla Buttercream over the cake; be sure to spread it all the way to the edge. Sprinkle the Skor bits over the buttercream and cover with the top cake layer. Frost the top and side of the cake with a thin, even layer of buttercream. Refrigerate the cake for 1 hour.

**4.** Dust a work surface with cornstarch and roll out the fondant to a 13½-inch round. Roll the fondant onto the rolling pin and unroll it over the cake. Smooth the surface of the fondant and trim around the base of the cake. Decorate the cake as desired. —*Margaret Braun*

**MAKE AHEAD** The chocolate-buttermilk cakes can be wrapped in plastic and then in foil and frozen for 1 month. The decorated fondant-covered cake can be refrigerated uncovered for up to 5 days.

WHITE CHOCOLATE CAKE WITH ORANGE MARMALADE FILLING

## VANILLA BUTTERCREAM

**TOTAL: 20 MIN**

**MAKES ABOUT 3 CUPS** ● ●

This is what's referred to as an Italian meringue buttercream—it's light and delicious. The softened butter is beaten into a fluffy meringue; it looks like it will never come together when you first start beating, but then it gradually turns into a silky, creamy frosting.

2½ sticks (10 ounces) unsalted butter, at room temperature

1 tablespoon pure vanilla extract

¾ cup sugar

3 large egg whites

**1.** In a medium bowl, using a wooden spoon, cream the butter with the vanilla extract.

**2.** In a large heatproof bowl, whisk the sugar with the egg whites. Set the bowl over a pan containing 1 inch of simmering water and whisk the egg whites constantly until the sugar is dissolved. Remove the bowl from the heat. Using an electric mixer, beat the whites at high speed until a medium-firm meringue forms, about 5 minutes.

**3.** Reduce the speed to moderate. Beat the creamed butter into the meringue ¼ cup at a time, beating until it is fully incorporated before adding more. Use the Vanilla Buttercream immediately or refrigerate for up to 1 day. —*M.B.*

## White Chocolate Cake with Orange Marmalade Filling

**ACTIVE: 25 MIN; TOTAL: 3 HR**

**12 SERVINGS** ● ●

2¼ cups all-purpose flour

2½ teaspoons baking powder

¼ teaspoon salt

1½ sticks (6 ounces) unsalted butter, softened

1½ cups sugar

4 large eggs

1 teaspoon pure vanilla extract

1¼ cups milk

8 ounces white chocolate, melted

2 tablespoons orange marmalade, very finely chopped if chunky

¼ cup confectioners' sugar

White Chocolate Buttercream (recipe follows)

½ cup Candied Orange Peels (recipe follows), dipped in melted white chocolate (optional), for garnish

**1.** Preheat the oven to 350°. Butter and flour two 9-inch round cake pans, making sure to tap out the excess flour.

**2.** Sift the flour with the baking powder and salt. In a large bowl, using an electric mixer, beat the butter at low speed until smooth. Add the sugar and beat until fluffy. Add the eggs 1 at a time, beating well after each addition. Add the vanilla. At low speed, alternately beat in the dry ingredients and the milk in 2 additions. Add the melted white chocolate and beat just until incorporated. Scrape the batter into the prepared cake pans and smooth the surfaces.

**3.** Bake the cakes in the center of the oven for 35 minutes, or until they are golden brown and a toothpick inserted into the center of each cake comes out clean. Let the cakes cool in the pans for 10 minutes, then invert them onto a wire rack and let cool completely.

**4.** In a small bowl, using a handheld electric mixer, beat the marmalade and the confectioners' sugar into 1 cup of the White Chocolate Buttercream. Set 1 cake layer right side up on a cake plate and spread the orange marmalade filling on top. Cover with the second cake layer. Frost the side and top of the cake with the remaining White Chocolate Buttercream. Garnish with white chocolate–dipped Candied Orange Peels and serve. —*Grace Parisi*

**MAKE AHEAD** The frosted cake can be refrigerated, covered with plastic wrap or a cake dome, for up to 2 days.

## WHITE CHOCOLATE BUTTERCREAM

**TOTAL: 10 MIN**

**MAKES 2¾ CUPS** ●

2 sticks (½ pound) unsalted butter, softened

12 ounces white chocolate, melted and cooled slightly

1 cup confectioners' sugar

1 teaspoon pure vanilla extract

In a large bowl, using a handheld electric mixer, beat the butter at medium speed until creamy. Beat in the melted white chocolate. Add the confectioners' sugar and vanilla and beat at low speed, scraping the side and bottom of the bowl, until light and fluffy. —*G.P.*

## CANDIED ORANGE PEELS

**ACTIVE: 45 MIN; TOTAL: 2 HR, PLUS OVERNIGHT DRYING**

**MAKES 4 CUPS** ●

The candied peels used to garnish the white chocolate cake are good to have on hand for baking during the holiday season. Dip the strips into melted chocolate to make candy, or mix them into cake batters and cookie or scone doughs to add a powerful orange flavor.

6 large organic navel oranges

4 cups sugar

3 tablespoons light corn syrup

**1.** Using a sharp paring knife, score the oranges lengthwise into quarters. Remove the peels and cut them lengthwise into ½-inch-wide strips.

**2.** In a medium saucepan, cover the orange peels with water and bring to a boil over moderately high heat. Boil for 5 minutes, then drain in a large colander. Repeat the blanching and draining process 2 more times to tenderize the orange peels and remove the bitterness.

**3.** In the saucepan, combine 2 cups of the sugar with the corn syrup and 1 cup of water. Bring to a boil over moderately high heat, occasionally washing down the side of the saucepan with a wet

# cakes, cookies + more

pastry brush. Add the orange peels to the syrup and cook, stirring occasionally, until the peels are somewhat transparent and most of the syrup has been absorbed, 40 to 50 minutes. During the last 10 minutes of cooking, stir the syrup frequently and watch carefully to prevent the peels from burning.

**4.** Spread 1 cup of the remaining sugar on each of 2 heavy, rimmed baking sheets. Drain the orange peels in a large colander. Using a fork or tongs, transfer each piece of orange peel to the sugar-coated baking sheets; do not clump the peels together. Let the orange peels cool for 15 minutes, then roll them in the sugar to coat completely. Let cool thoroughly in the sugar, then transfer the orange peels to a wire rack and let dry overnight. Discard the remaining sugar from the baking sheets. —*Peggy Cullen*

**MAKE AHEAD** The Candied Orange Peels can be stored in an airtight container for up to 1 month.

### Double Dark Chocolate Cupcakes with Peanut Butter Filling

**ACTIVE: 45 MIN; TOTAL: 3 HR**

**MAKES 2 DOZEN CUPCAKES** ● ◑

- ¾ cup plus 2 tablespoons cocoa powder (not Dutch-process)
- ½ cup boiling water
- 1 cup buttermilk
- 1¾ cups all-purpose flour
- 1¼ teaspoons baking soda
- ¼ teaspoon baking powder
- ¼ teaspoon salt
- 1½ sticks plus 3 tablespoons unsalted butter, softened
- 1½ cups granulated sugar
- 2 large eggs, at room temperature
- 1 teaspoon pure vanilla extract
- 1 cup creamy peanut butter
- ⅔ cup confectioners' sugar
- 1 cup heavy cream
- 8 ounces semisweet chocolate, chopped

**1.** Preheat the oven to 350° and position 2 racks in the lower and middle thirds of the oven. Line 24 muffin cups with paper or foil liners.

**2.** Put the cocoa powder in a medium heatproof bowl. Add the boiling water and whisk until a smooth paste forms. Whisk in the buttermilk until combined. In a medium bowl, sift the flour with the baking soda, baking powder and salt. In a large bowl, using an electric mixer, beat 1½ sticks of the butter with the granulated sugar until light and fluffy, about 3 minutes. Beat in the eggs and vanilla, then beat in the dry ingredients in 2 batches, alternating with the cocoa mixture. Carefully spoon the cupcake batter into the lined muffin cups, filling them about two-thirds full. Bake for 20 to 22 minutes, or until the cupcakes are springy. Let the cupcakes cool in the pans for 5 minutes, then transfer them to wire racks to cool completely.

**3.** In a medium bowl, beat the peanut butter with the remaining 3 tablespoons of butter until creamy. Sift the confectioners' sugar into the bowl and beat until light and fluffy, about 2 minutes. Spoon all but 3 tablespoons of the peanut butter filling into a pastry bag fitted with a ¼-inch star tip. Holding a cupcake in your hand, plunge the tip into the top of the cake, pushing it about ¾ inch deep. Gently squeeze the pastry bag to fill the cupcake, withdrawing it slowly as you squeeze; you will feel the cupcake expand slightly as you fill it. Scrape any filling from the top of the cupcake and repeat until all of the cupcakes are filled.

**4.** In a small saucepan, bring the heavy cream to a simmer. Off the heat, add the semisweet chocolate to the cream and let stand for 5 minutes, then whisk the melted chocolate into the cream until smooth. Let the chocolate icing stand until slightly cooled and thickened, about 15 minutes. Dip the tops of the

cupcakes into the icing, letting the excess drip back into the pan. Transfer the cupcakes to racks and let stand for 5 minutes. Dip the tops of the cupcakes again and transfer them to racks. Spoon the remaining 3 tablespoons of peanut butter filling into the pastry bag and pipe tiny rosettes on the tops of the cupakes. —*Peggy Cullen*

**MAKE AHEAD** The cupcakes are best served the same day they are made, but they can be refrigerated overnight in an airtight container.

### Chocolate Cream-Cheese Cupcakes

**TOTAL: 40 MIN**

**MAKES 2 DOZEN CUPCAKES** ●

These cupcakes from Anne Byrn, author of the *Cake Mix Doctor* cookbooks, are delicious even though they are made with a cake mix.

- One 18.25-ounce box devil's food cake mix
- ½ pound cream cheese, softened
- ½ cup water
- ½ cup vegetable oil
- ¼ cup light brown sugar
- 4 large eggs
- 1 teaspoon pure vanilla extract
- 1 cup granulated sugar
- 5 tablespoons unsalted butter
- ⅓ cup milk
- 1 cup semisweet chocolate chips
- 2 tablespoons chopped toasted almonds

**1.** Preheat the oven to 350°. Line two 12-cup muffin pans with paper liners. In a large bowl, beat the devil's food cake mix with the cream cheese, water, vegetable oil, brown sugar, eggs and vanilla at low speed until smooth.

**2.** Using an ice cream scoop, spoon the batter into the muffin cups, filling them two-thirds full. Bake the cupcakes until they are springy to the touch and a cake tester inserted in the center of a cupcake

DOUBLE DARK CHOCOLATE CUPCAKE WITH PEANUT BUTTER FILLING

# cakes, cookies + more

comes out clean, about 20 minutes. Transfer the muffin pans to a wire rack and let cool for 5 to 10 minutes.

3. Meanwhile, in a medium saucepan, combine the granulated sugar, butter and milk and bring to a boil over moderately high heat, stirring until dissolved. Remove from the heat and stir in the chocolate chips until melted. Transfer the frosting to a bowl and let cool until slightly thickened, about 5 minutes. Dip the top of each cupcake in the frosting and return to the wire rack. Garnish the cupcakes with the chopped almonds and let stand for 5 to 10 minutes, until the frosting is set, before serving.
—*Anne Byrn*

**MAKE AHEAD** The frosted cupcakes can be kept at cool room temperature in an airtight container overnight.

## Carrot Cupcakes with Caramel and Cream Cheese Frosting
**ACTIVE: 45 MIN; TOTAL: 1 HR 30 MIN**
**MAKES 2 DOZEN CUPCAKES** ● ●
The cream cheese frosting on these carrot cupcakes is intentionally undersweetened because of the sweet caramel topping.

CUPCAKES

- 8 carrots (1¼ pounds), peeled and coarsely shredded (4 cups)
- 1 cup golden raisins
- 1 cup pecans, coarsely chopped
- 2 cups all-purpose flour
- 2 teaspoons cinnamon
- 2 teaspoons baking powder
- ¼ teaspoon baking soda
- 1 teaspoon salt
- 1¼ cups canola oil
- 2 cups sugar
- 4 large eggs, at room temperature

TOPPINGS

- ½ cup sugar
- 2 tablespoons water
- Few drops of fresh lemon juice
- ¼ cup heavy cream

- 1 pound cream cheese, softened
- 2 sticks (½ pound) unsalted butter, softened
- ½ cup confectioners' sugar
- 1 teaspoon pure vanilla extract

1. **MAKE THE CUPCAKES:** Preheat the oven to 350°. Line two 12-cup muffin tins with paper liners. In a medium bowl, toss the carrots with the raisins and pecans. Onto a large sheet of wax paper, sift the flour with the cinnamon, baking powder, baking soda and salt.

2. In a large bowl, using an electric mixer, beat the canola oil with the sugar at medium-high speed until smooth. Add the eggs, 1 at a time, beating well between additions. Add the dry ingredients and beat at low speed until combined. Using a wooden spoon, stir in the carrot mixture.

3. Spoon the batter into the cups, filling them three-fourths full. Bake the cupcakes for about 25 minutes, or until the tops spring back when lightly pressed. Let cool in the pans for 10 minutes, then transfer the cupcakes to a wire rack to cool completely.

4. **MEANWHILE, MAKE THE TOPPINGS:** In a small, deep saucepan, combine the sugar, water and lemon juice. Using a wet pastry brush, wash down the side of the saucepan. Bring to a simmer over moderately high heat and cook, without stirring, until the caramel just begins to color around the edge, about 5 minutes. Gently swirl the pan and simmer until the caramel turns a medium amber color, about 2 minutes longer. Remove from the heat. Using a long-handled wooden spoon, stir in the heavy cream. Transfer the caramel to a small bowl and let cool.

5. In another bowl, beat the cream cheese at low speed until smooth. Beat in the butter, then beat in the confectioners' sugar and vanilla extract until the cream cheese frosting is smooth.

6. Spread 1 tablespoon of the cream cheese frosting over each cupcake. Fill a pastry bag fitted with a ¼-inch star tip with the remaining frosting. Pipe a ring around the top of each cupcake, leaving an empty space in the center. Spoon the caramel into the centers. Transfer to a platter and serve. —*Peggy Cullen*
**MAKE AHEAD** The cupcakes can be refrigerated in an airtight container for up to 3 days.

## Vanilla Cupcakes with Lemon Cream and Raspberries
**ACTIVE: 30 MIN; TOTAL: 3 HR 15 MIN**
**MAKES 14 CUPCAKES** ●

LEMON CREAM

- 2 large eggs
- ⅔ cup sugar
- ⅓ cup fresh lemon juice
- ¾ teaspoon finely grated lemon zest
- 1 stick plus 3 tablespoons unsalted butter, softened
- Pinch of salt

CUPCAKES

- 3 large egg whites
- ¾ cup milk
- 2½ teaspoons pure vanilla extract
- 1¾ cups plus 2 tablespoons cake flour
- 2½ teaspoons baking powder
- 1 stick plus 1 tablespoon unsalted butter, softened
- 1 cup plus 2 tablespoons sugar
- ½ teaspoon salt
- ½ cup seedless raspberry jam
- Fresh raspberries, for garnish

1. **MAKE THE LEMON CREAM:** In a saucepan, whisk the eggs with the sugar, lemon juice and zest. Stir constantly over moderate heat until thickened but still pourable, about 6 minutes. Transfer to a blender and let cool for 5 minutes. Add the butter and salt and blend until pale, about 1 minute. Transfer the lemon cream to a bowl, cover and refrigerate until cold.

**CARROT CUPCAKES WITH CARAMEL**

**VANILLA CUPCAKES WITH LEMON CREAM**

**2.** MAKE THE CUPCAKES: Preheat the oven to 350°. Line a 12-cup muffin pan with paper liners and set 2 foil muffin cups in a pie plate. In a small bowl, whisk the egg whites with 2 tablespoons of the milk and the vanilla. Whisk in the remaining milk. In another bowl, whisk the cake flour with the baking powder.

**3.** In a bowl, beat the butter, sugar and salt until fluffy. Add the dry ingredients in 2 batches, alternating with the milk mixture. Spoon into the muffin pan and foil cups and bake for 20 minutes, until golden and springy when lightly touched. Let cool in the pans for 5 minutes, then transfer to racks to cool completely.

**4.** Slice off the top of each cupcake and spread with the raspberry jam. Replace the tops. Spread the lemon cream on top, garnish with berries and serve.
—Bill Yosses

## Frozen Hazelnut Mousse Cakes with Armagnac

**TOTAL: 1 HR 15 MIN, PLUS OVERNIGHT FREEZING**

**MAKES TWO 9-INCH LOAF CAKES** ● ●

This sophisticated dessert was inspired by a recipe from Lindsey Shere, founding pastry chef at Chez Panisse in Berkeley, California.

**CAKES**

- 2 cups roasted skinned hazelnuts, chopped (7 ounces)
- 1 cup all-purpose flour
- ½ teaspoon cinnamon
- 8 large eggs, separated
- ¾ cup sugar
- Salt
- 1 stick unsalted butter, melted
- ¼ cup pure maple syrup
- 2 tablespoons Armagnac or Cognac

**MOUSSE**

- ¾ cup sugar
- ⅓ cup water
- 8 large egg yolks
- 1¾ cups heavy cream
- 2 tablespoons Armagnac or Cognac
- ½ teaspoon pure vanilla extract
- ½ cup roasted skinned hazelnuts, chopped
- 6 ounces bittersweet chocolate, chopped (1½ cups), 1 cup melted

**1.** MAKE THE CAKES: Preheat the oven to 375°. Butter an 11½-by-17-inch jelly roll pan and line the bottom with parchment paper. Lightly butter the parchment paper. In a food processor, finely grind the hazelnuts. In a medium bowl, combine the ground hazelnuts with the flour and cinnamon.

● FAST ● HEALTHY ● MAKE AHEAD ● STAFF FAVORITE

**2.** In a large bowl, using a handheld electric mixer, beat the egg yolks with ½ cup of the sugar at high speed until light yellow, about 3 minutes.

**3.** In another large bowl, using clean beaters, beat the egg whites with a pinch of salt with the electric mixer at high speed until soft peaks form. Gradually add the remaining ¼ cup of sugar and beat at high speed until the egg whites are firm and glossy.

**4.** With a large spatula, fold one-fourth of the dry ingredients into the egg yolk mixture. Fold in one-third of the beaten egg whites. Working in 2 batches, fold in the remaining dry ingredients and egg whites. Fold in the melted butter until just incorporated. Scrape the batter into the prepared jelly-roll pan and smooth the surface.

**5.** Bake for 10 minutes, or until the cake is golden and springs back when lightly touched. Transfer to a wire rack and let cool. Using the edges of the parchment paper, lift the cake out of the jelly-roll pan. Trim the edges and cut the cake into four 4½-by-8½-inch rectangles.

**6.** Line each of two 9-by-5-inch glass loaf pans with a cake rectangle. In a small bowl, mix the maple syrup with the Armagnac until blended; brush half of the syrup on the cakes in the loaf pans. Reserve the remaining syrup and cover the 2 remaining cake rectangles with plastic wrap.

**7.** MAKE THE MOUSSE: Prepare an ice water bath in a medium bowl. In a small saucepan, combine the sugar and water and bring to a boil. Simmer over moderately high heat until the sugar syrup reaches 220° on a candy thermometer, about 8 minutes.

**8.** In a heatproof medium bowl, beat the egg yolks with a handheld electric mixer until light yellow, about 3 minutes. While beating the yolks at high speed, carefully and slowly pour in the hot sugar syrup;

the mixture will thicken. Set the bowl in the ice water bath and beat the egg yolk mixture until chilled and very thick, about 4 minutes.

**9.** In large bowl, whip the cream to stiff peaks. Fold in the Armagnac and vanilla. Fold in the egg yolk mixture. Fold in the hazelnuts and chopped chocolate. Scrape the mousse into the loaf pans.

**10.** Brush one side of the remaining 2 cake rectangles with the rest of the maple-Armagnac syrup; set the cake rectangles brushed side down over the mousse. Cover with plastic and freeze overnight or for up to 5 days.

**11.** To serve, fill a large bowl with 4 inches of very hot water and dip the bottoms of the loaf pans in the water for 10 seconds. Dry the bottoms of the loaf pans and invert the cakes onto platters. With a sharp knife, slice the cakes crosswise 1 inch thick and transfer to plates. Drizzle the slices with the melted chocolate and serve. —*Marcia Kiesel*

**MAKE AHEAD** The cakes can be frozen for up to 1 week.

## Bittersweet Chocolate Mousse Refrigerator Cake

**TOTAL: 30 MIN, PLUS 8 HR CHILLING**
**6 TO 8 SERVINGS** ●

    2  cups chilled heavy cream
One 10-ounce jar bittersweet
        chocolate sauce (1 cup plus
        2 tablespoons)
One 9-ounce package chocolate
        wafers
Shaved bittersweet chocolate,
        for garnish

**1.** In a large chilled stainless steel or glass bowl, using a handheld electric mixer, beat the heavy cream with the chocolate sauce at medium speed until firm peaks form. Spread about ½ cup of the whipped chocolate cream on a long rectangular platter to form a 3-by-10-inch rectangle.

**2.** Using a small offset spatula, spread 1 tablespoon of the remaining chocolate cream on 35 chocolate wafers and arrange them in 5 stacks. Top each stack with a chocolate wafer (you will have 6 or 7 wafers left over). Arrange the wafer stacks on their sides as close together as possible on the chocolate cream on the platter. (The wafer stacks will lie lengthwise on the platter.) Spread all but about ½ cup of the remaining chocolate cream all over the cake, fixing any wafers that tilt or slide.

**3.** Press a long sheet of plastic wrap over the cake, flattening the top and sides gently. Refrigerate for at least 8 hours or for up to 2 days. Refrigerate the remaining chocolate cream.

**4.** Discard the plastic wrap and frost the cake with the remaining chocolate cream, smoothing the top and sides. Garnish with the chocolate shavings. Cut into slices, wiping the knife after each cut. —*Grace Parisi*

**MAKE AHEAD** The finished cake can be refrigerated for up to 2 days.

## Crispy Witches' Hats

**TOTAL: 1 HR 30 MIN, PLUS 2 HR CHILLING**

**MAKES 2 DOZEN COOKIES** ●
These Halloween cookies look like pointy hats. You can also use this recipe to make ganache-filled sandwiches, or even skip the ganache entirely.

    ¼  cup heavy cream
    9  ounces semisweet chocolate,
        coarsely chopped
    ½  cup plus 2 tablespoons
        pecan pieces
    ¼  cup all-purpose flour
    ½  teaspoon salt
    4  tablespoons unsalted butter,
        cut into pieces
    ¼  cup packed dark brown sugar
    ¼  cup light corn syrup
    ¼  teaspoon pure vanilla extract

BITTERSWEET CHOCOLATE MOUSSE REFRIGERATOR CAKE

# cakes, cookies + more

**1.** In a small saucepan, bring the cream to a boil. Off the heat, stir in 4 ounces of the chocolate and let stand for 1 minute, then whisk until smooth. Transfer to a bowl and let the ganache cool.

**2.** In a food processor, combine the pecans with the flour and salt and pulse until finely ground. In a medium saucepan, combine the butter, brown sugar and corn syrup and bring to a boil, stirring. Remove from the heat and add the vanilla and ground pecan mixture. Transfer the batter to a bowl and refrigerate until firm, about 2 hours.

**3.** Preheat the oven to 350°. Scoop 48 level teaspoons of the batter and roll each into a ball. Place 8 balls on a large ungreased cookie sheet 4 inches apart. Keep the rest of the balls refrigerated. Bake the cookies for 9 minutes, or until they stop bubbling. Set the baking sheet on a wire rack and let the cookies cool for 3 minutes. Working very quickly, form 4 of the cookies into cones: Carefully lift 1 cookie at a time with a spatula and roll it, bumpy side out, into a cone shape. Press the seam to close, transfer to a wire rack and let cool. Transfer the remaining 4 flat cookies to the rack. Repeat with the remaining balls, forming half into cones and transferring the remaining flat cookies to a wire rack to cool. Between batches, run the underside of the baking sheet under cool water and wipe it dry.

**4.** Line 2 baking sheets with wax paper. In a small saucepan, melt the remaining 5 ounces of chocolate. Using a small pastry brush, brush the chocolate all over the bumpy surface of the cones and the flat cookies and transfer them to the prepared sheets; warm the chocolate if it becomes too thick. Refrigerate the cookies just until the chocolate is set.

**5.** Fill a pastry bag fitted with a ⅛-inch plain tip with the chocolate ganache. Pipe a ring of ganache on a flat cookie,

about the size of the rim of a cone. Carefully place the cone on the ganache, holding it in place just until set. Repeat to make the remaining hats. Refrigerate just until chilled. Run a thin knife under the cookies to release them from the wax paper, transfer to a platter and serve. —*Peggy Cullen*

**MAKE AHEAD** The cookies can be refrigerated for up to 2 days.

## Chocolate Rosemary-Caramel Nut Bars

**ACTIVE: 30 MIN; TOTAL: 1 HR 30 MIN, PLUS 1 HR COOLING**

**MAKES 2 DOZEN BARS** ● ●

**CRUST**

- 2 **cups all-purpose flour**
- ½ **cup fine yellow cornmeal**
- ½ **cup sugar**
- ½ **teaspoon salt**
- 2 **sticks (½ pound) cold unsalted butter, cut into small pieces**
- 2 **large egg yolks**
- 3 **tablespoons heavy cream**

**TOPPING**

- 1 **cup walnuts (4 ounces)**
- 1 **cup unsalted, raw, shelled pistachios (4 ounces)**
- 2 **cups sugar**
- ½ **cup water**
- 1 **cup heavy cream**
- 1 **teaspoon finely chopped rosemary**
- ¼ **teaspoon salt**
- 1 **cup roasted skinned hazelnuts (4 ounces)**
- 8 **ounces bittersweet chocolate, coarsely chopped**

**1. MAKE THE CRUST:** Preheat the oven to 350°. In a large bowl, whisk the flour, cornmeal, sugar and salt. With a pastry blender, cut in the butter until the mixture resembles coarse meal. In a small bowl, beat the egg yolks with the cream; drizzle over the cornmeal mixture. With 2 forks, blend the dough lightly until combined. Using your hands, knead lightly.

**2.** On a lightly floured surface, roll out the dough to a 15½-by-10½-inch rectangle. Roll the dough onto the rolling pin, then transfer it to an ungreased 15-by-10-inch jelly-roll pan. Press the dough evenly over the bottom and up the sides of the pan. Freeze the crust until firm, about 30 minutes. Bake the crust for 12 minutes, or until pale and dry.

**3. MAKE THE TOPPING:** Spread the walnuts on a medium, rimmed baking sheet and bake for 8 minutes, or until lightly toasted. Repeat with the pistachios. Leave the oven on.

**4.** In a medium saucepan, combine the sugar and water and cook over moderately high heat, swirling the pan once or twice, until the sugar is dissolved. Simmer over moderate heat, brushing down the side of the pan with a wet pastry brush from time to time, until a deep golden brown caramel forms, about 18 minutes.

**5.** Meanwhile, in a small saucepan, bring the cream to a boil with the rosemary and salt. Remove from the heat. Carefully and slowly add the hot cream to the caramel, stirring constantly until smooth. Remove from the heat and stir in the hazelnuts, walnuts and pistachios.

**6.** Scrape the nut caramel over the crust and spread evenly with a spatula. Bake in the center of the oven for 25 minutes, or until the topping is golden and bubbling. Let cool.

**7.** In a glass bowl, melt the chocolate in a microwave oven at high power, stirring a few times. Let the melted chocolate cool until barely warm, about 15 minutes. Brush the chocolate over the caramel-nut topping. Let the chocolate cool until set, about 1 hour. Cut into 2-by-3-inch bars and serve. —*Mandy Groom Givler*

**MAKE AHEAD** The uncut bars can be covered with foil and stored at room temperature on the baking sheet for up to 1 week.

## Hazelnut Crescent Cookies

**ACTIVE: 25 MIN; TOTAL: 1 HR**

**MAKES 2 DOZEN COOKIES** ●

- 2 sticks (½ pound) unsalted butter, softened at room temperature
- 1 cup confectioners' sugar
- 3 large egg yolks
- 1½ teaspoons pure vanilla extract
- ½ teaspoon salt
- 1¾ cups all-purpose flour
- ¾ cup blanched skinned hazelnuts, finely ground

**1.** Preheat the oven to 350°. Line 2 baking sheets with parchment paper. In a large bowl, with an electric mixer, cream the butter with ½ cup of the confectioners' sugar at medium-high speed until pale and fluffy, about 1 minute. Add the egg yolks, vanilla extract and salt and beat at medium-high speed until blended, scraping down the side of the bowl as needed. Beat in the flour and ground hazelnuts at medium speed until just incorporated. Cover the dough with plastic wrap and refrigerate until firm, at least 30 minutes.

**2.** Using about 1½ tablespoons of the dough for each cookie, roll the dough into 3-inch-long cylinders with tapered ends. Form the cookies into crescents and transfer them to the prepared baking sheets, spacing them 1 inch apart. Bake the cookies for 18 minutes, or until light golden. Remove from the oven and let the cookies cool on the baking sheets for 10 minutes, or until just cool enough to handle.

**3.** Spread the remaining ½ cup of confectioners' sugar in a shallow bowl. Dip each warm cookie in the confectioners' sugar and coat evenly. Transfer the cookies to wire racks and let cool completely. *—Kurt Gutenbrunner*

**MAKE AHEAD** The cookies can be stored in an airtight container at room temperature for up to 3 days.

## Brown-Sugar Meringues

**ACTIVE: 15 MIN; TOTAL: 1 HR 25 MIN, PLUS 1 HR COOLING**

**MAKES 32 MERINGUES**

- 4 large egg whites, at room temperature
- 1 cup lightly packed light brown sugar

Pinch of salt

**1.** Preheat the oven to 250°. In a large bowl, beat the egg whites until soft peaks form. Beat in the brown sugar, 1 tablespoon at a time. Add the salt and beat until the meringue is thick and glossy, about 2 minutes longer.

**2.** Spoon 2-inch-wide mounds of the meringue onto 2 parchment-lined baking sheets. Bake in the center of the oven for 1 hour and 10 minutes, or until the meringues are no longer sticky to the touch. Turn off the oven, prop the door open 1 inch and let the meringues cool for 1 hour before serving. *—Russ Pillar*

## Meringue Phantom Cookies

**ACTIVE: 15 MIN; TOTAL: 1 HR, PLUS 3 HR COOLING**

**MAKES 2 DOZEN MERINGUES** ●

- 3 large egg whites, at room temperature
- ⅛ teaspoon cream of tartar
- ¾ cup superfine sugar
- 1 teaspoon finely grated lemon zest
- 1 teaspoon pure vanilla extract
- ¼ teaspoon almond extract
- 2 teaspoons cornstarch
- ¼ teaspoon ground ginger
- ¼ cup dried currants

**1.** Preheat the oven to 200° and position 2 racks in the middle. Line 2 large baking sheets with parchment paper.

**2.** In a large bowl, beat the egg whites at medium speed until frothy. Add the cream of tartar and beat at medium-high speed until very soft peaks form. Add the superfine sugar 1 tablespoon at a time, beating for 10 seconds between each

addition. Add the grated lemon zest and the vanilla and almond extracts and beat until the meringue is stiff and glossy, about 1 minute longer. Sift the cornstarch and ginger over the meringue and fold in with a large spatula.

**3.** Spoon the meringue onto the prepared baking sheets in walnut-size mounds, lifting the spoon each time to form little peaks. Place 2 currants in each for eyes. Bake the meringues for 45 minutes. Turn the oven off and let them stand in the oven until completely cool, at least 3 hours or overnight. Gently lift each meringue off the paper and transfer to a plate to serve. *—Peggy Cullen*

**MAKE AHEAD** The meringues can be stored in an airtight container for 2 days.

## Cinnamon-Ginger Cookies

**TOTAL: 35 MIN**

**MAKES 30 COOKIES** ●

- 1⅔ cups unbleached all-purpose flour
- 1 teaspoon baking soda
- 1 teaspoon cinnamon
- ¾ teaspoon ground ginger
- ½ teaspoon freshly grated nutmeg
- ¼ teaspoon ground cloves
- ¼ teaspoon ground cardamom
- ¼ teaspoon salt
- ⅛ teaspoon freshly ground black pepper
- 2 sticks (½ pound) unsalted butter, softened
- ⅓ cup packed dark brown sugar
- ¼ cup pure maple syrup
- 1 tablespoon vanilla soymilk or heavy cream

Granulated sugar, for rolling

**1.** Preheat the oven to 350° and position 2 racks in the upper and lower thirds of the oven. Line 2 baking sheets with parchment paper.

**2.** In a medium bowl, combine the flour with the baking soda, cinnamon, ginger, nutmeg, cloves, cardamom, salt and black pepper.

# cakes, cookies + more

**3.** In another medium bowl, using a handheld electric mixer, beat the butter until creamy. Add the brown sugar and maple syrup and beat at medium speed until light and fluffy. Add the soymilk, then beat in the dry ingredients at low speed until a soft dough forms.

**4.** Roll tablespoonfuls of the dough into balls, then roll them in the granulated sugar. Arrange the balls about 1½ inches apart on the prepared baking sheets. Bake for 20 minutes, or until golden and just set; shift the pans from top to bottom and front to back halfway through. —*Akasha Richmond*

**MAKE AHEAD** The cookies can be stored in an airtight container for up to 1 week or frozen for up to 1 month.

## Gingerbread Girls

**ACTIVE: 30 MIN; TOTAL: 3 HR**

MAKES 2 DOZEN 4-INCH

COOKIES ●

- 3 cups all-purpose flour
- 2 teaspoons ground ginger
- 2 teaspoons ground cinnamon
- ¾ teaspoon salt
- ¾ teaspoon ground cloves
- ½ teaspoon baking soda
- ½ teaspoon baking powder
- ¼ teaspoon freshly grated nutmeg
- ¼ teaspoon ground cardamom
- 1 stick (4 ounces) unsalted butter, at room temperature
- ½ cup packed dark brown sugar
- 1 large egg
- ½ cup molasses
- 1 teaspoon pure vanilla extract

Royal Icing (recipe follows)

**1.** In a bowl, whisk the flour with the ginger, cinnamon, salt, cloves, baking soda, baking powder, nutmeg and cardamom. In a large bowl, beat the butter with the brown sugar at medium speed until light and fluffy. Beat in the egg, molasses and vanilla until thoroughly blended, then beat in the dry ingredients at low speed. Pat

the gingerbread dough into 2 disks, wrap them in plastic and refrigerate until chilled, about 1 hour.

**2.** Preheat the oven to 350°. Line 2 large baking sheets with parchment paper. On a lightly floured surface, roll out 1 disk of dough about ⅛ inch thick. Using a 4-inch cookie cutter, stamp out cookies as close together as possible, then transfer the cookies to the baking sheet. Repeat with the remaining disk of dough. Gather all the dough scraps, stacking them in a pile, and refrigerate.

**3.** Bake the cookies until slightly puffed and very lightly browned on the bottoms, 12 to 13 minutes. Transfer to a rack and let cool completely. Reroll the scraps, then stamp out and bake the remaining cookies. Decorate the cookies with Royal Icing and let dry until set. —*Margaret Braun*

## ROYAL ICING

**TOTAL: 15 MIN**

MAKES ABOUT 2½ CUPS ● ●

To decorate the Gingerbread Girls, you'll want the icing to be fairly stiff for piping designs, trim, outlines or faces, or for gluing fondant shapes in place. For painting larger areas, thin the icing slightly with water so it's the consistency of paint.

- 2 large egg whites (see Note)
- 1 pound confectioners' sugar
- 1 tablespoon fresh lemon juice

Water (optional)

In a large bowl, beat the egg whites at medium speed until foamy. Add the confectioners' sugar 1 cup at a time, beating between additions until the sugar is completely incorporated. Add the lemon juice and beat at high speed until the icing holds its shape, about 5 minutes. Thin with water as needed. —*M.B.*

**NOTE** If you have any concerns about eating uncooked eggs, you can make this icing using pasteurized egg whites or powdered egg whites or with an instant royal-icing mix, sold at baking supply shops.

## Black-and-Orange Cookies

**ACTIVE: 30 MIN; TOTAL: 1 HR 30 MIN**

MAKES 3 DOZEN COOKIES ●

This recipe is a Halloween twist on a New York City classic: the black-and-white cookie. Topped with a soft, sugary icing, these sweets are more like small cakes than cookies.

COOKIES

- 1 cup plus 2 tablespoons cake flour
- ½ cup all-purpose flour
- 1 teaspoon baking powder
- ¼ teaspoon salt
- 1 stick (4 ounces) unsalted butter, at room temperature
- ¾ cup granulated sugar
- 2 large eggs, at room temperature
- 2 large egg yolks, at room temperature
- 2 teaspoons pure vanilla extract
- 2 teaspoons milk

ICING

- 2¾ cups confectioners' sugar
- ¼ cup boiling water
- 1 teaspoon pure vanilla extract

Orange food coloring, or red and yellow combined

- 2 ounces bittersweet chocolate, chopped

**1.** MAKE THE COOKIES: Preheat the oven to 350°; position 2 racks in the upper and middle thirds of the oven. Line 3 baking sheets with parchment paper.

**2.** Sift the cake flour, all-purpose flour, baking powder and salt onto a large sheet of wax paper. In a large bowl, using an electric mixer, beat the butter and granulated sugar at medium speed until light and fluffy, about 3 minutes. Add the whole eggs and yolks 1 at a time, beating well between additions. Beat in the vanilla and milk. At low speed, beat in the dry ingredients until just combined.

**3.** Spoon rounded tablespoons of the batter onto the baking sheets about 2 inches apart. Bake the cookies for about 12 minutes, until the centers spring back when lightly pressed. Be careful not to let the cookies brown or overbake, or they will be dry. Transfer the cookies, flat side up, to a wire rack and let cool completely.

4. MEANWHILE, MAKE THE ICING: In a medium bowl, whisk the confectioners' sugar with the boiling water until smooth. Add the vanilla extract and a few drops of food coloring and whisk until the icing is evenly colored. Using a small offset spatula, spread the orange-colored icing over half of the flat side of each cookie.

5. In a microwave oven, melt the chocolate in a small bowl. Stir the chocolate into the remaining orange icing. Spread the chocolate icing on the other half of each cookie and let stand until set, about 15 minutes. (If the icing becomes too thick, add hot water 1 teaspoon at a time until smooth and shiny.)
—*Peggy Cullen*

**MAKE AHEAD** The Black-and-Orange Cookies can be stored in an airtight container for up to 2 days.

## Pine Nut–Butter Cookies

**ACTIVE: 15 MIN; TOTAL: 1 HR 30 MIN**
**MAKES 2 DOZEN COOKIES ●**

- 1 stick plus 2 tablespoons (5 ounces) unsalted butter, softened
- ½ cup sugar
- ½ teaspoon ground fennel
- ¼ teaspoon salt
- 1 large egg yolk
- 1 teaspoon pure vanilla extract
- 1 cup all-purpose flour
- ¼ cup pine nuts

1. In a medium bowl, using a handheld electric mixer, beat the butter with the sugar, fennel and salt at medium speed until fluffy, 1 to 2 minutes. Add the egg yolk and vanilla extract and beat until combined. Add the flour and beat just until the dough comes together. Scrape

**GINGERBREAD GIRL**

**BLACK-AND-ORANGE COOKIES**

Black & Orange Cookies

# cakes, cookies + more

the dough onto a sheet of plastic wrap and form it into a log about 1½ inches in diameter. Wrap and refrigerate the dough until chilled, about 1 hour.

**2.** Preheat the oven to 350°. Cut the cookie dough into ¼-inch-thick slices. Arrange the cookies about 1½ inches apart on 2 ungreased baking sheets. Press 3 or 4 pine nuts into the center of each cookie. Bake the cookies for 13 to 14 minutes, or until they are golden brown around the edges. Let the cookies cool on the baking sheets for 5 minutes, then transfer them to a wire rack to cool completely. —*Geoffrey Zakarian*

**MAKE AHEAD** The cookies can be stored in an airtight container for up to 5 days or frozen for 1 month.

### Hazelnut–Pine Nut Cookies

**ACTIVE: 30 MIN; TOTAL: 1 HR 15 MIN**
**MAKES ABOUT 54 COOKIES** ● ●

- 2 cups blanched whole almonds (½ pound), finely ground in a food processor
- 1 cup roasted skinned hazelnuts (4 ounces), finely ground in a food processor
- 2 cups granulated sugar
- 6 tablespoons unsalted butter, at room temperature
- 1 teaspoon honey
- 2 large egg whites
- ¼ teaspoon salt
- 3 cups pine nuts (¾ pound)

Confectioners' sugar, for dusting

**1.** Preheat the oven to 400°. Line 2 large baking sheets with parchment paper. In a food processor, pulse the ground almonds and hazelnuts to blend. Pulse in the granulated sugar. Add the butter and honey and process until blended. Add the egg whites and salt and process just until incorporated. Scrape the dough into a bowl and roll tablespoons of it into balls. Roll each ball in the pine nuts, pressing lightly to help them adhere.

**2.** Arrange 12 balls on each baking sheet. Bake the cookies for 11 minutes, or until golden around the edges. Let cool on the baking sheets for 5 minutes, then slide the parchment onto racks to let the cookies cool completely. Repeat with more parchment paper and the remaining cookies. Dust the cooled cookies with confectioners' sugar and serve.
—*Mandy Groom Givler*

**MAKE AHEAD** The baked cookies can be stored at room temperature overnight or frozen for up to 1 week.

### Hazelnut Tuiles

**ACTIVE: 1 HR 10 MIN; TOTAL: 2 HR 10 MIN**
**MAKES 4 DOZEN TUILES** ●

- 7 tablespoons unsalted butter
- 1 cup cake flour
- 1 cup confectioners' sugar
- 3 large egg whites
- 1 tablespoon hazelnut oil

**1.** Preheat the oven to 300°. In a small skillet, cook the butter over moderately high heat until deep golden brown, about 2 minutes. Remove from the heat.

**2.** In a medium bowl, whisk the flour with the sugar and egg whites until smooth. Whisk in the butter and hazelnut oil. Let stand at room temperature for 1 hour.

**3.** Line a large baking sheet with a silicone mat. Spoon 6 teaspoons of the batter onto the baking sheet 3 inches apart. Spread the batter into 3 inch rounds. Bake the tuiles in the center of the oven, 2 baking sheets at a time, for 8 minutes, or until light golden, turning the baking sheets halfway through.

**4.** Drape the warm tuiles over a rolling pin immediately after removing them from the oven. Return the tuiles to the oven for 30 seconds if they become too brittle to bend. Repeat with the remaining batter. —*Margot Janse*

**MAKE AHEAD** The tuiles can be stored in an airtight container overnight or frozen for up to a month.

### Orange-Almond Shortbread with Strawberry Compote

**ACTIVE: 25 MIN; TOTAL: 50 MIN**
**6 SERVINGS** ●

- 1 cup sliced blanched almonds
- 1 orange
- ½ cup confectioners' sugar
- 1¼ cups all-purpose flour
- ½ teaspoon salt
- 1½ sticks (6 ounces) cold unsalted butter, cut into small pieces
- 1¼ teaspoons orange-flower water or pure vanilla extract
- 1 pint strawberries, hulled and thickly sliced
- ½ cup granulated sugar
- ¾ cup chilled crème fraîche, lightly whipped

**1.** Preheat the oven to 325°. Spread the almonds in a pie plate or on a small baking sheet and bake for 8 minutes, or until lightly toasted. Transfer the toasted almonds to a plate and let cool completely. Lightly oil a 9-inch round springform pan.

**2.** Finely grate 1¼ teaspoons of the zest from the orange. In a food processor, pulse the toasted almonds with the confectioners' sugar until the nuts are finely ground. Add the flour, ¾ teaspoon of the orange zest and the salt, then pulse the mixture until combined. Add the cold butter and pulse just until the mixture resembles large crumbs; stop pulsing before the dough begins to clump together. Add the orange-flower water and pulse just until the dough forms large clumps.

**3.** Scrape the shortbread dough into the prepared springform pan. Using floured hands, firmly press the dough into an even layer on the bottom of the pan and prick it all over the top with a fork. Bake for about 25 minutes, or until the shortbread is golden brown around the edge; rotate the pan halfway through baking for even browning.

**4.** Transfer the pan to a wire rack and immediately cut the shortbread into 12 wedges. Let the shortbread wedges cool in the pan.

**5.** Meanwhile, with a sharp knife, peel the orange, removing all of the bitter white pith. Working over a medium saucepan, cut in between the membranes to release the orange sections into the saucepan. Squeeze the juice from the orange membranes into the pan. Add the sliced strawberries, granulated sugar and the remaining ½ teaspoon of orange zest and bring to a simmer.

**6.** Cook the fruit over moderate heat, stirring occasionally, until the strawberries and oranges are softened and syrupy, about 8 minutes. The fruit compote should be slightly thinner than jam. Transfer the compote to a bowl and let cool to room temperature.

**7.** Remove the springform ring and arrange the shortbread wedges on plates. Serve with the strawberry compote and the crème fraîche. —*Melissa Clark*

**MAKE AHEAD** The shortbreads can be stored in an airtight container for up to 2 days. The compote can be refrigerated for up to 2 days.

## Sugar-Dusted Vanilla Ricotta Fritters

**TOTAL: 30 MIN**
**8 SERVINGS** ● ●
The fritters are also good sprinkled with cinnamon sugar or dipped in jelly.

Vegetable oil, for frying
3 large eggs
¼ cup granulated sugar
½ teaspoon pure vanilla extract
½ pound whole milk ricotta cheese (1 cup)
1¼ cups all-purpose flour
2 teaspoons baking powder
Confectioners' sugar, for dusting

**1.** In a large saucepan, heat 2 inches of vegetable oil to 375°. Set a large wire rack over a baking sheet, top with paper towels and position it near the saucepan.

**2.** Meanwhile, in a large bowl, beat the eggs, granulated sugar and vanilla with a wooden spoon. Add the ricotta and beat until smooth. Add the flour and baking powder and beat just until blended.

**3.** Using a very small ice cream scoop or 2 teaspoons, slide 8 walnut-size rounds of batter into the hot oil. Fry over moderate heat until deep golden all over and cooked through, 3 to 4 minutes. Using a slotted spoon, transfer the fritters to the rack to drain. Fry the remaining fritters in batches of 8. Transfer to a platter and dust with confectioners' sugar. —*Gale Gand*

**MAKE AHEAD** The fritter batter can be refrigerated for up to 6 hours.

## Fried Milk

**TOTAL: 45 MIN, PLUS 3 HR CHILLING**
**6 SERVINGS** ● ●
In Spain's Asturias region, this creamy custard is served as a starter or as a light dessert.

¾ cup cornstarch
1 cup sugar
4 cups plus 2 tablespoons whole milk
3 egg yolks
3 whole eggs, at room temperature
2 tablespoons plus ¼ teaspoon cinnamon
1 teaspoon pure vanilla extract
1 cup all-purpose flour
Vegetable oil, for frying

**1.** Lightly oil an 8-by-11-inch glass baking dish. In a medium heatproof bowl, mix the cornstarch with ½ cup of the sugar. Slowly whisk in 1 cup of the milk. Add the egg yolks and 1 of the whole eggs and whisk until smooth. Whisk in ¼ teaspoon of the cinnamon.

**2.** In a medium saucepan, heat 3 cups of the milk over moderate heat until small bubbles begin to form around the edge

of the surface. Gradually whisk the hot milk into the egg mixture. Return the mixture to the saucepan and cook over moderate heat, whisking constantly, until it becomes slightly thicker than mayonnaise, about 5 minutes. Stir in the vanilla extract.

**3.** Scrape the custard into the prepared baking dish and smooth the surface; let cool slightly. Refrigerate until very firm, at least 3 hours or overnight.

**4.** In a bowl, mix the remaining ½ cup of sugar with the remaining 2 tablespoons of cinnamon. In a pie plate, whisk the remaining 2 eggs with the remaining 2 tablespoons of milk. Spread the flour in another pie plate.

**5.** Cut the custard into 24 rectangles. In a large nonstick skillet, heat ½ inch of vegetable oil until shimmering. Working with 6 pieces of custard at a time and keeping the rest refrigerated, dip the custard rectangles in the beaten eggs, then dredge in the flour. Fry the custard over moderate heat, turning once or twice, until golden and crisp, about 5 minutes. Transfer to a rack lined with paper towels and immediately sift cinnamon sugar over them. Repeat with the remaining pieces of custard. Serve warm or at room temperature. —*José Andrés*

## Cookie Cannoli with Coffee Cream

**TOTAL: 1 HR 30 MIN**
**6 SERVINGS**
4 tablespoons unsalted butter, at room temperature
⅔ cup sugar
2 egg whites, at room temperature
½ cup all-purpose flour
½ teaspoon grated orange zest
¾ teaspoon pure vanilla extract
Pinch of salt
1 cup mascarpone
1 cup heavy cream
1 teaspoon pure coffee extract
Confectioners' sugar, for dusting

# cakes, cookies + more

**1.** Preheat the oven to 375°. Line 2 baking sheets with parchment paper. Trace three 4-inch circles on each with a pencil; turn the parchment over.

**2.** In a medium bowl, using an electric mixer, beat the butter with ⅓ cup of the sugar until fluffy. Add the egg whites and beat until blended. Add the flour, orange zest, ¼ teaspoon of the vanilla and the salt and beat until smooth.

**3.** Using a small offset spatula, evenly spread 1 tablespoon of the batter into each circle. Bake the cookies, 1 sheet at a time, for 8 to 9 minutes, or until lightly golden and browned around the edges. Immediately roll each cookie around a 1-inch-wide tube or dowel and let cool until crisp. Carefully remove the cannoli from the tubes and transfer to a wire rack. Repeat twice with the remaining batter to make 18 cookies.

**4.** In a bowl, using an electric mixer, beat the mascarpone at medium speed with the cream, the coffee extract and the remaining ⅓ cup sugar and ½ teaspoon of vanilla until firm peaks form.

**5.** Fill a pastry bag fitted with a ½-inch star tip with the coffee cream. Carefully pipe the coffee cream into both ends of the cookies, finishing with a small rosette at each end. Transfer the cannoli to a platter, dust them with confectioners' sugar and serve. —*Gina DePalma*

**MAKE AHEAD** The unfilled cookies can be stored in an airtight container at room temperature for up to 3 days.

## Chocolate Cream Squares

**ACTIVE: 1 HR; TOTAL: 2 HR, PLUS 4 HR CHILLING**

**MAKES 18 SQUARES** ● ●

This superrich dessert contains chocolate whipped cream between layers of bittersweet chocolate cake topped with a fudgy chocolate glaze. It's best made a day ahead and refrigerated overnight so that it sets firmly.

### CAKE
- ½ **pound bittersweet chocolate, cut into ½-inch pieces**
- 2 **teaspoons instant espresso powder dissolved in ⅓ cup hot water**
- 6 **large eggs, separated**
- ⅔ **cup granulated sugar**
- 2 **teaspoons pure vanilla extract**
- ¼ **teaspoon cream of tartar**

**Pinch of salt**

- ¼ **cup all-purpose flour**

**Unsweetened cocoa powder, for dusting**

### FILLING
- 6 **ounces bittersweet chocolate, cut into ½-inch pieces**
- 2 **tablespoons unsalted butter**
- 2 **tablespoons water**
- 1½ **cups heavy cream**
- 3 **tablespoons confectioners' sugar**
- 1 **teaspoon pure vanilla extract**

### GLAZE
- 1 **tablespoon solid vegetable shortening**
- ¼ **cup granulated sugar**
- ⅓ **cup water**
- 4 **ounces bittersweet chocolate, cut into ½-inch pieces**
- 1 **ounce unsweetened chocolate, finely chopped**
- 1 **teaspoon pure vanilla extract**

**1. MAKE THE CAKE:** Preheat the oven to 375°. Butter an 18-by-12-inch rimmed baking sheet and line the bottom with parchment or wax paper. Butter the paper and dust with flour, tapping out any excess. In a small saucepan, combine the chocolate with the dissolved espresso and cook over low heat, stirring constantly, until melted, about 2 minutes. Let cool slightly.

**2.** In a medium bowl, using an electric mixer, beat the egg yolks at high speed until pale, 2 to 3 minutes. At medium speed, gradually beat in ⅓ cup of the granulated sugar. Increase the speed to high and beat until very thick and pale, about 5 minutes. Add the vanilla and the chocolate mixture and beat at low speed until blended.

**3.** In a large bowl, using clean beaters, beat the egg whites with the cream of tartar and salt until soft peaks form. Gradually add the remaining ⅓ cup of granulated sugar and beat at high speed until the whites are stiff and glossy. Using a large rubber spatula, fold the chocolate mixture and the flour into the whites in 2 batches, until no streaks remain. Gently spread the batter evenly in the prepared baking sheet. Bake for 12 minutes, or until the cake has risen and is slightly springy to the touch. Transfer to a rack and let cool.

**4.** Run the tip of a knife around the cake and sift cocoa over the surface. Cover the cake with wax paper and top with a cutting board. Invert the cake onto the cutting board. Lift off the pan and peel off the paper. Cut the cake in half crosswise, forming 2 rectangles. Chill until firm, about 30 minutes.

**5. MEANWHILE, MAKE THE FILLING:** In a small saucepan, combine the chocolate with the butter and water. Cook over very low heat, stirring constantly, until melted and shiny. Scrape into a bowl and let cool. Using an electric mixer, beat the heavy cream with the confectioners' sugar and vanilla extract until firm peaks form. Using a rubber spatula, gently fold in the cooled chocolate.

**6. MAKE THE GLAZE:** In a small saucepan, combine the shortening with the granulated sugar and water and bring to a simmer. Remove the saucepan from the heat, add the bittersweet and unsweetened chocolate and let stand, without stirring, until the chocolate is melted, about 2 minutes. Whisk in the vanilla extract. Let the glaze cool until slightly thickened, about 30 minutes.

**7.** Spread the cream filling over one half of the cake and top with the other half, cocoa side up. Press down lightly and run a cake spatula all around to smooth the edges. Pour the glaze down the center of the cake and gently spread it so that it covers the top and drizzles down the sides. Freeze the cake for 4 hours or overnight. Let stand at room temperature until just soft enough to cut. Cut the cake into 3 long strips, then cut each strip into 6 squares. Transfer to plates and serve. —*Greg Patent*

**MAKE AHEAD** The cake can be frozen for 1 week.

## Pistachio-Cranberry Biscotti

**ACTIVE: 20 MIN; TOTAL: 1 HR 30 MIN**
MAKES ABOUT 42 BISCOTTI ● ●

- 1 cup shelled raw pistachios
- 2 cups all-purpose flour
- 1 teaspoon baking powder
- ¼ teaspoon baking soda
- ¼ teaspoon salt
- 4 ounces unsalted butter, softened
- ¾ cup sugar
- 2 large eggs
- 1 teaspoon pure vanilla extract
- 1 cup dried cranberries
- 2 ounces white chocolate, melted

**1.** Preheat the oven to 350°. Spread the pistachios in a pie plate and bake until golden, about 6 minutes; let cool. Turn the oven down to 325°.

**2.** In a small bowl, whisk the flour, baking powder, baking soda and salt. In a medium bowl, beat the butter with the sugar until light and fluffy. Beat in the eggs 1 at a time, followed by the vanilla. At low speed, beat in the dry ingredients. With a spoon, stir in the pistachios and cranberries.

**3.** Butter and flour a large cookie sheet. Pat the dough out on the sheet into two 14-inch-long logs 1 inch wide and 1 inch high; leave 3 inches between them. Bake the logs in the lower third of the oven until golden, about 20 minutes. Transfer the cookie sheet to a rack; let the logs cool for 5 minutes. Using a serrated knife, slice the logs on the diagonal ½ inch thick.

**4.** Bake the slices for 7 minutes on each side. Transfer the biscotti to a rack to cool completely. Drizzle with the melted white chocolate and refrigerate until set, about 10 minutes. —*Lou Seibert Pappas*

**MAKE AHEAD** The biscotti can be kept in an airtight container for 1 week.

## Ice Cream in Crispy Chocolate-Coconut Cones

**TOTAL: 1 HR 30 MIN**
MAKES 10 CONES ●

- 1 tablespoon unsalted melted butter, plus more for brushing
- 1¼ cups unsweetened shredded coconut (3 ounces)
- ½ cup sugar
- 2 large eggs
- ½ pound bittersweet chocolate, chopped and melted

Dulce de leche ice cream, for serving

**1.** Preheat the oven to 350°. Trace a 6-inch circle onto 5 separate sheets of parchment paper. Turn the sheets over and brush butter inside the rounds and 1 inch beyond the traced rims. Form a 12-inch sheet of foil into a 6-inch-long cone. Wrap another sheet of foil around the cone to smooth the surface.

**2.** In a food processor, pulse the coconut until fine. Add the sugar, eggs and the 1 tablespoon of melted butter; process until combined. Transfer the batter to a bowl.

**3.** Set 1 of the prepared sheets of parchment on a baking sheet. Spoon 1½ tablespoons of the batter onto the buttered round. Using an offset spatula, spread the batter to the edge of the circle in a thin and even layer. Bake the tuile for 6 minutes, or until golden all over.

**4.** Immediately transfer the parchment paper to a work surface. Carefully roll the tuile around the aluminum-foil cone, pressing it into a cone shape; let cool for 1 to 2 minutes before removing the foil cone from inside the tuile. Repeat with the remaining batter, using each piece of parchment paper twice and buttering the rounds between batches.

**5.** Using a small pastry brush, coat the inside of each cone with melted chocolate. Brush the outer rim of the cone with a ½-inch band of melted chocolate. Transfer the cones to a baking sheet lined with wax paper and chill until set. Fill with scoops of ice cream and serve at once. —*Jacques Torres*

**MAKE AHEAD** The cones can be kept at room temperature in an airtight container for up to 2 days.

## Frozen Lemon Cream Sandwiches

**TOTAL: 20 MIN, PLUS 4 HR FREEZING**
6 SERVINGS ●

English lemon curd from a jar plus high-quality store-bought Belgian butter cookies become an impressive dessert that can be made well ahead.

One 7-ounce container chilled crème fraîche
- ¼ cup lemon curd
Finely grated zest of 1 lemon
- 12 crisp butter waffle cookies
- ¼ cup chopped unsalted pistachios

**1.** Line a small baking sheet with wax paper. In a chilled bowl, using a hand-held electric mixer, beat the crème fraîche with the lemon curd and lemon zest until firm peaks form.

**2.** Arrange half of the waffle cookies on the baking sheet and spoon the lemon cream onto the centers, letting it ooze to the edges. Top with the remaining cookies, pressing down gently. Freeze the sandwiches until firm, at least 4 hours.

**3.** Spread the nuts on a plate and roll the edges of the sandwiches in them. Serve at once. —*Grace Parisi*

**MAKE AHEAD** The lemon cream sandwiches can be frozen in an airtight container for up to 1 week.

**FROZEN FRUIT NOUGAT WITH CITRUS SAUCE**

**MOROCCAN RICE PUDDING WITH ALMONDS**

## Frozen Fruit Nougat with Citrus Sauce

**ACTIVE: 1 HR 15 MIN; TOTAL: 2 HR 30 MIN, PLUS OVERNIGHT FREEZING**

**10 SERVINGS** ●

**FROZEN NOUGAT**

- ¼ cup dried cranberries, coarsely chopped (1¼ ounces)
- ¼ cup finely chopped dried apricots (2 ounces)
- ¼ cup dried currants (1¼ ounces)
- ⅛ cup finely diced candied orange rind (1 ounce)
- ¼ cup plus 2 tablespoons kirsch
- ½ cup plus 2 tablespoons sliced blanched almonds (2 ounces)
- ¼ cup plus 2 tablespoons shelled unsalted pistachios (2 ounces)
- 1 cup sugar
- 1½ teaspoons water
- 1½ cups plus 1½ tablespoons heavy cream
- 2 large egg whites

**CITRUS SAUCE**

- ½ cup honey
- 1 vanilla bean, split, seeds scraped
- 6 tablespoons fresh orange juice
- ¼ cup fresh lemon juice
- 1½ teaspoons grated orange zest
- 5 small seedless tangerines

**1.** MAKE THE FROZEN NOUGAT: In a large bowl, combine the cranberries, apricots, currants, candied orange rind and kirsch and let stand for 2 hours.

**2.** Preheat the oven to 350°. Line a large baking sheet with parchment paper. On a pie plate, spread the almonds and pistachios and toast for 7 to 8 minutes, until golden; let cool.

**3.** In a medium saucepan, combine ½ cup of the sugar with the water and cook over high heat until a medium amber caramel forms, about 7 minutes. Add 1½ tablespoons of the cream and boil for 2 minutes. Off the heat, add the nuts and stir to coat them evenly with the caramel. Pour the nuts onto the prepared baking sheet and spread in a thin layer. Cover with another sheet of parchment and, using a rolling pin, roll the brittle flat; let cool. Break the brittle into 1-inch pieces. Transfer to a food processor and pulse until coarsely ground.

**4.** Line a 9-by-5-inch loaf pan with plastic wrap, leaving 4 inches of overhang all around. Drain the dried fruits, pressing to remove as much of the liquid as possible. In a large bowl, using an electric mixer, beat the egg whites until soft peaks form. Gradually beat in the remaining ½ cup of sugar at high speed and continue to beat until the whites are firm and glossy. In another large bowl, beat the remaining 1½ cups of cream until firm peaks form. Carefully fold the cream into the beaten egg whites. Fold in the dried fruits and the ground brittle until evenly distributed. Spoon the nougat into the prepared loaf pan and smooth the top. Fold the plastic over and freeze until firm, at least 8 hours.

**5. MEANWHILE, MAKE THE SAUCE:** In a small saucepan, combine the honey with the vanilla bean and seeds and bring to a boil. Off the heat, add the orange juice, lemon juice and orange zest and let cool.

**6.** Peel the small tangerines. Working over a bowl, cut in between the membranes, releasing the segments into the bowl. Add the segments to the sauce.

**7.** Unmold the nougat; remove the plastic wrap. Cut into 10 slices, spoon the citrus sauce on the side and serve.
—*Gabriel Kreuther*

**MAKE AHEAD** The nougat can be frozen, and the sauce refrigerated, for 2 days.

## Candy Corn Ice Pops
**ACTIVE: 10 MIN; TOTAL: 6 HR**
**MAKES 16 POPS** ● ●
These tricolored pops are made by freezing layers of juice in a mold. Use a white, an orange and a yellow juice to match the colors of candy corn.

**About ½ cup white-colored fruit juice, such as a pineapple-coconut blend**
**About 1 cup orange-colored juice, such as mango juice**
**About 2 cups deep-yellow-colored juice, such as orange juice**

**1.** Pour the white juice into ice-pop molds (see Note) and freeze until solid, about 2 hours. Add the orange-colored juice to the pops and freeze until solid; follow with the yellow juice. Insert the sticks and cover with the lids; freeze until solid.

**2.** Unmold the pops and serve at once.
—*Peggy Cullen*

**NOTE** You can buy "Tiered Castle" ice-pop molds, which include wooden sticks and a lid, from Kitchen Krafts ($16 per 8-pop mold; kitchenkrafts.com or 800-776-0575).

**MAKE AHEAD** The pops can be frozen in their molds for up to 1 week.

## Moroccan Rice Pudding with Toasted Almonds
**ACTIVE: 25 MIN; TOTAL: 1 HR, PLUS 1 HR COOLING**
**6 SERVINGS** ●
Rice pudding is prepared in one form or another all over the eastern Mediterranean. This Moroccan version is particularly delicious, perhaps because the rice is cooked in two stages: First it's boiled in water, then it's simmered in milk.

¾ **cup arborio rice**
1½ **cups water**
¼ **teaspoon salt**
2 **tablespoons plus 1 teaspoon unsalted butter**
2½ **cups whole milk**
¾ **cup confectioners' sugar**
1 **tablespoon orange-flower water (optional)**
½ **cup blanched almonds**

**1.** In a fine-mesh sieve, rinse the rice under cold water until the water runs clear. Transfer the rice to a medium

saucepan. Add the 1½ cups of water and the salt and bring to a boil. Add 2 tablespoons of the butter, cover and cook over low heat until the water is almost completely absorbed, about 15 minutes.

**2.** Stir in the milk and sugar and bring to a boil over moderate heat. Cook, stirring occasionally, until the rice is tender, about 7 minutes. Stir in the orange-flower water and simmer for 1 minute. Transfer the rice pudding to a bowl and let cool; the pudding will firm up.

**3.** Meanwhile, in a small skillet, melt the remaining 1 teaspoon of butter. Add the almonds and cook over moderately high heat, stirring, until golden, about 6 minutes. Transfer the almonds to a plate to cool. Sprinkle the almonds over the pudding and serve. —*Anissa Helou*

**MAKE AHEAD** The rice pudding can be refrigerated overnight. Serve chilled or at room temperature.

## Brûléed Rice Pudding
**ACTIVE: 45 MIN; TOTAL: 2 HR**
**6 SERVINGS** ●
6 **cups whole milk**
**Zest of 1 lemon, in wide strips**
1 **cinnamon stick, broken in half**
1 **cup medium-grain rice (7 ounces), such as bomba, Valencia or arborio**
¾ **cup heavy cream**
½ **cup granulated sugar**
6 **tablespoons light brown sugar**

**1.** In a medium enameled cast-iron casserole, combine the milk with the lemon zest and cinnamon stick and bring to a simmer over moderate heat. Add the rice and cook over low heat for 20 minutes, stirring occasionally. Discard the lemon zest and the cinnamon stick. Continue to cook the rice, stirring often, until it is just tender, about 50 minutes. Add the cream and simmer, stirring often, until the rice is very tender and the pudding is creamy, about 15 minutes.

# cakes, cookies + more

**2.** Stir in the granulated sugar and simmer over moderate heat until dissolved, about 2 minutes. Spoon the pudding into six 1-cup ramekins and let cool to room temperature, about 30 minutes.

**3.** Preheat the broiler. Using a coarse sieve, sift 1 tablespoon of brown sugar over each pudding. Set 3 ramekins on a small baking sheet and broil 4 inches from the heat for 20 seconds, or until the sugar is bubbling; repeat with the remaining ramekins. Let cool until the sugar hardens, then serve. —*José Andrés*

## Bread Pudding Soufflé with Bourbon Sauce

**ACTIVE: 1 HR; TOTAL: 2 HR**

2 SERVINGS

SOUFFLÉ

1½ tablespoons raisins

½ cup sugar, plus more for
    sprinkling

Scant ¼ teaspoon cinnamon

Pinch of freshly grated nutmeg

  1 large egg, lightly beaten

½ cup heavy cream

½ teaspoon pure vanilla extract

  2 cups day-old crustless French or
    challah bread cubes (½ inch)

  3 large egg whites

Pinch of cream of tartar

BOURBON SAUCE

½ cup heavy cream

¾ teaspoon cornstarch dissolved
    in 1 tablespoon water

1½ tablespoons sugar

1½ tablespoons bourbon

**1. MAKE THE SOUFFLÉ:** Preheat the oven to 350°. Butter an 8-by-4-inch loaf pan. Sprinkle the raisins on the bottom. In a bowl, combine ¼ cup of the sugar, the cinnamon and the nutmeg. Whisk in the egg, cream and vanilla. Add the bread. Let stand for 5 minutes, stirring occasionally, until the liquid is absorbed.

**2.** Spoon the bread into the prepared loaf pan and smooth the top. Bake for 25 minutes, or until golden and set. Let cool slightly, then turn the bread pudding out onto a cutting board; coarsely chop.

**3.** Butter a 3-cup ramekin or soufflé dish and coat it with sugar. In a clean bowl, using an electric mixer, beat the egg whites with the cream of tartar until frothy. Increase the speed to high and beat until soft peaks form. Gradually add the remaining ¼ cup of sugar and beat until stiff and glossy. Put half of the bread pudding in a medium bowl. Fold in one-fourth of the beaten egg whites until just combined. Spoon the mixture into the ramekin. Add the remaining bread pudding to the bowl and fold in the remaining egg whites. Spoon the mixture into the ramekin, mounding it about 1 inch above the rim. Bake the soufflé for 25 minutes, or until golden and puffed.

**4. MEANWHILE, MAKE THE BOURBON SAUCE:** In a saucepan, bring the cream to a boil. Whisk in the dissolved cornstarch and cook until slightly thickened, 1 minute. Off the heat, add the sugar and bourbon. Return to the heat and simmer over moderately low heat for 1 minute.

**5.** As soon as the soufflé is done, poke a hole in the center and pour in half of the bourbon sauce. Serve at once, passing extra sauce on the side. —*Tory McPhail*

## Pumpkin Pudding with Candied Ginger Whipped Cream

**TOTAL: 30 MIN, PLUS 4 HR CHILLING**

12 SERVINGS ● ●

PUDDING

  4 large egg yolks

  1 cup sugar

¼ cup cornstarch

  1 teaspoon ground cinnamon

¼ teaspoon freshly
    grated nutmeg

Pinch of ground cloves

Pinch of salt

1½ cups whole milk

1½ cups half-and-half

One 15-ounce can unsweetened
    pumpkin puree (1¾ cups)

  4 tablespoons (2 ounces)
    unsalted butter

  1 tablespoon pure vanilla extract

TOPPING

  2 cups heavy cream

¼ cup confectioners' sugar

  2 tablespoons minced
    crystallized ginger

  1 cup coarsely crumbled
    store-bought gingersnap cookies

**1. MAKE THE PUDDING:** In a medium bowl, combine the egg yolks, sugar, cornstarch, cinnamon, nutmeg, cloves and salt. Using a handheld electric mixer, beat at medium speed until the egg yolk mixture is thickened and light yellow, about 4 minutes.

**2.** In a medium saucepan, heat the milk and half-and-half until small bubbles appear around the rim. Gradually beat 1 cup of the hot milk mixture into the egg yolk mixture, then add the egg yolk mixture to the saucepan. Cook over moderate heat, stirring constantly with a heatproof rubber spatula, until the pudding is gently boiling and as thick as mayonnaise, 6 minutes. Remove from the heat.

**3.** In a small skillet, cook the pumpkin puree over high heat, stirring constantly, until slightly dry, about 3 minutes. Add the puree to the pudding along with the butter and vanilla and stir until the butter melts. Transfer the pudding to a large bowl and press a sheet of plastic wrap directly onto the surface. Refrigerate until very cold, about 4 hours.

**4. MAKE THE TOPPING:** In a large bowl, using an electric mixer, beat the heavy cream with the confectioners' sugar and minced crystallized ginger at high speed until firm peaks form.

**5.** Spoon the pudding into wine glasses or bowls and dollop the ginger whipped cream on top. Sprinkle with the gingersnaps and serve. —*Grace Parisi*

# coconut milk

**Unsweetened coconut milk can add a rich texture and exotic flavor to all kinds of recipes—from savory to sweet. The chewy candy bars here, which are layered with a mixture of unsweetened shredded coconut and coconut milk and then spread with bittersweet chocolate, show one of the many uses for this ingredient.**

### Coconut Chocolate Candy Bars

**ACTIVE: 1 HR; TOTAL: 2 HR**

MAKES ABOUT FORTY 1¼-INCH SQUARES ● ○

- 1½ cups unsweetened shredded coconut
- One 14-ounce can unsweetened coconut milk
- ½ cup sugar
- 2 tablespoons light corn syrup
- 6 tablespoons unsalted butter
- 11 ounces bittersweet chocolate, chopped and melted

1. Preheat the oven to 350° and set the rack in the middle of the oven. Spread the shredded coconut on a large, rimmed baking sheet and toast until lightly golden, about 4 minutes. Let the shredded coconut cool completely.

2. Stir the coconut milk in the can until it comes together. In a medium saucepan, combine the coconut milk with the sugar, light corn syrup and 4 tablespoons of the butter. Cook the coconut milk mixture over moderately low heat, stirring frequently, until it is as thick as jam, about 40 minutes. Remove the coconut milk mixture from the heat and whisk in the remaining 2 tablespoons of butter and the toasted coconut. Transfer to a bowl and let cool completely .

3. Cover a large baking sheet with wax paper. Using an offset spatula, carefully spread half of the melted bittersweet chocolate on the wax paper in a 10-by-7-inch rectangle. Refrigerate the chocolate until firm, about 10 minutes. Spread the coconut mixture over the chocolate and refrigerate until set, about 10 minutes. Carefully spread the remaining melted chocolate over the coconut and refrigerate the candy until firm, about 20 minutes. Using a long, sharp knife, trim the edges of the rectangle, then cut the candy bars into 40 squares. Cover and refrigerate the coconut chocolate candy bars until ready to serve. —*Grace Parisi*

**MAKE AHEAD** The candy bars can be refrigerated for up to 1 week.

---

### TASTE TEST: CANNED COCONUT MILK

F&W editors tested almost a dozen brands of unsweetened coconut milk to find the three with the purest flavor.

**BALI SPICE ALL-NATURAL PREMIUM COCONUT MILK** From an all-female-owned-and-run factory in Indonesia, it has a light and pourable consistency.

**THAI KITCHEN PREMIUM COCONUT MILK** Made from the first pressing of fresh coconut; natural emulsifiers account for its rich texture.

**CHAOKOH COCONUT MILK** This Thai-produced coconut milk has a thick, puddinglike consistency; you scoop it from the can rather than pour it.

# cakes, cookies + more

## Aunt Ruthie's Coconut Snowballs

**TOTAL: 2 HR 50 MIN, PLUS 1 HR CHILLING**

**MAKES 14 SNOWBALLS** ●

1½ cups all-purpose flour

1½ cups confectioners' sugar

16 large egg whites

¼ teaspoon fresh lemon juice

¼ teaspoon salt

Two 14-ounce cans unsweetened coconut milk

1 cup granulated sugar

6 cups sweetened shredded coconut (three 7-ounce packages)

Marshmallow Frosting (recipe follows)

**1.** Preheat the oven to 350°. Line the bottoms of two 9-inch cake pans with parchment paper. In a bowl, whisk the flour with ½ cup of the confectioners' sugar.

**2.** In a very large bowl, beat the egg whites with the lemon juice and salt at high speed until soft peaks form. Beat in the remaining 1 cup of confectioners' sugar, ¼ cup at a time, and continue beating until firm peaks form. Sift the dry ingredients over the egg whites and fold in completely. Divide the batter between the pans and smooth the tops. Bake for 25 minutes, or until they are golden and the tops spring back when lightly tapped. Invert the cake pans onto a rack and let cool completely.

**3.** Run a knife around the edge of each cake and unmold. Peel off the parchment paper. Using a 3-inch round cookie cutter, stamp out 14 rounds total.

**4.** In a saucepan, combine the coconut milk and granulated sugar and cook over moderate heat, stirring, until the sugar is dissolved. Transfer to a large, shallow glass baking dish and let cool. Add the cake rounds and let soak for 5 minutes. Transfer the soaked cake rounds to a wire rack set over a baking sheet and let the cakes drain for 10 minutes.

**5.** Line a baking sheet with wax paper. Spread half of the shredded coconut on a large platter. Fill a pastry bag fitted with a large round tip or a large, sturdy plastic bag with a corner snipped off with some of the Marshmallow Frosting. Pipe frosting onto 2 of the soaked cake rounds, covering the entire tops. Invert the rounds into the shredded coconut and press lightly. Pipe frosting onto the tops and sides of the rounds and sprinkle some of the remaining coconut all over. Tap off any excess. Transfer the snowballs to the wax paper–lined baking sheet and continue making snowballs. Refrigerate them until set, about 1 hour. —*Daniel Orr*

## MARSHMALLOW FROSTING

**TOTAL: 30 MIN**

**MAKES 9 CUPS** ●

4 teaspoons unflavored gelatin (from 2 envelopes)

¼ cup plus 2 tablespoons water

2 cups sugar

¾ cup light corn syrup

6 large egg whites

¼ teaspoon fresh lemon juice

⅛ teaspoon salt

**1.** In a small microwavable bowl, sprinkle the gelatin over 3 tablespoons of the water and let stand until softened.

**2.** In a medium saucepan, combine 1½ cups of the sugar with the corn syrup and the remaining 3 tablespoons of water. Bring to a boil, stirring, until the sugar is dissolved. Keep warm.

**3.** Meanwhile, in a standing electric mixer fitted with a whisk, beat the egg whites, lemon juice and salt until soft peaks form. Gradually add the remaining ½ cup of sugar, beating at high speed until stiff and glossy. At medium speed, carefully add the hot sugar syrup in a thin stream. When all of the syrup has been added, beat the meringue at medium-high speed until slightly cooled, about 5 minutes. Microwave the gelatin until melted, about 15 seconds. With the mixer on, beat the melted gelatin into the meringue. Use right away. —*D.O.*

## Espresso Jell-O

**TOTAL: 10 MIN, PLUS 3 HR CHILLING**

**4 SERVINGS** ●

1 envelope unflavored gelatin

¼ cup cold water

1½ cups hot brewed espresso

¼ cup plus 2 tablespoons sugar

½ cup heavy cream, chilled

Coarsely ground coffee, for garnish

**1.** In a medium bowl, sprinkle the gelatin over the water and let stand for 5 minutes. Add the espresso and ¼ cup of the sugar and stir until thoroughly dissolved. Pour into four ½-cup molds or a loaf pan, cover with plastic wrap and refrigerate until set, 2 to 3 hours.

**2.** Meanwhile, in another bowl, whip the cream with the remaining 2 tablespoons of sugar until it holds soft peaks.

**3.** Dip the molds in warm water and turn the desserts out onto plates or cut the gelatin into 1-inch squares and mound in wineglasses or bowls. Garnish each serving with whipped cream and sprinkle with ground coffee. —*Lauren Chattman*

**MAKE AHEAD** The Espresso Jell-O can be refrigerated for up to 3 days.

## Chocolate-Coated Almonds

**ACTIVE: 20 MIN; TOTAL: 1 HR**

**MAKES 3 CUPS** ●

⅓ cup granulated sugar

3 tablespoons water

1¼ cups blanched almonds, toasted

5 ounces bittersweet chocolate, melted

**1.** In a saucepan, combine the sugar and water and boil over moderate heat without stirring until the syrup reaches 248° on a candy thermometer, 10 minutes. Add the almonds and stir to coat. Spread the nuts in a single layer on a parchment-lined baking sheet; let cool.

**2.** Drizzle the melted chocolate over the almonds and refrigerate until the chocolate is set, about 15 minutes. Serve cold or at room temperature. —*Carrie Pillar*

ESPRESSO JELL-O

SHALLOT-LEMON CONFIT, P. 348

# sauces+
# condiments

16

**BOURBON, ORANGE AND MOLASSES RUB**

**INGREDIENTS FOR GLOBAL RUBS**

### Bourbon, Orange and Molasses Rub

**TOTAL: 25 MIN**

**MAKES ABOUT 1 CUP** ● ● ●

2 tablespoons canola oil
1 medium shallot, minced
1 garlic clove, minced
½ cup bourbon
¾ cup fresh orange juice
¼ cup unsulfured molasses
2 tablespoons sherry vinegar
1 tablespoon finely grated orange zest
1 tablespoon chopped thyme
½ teaspoon cinnamon
½ teaspoon salt

In a saucepan, heat the oil. Add the shallot and garlic and cook over moderate heat until softened, 3 minutes. Add the bourbon and carefully ignite it. Add the orange juice, molasses, vinegar, orange zest, thyme, cinnamon and salt and simmer over moderate heat until reduced to a scant cup, 15 minutes. Let cool.
—*David Walzog*

**MAKE AHEAD** The rub can be refrigerated for up to 1 week.

**IDEAL MATCH** Pork, duck breasts.

### Herb, Garlic and Lemon Rub

**TOTAL: 10 MIN**

**MAKES ABOUT ½ CUP** ● ● ●

¼ cup extra-virgin olive oil
2 garlic cloves, minced
2 tablespoons fresh lemon juice
1 tablespoon chopped parsley
1 tablespoon chopped cilantro
1 tablespoon chopped chives
1 tablespoon grated lemon zest
1 teaspoon chopped thyme
1 teaspoon chopped rosemary
1 teaspoon kosher salt

In a bowl, blend all of the ingredients.
—*David Walzog*

**IDEAL MATCH** White-fleshed fish, chicken.

### Moroccan Spice Rub

**TOTAL: 5 MIN**

**MAKES 3 TABLESPOONS** ● ● ●

1 teaspoon granulated garlic
1 teaspoon freshly ground black pepper
1 teaspoon ground fennel
1 teaspoon dry mustard
1 teaspoon kosher salt
¾ teaspoon ground cumin
½ teaspoon cayenne pepper
¼ teaspoon rubbed sage
¼ teaspoon freshly grated nutmeg

In a small bowl, blend the ingredients.
—*David Walzog*

**IDEAL MATCH** Pork, chicken.

### Sesame-Soy Rub

**TOTAL: 10 MIN**

**MAKES ABOUT ⅔ CUP** ● ● ●

- ¼ cup sesame seeds
- 2 tablespoons soy sauce
- 2 tablespoons Japanese mirin
- 2 tablespoons canola oil
- 1 tablespoon Asian sesame oil
- 1 tablespoon fresh lemon juice
- 1 tablespoon fresh orange juice
- 1 teaspoon grated orange zest
- ¼ teaspoon cayenne pepper

In a mini food processor, grind the sesame seeds to a coarse powder. Transfer the sesame powder to a bowl and stir in the soy sauce, mirin, canola and sesame oils, lemon and orange juices, orange zest and cayenne. —*David Walzog*

**MAKE AHEAD** The rub can be refrigerated for up to 1 week.

**IDEAL MATCH** White-fleshed fish, chicken.

### Red Wine–Carrot Sauce

**ACTIVE: 15 MIN; TOTAL: 45 MIN**

**MAKES ABOUT ¾ CUP**

The slightly sweet taste of this sauce evokes the flavor of boeuf bourguignon.

- Salt
- 1 large carrot, peeled and cut into 1-inch pieces
- 2 cups full-bodied dry red wine
- 1 medium shallot, minced
- 6 tablespoons unsalted butter, cut into tablespoons and chilled
- Feshly ground pepper

1. Bring a saucepan of salted water to a boil. Add the carrot, cover and simmer until tender, about 15 minutes. Drain, transfer the carrot to a mini processor and puree.

2. In the same saucepan, bring the red wine to a boil. Ignite the wine and let the alcohol burn off. Add the minced shallot and boil over high heat until the wine is reduced by three-quarters, about 8 minutes. Stir in the carrot puree and bring the sauce to a boil.

3. Remove the pan from the heat and whisk in the chilled butter, 1 tablespoon at a time, until the butter, is incorporated and the sauce is smooth. Return the pan to low heat now and then to keep the sauce hot enough to melt the butter, but do not let it boil. Season with salt and pepper; the sauce should be peppery. —*Jean-Georges Vongerichten*

**MAKE AHEAD** The sauce, without the butter, can be refrigerated for up to 3 days. Bring to a boil and proceed.

**SERVE WITH** Steaks, poached eggs, roast chicken.

### Red Chile BBQ Sauce

**ACTIVE: 25 MIN; TOTAL: 45 MIN**

**MAKES ABOUT 1¼ CUPS** ● ● ●

- 2 tablespoons canola oil
- ¼ cup minced onion
- 2 large garlic cloves, minced
- 2 dried ancho chiles, stems and seeds discarded, chiles cut into ½-inch pieces
- 1 cup canned crushed tomatoes
- ½ cup red wine vinegar
- ⅓ cup light brown sugar
- ⅓ cup Worcestershire sauce
- 2 tablespoons fresh orange juice
- 1 tablespoon finely grated orange zest
- 1 teaspoon chopped thyme
- ½ teaspoon cayenne pepper
- Salt

In a small saucepan, heat the oil. Add the onion, garlic and ancho chiles and cook over moderate heat until fragrant, about 4 minutes. Add the tomatoes, vinegar, brown sugar, Worcestershire sauce, orange juice, orange zest, thyme and cayenne. Simmer over moderate heat, stirring occasionally, until thickened and flavorful, about 20 minutes. Season with salt. —*David Walzog*

**MAKE AHEAD** The barbecue sauce can be refrigerated for up to 2 weeks.

**IDEAL MATCH** Pork, chicken.

### Rhubarb Ketchup

**ACTIVE: 15 MIN; TOTAL: 45 MIN**

**MAKES ABOUT 5 CUPS** ● ●

- 2 pounds rhubarb stalks, cut into ½-inch dice
- ⅓ cup ruby port
- ¼ cup red wine vinegar
- 1 cup sugar
- Zest of 1 orange, peeled in wide strips
- Salt
- Cayenne pepper

In a saucepan, combine the rhubarb with the port, vinegar, sugar and orange zest and bring to a boil. Remove from the heat and let steep for 30 minutes. Cover and simmer over moderately low heat, stirring often, until the rhubarb is tender, 5 minutes. Discard the zest. Transfer to a blender and puree. Season with salt and cayenne. —*Jean-Georges Vongerichten*

**MAKE AHEAD** The ketchup can be refrigerated for up to 2 weeks.

**SERVE WITH** Steaks, pork or veal chops.

# ingredient

**GLOBAL RUBS DEFINED**   **TIP**

**INDIAN GARAM MASALA** A mix of cardamom, pepper, cloves, cinnamon and other spices.

**JAMAICAN JERK** A fiery rub containing allspice and Scotch bonnet chiles.

**MEXICAN ADOBO** A thick red paste of garlic, ancho or guajillo chiles and vinegar.

**MOROCCAN RAS EL HANOUT** A complex mix of ginger, cumin, coriander, turmeric, cardamom, nutmeg and dried rose petals.

**THAI CURRY** An intense mix of chiles ground with lemongrass, shallots, garlic, cilantro, kaffir lime and shrimp paste.

# sauces + condiments

## Garlic-Soy Sauce

**TOTAL: 15 MIN**
**MAKES ABOUT 1¼ CUPS** ●

- 2 tablespoons extra-virgin olive oil
- 6 garlic cloves, very thinly sliced
- ½ cup low-sodium soy sauce
- 1½ sticks (6 ounces) unsalted butter, cut into tablespoons and chilled
- Freshly ground pepper

**1.** In a medium saucepan, heat the olive oil until shimmering. Add the garlic and cook over moderately low heat, stirring constantly, until golden, 3 to 5 minutes. Transfer the garlic to a blender, add the soy sauce and puree.

**2.** Return the garlic-soy mixture to the saucepan and bring to a boil. Reduce the heat to low. Remove the saucepan from the heat and whisk in the chilled butter, 1 tablespoon at a time, until it is incorporated and the sauce is smooth. Return the saucepan to the heat now and then to keep the sauce hot enough to melt the butter, but do not let the sauce boil. Generously season the Garlic-Soy Sauce with freshly ground pepper.

*—Jean-Georges Vongerichten*

**MAKE AHEAD** The recipe can be prepared through Step 1 and refrigerated for up to 2 days. Bring the garlic-soy mixture to a boil and proceed.
**SERVE WITH** Steaks, fish, chicken breasts, shrimp, steamed spinach or broccoli.

## Charred Poblano and Garlic Pesto

**TOTAL: 20 MIN**
**MAKES ABOUT 1 CUP** ● ● ●

- 2 large poblanos (6 ounces each), halved lengthwise and cored
- Canola oil
- 4 large unpeeled garlic cloves, lightly smashed
- 2 scallions
- ¼ cup cilantro leaves
- ⅓ cup crumbled queso fresco or feta cheese
- Salt and freshly ground pepper

Heat a cast-iron skillet. Rub the chiles with canola oil and set them in the skillet skin side down. Add the garlic and scallions and cook over moderately high heat, flattening the chiles with a spatula, until charred all over, about 6 minutes. Transfer to a plate and let cool slightly. Peel the chiles and garlic and coarsely chop them, then transfer to a mini food processor. Add the scallions and cilantro; pulse until minced. With the machine on, add 3 tablespoons of oil and process the mixture to a coarse paste. Add the cheese and pulse until just blended. Season the pesto with salt and pepper.

*—Grace Parisi*

**MAKE AHEAD** The pesto can be refrigerated for up to 1 week.
**SERVE WITH** Grilled chicken or roasted vegetable sandwiches, or mixed into meatballs, rice, soup or pasta.

## Mediterranean Country Sachets

**TOTAL: 15 MIN**
**MAKES 10 SACHETS** ● ●

Drop one of these sachets into a pork, lamb or beef stew, fish or chicken stock or chicken or turkey noodle soup.

- 3 tablespoons plus 1 teaspoon each of dried rosemary and dried chives
- 1¼ teaspoons dried lavender flowers
- Ten 7-inch 2-ply squares of cheesecloth
- 3 tablespoons plus 1 teaspoon whole black peppercorns
- Ten 6-inch lengths of kitchen string

In a medium bowl, combine the rosemary with the chives and lavender and stir to blend. Lay the cheesecloth on a work surface. Spoon 2 rounded teaspoons of the dried herbs in the center of each square. Add 1 teaspoon of the black peppercorns to each sachet. Gather each square into a neat bundle and secure with kitchen string. *—Alisa Barry*

## Tuscan Herb Sachets

**TOTAL: 15 MIN**
**MAKES 10 SACHETS** ● ●

Use a sachet in beef or pork stew, or sprinkle the contents into tomato sauce as it cooks. Or mix the seasonings into meatballs or meat loaf.

- 3 tablespoons plus 1 teaspoon each of dried basil, dried oregano, dried marjoram and dried parsley
- Ten 7-inch 2-ply squares of cheesecloth
- Ten 6-inch lengths of kitchen string

In a medium bowl, combine the dried basil, oregano, marjoram and parsley and stir to blend. Lay the cheesecloth on a work surface. Spoon 1 tablespoon plus 1 teaspoon of the dried herbs in the center of each square. Gather each square into a neat bundle and secure with kitchen string.

*—Alisa Barry*

# ingredient

**TIP**  **HERB + SPICE SACHETS**

The aromatic sachets on these pages are incredibly simple to use—just toss one into a pot if you're making a stock, soup, stew or braise. Alternatively, stuff a sachet into a whole chicken; as the bird roasts, it will flavor the juices. Most everything you need for the sachets—cheesecloth, kitchen string, whole spices, dried herbs—can be found in the supermarket. If you're making a lot, consider buying dried herbs and spices in bulk. You can keep the sachets in an airtight container for up to six months.

## Moroccan Spice Sachets

**TOTAL: 45 MIN**

**MAKES 10 SACHETS** ●

These sachets complement both sweet and savory dishes: Drop one into lamb stew or soup, into the poaching liquid for pears or apples or stuff one into a chicken cavity before roasting.

- 1¼ cups finely grated orange zest (from 20 medium oranges)
- Ten 7-inch 2-ply squares of cheesecloth
- 40 whole cloves
- 10 cinnamon sticks, broken in half
- 10 whole star anise pods
- 2½ teaspoons dried mint
- Ten 6-inch lengths of kitchen string

**1.** Preheat the oven to 250°. Spread the grated orange zest in a thin, even layer on a medium, rimmed baking sheet and bake for 15 minutes, or until completely dry, stirring halfway through to break up any clumps of zest.

**2.** Lay the squares of cheesecloth on a clean, dry work surface. Spoon 2 tablespoons of the dried orange zest in the center of each square and top with 4 cloves, 2 cinnamon stick halves, 1 star anise pod and ¼ teaspoon dried mint. Gather each cheesecloth square into a neat bundle and secure tightly with kitchen string.
—*Alisa Barry*

## Lavender-Rosemary Salt

**TOTAL: 20 MIN, PLUS OVERNIGHT STANDING**

**MAKES ABOUT 2½ CUPS** ●

Seasoned salts add quick flavor to just about anything: Sprinkle flavored salts over poultry, meat or fish before roasting or grilling, toss with homemade croutons, mix into burgers, stir into stews or use to season cooked vegetables and pizzas. This Lavender-Rosemary Salt works best with beef, chicken or pork. It also tastes great with artichokes.

- 1¾ cups kosher salt
- ½ cup plus 2 tablespoons coarse sea salt
- 6 tablespoons plus 2 teaspoons dried rosemary
- 3 tablespoons plus 1 teaspoon dried lavender flowers

In a medium bowl, combine the kosher salt and sea salt. In a mortar or a food processor, combine the salt mixture with the dried rosemary and lavender flowers. Grind the ingredients with a pestle or pulse until very coarsely crushed. Transfer the flavored salt to an airtight container. Let the flavored salt stand overnight before using. —*Alisa Barry*

**MAKE AHEAD** The salt can be stored in an airtight container for up to 1 year.

## Peppercorn Salt

**TOTAL: 20 MIN, PLUS OVERNIGHT STANDING**

**MAKES ABOUT 2⅔ CUPS** ●

This Peppercorn Salt is delicious with roasted or grilled beef and lamb as well as with pork. It's also fabulous when sprinkled into creamy soups and over fattier types of fish such as salmon, bluefish or mackerel.

- 1¾ cups kosher salt
- ½ cup plus 2 tablespoons coarse sea salt
- 3 tablespoons plus 1 teaspoon whole black peppercorns

In a medium bowl, combine the kosher salt and sea salt. In a mortar or a food processor, combine the salt mixture with the whole peppercorns. Grind the ingredients with a pestle or pulse until very coarsely crushed. Transfer the flavored salt to an airtight container. Let the flavored salt stand overnight before using. —*Alisa Barry*

**VARIATION** Mix in colored peppercorns for a slightly different flavor and look.

**MAKE AHEAD** The salt can be stored in an airtight container for up to 1 year.

## Citrus-Fennel Salt

**TOTAL: 20 MIN, PLUS OVERNIGHT STANDING**

**MAKES ABOUT 2½ CUPS** ● ●

- 6 tablespoons plus 2 teaspoons finely grated lemon zest (from 10 lemons)
- 1¾ cups kosher salt
- ½ cup plus 2 tablespoons coarse sea salt
- 3 tablespoons plus 1 teaspoon fennel seeds

**1.** Preheat the oven to 250°. Spread the lemon zest on a medium baking sheet. Bake for 15 minutes, or until completely dry, stirring halfway through baking to break up any clumps. Let cool slightly.

**2.** In a medium bowl, combine the kosher and sea salts. In a mortar or a food processor, combine the salt mixture with the lemon zest and the fennel. Grind with a pestle or pulse until very coarsely crushed. Transfer to an airtight container. Let stand overnight before using. —*Alisa Barry*

**MAKE AHEAD** The salt can be stored in an airtight container for up to 1 year.

# equipment

**NONSLIP BOWLS**      **TIP**

**OXO** These nesting bowls coated in rubber won't slip on the counter (from $15 for a 1.5-quart bowl; 800-545-4411 or oxo.com).

# sauces + condiments

## Sugar Syrup

ACTIVE: 5 MIN; TOTAL: 35 MIN
MAKES ABOUT 1¼ CUPS ●

This syrup is the base for the three recipes that follow. Use it for flavored syrups of your own creation as well.

- 1 cup water
- 1 cup sugar

1. In a saucepan, combine the water and sugar. Bring to a simmer over moderately high heat, stirring occasionally to dissolve the sugar. Cover and remove from the heat. Let stand for 30 minutes.
2. Strain the syrup into a clean bottle or jar and refrigerate. —Alisa Barry

MAKE AHEAD The syrup can be refrigerated for up to 3 months.

## Orange and Cranberry Syrup

ACTIVE: 5 MIN; TOTAL: 35 MIN
MAKES ABOUT 1¼ CUPS ● ●

Add infused syrups—like this Orange and Cranberry Syrup—to hot or iced tea, mix them with vodka or a crisp, dry white wine like Pinot Grigio, or use them as a poaching liquid for apples, pears, prunes or dried apricots. You can flavor syrups with fruit, tea, citrus zest, flowers, spices and herbs, all of which give the syrups a lovely color.

- 1 cup water
- 1 cup sugar
- Zest of 1 organic orange,
    removed in large strips
    with a vegetable peeler
- ¼ cup fresh or frozen cranberries

1. In a medium saucepan, combine the water and sugar. Bring the mixture to a simmer over moderately high heat, stirring occasionally to dissolve the sugar. Add the strips of orange zest and the cranberries to the saucepan, cover the pan and remove it from the heat. Let the syrup stand for 30 minutes.
2. Strain the syrup into a clean bottle or jar and refrigerate. —Alisa Barry

MAKE AHEAD The infused syrup can be refrigerated for up to 3 months.

## Minted Lime Syrup

ACTIVE: 5 MIN; TOTAL: 35 MIN
MAKES ABOUT 1¼ CUPS ● ●

- 1 cup water
- 1 cup sugar
- Zest of 2 organic limes,
    removed in large strips
    with a vegetable peeler
- 3 mint sprigs

1. In a medium saucepan, combine the water and sugar. Bring to a simmer over moderately high heat, stirring occasionally to dissolve the sugar. Add the lime zest and mint sprigs, cover and remove from the heat. Let stand for 30 minutes.
2. Strain the syrup into a clean bottle or jar and refrigerate. —Alisa Barry

MAKE AHEAD The infused syrup can be refrigerated for up to 3 months.

## Green Tea–Honey Syrup

ACTIVE: 5 MIN; TOTAL: 35 MIN
MAKES ABOUT 1¼ CUPS ● ●

- 1 cup water
- 1 cup sugar
- 2 bags of green tea
- 1 tablespoon orange-blossom honey

1. In a saucepan, bring the water and sugar to a simmer over moderately high heat, stirring occasionally to dissolve the sugar. Add the tea bags, cover and remove from the heat. Let stand for 30 minutes.
2. Stir the honey into the tea-infused syrup. Strain the syrup into a clean bottle or jar and refrigerate. —Alisa Barry

MAKE AHEAD The infused syrup can be refrigerated for up to 3 months.

## Shallot-Lemon Confit

ACTIVE: 20 MIN; TOTAL: 50 MIN
MAKES ABOUT 2½ CUPS ● ●

- 1 pound small or medium
    shallots, peeled
- ¼ cup vegetable oil
- 12 coriander seeds
- 6 whole black peppercorns
- 2 garlic cloves, halved

- Zest of 4 lemons, julienned
- Juice of 2 lemons
- 1 celery rib, finely chopped
- 1 bay leaf
- 1 thyme sprig
- 1 parsley sprig
- 1 teaspoon sugar
- 1 large scallion, julienned
- Salt

In a medium saucepan of boiling water, blanch the shallots for 3 minutes; drain. Return the shallots to the pan, add the oil, coriander seeds, peppercorns, garlic, lemon zest and juice, celery, bay leaf, thyme, parsley and sugar and simmer over moderately low heat, stirring a few times, until the shallots are very tender, about 30 minutes. Fold in the scallion and season with salt.

—Jean-Georges Vongerichten

MAKE AHEAD The Shallot-Lemon Confit can be refrigerated for up to 2 days. Reheat gently.

SERVE WITH Steaks, tuna steaks, pork or veal chops, country terrines, bluefish, mackerel, cold roast pork.

## Sichuan Pickled Cucumbers

TOTAL: 20 MIN, PLUS 24 HR
MARINATING
8 SERVINGS ● ●

- 2 large seedless cucumbers, cut
    into 2-by-¼-inch matchsticks
- ¾ cup rice vinegar
- ¾ cup water
- 6 dried red chiles
- 1 tablespoon salt
- 1 tablespoon sugar

Put the cucumbers in a large heatproof bowl. In a small saucepan, bring the vinegar, water, chiles, salt and sugar to a boil, stirring. Pour over the cucumbers, then let cool. Tightly cover and refrigerate for 24 hours. Drain before serving. —Zak Pelaccio

MAKE AHEAD The drained cucumbers can be refrigerated for up to 2 days.

INFUSED SUGAR SYRUPS

# sauces + condiments

## Almost Instant Heirloom Tomato–Basil Relish

**TOTAL: 15 MIN**
MAKES ABOUT 1½ CUPS ● ● ●

- 2 pounds heirloom tomatoes— peeled, seeded and cut into small dice
- 2 tablespoons Champagne vinegar or white wine vinegar
- 2 tablespoons sugar
- Salt and freshly ground black pepper
- 2 tablespoons extra-virgin olive oil
- ¼ cup finely shredded basil leaves

# superfast

## CONDIMENTS

**GOAT CHEESE AND ARTICHOKE SPREAD** Mix softened goat cheese with chopped scallions, thinly sliced marinated artichokes and olive oil, and season with salt and pepper. Delicious on toasted rosemary or olive bread.

**HORSERADISH MUSTARD TOPPING** Blend equal parts grainy mustard and mayonnaise and add freshly grated or prepared horseradish to taste. Serve with roast beef.

**ITALIAN SUB DRESSING** Mix equal parts finely chopped pepperoncini and cornichons with minced garlic, red wine vinegar, mustard and olive oil. Great with cold cuts.

**PEACH BUTTER** Stir ripe but firm finely chopped peaches and honey into softened unsalted butter. Spread on biscuits or French toast, or on a baguette topped with prosciutto.

Heat a large skillet. Add the tomatoes and cook over high heat until sizzling, 1 minute. Add the vinegar and sugar and a pinch each of salt and pepper and bring to a boil; transfer the tomatoes to a bowl. Boil the juices over high heat until reduced to ¼ cup, 5 minutes. Stir the juices, olive oil and basil into the tomatoes and season with salt and pepper. Serve the relish warm or at room temperature. —*Warren Schwartz*

**MAKE AHEAD** The relish can be refrigerated for up to 3 days; let return to room temperature before serving.

**SERVE WITH** Grilled or roast chicken or meaty white-fleshed fish like halibut or mahimahi.

## Kumquat and Pineapple Chutney

**TOTAL: 35 MIN**
MAKES ABOUT 1 CUP ● ●

- 1 rounded cup kumquats (5 ounces)
- 1 cup finely diced peeled pineapple (¼ pound)
- 3 tablespoons fresh lemon juice
- 3 tablespoons light brown sugar
- 2 tablespoons fresh orange juice
- 2 tablespoons Madeira

1. In a small saucepan of boiling water, blanch the kumquats for 1 minute. Drain and repeat 3 times. Halve each kumquat and squeeze out and reserve any juice; discard the pulp and seeds. Finely dice the skin.
2. In the same saucepan, combine the diced kumquats with the pineapple, lemon juice, brown sugar, orange juice, kumquat juice and Madeira and bring to a boil. Simmer the chutney over moderate heat, stirring occasionally, until it is thickened, about 8 minutes.
—*Jean-Georges Vongerichten*

**MAKE AHEAD** The chutney can be refrigerated for up to 1 week.

**SERVE WITH** Pork or veal chops, duck breasts, cold leftover roasts, cheese plates, country terrines.

## Spiced Prune Chutney

**TOTAL: 30 MIN**
MAKES ABOUT 1½ CUPS ● ● ●

- 1 cup dried pitted prunes, chopped
- 1 cup water
- 1½ tablespoons extra-virgin olive oil
- 1 small red onion, minced
- 1 medium plum tomato, seeded and chopped
- 1½ teaspoons yellow or brown mustard seeds
- ¼ teaspoon cinnamon
- ¼ teaspoon freshly grated nutmeg
- ¼ teaspoon crushed red pepper
- 2 tablespoons sherry vinegar
- 2 tablespoons light brown sugar
- Pinch of salt

1. In a glass bowl, combine the prunes and water. Cover with plastic wrap and microwave at high power for 2 minutes, or until the prunes are plumped. Let cool.
2. In a medium saucepan, heat the oil until shimmering. Add the onion and cook over moderately high heat until softened, about 5 minutes. Add the tomato and cook until slightly softened, about 4 minutes. Add the mustard seeds, cinnamon, nutmeg and crushed red pepper and cook until fragrant, about 1 minute. Stir in the prunes and their liquid, the vinegar, brown sugar and salt and simmer over moderately low heat, stirring occasionally, until jamlike, about 20 minutes. —*Tommy Habetz*

**MAKE AHEAD** The chutney can be refrigerated for up to 2 weeks.

## Cranberry, Quince and Pear Chutney

**ACTIVE: 15 MIN; TOTAL: 45 MIN**
MAKES 4½ CUPS ● ●

With its depth and complexity, this chutney makes a delicious alternative to the usual cranberry sauce.

- 1⅔ cups verjus (see Note) or white wine
- 1 cup sugar
- 2 cups fresh cranberries

3 large Bartlett pears, peeled and finely diced

2 medium quinces (7 ounces each), peeled and finely diced

2 teaspoons grappa or brandy

**1.** In a medium saucepan, combine 1 cup of the verjus with the sugar and bring to a boil. Cook over moderate heat, stirring occasionally, until reduced by one-third, about 10 minutes. Add the cranberries and cook until softened, gently smashing the cranberries against the side of the pan, about 15 minutes.

**2.** Meanwhile, in another medium saucepan, combine the pears with the quinces and remaining ⅔ cup of verjus and bring to a boil. Cover and cook the fruit over moderately low heat until the pears are softened, about 20 minutes; let cool.

**3.** In a medium bowl, combine the cranberry sauce with the pears, quinces and grappa. Refrigerate until chilled.

—*Lee Hefter*

**NOTE** Verjus, the juice of unripe grapes, has a tart, applelike flavor. You can buy it at specialty markets. The F&W Test Kitchen especially likes Wölffer Estate's verjus (631-537-5106 or wolffer.com).

**MAKE AHEAD** The chutney can be refrigerated for up to 1 month.

### Icebox Strawberry Jam
**ACTIVE: 5 MIN; TOTAL: 45 MIN**
**MAKES 1 CUP** ● ●

This simple recipe doesn't require sterilized jars, a thermometer or a pressure canner. Ripe fruit is simply cooked with honey and spices to create a jam that lasts two weeks in the fridge.

1 pint strawberries, thickly sliced (2 cups)

¼ cup honey

¼ teaspoon finely grated lemon zest

Small pinch of five-spice powder (optional)

Salt and freshly ground pepper

In a medium saucepan, combine the strawberries with the honey, lemon zest and five-spice powder and season lightly with salt and pepper. Bring to a boil. Simmer over moderately low heat, stirring occasionally, until thickened, about 40 minutes. Let cool, then refrigerate until chilled. —*Daniel Orr*

**SERVE WITH** Gramma's Buttermilk Biscuits (p. 295).

### Three-Cranberry Conserve
**TOTAL: 15 MIN**
**MAKES ABOUT 3 CUPS** ● ● ● ●

1 cup cranberry juice

1 cup sugar

Zest of 1 orange, removed in large strips with a vegetable peeler

4 cups fresh or frozen cranberries (1 pound)

1 cup dried cranberries (4 ounces)

In a medium saucepan, combine the cranberry juice with the sugar and orange zest and bring to a boil, stirring until the sugar dissolves. Add the fresh and the dried cranberries and cook over moderate heat, gently crushing the fresh berries against the side of the pan, until the conserve is thick and jamlike, about 10 minutes. Transfer the conserve to a serving bowl and let cool, then discard the orange zest. —*Grace Parisi*

**MAKE AHEAD** The cranberry conserve can be refrigerated for up to 2 weeks.

### Brandied Apricot Butter
**TOTAL: 20 MIN**
**MAKES ABOUT 1¼ CUPS** ● ●

This fruit-filled butter is wonderful on crusty bread. It's also great with warm popovers, pancakes, waffles and muffins.

½ cup dried apricots, chopped

¼ cup Cognac or other brandy

2 tablespoons light brown sugar

2 sticks unsalted butter, softened

Salt

Crusty country bread, for serving

In a small saucepan, soak the dried apricots in the Cognac for 10 minutes. Bring to a boil, then carefully ignite with a long match. When the flames subside, add the brown sugar and cook over moderate heat, stirring occasionally, until the sugar is dissolved. Transfer the apricots and their liquid to a food processor and let cool. Add the butter and process until fairly smooth. Lightly season the butter with salt. Scrape the apricot butter into a large ramekin and serve with crusty bread.

—*Naomi Hebberoy*

**MAKE AHEAD** The apricot butter can be frozen for up to 2 weeks.

### Toasted Nuts in Honey
**TOTAL: 15 MIN**
**MAKES ONE 12-OUNCE JAR OR TWO 6-OUNCE JARS** ● ● ● ●

Spoon these sweet and sticky toasted nuts over ice cream or yogurt, serve with ricotta or sheep's-milk cheese or mix into chicken or pork stir-fries.

1 cup mixed unsalted nuts, such as almonds, cashews, pecans, hazelnuts and walnuts

1¼ cups clover honey

**1.** Preheat the oven to 350°. Spread the nuts on a rimmed baking sheet. Bake for 10 minutes, or until fragrant and lightly toasted. Transfer to a plate and let cool.

**2.** Pour half of the honey into a 12-ounce clear-glass jar or into two 6-ounce jars. Add the cooled toasted nuts and top with the remaining honey. Seal the jar or jars.

—*Alisa Barry*

**DRIED FRUIT AND TOASTED NUTS IN CHESTNUT HONEY VARIATION** For a more intense flavor, replace ¼ cup of the clover honey with earthy chestnut honey. Replace 2 tablespoons of the toasted nuts with dried cherries, cranberries or currants.

**MAKE AHEAD** The sealed jars of toasted nuts can be stored at room temperature for up to 1 month.

SAFFRON COOLER, P. 357

# drinks

17

SALUKI

CHEVAL

### Saluki

**TOTAL: 5 MIN**

**MAKES 1 DRINK** ●

Ice cubes

¼ cup fresh pink grapefruit juice

3 tablespoons vodka

Pinch of salt

½ cup tonic

Fill an 8-ounce highball glass with ice. Add the grapefruit juice, vodka and salt and stir. Pour in the tonic and serve. —*Pete Wells*

### Cheval

**TOTAL: 5 MIN**

**MAKES 1 DRINK** ●

¼ seedless cucumber, thinly sliced

2 lime quarters

3 tablespoons vodka

Ice cubes

2 to 3 tablespoons ginger beer

In a cocktail shaker, muddle all but 1 of the cucumber slices with the lime quarters. Add the vodka and ice, shake well and strain into a highball glass over ice. Top with the ginger beer and garnish with the reserved cucumber slice.

—*Chuck Avery*

### Dry Toast

**TOTAL: 5 MIN**

**MAKES 1 DRINK** ●

Ice cubes

3 tablespoons vodka

1½ tablespoons fresh lemon juice

1 teaspoon Cointreau

1 teaspoon apricot jam

Fill a cocktail shaker with ice. Add the vodka, lemon juice, Cointreau and apricot jam and shake for at least 1 minute to break up the jam. Strain into a chilled cocktail glass and serve. —*Pete Wells*

### Hollow Hills

**ACTIVE: 5 MIN; TOTAL: 2 HR**

**MAKES 8 DRINKS** ● ●

1½ cups vodka

1 cup Tuaca

1 cup apricot nectar or juice

1 cup apple juice

½ cup pomegranate juice

Ice cubes

In a pitcher, combine all of the ingredients and chill for 2 hours. Stir and pour into large wine glasses over ice. —*Kevin Delk*

### Vanilla Pear Mimosa

**TOTAL: 5 MIN**

**MAKES 1 DRINK** ●

1½ tablespoons vanilla-flavored vodka

3 tablespoons pear nectar or juice

½ cup chilled Prosecco

Pour the vodka into a flute. Top with the nectar and Prosecco. —*Twenty Manning*

## Bitter Queen

**TOTAL: 5 MIN**

**MAKES 1 DRINK** ●●

Ice cubes

¼ cup vodka

2 tablespoons Campari

2 tablespoons limoncello

¼ cup fresh orange juice

1 lime slice

Fill a cocktail shaker with ice cubes. Add the vodka, Campari and limoncello and shake well. Strain into a chilled martini glass, then top with the fresh orange juice. Garnish with the lime slice.
—*Crispy Soloperto*

## Roof Garden

**TOTAL: 5 MIN**

**MAKES 1 DRINK** ●

10 mint leaves

2 thyme sprigs

2 teaspoons sugar

Ice cubes

¼ cup vodka

2 tablespoons Simple Syrup (recipe follows)

2 tablespoons fresh lemon juice

¼ to ⅓ cup chilled club soda

In a cocktail shaker, muddle the mint leaves and thyme sprigs with the sugar. Add ice cubes and the vodka, Simple Syrup and fresh lemon juice and shake well; strain into a highball glass over ice and top with the club soda.
—*Jeremiah Doherty*

**SIMPLE SYRUP**

**TOTAL: 5 MIN**

**MAKES ABOUT 1¼ CUPS** ●●●

1 cup sugar

1 cup water

In a small saucepan, bring the sugar and water to a boil; let simmer for 3 minutes, until the sugar is dissolved.
—*F&W Test Kitchen*

**MAKE AHEAD** The syrup can be refrigerated for up to 3 weeks.

## Orange Fizz

**TOTAL: 10 MIN**

**MAKES 2 DRINKS** ●

½ cup orange-flavored vodka

¼ cup Cointreau

1 tablespoon fresh orange juice

4 drops orange-flower water (see Note)

One 3-inch strip of orange zest

Ice cubes

1 cup club soda

In a cocktail shaker, mix the vodka, Cointreau, orange juice and orange-flower water. Add the orange zest and ice cubes and shake. Strain into 2 tall glasses over ice. Add the club soda and serve.
—*Sylvie Chantecaille*

**NOTE** Orange-flower water is available at Middle Eastern and specialty food shops.

## Sugar Baby

**TOTAL: 5 MIN, PLUS 5 DAYS MARINATING**

**MAKES 2 DOZEN DRINKS** ●

½ ripe pineapple—peeled, cored and cubed (about 1 pound)

2 vanilla beans, split

2 cinnamon sticks, broken up

1 liter vodka

Ice cubes

About 1½ liters Sprite

In a large container or pitcher, combine all of the ingredients except for the ice and Sprite; mash the pineapple cubes and vanilla bean with a wooden spoon. Cover and refrigerate for 5 to 7 days. Strain the infused vodka into ice-filled glasses and top with Sprite. —*The Sam Bar, Houston*

## Citrus-Mint Cocktails

**ACTIVE: 20 MIN; TOTAL: 45 MIN**

**MAKES 10 DRINKS**

This drink can be prepared with vodka and white wine for a cocktail, as it is in the recipe below; if you prefer a virgin version, you can omit the alcohol and substitute club soda.

1½ cups sugar

2 cups loosely packed mint leaves, plus 8 large, lightly crushed mint sprigs

1½ cups water

2 cups loosely packed cilantro leaves, lightly crushed

1 cup fresh lemon juice

1 cup fresh lime juice

3 cups vodka

2 cups dry white wine

Ice cubes and chilled club soda, for serving

**1.** In a medium saucepan, combine the sugar and the crushed mint sprigs with the water and bring to a boil over moderately high heat. Remove the mint syrup from the heat and let it stand until cool. Strain the syrup into a medium pitcher or glass measuring cup and discard the mint sprigs.

**2.** In a large pitcher, using a wooden pestle or the back of a wooden spoon, muddle the 2 cups of mint leaves with the crushed cilantro, the lemon juice and lime juice. Add the cooled mint syrup, the vodka and the white wine and stir the cocktail to combine. Strain the Citrus-Mint Cocktail into tall glasses filled with ice cubes, top each drink with a splash of club soda and serve.
—*Alexandra and Eliot Angle*

**MAKE AHEAD** The mint syrup can be refrigerated for up to 2 days.

## The Vamp

**TOTAL: 5 MIN**

**MAKES 1 DRINK** ●

Splash of bourbon

Ice cubes

2 tablespoons vodka

1 tablespoon ruby port

1 tablespoon crème de cassis

Rinse a chilled martini glass with the bourbon. Fill a cocktail shaker with ice. Add the vodka, port and cassis and shake well. Strain into the martini glass. —*Mi Suk Ahn*

# drinks

## Rose Martinis

**TOTAL: 20 MIN**
**MAKES 8 DRINKS** ●

½ cup water
2 tablespoons sugar
3½ cups vodka
4 teaspoons fresh lemon juice
½ teaspoon rose water
Ice cubes
24 edible rose petals
(optional; see Note)

**1.** In a small saucepan, combine the water and sugar and bring to a boil. Simmer over low heat, stirring, until the sugar dissolves. Let cool, then stir in the vodka, lemon juice and rose water.

**2.** Fill a cocktail shaker with ice cubes. Add one-fourth of the martini mixture and shake. Strain into 2 martini glasses, garnish with rose petals and serve. Repeat to make the remaining drinks. —*Sylvie Chantecaille*

**NOTE** Edible rose petals are available from Quail Mountain Herbs (831-722-8456).

# equipment

This sturdy aluminum juicer turns citrus halves inside out, pressing out juice and leaving behind seeds and pulp (from $15; 800-243-0852 or surlatable.com).

## Red Grape and Coconut Refresher

**TOTAL: 5 MIN**
**MAKES 1 DRINK** ● ●

12 seedless red grapes, plus
3 grapes for garnish
1 teaspoon dark brown sugar
¼ cup vodka
¼ cup unsweetened coconut water
(see Note)
Crushed ice
¼ cup Champagne or sparkling wine

In a cocktail shaker, muddle 12 of the red grapes with the brown sugar. Add the vodka and coconut water, stir and pour into a highball glass over crushed ice; don't strain. Top with the Champagne and garnish with 3 grapes. —*Albert Trummer*

**NOTE** Unsweetened coconut water is available at many supermarkets and Latin American food stores.

## Louisville Limeade

**TOTAL: 25 MIN**
**MAKES 8 DRINKS** ●

This delicious take on the Cuban mojito is made with Kentucky bourbon instead of rum.

1 cup water
⅔ cup sugar
2 limes, each cut into 8 wedges, plus more wedges for garnish
24 mint sprigs, plus more for garnish
Ice cubes
1 cup Rose's lime juice
3 cups bourbon
Seltzer

**1.** In a small saucepan, simmer the water and sugar, stirring, until the sugar is dissolved. Transfer the sugar syrup to a bowl and refrigerate until chilled.

**2.** In a large pitcher, combine the sugar syrup with the 16 lime wedges and the 24 mint sprigs. Using a wooden spoon, mash everything together. Strain the syrup into a clean pitcher.

**3.** Fill a large cocktail shaker with ice. Add half of the lime-mint syrup, ½ cup of the Rose's lime juice and 1½ cups of the bourbon and shake vigorously. Fill 4 highball glasses with ice cubes. Strain the limeade into the glasses and add a splash of seltzer to each drink. Garnish with a lime wedge and a mint sprig. Repeat with the remaining ingredients to make 4 more drinks. —*Daniel Orr*

**MAKE AHEAD** The sugar syrup can be refrigerated for up to 5 days.

## Sawtooth Mountain Breezes

**TOTAL: 5 MIN**
**MAKES 8 DRINKS** ●

2 cups grapefruit juice
2 cups cranberry juice
16 ounces (2 cups) vodka
Sugar, for glass rims
Crushed ice
8 lime slices, for serving

In a large glass pitcher, stir together the grapefruit and cranberry juices and the vodka. Pour the cocktail into 8 tall sugar-rimmed, ice-filled glasses. Add a lime slice to each glass and serve. —*Russ Pillar*

## Pomegranate Margaritas

**TOTAL: 20 MIN**
**MAKES 8 DRINKS** ● ●

One 1-liter bottle tequila
2 cups Cointreau
2 cups unsweetened pomegranate juice
1 cup fresh lime juice
Ice cubes

In a large glass pitcher, combine the tequila, Cointreau, pomegranate juice and lime juice. Fill a cocktail shaker with ice, pour in 1 cup of the margarita mix and shake well. Strain into a cocktail glass and serve. Repeat with the remaining mix. —*Nadia Roden*

**MAKE AHEAD** The margarita mix can be refrigerated overnight.

# drinks

## Sparkling Lemongrass Coolers

**ACTIVE: 5 MIN; TOTAL: 3 HR**

**MAKES 8 DRINKS** ●

- 4 plump lemongrass stalks, cut into 2-inch lengths, lightly crushed
- 4 cups water
- 1 cup sugar
- ¼ cup fresh lime juice

Ice cubes

Ginger beer or seltzer

Rum

**1.** In a medium saucepan, combine the lemongrass pieces, water and sugar; bring to a boil, stirring, until the sugar dissolves. Remove the pan from the heat, cover and let steep until cool, about 3 hours. Strain the syrup through a fine-mesh sieve and discard the lemongrass pieces. Stir in the fresh lime juice. **2.** Fill 8 tall glasses with ice. Add ½ cup of the syrup to each glass. Top off with ginger beer or seltzer and a shot of rum. —*Grace Parisi*

## Coquito

**ACTIVE: 5 MIN; TOTAL: 2 HR 15 MIN**

**MAKES 2 DOZEN DRINKS** ●

2¼ cups water

Thick strips of zest from 2 limes

- 1 cinnamon stick

2⅓ cups (1 pound) sugar

One 14-ounce can unsweetened coconut milk

One 12-ounce can evaporated milk

- ¼ cup pure vanilla extract
- 3 large egg yolks (optional)

2¼ cups (½ liter) light rum

In a saucepan, simmer the water, lime zest and cinnamon over moderate heat until the water turns golden, 15 minutes. Strain into a heatproof bowl and refrigerate until chilled, 1 hour or up to 1 week. Whisk in the sugar, coconut milk, evaporated milk, vanilla, egg yolks (if using) and rum until the sugar dissolves. Refrigerate until chilled, about 1 hour. Stir and serve in small glasses. —*Carmen Gonzalez*

## Sudden Headache

**TOTAL: 5 MIN**

**MAKES 1 DRINK** ●

Ice cubes

- 2 tablespoons silver tequila
- 1½ tablespoons orange liqueur
- 3 tablespoons mango nectar or juice
- 1½ tablespoons fresh lime juice
- 1½ tablespoons Simple Syrup (p. 355)
- ¼ cup plus 1 tablespoon demi sec Champagne

Fill a cocktail shaker with ice. Add all of the ingredients except the Champagne and shake well. Strain into a flute and top with the demi sec.
—*Chris Dexter and Matt Eisler*

## Saffron Cooler

**ACTIVE: 10 MIN; TOTAL: 3 HR**

**MAKES 2 QUARTS** ●

This is a more complex and food-friendly alternative to the classic wine spritzer.

- 1 quart water
- 1 bottle dry white wine
- ¾ cup honey

One 3-inch piece of fresh ginger, thinly sliced

- 5 cardamom pods, lightly crushed
- 3 allspice berries
- 2 cinnamon sticks
- 2 star anise pods
- 1 stalk of lemongrass, thinly sliced
- 1 teaspoon saffron threads
- ½ teaspoon whole black peppercorns
- ½ teaspoon fennel seeds
- ¼ teaspoon hot sauce
- 1½ lemons, thinly sliced
- ½ cup packed mint leaves

**1.** In a large saucepan, combine the water with the wine, honey, ginger, cardamom, allspice, cinnamon, star anise, lemongrass, saffron, peppercorns, fennel seeds, hot sauce and half of the lemon slices and bring to a boil. Transfer to a bowl and refrigerate until chilled, about 3 hours.

**2.** In a very large pitcher, lightly crush the mint leaves with a wooden spoon. Add the chilled spiced mixture and stir. Strain the cooler before serving. Garnish with the remaining lemon slices and serve. —*Daniel Orr*

**MAKE AHEAD** The cooler can be refrigerated after straining for up to 2 days.

## Stone Wall

**TOTAL: 5 MIN**

**MAKES 1 DRINK** ●

One 1-inch piece of fresh ginger, peeled and thinly sliced

- ½ tablespoon Simple Syrup (p. 355)

Ice cubes

- 3 tablespoons apple cider
- 3 tablespoons aged rum
- 3 tablespoons ginger beer
- 1 lime wedge
- 1 thin tart apple slice, for garnish

In a cocktail shaker, muddle the slices of ginger and the Simple Syrup. Add ice and the cider and rum, shake well and strain into a rocks glass over ice. Top the drink with the ginger beer and a squeeze of lime and garnish with the apple slice.
—*Dale DeGroff*

## Star of India

**TOTAL: 5 MIN**

**MAKES 1 DRINK** ●

Ice cubes

- 3 tablespoons aged rum
- 1 tablespoon orange liqueur
- 1½ tablespoons passion fruit nectar or juice
- ½ tablespoon Sambuca

Splash of Sprite

- 1 organic rose petal, for garnish (optional)

Fill a cocktail shaker with ice. Add the rum, orange liqueur, passion fruit nectar and Sambuca and shake well. Strain into a chilled martini glass, top with Sprite and garnish with the rose petal.
—*Jeremy Campbell*

● **FAST**   ● **HEALTHY**   ● **MAKE AHEAD**   ● **STAFF FAVORITE**

357

# drinks

## Watermelon Coolers

**TOTAL: 30 MIN**
**MAKES 2½ QUARTS ● ●**

¾ cup sugar
¾ cup water
1 cup fresh lime juice
3 cups white rum
4 cups seedless watermelon chunks
   (one-quarter of a watermelon)
8 cups crushed ice
**Watermelon spears and mint sprigs,**
   **for garnish**

**1.** In a saucepan, combine the sugar and water. Bring to a simmer over moderate heat, stirring, until the sugar dissolves. Remove from the heat and let cool.
**2.** In a blender, combine half of the sugar syrup with half of the lime juice, rum and watermelon chunks and blend until combined. Add half of the ice and blend until smooth, then pour into a large pitcher. Repeat with the remaining sugar syrup, lime juice, rum, watermelon chunks and ice. Serve in chilled glasses, garnished with watermelon spears and topped with mint sprigs. —*Susan Mason*
**MAKE AHEAD** The watermelon mixture can be prepared earlier in the day. Blend with ice just before serving.

## Thai Martini

**TOTAL: 5 MIN**
**MAKES 1 DRINK ●**

½ Granny Smith apple, diced, plus
   1 thin apple slice for garnish
1 teaspoon sliced fresh lemongrass
   (tender inner bulb only)
**Ice cubes**
¼ cup plus 1 tablespoon coconut-
   flavored rum
2 tablespoons sour apple liqueur

In a cocktail shaker, muddle the diced apple with the lemongrass. Add ice and the rum and sour apple liqueur. Shake well, then strain into a chilled martini glass and garnish with the apple slice. —*Clif Travers*

## Ice Wine Martini

**TOTAL: 5 MIN**
**MAKES 1 DRINK ●**

11 large green seedless grapes,
   1 sliced crosswise for garnish
¼ cup ice wine
¼ cup vodka
**Ice cubes**

In a blender, puree the 10 whole grapes with the ice wine and vodka. Pass through a tea strainer into an ice-filled cocktail shaker. Shake well, strain again into a chilled martini glass and garnish with the grape slices. —*David Ward*

## Spice

**TOTAL: 5 MIN**
**MAKES 1 DRINK ●**

2 large mint sprigs
**Ice cubes**
2 tablespoons pear nectar or juice
3 tablespoons spiced rum
1½ tablespoons fresh lime juice
1½ tablespoons Simple Syrup (p. 355)
**Pinch of freshly grated nutmeg**
1 thin pear slice, for garnish

Crush the mint sprigs; add to a cocktail shaker with ice and the pear nectar, rum, lime juice, Simple Syrup and nutmeg. Shake well, strain into a chilled martini glass and garnish with a pear slice. —*Ryan Magarian*

## Fahrenheit 5

**TOTAL: 5 MIN**
**MAKES 1 DRINK ● ●**

**Ice cubes**
1½ tablespoons coconut-flavored rum
1½ tablespoons orange liqueur
2½ tablespoons cranberry juice
1½ tablespoons pineapple juice
**Splash of Sprite**

Fill a cocktail shaker with ice. Add the rum, orange liqueur and cranberry and pineapple juices; shake well. Strain into a chilled martini glass and top with Sprite. —*Michael Brown*

## Midtown Sangria

**ACTIVE: 5 MIN; TOTAL: 2 HR**
**MAKES 8 DRINKS ●**

1½ cups water
3 tablespoons orange clover honey
¼ teaspoon ground cinnamon
**One 750-ml bottle dry but fruity white**
   **wine, such as Sauvignon Blanc**
1½ cups apple juice
**Ice cubes**
**Thin orange slices, for garnish**

In a glass measuring cup or glass bowl, combine the water, honey and ground cinnamon and microwave at high power for 40 seconds. Stir well, then pour into a pitcher and add the white wine and apple juice. Refrigerate the sangria until chilled, about 2 hours. Stir the mixture well and pour into ice-filled wine glasses. Garnish with the orange slices. —*Gina Word*

## Bubbling Cauldron Cocktails

**TOTAL: 15 MIN**
**MAKES 8 DRINKS ●**

This recipe was created for a Halloween party. The pear balls garnishing each drink are studded with currants so they resemble eyeballs.

½ lemon
2 ripe Bartlett pears
1 tablespoon dried currants
½ cup pear nectar
**One 750-ml bottle Champagne or**
   **other sparkling white wine**

**1.** Fill a bowl with water and squeeze the lemon half into it. Peel the pears and add them to the lemon water. Using a small melon baller, scoop out balls from each pear; return the balls to the lemon water. You will need 16 pear balls. Using a toothpick, make a small hole in each pear ball and tuck a currant into each hole.
**2.** Pour 1 tablespoon of the pear nectar into each of 8 Champagne flutes. Fill the flutes with Champagne. Spear 2 pear "eyeballs" on a toothpick, put in each flute and serve at once. —*Grace Parisi*

WATERMELON COOLERS

# drinks

## Coconut-Pineapple Batida

**TOTAL: 15 MIN**

**MAKES 4 DRINKS** ●

Add 1 cup of white rum to this rich and tangy Latin shake for an equally refreshing cocktail.

- ½ fresh pineapple—peeled, cored and cut into 1-inch chunks (about 3 cups)
- ½ cup unsweetened coconut milk, stirred
- 3 tablespoons fresh lime juice
- 1 tablespoon sugar
- 1½ cups crushed ice

In a blender, combine the fresh pineapple chunks with the coconut milk, lime juice and sugar and puree until smooth. Add the crushed ice and blend until frosty. Serve at once. —*Grace Parisi*

## Spiced Red Wine Punch

**ACTIVE: 10 MIN; TOTAL: 40 MIN**

**MAKES 8 DRINKS** ●

- 2 cups water
- 1 cup sugar
- 2 cinnamon sticks
- 12 cloves
- 12 allspice berries
- ½ teaspoon fenugreek seeds
- Four ¼-inch-thick slices of fresh ginger, lightly crushed
- Zest of 1 orange, removed with a vegetable peeler in 1-inch-wide strips
- ½ cup fresh orange juice
- One 750-ml bottle Syrah or other full-bodied red wine
- Orange slices, for garnish

**1.** In a medium saucepan, combine the water with the sugar, cinnamon sticks, cloves, allspice berries, fenugreek seeds, crushed ginger and orange zest. Bring the mixture to a boil over moderate heat, stirring, until the sugar dissolves. Lower the heat and simmer the syrup for 5 minutes. Remove from the heat and let the syrup steep for 25 minutes.

**2.** Add the orange juice, then strain the syrup into a medium bowl. Wipe out the saucepan, add the red wine and spiced syrup and heat over moderately low heat until simmering. Pour the spiced wine into heatproof glasses and garnish with orange slices. Serve the punch warm. —*Grace Parisi*

**MAKE AHEAD** The red wine punch can be refrigerated overnight. Gently reheat it before serving.

## Green My Eyes

**TOTAL: 5 MIN**

**MAKES 1 DRINK** ●

- 4 thin cucumber slices
- Ice cubes
- 3 tablespoons dry sake
- ½ tablespoon Simple Syrup (p. 355)

In a cocktail shaker, muddle 3 of the cucumber slices. Add ice and the sake and Simple Syrup; shake well. Strain the mixture into a chilled martini glass and garnish with the remaining cucumber slice. —*Kyle Withrow*

## Starlight

**ACTIVE: 5 MIN; TOTAL: 2 HR**

**MAKES 8 DRINKS** ●

- 1½ cups Campari
- ¾ cup orange liqueur
- ¼ cup Cognac
- ½ cup fresh lemon juice
- ⅓ cup Simple Syrup (p. 355)
- 1 cup fresh orange juice
- Ice cubes
- 2 cups chilled club soda
- Lemon and lime slices, for garnish

In a pitcher, combine all of the ingredients except the ice, club soda and citrus slices. Refrigerate until chilled, about 2 hours. Stir and pour into highball glasses over ice cubes. Top off with club soda and garnish with the lemon and lime slices. —*The Bellagio, Las Vegas*

## Jade Cocktail

**TOTAL: 5 MIN**

**MAKES 1 DRINK** ●

- Ice cubes
- 3 tablespoons vanilla-flavored vodka
- 1 tablespoon melon-flavored liqueur
- ¼ cup pineapple juice
- 2 tablespoons fresh lime juice
- 1 tablespoon fresh lemon juice
- 1 tablespoon Simple Syrup (p. 355)

Fill a cocktail shaker with ice. Add all of the ingredients, shake well and strain into a chilled martini glass. —*Ryan Buenning*

## Almond Saketini

**TOTAL: 5 MIN**

**MAKES 1 DRINK** ●

- Ice cubes
- ½ cup sake
- 1½ tablespoons almond syrup
- Splash of Lillet
- 1 toasted almond

Fill a cocktail shaker with ice. Add the sake, syrup and Lillet. Shake well and strain into a chilled martini glass. Garnish with the almond and serve. —*Richard Terzaghi*

## Iced Pomegranate-Fennel Green Tea

**ACTIVE: 15 MIN; TOTAL: 1 HR**

**MAKES 3 QUARTS** ● ●

This refreshing tonic combines two popular Indian beverages—freshly squeezed pomegranate juice and fennel-seed tea.

- 8 cups water
- ¼ cup fennel seeds
- 8 green-tea bags
- ½ cup sugar
- 1 quart pure pomegranate juice
- ¼ cup fresh lemon juice
- 1 lemon, thinly sliced
- 1 navel orange, thinly sliced
- Ice cubes

In a large saucepan, bring the water and fennel seeds to a boil. Reduce the heat to low; simmer for 20 minutes. Remove from the heat, add the tea bags and let

steep for 10 minutes. Strain the tea into a heatproof bowl. Stir in the sugar and let cool. Add the pomegranate juice, lemon juice and lemon and orange slices. Serve in tall glasses over ice.
—*Akasha Richmond*

**MAKE AHEAD** The tea can be refrigerated for up to 6 hours.

### Iced Hibiscus Tea

**TOTAL: 25 MIN**

**MAKES 2 QUARTS** ● ● ●

Nadia Roden, the daughter of cookbook author Claudia Roden, discovered this tangy and sweet red-colored beverage in Egypt, where people stop at street vendors to drink and chat all day long.

 2 **quarts plus ½ cup water**
1½ **cups dried hibiscus flowers (1½ ounces; see Note)**
 1 **cup sugar**
**Ice cubes**

In a medium saucepan, bring the water and hibiscus flowers to a boil. Simmer over moderate heat for 5 minutes. Add the sugar and cook, stirring, until dissolved. Pour the drink into a medium bowl. Fill a larger bowl with ice water and set the smaller bowl inside. Stir the drink occasionally until chilled, about 10 minutes. Strain the tea into a pitcher; serve in tall glasses over ice. —*Nadia Roden*

**NOTE** Dried hibiscus flowers, which have a cranberry-like flavor, can be found at specialty food stores and at Latin and Caribbean markets, where they are called sorrel or *flor de Jamaica*.

**MAKE AHEAD** The iced tea can be refrigerated overnight.

### Gingery Soymilk Chai

**ACTIVE: 5 MIN; TOTAL: 45 MIN**

**MAKES 3½ QUARTS** ●

Chai is a classic hot Indian drink made with tea, milk, cardamom and cloves. But this is not your typical chai: The tea in this recipe is optional.

2½ **quarts water**
 ½ **pound fresh ginger, very thinly sliced**
 2 **cinnamon sticks**
 ¾ **teaspoon whole black peppercorns**
 1 **quart vanilla soymilk**
 8 **black-tea bags (optional)**
**Sugar or honey, for serving**

In a large saucepan, bring the water, ginger, cinnamon and peppercorns to a boil. Reduce the heat to low and simmer for 30 minutes. Strain into a heatproof bowl and discard the spices. Wipe out the saucepan and return the liquid to it. If using tea, add the soymilk and tea bags and bring to a simmer. Remove from the heat, cover and let steep for 10 minutes. Discard the tea bags and serve hot with sugar. If not using tea, add the soymilk, bring to a simmer and serve hot with sugar. —*Akasha Richmond*

### Almond-Tea Milk Shakes

**TOTAL: 15 MIN, PLUS OVERNIGHT STEEPING AND 3 HR FREEZING**

**MAKES 8 SHAKES**

This sweet and refreshing milk shake was inspired by Chinese bubble tea and the "bubbly" foam that's created when freshly brewed tea is shaken with ice, milk, sugar and other flavorings.

1½ **cups blanched slivered almonds**
 ⅓ **cup sugar**
 ⅔ **cup water**
 4 **cups milk**
 ¾ **cup light corn syrup**
 1 **cup cold brewed black tea**

**1.** Preheat the oven to 350°. Spread the almonds in a pie plate and toast for about 8 minutes, or until golden. In a small saucepan, combine the sugar and water and bring to a boil, stirring until the sugar dissolves. Add the milk, light corn syrup and toasted almonds and refrigerate overnight.

**2.** Puree the almond mixture in a blender until smooth. Strain through a fine sieve, pressing hard on the almonds; discard the almonds. Transfer the liquid to a roasting pan and freeze, stirring occasionally, until semi-solid, about 3 hours.
**3.** Transfer half of the ice milk to a blender. Add half of the tea; blend and pour into small glasses. Repeat with the remaining ingredients. —*Nick Morgenstern*

### Warm Almond Milk with Bananas and Honey

**ACTIVE: 10 MIN; TOTAL: 30 MIN**

**MAKES 4 DRINKS** ● ●

 ½ **pound roasted unsalted almonds, with skin (1½ cups)**
 1 **quart skim milk**
 ¼ **cup honey**
 1 **teaspoon cardamom seeds**
 2 **bananas, sliced ¼ inch thick**

**1.** In a food processor, grind the almonds to a coarse powder. Transfer to a saucepan. Add the milk, 1 tablespoon of the honey and the cardamom. Warm over moderate heat. Off the heat, cover and let stand for 20 minutes, then strain. Discard the solids.
**2.** In a medium nonstick skillet, warm the remaining 3 tablespoons of honey. Add the bananas and cook over moderately high heat, stirring, for 2 minutes. Scrape into bowls, pour in the warm almond milk and serve with spoons. —*Jeff Orr*

# beverage

**WHAT IS SAKE, EXACTLY?**　　**TIP**

It's an alcoholic drink brewed from rice, and it has the highest naturally occurring alcohol content of any brewed beverage. It's not a beer, as some insist, even though it's made from a grain. And it's not a rice wine, either.

# wine pairings

Elin McCoy, a contributing editor at FOOD & WINE, has created the ultimate user-friendly guide to pairing wine and food. Her glossary here, with descriptions of the key wine varieties and advice on pairing specific bottles with specific recipes, is both flexible and focused. We know you'll find it handy.

## champagne + sparkling wine

The most famous sparkling wine is, of course, Champagne, which comes from the region of the same name northeast of Paris. Champagne is usually a blend of Pinot Noir, Chardonnay and sometimes Pinot Meunier grapes, and it's produced in a wide spectrum of styles, ranging from dry (Brut) to sweet (Doux), and from austere and light-bodied to full, toasty and rich.

The very best French Champagnes have both more elegance and more complexity than the sparkling wines produced elsewhere in the world. Nevertheless, California, the Pacific Northwest and Australia all make wonderful New World versions using the same grapes and the same method as the French. Italian Prosecco and Spanish Cava are good, inexpensive alternatives.

The brisk acidity of sparkling wine makes it an ideal aperitif. It pairs nicely with salty, smoky and spicy dishes.

### DRY, LIGHT, CRISP CHAMPAGNE
Piper-Heidsieck Brut (France)
Lanson Black Label (France)
**PAIRINGS**
- Warm Crab Dip with Fresh Herbs, 11
- Caviar and Potato Salad Tartlets, 16
- Smoked Salmon–Stuffed Puffs, 21
- Red Snapper with Mussels, Potatoes and Chorizo, 175

### DRY, RICH CHAMPAGNE
Louis Roederer Brut Premier (France)
Pol Roger Brut (France)
**PAIRINGS**
- Smoky Deviled Eggs, 14
- Smoked Salmon Spirals, 21
- Dulce de Leche–Glazed Ham, 157
- Roasted Whole Snapper with Tomato-Bread Salad, 175

### DRY, FRUITY SPARKLING WINE
### DRY, FRUITY SPARKLING WINE
Roederer Estate (California)
Schramsberg Blanc de Noirs (California)
**PAIRINGS**
- Crudités with Creamy Pistachio Dip, 11
- Stuffed Shiitake Mushrooms, 15
- Asian Watercress Salad with Salmon, 163
- Sweet-and-Sour Swordfish, 168

### DRY, CRISP SPARKLING WINE
Chandon Brut Classic (California)
Mionetto DOC Prosecco (Italy)
Bodegas Jaume Serra Cristalino Cava (Spain)
**PAIRINGS**
- Armagnac-Doused Shrimp, 22
- Spicy King Prawns, 186
- Indian-Style Shrimp and Rice Pilaf, 187
- Chile-Steamed Mussels with Green Olive Crostini, 198

## whites

### ALBARIÑO + VINHO VERDE
Spain's most exciting white wine, and one of its most fashionable, is the zesty and aromatic Albariño. Made predominantly in the Rías Baixas region, the wine has seductive aromas of citrus, honey and kiwi and flavors of fresh ginger, lemon and almond. The texture is creamy and at the same time crisp and light—all complete with a lively acidity. These traits make it a perfect partner for scallops and other seafood. The Albariño grape is called Alvarinho in Portugal, where it's used to make the best Vinho Verdes. These slightly fizzy bottlings are light and refreshing and go beautifully with oily fish like sardines.

### AROMATIC, ZESTY ALBARIÑO/VINHO VERDE
Vionta Albariño (Spain)
Bodega Salnesur Condes de Albarei Albariño (Spain)
Aveleda Quinta da Aveleda Vinho Verde Alvarinho (Portugal)
Sogrape Morgadio da Torre Vinho Verde Alvarinho (Portugal)
Havens Albariño (California)
**PAIRINGS**
- Spanish Cod with Chickpeas and Sherry, 173
- Spice-Crusted Scallops with Crisp Capers, 193
- Mussels in Sailor's Sauce, 196

### CHARDONNAY + WHITE BURGUNDY
The world's most popular white wine originally came from the Burgundy region of eastern France, but it's now made successfully in just about every wine-producing country in the world, in an enormous range of styles and flavors. In France, the best white Burgundies are elegant, complex and rich, with flavors of earth, nuts and minerals; the simpler wines from Mâcon and Rully suggest green apples and lemons. Californian and Australian versions are often higher in alcohol and lush with tropical fruit flavors. Most Chardonnays (Chablis is generally an exception) are aged in oak barrels, which tend to give them a buttery richness and toasty vanilla aromas and flavors. The biggest and oakiest Chardonnays can be tricky to match with food, but they are marvelous partners for sweet corn, rich fish and poultry dishes made with cream, butter, cheese or coconut. Minimally oaked—or even unoaked—Chardonnay is a new trend, as winemakers in California, Australia and elsewhere create bottlings that emphasize the grape's crisp fruitiness. These are particularly good with seafood, as some of the latest examples from Italy and especially New Zealand aptly demonstrate.

### SUBTLE, COMPLEX WHITE BURGUNDY
Joseph Drouhin Chassagne-Montrachet (France)
Louis Jadot Meursault-Genevrières (France)
**PAIRINGS**
- Grilled Salmon with Mustard Sauce, 163
- Halibut and Fall Harvest Sauté, 178
- Sautéed Trout Fillets with a Pumpkin Seed Crust, 178

### FLINTY, HIGH-ACID CHABLIS
Château de Maligny (France)
William Fevre (France)
**PAIRINGS**
- Pan-Fried Pompano with Tomato-Caraway Glaze, 179
- Sautéed Shrimp and Tarragon with Parsnip Purée, 190
- Celery Root Remoulade with Scallops and Caviar, 195
- Sake-Steamed Clams, 196

### RIPE, OAKY CHARDONNAY
Newton (California)
Rosemount Estate Show Reserve (Australia)
Morgan (California)

# wine pairings

**PAIRINGS**

- Crispy Fried Chicken Livers, 14
- Caramelized Onion and Gruyère Tart, 18
- Farfalle with Creamy Smoked Salmon and Vodka Sauce, 84
- Chicken Breasts with Spinach, Leek and Saffron Sauce, 90
- Sautéed Chicken with Fresh Herbs and Wilted Greens, 92
- Crispy Roast Chicken and Shallots with Miso Gravy, 107
- Easter Veal Loin with Fennel–Lima Bean Puree, 158
- Swordfish Steaks with Mint and Garlic, 168
- Grilled Shrimp and Chayote Salad with Chili-Garlic Dressing, 186

### FRUITY, LOW-OAK CHARDONNAY

Louis Latour Pouilly-Fuissé (France)
Kim Crawford Unoaked (New Zealand)
Ruffino Libaio (Italy)

**PAIRINGS**

- Sheep's-Milk Ricotta Gnocchi with Mushrooms and Corn, 77
- Spaghetti with Browned Butter and Crispy Bread Crumbs, 79
- Buttermilk-Roasted Chicken with Date Butter, 93
- Lemon Confit Chicken with Calamata Olives, 96
- Chicken with Leafy Greens and Lemon, 98
- Chile-Rubbed Swordfish Kebabs with Cucumber Salad, 167
- Seared Scallops with Braised Collard Greens and Cider Sauce, 194
- Clams with Spicy Sausage, 195

## CHENIN BLANC

This underappreciated grape is grown widely in the Loire region of France, where it's used to make dry Vouvray and Savennières, as well as delicious sweet wines and a few sparkling ones. But it has also found a home in South Africa, California and Washington State, which typically turn it into a light dry or semidry white with overtones of green apples and peaches and an acidity that can range from soft to zesty. It's an interesting aperitif and a good partner for light fish dishes. Distinguished dry examples have a pleasant underlying mineral chalkiness.

### LIGHT, SOFT CHENIN BLANC

Sutter Home (California)
Dry Creek Vineyard (California)

**PAIRINGS**

- Chickpea Blinis with Pineapple-Mint Relish, 12
- Fresh Pasta with Spicy Corn and Asparagus, 78
- Hoosier Chicken with Potato Chip Crust, 92
- Pan-Fried Salmon Burgers with Cabbage Slaw and Avocado Aioli, 164
- Grilled Shrimp and Corn Wraps, 186
- Shrimp and Lemon Skewers with Feta-Dill Sauce, 189

### DRY, MINERAL-FLAVORED CHENIN BLANC

Kanu (South Africa)
Chappellet (California)
Gaston Huët Vouvray Sec (France)

**PAIRINGS**

- Sesame-Coated Sweet Potato Croquettes, 12
- Spicy Tuna Rillettes, 27
- Turkey Burgers with Pesto Mayonnaise, 106
- Matzo Meal–Crusted Trout, 178
- Grilled Whole Fish with Curried Yogurt Marinade, 180
- Curried Shrimp and Carrot Bouillabaisse, 190
- Scallops, Corn and Basil Steamed in Foil, 192
- Pan-Fried Asian-Style Crab Burgers, 198

## GEWÜRZTRAMINER

The great examples of this flamboyant, fragrant white wine come from Alsace; most of them are bone-dry, but they can range all the way to very sweet (labeled *vendange tardive*—late harvest). Regardless of style, they have an irresistible, heady scent of lychees and cloves; concentrated, spicy (*Gewürz* is the German word for "spice") apricot and ginger flavors; and a rich, low-acid texture. They are superb companions for Muenster cheese, chicken liver pâté, smoked fish and baked ham. New World bottlings from California and Washington State are usually lighter, with a hint of sweetness; they go well with curries and dishes flavored with ginger, coriander, cloves or lemongrass.

### SPICY ALSACE GEWÜRZTRAMINER

Muré (France)
Hugel (France)

**PAIRINGS**

- Chicken with Almonds and Honey, 96
- Roast Pork Loin with Armagnac-Prune Sauce, 144
- Tandoori Pork with Gingered Mango Salad, 145

- Salmon Rolls with Fennel and Creole Mustard Spaetzle, 162

### SPICY NEW WORLD GEWÜRZTRAMINER

Beringer (California)
Navarro Vineyards Anderson Valley (California)

**PAIRINGS**

- Asian-Style Grilled Chicken, 98
- Korean-Style Chicken Wraps, 101
- Grilled Maple-Brined Pork Chops, 147
- Indian-Spiced Sea Bass with Spinach, Peas and Carrots, 172

## GRÜNER VELTLINER

Grüner Veltliner, Austria's fresh, peppery, spicy white, has become a popular U.S. import, and for good reason: It's extremely versatile at the table. Some bottlings can hint of celery or citrus, while others show roundness and depth. It's best enjoyed young, as a refreshing, uncomplicated foil for fish, cold cuts, poultry and mildly spiced dishes. Grander bottlings, however, can be aged, developing complexity that rivals white Burgundy. The grape is also grown in Hungary and the Czech Republic, where it makes an attractively fruity white.

### TART, PEPPERY GRÜNER VELTLINER

Jamek (Austria)
Nigl (Austria)

**PAIRINGS**

- Creamy Fried Mozzarella Balls, 14
- Cold Noodles with Tofu in Peanut Sauce, 80
- Chicken Skewers with Lemon-Mint Vinaigrette, 101
- Creole-Style Sea Bass Fillets, 171
- Steamed Cod with Crisp Vegetables, 174

## PINOT BLANC

Sometimes called the poor man's Chardonnay, Pinot Blanc is undervalued in its French stronghold, Alsace, and overlooked elsewhere—which is too bad, because this mild wine is dependable, easy to like and reasonably priced. As with most Alsace wines, there's no oak or excessive alcohol screaming for attention. In Austria, Pinot Blanc is called Weissburgunder; it's also produced, on a small scale, in California, Oregon and Italy (where it's dry, light and leafy and known as Pinot Bianco). Pinot Blanc's apple and pear flavors, mineral edge and crisp acidity marry well with vegetables and fish dishes.

### MEDIUM-BODIED, ROUND PINOT BLANC

Domaine Marcel Deiss Bergheim (France)
Pierre Sparr Réserve (France)
Steele (California)

**PAIRINGS**

- Shrimp BLTs, 23
- Pasta with Borlotti Beans, Olives and Cherry Tomatoes, 74
- Creamy Chicken Stew, 104
- Striped Bass with Wild Mushrooms, 173
- Seared Cod with Spicy Mussel Aioli, 173
- Winter Shrimp Salad with Fennel and Ruby Grapefruit, 185

## PINOT GRIS + PINOT GRIGIO

The region or country where the Pinot Gris grape grows makes all the difference in the wine's style and flavor. In Alsace, it's a high-impact wine with a musky aroma and bold, concentrated flavors of bitter almonds, spice and honey. It's available in dry and opulently sweet (*vendange tardive*) versions; the dry ones are good with smoky and creamy dishes. In Oregon, where the grape is an emerging star, pear and mango flavors prevail, along with a scent of honeysuckle. The best bottlings here are lighter and less intense than those from Alsace, with a creamy yet slightly crisp character that's versatile with food and ideal with salmon. The Italian version, the popular Pinot Grigio, is simple and crisp, with bright, clean, lightly spicy flavors. It works best as an aperitif or with seafood.

### DRY, MEDIUM-BODIED PINOT GRIS

Domaine Schlumberger Les Princes Abbés (France)
Domaine Weinbach Cuvée Laurence (France)
King Estate (Oregon)
Sokol Blosser (Oregon)

**PAIRINGS**

- Smoked Salmon Soufflés with Gingered Salad, 22
- Spaghetti with Curried Seafood Marinara, 83
- Chicken Salad with Poblano Vinaigrette, 102
- Salt-Baked Sea Bass with Warm Tomato Vinaigrette, 171
- Monkfish and Chorizo Kebabs, 175

### LIGHT, SPICY PINOT GRIGIO

Mezzacorona (Italy)
Campanile (Italy)
Alois Lageder (Italy)

# wine pairings

- Prosciutto, Tomato and Olive Bruschetta, 15
- Roasted Persimmons Wrapped in Pancetta, 28
- Penne all'Arrabbiata, 75
- Spaghetti with Shrimp and Spicy Tomato Sauce, 80
- Seafood Capellini with Saffron, 83
- Chicken, Tomato and Mozzarella Salad with Spicy Basil Dressing, 92
- Very Soft Polenta with Rock Shrimp Ragout, 189
- Sea Scallops with Spinach and Grape Tomatoes, 191

## RIESLING

The versatile Riesling grape produces striking wines that range from pale, dry and delicate to apricot-scented and honey-sweet; the latter can age for decades. The lighter German ones have a pinpoint balance of fruitiness and mouthwatering acidity. Those from Alsace are weightier and very dry, with steel and mineral flavors. Other regions also make good, if less complex, Rieslings. Austria's are vibrant and powerful; Australia's have zingy lime scents and flavors; Washington State's are soft, with a touch of sweetness. Riesling's fruit, acidity, low alcohol and lack of oak make it one of the most food-friendly of wines, a lovely complement to delicate fish, to spicy Asian and Latin dishes and to all smoked and salty foods. Riesling's versatility at the table has made it increasingly fashionable in restaurants that emphasize fusion cuisines.

### BRIGHT, CITRUSY RIESLING

Dr. Bürklin-Wolf (Germany)
Annie's Lane Clare Valley (Australia)
Chateau Ste. Michelle Eroica (Washington State)

PAIRINGS

- Tuna Rolls with Roasted Shallot–Wasabi Sauce, 20
- Scallops Steamed in Sake and Riesling, 26
- Spicy Poached Chicken Burgers, 102
- Grilled Quick-Cured Trout with Mustard-Olive Dressing, 179
- Spicy Shrimp with Garlic-Almond Sauce, 184
- Shrimp and Broccoli with Honey-Walnut Caramel Sauce, 184

### SOFT, OFF-DRY RIESLING

Trefethen (California)
Dr. Loosen Erdener Treppchen Kabinett (Germany)

PAIRINGS

- Shrimp and Chicken Summer Rolls, 24
- Cider-Braised Chicken with Onion-Raisin Sauce, 97
- Pan-Roasted Pork with Apple Chutney and Pepper Relish, 146
- Pan-Roasted Halibut with Jalapeño Vinaigrette, 176
- Four Pea Salad with Scallops, 192

### DRY, FULL-FLAVORED ALSACE RIESLING

Domaine Trimbach (France)
Domaine Zind Humbrecht (France)

PAIRINGS

- Mini Tartes Flambées, 18
- Lemony Smoked Trout Salad in Red Endive Scoops, 26
- Crab and Corn Beignets, 28
- Cavatelli with Spicy Winter Squash, 74
- Alsatian-Brined Turkey with Riesling Gravy, 111
- Salmon with Saffron-Braised Cucumber and Fennel, 162
- Poached Salmon in a Fresh Herb and Spring Pea Broth, 164
- Salmon with Scotch Bonnet–Herb Sauce and Onion Toasts, 167
- Steamed Ginger Salmon with Stir-Fried Bok Choy, 167

## SAUVIGNON BLANC

Tart acidity, aromas of fresh-cut grass and herbs and flavors of green pepper and sometimes citrus give Sauvignon Blancs the world over a character people either love or hate. Sancerre and Pouilly-Fumé from France's Loire Valley have flint and mineral flavors. Lively New Zealand bottlings taste of passion fruit and gooseberries. South Africa's are elegant and bright, California's are lighter and all are fresh and crisp. When the grape is blended with rounder, heavier Sémillon, as it typically is in Bordeaux, the result is mellow and full-bodied. The riper, oak-aged Sauvignon Blancs hint of melons and toast. The lighter versions of the wine go well with salads and with almost all fish and green vegetables—even hard-to-pair asparagus.

### LIVELY, ASSERTIVE SAUVIGNON BLANC

Brancott Estate (New Zealand)
Neil Ellis (South Africa)
St. Supéry (California)
Pascal Jolivet Pouilly-Fumé (France)
La Poussie Sancerre (France)

## PAIRINGS
- Zucchini "Sandwiches" with Herbed Goat Cheese, 15
- Tuna and Green Olive Empanadas, 24
- Broiled Sardines with Mustard-Shallot Crumbs, 26
- Mascarpone-Stuffed Roast Chicken with Spring Herb Salad, 94
- Seared Tuna with Chimichurri Sauce and Greens, 170
- Grilled Dorado with Walnut and Parsley Pesto, 180
- Spicy Orange Shrimp Seviche, 185
- Grilled Yucatán Shrimp, 190
- Mussels with Tomatoes and Feta, 198

### ROUND, RICH SAUVIGNON BLANC
Matanzas Creek Winery (California)
Château Carbonnieux Blanc (France)
## PAIRINGS
- Fettuccine with Shrimp, Asparagus and Peas, 82
- Braised Swordfish with Black Olives, Tomatoes and Marjoram, 168
- Roasted Halibut with Green Olive Sauce, 177
- Sautéed Shrimp with Green Olives, Scallions and Anchovies, 189
- Sautéed Sea Scallops and Mâche Salad with Moutarde Violette, 191

## SÉMILLON
Often blended with Sauvignon Blanc to add weight and richness, the Sémillon grape has a round flavor and an almost waxy texture on its own. The wine's stony, mineral and melon-like attributes are a perfect foil for crab and rich seafood dishes that are prepared with cream-based sauces. The grape is widely planted in France, where it makes both dry and sweet whites. In Australia, Sémillon has come into its own in a rich, oak-aged style. Likewise, both Napa Valley and Washington State have produced distinguished examples of this wine.

### ROUND-TEXTURED SÉMILLON
Moss Wood (Australia)
Château de Chantegrive Blanc Cuvée Caroline (France)
Clos du Val Ariadne (California)
L'Ecole No. 41 (Washington State)
## PAIRINGS
- Celery Root–Potato Pancakes with Green Apple Sour Cream, 12
- Goat Cheese Panna Cotta with Tomato Salad, 16
- Orecchiette with Hazelnuts and Goat Cheese, 79

- Chicken Piccata with Artichokes and Olives, 91
- Roasted Fish with Charmoula, Tomatoes and Potatoes, 174
- Scallops with Orzo, Tomatoes and Ginger, 192

## SOAVE, VERDICCHIO + GAVI
Italy produces many delicious light white wines; three of them are particularly well known and universally loved. Soave, from Veneto, is a pleasant, fruity—as well as inexpensive—wine. Verdicchio, from the Marches, has a sharp acidity followed by a tangy finish. Finally, Gavi, from Piedmont, is a delicate wine marked by citrus and mineral notes. All three pair well with pesto pasta as well as fish and shellfish prepared with fresh herbs.

### LIGHT, DRY SOAVE OR SIMILAR WHITE
Anselmi "San Vincenzo" Soave (Italy)
Pieropan Soave Classico (Italy)
Verdicchio San Floriano Monte Schiavo (Italy)
Principessa Gavia Gavi (Italy)
## PAIRINGS
- Turkish Cigars, 19
- Penne with Zucchini and Basil, 76
- Campofilone Pasta with Lobster and Tomato, 82
- Midnight Pasta with Tuna, Pancetta and Spinach, 83
- Chicken Breasts with Red Onions and Thyme, 91

## VERMENTINO
Vermentino is assertive and savory, with a salty, lemony edge and razorlike acidity—all of which make it a perfect partner for any kind of shellfish. Though the Vermentino grape grows throughout Italy, the Vermentinos of Tuscany and Sardinia generally have the most character and the most complexity.

### HIGH-ACID, SAVORY VERMENTINO
Antinori Vermentino (Italy)
Argiolas Costamolino Vermentino (Italy)
## PAIRINGS
- Mexican Shrimp Cocktail, 23
- Gemelli with Shrimp and Green Peppercorns, 80
- Pasta Shells with Swordfish, 84
- Vermentino-Braised Sea Bass, 170
- Grilled Calamari with Parsley, 180
- Sardinian Clams with Fregola, 195

# wine pairings

### VERNACCIA DI SAN GIMIGNANO

Vernaccia di San Gimignano is, according to Tuscan tradition, "the wine that kisses, bites and stings." It's also the best known of the many wines made from the Vernaccia grape that flourishes throughout Italy. The grapes for this version—generally considered Tuscany's finest white wine—grow on the hillsides surrounding San Gimignano, the medieval town famous for its picturesque bell towers. The wine is fresh and reliable, with no oak. Its tangy mineral and citrus flavors and crisp acidity pair beautifully with pasta and shellfish.

#### TANGY, CRISP VERNACCIA DI SAN GIMIGNANO
Falchini (Italy)
Fattoria San Quirico (Italy)
Melini Lydia (Italy)
**PAIRINGS**
- Tangy Spinach Pastries, 17
- Roasted Tomatoes with Penne and Ricotta Salata, 75
- Garlicky Lemongrass Chicken, 102

### VIOGNIER

Whether it's the classic bottling from the northern Rhône Valley appellation of Condrieu in France or one of the newer versions from California, the East Coast and now, Australia, Viognier stands out for is its exotic honeysuckle aroma, its intense ripe-peach and ripe-apricot flavors and, most of all, its fleshy, mouth-filling texture. The aroma leads you to expect sweetness, but in the mouth it's bone-dry. Low in acid and often high in alcohol, Viognier is typically rich and powerful. Opulent dishes with tropical or dried fruit and those with curry or smoky flavors are good matches.

#### FULL-BODIED, FRAGRANT VIOGNIER
Bonterra Mendocino County (California)
Arrowood Saralee's Vineyard (California)
Stag's Leap (California)
Calera Mount Harlan (California)
Yalumba Eden Valley (Australia)
Jean-Luc Colombo Côtes-du-Rhône Blanc,
    Les Figuières (France)
**PAIRINGS**
- Shrimp Tempura with Miso Mayonnaise, 23

- Spicy Chinese Noodles with Shrimp, 80
- Stir-Fried Pork with Ginger and Basil, 149
- Sea Bass with Rice Noodles in Tomato-Pineapple Broth, 172
- Pan-Fried Shrimp with Lemon and Ouzo, 190
- Warm Lobster Salad with Gazpacho Consommé, 199

## rosés

Rosés are as refreshing as white wines while offering the body and fruit of light reds. They come from many countries and from many different grapes and range in style from simple summer thirst-quenchers to sophisticated marvels. The best, from Provence and the Tavel appellation of the Rhône Valley, are savory, bone-dry bottlings made from Syrah, Grenache and Cinsaut grapes. Italy, Spain and California produce their own delectable versions. What they all have in common is zesty fruit and acidity that make them delightful with the smoky, sweet and hot spices of Chinese, Thai, Middle Eastern, Cajun and Southwestern dishes.

#### BRIGHT, FRUITY ROSÉ
Château Routas Côteau Varois Rosé Rouvière (France)
Château d'Acqueria Tavel (France)
Mas de Gourgonnier Rosé (France)
Bonny Doon Vineyard Vin Gris de Cigare (California)
Castello di Ama Rosato (Italy)
La Palma Rosé Rapel Valley (Chile)
**PAIRINGS**
- Roast Chickens with Lebanese Rice and Pomegranate Jus, 94
- Turkey-Date Meatballs with Lentils and Yogurt Sauce, 108
- Turkey Breast Fajitas with Strawberry-Jalapeño Salsa, 109
- Moroccan-Spiced Lamb Chops, 133
- Lamb Meatballs in Sour-Cherry Sauce, 137
- Ground Pork Satay on Lemongrass Skewers, 149
- Mussel and Fingerling Potato Salad, 196

# reds

## BARBERA

The second-most-planted grape in Italy (after Sangiovese), Barbera produces its finest wines—tart, bright and medium-bodied, with very little tannin—in the Piedmont areas of Asti and Alba. (A few California wineries also make Barbera, with mixed results.) Both simple styles (fresh, fruity and without oak) and more serious bottlings (plummy and oaky) have a deep, ruby color and a high acidity that gives this versatile wine vibrancy and zip. Licorice, berries and cherries are typical flavors; the taste is straightforward, mouth-filling and, for a red, quite refreshing. Barbera's tartness combines superbly with antipasti, tomato-sauced pastas and bitter greens.

### TART, LOW-TANNIN BARBERA

Michele Chiarlo Barbera d'Asti (Italy)
Bruno Giacosa Barbera d'Alba (Italy)
Renato Ratti Barbera d'Alba (Italy)

### PAIRINGS

- Rustic Chicken Liver Mousse, 14
- Tagliolini with Eggplant and Mint, 76
- Fettuccine with Mushrooms and Prosciutto, 85
- Crisp Chicken with Garlic, 93
- Turkey and Green Bean Stir-Fry with Peanuts, 108
- Cornish Hens with Shiitake and Watercress, 117
- Braised Veal Chops with Honey and Red Grapes, 157
- Lemon-Parmesan Veal Rolls with Arugula Salad, 158

## BEAUJOLAIS

This fruity and famously charming wine is made from the Gamay grape in the Beaujolais region of France. Bottlings range from the simple Beaujolais-Villages, best when it's young, to deeper, more complex *cru* examples from villages with their own appellations, such as Moulin-à-Vent, which age well. What they all share is a smooth texture and an exuberant juicy fruitiness, with strawberry-cherry flavors. Though Beaujolais isn't as fashionable as it once was, its low tannin, fresh, enticing acidity and lack of oak still enable it to pair well with a variety of foods. It traditionally accompanies roast chicken, and it's also excellent with turkey and most cheeses.

### LIGHT, FRUITY BEAUJOLAIS

Georges Duboeuf Beaujolais Nouveau (France)
Château de La Chaize Brouilly (France)
Louis Jadot Beaujolais-Villages (France)

### PAIRINGS

- Warm Onion Flans with Fresh Tomato Sauce, 17
- Roast Chickens with Lemon and Orange, 94
- Arrowhead Farms Fried Chicken, 104
- Paprika-Glazed Turkey, 112
- Moroccan Lamb Burgers with Mint-Yogurt Sauce, 140
- Pork Medallions with Tangerine-Chile Pan Sauce, 145

## CABERNET SAUVIGNON + BORDEAUX

Cabernet Sauvignon is not merely the classic grape of Bordeaux; it is really the king of grapes, producing some of the world's most complex, elegant, powerful and long-lived red wines. In Bordeaux, where it's often blended with Merlot and Cabernet Franc, it dominates the wines of the Médoc and Graves regions, playing a smaller role in St-Émilion and Pomerol. Those made with a larger proportion of Cabernet Sauvignon typically have black currant and plum aromas and flavors; herbal, olivelike and even minty elements all add complexity. Mouth-puckering tannins, enhanced by aging in oak barrels, give the wines astringency and bite when they're young; aging smooths out the tannins and brings out aromas and flavors of cedar and cigar boxes. Many California bottlings are also blends. The fruit in New World Cabernets tends to be sweeter and riper than in the classic Bordeaux. Cabernet Sauvignon has a particular affinity for the pungent flavors of lamb; it also pairs well with roasts and steaks.

### TANNIC, COMPLEX CABERNET

Joseph Phelps Vineyards (California)
Gallo of Sonoma (California)
Wynns Coonawarra Estate (Australia)
Casa Lapostolle Cuvée Alexandre (Chile)
Château Beycheville (France)
Château Gruaud Larose (France)

### PAIRINGS

- Beef Tenderloin Steaks with Fontina Fonduta, 124
- Seared Steaks with Porcini Mushroom Cream Sauce, 124
- Beef and Vegetable Daube with Celery Root Purée, 129
- Braised Lamb with Giant White Beans, 131
- Lamb Schnitzel with Aioli, 134

# wine pairings

- Herb-Roasted Rack of Lamb with Smoky Cabernet Sauce, 135
- Standing Rib Roast of Pork with Tuscan Herb Sauce, 152

### CHIANTI + SANGIOVESE

Italy's best-known wine—a medium-bodied, brightly flavored, smooth-textured red—is made primarily from the Sangiovese grape in the Chianti region of Tuscany (although a growing number of bottles of Sangiovese are from California). Wines from Italy simply labeled "Chianti" tend to be soft and simple, with cherry flavors and a touch of fresh thyme; those from the Chianti Classico region and Riserva bottlings, which are aged longer before release, are more intense, with licorice, sweet-sour dried cherry and earthy flavors and considerable tannin. Chianti's acidity and its suggestion of saltiness make it an excellent partner for many foods, especially olives and garlic, tomato-sauced pastas, grilled steaks and pecorino and other tangy cheeses. A clone of the Sangiovese grape is the base for Brunello di Montalcino, which is deep, rich and marvelously full-bodied. Many producers also make big, rich Sangiovese–Cabernet Sauvignon blends, which are known as Super-Tuscans.

#### SIMPLE, FRUITY CHIANTI OR SANGIOVESE

Castello di Gabbiano Chianti (Italy)
Selvapiana Chianti Rufina (Italy)
Atlas Peak Sangiovese (California)
**PAIRINGS**
- Parmesan-Dusted Meatballs, 28
- Whole Wheat Spaghetti with Fresh Ricotta and Lemon Zest, 75
- Tuscan Chicken Under a Brick, 100
- Moussaka with Yogurt Béchamel, 139

#### COMPLEX, SAVORY CHIANTI CLASSICO OR RISERVA

Castello di Ama Chianti Classico (Italy)
Frescobaldi Chianti Rufina Nipozzano Riserva (Italy)
**PAIRINGS**
- Tagliarini with Almond-Arugula Pesto and Meatballs, 86
- Pappardelle with Red Wine and Meat Ragù, 86
- Garlicky Broccoli Rabe with Chicken Sausage and Peppers, 103
- Shepherd's Pie with Parsnip Puree Topping, 112
- Tuscan-Style Spareribs with Balsamic Glaze, 151
- Tuscan Baby Back Ribs, 152

### DOLCETTO

Italy's answer to Beaujolais: a plummy, grapey, delicious low-acid wine from Piedmont. It is light and spicy, with a juiciness reminiscent of cranberries, and best when it's young (most of these wines are designed to be drunk when they are two or three years old). It's a versatile wine that's lovely with osso buco and most meaty pasta dishes as well as many creamy cheeses.

#### LIGHT, ZESTY, FRUITY DOLCETTO

Roberto Voerzio Dolcetto d'Alba Priavino (Italy)
Aldo Conterno Dolcetto d'Alba (Italy)
Giuseppe Cortese Dolcetto d'Alba (Italy)
**PAIRINGS**
- Fettuccine with Walnut-Parsley Pesto, 76
- Spinach and Ricotta Gnocchi, 78
- Roasted Chicken Legs with Garlicky Potatoes and Peppers, 97
- Tina's Turkey Chili, 106
- Pork and Chickpea Stew with Orange and Cumin, 148

### GRENACHE

Although Grenache is the world's most widely planted red grape variety, few wine lovers give it much thought. But it's a mistake to overlook Grenache. Rhône wine enthusiasts know it as one of the main grapes used in sturdy, deep-flavored Châteauneuf-du-Pape and the delicious rosés of the Tavel region. France's plantings, however, are dwarfed by Spain's. There the grape is known as Garnacha Tinta, important in Rioja blends; it also makes the concentrated, high-alcohol, heady, powerful reds of Priorat. In California, South Africa and Australia, it has been used to make everything from port-style wines to simple rosés, though many of these are undistinguished. Recently, however, some Australian winemakers have sought out top old-vine Grenache vineyards to make mouth-filling, assertively fruity versions that are best enjoyed young in their lusty prime and are superb with grilled meats.

#### ASSERTIVE, HEADY GRENACHE

Clos Mogador Priorat (Spain)
Clarendon Hills Clarendon (Australia)
D'Arenberg The Custodian (Australia)
Château de Beaucastel Châteauneuf-du-Pape (France)
**PAIRINGS**
- Cape Malay Meat Loaf, 127
- Moroccan-Spiced Lamb-and-Rice Meatballs, 138

- Lamb Burgers with Cilantro-Yogurt Sauce, 140
- Asturian Pork and Beans, 154

## MALBEC

Malbec is the French grape that's put Argentina on the wine map. In Bordeaux, Malbec used to be a minor part of the traditional mix of grapes that make that area's château wines, and it's still used in Cahors in southwest France to make sturdy, inky-dark reds with wild-berry flavors. But where Malbec really shines is in the high-altitude vineyards of Argentina, especially from old-vine plantings in the Mendoza region. There, the warm, dry, sunny climate gives the wine a deep, dark, plummy character, with faint hints of chocolate, leather and licorice—the perfect hearty red. Until recently, Argentina mainly kept Malbecs for itself. But in the past few years a strong export market has developed, driven by international interest in this dark, gutsy and often bargain-priced red that pairs beautifully with grilled steaks, hearty stews and full-flavored cheeses.

### PLUMMY, EARTHY MALBEC

Doña Paula (Argentina)
Valentín Bianchi (Argentina)
Terrazas de los Andes (Argentina)
Domaine de Lagrézette Château Lagrézette (France)

**PAIRINGS**

- Skirt Steak Burgers with Tomatillo-Corn Relish, 122
- Grilled Skirt Steak with Chimichurri Sauce, 123
- Grilled Flank Steak with Soy-Chile Glaze, 125
- Meat Loaf Stuffed with Prosciutto and Spinach, 126
- Sausage Burgers with Grilled Green Chiles, 155

## MERLOT

Merlot, Bordeaux's major red grape variety after Cabernet Sauvignon, is similar in flavor but less assertive; because of its softer texture, it's often used in blends to tame Cabernet's hard tannins. When Merlot is the dominant grape, as in Bordeaux's Pomerol and St-Émilion, or when it's bottled on its own, the result has a rich, velvety texture and juiciness, with aromas and flavors of plums and black cherries. The luscious fruit combines well with medium-weight meats—duck, pork, veal—especially in dishes with a hint of sweetness. Washington State and California's Napa and Sonoma regions also make delightful Merlots.

### RICH, VELVETY MERLOT

Swanson (California)
Duckhorn Vineyards (California)
Waterbrook (Washington State)
Château Simard (France)

**PAIRINGS**

- Chicken Stuffed with Prosciutto, Spinach and Boursin, 96
- Soy-Marinated Chicken Thighs with Shiitake Mushrooms, 100
- Herb-and-Cheese-Filled Chicken Thighs, 102
- Duck Two Ways with Chickpea Crêpes and Fennel Compote, 114
- Sirloin Burgers with Wasabi Mayo and Ginger-Pickled Onions, 122
- Beef Stew with Belgian-Style Pale Ale, 130
- Lemony Lamb Chops with Asparagus, 133

## NEBBIOLO, BAROLO + BARBARESCO

Barolo and Barbaresco are the most famous reds of Italy's Piedmont region. Made from the Nebbiolo grape, these big, dry, tannic wines are named for the districts where the fruit is grown. Barolo is heavier and more pungent than Barbaresco, but both share distinctive aromas of berries and mushrooms and a hint of tar or licorice that carries through in the flavor. Often, a scent of violets adds elegance to their earthiness. Mouth-puckering tannins contribute to the impression of dryness, making these reds ideal with Italian dishes—game, saltimbocca, garlicky roasts and strong cheeses—whose richness needs the balance of a dry, astringent wine. These grand, powerful wines are good at four to six years of age, but the most concentrated bottlings can develop for a decade or more. Nebbiolo is also produced as a varietal wine in Piedmont, but in a lighter style than Barolo or Barbaresco. California has experimented with Nebbiolo, with mixed results.

### DEEP, PUNGENT, TANNIC BAROLO

Ceretto (Italy)
Elio Grasso (Italy)
Pio Cesare (Italy)

**PAIRINGS**

- Slow-Braised Lamb Shanks, 130
- Lamb Braised in Milk with Garlic and Fennel, 131
- Grilled Ouzo-and-Nutmeg Lamb Chops, 133
- Lamb Steaks with Milk, Honey and Cumin Marinade, 134

# wine pairings

### TANNIC, FULL-BODIED BARBARESCO

Pelissero (Italy)
Prunotto (Italy)
Vietti (Italy)

**PAIRINGS**

- Lamb Chops with Mint-Cilantro Relish, 133
- Lamb Stew with Lemon, 135
- Eggplants Stuffed with Tarragon Lamb, 138
- Roast Bacon-Wrapped Pork, 145

## PINOT NOIR + RED BURGUNDY

The most sensual and beguiling of all red wines, the best Pinot Noirs are from Burgundy, but California, Oregon and New Zealand have all done wonders with this difficult grape. Though Pinot Noir appears in many different styles, its hallmarks are seductive scents and flavors that suggest cherries, strawberries and damp earth or mushrooms, and, above all, a silky texture. Bottlings range from light- to medium-bodied and from simple to complex, but very few are tannic, and almost all can be drunk young. California's Pinot Noirs are beginning to rival Burgundy's for elegance and complexity as new areas, like the Santa Lucia Highlands, are being planted with this famously fussy grape. While California Pinots can be stylistically heavy and alcoholic, Oregon's generally have delicacy, charm and bright cherry fruit. Pinot Noir's low tannin, tart fruitiness and subtle flavors make it flexible with food. Fruity styles work well with Asian flavors and fish; earthier ones respond beautifully to mushrooms and game.

### LIGHT, FRUITY PINOT NOIR

Elk Cove Vineyards (Oregon)
Estancia Pinnacles (California)

**PAIRINGS**

- Honey-Glazed Pork Shoulder with Braised Leeks, 149
- Crispy Fresh Ham with Rum Sauce, 156
- Sesame-Crusted Tuna Steaks, 170
- Lobster with Pinot Noir Sauce, Salsify Puree and Frizzled Leeks, 200

### RICH, EARTHY PINOT NOIR

Wild Horse (California)
Au Bon Climat (California)
Ponzi (Oregon)

**PAIRINGS**

- Spiced Turkey Tagine with Prunes, 106
- Herb-Roasted Turkey with Maple Gravy, 111

- Seared Duck Breasts with Port-Fruit Chutney, 117
- Quail with Sweet Pea Oatmeal and Summer Vegetable Ragout, 118

### COMPLEX, SILKY RED BURGUNDY

Bouchard Père & Fils Beaune-Grèves Vigne de l'Enfant Jésus (France)
Domaine Faiveley Nuits-St-Georges Les Porets (France)

**PAIRINGS**

- Roast Chickens with Black Pepper–Maple Glaze, 93
- Roasted Quail with Corn Bread Stuffing and Port-Orange Sauce, 117
- Beef Tenderloin with Bacon and Creamed Leeks, 124
- Herbed Pork Rib Roast, 145

## RIOJA + TEMPRANILLO

Tempranillo, which reigns supreme among Spanish grapes, gives the renowned red blends of the Rioja region their herbal scent, earthy flavor and elegant texture. Riojas made in a modern style have forward fruit and just a little oak; the more traditional, more complex ones are mellower and oakier. The newly fashionable Ribera del Duero region produces delicious blends in a bigger, richer, fruitier style. In both places, the younger versions, labeled "Crianza," are spicy, easy-drinking wines; "Reservas" and "Gran Reservas" are more subtle and refined, with flavors of leather and earth. These are big wines, apt matches for hearty bean and spicy sausage stews, grilled meats and earthy dishes (for instance, those with wild mushrooms).

### SOFT, EARTHY RIOJA

Muga Reserva (Spain)
Marqués de Cáceres (Spain)
Cune Imperial Gran Reserva (Spain)
Montecillo Reserva (Spain)

**PAIRINGS**

- Basque Chicken and Chorizo Sauté, 98
- Duck Confit Potpie, 115
- Chorizos Braised in Hard Cider, 156

## SHIRAZ + SYRAH

The intense and concentrated wines that are made from Syrah grapes are packed with blueberry and blackberry fruit and with spicy, peppery, sometimes smoky accents.

Syrah is the star grape in France's northern Rhône Valley, where it goes into dense, powerful wines that take on a chocolaty, leathery character. Elsewhere in the Rhône, it is one of several grapes in softer, rounder, less tannic blends such as the much-loved Châteauneuf-du-Pape. In California, where the grape is deservedly popular, it may be blended with other Rhône varieties. In Washington State, it has become an unexpected success, producing rich, striking wines. It's also widely planted in Australia, where it goes by the name Shiraz and yields wines that range from solid all the way to superb. Many of the Australian bottlings are thick, chocolaty and jammy, with notes of sweet vanilla from oak aging. Syrah's big, spicy-peppery flavors demand robust, flavorful foods. Grilled meat and game are a match, and the Rhône blends pair with spicy dishes and barbecued meats.

### RICH, SMOKY-PLUMMY SHIRAZ
Woop Woop Shiraz (Australia)
Grant Burge Miamba (Australia)
**PAIRINGS**
- Beef Rib Eye and Vegetable Stew, 129
- Grandma Selma's Brisket, 130
- Lamb and Two-Cheese Quesadillas, 140

### ROUND, SUPPLE, FRUITY SYRAH AND BLENDS
Paul Jaboulet Aîné Côtes-du-Rhône (France)
Ravenswood Icon (California)
**PAIRINGS**
- Lemon Chicken with Potatoes and Tomatoes, 91
- Turkey Leg Confit with Garlic Gravy, 113
- Vietnamese Grilled Pork
  Meatball Sandwiches, 153

### POWERFUL, SPICY SYRAH
Domaine Santa Duc Gigondas (France)
Jade Mountain (California)
Covey Run (Washington State)
**PAIRINGS**
- Pecan-Crusted Beef Tenderloin
  with Juniper Jus, 125
- Coconut Lamb Curry, 134
- Citrus-Scented Lamb Stew, 134
- Roast Leg of Lamb with Dried-Cherry
  Sauce, 137
- Cassoulet with Bacon, Andouille and
  Country Ribs, 146

## ZINFANDEL
Though it's generally believed to have first traveled over to the United States from Italy, Zinfandel is really California's own grape. And it's an enormously versatile one that is used to make everything from bland, semisweet blush wines to jammy, highly intense reds. The Zinfandels that go best with most foods are the medium- to full-bodied bottlings that emphasize the grape's characteristic raspberry-boysenberry, often spicy, fruit. These bright berry flavors and the wine's lively acidity make it a good partner for hearty food. Grilled or barbecued meats are excellent choices, as are spicy, salty dishes.

### INTENSE, BERRY-FLAVORED ZINFANDEL
Cline (California)
Ridge Geyserville (California)
St. Francis Old Vines (California)
Seghesio Sonoma County (California)
**PAIRINGS**
- Spaghetti with Creamy Pancetta Sauce, 85
- Seared Duck with Fig Sauce, 113
- Pancetta-Beef Burgers with Horseradish
  Ketchup, 123
- Peppercorn Beef with Gorgonzola Cheese, 125
- Meat-Stuffed Poblanos with Cilantro-Lime Sauce, 127
- Grilled Lamb Kebabs with Smoky Tomato Sauce, 132
- Sweet-and-Spicy Pork Ribs, 151
- Sausage and Broccoli Rabe Burgers, 154

# recipes

## a

Aioli, Avocado, 164

**almonds**

Almond Saketini, 360

Almond-Tea Milk Shakes, 361

Apple Salad with Cabrales Cheese and
Toasted Almonds, 36

Apricot and Almond Soufflés,
304, **305**

Chicken with Almonds and Honey, 96

Chocolate-Coated Almonds, 340

Creamy Tomato Soup with Toasted
Almonds, 55

Date and Fig *Pastilla,* 302

Frozen Fruit Nougat with Citrus
Sauce, 336, **336**

Hazelnut–Pine Nut Cookies, 332

Mixed Greens with Spiced Pears and
Almonds, 35

Moroccan Rice Pudding with Toasted
Almonds, **336,** 337

Orange-Almond Shortbread with
Strawberry Compote, 332

Romesco Sauce, 268

Spicy Shrimp with Garlic-Almond
Sauce, 184, **184**

Tagliarini with Almond-Arugula Pesto

and Meatballs, 86

Warm Almond Milk with Bananas and
Honey, 361

Yellow Pepper and Almond Soup, 54

**appetizers.** *See* starters

**apples + apple juice**

Apple and Mixed Berry Crumble, 294

Apple Crisp with Sweet Ginger and
Macadamia Nuts, 291

Apple Salad with Cabrales Cheese and
Toasted Almonds, 36

Apple Skillet Cake, 291

Bread Stuffing with Apple, Raisins and
Marmalade, 250

Caramel Lady Apples, 290

Celery Root and Green Apple
Puree, 220

Celery Root–Potato Pancakes with
Green Apple Sour Cream, 12, **13**

Cider–Caramelized Apple Pound
Cake, 312

Crab Salad with Apple, Endives and
Pecans, 47

Eli's Golden Apple Turnovers, 294

Escarole and Fresh Herb Salad with
Apples and Pomegranates, **30,** 35

Green Cabbage and Apple Sauté, 216

Hollow Hills, 354

Lattice-Topped Apple Pie, **282,** 283

Pan-Roasted Pork with Apple Chutney
and Pepper Relish, 146, **147**

Phyllo Apple-Plum Strudel, 291

**apricots + apricot juice**

Apricot and Almond Soufflés, 304, **305**

Apricot Pavlova with Chamomile
Cream, 303

Brandied Apricot Butter, 351

Frozen Fruit Nougat with Citrus Sauce,
336, **336**

Hollow Hills, 354

Armagnac-Doused Shrimp, 22

**artichokes**

Artichoke Bread Pudding, 250

Artichokes Simmered with Green
Beans and Bacon, 208

Basque Chicken and Chorizo
Sauté, 98, **99**

Braised Artichoke Hearts with
Parsley, 207

Braised Artichokes with Red and White
Pearl Onions, 207

Chestnut and Artichoke Roast, 208

Chicken Piccata with Artichokes and
Olives, 91
Ham and Artichoke Panini, 262, **262**
Spinach and Artichoke
Pizzas, 254

arugula
Arugula, Fennel and Orange
Salad, 37
Lemon and Arugula Salad with
Parmesan Cheese, 37
Lemon-Parmesan Veal Rolls with
Arugula Salad, 158
Lentil Soup with Serrano Ham and
Arugula, **50,** 62
Mixed Salad with Bacon, Blue Cheese
and Pecans, 37
Shrimp BLTs, 23
Tagliarini with Almond-Arugula Pesto
and Meatballs, 86
Tricolore Salad with Walnuts and
Prosciutto, 37

asparagus
Asparagus and Potato Salad with
Riesling-Tarragon Vinaigrette, 212
Asparagus and Smoked Salmon
Tart, 276
Asparagus Glazed with White Truffle
Fondue, 212, **213**
Asparagus Salad with Toasted Walnuts
and Goat Cheese, **34,** 35
Asparagus Soup with Lemon-Herb
Crème Fraîche, 55
Fettuccine with Shrimp, Asparagus
and Peas, 82
Fresh Pasta with Spicy Corn and
Asparagus, **72,** 78
Lemony Lamb Chops with
Asparagus, 133
Steamed Cod with Crisp
Vegetables, 174
Asturian Pork and Beans, 154, **154**

avocados
Avocado Aioli, 164
Spicy Chicken, Avocado and Mango
Salad, 49, **49**
Spicy Poached Chicken Burgers,
102, **103**

# b

bacon. *See also* pancetta
Artichokes Simmered with Green
Beans and Bacon, 208
Baby Peas with Bacon and Crispy
Leeks, **218,** 219
Bacon-Wrapped Enoki, 221, **221**
Beef Tenderloin with Bacon and
Creamed Leeks, 124
BLTs on Toasted Brioche with Aioli and
Basil, 256
Brussels Sprouts with Chestnuts and
Bacon, **210,** 211
Cassoulet with Bacon, Andouille and
Country Ribs, 146
Choucroute Bread Pudding, 251
Mini Tartes Flambées, 18
Mixed Salad with Bacon, Blue Cheese
and Pecans, 37
Mussel Chowder with Bacon and
Shiitake Mushrooms, 67
Potato Salad with Bacon and
Tomatoes, 231
Roast Bacon-Wrapped Pork, **142,** 145
Smoked Trout and Bacon Pitas, 256
Smoky Sautéed Bacon and Leeks, 216
Baked Alaskas, Mango-Raspberry,
302, **303**

bananas
Crispy Fresh Ham with Rum
Sauce, 156
Dulce de Leche Roasted Banana
Split, 301
Warm Almond Milk with Bananas and
Honey, 361

beans. *See also chickpeas; lentils*
Artichokes Simmered with Green
Beans and Bacon, 208
Asturian Pork and Beans, 154, **154**
Braised Lamb with Giant
White Beans, 131
Cannellini Bean and Escarole
Soup, 60
Caribbean Rice and Beans, 237
Cassoulet with Bacon, Andouille and
Country Ribs, 146

Chipotle-Spiked Winter Squash and
Black Bean Salad, 224, **225**
Chunky Summer Minestrone, 64
Cranberry Bean Stew with Potatoes
and Bell Peppers, 230, **230**
Curried Mixed Vegetables, 223
Easter Veal Loin with Fennel–Lima
Bean Puree, 158, **159**
Garlicky Broccoli Rabe with Chicken
Sausage and Peppers, 103
Green Bean Ragout with Tomatoes and
Mint, 212
Green Beans in Cherry Tomato
Sauce, 215
Green Beans with Onions
and Capers, 215
Indian-Spiced Edamame, 11
Pasta with Borlotti Beans, Olives and
Cherry Tomatoes, 74, **74**
Salade Niçoise with Fennel-Dusted
Tuna, 47
Smoky Black-Eyed Peas, 242
Tangy Mung Bean Salad, 242
Tina's Turkey Chili, 106
Turkey and Green Bean Stir-Fry with
Peanuts, 108, **109**
Warm Succotash Salad, 49, **49**
White Bean Soup with Cauliflower,
60, **61**

beef
Beef and Vegetable Daube with Celery
Root Puree, 129
Beef Rib Eye and Vegetable Stew,
**128,** 129
Beef Stew with Belgian-Style Pale
Ale, 130
Beef Tenderloin Steaks with Fontina
Fonduta, 124
Beef Tenderloin with Bacon and
Creamed Leeks, 124
Bread Stuffing with Apple, Raisins and
Marmalade, 250
Grandma Selma's Brisket, 130
Grilled Chili-Rubbed Steak Salad with
Roasted Shallot Vinaigrette, 48
Grilled Flank Steak with Soy-Chile
Glaze, 124

# index

Grilled Skirt Steak and Gorgonzola
Sandwiches, 257
Grilled Skirt Steak with Chimichurri
Sauce, **122**, 123
Hearty Goulash Soup, 70
Meat Loaf Stuffed with Prosciutto and
Spinach, 126
Meat-Stuffed Poblanos with Cilantro-
Lime Sauce, 127
Moussaka with Yogurt Béchamel, 139
Pancetta-Beef Burgers with
Horseradish Ketchup, 123
Pappardelle with Red Wine and Meat
Ragù, 86, **87**
Pecan-Crusted Beef Tenderloin with
Juniper Jus, **120**, 125
Peppercorn Beef with Gorgonzola
Cheese, 125
Roast Beef with Braised-Celery-and-
Chile Relish on Ciabatta, 256
Sausage and Broccoli Rabe Burgers,
154, **154**
Seared Steak with Porcini Mushroom
Cream Sauce, 124
Sirloin Burgers with Wasabi Mayo and
Ginger-Pickled Onions, 122
Skirt Steak Burgers with Tomatillo-
Corn Relish, 122, **122**
Star Anise–Beef Soup, 71
Winter Borscht with Brisket, 70
**beets**
Mâche Salad with Beets, 44
Winter Borscht with Brisket, 70
**berries.** *See also* cranberries; raspber-
ries; strawberries
Apple and Mixed Berry Crumble, 294
Blackberry Cobbler, 294, **295**
Blueberry Corn Cakes with Maple
Syrup, 274, **275**
Lattice-Topped Blackberry Tart, 287
Peach and Berry Croustades, **292**, 293
**biscotti**
Parmesan-Prosciutto Biscotti, 250
Pistachio-Cranberry Biscotti, 335
**biscuits**
Buttermilk Ham and Cheese
Biscuits, 276

Clinton Street Biscuits, **248**, 249
Gramma's Buttermilk Biscuits with
Berries and Ice Cream, 295, **295**
**blackberries**
Blackberry Cobbler, 294, **295**
Lattice-Topped Blackberry Tart, 287
Peach and Berry Croustades, **292**, 293
Black-Eyed Peas, Smoky, 242
Blinis, Chickpea, with Pineapple Relish, 12
**blueberries**
Apple and Mixed Berry Crumble, 294
Blueberry Corn Cakes with Maple
Syrup, 274, **275**
**blue cheese**
Frisée and Endive Salad with Pears and
Blue Cheese, 36
Frisée Salad with Pears, Blue Cheese
and Hazelnuts, 36
Grilled Skirt Steak and Gorgonzola
Sandwiches, 257
Iceberg Wedges with Blue Cheese
Dressing, 32, **32**
Mixed Salad with Bacon, Blue Cheese
and Pecans, 37
Peppercorn Beef with Gorgonzola
Cheese, 125
Roquefort Bread Puddings, 251
**bok choy**
Steamed Ginger Salmon with Stir-
Fried Bok Choy, 167
Warm Bok Choy with Soy Dressing, 223
Borscht, Winter, with Brisket, 70
Bouillabaisse, Curried Shrimp and
Carrot, 190
**bourbon**
Bourbon, Orange and Molasses Rub,
344, **344**
Louisville Limeade, 356
The Vamp, 355
**bread puddings**
Artichoke Bread Pudding, 250
Bread Pudding Soufflé with Bourbon
Sauce, 338
Choucroute Bread Pudding, 251
Lemon Curd Bread Pudding, 298
Roquefort Bread Puddings, 251
Tomato Bread Pudding, 252

**breads**
Auntie Buck's Light and Buttery
Dinner Rolls, 249
Bread Stuffing with Apple, Raisins and
Marmalade, 250
Buttermilk Corn Bread, 249
Buttermilk Ham and Cheese
Biscuits, 276
Clinton Street Biscuits, **248**, 249
Corn Bread Salad with Tomatoes and
Pepper Jack Cheese, 45
Crispy Cornmeal-Gruyère Muffins, 271
Fresh Corn Muffins, 269, **269**
Garlicky Cherry Tomato and Bread
Gratin, 252, 253
Gramma's Buttermilk Biscuits with
Berries and Ice Cream, 295, **295**
Greek Salad with Garlicky Pita
Toasts, 40
Green Olive Crostini, 198
Orange-Rosemary Scones, **270**, 271
Parmesan-Prosciutto Biscotti, 250
Prosciutto, Tomato and Olive
Bruschetta, 15
Pumpkin Seed Bread Salad, 255
Roasted Whole Snapper with Tomato-
Bread Salad, 175
Robin's Whole Wheat Bread, 248, **248**
Sour Cream–Pecan Scones, 271
Zucchini Bread, 273
Zucchini Bread French Toast with
Maple-Bourbon Butter, 273
**broccoli rabe**
Garlicky Broccoli Rabe with Chicken
Sausage and Peppers, 103
Sausage and Broccoli Rabe
Burgers, 154, **154**
Spicy Broccoli Rabe, 222
Bruschetta, Prosciutto, Tomato and
Olive, 15
**brussels sprouts**
Brussels Sprouts with Chestnuts and
Bacon, **210**, 211
Roasted Brussels Sprout and Potato
Gratin, 232
Bulgur, Pomegranate and Walnut
Salad, 234, **235**

**burgers**

Lamb Burgers with Cilantro-Yogurt Sauce, 140, **141**

Moroccan Lamb Burgers with Mint-Yogurt Sauce, 140

Pancetta-Beef Burgers with Horseradish Ketchup, 123

Pan-Fried Asian-Style Crab Burgers, 198

Pan-Fried Salmon Burgers with Cabbage Slaw and Avocado Aioli, 164, **165**

Sausage and Broccoli Rabe Burgers, 154, **154**

Sausage Burgers with Grilled Green Chiles, 155

Sirloin Burgers with Wasabi Mayo and Ginger-Pickled Onions, 122

Skirt Steak Burgers with Tomatillo-Corn Relish, 122, **122**

Spicy Poached Chicken Burgers, 102, **103**

Turkey Burgers with Pesto Mayonnaise, 106

Butter, Brandied Apricot, 351

**buttercream frostings**

Vanilla Buttercream, 321

White Chocolate Buttercream, 321

**buttermilk**

Buttermilk Corn Bread, 249

Buttermilk Ham and Cheese Biscuits, 276

Buttermilk-Roasted Chicken with Date Butter, 93

Chocolate-Buttermilk Layer Cake with Vanilla Buttercream, 319

Gramma's Buttermilk Biscuits with Berries and Ice Cream, 295, **295**

Oatmeal Pancakes, 274

**butternut squash**

Butternut Squash–Polenta Gratin, 224

Buttery Root Vegetable Ragout, 226

Cavatelli with Spicy Winter Squash, 74, **74**

Chipotle-Spiked Winter Squash and Black Bean Salad, 224, **225**

Halibut and Fall Harvest Sauté, 178

Roasted Winter Squash and Onion Turnovers, 272

Seven-Vegetable Couscous, 242

Winter Squash Soup with Pie Spices, **62**, 63

Butterscotch Mousse Pie, 280, **280**

# C

**cabbage**

Asian Coleslaw with Miso-Ginger Dressing, 40

Buttery Root Vegetable Ragout, 226

Curried Kaleslaw, 223

Green Cabbage and Apple Sauté, 216

Grilled Shrimp and Corn Wraps, 186, **187**

Pan-Fried Salmon Burgers with Cabbage Slaw and Avocado Aioli, 164, **165**

Savoy Cabbage and Pancetta, 216

Sour Fish Soup with Napa Cabbage and Enoki Mushrooms, **66**, 67

Steamed Ginger Salmon with Stir-Fried Bok Choy, 167

Warm Bok Choy with Soy Dressing, 223

Winter Borscht with Brisket, 70

**cakes**

Apple Skillet Cake, 291

Bittersweet Chocolate Mousse Refrigerator Cake, 326, **327**

Breton Butter Cake, 312

Cappuccino Cheesecakes, 314

Carrot Cupcakes with Caramel and Cream Cheese Frosting, 324, **325**

Chocolate-Buttermilk Layer Cake with Vanilla Buttercream, 319

Chocolate–Cream Cheese Cupcakes, 322

Chocolate-Pecan Brownie Cake with Glossy Chocolate Glaze, 316

Chocolate Spider Cake with Caramel-Coffee Mousse, **308**, 309

Cider–Caramelized Apple Pound Cake, 312

Citrus Chiffon Cake, 313

Crème Caramel Loaf, 311

Double Dark Chocolate Cupcakes with Peanut Butter Filling, 322, **323**

Earl Grey Devil's Food Cakes with Cherries, 319

Frozen Hazelnut Mousse Cakes with Armagnac, 325

Guinness Ginger Cake, 313

Lemon Cheesecake with Olive Oil, 314

Lemon–Poppy Seed Cake, 274

Lemon Ricotta Cheesecake, 313

Molten Chocolate Cakes, 316

Nono's Mocha Praline Cake, 315

Pecan-Spice Cake with Caramel Frosting, 310, **311**

Rum-Mocha Walnut Layer Cake, 316, **317**

Salted Caramel Cheesecakes, 310, **311**

Semolina Cakes with Fig Compote, 308, **308**

Triple-Layer Chocolate Macaroon Cake, **306**, 315

Vanilla Cupcakes with Lemon Cream and Raspberries, 324, **325**

White Chocolate Cake with Orange Marmalade Filling, **320**, 321

Calamari, Grilled, with Parsley, 180, **181**

Calzones, Grilled Radicchio and Cheese, 255

Candy Corn Ice Pops, 337

Cannoli, Cookie, with Coffee Cream, 333

Cantaloupe and Prosciutto Salad with Ice Wine Vinaigrette, 37

Cappuccino Cheesecakes, 314

**caramel**

Caramel Frosting, 310

Caramel Lady Apples, 290

Carrot Cupcakes with Caramel and Cream Cheese Frosting, 324, **325**

**carrots**

Buttery Root Vegetable Ragout, 226

Carrot Cupcakes with Caramel and Cream Cheese Frosting, 324, **325**

Carrots with Sausage and Rosemary, 217, **218**

Curried Mixed Vegetables, 223

Curried Shrimp and Carrot Bouillabaisse, 190

# index

Fiery Carrot Dip, 10, **10**

Gingered Carrot Soup with Crème Fraîche, 58, **59**

Indian-Spiced Sea Bass with Spinach, Peas and Carrots, 172

Pickled Carrots, 153

Red Wine–Carrot Sauce, 345

Roasted Carrots and Fennel with Tomato and Olive Pesto, 217

Sautéed Turnips and Carrots with Rosemary-Ginger Honey, 217

Seven-Vegetable Couscous, 242

Spicy Carrots with Peperoncini, 216

Cassoulet with Bacon, Andouille and Country Ribs, 146

**cauliflower**

Caramelized Cauliflower with Pancetta and Spinach, 219

Cauliflower with Pine Nut Crumble, 219

Mushrooms à la Grecque, **210**, 211

White Bean Soup with Cauliflower, 60, **61**

Cavatelli with Spicy Winter Squash, 74, **74**

Caviar and Potato Salad Tartlets, 16

**celery**

Herb-Marinated Mushroom and Celery Salad, 44

Roast Beef with Braised-Celery-and-Chile Relish on Ciabatta, 256

**celery root**

Celery Root and Green Apple Puree, 220

Celery Root–Leek Gratin, 220

Celery Root–Potato Pancakes with Green Apple Sour Cream, 12, **13**

Celery Root Puree, 220

Celery Root Remoulade with Scallops and Caviar, 195

Smoked Salmon and Celery Root Bisque, 68

**cereal.** *See* Granola

Chai, Gingery Soymilk, 361

Chayote and Shrimp, Grilled, Salad with Chili-Garlic Dressing, 186

**champagne**

Bubbling Cauldron Cocktails, 358

Red Grape and Coconut Refresher, 356

Sudden Headache, 357

**cheese.** *See also* blue cheese; feta cheese; goat cheese; mozzarella cheese; Parmesan cheese; ricotta cheese

Apple Salad with Cabrales Cheese and Toasted Almonds, 36

Apple Salad with Cabrales Cheese and Toasted Almonds, 36

Artichoke Bread Pudding, 250

Beef Tenderloin Steaks with Fontina Fonduta, 125

Buttermilk Ham and Cheese Biscuits, 276

Cappuccino Cheesecakes, 314

Caramelized Onion and Gruyère Tart, 18, **19**

Carrot Cupcakes with Caramel and Cream Cheese Frosting, 324, **325**

Chicken Stuffed with Prosciutto, Spinach and Boursin, 96

Chocolate–Cream Cheese Cupcakes, 322

Cookie Cannoli with Coffee Cream, 333

Corn Bread Salad with Tomatoes and Pepper Jack Cheese, 45

Crispy Cornmeal-Gruyère Muffins, 271

Escarole and Tomato Salad with Shaved Piave Cheese, 45

Golden Gratinéed Onion Soup, 56

Grilled Cheese and Chorizo Sandwiches, **246**, 259

Grilled Corn with Chiles, Cheese and Lime, 224, **225**

Ham and Artichoke Panini, 262, **262**

Hearty Fennel Soup with Sausage and Gouda Croutons, 58, **59**

Lamb and Two-Cheese Quesadillas, 140, **141**

Lemon Cheesecake with Olive Oil, 314

Mascarpone-Stuffed Roast Chicken with Spring Herb Salad, **88**, 94

Meat Loaf Stuffed with Prosciutto and Spinach, 126

Nectarine and Cream Cheese Monte Cristos, 273

Rich and Creamy Salsify Gratin, 220

Roasted Tomatoes with Penne and Ricotta Salata, 75

Roasted Winter Squash and Onion Turnovers, 272

Salted Caramel Cheesecakes, 310, **311**

Seared Pork and Pickled Eggplant Panini, 258

Sesame-Coated Sweet Potato Croquettes, 12, **13**

Spaghetti with Browned Butter and Crispy Bread Crumbs, 79

Strawberry and Mascarpone Trifles with Riesling Syrup, 297

Summer Squash Sandwiches with Pecorino Butter, 263

Zucchini Gratin with Gruyère Cheese, 206

**cheesecakes**

Cappuccino Cheesecakes, 314

Lemon Cheesecake with Olive Oil, 314

Lemon Ricotta Cheesecake, 313

Salted Caramel Cheesecakes, 310, **311**

**cherries**

Earl Grey Devil's Food Cakes with Cherries, 319

Lamb Meatballs in Sour-Cherry Sauce, 137

Market Radish Soup with Balsamic Cherries, 52, **52**

Roast Leg of Lamb with Dried-Cherry Sauce, **136**, 137

**chestnuts**

Brussels Sprouts with Chestnuts and Bacon, **210**, 211

Chestnut and Artichoke Roast, 208

Frozen Chocolate-Chestnut Pie, 284

Roasted Chestnut Soup, 60

Wild Rice with Chestnuts and Dried Cranberries, 237

**chicken.** *See also* chicken sausages

Arrowhead Farms Fried Chicken, 104, **105**

Asian-Style Grilled Chicken, 98

Basque Chicken and Chorizo Sauté, 98, **99**

Buttermilk-Roasted Chicken with Date Butter, 93

Chicken, Tomato and Mozzarella Salad with Spicy Basil Dressing, 92

Chicken and Potato Soup with Lemongrass, 69

Chicken Breasts with Red Onions and Thyme, **90**, 91

Chicken Breasts with Spinach, Leek and Saffron Sauce, 90, **90**

Chicken Piccata with Artichokes and Olives, 91

Chicken Salad with Poblano Vinaigrette, 102

Chicken Skewers with Lemon-Mint Vinaigrette, 101

Chicken Soup with Passatelli, 64

Chicken Stuffed with Prosciutto, Spinach and Boursin, 96

Chicken with Almonds and Honey, 96

Chicken with Leafy Greens and Lemon, 98

Cider-Braised Chicken Legs with Onion-Raisin Sauce, 97

Creamy Chicken Stew, 104

Crisp Chicken with Garlic, 93

Crispy Fried Chicken Livers, 14

Crispy Roast Chicken and Shallots with Miso Gravy, 107

Garlicky Lemongrass Chicken, 102

Grilled Chicken Sandwiches with Remoulade and Shaved Lemon, 257

Herb-and-Cheese-Filled Chicken Thighs, 102, **103**

Hoosier Chicken with Potato Chip Crust, 92

Indian-Spiced Chicken Salad Sandwiches, 257

Korean-Style Chicken Wraps, 101

Lemon Chicken with Potatoes and Tomatoes, 91

Lemon Confit Chicken with Calamata Olives, 96

Mascarpone-Stuffed Roast Chicken with Spring Herb Salad, **88**, 94

Roast Chickens with Lebanese Rice and Pomegranate Jus, 94

Roast Chicken with Black Pepper–Maple Glaze, 93

Roasted Chicken Legs with Garlicky Potatoes and Peppers, 97

Roast Chickens with Lemon and Orange, 94, **95**

Rustic Chicken Liver Mousse, 14

Sautéed Chicken with Fresh Herbs and Wilted Greens, 92

Seven-Vegetable Couscous, 242

Shrimp and Chicken Summer Rolls, 24

Soy-Marinated Chicken Thighs with Shiitake Mushrooms, 100

Spicy Chicken, Avocado and Mango Salad, 49, **49**

Spicy Poached Chicken Burgers, 102, **103**

Tuscan Chicken Under a Brick, 100

chicken sausages

Asian Spinach Salad with Sausage and Pears, 48

Garlicky Broccoli Rabe with Chicken Sausage and Peppers, 103

chickpeas

Chickpea Blinis with Pineapple Relish, 12

Chickpea Crêpes, 115

Chickpea Puree with Fennel Salad, 38

Garbanzo Soup with Chorizo and Smoked Paprika, **62**, 63

Pork and Chickpea Stew with Orange and Cumin, 148, **148**

Seven-Vegetable Couscous, 242

Spanish Cod with Chickpeas and Sherry, 173

Spiced Turkey Tagine with Prunes, 106

Tangy Chickpea Soup with Olives and Anise, 64

Zucchini Musakka with Chickpeas and Spiced Lamb, **204**, 205

chiles

Charred Poblano and Garlic Pesto, 346

Chicken Salad with Poblano Vinaigrette, 102

Chile-Rubbed Swordfish Kebabs with Cucumber Salad, 167

Chile-Steamed Mussels with Green Olive Crostini, 198

Chipotle-Spiked Winter Squash and

Black Bean Salad, 224, **225**

Corn Soup with Chiles and Manchego, 56, **57**

Creamy Green Chile Soup, 56

Deviled Crab Omelets, 267

Grilled Corn with Chiles, Cheese and Lime, 224, 225

Meat-Stuffed Poblanos with Cilantro-Lime Sauce, 127

Pan-Roasted Halibut with Jalapeño Vinaigrette, 176, **177**

Red Chile BBQ Sauce, 345

Roast Beef with Braised-Celery-and-Chile Relish on Ciabatta, 256

Romesco Sauce, 268

Salmon with Scotch Bonnet Herb Sauce and Onion Toasts, **166**, 167

Sausage Burgers with Grilled Green Chiles, 155

Sichuan Pickled Cucumbers, 348

Spicy Carrots with Peperoncini, 216

Tina's Turkey Chili, 106

Turkey Breast Fajitas with Strawberry-Jalapeño Salsa, 109, 109

Chili, Tina's Turkey, 106

chocolate

Bittersweet Chocolate Mousse Refrigerator Cake, 326, 327

Black-and-Orange Cookies, 330, **331**

Blood Orange and Chocolate Trifles, 297

Chocolate-Buttermilk Layer Cake with Vanilla Buttercream, 319

Chocolate-Caramel Hazelnut Tart, 288

Chocolate-Coated Almonds, 340

Chocolate–Cream Cheese Cupcakes, 322

Chocolate Cream Squares, 334

Chocolate-Pecan Brownie Cake with Glossy Chocolate Glaze, 316

Chocolate Rosemary-Caramel Nut Bars, 328

Chocolate Spider Cake with Caramel-Coffee Mousse, **308**, 309

Coconut Chocolate Candy Bars, 340

Crispy Witches' Hats, 326

Double Dark Chocolate Cupcakes with

# index

Peanut Butter Filling, 322, **323**

Earl Grey Devil's Food Cakes with Cherries, 319

Frozen Chocolate-Chestnut Pie, 284

Frozen Hazelnut Mousse Cakes with Armagnac, 325

Ice Cream in Crispy Chocolate-Coconut Cones, 335

Molten Chocolate Cakes, 316

Triple-Layer Chocolate Macaroon Cake, **306**, 315

White Chocolate Buttercream, 321

White Chocolate Cake with Orange Marmalade Filling, **320**, 321

chorizos

Asturian Pork and Beans, 154, **154**

Basque Chicken and Chorizo Sauté, 98, **99**

Chorizos Braised in Hard Cider, 156

Garbanzo Soup with Chorizo and Smoked Paprika, **62**, 63

Grilled Cheese and Chorizo Sandwiches, **246**, 259

Monkfish and Chorizo Kebabs, **174**, 175

Mushroom Soup with Chorizo and Scallions, 58

Red Snapper with Mussels, Potatoes and Chorizo, **174**, 175

Choucroute Bread Pudding, 251

chowders

Cherrystone Clam Chowder with Corn, 65

Mussel Chowder with Bacon and Shiitake Mushrooms, 67

Spicy Kale Chowder with Andouille Sausage, 67

chutneys

Cranberry, Quince and Pear Chutney, 350

Kumquat and Pineapple Chutney, 350

Spiced Prune Chutney, 350

cider

Cider-Braised Chicken Legs with Onion-Raisin Sauce, 97

Cider–Caramelized Apple Pound Cake, 312

Cinnamon-Ginger Cookies, 329

clams

Cherrystone Clam Chowder with Corn, 65

Clams with Spicy Sausage, **194**, 195

Fresh Clam and Noodle Soup, 65

Sake-Steamed Clams, **194**, 196

Sardinian Clams with Fregola, 195

Cobbler, Blackberry, 294, **295**

coconut

Aunt Ruthie's Coconut Snowballs, 339

Coconut Chocolate Candy Bars, 340

Coconut-Creamed Spinach, 222

Coconut-Pineapple Batida, 360

Coquito, 357

Ice Cream in Crispy Chocolate-Coconut Cones, 335

Lemon-Coconut Tart with Brown-Sugar Cream, 287

Red Grape and Coconut Refresher, 356

Triple-Layer Chocolate Macaroon Cake, **306**, 315

cod

Mediterranean Fish Soup with Garlicky Rouille, 68

Roasted Fish with Charmoula, Tomatoes and Potatoes, 174

Seared Cod with Spicy Mussel Aioli, 173

Spanish Cod with Chickpeas and Sherry, 173

Steamed Cod with Crisp Vegetables, 174

coffee

Cappuccino Cheesecakes, 314

Cookie Cannoli with Coffee Cream, 333

Espresso Jell-O, 340, **341**

Nono's Mocha Praline Cake, 315

Rum-Mocha Walnut Layer Cake, 316, **317**

cognac

Starlight, 360

Coleslaw, Asian, with Miso-Ginger Dressing, 41

Collard Greens, Braised, and Cider Sauce, Seared Scallops with, 194

condiments. *See also* sauces

Almost-Instant Heirloom

Tomato–Basil Relish, 350

Avocado Aioli, 164

Bourbon, Orange and Molasses Rub, 344, **344**

Brandied Apricot Butter, 351

Citrus-Fennel Salt, 347

Cranberry, Quince and Pear Chutney, 350

Green-Tomato Pickle, 227

Herb, Garlic and Lemon Rub, 344

Icebox Strawberry Jam, 351

Kumquat and Pineapple Chutney, 350

Lavender-Rosemary Salt, 347

Mediterranean Country Sachets, 346

Moroccan Spice Rub, 344

Moroccan Spice Sachets, 347

Oregano Oil, 178

Peppercorn Salt, 347

Pineapple-Mint Relish, 13

Quick Pickled Carrots, 153

Rhubarb Ketchup, 345

Sesame-Soy Rub, 345

Shallot-Lemon Confit, **342**, 348

Sichuan Pickled Cucumbers, 348

Spiced Prune Chutney, 350

Three-Cranberry Conserve, 351

Toasted Nuts in Honey, 351

Tuscan Herb Sachets, 347

cookies + bars

Black-and-Orange Cookies, 330, **331**

Brown-Sugar Meringues, 329

Chocolate Rosemary-Caramel Nut Bars, 328

Cinnamon-Ginger Cookies, 329

Cookie Cannoli with Coffee Cream, 333

Crispy Witches' Hats, 326

Gingerbread Girls, 330, **331**

Hazelnut Crescent Cookies, 329

Hazelnut–Pine Nut Cookies, 332

Hazelnut Tuiles, 332

Meringue Phantom Cookies, 329

Orange-Almond Shortbread with Strawberry Compote, 332

Pine Nut–Butter Cookies, 331

corn

Cherrystone Clam Chowder with Corn, 65

Corn and Pea Risotto, 245, **245**

Corn Soup with Chiles and
  Manchego, 56, **57**

Crab and Corn Beignets, 28, **29**

Fresh Corn and Blue Potato Hash, 233

Fresh Corn Muffins, 269, **269**

Fresh Pasta with Spicy Corn and
  Asparagus, **72**, 78

Grilled Corn with Chiles, Cheese and
  Lime, 224, **225**

Grilled Shrimp and Corn Wraps,
  186, **187**

Red Apple Inn Corn Pudding, 225

Sautéed Corn and Shiitake Frittata
  with Parmesan, 267

Scallops, Corn and Basil Steamed in
  Foil, 192

Sheep's-Milk Ricotta Gnocchi with
  Mushrooms and Corn, 77, **77**

Skirt Steak Burgers with Tomatillo-
  Corn Relish, 122, **122**

Warm Succotash Salad, 49, **49**

corn bread

Buttermilk Corn Bread, 249

Corn Bread Salad with Tomatoes and
  Pepper Jack Cheese, 45

Roasted Quail with Corn Bread Stuffing and Port-Orange Sauce, 117

Cornish Hens with Shiitake and
  Watercress, 117

cornmeal

Blueberry Corn Cakes with Maple
  Syrup, 274, **275**

Buttery Cornmeal Pastry, 249

Crispy Cornmeal-Gruyère Muffins, 271

Fresh Corn Muffins, 269, **269**

couscous

Couscous with Red Lentils and Easy
  Preserved Lemons, 243, **245**

Israeli Couscous with Peas and
  Mint, 243

Seven-Vegetable Couscous, 242

crabmeat

Crab and Corn Beignets, 28, **29**

Crab Salad with Apple, Endives and
  Pecans, 47

Deviled Crab Omelets, 267

Pan-Fried Asian-Style Crab
  Burgers, 198

Warm Crab Dip with Fresh Herbs, 11

cranberries + cranberry juice

Cranberry, Quince and Pear
  Chutney, 350

Frozen Fruit Nougat with Citrus Sauce,
  336, **336**

Mixed Greens with Nuts and Dried
  Fruit, 33

Orange and Cranberry Syrup, 348, **349**

Pistachio-Cranberry Biscotti, 335

Sawtooth Mountain Breezes, 356

Seared Duck Breasts with Port Fruit
  Chutney, **116**, 117

Three-Cranberry Conserve, 351

Wild Rice with Chestnuts and Dried
  Cranberries, 237

cream cheese

Cappuccino Cheesecakes, 314

Carrot Cupcakes with Caramel and
  Cream Cheese Frosting, 324, **325**

Chocolate–Cream Cheese
  Cupcakes, 322

Lemon Cheesecake with Olive Oil, 314

Nectarine and Cream Cheese Monte
  Cristos, 273

Salted Caramel Cheesecakes, 310, **311**

Crème Caramel Loaf, 311

crêpes

Chickpea Crêpes, 115

Crêpes with Smoked Trout and
  Caviar, 277

Croquettes, Sesame-Coated Sweet
  Potato, 12, **13**

Crostatas, Ricotta and Prosecco-Poached
  Pear, 293

Crostini, Green Olive, 198

Croustades, Peach and Berry, **292**, 293

Crudités with Creamy Pistachio Dip, 11

cucumbers

Cheval, 354, **354**

Chile-Rubbed Swordfish Kebabs with
  Cucumber Salad, 167

Chilled Cucumber Soup with Pickled
  Red Onion, 54

Cucumber Salad with Mint and Crème

Fraîche, 44

Cucumber Soup with Seared Tuna
  Tartare, 54

Fattoush, 40

Greek Salad with Garlicky Pita
  Toasts, 40

Green My Eyes, 360

Salmon with Saffron-Braised Cucumber and Fennel, 162, **162**

Sichuan Pickled Cucumbers, 348

Summer Tomato Soup with Herbed
  Goat Cheese, 52, **52**

Turkish Chopped Salad, 39

cupcakes

Carrot Cupcakes with Caramel and
  Cream Cheese Frosting, 324, **325**

Chocolate–Cream Cheese
  Cupcakes, 322

Double Dark Chocolate Cupcakes with
  Peanut Butter Filling, 322, **323**

Vanilla Cupcakes with Lemon Cream
  and Raspberries, 324, **325**

Curd, Lemon, 300

curried dishes

Coconut Lamb Curry, 134

Curried Kaleslaw, 223

Curried Mixed Vegetables, 223

Curried Shrimp and Carrot
  Bouillabaisse, 190

Grilled Whole Fish with Curried Yogurt
  Marinade, 180

Spaghetti with Curried Seafood
  Marinara, 83

# d

Dal, Yellow Lentil, 236

dates

Buttermilk-Roasted Chicken with Date
  Butter, 93

Date, Goat Cheese and Pancetta on
  Walnut Bread, 260, 261

Date and Fig Pastilla, 302

Tamarind-Date Dipping Sauce, 234

Turkey-Date Meatballs with Lentils and
  Yogurt Sauce, 108

desserts. *See also* cakes; cookies; pies

# index

and tarts (sweet)
Apple and Mixed Berry Crumble, 294
Apple Crisp with Sweet Ginger and
Macadamia Nuts, 291
Apricot and Almond Soufflés,
304, **305**
Apricot Pavlova with Chamomile
Cream, 303
Aunt Ruthie's Coconut Snowballs, 339
Blackberry Cobbler, 294, **295**
Blood Orange and Chocolate
Trifles, 297
Bread Pudding Soufflé with Bourbon
Sauce, 338
Brûléed Rice Pudding, 337
Candy Corn Ice Pops, 337
Caramel Lady Apples, 290
Chocolate-Coated Almonds, 340
Chocolate Cream Squares, 334
Coconut Chocolate Candy Bars, 340
Date and Fig Pastilla, 302
Dulce de Leche Roasted Banana
Split, 301
Eli's Golden Apple Turnovers, 294
Espresso Jell-O, 340, **341**
Fried Milk, 333
Frozen Fruit Nougat with Citrus Sauce,
336, **336**
Frozen Lemon Cream Sandwiches, 335
Gramma's Buttermilk Biscuits with
Berries and Ice Cream, 295, **295**
Ice Cream in Crispy Chocolate-
Coconut Cones, 335
Lemon Curd, 300
Lemon Curd Bread Pudding, 298
Lemon Panna Cottas with Peach
Compote and Ginger Syrup, 298
Mango-Raspberry Baked Alaskas,
302, **303**
Mango Sticky Rice, 301
Moroccan Rice Pudding with Toasted
Almonds, **336**, 337
Muscat-Poached Peaches with Lemon
Verbena, 298, **299**
Neapolitan Lemon Granita, 300
Oranges in Citrus Syrup, 297
Peach and Berry Croustades, **292**, 293

Phyllo Apple-Plum Strudel, 291
Pineapple Shortcakes with Dulce de
Leche Whipped Cream, 301
Pistachio-Cranberry Biscotti, 335
Pumpkin Pudding with Candied Ginger
Whipped Cream, 338
Rice Pudding with Strawberries, 297
Ricotta and Prosecco-Poached Pear
Crostatas, 293
Strawberry and Mascarpone Trifles
with Riesling Syrup, 297
Strawberry and Sweet Wine Gelées
with Candied Pistachios, 296
Strawberry Granita, 300
Strawberry-Rhubarb Galette, 296
Sugar-Dusted Vanilla Ricotta
Fritters, 333
White Grapefruit and Star Anise
Granita, 300
Yogurt and Sautéed Dried Fruits and
Nuts, 302, **303**
dips + spreads
Crudités with Creamy Pistachio Dip, 11
Fiery Carrot Dip, 10, **10**
Rustic Chicken Liver Mousse, 14
Spicy Tuna Rillettes, 27, **27**
Warm Crab Dip with Fresh Herbs, 11
drinks, 352–361
Almond Saketini, 360
Almond-Tea Milk Shakes, 361
Bitter Queen, 355
Bubbling Cauldron Cocktails, 358
Cheval, 354, **354**
Citrus-Mint Cocktails, 355
Coconut-Pineapple Batida, 360
Coquito, 357
Dry Toast, 354
Fahrenheit 5, 358
Gingery Soymilk Chai, 361
Green My Eyes, 360
Hollow Hills, 354
Iced Hibiscus Tea, 361
Iced Pomegranate-Fennel Green
Tea, 360
Ice Wine Martini, 358
Jade Cocktail, 360
Louisville Limeade, 356

Midtown Sangria, 358
Orange Fizz, 355
Pomegranate Margaritas, 356
Red Grape and Coconut Refresher, 356
Roof Garden, 355
Rose Martinis, 356
Saffron Cooler, **352**, 357
Saluki, 354, **354**
Sawtooth Mountain Breeze, 356
Sparkling Lemongrass Coolers, 357
Spice, 358
Spiced Red Wine Punch, 360
Starlight, 360
Star of India, 357
Stone Wall, 357
Sudden Headache, 357
Sugar Baby, 355
Thai Martini, 358
The Vamp, 355
Vanilla Pear Mimosa, 354
Warm Almond Milk with Bananas and
Honey, 361
Watermelon Coolers, 358, **359**
duck
Duck Confit Potpie, 115, **116**
Duck Two Ways with Chickpea Crêpes
and Fennel Compote, 114
Seared Duck Breasts with Port-Fruit
Chutney, **116**, 117
Seared Duck with Fig Sauce, 113
Three-Pepper Duck Confit, 116
dulce de leche
Dulce de Leche–Glazed Ham, 157
Dulce de Leche Roasted Banana
Split, 301
Pineapple Shortcakes with Dulce de
Leche Whipped Cream, 301

# e

edamame
Curried Mixed Vegetables, 223
Indian-Spiced Edamame, 11
Warm Succotash Salad, 49, **49**
eggplant
Asian Eggplant Salad, 44
Eggplant and Lentil Stew with

Pomegranate Molasses, 240, 241

Eggplant Salad with Cumin and Fresh
Herbs, 204

Eggplants Stuffed with Tarragon
Lamb, 138

Eggplant Tempura Fans, 204

Grilled Eggplant and Fresh Herb Salad
Subs with Parmesan, 260

Grilled Eggplants with Cumin-Yogurt
Sauce, **204**, 205

Moussaka with Yogurt Béchamel, 139

Seared Pork and Pickled Eggplant
Panini, 258

Stir-Fried Pork with Ginger and
Basil, 149

Tagliolini with Eggplant and Mint, 76

eggs

Crusty Potato Frittatas with Romesco
Sauce, 268

Deviled Crab Omelets, 267

Egg Salad with Capers and Spinach on
Toasted Brioche, 263

Herb and Onion Frittata, 268, **269**

Poached Eggs with Pancetta and
Tossed Mesclun, 267

Sautéed Corn and Shiitake Frittata
with Parmesan, 267

Shirred Eggs with Mushrooms and
Swiss Chard, 266, **266**

Smoked Salmon Soufflés with Gingered Salad, 22

Smoky Deviled Eggs, **8**, 14

Spinach and Goat Cheese Frittata,
266, 266

Empanadas, Tuna and Green Olive, 24, **25**

endives

Crab Salad with Apple, Endives and
Pecans, 47

Crisp Winter Salad with Ginger-Garlic
Vinaigrette, **32**, 33

Crudités with Creamy Pistachio Dip, 11

Endive Salad with Grainy-Mustard
Vinaigrette, 33

Frisée and Endive Salad with Pears and
Blue Cheese, 36

Frisée Salad with Pears, Blue Cheese
and Hazelnuts, 36

Lemony Smoked Trout Salad in Red
Endive Scoops, 26, 27

Roasted Endives with Prosciutto, 223

Tricolore Salad with Walnuts and
Prosciutto, 37

escarole

Cannellini Bean and Escarole Soup, 60

Escarole and Fresh Herb Salad with
Apples and Pomegranates, **30**, 35

Escarole and Tomato Salad with
Shaved Piave Cheese, 45

f

Fajitas, Turkey Breast, with Strawberry-
Jalapeño Salsa, 109, **109**

Farfalle with Creamy Smoked Salmon
and Vodka Sauce, 84, **84**

Fattoush, 40

fennel

Arugula, Fennel and Orange Salad, 37

Chickpea Puree with Fennel Salad, 38

Chopped Fennel and Olive Salad, 38

Duck Two Ways with Chickpea Crêpes
and Fennel Compote, 114

Easter Veal Loin with Fennel–Lima
Bean Puree, 158, 159

Fennel Salad with Parmesan, 38

Hearty Fennel Soup with Sausage and
Gouda Croutons, 58, 59

Hobo Potatoes with Fennel and
Herbs, 232

Iced Pomegranate-Fennel Green
Tea, 360

Radicchio Salad with Oranges and
Fennel, 38

Roasted Carrots and Fennel with
Tomato and Olive Pesto, 217

Salmon Rolls with Fennel and Creole
Mustard Spaetzle, 162, **162**

Salmon with Saffron-Braised
Cucumber and Fennel, 162, **162**

Seven-Vegetable Couscous, 242

Winter Shrimp Salad with Fennel and
Ruby Grapefruit, 185

feta cheese

Feta, Tomato and Red Onion
Salad, 39, **41**

Fried Zucchini Blossoms, 207

Lamb and Two-Cheese Quesadillas,
140, **141**

Mussels with Tomatoes and Feta, 198

Shrimp and Lemon Skewers with
Feta-Dill Sauce, 189

Turkish Cigars, 19, **19**

Zucchini Pappardelle with Tomatoes
and Feta, 202, **206**

fettuccine

Fettuccine with Mushrooms and
Prosciutto, 85

Fettuccine with Shrimp, Asparagus
and Peas, 82

Fettuccine with Walnut-Parsley
Pesto, 76

figs

Date and Fig Pastilla, 302

Seared Duck Breasts with Port Fruit
Chutney, **116**, 117

Seared Duck with Fig Sauce, 113

Semolina Cakes with Fig Compote,
308, **308**

fish, 160–181. *See also* salmon; tuna

Braised Swordfish with Black Olives,
Tomatoes and Marjoram, 168

Broiled Sardines with Mustard-Shallot
Crumbs, 26

Chile-Rubbed Swordfish Kebabs with
Cucumber Salad, 167

Creole-Style Sea Bass Fillets, 171

Crêpes with Smoked Trout and
Caviar, 277

Grilled Calamari with Parsley, 180, **181**

Grilled Dorado with Walnut and Parsley
Pesto, 180

Grilled Quick-Cured Trout with Mustard-Olive Dressing, 179

Grilled Whole Fish with Curried Yogurt
Marinade, 180

Halibut and Fall Harvest Sauté, 178

Indian-Spiced Sea Bass with Spinach,
Peas and Carrots, 172

Lemony Smoked Trout Salad in Red
Endive Scoops, 26, **27**

Matzo Meal–Crusted Trout, 178

# index

Mediterranean Fish Soup with Garlicky
Rouille, 68

Monkfish and Chorizo Kebabs, **174**, 175

Pan-Fried Pompano with
Tomato-Caraway Glaze, 179

Pan-Roasted Halibut with Jalapeño
Vinaigrette, 176, **177**

Pasta Shells with Swordfish, **84**, 85

Red Snapper with Mussels, Potatoes
and Chorizo, **174**, 175

Roasted Fish with Charmoula,
Tomatoes and Potatoes, 174

Roasted Halibut with Green Olive
Sauce, 177, **177**

Roasted Whole Snapper with
Tomato-Bread Salad, 175

Salt-Baked Sea Bass with Warm
Tomato Vinaigrette, 171

Sautéed Trout Fillets with a Pumpkin
Seed Crust, 178

Sea Bass with Rice Noodles in
Tomato-Pineapple Broth, 172

Seafood Capellini with Saffron, 83

Seared Cod with Spicy Mussel
Aioli, 173

Smoked Trout and Bacon Pitas, 256

Sour Fish Soup with Napa Cabbage
and Enoki Mushrooms, **66**, 67

Spanish Cod with Chickpeas and
Sherry, 173

Steamed Cod with Crisp
Vegetables, 174

Striped Bass with Wild Mushrooms, 173

Sweet-and-Sour Swordfish, **160**, 168

Swordfish Steaks with Mint and Garlic,
168, **169**

Vermentino-Braised Sea Bass, 170

French Toast, Zucchini Bread, with
Maple-Bourbon Butter, 273

frittatas

Crusty Potato Frittatas with Romesco
Sauce, 268

Herb and Onion Frittata, 268, **269**

Sautéed Corn and Shiitake Frittata
with Parmesan, 267

Spinach and Goat Cheese
Frittata, 266, **266**

Fritters, Sugar-Dusted Vanilla
Ricotta, 333

frostings + icing

Caramel Frosting, 310

Marshmallow Frosting, 338

Royal Icing, 330

Vanilla Buttercream, 321

White Chocolate Buttercream, 321

fruits. *See also specific fruits*

Dried Fruit and Toasted Nuts in
Chestnut Honey (variant), 351

Frozen Fruit Nougat with Citrus Sauce,
336, **336**

Mix-and-Match Granola, **264**, 277

Yogurt and Sautéed Dried Fruits and
Nuts, 302, **303**

# g

Galette, Strawberry-Rhubarb, 296

garbanzos. *See* chickpeas

garlic

Charred Poblano and Garlic Pesto, 346

Crisp Chicken with Garlic, 93

Garlicky Broccoli Rabe with Chicken
Sausage and Peppers, 103

Garlicky Cherry Tomato and Bread
Gratin, 252, **253**

Garlicky Lemongrass Chicken, 102

Garlicky Potato and Baby Spinach
Gratin, 222

Garlic-Soy Sauce, 346

Herb, Garlic and Lemon Rub, 344

Mediterranean Fish Soup with Garlicky
Rouille, 68

Spicy Shrimp with Garlic-Almond
Sauce, 184, **184**

Gemelli with Shrimp and Green
Peppercorns, 80, **81**

ginger

Apple Crisp with Sweet Ginger and
Macadamia Nuts, 291

Cinnamon-Ginger Cookies, 329

Gingerbread Girls, 330, **331**

Gingered Carrot Soup with Crème
Fraîche, 58, **59**

Gingery Soymilk Chai, 361

Guinness Ginger Cake, 313

Lemon Panna Cottas with Peach
Compote and Ginger Syrup, 298

Stone Wall, 357

ginger beer

Sparkling Lemongrass Coolers, 357

Stone Wall, 357

gnocchi

Sheep's-Milk Ricotta Gnocchi with
Mushrooms and Corn, 77, **77**

Spinach and Ricotta Gnocchi, 78

goat cheese

Asparagus Salad with Toasted Walnuts
and Goat Cheese, **34**, 35

Date, Goat Cheese and Pancetta on
Walnut Bread, 260, **261**

Gaucho Pizzas, 252, **253**

Goat Cheese Panna Cotta with Tomato
Salad, 16

Orecchiette with Hazelnuts and Goat
Cheese, 79

Spinach and Goat Cheese Frittata,
266, **266**

Summer Tomato Soup with Herbed
Goat Cheese, 52, **52**

Zucchini "Sandwiches" with Herbed
Goat Cheese, 15

Goulash Soup, Hearty, 70

grains. *See also* rice

Apple and Mixed Berry Crumble, 294

Blueberry Corn Cakes with Maple
Syrup, 274, **275**

Bulgur, Pomegranate and Walnut
Salad, 234, **235**

Buttery Cornmeal Pastry, 249

Crispy Cornmeal-Gruyère Muffins, 271

Fresh Corn Muffins, 269, **269**

Kasha and Noodles with Caramelized
Onions, 236

Mix-and-Match Granola, 264, **277**

Oatmeal Pancakes, 274

Quail with Sweet Pea Oatmeal and
Summer Vegetable Ragout, 118, **119**

granitas

Neapolitan Lemon Granita, 300

Strawberry Granita, 300

White Grapefruit and Star Anise
Granita, 300
Granola, Mix-and-Match, **264,** 277
**grapefruit + grapefruit juice**
Fresh Green Salad with Citrus
Vinaigrette, 32
Saluki, 354, **354**
Sawtooth Mountain Breezes, 356
White Grapefruit and Star Anise
Granita, 300
Winter Shrimp Salad with Fennel and
Ruby Grapefruit, 185
**grapes**
Braised Veal Chops with Honey and
Red Grapes, 157
Ice Wine Martini, 358
Red Grape and Coconut
Refresher, 356
**gratins**
Butternut Squash–Polenta
Gratin, 224
Celery Root–Leek Gratin, 220
Garlicky Cherry Tomato and Bread
Gratin, 252, **253**
Garlicky Potato and Baby Spinach
Gratin, 222
Rich and Creamy Salsify Gratin, 220
Roasted Brussels Sprout and Potato
Gratin, 232
Zucchini Gratin with Gruyère
Cheese, 206
**green beans**
Artichokes Simmered with Green
Beans and Bacon, 208
Green Bean Ragout with Tomatoes
and Mint, 212
Green Beans in Cherry Tomato
Sauce, 215
Green Beans with Onions and
Capers, 215
Salade Niçoise with Fennel-Dusted
Tuna, 47
Turkey and Green Bean Stir-Fry with
Peanuts, 108, **109**
**greens.** *See also* arugula; cabbage;
endives; escarole; lettuce; raddichio;
spinach

Asian Watercress Salad with
Salmon, 163
Chicken with Leafy Greens and
Lemon, 98
Cornish Hens with Shiitake and
Watercress, 117
Crisp Winter Salad with Ginger-Garlic
Vinaigrette, **32,** 33
Curried Kaleslaw, 223
Fresh Green Salad with Citrus
Vinaigrette, 32
Frisée Salad with Pears, Blue Cheese
and Hazelnuts, 36
Garlicky Broccoli Rabe with Chicken
Sausage and Peppers, 103
Lefty's Green Salad, 33
Mâche Salad with Beets, 44
Mixed Greens with Nuts and Dried
Fruit, 33
Mixed Greens with Spiced Pears and
Almonds, 35
Mixed Salad with Bacon, Blue Cheese
and Pecans, 37
Papaya, Orange and Watercress Salad
with Pancetta, 42
Pickled Asian Pear Salad with Creamy
Lemon Dressing, 41
Poached Eggs with Pancetta and
Tossed Mesclun, 267
Sautéed Sea Scallops and Mâche
Salad with Moutarde Violette, 191
Seared Scallops with Braised Collard
Greens and Cider Sauce, 194
Seared Tuna with Chimichurri Sauce
and Greens, 170, **171**
Shirred Eggs with Mushrooms and
Swiss Chard, 266, **266**
Sour Fish Soup with Napa Cabbage
and Enoki Mushrooms, **66,** 67
Spicy Kale Chowder with Andouille
Sausage, 67
Spring Peas with New Potatoes, Herbs
and Watercress, 218
Swiss Chard Salad with Garlicky
Yogurt, 39
Tricolore Salad with Walnuts and
Prosciutto, 37

# h

**halibut**
Halibut and Fall Harvest Sauté, 178
Pan-Roasted Halibut with Jalapeño
Vinaigrette, 176, **177**
Roasted Halibut with Green Olive
Sauce, 177, **177**
Seafood Capellini with Saffron, 83
**ham.** *See also* prosciutto
Asturian Pork and Beans, 154, **154**
Buttermilk Ham and Cheese
Biscuits, 276
Choucroute Bread Pudding, 251
Crispy Fresh Ham with Rum
Sauce, 156
Dulce de Leche–Glazed Ham, 157
Ham and Artichoke Panini, 262, **262**
Ham and Cheese Pizza Rustica, 254
Lentil Soup with Serrano Ham and
Arugula, **50,** 62
Porcini Risotto with Serrano Ham, 244
Hash, Fresh Corn and Blue Potato, 233
**hazelnuts**
Chocolate-Caramel Hazelnut Tart, 288
Chocolate Rosemary-Caramel Nut
Bars, 328
Frisée Salad with Pears, Blue Cheese
and Hazelnuts, 36
Frozen Hazelnut Mousse Cakes with
Armagnac, 325
Hazelnut Crescent Cookies, 329
Hazelnut–Pine Nut Cookies, 332
Nono's Mocha Praline Cake, 315
Orecchiette with Hazelnuts and Goat
Cheese, 79
Hazelnut Tuiles, 332
**herbs.** *See also specific herbs*
Escarole and Fresh Herb Salad with
Apples and Pomegranates, **30,** 35
Grilled Eggplant and Fresh Herb Salad
Subs with Parmesan, 260
Herb, Garlic and Lemon Rub, 344
Herb-and-Cheese-Filled Chicken
Thighs, 102, **103**
Herb and Onion Frittata, 268, **269**
Herbed Pork Rib Roast, **144,** 145

# index

Herb-Marinated Mushroom and Celery
Salad, 44
Herb-Roasted Rack of Lamb with
Smoky Cabernet Sauce, 135
Herb-Roasted Turkey with Maple
Gravy, **110**, 111
Mascarpone-Stuffed Roast Chicken
with Spring Herb Salad, **88**, 94
Mediterranean Country Sachets, 346
Poached Salmon in a Fresh Herb and
Spring Pea Broth, 164, **165**
Rice with Fresh Herbs, 237
Standing Rib Roast of Pork with
Tuscan Herb Sauce, 152
Tuscan Herb Sachets, 346

**honey**
Honey-Glazed Pork Shoulder with
Braised Leeks, **148**, 149
Toasted Nuts in Honey, 351

**hors d'oeuvres.** *See* starters
Hummus and Roasted Pepper
Sandwiches, Open-Faced, 262, **262**

## i

Ice Cream in Crispy Chocolate-Coconut
Cones, 335
Ice Pops, Candy Corn, 337
Ice Wine Martini, 358
Icing, Royal, 330

## j

Jam, Icebox Strawberry, 351
Jell-O, Espresso, 340, **341**

## k

**kale**
Curried Kaleslaw, 223
Spicy Kale Chowder with Andouille
Sausage, 67
Kasha and Noodles with Caramelized
Onions, 236
Ketchup, Rhubarb, 345
Kumquat and Pineapple Chutney, 350

## l

**lamb**
Braised Lamb with Giant White
Beans, 131
Cape Malay Meat Loaf, 127
Citrus-Scented Lamb Stew, 134
Coconut Lamb Curry, 134
Eggplants Stuffed with Tarragon
Lamb, 138
Gaucho Pizzas, 252, **253**
Grilled Lamb Kebabs with Smoky
Tomato Sauce, 132, **132**
Grilled Ouzo-and-Nutmeg Lamb
Chops, 133
Herb-Roasted Rack of Lamb with
Smoky Cabernet Sauce, 135
Lamb and Two-Cheese
Quesadillas, 140, **141**
Lamb Braised in Milk with Garlic and
Fennel, 131
Lamb Burgers with Cilantro-Yogurt
Sauce, 140, **141**
Lamb Chops with Mint-Cilantro
Relish, 133
Lamb Meatballs in Sour-Cherry
Sauce, 137
Lamb Schnitzel with Aioli, 134
Lamb Steaks with Milk, Honey and
Cumin Marinade, 134
Lamb Stew with Lemon, 135
Lemony Lamb Chops with
Asparagus, 133
Moroccan Lamb Burgers with
Mint-Yogurt Sauce, 140
Moroccan-Spiced Lamb-and-Rice
Meatballs, 138
Moroccan-Spiced Lamb Chops,
**132**, 133
Moussaka with Yogurt Béchamel, 139
Roast Leg of Lamb with Dried-Cherry
Sauce, **136**, 137
Slow-Braised Lamb Shanks, 130
Tagliarini with Almond-Arugula Pesto
and Meatballs, 86
Zucchini Musakka with Chickpeas and
Spiced Lamb, **204**, 205

Latkes, Supercrispy Potato, 235
Lavender-Rosemary Salt, 347

**leeks**
Baby Peas with Bacon and Crispy
Leeks, **218**, 219
Beef Tenderloin with Bacon and
Creamed Leeks, 124
Celery Root–Leek Gratin, 220
Chicken Breasts with Spinach, Leek
and Saffron Sauce, 90, **90**
Crispy Potato-Leek Rösti, 232
Honey-Glazed Pork Shoulder with
Braised Leeks, **148**, 149
Lobster with Pinot Noir Sauce, Salsify
Puree and Frizzled Leeks, 200, **201**
Smoky Sautéed Bacon and Leeks, 216

**lemongrass**
Chicken and Potato Soup with
Lemongrass, 69
Garlicky Lemongrass Chicken, 102
Ground Pork Satay on Lemongrass
Skewers, 149
Lemongrass-Scented Noodle Soup
with Shrimp, 69
Sparkling Lemongrass Coolers, 357

**lemons + lemon juice**
Citrus Chiffon Cake, 313
Citrus-Fennel Salt, 347
Citrus-Mint Cocktails, 355
Couscous with Red Lentils and Easy
Preserved Lemons, 243, **245**
Frozen Lemon Cream Sandwiches, 335
Herb, Garlic and Lemon Rub, 344
Lemon and Arugula Salad with
Parmesan Cheese, 37
Lemon Cheesecake with Olive Oil, 314
Lemon Chicken with Potatoes and
Tomatoes, 91
Lemon-Coconut Tart with Brown-
Sugar Cream, 287
Lemon Confit Chicken with Calamata
Olives, 96
Lemon Curd, 300
Lemon Curd Bread Pudding, 298
Lemon Panna Cottas with Peach
Compote and Ginger Syrup, 298
Lemon-Parmesan Veal Rolls with

Arugula Salad, 158

Lemon–Poppy Seed Cake, 274

Lemon Ricotta Cheesecake, 313

Neapolitan Lemon Granita, 300

Roast Chickens with Lemon and
Orange, 94, **95**

Roasted Peppers with Preserved
Lemon and Capers, 215

Shallot-Lemon Confit, **342**, 348

Shrimp and Lemon Skewers with
Feta-Dill Sauce, 189

Vanilla Cupcakes with Lemon Cream
and Raspberries, 324, **325**

**lentils**

Couscous with Red Lentils and Easy
Preserved Lemons, 243, **245**

Eggplant and Lentil Stew with
Pomegranate Molasses, **240**, 241

Indian Rice and Lentils with
Raita, 238

Lentil Soup with Serrano Ham and
Arugula, **50**, 62

Turkey-Date Meatballs with Lentils and
Yogurt Sauce, 108

Warm Lentils with Radishes, 241

Yellow Lentil Dal, 236

**lettuce**

BLTs on Toasted Brioche with Aioli and
Basil, 256

Fresh Green Salad with Citrus
Vinaigrette, 32

Frisée and Endive Salad with Pears and
Blue Cheese, 36

Frisée Salad with Pears, Blue Cheese
and Hazelnuts, 36

Iceberg Wedges with Blue Cheese
Dressing, 32, **32**

Korean-Style Chicken Wraps, 101

Mâche Salad with Beets, 44

Mixed Lettuces with Orange
Vinaigrette and Candied Pecans, 33

Mixed Salad with Bacon, Blue Cheese
and Pecans, 37

Pickled Asian Pear Salad with Creamy
Lemon Dressing, 41

**limes + lime juice**

Cheval, 354, **354**

Citrus Chiffon Cake, 313

Citrus-Mint Cocktails, 355

Louisville Limeade, 356

Minted Lime Syrup, 348, **349**

Pomegranate Margaritas, 356

**liver**

Crispy Fried Chicken Livers, 14

Rustic Chicken Liver Mousse, 14

**lobster**

Campofilone Pasta with Lobster and
Tomato, 82

Lobster with Pinot Noir Sauce, Salsify
Puree and Frizzled Leeks, 200, **201**

Warm Lobster Salad with Gazpacho
Consommé, 199

# m

Macadamia Nuts and Sweet Ginger,
Apple Crisp with, 291

Mâche Salad with Beets, 44

**mangoes**

Mango-Raspberry Baked Alaskas,
302, **303**

Mango Sticky Rice, 301

Spicy Chicken, Avocado and Mango
Salad, 49, **49**

Spicy Green Papaya Salad, 42, **43**

Tandoori Pork with Gingered Mango
Salad, 145

**maple syrup**

Grilled Maple-Brined Pork
Chops, 147, **147**

Maple-Pear Kuchen, 289

Roast Chicken with Black
Pepper–Maple Glaze, 93

Zucchini Bread French Toast with
Maple-Bourbon Butter, 273

Margaritas, Pomegranate, 356

Marshmallow Frosting, 338

**martinis**

Ice Wine Martini, 358

Rose Martinis, 356

Thai Martini, 358

Mascarpone-Stuffed Roast Chicken with
Spring Herb Salad, **88**, 94

Matzo Meal–Crusted Trout, 178

**meatballs**

Lamb Meatballs in Sour-Cherry
Sauce, 137

Moroccan-Spiced Lamb-and-Rice
Meatballs, 138

Parmesan-Dusted Meatballs, 28

Sweet-and-Sour Meatball Soup, 70

Tagliarini with Almond-Arugula Pesto
and Meatballs, 86

Turkey-Date Meatballs with Lentils and
Yogurt Sauce, 108

Vietnamese Grilled Pork Meatball
Sandwiches, 153

**meat loaf**

Cape Malay Meat Loaf, 127

Meat Loaf Stuffed with Prosciutto and
Spinach, 126

**melon**

Cantaloupe and Prosciutto Salad with
Ice Wine Vinaigrette, 37

Tomato and Mozzarella Salad with
Frozen Balsamic Vinaigrette, 46, **46**

Watermelon Coolers, 358, **359**

**meringues**

Brown-Sugar Meringues, 329

Meringue Phantom Cookies, 329

**milk**

Almond-Tea Milk Shakes, 361

Fried Milk, 333

Warm Almond Milk with Bananas and
Honey, 361

Minestrone, Chunky Summer, 64

**mint**

Citrus-Mint Cocktails, 355

Cucumber Salad with Mint and Crème
Fraîche, 44

Fattoush, 40

Lamb Chops with Mint-Cilantro
Relish, 133

Louisville Limeade, 356

Minted Lime Syrup, 348, **349**

Moroccan Lamb Burgers with Mint-
Yogurt Sauce, 140

Roof Garden, 355

Swordfish Steaks with Mint and
Garlic, 168, **169**

Tomato and Mint Pesto Risotto, 244

# index

miso
  Asian Coleslaw with Miso-Ginger
    Dressing, 40
  Crispy Roast Chicken and Shallots
    with Miso Gravy, 107
  Shrimp Tempura with Miso
    Mayonnaise, 23
  Wild Mushrooms with Miso, Fresh
    Herbs and Madeira, 221
molasses
  Bourbon, Orange and Molasses
    Rub, 344, **344**
  Gingerbread Girls, 330, **331**
  Guinness Ginger Cake, 313
monkfish
  Mediterranean Fish Soup with Garlicky
    Rouille, 68
  Monkfish and Chorizo Kebabs, **174**, 175
Moussaka with Yogurt Béchamel, 139
mozzarella cheese
  Cantaloupe and Prosciutto Salad with
    Ice Wine Vinaigrette, 37
  Chicken, Tomato and Mozzarella Salad
    with Spicy Basil Dressing, 92
  Creamy Fried Mozzarella Balls, 14
  Grilled Radicchio and Cheese
    Calzones, 255
  Ham and Artichoke Panini, 262, **262**
  Ham and Cheese Pizza Rustica, 254
  Lamb and Two-Cheese
    Quesadillas, 140, **141**
  Tomato and Mozzarella Salad with
    Frozen Balsamic Vinaigrette, 46, **46**
muffins
  Crispy Cornmeal-Gruyère Muffins, 271
  Fresh Corn Muffins, 269, **269**
Mung Bean Salad, Tangy, 242
Musakka, Zucchini, with Chickpeas and
  Spiced Lamb, **204**, 205
Muscat-Poached Peaches with Lemon
  Verbena, 298, **299**
mushrooms
  Bacon-Wrapped Enoki, 221, **221**
  Cornish Hens with Shiitake and
    Watercress, 117
  Creamed Cipollini Onions and
    Mushrooms, 208, **209**

Creamy Polenta with Wild Mushroom
  Ragout, 238, **239**
Fettuccine with Mushrooms and
  Prosciutto, 85
Herb-Marinated Mushroom and Celery
  Salad, 44
Mushrooms à la Grecque, **210**, 211
Mushroom Soup with Chorizo and
  Scallions, 58
Mussel Chowder with Bacon and
  Shiitake Mushrooms, 67
Porcini Risotto with Serrano Ham, 244
Potato and Wild Mushroom Soup, 59
Sautéed Corn and Shiitake Frittata
  with Parmesan, 267
Seared Steaks with Porcini Mushroom
  Cream Sauce, 124
Sheep's-Milk Ricotta Gnocchi with
  Mushrooms and Corn, 77, **77**
Shirred Eggs with Mushrooms and
  Swiss Chard, 266, **266**
Sour Fish Soup with Napa Cabbage
  and Enoki Mushrooms, **66**, 67
Soy-Marinated Chicken Thighs with
  Shiitake Mushrooms, 100
Striped Bass with Wild Mushrooms, 173
Stuffed Shiitake Mushrooms, 15
Wild Mushroom Ragout, 221
Wild Mushrooms with Miso, Fresh
  Herbs and Madeira, 221
mussels
  Chile-Steamed Mussels with Green
    Olive Crostini, 198
  Mussel and Fingerling Potato
    Salad, 196
  Mussel Chowder with Bacon and
    Shiitake Mushrooms, 67
  Mussels in Sailor's Sauce, 196, **197**
  Mussels with Tomatoes and Feta, 198
  Red Snapper with Mussels, Potatoes
    and Chorizo, **174**, 175
  Seared Cod with Spicy Mussel
    Aioli, 173
mustard
  Creole Mustard Spaetzle, **162**, 163
  Endive Salad with Grainy-Mustard
    Vinaigrette, 33

Grilled Quick-Cured Trout with
  Mustard-Olive Dressing, 179
Grilled Salmon with Mustard
  Sauce, 163
Sautéed Sea Scallops and Mâche
  Salad with Moutarde Violette, 191

# n

Nectarine and Cream Cheese Monte
  Cristos, 273
noodles. *See also* pasta
  Cold Noodles with Tofu in Peanut
    Sauce, 80
  Fresh Clam and Noodle Soup, 65
  Hot and Sour Noodle Soup with
    Pork, 64
  Kasha and Noodles with Caramelized
    Onions, 236
  Lemongrass-Scented Noodle Soup
    with Shrimp, 69
  Sea Bass with Rice Noodles in Tomato-
    Pineapple Broth, 172
  Spicy Chinese Noodles with Shrimp, 80
  Star Anise–Beef Soup, 71
  Warm Soba in Broth with Spinach and
    Tofu, 66, **66**
nuts. *See also* almonds; hazelnuts;
pecans; pine nuts; pistachios;
walnuts
  Apple Crisp with Sweet Ginger and
    Macadamia Nuts, 291
  Brussels Sprouts with Chestnuts and
    Bacon, **210**, 211
  Chestnut and Artichoke Roast, 208
  Chocolate Rosemary-Caramel Nut
    Bars, 328
  Crudités with Creamy Pistachio Dip, 11
  Dried Fruit and Toasted Nuts in Chest-
    nut Honey, 351
  Frozen Chocolate-Chestnut Pie, 284
  Mix-and-Match Granola, **264**, 277
  Mixed Greens with Nuts and Dried
    Fruit, 33
  Roasted Chestnut Soup, 60
  Strawberry and Sweet Wine Gelées
    with Candied Pistachios, 296

Toasted Nuts in Honey, 351
Wild Rice with Chestnuts and Dried
Cranberries, 237
Yogurt with Sautéed Dried Fruits and
Nuts, 302, **303**

## O

oats
Apple and Mixed Berry Crumble, 294
Mix-and-Match Granola, **264,** 277
Oatmeal Pancakes, 274
Quail with Sweet Pea Oatmeal and
Summer Vegetable Ragout, 118, **119**
Oil, Oregano, 178
okra
Okra and Tomato Stew with
Cilantro, 227
Okra in Tomato Sauce, 226
olives
Braised Swordfish with Black Olives,
Tomatoes and Marjoram, 168
Chicken Piccata with Artichokes and
Olives, 91
Chopped Fennel and Olive Salad, 38
Fennel Salad with Parmesan, 38
Green Olive Crostini, 198
Grilled Quick-Cured Trout with
Mustard-Olive Dressing, 179
Lemon Confit Chicken with Calamata
Olives, 96
Lemony Greens with Olive Oil and
Olives, 33
Pasta with Borlotti Beans, Olives and
Cherry Tomatoes, 74, **74**
Prosciutto, Tomato and Olive
Bruschetta, 15
Roasted Halibut with Green Olive
Sauce, 177, **177**
Sautéed Shrimp with Green Olives,
Scallions and Anchovies, **184,** 189
Tangy Chickpea Soup with Olives and
Anise, 64
Tuna and Green Olive Empanadas,
24, **25**
onions
Braised Artichokes with Red and White

Pearl Onions, 207
Caramelized Onion and Gruyère
Tart, 18, **19**
Caramelized Onion and Polenta
Tart, 238
Chicken Breasts with Red Onions and
Thyme, **90,** 91
Cider-Braised Chicken Legs with
Onion-Raisin Sauce, 97
Creamed Cipollini Onions and
Mushrooms, 208, **209**
Golden Gratinéed Onion Soup, 56
Green Beans with Onions and
Capers, 215
Herb and Onion Frittata, 268, **269**
Kasha and Noodles with Caramelized
Onions, 236
Mini Tartes Flambées, 18
Stuffed Onions, 210
Warm Onion Flans with Fresh Tomato
Sauce, 17
oranges + orange juice
Arugula, Fennel and Orange Salad, 37
Bitter Queen, 355
Blood Orange and Chocolate
Trifles, 297
Bourbon, Orange and Molasses Rub,
344, **344**
Candied Orange Peels, 321
Citrus Chiffon Cake, 313
Fresh Green Salad with Citrus
Vinaigrette, 32
Frozen Fruit Nougat with Citrus Sauce,
336, **336**
Orange-Almond Shortbread with
Strawberry Compote, 332
Orange and Cranberry Syrup, 348, **349**
Orange Fizz, 355
Orange-Rosemary Scones, **270,** 271
Oranges in Citrus Syrup, 297
Papaya, Orange and Watercress Salad
with Pancetta, 42
Radicchio Salad with Oranges and
Fennel, 38
Spicy Orange Shrimp Seviche, 185
Starlight, 360
Orecchiette with Hazelnuts and Goat

Cheese, 79
Oregano Oil, 178
Orzo, Tomatoes and Ginger, Scallops
with, 192, **193**
Oyster, Smoked, Po'Boys, 258

## P

pancakes
Blueberry Corn Cakes with Maple
Syrup, 274, **275**
Celery Root–Potato Pancakes with
Green Apple Sour Cream, 12, **13**
Oatmeal Pancakes, 274
Supercrispy Potato Latkes, 235
Zucchini Cakes, 207
pancetta
Caramelized Cauliflower with Pancetta
and Spinach, 219
Date, Goat Cheese and Pancetta on
Walnut Bread, 260, **261**
Midnight Pasta with Tuna, Pancetta
and Spinach, 83
Pancetta-Beef Burgers with
Horseradish Ketchup, 123
Papaya, Orange and Watercress Salad
with Pancetta, 42
Poached Eggs with Pancetta and
Tossed Mesclun, 267
Roasted Persimmons Wrapped in
Pancetta, 28
Sausage and Broccoli Rabe Burgers,
154, **154**
Savoy Cabbage and Pancetta, 216
Shrimp BLTs, 23
Spaghetti with Creamy Pancetta
Sauce, 85
panna cotta
Goat Cheese Panna Cotta with Tomato
Salad, 16
Lemon Panna Cottas with Peach
Compote and Ginger Syrup, 298
papaya
Papaya, Orange and Watercress Salad
with Pancetta, 42
Spicy Green Papaya Salad, 42, **43**

# index

Pappardelle with Red Wine and Meat Ragù, 86, **87**

Paprika-Glazed Turkey, 112

**Parmesan cheese**

Butternut Squash–Polenta Gratin, 224

Celery Root–Leek Gratin, 220

Chopped Fennel and Olive Salad, 38

Fennel Salad with Parmesan, 38

Grilled Eggplant and Fresh Herb Salad Subs with Parmesan, 260

Herb-and-Cheese-Filled Chicken Thighs, 102, **103**

Lemon and Arugula Salad with Parmesan Cheese, 37

Lemon-Parmesan Veal Rolls with Arugula Salad, 158

Parmesan-Dusted Meatballs, 28

Parmesan-Prosciutto Biscotti, 250

Spaghetti with Browned Butter and Crispy Bread Crumbs, 79

**parsley**

Fattoush, 40

Fettuccine with Walnut-Parsley Pesto, 76

Grilled Dorado with Walnut and Parsley Pesto, 180

Grilled Skirt Steak with Chimichurri Sauce, **122**, 123

Seared Tuna with Chimichurri Sauce and Greens, 170, **171**

**parsnips**

Buttery Root Vegetable Ragout, 226

Roasted Parsnips with Horseradish-Herb Butter, 226

Sautéed Shrimp and Tarragon with Parsnip Puree, 190

Shepherd's Pie with Parsnip Puree Topping, 112

**pasta**, 72–88. *See also* couscous, noodles

Campofilone Pasta with Lobster and Tomato, 82

Cavatelli with Spicy Winter Squash, 74, **74**

Farfalle with Creamy Smoked Salmon and Vodka Sauce, 84, **84**

Fettuccine with Mushrooms and Prosciutto, 85

Fettuccine with Shrimp, Asparagus and Peas, 82

Fettuccine with Walnut-Parsley Pesto, 76

Fresh Pasta with Spicy Corn and Asparagus, **72**, 78

Gemelli with Shrimp and Green Peppercorns, 80, **81**

Midnight Pasta with Tuna, Pancetta and Spinach, 83

Orecchiette with Hazelnuts and Goat Cheese, 79

Pappardelle with Red Wine and Meat Ragù, 86, **87**

Pasta Shells with Swordfish, **84**, 85

Pasta with Borlotti Beans, Olives and Cherry Tomatoes, 74, **74**

Penne all'Arrabbiata, 75

Penne with Zucchini and Basil, 76, **77**

Roasted Tomatoes with Penne and Ricotta Salata, 75

Sardinian Clams with Fregola, 195

Scallops with Orzo, Tomatoes and Ginger, 192, **193**

Seafood Capellini with Saffron, 83

Sheep's-Milk Ricotta Gnocchi with Mushrooms and Corn, 77, **77**

Spaghetti with Browned Butter and Crispy Bread Crumbs, 79

Spaghetti with Creamy Pancetta Sauce, 85

Spaghetti with Curried Seafood Marinara, 83

Spaghetti with Shrimp and Spicy Tomato Sauce, 80

Spinach and Ricotta Gnocchi, 78

Tagliarini with Almond-Arugula Pesto and Meatballs, 86

Tagliolini with Eggplant and Mint, 76

Whole Wheat Spaghetti with Fresh Ricotta and Lemon Zest, 75

**pastry**

Buttery Cornmeal Pastry, 249

Crème Fraîche Pastry, 294

Flaky Turnover Pastry, 272

Tender-Flaky Pastry, 296

**peaches**

Lemon Panna Cottas with Peach Compote and Ginger Syrup, 298

Muscat-Poached Peaches with Lemon Verbena, 298, **299**

Peach and Berry Croustades, **292**, 293

**peanut butter**

Cold Noodles with Tofu in Peanut Sauce, 80

Double Dark Chocolate Cupcakes with Peanut Butter Filling, 322, **323**

**pears + pear juice**

Asian Spinach Salad with Sausage and Pears, 48

Bubbling Cauldron Cocktails, 358

Cranberry, Quince and Pear Chutney, 350

Frisée and Endive Salad with Pears and Blue Cheese, 36

Frisée Salad with Pears, Blue Cheese and Hazelnuts, 36

Maple-Pear Kuchen, 289

Mixed Greens with Nuts and Dried Fruit, 33

Mixed Greens with Spiced Pears and Almonds, 35

Pickled Asian Pear Salad with Creamy Lemon Dressing, 41

Ricotta and Prosecco-Poached Pear Crostatas, 293

Vanilla Pear Mimosa, 354

**peas**

Baby Peas with Bacon and Crispy Leeks, **218**, 219

Chilled Tomato Soup with Sweet Pea Puree, 53

Chunky Summer Minestrone, 64

Corn and Pea Risotto, 245, **245**

Fettuccine with Shrimp, Asparagus and Peas, 82

Four Pea Salad with Scallops, 192

Indian-Spiced Sea Bass with Spinach, Peas and Carrots, 172

Israeli Couscous with Peas and Mint, 243

Poached Salmon in a Fresh Herb and Spring Pea Broth, 164, **165**

Quail with Sweet Pea Oatmeal and
    Summer Vegetable Ragout, 118, **119**
Smoky Black-Eyed Peas, 242
Spring Peas with New Potatoes, Herbs
    and Watercress, 218
pecans
    Carrot Cupcakes with Caramel and
        Cream Cheese Frosting, 324, **325**
    Chocolate-Pecan Brownie Cake with
        Glossy Chocolate Glaze, 316
    Crab Salad with Apple, Endives and
        Pecans, 47
    Crispy Witches' Hats, 326
    Georgia Pecan Pie, 280, **280**
    Mixed Greens with Nuts and Dried
        Fruit, 33
    Mixed Lettuces with Orange
        Vinaigrette and Candied Pecans, 33
    Mixed Salad with Bacon, Blue Cheese
        and Pecans, 37
    Pecan-Crusted Beef Tenderloin with
        Juniper Jus, **120**, 125
    Pecan-Spice Cake with Caramel
        Frosting, 310, **311**
    Sour Cream–Pecan Scones, 271
    Toasted Rosemary Pecans, 11
Penne all'Arrabbiata, 75
Penne with Zucchini and Basil, 76, **77**
Peppercorn Beef with Gorgonzola
    Cheese, 125
Peppercorn Salt, 347
peppers. *See also* chiles
    Basque Chicken and Chorizo Sauté,
        98, **99**
    Cranberry Bean Stew with Potatoes
        and Bell Peppers, 230, **230**
    Crispy Fresh Ham with Rum Sauce, 156
    Garlicky Broccoli Rabe with Sausage
        and Peppers, 103
    Greek Salad with Garlicky Pita
        Toasts, 40
    Open-Faced Roasted Pepper and Hum-
        mus Sandwiches, 262, **262**
    Pan-Roasted Pork with Apple Chutney
        and Pepper Relish, 146, **147**
    Roasted Chicken Legs with Garlicky
        Potatoes and Peppers, 97

Roasted Peppers with Preserved
    Lemon and Capers, 215
Romesco Sauce, 268
Sofrito, 157
Sweet-and-Sour Swordfish, **160**, 168
Tiny Peppers in Cherry Tomato Sauce,
    **214**, 215
Turkish Chopped Salad, 39
Warm Lobster Salad with Gazpacho
    Consommé, 199
Yellow Pepper and Almond Soup, 54
Persimmons, Roasted, Wrapped in
    Pancetta, 28
pesto
    Charred Poblano and Garlic Pesto, 346
    Fettuccine with Walnut-Parsley
        Pesto, 76
    Grilled Dorado with Walnut and Parsley
        Pesto, 180
    Tagliarini with Almond-Arugula Pesto
        and Meatballs, 86
    Tomato and Mint Pesto Risotto, 244
Phyllo Apple-Plum Strudel, 291
pickles
    Green-Tomato Pickle, 227
    Quick Pickled Carrots, 153
    Sichuan Pickled Cucumbers, 348
pies and tarts (savory)
    Asparagus and Smoked Salmon
        Tart, 276
    Caramelized Onion and Gruyère
        Tart, 18, **19**
    Caramelized Onion and Polenta
        Tart, 238
    Caviar and Potato Salad Tartlets, 16
    Duck Confit Potpie, 115, **116**
    Mini Tartes Flambées, 18
    Shepherd's Pie with Parsnip Puree
        Topping, 112
pies and tarts (sweet). *See also* desserts
    Butterscotch Mousse Pie, 280, **280**
    Chocolate-Caramel Hazelnut Tart, 288
    Fresh Raspberry Tart, **278**, 286
    Frozen Chocolate-Chestnut Pie, 284
    Georgia Pecan Pie, 280, **280**
    Lattice-Topped Apple Pie, **282**, 283
    Lattice-Topped Blackberry Tart, 287

Lemon-Coconut Tart with Brown-
    Sugar Cream, 287
Maple-Pear Kuchen, 289
Prune-Custard Tart, 288
Pumpkin Meringue Puff Pie, 284, **285**
Sweet Potato Chiffon Pie, 281
pineapples + pineapple juice
    Coconut-Pineapple Batida, 360
    Jade Cocktail, 360
    Kumquat and Pineapple Chutney, 350
    Pineapple-Mint Relish, 13
    Pineapple Shortcakes with Dulce
        de Leche Whipped Cream, 301
    Sea Bass with Rice Noodles in Tomato-
        Pineapple Broth, 172
    Sugar Baby, 355
pine nuts
    Cauliflower with Pine Nut Crumble, 219
    Hazelnut–Pine Nut Cookies, 332
    Pine Nut–Butter Cookies, 331
pistachios
    Chocolate Rosemary-Caramel Nut
        Bars, 328
    Crudités with Creamy Pistachio Dip, 11
    Frozen Fruit Nougat with Citrus
        Sauce, 336, **336**
    Frozen Lemon Cream Sandwiches, 335
    Pistachio-Cranberry Biscotti, 335
    Strawberry and Sweet Wine Gelées
        with Candied Pistachios, 296
pizzas and calzones
    Crispy Pizza Dough, 254
    Gaucho Pizzas, 252, 253
    Grilled Radicchio and Cheese
        Calzones, 255
    Ham and Cheese Pizza Rustica, 254
    Spinach and Artichoke Pizzas, 254
plums
    Phyllo Apple-Plum Strudel, 291
    Po'Boys, Smoked Oyster, 258
polenta
    Butternut Squash–Polenta Gratin, 224
    Caramelized Onion and Polenta
        Tart, 238
    Creamy Polenta with Wild Mushroom
        Ragout, 238, **239**
    Very Soft Polenta with Rock Shrimp

# index

Ragout, **188,** 189

**pomegranate molasses**

Bulgur, Pomegranate and Walnut
Salad, 234, **235**

Eggplant and Lentil Stew with
Pomegranate Molasses, **240,** 241

Roast Chickens with Lebanese Rice
and Pomegranate Jus, 94

Tangy Mung Bean Salad, 242

Turkish Chopped Salad, 39

**pomegranates + pomegranite juice**

Bulgur, Pomegranate and Walnut
Salad, 234, **235**

Escarole and Fresh Herb Salad with
Apples and Pomegranates, **30,** 35

Hollow Hills, 354

Iced Pomegranate-Fennel Green
Tea, 360

Pomegranate Margaritas, 356

Pompano, Pan-Fried, with Tomato-
Caraway Glaze, 179

**poppy seeds**

Lemon—Poppy Seed Cake, 274

Porcini Risotto with Serrano Ham, 244

**pork.** *See also* bacon; ham; pork
sausages

Cassoulet with Bacon, Andouille and
Country Ribs, 146

Grilled Maple-Brined Pork Chops,
147, **147**

Ground Pork Satay on Lemongrass
Skewers, 149

Herbed Pork Rib Roast, **144,** 145

Honey-Glazed Pork Shoulder with
Braised Leeks, **148,** 149

Hot and Sour Noodle Soup with
Pork, 64

Meat Loaf Stuffed with Prosciutto and
Spinach, 126

Meat-Stuffed Poblanos with Cilantro-
Lime Sauce, 127

Mini Vietnamese Pork and Pickle
Sandwiches, 259

Pan-Roasted Pork with Apple Chutney
and Pepper Relish, 146, **147**

Parmesan-Dusted Meatballs, 28

Pork and Chickpea Stew with Orange

and Cumin, 148, **148**

Pork Medallions with Tangerine-Chile
Pan Sauce, 145

Roast Bacon-Wrapped Pork, **142,** 145

Roast Pork Loin with Armagnac-Prune
Sauce, 144, **144**

Seared Pork and Pickled Eggplant
Panini, 258

Standing Rib Roast of Pork with
Tuscan Herb Sauce, 152

Stir-Fried Pork with Ginger and
Basil, 149

Sweet-and-Sour Meatball Soup, 70

Sweet-and-Spicy Pork Ribs, 151

Tagliarini with Almond-Arugula Pesto
and Meatballs, 86

Tandoori Pork with Gingered Mango
Salad, 145

Tuscan Baby Back Ribs, 152

Tuscan-Style Spareribs with Balsamic
Glaze, **150,** 151

Vietnamese Grilled Pork Meatball
Sandwiches, 153

**pork sausages**

Asturian Pork and Beans, 154, **154**

Basque Chicken and Chorizo
Sauté, 98, **99**

Carrots with Sausage and Rosemary,
217, **218**

Cassoulet with Bacon, Andouille and
Country Ribs, 146

Chorizos Braised in Hard Cider, 156

Choucroute Bread Pudding, 251

Clams with Spicy Sausage, **194,** 195

Garbanzo Soup with Chorizo and
Smoked Paprika, **62,** 63

Grilled Cheese and Chorizo
Sandwiches, **246,** 259

Hearty Fennel Soup with Sausage and
Gouda Croutons, 58, **59**

Mini Vietnamese Pork and Pickle
Sandwiches, 259

Monkfish and Chorizo Kebabs, **174,** 175

Mushroom Soup with Chorizo and
Scallions, 58

Red Snapper with Mussels, Potatoes
and Chorizo, **174,** 175

Sausage and Broccoli Rabe Burgers,
154, **154**

Sausage Burgers with Grilled Green
Chiles, 155

Spicy Kale Chowder with Andouille
Sausage, 67

Potato Chip Crust, Hoosier Chicken
with, 92

**potatoes.** *See also* sweet potatoes

Asparagus and Potato Salad with
Riesling-Tarragon Vinaigrette, 212

Caviar and Potato Salad Tartlets, 16

Celery Root–Potato Pancakes with
Green Apple Sour Cream, 12, **13**

Cherrystone Clam Chowder with
Corn, 65

Chicken and Potato Soup with Lemongrass, 69

Cranberry Bean Stew with Potatoes
and Bell Peppers, 230, **230**

Crisp Herb-Roasted Fingerlings with
Scallions, **228,** 231

Crispy Potato-Leek Rösti, 232

Crusty Potato Frittatas with Romesco
Sauce, 268

Fresh Corn and Blue Potato Hash, 233

Garlicky Potato and Baby Spinach
Gratin, 222

Grilled Potatoes with Garlic Aioli, 231

Hobo Potatoes with Fennel and
Herbs, 232

Idaho Potato Chips, 10, **10**

Ikarian Potato Salad with Purslane, 231

Lemon Chicken with Potatoes and
Tomatoes, 91

Mashed Yukon Golds with Chives, 233

Mussel and Fingerling Potato Salad, 196

Oven Fries with Garlic and Parsley,
230, **230**

Pan-Fried Potato Samosas, 233

Potato and Wild Mushroom Soup, 59

Potato Salad with Bacon and
Tomatoes, 231

Red Skin Potato Mash, 233

Red Snapper with Mussels, Potatoes
and Chorizo, **174,** 175

Roasted Brussels Sprout and Potato

Gratin, 232

Roasted Chestnut Soup, 60

Roasted Chicken Legs with Garlicky
Potatoes and Peppers, 97

Roasted Fish with Charmoula,
Tomatoes and Potatoes, 174

Salade Niçoise with Fennel-Dusted
Tuna, 47

Spring Peas with New Potatoes, Herbs
and Watercress, 218

Supercrispy Potato Latkes, 235

poultry, 88–119. *See also* chicken; duck;
turkey

Cornish Hens with Shiitake and
Watercress, 117

Quail with Sweet Pea Oatmeal and
Summer Vegetable Ragout, 118, **119**

Roasted Quail with Corn Bread Stuffing and Port-Orange Sauce, 117

Prawns, King, Spicy, 186

prosciutto

Cantaloupe and Prosciutto Salad with
Ice Wine Vinaigrette, 37

Chicken Stuffed with Prosciutto,
Spinach and Boursin, 96

Fettuccine with Mushrooms and
Prosciutto, 85

Meat Loaf Stuffed with Prosciutto and
Spinach, 126

Parmesan-Prosciutto Biscotti, 250

Prosciutto, Tomato and Olive
Bruschetta, 15

Roasted Endives with Prosciutto, 223

Tricolore Salad with Walnuts and
Prosciutto, 37

prosecco

Ricotta and Prosecco-Poached Pear
Crostadas, 293

Vanilla Pear Mimosa, 354

prunes

Prune-Custard Tart, 288

Roast Pork Loin with Armagnac-Prune
Sauce, 144, **144**

Spiced Prune Chutney, 350

Spiced Turkey Tagine with Prunes, 106

puddings. *See also* bread puddings

Brûléed Rice Pudding, 337

Moroccan Rice Pudding with Toasted
Almonds, **336,** 337

Pumpkin Pudding with Candied Ginger
Whipped Cream, 338

Red Apple Inn Corn Pudding, 225

Rice Pudding with Strawberries, 297

pumpkin

Pumpkin Meringue Puff Pie, 284, **285**

Pumpkin Pudding with Candied Ginger
Whipped Cream, 338

pumpkin seeds

Pumpkin Seed Bread Salad, 255

Sautéed Trout Fillets with a Pumpkin
Seed Crust, 178

Purslane, Ikarian Potato Salad with, 231

q

quail

Quail with Sweet Pea Oatmeal and
Summer Vegetable Ragout, 118, **119**

Roasted Quail with Corn Bread
Stuffing and Port-Orange Sauce, 117

Quesadillas, Lamb and Two-Cheese,
140, **141**

Quince, Cranberry and Pear Chutney, 350

r

radicchio

Crisp Winter Salad with Ginger-Garlic
Vinaigrette, **32,** 33

Frisée Salad with Pears, Blue Cheese
and Hazelnuts, 36

Grilled Radicchio and Cheese
Calzones, 255

Radicchio Salad with Oranges and
Fennel, 38

Tricolore Salad with Walnuts and
Prosciutto, 37

radishes

Market Radish Soup with Balsamic
Cherries, 52, 52

Warm Lentils with Radishes, 241

raisins

Bread Stuffing with Apple, Raisins and

Marmalade, 250

Carrot Cupcakes with Caramel and
Cream Cheese Frosting, 324, **325**

Cider-Braised Chicken Legs with
Onion-Raisin Sauce, 97

Mushrooms à la Grecque, **210,** 211

raspberries

Apple and Mixed Berry Crumble, 294

Fresh Raspberry Tart, **278,** 286

Gramma's Buttermilk Biscuits with
Berries and Ice Cream, 295, **295**

Mango-Raspberry Baked Alaskas,
302, **303**

Peach and Berry Croustades, **292,** 293

Vanilla Cupcakes with Lemon Cream
and Raspberries, 324, **325**

red snapper

Red Snapper with Mussels, Potatoes
and Chorizo, **174,** 175

Roasted Whole Snapper with Tomato-
Bread Salad, 175

Sour Fish Soup with Napa Cabbage
and Enoki Mushrooms, **66,** 67

relishes

Almost-Instant Heirloom
Tomato–Basil Relish, 350

Pineapple-Mint Relish, 13

rhubarb

Rhubarb Ketchup, 345

Strawberry-Rhubarb Galette, 296

rice

Brûléed Rice Pudding, 337

Caribbean Rice and Beans, 237

Corn and Pea Risotto, 245, **245**

Fragrant Basmati Rice, 237

Indian Rice and Lentils with Raita, 238

Indian-Style Shrimp and Rice Pilaf,
187, **187**

Mango Sticky Rice, 301

Moroccan Rice Pudding with Toasted
Almonds, **336,** 337

Moroccan-Spiced Lamb-and-Rice
Meatballs, 138

Porcini Risotto with Serrano Ham, 244

Rice-and-Dill-Stuffed Zucchini, 205

Rice Pudding with Strawberries, 297

Rice with Fresh Herbs, 237

# index

Roast Chickens with Lebanese Rice and Pomegranate Jus, 94

Summer Vegetable Rice, 237

Tomato and Mint Pesto Risotto, 244

Wild Rice with Chestnuts and Dried Cranberries, 237

**ricotta cheese**

Blood Orange and Chocolate Trifles, 297

Ham and Cheese Pizza Rustica, 254

Lemon Ricotta Cheesecake, 313

Ricotta and Prosecco-Poached Pear Crostatas, 293

Sheep's-Milk Ricotta Gnocchi with Mushrooms and Corn, 77, **77**

Spinach and Ricotta Gnocchi, 78

Sugar-Dusted Vanilla Ricotta Fritters, 333

Whole Wheat Spaghetti with Fresh Ricotta and Lemon Zest, 75

**ricotta salata cheese**

Roasted Tomatoes with Penne and Ricotta Salata, 75

**risotto**

Corn and Pea Risotto, 245, **245**

Porcini Risotto with Serrano Ham, 244

Tomato and Mint Pesto Risotto, 244

Rolls, Dinner, Light and Buttery, Auntie Buck's, 249

Romesco Sauce, 268

Roquefort Bread Puddings, 251

**rosemary**

Lavender-Rosemary Salt, 347

Orange-Rosemary Scones, **270**, 271

Toasted Rosemary Pecans, 11

Rösti, Crispy Potato-Leek, 232

**rubs**

Bourbon, Orange and Molasses Rub, 344, **344**

Herb, Garlic and Lemon Rub, 344

Moroccan Spice Rub, 344

Sesame-Soy Rub, 345

**rum**

Crispy Fresh Ham with Rum Sauce, 156

Fahrenheit 5, 358

Rum-Mocha Walnut Layer

Cake, 316, **317**

Sparkling Lemongrass Coolers, 357

Spice, 358

Star of India, 357

Stone Wall, 357

Thai Martini, 358

Watermelon Coolers, 358

# S

**sachets**

Mediterranean Country Sachets, 346

Moroccan Spice Sachets, 347

Tuscan Herb Sachets, 347

Saffron Cooler, **352**, 357

**sake**

Green My Eyes, 360

Sake-Steamed Clams, **194**, 196

Saketini, Almond, 360

**salads, 30–49**

Apple Salad with Cabrales Cheese and Toasted Almonds, 36

Arugula, Fennel and Orange Salad, 37

Asian Coleslaw with Miso-Ginger Dressing, 40

Asian Eggplant Salad, 44

Asian Spinach Salad with Sausage and Pears, 48

Asian Watercress Salad with Salmon, 163

Asparagus and Potato Salad with Riesling-Tarragon Vinaigrette, 212

Asparagus Salad with Toasted Walnuts and Goat Cheese, **34**, 35

Bulgur, Pomegranate and Walnut Salad, 234, **235**

Cantaloupe and Prosciutto Salad with Ice Wine Vinaigrette, 37

Chicken, Tomato and Mozzarella Salad with Spicy Basil Dressing, 92

Chicken Salad with Poblano Vinaigrette, 102

Chickpea Puree with Fennel Salad, 38

Chipotle-Spiked Winter Squash and Black Bean Salad, 224, **225**

Chopped Fennel and Olive Salad, 38

Corn Bread Salad with Tomatoes and

Pepper Jack Cheese, 45

Crab Salad with Apple, Endives and Pecans, 47

Crisp Winter Salad with Ginger-Garlic Vinaigrette, **32**, 33

Cucumber Salad with Mint and Crème Fraîche, 44

Curried Kaleslaw, 223

Eggplant Salad with Cumin and Fresh Herbs, 204

Endive Salad with Grainy-Mustard Vinaigrette, 33

Escarole and Fresh Herb Salad with Apples and Pomegranates, **30**, 35

Escarole and Tomato Salad with Shaved Piave Cheese, 45

Fattoush, 40

Fennel Salad with Parmesan, 38

Feta, Tomato and Red Onion Salad, 39, **41**

Four Pea Salad with Scallops, 192

Fresh Green Salad with Citrus Vinaigrette, 32

Frisée and Endive Salad with Pears and Blue Cheese, 36

Frisée Salad with Pears, Blue Cheese and Hazelnuts, 36

Greek Salad with Garlicky Pita Toasts, 40

Grilled Chili-Rubbed Steak Salad with Roasted Shallot Vinaigrette, 48

Grilled Shrimp and Chayote Salad with Chili-Garlic Dressing, 186

Herb-Marinated Mushroom and Celery Salad, 44

Iceberg Wedges with Blue Cheese Dressing, 32, **32**

Ikarian Potato Salad with Purslane, 231

Lefty's Green Salad, 33

Lemon and Arugula Salad with Parmesan Cheese, 37

Lemony Greens with Olive Oil and Olives, 33

Mâche Salad with Beets, 44

Mixed Greens with Nuts and Dried Fruit, 33

Mixed Greens with Spiced Pears and

Almonds, 35

Mixed Lettuces with Orange Vinaigrette and Candied Pecans, 33

Mixed Salad with Bacon, Blue Cheese and Pecans, 37

Mussel and Fingerling Potato Salad, 196

Papaya, Orange and Watercress Salad with Pancetta, 42

Pickled Asian Pear Salad with Creamy Lemon Dressing, 41

Potato Salad with Bacon and Tomatoes, 231

Radicchio Salad with Oranges and Fennel, 38

Salade Niçoise with Fennel-Dusted Tuna, 47

Sautéed Sea Scallops and Mâche Salad with Moutarde Violette, 191

Sesame-Crusted Tofu Salad with Citrus Vinaigrette, 41, **41**

Spicy Chicken, Avocado and Mango Salad, 49, **49**

Spicy Green Papaya Salad, 42, **43**

Swiss Chard Salad with Garlicky Yogurt, 39

Tangy Mung Bean Salad, 242

Tangy Tomatillo Salad with Sun-Dried Tomatoes, 46, **46**

Tomato and Mozzarella Salad with Frozen Balsamic Vinaigrette, 46, **46**

Tomato Salad with Scallions and Balsamic Dressing, 45

Tricolore Salad with Walnuts and Prosciutto, 37

Turkish Chopped Salad, 39

Warm Lobster Salad with Gazpacho Consommé, 199

Warm Succotash Salad, 49, **49**

Winter Shrimp Salad with Fennel and Ruby Grapefruit, 185

**salmon**

Asian Watercress Salad with Salmon, 163

Asparagus and Smoked Salmon Tart, 276

Farfalle with Creamy Smoked Salmon

and Vodka Sauce, 84, **84**

Grilled Salmon with Mustard Sauce, 163

Pan-Fried Salmon Burgers with Cabbage Slaw and Avocado Aioli, 164, **165**

Poached Salmon in a Fresh Herb and Spring Pea Broth, 164, **165**

Salmon Niçoise Sandwiches, 258

Salmon Rolls with Fennel and Creole Mustard Spaetzle, 162, **162**

Salmon with Saffron-Braised Cucumber and Fennel, 162, **162**

Salmon with Scotch Bonnet–Herb Sauce and Onion Toasts, **166**, 167

Smoked Salmon and Celery Root Bisque, 68

Smoked Salmon Soufflés with Gingered Salad, 22

Smoked Salmon Spirals, 21

Smoked Salmon–Stufffed Puffs, **20**, 21

Steamed Ginger Salmon with Stir-Fried Bok Choy, 167

**salsify**

Lobster with Pinot Noir Sauce, Salsify Puree and Frizzled Leeks, 200, **201**

Rich and Creamy Salsify Gratin, 220

**salts**

Citrus-Fennel Salt, 347

Lavender-Rosemary Salt, 347

Peppercorn Salt, 347

Samosas, Pan-Fried Potato, 233

**sandwiches.** *See also* burgers

BLTs on Toasted Brioche with Aioli and Basil, 256

Date, Goat Cheese and Pancetta on Walnut-Raisin Bread, 260, **261**

Egg Salad with Capers and Spinach on Toasted Brioche, 263

Grilled Cheese and Chorizo Sandwiches, **246**, 259

Grilled Chicken Sandwiches with Remoulade and Shaved Lemon, 257

Grilled Chili-Steak Salad Sandwich (variation), 48

Grilled Eggplant and Fresh Herb Salad Subs with Parmesan, 260

Grilled Skirt Steak and Gorgonzola Sandwiches, 257

Ham and Artichoke Panini, **262**, 262

Indian-Spiced Chicken Salad Sandwiches, 257

Mini Vietnamese Pork and Pickle Sandwiches, 259

Nectarine and Cream Cheese Monte Cristos, 273

Open-Faced Roasted Pepper and Hummus Sandwiches, 262, **262**

Roast Beef with Braised-Celery-and-Chile Relish on Ciabatta, 256

Salmon Niçoise Sandwiches, 258

Seared Pork and Pickled Eggplant Panini, 258

Smoked Oyster Po'Boys, 258

Smoked Trout and Bacon Pitas, 256

Summer Squash Sandwiches with Pecorino Butter, 263

Vietnamese Grilled Pork Meatball Sandwiches, 153

Sangria, Midtown, 358

Sardines, Broiled, with Mustard-Shallot Crumbs, 26

**sauces**

Charred Poblano and Garlic Pesto, 346

Garlic-Soy Sauce, 346

Red Chile BBQ Sauce, 345

Red Wine–Carrot Sauce, 345

Rhubarb Ketchup, 345

Romesco Sauce, 268

Tamarind-Date Dipping Sauce, 234

**sausages.** *See* chicken sausages; pork sausages

**scallops**

Celery Root Remoulade with Scallops and Caviar, 195

Four Pea Salad with Scallops, 192

Sautéed Sea Scallops and Mâche Salad with Moutarde Violette, 191

Scallops, Corn and Basil Steamed in Foil, 192

Scallops Steamed in Sake and Riesling, 26

Scallops with Orzo, Tomatoes and Ginger, 192, **193**

# index

Seared Scallops with Braised Collard
Greens and Cider Sauce, 194
Sea Scallops with Spinach and Grape
Tomatoes, 191
Spaghetti with Curried Seafood
Marinara, 83
Spice-Crusted Scallops with Crisp
Capers, 193, **193**

**scones**
Orange-Rosemary Scones, **270**, 271
Sour Cream–Pecan Scones, 271

**sea bass**
Creole-Style Sea Bass Fillets, 171
Grilled Whole Fish with Curried Yogurt
Marinade, 180
Indian-Spiced Sea Bass with Spinach,
Peas and Carrots, 172
Salt-Baked Sea Bass with Warm
Tomato Vinaigrette, 171
Sea Bass with Rice Noodles in Tomato-
Pineapple Broth, 172
Vermentino-Braised Sea Bass, 170

**seafood.** *See* fish; shellfish
Semolina Cakes with Fig Compote,
308, **308**

**sesame seeds**
Sesame-Coated Sweet Potato
Croquettes, 12, **13**
Sesame-Crusted Tofu Salad with
Citrus Vinaigrette, 41
Sesame-Crusted Tuna Steaks, 170, **171**
Sesame-Soy Rub, 345

Seviche, Spicy Orange Shrimp, 185

**shallots**
Crispy Roast Chicken and Shallots
with Miso Gravy, 107
Grilled Chili-Rubbed Steak Salad with
Roasted Shallot Vinaigrette, 48
Shallot-Lemon Confit, **342**, 348
Tuna Rolls with Roasted
Shallot–Wasabi Sauce, 20, **20**

**shellfish, 182–201.** *See also* scallops;
shrimp
Campofilone Pasta with Lobster and
Tomato, 82
Cherrystone Clam Chowder with
Corn, 65

Chile-Steamed Mussels with Green
Olive Crostini, 198
Clams with Spicy Sausage, **194**, 195
Crab and Corn Beignets, 28, **29**
Crab Salad with Apple, Endives and
Pecans, 47
Deviled Crab Omelets, 267
Fresh Clam and Noodle Soup, 65
Lobster with Pinot Noir Sauce, Salsify
Puree and Frizzled Leeks, 200, **201**
Mussel and Fingerling Potato
Salad, 196
Mussel Chowder with Bacon and
Shiitake Mushrooms, 67
Mussels in Sailor's Sauce, 196, **197**
Mussels with Tomatoes and Feta, 198
Pan-Fried Asian-Style Crab
Burgers, 198
Red Snapper with Mussels, Potatoes
and Chorizo, **174**, 175
Sake-Steamed Clams, **194**, 196
Sardinian Clams with Fregola, 195
Seared Cod with Spicy Mussel
Aioli, 173
Smoked Oyster Po'Boys, 258
Spaghetti with Curried Seafood
Marinara, 83
Warm Crab Dip with Fresh Herbs, 11
Warm Lobster Salad with Gazpacho
Consommé, 199

Shepherd's Pie with Parsnip Puree
Topping, 112
Shortbread, Orange-Almond, with
Strawberry Compote, 332
Shortcakes, Pineapple, with Dulce de
Leche Whipped Cream, 301

**shrimp**
Armagnac-Doused Shrimp, 22
Curried Shrimp and Carrot
Bouillabaisse, 190
Fettuccine with Shrimp, Asparagus
and Peas, 82
Gemelli with Shrimp and Green
Peppercorns, 80, **81**
Grilled Shrimp and Chayote Salad with
Chili-Garlic Dressing, 186
Grilled Shrimp and Corn

Wraps, 186, **187**
Grilled Yucatán Shrimp, 190
Indian-Style Shrimp and Rice
Pilaf, 187, **187**
Lemongrass-Scented Noodle Soup
with Shrimp, 69
Mexican Shrimp Cocktail, 23
Pan-Fried Shrimp with Lemon and
Ouzo, 190
Sautéed Shrimp and Tarragon with
Parsnip Puree, 190
Sautéed Shrimp with Green Olives,
Scallions and Anchovies, **184**, 189
Seafood Capellini with Saffron, 83
Shrimp and Broccoli with Honey-
Walnut Caramel Sauce, **182**, 184
Shrimp and Chicken Summer Rolls, 24
Shrimp and Lemon Skewers with
Feta-Dill Sauce, 189
Shrimp BLTs, 23
Shrimp Tempura with Miso
Mayonnaise, 23
Spaghetti with Curried Seafood
Marinara, 83
Spaghetti with Shrimp and Spicy
Tomato Sauce, 80
Spicy Chinese Noodles with
Shrimp, 80
Spicy King Prawns, 186
Spicy Orange Shrimp Seviche, 185
Spicy Shrimp with Garlic-Almond
Sauce, 184, **184**
Very Soft Polenta with Rock Shrimp
Ragout, **188**, 189
Winter Shrimp Salad with Fennel and
Ruby Grapefruit, 185

**slaws**
Asian Coleslaw with Miso-Ginger
Dressing, 40
Curried Kaleslaw, 223

Sofrito, 157

**soufflés**
Apricot and Almond Soufflés,
304, **305**
Bread Pudding Soufflé with Bourbon
Sauce, 338
Smoked Salmon Soufflés with

Gingered Salad, 22

soups, 50–71

Asparagus Soup with Lemon-Herb
Crème Fraîche, 55

Cannellini Bean and Escarole Soup, 60

Cherrystone Clam Chowder with
Corn, 65

Chicken and Potato Soup with
Lemongrass, 69

Chicken Soup with Passatelli, 64

Chilled Cucumber Soup with Pickled
Red Onion, 54

Chilled Tomato Soup with Sweet Pea
Puree, 53

Chunky Summer Minestrone, 64

Corn Soup with Chiles and
Manchego, 56, **57**

Creamy Green Chile Soup, 56

Creamy Tomato Soup with Buttery
Croutons, 55

Creamy Tomato Soup with Toasted
Almonds, 55

Cucumber Soup with Seared Tuna
Tartare, 54

Fresh Clam and Noodle Soup, 65

Garbanzo Soup with Chorizo and
Smoked Paprika, **62**, 63

Gingered Carrot Soup with Crème
Fraîche, 58, **59**

Golden Gratinéed Onion Soup, 56

Hearty Fennel Soup with Sausage and
Gouda Croutons, 58, **59**

Hearty Goulash Soup, 70

Hot and Sour Noodle Soup with
Pork, 64

Hot 'n' Cold Tomato Soup, 53

Lemongrass-Scented Noodle Soup
with Shrimp, 69

Lentil Soup with Serrano Ham and
Arugula, **50**, 62

Market Radish Soup with Balsamic
Cherries, 52, **52**

Mediterranean Fish Soup with Garlicky
Rouille, 68

Mushroom Soup with Chorizo and
Scallions, 58

Mussel Chowder with Bacon and

Shiitake Mushrooms, 67

Potato and Wild Mushroom Soup, 59

Roasted Chestnut Soup, 60

Smoked Salmon and Celery Root
Bisque, 68

Sour Fish Soup with Napa Cabbage
and Enoki Mushrooms, **66**, 67

Spicy Kale Chowder with Andouille
Sausage, 67

Star Anise–Beef Soup, 71

Summer Tomato Soup with Herbed
Goat Cheese, 52, **52**

Sweet-and-Sour Meatball Soup, 70

Tangy Chickpea Soup with Olives and
Anise, 64

Warm Soba in Broth with Spinach and
Tofu, 66, **66**

White Bean Soup with Cauliflower,
60, **61**

Winter Borscht with Brisket, 70

Winter Squash Soup with Pie Spices,
**62**, 63

Yellow Pepper and Almond Soup, 54

Sour Cream–Pecan Scones, 271

soybeans. See edamame

Spaetzle, Creole Mustard, **162**, 163

spaghetti

Fresh Clam and Noodle Soup, 65

Midnight Pasta with Tuna, Pancetta
and Spinach, 83

Spaghetti with Browned Butter and
Crispy Bread Crumbs, 79

Spaghetti with Creamy Pancetta
Sauce, 85

Spaghetti with Curried Seafood
Marinara, 83

Spaghetti with Shrimp and Spicy
Tomato Sauce, 80

Whole Wheat Spaghetti with Fresh
Ricotta and Lemon Zest, 75

spinach

Asian Spinach Salad with Sausage and
Pears, 48

Caramelized Cauliflower with Pancetta
and Spinach, 219

Chicken Breasts with Spinach, Leek
and Saffron Sauce, 90, **90**

Chicken Stuffed with Prosciutto,
Spinach and Boursin, 96

Coconut-Creamed Spinach, 222

Egg Salad with Capers and Spinach on
Toasted Brioche, 263

Garlicky Potato and Baby Spinach
Gratin, 222

Indian-Spiced Sea Bass with Spinach,
Peas and Carrots, 172

Lemony Greens with Olive Oil and
Olives, 33

Meat Loaf Stuffed with Prosciutto and
Spinach, 126

Midnight Pasta with Tuna, Pancetta
and Spinach, 83

Sautéed Chicken with Fresh Herbs and
Wilted Greens, 92

Scallops, Corn and Basil Steamed in
Foil, 192

Sea Scallops with Spinach and Grape
Tomatoes, 191

Spinach and Artichoke Pizzas, 254

Spinach and Goat Cheese Frittata,
266, **266**

Spinach and Ricotta Gnocchi, 78

Tangy Spinach Pastries, 17

Tuna Rolls with Roasted
Shallot–Wasabi Sauce, 20, **20**

Warm Soba in Broth with Spinach and
Tofu, 66, **66**

Winter Shrimp Salad with Fennel and
Ruby Grapefruit, 185

squash. See also zucchini

Butternut Squash–Polenta Gratin, 224

Buttery Root Vegetable Ragout, 226

Cavatelli with Spicy Winter
Squash, 74, **74**

Chipotle-Spiked Winter Squash and
Black Bean Salad, 224, **225**

Grilled Shrimp and Chayote Salad with
Chili-Garlic Dressing, 186

Halibut and Fall Harvest Sauté, 178

Hot 'n' Cold Tomato Soup, 53

Pumpkin Meringue Puff Pie, 284, **285**

Pumpkin Pudding with Candied Ginger
Whipped Cream, 338

Roasted Winter Squash and Onion

# index

Turnovers, 272

Seven-Vegetable Couscous, 242

Summer Squash Sandwiches with
Pecorino Butter, 263

Summer Vegetable Rice, 237

Winter Squash Soup with Pie
Spices, **62,** 63

**squid**

Grilled Calamari with Parsley, 180, **181**

Spaghetti with Curried Seafood
Marinara, 83

**star anise**

Star Anise–Beef Soup, 71

White Grapefruit and Star Anise
Granita, 300

**starters, 8–29**

Armagnac-Doused Shrimp, 22

Bacon-Wrapped Enoki, 221, **221**

Broiled Sardines with Mustard-Shallot
Crumbs, 26

Caramelized Onion and Gruyère
Tart, 18, **19**

Caviar and Potato Salad Tartlets, 16

Celery Root–Potato Pancakes with
Green Apple Sour Cream, 12, **13**

Chickpea Blinis with Pineapple-Mint
Relish, 12

Crab and Corn Beignets, 28, **29**

Creamy Fried Mozzarella Balls, 14

Crispy Fried Chicken Livers, 14

Crudités with Creamy Pistachio Dip, 11

Fiery Carrot Dip, 10, **10**

Goat Cheese Panna Cotta with Tomato
Salad, 16

Idaho Potato Chips, 10, **10**

Indian-Spiced Edamame, 11

Lemony Smoked Trout Salad in Red
Endive Scoops, 26, **27**

Mexican Shrimp Cocktail, 23

Mini Tartes Flambées, 18

Parmesan-Dusted Meatballs, 28

Prosciutto, Tomato and Olive
Bruschetta, 15

Roasted Persimmons Wrapped in
Pancetta, 28

Rustic Chicken Liver Mousse, 14

Scallops Steamed in Sake and

Riesling, 26

Sesame-Coated Sweet Potato
Croquettes, 12, 13

Shrimp and Chicken Summer Rolls, 24

Shrimp BLTs, 23

Shrimp Tempura with Miso
Mayonnaise, 23

Smoked Salmon Soufflés with
Gingered Salad, 22

Smoked Salmon Spirals, 21

Smoked Salmon–Stufffed Puffs, **20,** 21

Smoky Deviled Eggs, **8,** 14

Spicy Tuna Rillettes, 27, **27**

Stuffed Shiitake Mushrooms, 15

Tangy Spinach Pastries, 17

Toasted Rosemary Pecans, 11

Tuna and Green Olive Empanadas,
24, **25**

Tuna Rolls with Roasted
Shallot–Wasabi Sauce, 20, **20**

Turkish Cigars, 19, **19**

Warm Crab Dip with Fresh Herbs, 11

Warm Onion Flans with Fresh Tomato
Sauce, 17

Zucchini "Sandwiches" with Herbed
Goat Cheese, 15

**stews**

Beef and Vegetable Daube with Celery
Root Puree, 129

Beef Rib Eye and Vegetable Stew,
**128,** 129

Beef Stew with Belgian-Style Pale
Ale, 130

Citrus-Scented Lamb Stew, 134

Cranberry Bean Stew with Potatoes
and Bell Peppers, 230, **230**

Creamy Chicken Stew, 104

Curried Shrimp and Carrot
Bouillabaisse, 190

Eggplant and Lentil Stew with
Pomegranate Molasses, **240,** 241

Lamb Stew with Lemon, 135

Okra and Tomato Stew with
Cilantro, 227

Pork and Chickpea Stew with Orange
and Cumin, 148, **148**

Spiced Turkey Tagine with Prunes, 106

Tina's Turkey Chili, 106

Stir-Fried Pork with Ginger and Basil, 149

Stock, Rich Turkey, 112

**strawberries**

Gramma's Buttermilk Biscuits with
Berries and Ice Cream, 295, **295**

Icebox Strawberry Jam, 351

Orange-Almond Shortbread with
Strawberry Compote, 332

Rice Pudding with Strawberries, 297

Strawberry and Mascarpone Trifles
with Riesling Syrup, 297

Strawberry and Sweet Wine Gelées
with Candied Pistachios, 296

Strawberry Granita, 300

Strawberry-Rhubarb Galette, 296

Turkey Breast Fajitas with Strawberry-
Jalapeño Salsa, 109, **109**

Striped Bass with Wild Mushrooms, 173

Strudel, Phyllo Apple-Plum, 291

Stuffing, Bread, with Apple, Raisins and
Marmalade, 250

Succotash Salad, Warm, 49, **49**

Summer Rolls, Shrimp and Chicken, 24

**sweet potatoes**

Coconut Lamb Curry, 134

Duck Confit Potpie, 115, **116**

Sesame-Coated Sweet Potato
Croquettes, 12, **13**

Sweet Potato Chiffon Pie, 281

**Swiss chard**

Shirred Eggs with Mushrooms and
Swiss Chard, 266, **266**

Swiss Chard Salad with Garlicky
Yogurt, 39

**swordfish**

Braised Swordfish with Black Olives,
Tomatoes and Marjoram, 168

Chile-Rubbed Swordfish Kebabs with
Cucumber Salad, 167

Pasta Shells with Swordfish, **84,** 85

Sweet-and-Sour Swordfish, **160,** 168

Swordfish Steaks with Mint and
Garlic, 168, **169**

**syrups**

Green Tea–Honey Syrup, 348, **349**

Minted Lime Syrup, 348, **349**

Orange and Cranberry Syrup, 348, **349**

Simple Syrup, 355

Sugar Syrup, 348

# t

Tagliarini with Almond-Arugula Pesto and
Meatballs, 86

Tagliolini with Eggplant and Mint, 76

Tamarind-Date Dipping Sauce, 234

Tandoori Pork with Gingered Mango
Salad, 145

tangerines

Frozen Fruit Nougat with Citrus
auce, 336, **336**

Pork Medallions with Tangerine-Chile
Pan Sauce 145

tarts, savory. *See* pies and tarts (savory)

tarts, sweet. *See* pies and tarts (sweet)

tea

Almond-Tea Milk Shakes, 361

Earl Grey Devil's Food Cakes with
Cherries, 319

Gingery Soymilk Chai, 361

Green Tea–Honey Syrup, 348, **349**

Iced Hibiscus Tea, 361

Iced Pomegranate-Fennel Green
Tea, 360

Tempura, Shrimp, with Miso
Mayonnaise, 23

tequila

Pomegranate Margaritas, 356

tofu

Cold Noodles with Tofu in Peanut
Sauce, 80

Sesame-Crusted Tofu Salad with
Citrus Vinaigrette, 41, **41**

Warm Soba in Broth with Spinach and
Tofu, 66, **66**

tomatillos

Creamy Green Chile Soup, 56

Skirt Steak Burgers with Tomatillo-
Corn Relish, 122, **122**

Tangy Tomatillo Salad with Sun-Dried
Tomatoes, 46, **46**

tomatoes

Almost-Instant Heirloom

Tomato–Basil Relish, 350

BLTs on Toasted Brioche with Aioli and
Basil, 256

Braised Swordfish with Black Olives,
Tomatoes and Marjoram, 168

Chicken, Tomato and Mozzarella Salad
with Spicy Basil Dressing, 92

Chilled Tomato Soup with Sweet Pea
Puree, 53

Corn Bread Salad with Tomatoes and
Pepper Jack Cheese, 45

Creamy Tomato Soup with Buttery
Croutons, 55

Creamy Tomato Soup with Toasted
Almonds, 55

Escarole and Tomato Salad with
Shaved Piave Cheese, 45

Feta, Tomato and Red Onion
Salad, 39, **41**

Garlicky Cherry Tomato and Bread
Gratin, 252, **253**

Goat Cheese Panna Cotta with Tomato
Salad, 16

Greek Salad with Garlicky Pita
Toasts, 40

Green Bean Ragout with Tomatoes
and Mint, 212

Green Beans in Cherry Tomato
Sauce, 215

Green-Tomato Pickle, 227

Grilled Lamb Kebabs with Smoky
Tomato Sauce, 132, **132**

Hot 'n' Cold Tomato Soup, 53

Mussels with Tomatoes and
Feta, 198

Okra and Tomato Stew with
Cilantro, 227

Okra in Tomato Sauce, 226

Pan-Fried Pompano with Tomato-
Caraway Glaze, 179

Pasta with Borlotti Beans, Olives and
Cherry Tomatoes, 74, **74**

Penne all'Arrabbiata, 75

Potato Salad with Bacon and
Tomatoes, 231

Prosciutto, Tomato and Olive
Bruschetta, 15

Roasted Fish with Charmoula,
Tomatoes and Potatoes, 174

Roasted Tomatoes with Penne and
Ricotta Salata, 75

Roasted Whole Snapper with Tomato-
Bread Salad, 175

Salt-Baked Sea Bass with Warm
Tomato Vinaigrette, 171

Scallops with Orzo, Tomatoes and
Ginger, 192, **193**

Sea Scallops with Spinach and Grape
Tomatoes, 191

Shrimp BLTs, 23

Sofrito, 157

Spaghetti with Shrimp and Spicy
Tomato Sauce, 80

Summer Tomato Soup with Herbed
Goat Cheese, 52, **52**

Tangy Tomatillo Salad with Sun-Dried
Tomatoes, 46, **46**

Tiny Peppers in Cherry Tomato Sauce,
**214**, 215

Tomato and Mint Pesto Risotto, 244

Tomato and Mozzarella Salad with
Frozen Balsamic Vinaigrette, 46, **46**

Tomato Bread Pudding, 252

Tomato Salad with Scallions and
Balsamic Dressing, 45

Turkish Chopped Salad, 39

Warm Lobster Salad with Gazpacho
Consommé, 199

Warm Onion Flans with Fresh Tomato
Sauce, 17

Zucchini Pappardelle with Tomatoes
and Feta, **202**, 206

tortillas

Grilled Shrimp and Corn Wraps,
186, **187**

Lamb and Two-Cheese Quesadillas,
140, **141**

Turkey Breast Fajitas with Strawberry-
Jalapeño Salsa, 109, **109**

trifles

Blood Orange and Chocolate
Trifles, 297

Strawberry and Mascarpone Trifles
with Riesling Syrup, 297

# index

**trout**

Crêpes with Smoked Trout and
Caviar, 277

Grilled Quick-Cured Trout with
Mustard-Olive Dressing, 179

Lemony Smoked Trout Salad in Red
Endive Scoops, 26, **27**

Matzo Meal–Crusted Trout, 178

Sautéed Trout Fillets with a Pumpkin
Seed Crust, 178

Smoked Trout and Bacon Pitas, 256

Tuiles, Hazelnut, 332

**tuna**

Cucumber Soup with Seared Tuna
Tartare, 54

Mediterranean Fish Soup with Garlicky
Rouille, 68

Midnight Pasta with Tuna, Pancetta
and Spinach, 83

Salade Niçoise with Fennel-Dusted
Tuna, 47

Seared Tuna with Chimichurri Sauce
and Greens, 170, **171**

Sesame-Crusted Tuna Steaks,
170, **171**

Spicy Tuna Rillettes, 27, **27**

Tuna and Green Olive Empanadas,
24, **25**

Tuna Rolls with Roasted
Shallot–Wasabi Sauce, 20, **20**

**turkey**

Alsatian-Brined Turkey with Riesling
Gravy, 111

Herb-Roasted Turkey with Maple
Gravy, **110**, 111

Pappardelle with Red Wine and Meat
Ragù, 86, **87**

Paprika-Glazed Turkey, 112

Rich Turkey Stock, 112

Shepherd's Pie with Parsnip Puree
Topping, 112

Spiced Turkey Tagine with Prunes, 106

Tina's Turkey Chili, 106

Turkey and Green Bean Stir-Fry with
Peanuts, 108, **109**

Turkey Breast Fajitas with Strawberry-
Jalapeño Salsa, 109, **109**

Turkey Burgers with Pesto
Mayonnaise, 106

Turkey-Date Meatballs with Lentils and
Yogurt Sauce, 108

Turkey Leg Confit with Garlic
Gravy, 113

**turnips**

Sautéed Turnips and Carrots with
Rosemary-Ginger Honey, 217

Seven-Vegetable Couscous, 242

**turnovers**

Eli's Golden Apple Turnovers, 294

Flaky Turnover Pastry, 272

Roasted Winter Squash and Onion
Turnovers, 272

# V

**veal**

Braised Veal Chops with Honey and
Red Grapes, 157

Easter Veal Loin with Fennel–Lima
Bean Puree, 158, **159**

Lemon-Parmesan Veal Rolls with
Arugula Salad, 158

Sausage and Broccoli Rabe Burgers,
154, **154**

Seven-Vegetable Couscous, 242

**vegetables, 202–227.** *See also* specific
vegetables

Beef and Vegetable Daube with Celery
Root Puree, 129

Beef Rib Eye and Vegetable Stew,
**128**, 129

Buttery Root Vegetable Ragout, 226

Crudités with Creamy Pistachio
Dip, 11

Curried Mixed Vegetables, 223

Halibut and Fall Harvest Sauté, 178

Quail with Sweet Pea Oatmeal and
Summer Vegetable Ragout,
118, **119**

Shrimp and Broccoli with Honey-
Walnut Caramel Sauce, 184

Seven-Vegetable Couscous, 242

Steamed Cod with Crisp Vegetables,
174

Summer Vegetable Rice, 237

Vermentino-Braised Sea Bass, 170

**vodka**

Bitter Queen, 355

Cheval, 354, **354**

Citrus-Mint Cocktails, 355

Dry Toast, 354

Hollow Hills, 354

Ice Wine Martini, 358

Jade Cocktail, 360

Orange Fizz, 355

Red Grape and Coconut Refresher, 356

Roof Garden, 355

Rose Martinis, 356

Saluki, 354, **354**

Sawtooth Mountain Breezes, 356

Sugar Baby, 355

The Vamp, 355

Vanilla Pear Mimosa, 354

# W

**walnuts**

Asparagus Salad with Toasted Walnuts
and Goat Cheese, **34,** 35

Bread Stuffing with Apple, Raisins and
Marmalade, 250

Bulgur, Pomegranate and Walnut Salad, 234, **235**

Chocolate Rosemary-Caramel Nut
Bars, 328

Fettuccine with Walnut-Parsley
Pesto, 76

Grilled Dorado with Walnut and Parsley
Pesto, 180

Mixed Greens with Nuts and Dried
Fruit, 33

Rum-Mocha Walnut Layer Cake,
316, **317**

Shrimp and Broccoli with Honey-
Walnut Caramel Sauce, **182,** 184

Tricolore Salad with Walnuts and
Prosciutto, 37

**watercress**

Asian Watercress Salad with
Salmon, 163

Cornish Hens with Shiitake and

Watercress, 117

Mixed Salad with Bacon, Blue Cheese and Pecans, 37

Papaya, Orange and Watercress Salad with Pancetta, 42

Pickled Asian Pear Salad with Creamy Lemon Dressing, 41

Spring Peas with New Potatoes, Herbs and Watercress, 218

**watermelon**

Tomato and Mozzarella Salad with Frozen Balsamic Vinaigrette, 46, **46**

Watermelon Coolers, 358, **359**

**wine**

Citrus-Mint Cocktails, 355

Ice Wine Martini, 358

Midtown Sangria, 358

Red Wine–Carrot Sauce, 345

Saffron Cooler, **352,** 357

Spiced Red Wine Punch, 360

Strawberry and Sweet Wine Gelées with Candied Pistachios, 296

# y

**yogurt**

Chilled Cucumber Soup with Pickled Red Onion, 54

Grilled Eggplants with Cumin-Yogurt Sauce, **204,** 205

Grilled Whole Fish with Curried Yogurt Marinade, 180

Indian Rice and Lentils with Raita, 238

Lamb Burgers with Cilantro-Yogurt Sauce, 140, **141**

Lamb and Two-Cheese Quesadillas, 140, **141**

Moroccan Lamb Burgers with Mint-Yogurt Sauce, 140

Swiss Chard Salad with Garlicky Yogurt, 39

Turkey-Date Meatballs with Lentils and Yogurt Sauce, 108

Yogurt with Sautéed Dried Fruits and Nuts, 302, **303**

# Z

**zucchini**

Chunky Summer Minestrone, 64

Curried Mixed Vegetables, 223

Fried Zucchini Blossoms, 207

Hot 'n' Cold Tomato Soup, 53

Penne with Zucchini and Basil, 76, **77**

Rice-and-Dill-Stuffed Zucchini, 205

Seven-Vegetable Couscous, 242

Steamed Cod with Crisp Vegetables, 174

Summer Squash Sandwiches with Pecorino Butter, 263

Summer Vegetable Rice, 237

Zucchini Bread, 273

Zucchini Bread French Toast with Maple-Bourbon Butter, 273

Zucchini Cakes, 207

Zucchini Gratin with Gruyère Cheese, 206

Zucchini Musakka with Chickpeas and Spiced Lamb, **204,** 205

Zucchini Pappardelle with Tomatoes and Feta, **202,** 206

Zucchini "Sandwiches" with Herbed Goat Cheese, 15

# chefs + cooks

Mi Suk Ahn is the bar manager at the restaurant Brasa in Seattle.

Bruce Aidells, a food writer, cooking teacher and author of *Bruce Aidells's Complete Book of Pork,* founded Aidells Sausage Company.

Engin Akin is a food journalist living in Istanbul.

Jeffrey Alford is a cook, photographer and co-author, with his wife, Naomi Duguid, of several cookbooks, including *Home Baking: The Artful Mix of Flour and Tradition Around the World* and *Hot Sour Salty Sweet.*

Michael Allemeier is executive winery chef at the Mission Hill Terrace restaurant in the Okanagan Valley in British Columbia, Canada.

José Andrés is a chef and restaurateur who owns Jaleo, Café Atlántico, Minibar at Café Atlántico, Zaytinya and Oyamel, all in the Washington, D.C., area.

Alexandra and Eliot Angle are the owners of Aqua Vitae Design, a Los Angeles–based event and interior design company. They are also the authors of *Cocktail Parties with a Twist.*

Valentina Argiolas manages public relations for Argiolas Winery in Sardinia, Italy.

Chuck Avery is the director of bar operations at Loa in the International House hotel in New Orleans.

Karen Barker is the pastry chef and co-owner, with her husband, Ben, of Magnolia Grill in Durham, North Carolina. She is the author of *Not Afraid of Flavor* and *Sweet Stuff: Karen Barker's American Desserts.*

Alisa Barry is the founder of Bella Cucina Artful Food, a specialty food shop in Atlanta, Georgia, and the author of *La Bella Vita: Inspiration and Recipes from the Creator of Bella Cucina.*

Mario Batali is the host of Food Network's *Molto Mario,* and the chef, co-owner and partner of several New York City restaurants, among them Babbo, Lupa and Casa Mono. He is also the author of several cookbooks.

Peter Berley is a private chef, caterer and cooking instructor who made his name as chef at New York City's Angelica Kitchen. He is the author of *Fresh Food Fast* and *The Modern Vegetarian Kitchen.*

Paul Bertolli is the chef and co-owner of Oliveto Café & Restaurant in Oakland, California, and the author of *Cooking by Hand.*

Mark Bittman writes "The Minimalist," a weekly column for the *New York Times.* He is the author of the best-selling *How to Cook Everything.*

Jim Botsacos is the chef and partner at Molyvos and a partner at Abboccato, both in New York City.

David Bouley is the chef and owner of Bouley and Danube, both in New York City, and author of *East of Paris*.

Daniel Boulud, an F&W Best New Chef 1988, is the chef and owner of Daniel, Café Boulud and db Bistro Moderne restaurants in New York City and Café Boulud Palm Beach at the Brazilian Court in Palm Beach, Florida. He is also the author of several cookbooks, including *Daniel's Dish: Entertaining at Home with a Four-Star Chef*.

Graham Elliot Bowles, an F&W Best New Chef 2004, is the *chef de cuisine* at Avenues in The Peninsula Hotel in Chicago.

James Boyce is the executive chef at Studio in the Montage Resort & Spa in Laguna Beach, California.

Michel Bras is the chef and owner of the Michelin-rated three-star restaurant Michel Bras in Laguiole, France.

Margaret Braun is an artist, cake designer and the author of *Cakewalk*.

Michael Brown is the bartender at Degrees, the bar in the Ritz-Carlton Georgetown in Washington, D.C.

Morgan Brownlow is the chef and co-owner of clarklewis in Portland, Oregon.

Ryan Buenning is a managing partner and chief mixologist at Jade Bar in San Francisco.

Marisol Bueno is the owner of Pazo de Senorans, a winery in Spain's Galicia region.

Anne Byrn is the author of *The Cake Mix Doctor* series of cookbooks and food writer for Nashville's *Tennessean*.

Dolores Cakebread and her husband, Jack, own Cakebread Cellars Winery in Napa Valley.

Jeremy Campbell is the bar manager at Monsoon in Chicago.

Ian Chalermkittichai is the executive chef at Kittichai, a Thai restaurant in New York City.

Sylvie Chantecaille is the owner and founder of Chantecaille Beauté.

Lauren Chattman is a former pastry chef and the author of six cookbooks, including *Icebox Pies*.

Ashley Christensen is the chef at Enoteca Vin in Raleigh, North Carolina.

Josiah Citrin, an F&W Best New Chef 1997, is the chef and owner of Melisse in Santa Monica, California, and co-owner of Lemon Moon in Los Angeles.

Melissa Clark is a freelance food writer. She has authored and co-authored 16 cookbooks, including *East of Paris* with David Bouley.

Jim Clendenen founded Au Bon Climat winery in Santa Barbara County, California. He earned an F&W American Wine Award as 2001's Winemaker of the Year.

Scott Conant, an F&W Best New Chef 2004, is the executive chef and co-owner of L'Impero and Bar Tonno, both in New York City.

Paul Condron is the chef at the New Zealand winery Sileni Estates.

Peggy Cullen is a baker, candy maker and the author of *Got Milk?*, *The Cookie Book* and *Caramel*. She is also the owner of Lucky Star Sweets, a confectionery company.

Musa Dagdeviren is the chef at Ciya in Istanbul.

Josh DeChellis is the chef at Sumile in New York City.

Dale DeGroff, a former bartender at The Rainbow Room, wrote *The Craft of the Cocktail*. He created the cocktails for the Silver Leaf Tavern in the Kimpton Hotel in New York City.

Kevin Delk is the owner of Mario's Double Daughter's Salotto bar in Denver.

Erica De Mane is the author of several books on Italian cooking, including *The Flavors of Southern Italy* and *Pasta Improvvisata*.

Jody Denton is the chef and owner of Merenda in Bend, Oregon.

Gina DePalma is the pastry chef at Babbo in New York City.

Portia de Smidt is a chef and co-owner of the Africa Café in Cape Town, South Africa. She is the author of *The Africa Café Experience*.

Chris Dexter co-owns Elm Street Liquors in Chicago.

Jeremiah Doherty manages the bar at Grace in Los Angeles.

Scott Dolich, an F&W Best New Chef 2004, is the chef and owner of Park Kitchen in Portland, Oregon.

Tom Douglas is the chef and owner of Dahlia Lounge, Palace Kitchen, Etta's and Lola's, all in Seattle. He is also the author of *Tom Douglas' Seattle Kitchen* and *Tom's Big Dinners*.

Celestino Drago is the owner and executive chef of Drago and Enoteca Drago, both in Los Angeles.

Naomi Duguid is a cook, photographer and co-author, with her husband, Jeffrey Alford, of several cookbooks, including *Home Baking: The Artful Mix of Flour and Tradition Around the World* and *Hot Sour Salty Sweet*.

Matt Eisler co-owns Elm Street Liquors in Chicago.

Chris Erasmus is the executive sous chef at Le Quartier Français in Franschhoek, South Africa.

Duskie Estes is the chef and co-owner of Zazu in Santa Rosa, California.

# chefs + cooks

**Rob Evans,** an F&W Best New Chef 2004, is the chef and owner of Hugo's in Portland, Maine.

**Dimitri Fayard** is the co-chef and co-owner of Vanille Pâtisserie in Chicago.

**Dominique Filoni,** an F&W Best New Chef 2004, is the chef at Savona in Gulph Mills, Pennsylvania, and chef and owner of Bianca in nearby Bryn Mawr.

**Claudia Fleming** is the author of *The Last Course* and consulting pastry chef at Amuse in New York City.

**Alex Freij** is the owner of Diner 24 in New York City.

**Nobuo Fukuda,** an F&W Best New Chef 2003, is the chef and co-owner of Sea Saw in Scottsdale, Arizona.

**Tom Fundaro** is the executive chef at Villa Creek in Paso Robles, California.

**Gina Gallo** is a third-generation winemaker at Gallo in Sonoma County, California.

**Gale Gand** is the executive pastry chef and partner of Tru restaurant in Chicago and the host of Food Network's *Sweet Dreams.* She has written several cookbooks, including *TRU: A Cookbook from the Legendary Chicago Restaurant.*

**Marcella Giamundo** is a former vice president at Richard Ginori, the Italian china company.

**Rafaella Giamundo** is an avid home cook living in Italy.

**Mandy Groom Givler** is the executive pastry chef for Gotham Bldg Tavern and Family Supper.

**Suzanne Goin,** an F&W Best New Chef 1999, is the chef and co-owner of Lucques and A.O.C., both in Los Angeles.

**Carmen Gonzalez** is the chef and owner of Carmen the Restaurant in Coral Gables, Florida.

**Koren Grieveson** is the chef at Avec in Chicago.

**Kurt Gutenbrunner** is the executive chef and owner of Wallsé and executive chef of Café Sabarsky, both in New York City.

**Tommy Habetz** is co-chef and co-owner of Gotham Bldg Tavern in Portland, Oregon.

**Naomi Hebberoy** is co-chef and co-owner of Gotham Bldg Tavern and co-founder of Ripe and Family Supper, all in Portland, Oregon.

**Kate Heddings** is the editor of F&W Cookbooks and a senior editor at F&W Magazine.

**Lee Hefter,** an F&W Best New Chef 1998, is the executive chef and managing partner at Spago Beverly Hills and Brasserie Vert in Hollywood.

**Anissa Helou** is the London-based author of *Lebanese Cuisine, Café Morocco* and *Mediterranean Street Food.*

**Christophe Hille** is the executive chef and co-owner of A16 in San Francisco.

**Barak Hirschowitz** is the executive chef at Tides at the Bay Hotel in Cape Town, South Africa.

**Marion Hoezel** is a former pastry chef at clarklewis in Portland, Oregon.

**Ben Hussman** is an avid home cook and a community volunteer in Little Rock, Arkansas.

**Bob Isaacson** is the culinary consultant for the Smith Fork Ranch in Crawford, Colorado.

**Mohammad Islam** is the executive chef at Chateau Marmont and The Standard, both in Hollywood, California.

**Johnny Iuzzini** is the executive pastry chef at New York City's Jean Georges.

**Dana Jacobi** has written several cookbooks, including *The 12 Best Foods Cookbook, Amazing Soy* and *The Best of Clay Pot Cooking.*

**Sally James** is the consulting chef at d'Arenberg winery in Australia's McLaren Vale.

**Margot Janse** is the executive chef at Le Quartier Français in Franschhoek, South Africa.

**Linda Japngie** is the chef at Ixta, a Latin American restaurant in New York City.

**Kimball Jones,** a food and wine consultant based in Napa Valley, is the former chef of Wente Vineyards in Livermore, California, and co-author of the winery's cookbooks.

**Zov Karamardian** is the chef and owner of Zov's Bistro in Tustin, California, and author of *Zov! Recipes and Stories from the Heart.*

**Trevor Kaufman** is an avid home cook who spent summers during college working at Bouley in New York City. He is the CEO of Schematic, a Web development company in Los Angeles.

**Hubert Keller** is the chef and owner of San Francisco's Fleur de Lys as well as Burger Bar and Fleur de Lys Las Vegas in the Mandalay Bay Hotel.

**Melissa Kelly** is the executive chef and co-owner of Primo in Rockland, Maine, and Orlando, Florida.

**Marcia Kiesel** is the F&W Test Kitchen supervisor and co-author of *The Simple Art of Vietnamese Cooking.*

**Eric Michel Klein,** an F&W Best New Chef 2004, is the executive chef at Wynn property in Las Vegas.

**Neil Kleinberg** is the chef and co-owner of Clinton St. Baking Company in New York City.

**Diane Kochilas** has written four books on Greek cuisine, including *Meze: Small Plates to Savor* and *Share from the Mediterranean Table,* and is the weekly food columnist for Greece's largest daily newspaper, *Ta Nea.* She runs the Glorious Greek Kitchen cooking school on the island of Ikaria.

**Aglaia Kremezi** is an Athens-born journalist, writer, menu consultant, photographer and author of several books, including *The Foods of Greece, The Mediterranean Pantry* and *The Cooking of the Greek Islands.*

**Gabriel Kreuther,** an F&W Best New Chef 2003, is the chef at The Modern in the Museum of Modern Art in New York City.

**Leslie Kunde** is the matriarch of the Kunde family, owners of the Kunde Estate Winery Vineyards in Sonoma, California.

**Donald Link** is the chef and partner of Herbsaint in New Orleans.

**Alessandro Lunardi** is the East Coast sales director for Robert Mondavi Imports.

**Barbara Lynch,** an F&W Best New Chef 1996, is the chef and owner of Boston's No. 9 Park and The Butcher Shop, a combination charcuterie market and wine bar.

**Stephanie Lyness** is the Connecticut food critic for the *New York Times.* She has collaborated on several cookbooks, including *Indian Home Cooking* with Suvir Saran.

**Ryan Magarian** is the mixologist at Jäger in Seattle.

**Waldy Malouf** is the executive chef and co-owner of Beacon in New York City and author of *The Hudson River Valley Cookbook* and *High Heat.*

**Walter Manzke** is the executive chef at Bouchee in Carmel-by-the-Sea, California.

**Susan Mason** owns Susan Mason Catering in Savannah, Georgia.

**Shawn McClain** is the executive chef and co-owner of Chicago's Spring and Green Zebra restaurants.

**Tory McPhail** is the executive chef at Commander's Palace in New Orleans.

**Elizabeth Mendez** is the *chef de cuisine* at the Kinara Day Spa and Café in Los Angeles.

**Annie Miler** is the chef and owner of Clementine in Los Angeles.

**Martin Molteni** is a consultant at Terrazas de los Andes winery in Mendoza, Argentina.

**Michael Moorhouse** is the pastry chef at Blue Hill at Stone Barns in Pocantico Hills, New York.

**Nick Morgenstern** is the pastry chef at Marseille and Nice Matin, both in New York City.

**Masaharu Morimoto** is the executive chef and owner of Morimoto in Philadelphia and a former star of Food Network's *Iron Chef.*

**Marc Orfaly,** an F&W Best New Chef 2004, is the chef and owner of Pigalle in Boston.

**Daniel Orr** is the executive chef at the CuisinArt Resort & Spa on Anguilla.

**Jeff Orr** is the chef and owner of Harvest in Madison, Wisconsin.

**Marie Paillard** is the wife of Bruno Paillard, a winemaker and owner of Champagne Bruno Paillard in Reims, France.

**Grace Parisi** is the F&W Test Kitchen senior associate and author of *Get Saucy.*

**Greg Patent** has written several cookbooks, including *Baking in America,* a 2003 James Beard Award winner.

**François Payard** is a third-generation French pastry chef and the author of *Simply Sensational Desserts.* He is the chef and owner of Payard Pâtisserie & Bistro in New York City.

**Zak Pelaccio** is the executive chef at 5 Ninth in New York City.

**Jacques Pépin** is an F&W Magazine contributing editor, master chef, TV personality and cooking teacher. He is the author of a memoir, *The Apprentice: My Life in the Kitchen,* and 23 cookbooks, including *Jacques Pépin: Fast Food My Way,* which is the companion to the public television series of the same name. Personal chef to three French heads of state, including Charles de Gaulle, before moving to the United States in 1959, Pépin is a 2004 recipient of the French Legion of Honor.

**Melissa Perello,** an F&W Best New Chef 2004, is the executive chef at Fifth Floor in San Francisco.

**Iñigo Pérez** is a consultant to Carlos Falco, founder and chief winemaker of Marqués de Griñón winery, and the chef and owner of Urrechu and El Fogón de Zein, both in Madrid.

**Guillermo Pernot,** an F&W Best New Chef 1998, is the executive chef and owner of ¡Pasión! in Philadelphia and the author of *¡Ceviche!*

**Charles Phan** is the chef and owner of The Slanted Door, a Vietnamese restaurant in San Francisco.

**Carrie Pillar** is a former pastry cook at Spago and Patina, both in Los Angeles.

**Russ Pillar,** an avid home cook, co-founded the brand investment firm Critical Mass.

**Maggie Pond** is the chef at César in Berkeley, California.

# chefs + cooks

**Rachael Ray** is the host of Food Network's *30 Minute Meals, $40 a Day* and *Inside Dish* and the author of several cookbooks including, *30-Minute Meals for the Carb-Frustrated.*

**Shelly Register** is a former pastry chef at Aubergine restaurant in Newport Beach, California.

**Victoria Abbott Riccardi** is the author of *Untangling My Chopsticks: A Culinary Sojourn in Kyoto.*

**Akasha Richmond** is a caterer, personal chef and owner of Akasha's Visionary Cuisine in Los Angeles.

**Julie Ridlon** is the chef and owner of Chanterelle Catering and co-founder of the Clayton Farmers' Market in St. Louis, Missouri.

**Bruce Riezenman** is a chef at E. & J. Gallo Winery and owner and executive chef of Park Avenue Catering Co. in Sonoma County, California.

**Pascal Rigo** owns bakeries and restaurants in San Francisco, including Chez Nous and Le Petit Robert. In addition, he oversees the menu at La Table O&CO and is the author of *The American Boulangerie.*

**Eric Ripert** is the executive chef and co-owner of Le Bernardin in New York City and co-author of two cookbooks, *Le Bernardin Cookbook: Four-Star Simplicity* and *A Return to Cooking.*

**Nadia Roden** is an artist, textile designer and animator. She wrote and illustrated the cookbook *Granita Magic.*

**Ilene Rosen** is the savory chef at City Bakery in New York City.

**Jamie Samford** is the executive chef at Central Market in Dallas.

**Suvir Saran** is co-author of *Indian Home Cooking* and co-executive chef of Devi in New York City.

**Warren Schwartz** is the executive chef at Whist in Santa Monica, California.

**Lou Seibert Pappas** is the author of *Biscotti.*

**Christian Shaffer** is the chef and owner of two California restaurants, Chloe in Playa del Rey and Avenue in Manhattan Beach.

**Jane Sigal** is a cookbook author and senior food editor at F&W Magazine.

**Maria Helm Sinskey,** an F&W Best New Chef 1996, is the culinary director of Robert Sinskey Vineyards in Napa Valley and author of *The Vineyard Kitchen.*

**Charmaine Solomon** has written more than 31 cookbooks, including *Complete Vegetarian Cookbook.*

**Crispy Soloperto** manages the Raleigh restaurant in the Raleigh Hotel, Miami.

**Barbara Spencer** grows certified organic fruits, vegetables and beans with her husband, Bill Spencer, at Windrose Farm near Paso Robles, California.

**John Stewart** is the chef and co-owner of Zazu in Santa Rosa, California.

**Frank Stitt** is the executive chef and owner of several restaurants, including Highlands Bar and Grill in Birmingham, Alabama.

**Jean-Claude Szurdak** is the former owner of Jean-Claude Caterers and three pastry shops, all in New York City. He was the chef and back-kitchen manager on Jacques Pépin's television series *Fast Food My Way.*

**Bill Telepan** is a chef and author of *Inspired by Ingredients: Market Menus and Family Favorites from a Three-Star Chef.*

**Richard Terzaghi** is a co-owner of Baraka in San Francisco.

**Bradford Thompson,** an F&W Best New Chef 2004, is the *chef de cuisine* at Mary Elaine's in Scottsdale, Arizona.

**Jacques Torres** is the Dean of Pastry Arts at the French Culinary Institute in New York City, a television host and cookbook author. He owns Jacques Torres Chocolate and Jacques Torres Chocolate Haven, both in New York City.

**Fabio Trabocchi,** an F&W Best New Chef 2002, is the chef at Maestro at the Ritz-Carlton Tysons Corner in McLean, Virginia.

**Clif Travers** is the head bartender at Cuchi Cuchi in Cambridge, Massachusetts.

**Albert Trummer** is a cocktail consultant, notably at Town and Kittichai, both in New York City.

**Tina Ujlaki** is the executive food editor at F&W Magazine.

**Marie van der Merwe** is the chef and owner of Strandkombuis restaurant in Yzerfontein, South Africa.

**Mary Lynn Van Wyck** co-owns Van Wyck & Van Wyck, a floral and event design company based in New York City.

**Marc Vetri,** an F&W Best New Chef 1999, is the chef and co-owner of Vetri in Philadelphia.

**John Villa** is the executive chef of Patroon and executive chef and co-owner of Dominic, both in New York City.

**John Vlandis** is the former executive chef at the Hess Collection Winery in Napa.

**Anya von Bremzen** is a food writer and the author of several cookbooks, including *Please to the Table: The Russian Cookbook* and *The Greatest Dishes! Around the World in 80 Recipes.*

**Jean-Georges Vongerichten,** an F&W Magazine contributing editor, is the chef and co-owner of numerous restaurants around the world, including Jean Georges, Spice Market and V Steakhouse, all in New York City. He has co-authored *Simple Cuisine, Cooking at Home with a Four-Star Chef* and *Simple to Spectacular.*

Bob Waggoner is the executive chef at Charleston Grill in the Charleston Place Hotel in Charleston, South Carolina.

Steven Wagner, owner of Steven Wagner Design, is a former editor of Bell'Italia, an Italian travel and food magazine.

David Walzog is the executive chef of Michael Jordan's The Steak House NYC, The Steakhouse at Monkey Bar and Strip House, all in New York City.

David Ward is the owner of Blue Martini, a bar in Birmingham, Michigan.

Lucia Watson is the chef and owner of Lucia's Restaurant and Wine Bar in Minneapolis and co-author of Savoring the Seasons of the Northern Heartland.

Pete Wells, a former F&W Magazine editor, is the articles editor at Details and the winner of three James Beard Foundation Journalism Awards.

Kyle Withrow is the bartender at Levende Lounge in San Francisco.

Mat Wolf, an F&W Best New Chef 2004, is the chef at Gautreau's in New Orleans.

Paula Wolfert, an F&W Magazine contributing editor, is the author of many award-winning cookbooks, including Mediterranean Cooking, Mediterranean Grain and Greens and The Slow Mediterranean Kitchen.

Gina Word is a former head bartender for Spice in Atlanta.

Jean-Pierre Xiradakis is the chef and owner of La Tupina in Bordeaux, France.

Bill Yosses is the chef at New York City's Josephs and co-author of Desserts for Dummies.

Eli Zabar is the owner and founder of Eli's, a specialty food store, bread company and restaurant in New York City.

Geoffrey Zakarian is the chef and proprietor of Town in the Chambers Hotel in New York City.

Galen Zamarra is the chef and co-owner at Mas in New York City.

Terry Zarikian is a Miami-based publicist and food editor of Selecta magazine.

# photographers

Achilleos, Antonis 52 (left), 202, 204 (left)

Bacon, Quentin 10 (right), 19 (right), 20 (bottom), 30, 74 (right), 99, 103 (left), 120, 188, 197, 253 (bottom), 325 (right), 336 (top)

Baigrie, James 32 (left), 46 (right), 74 (left), 90 (right), 147 (top), 177 (top), 184 (left), 210 (right), 225 (top), 295 (bottom), 352

Franco, Jim 66 (top), 235, 305

Gallagher, Dana 59 (top), 90 (left), 148 (left), 166, 184 (right), 280 (right), 282, 311 (bottom), 317, 323, 341, 344

Halenda, Gregor 179, 222, 289, 347

Hirsheimer, Christopher 32 (right), 61, 248 (left)

Howard, Rob 253 (top)

Janisch, Frances 13 (bottom), 25, 49 (left), 57, 132 (left), 144 (left), 177 (bottom), 194 (bottom), 201, 204 (right), 218, 230 (right), 240, 245 (bottom), 248 (right), 264, 269 (bottom), 275, 303 (top), 320, 342, 349

Jones, Deborah 292

Kachatorian, Ray 46 (left), 109 (bottom)

Keller & Keller 100, 174 (right), 278, 286

Kernick, John 10 (left), 27 (right), 62 (top), 84 (bottom), 110, 122 (left), 209, 210 (left), 228, 280 (left), 285, 308 (right), 325 (left), 331

Loftus, David 81, 84 (top), 87, 116 (left), 188, 225 (bottom)

McCaul, Andrew 107 (bottom), 259

McEvoy, Maura 43, 66 (bottom), 95, 105, 142, 148 (right), 295 (top), 311 (top), 359

Mentis, Anastassios 126, 155, 172, 236, 272

Meppem, William 27 (left), 29, 303 (bottom), 354 (left), 408

Miller, Ellie 373

Pearson, Victoria 77 (top), 169, 181, 214, 270

Pedersen, Pernille 41 (left), 187 (top), 230 (left), 246, 262

Piasecki, Eric 69, 356

Resen, Laura 159

Rossi, Aldo 136

Rupp, Tina 13 (top), 20 (top), 34, 49 (right), 50, 59 (bottom), 62 (bottom), 72, 77 (bottom), 88, 103 (right), 109 (top), 119, 122 (right), 128, 132 (right), 141, 144 (right), 147 (bottom), 150, 154 (right), 162, 165, 171, 174 (left), 187 (bottom), 193, 194 (top), 239, 245 (top), 266, 354 (right)

Salas, Javier 154 (left)

Sanchez, Hector 107 (top), 221

Schroff, Zubin 41 (right), 336 (bottom)

Smith, Mel 115

Stone, Brittain 5, 269 (top)

Tinslay, Petrina 52 (right), 160, 182, 213, 299, 327

Webber, Wendell T. 45, 339

Williams, Anna 261, 306, 308 (left)

Woffinden, Andrew 36

Wright, Robert 8, 19 (left), 116 (right)